本年鉴已经审核，未涉及保密问题，可以公开出版发行。

西安市统计局局长：

李利民

This yearbook is an open publication.All data on this yearbook have been examined without any secret.

Li Limin

Commissioner for xi'an Municipal Bureau of Statistics

中国统计出版社
China Statistics Press

西安统计年鉴

XI'AN STATISTICS YEARBOOK

2004年（总第12期 NO.12）

西安市统计局 编
XI'AN MUNICIPAL BUREAU STATISTICS

(京)新登字041号

图书在版编目（CIP）数据

西安统计年鉴.2004/西安市统计局编.—北京：中国统计出版社，2004.6

ISBN 7-5037-4360-3

Ⅰ.西…

Ⅱ.西…

Ⅲ.统计资料—西安市—2004—年鉴

Ⅳ.C832.411-54

中国版本图书馆CIP数据核字（2004）第041471号

西安统计年鉴—2004

作　者/西安市统计局

责任编辑/蔡启新

责任校对/西安市统计局

封面设计/贾　石　师爱平

出版发行/中国统计出版社

通信地址/北京市西城区三里河月坛南街75号　中国统计出版社

邮　编/100826

电　话/(010)63262295

印　刷/西安合鑫统计资料印刷厂

经　销/新华书店

开　本/890x1240毫米 1/16开本

字　数/112万字

印　张/39.5印张

印　数/1200册

版　别/2004年6月第1版

版　次/2004年6月第1次印刷

书　号/ISBN 7-5037-4360-3/F·1824

定　价/260元

XI'AN Statistical Yearbook-2004

《西安统计年鉴—2004》
编　辑　部

XI'AN Statistical Yearbook-2004

EDITORLAL STAFF

编者说明

一、《西安统计年鉴—2004》由西安市统计局编辑、中国统计出版社出版，是全面系统综合反映西安国民经济、社会和科技发展状况的大型工具书。该书具有信息量大、覆盖面广的特点，融权威性、实用性于一体，它不仅向各级党政领导提供决策依据，而且还及时向社会公众提供经济信息，同时也是向世界宣传西安，让世界了解西安，让西安走向世界的一本宣传资料。

二、全书共分十九部分，主要包括：1、综合；2、国民经济核算；3、人口、从业人员与职工工资；4、固定资产投资；5、财政；6、物价指数；7、人民生活；8、城市公用事业及环境保护；9、农业；10、工业；11、建筑业；12、运输和邮电；13、国内贸易；14、对外经济贸易和旅游；15、金融和保险；16、教育和科技；17、文化、体育、卫生、社会福利和其他；18、企业调查；19.附录。

三、《西安统计年鉴—2004》继续采用中英文对照编排，版式和表式在此前基础上仍有所调整。年鉴数据以2003年为主，主要指标列示了建国以来重点年份和就近连续年份的统计资料。对个别年份的历史资料进行了修正。

四、本年鉴中符号使用说明："–"表示无经济活动；"…"表示数据不足本表最小单位数；"空格"表示该项统计指标数据不详；"#"表示其中的主要项。

《西安统计年鉴》从1993年由中国统计出版社正式出版以来的十二年间，一直得到了全市各部门和驻市各单位的热情支持，在此，谨向这些部门和单位表示衷心感谢。

PREFACE

Ⅰ.Compiled by Xi'an Municipal Statistic Bureau and published by State Statistics Press, Xi'an Statistical Yearbook 2004 is a large volume publication which provides comprehensive and systematic data covering national economy and social and technological development in Xi'an. Owing to its features of large information quantity, wide covering area and integrity of authority with practical applicability, it can be used not only to provide party and government leadership at different levels with decision basis, but to provide the public at large with economic information in time. Furthermore, it is an excellent publicity material to introduce Xi'an City and accelerate Xi'an to go into the world arena.

Ⅱ.The yearbook is comprised of 19 parts as follows,1.General Survey; 2.National EconomicAccounts; 3.Population, Employment and Wages; 4.Investment in Fixed Assets;5.Government Finance; 6.Price Indices; 7.People's Livelihood; 8.Urban Public Utilities and Environment Protection; 9.Agriculture; 10.Industry; 11.Construction; 12.Transportation,Post and Telecommunication Service 13.Domestic Trade; 14.Foreign Trade and Economic Cooperation, Tourism; 15.Banking and Insurance; 16.Education,Science and Technology; 17.Culture, Sports, Public Health , Social Welfare Institutions and Other social Activities; 18.Enterprises Investigation; 19.Appendix.

Ⅲ.As it is Chinese-English bilingual edition for the yearbook, the formal and list formation of the book has been adjusted . The content of this yearbook are comprised of mainly the statistic of 2003 and statistical data of the representative years after 1949 and previous successive years. Some corrections have been made to historic data in a few years.

Ⅳ.Explanations on symbols used in this yearbook:

'-' indicates no economic activity;

'…' indicates that the datum is not large enough to be rounded into the minimal unit;

Space indicates that the datum is unknown;

'#' indicates the major component item.

Here we would like to express our sincere thanks to the departments of municipal government and enterprises in Xi'an who have provided us with much enthusiastic support since the publication of Xi'an Statistical Yearbook by China statistics Press in 1993.

西安市生产总值

Gross Product of Xi'an City

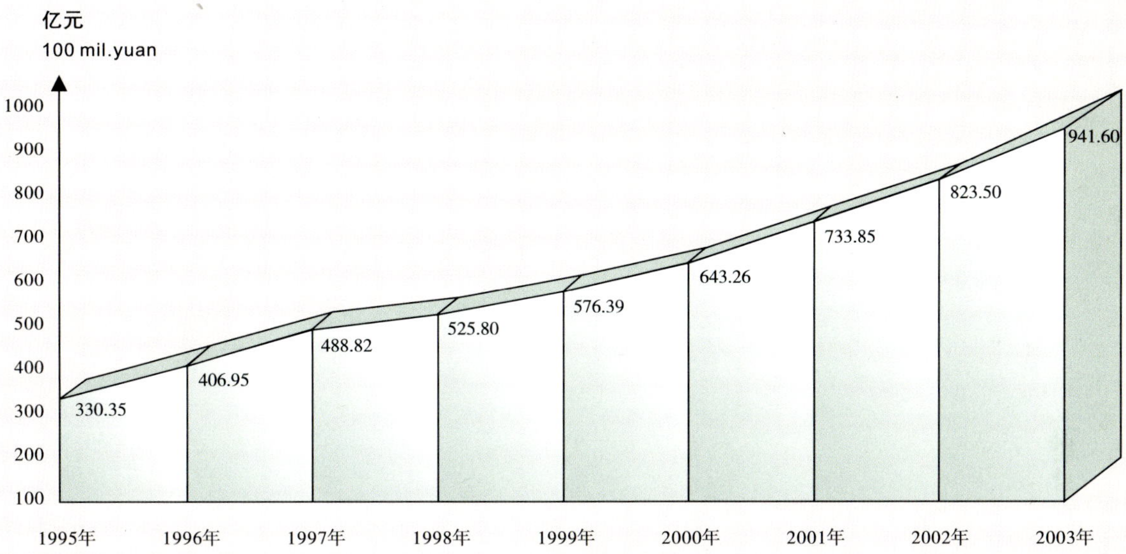

2003年GDP构成

Structure of Gross Domestic Product in 2003

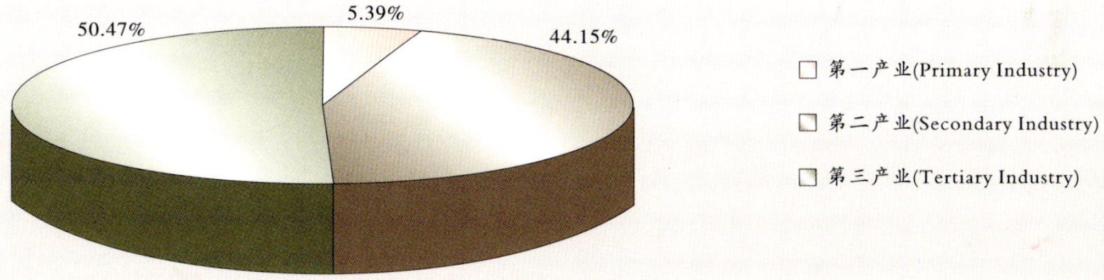

1995年GDP构成

Structure of Gross Domestic Product in 1995

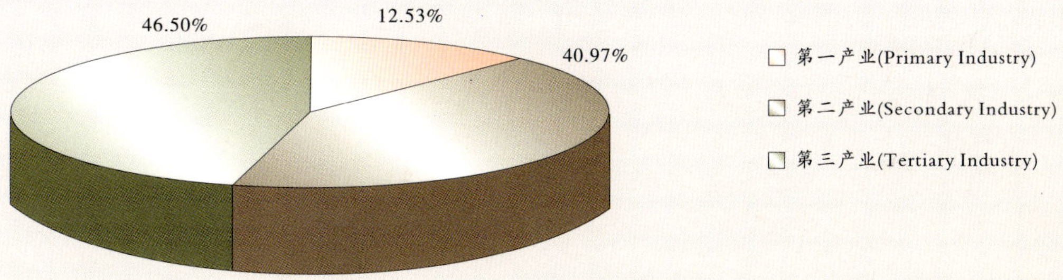

总人口
Total Population

万人
10 000 Persons

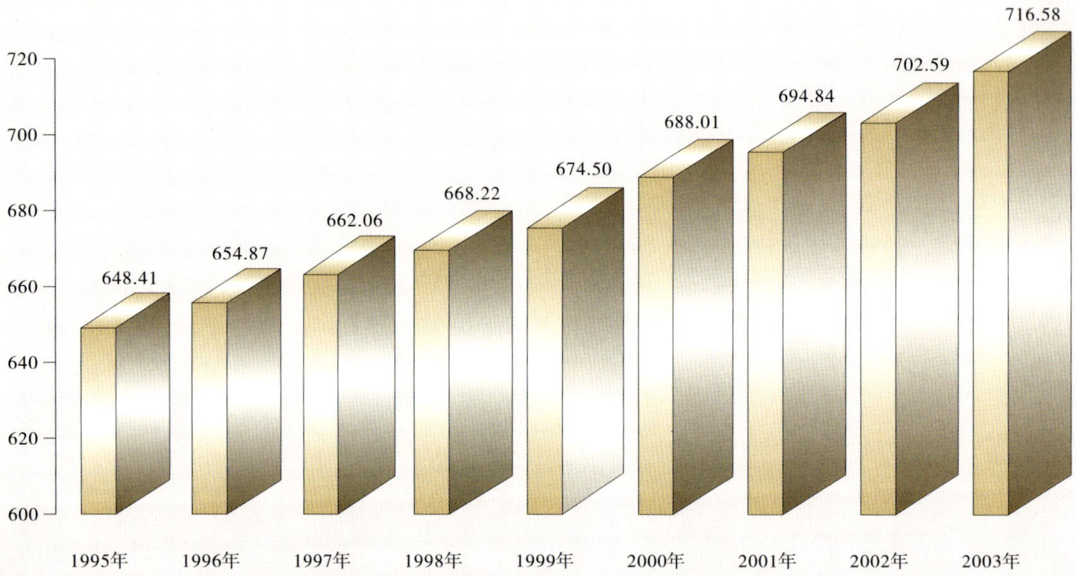

全部工业总产值
Gross Output Value of Whole Industry

亿元
100 mil. Yuan

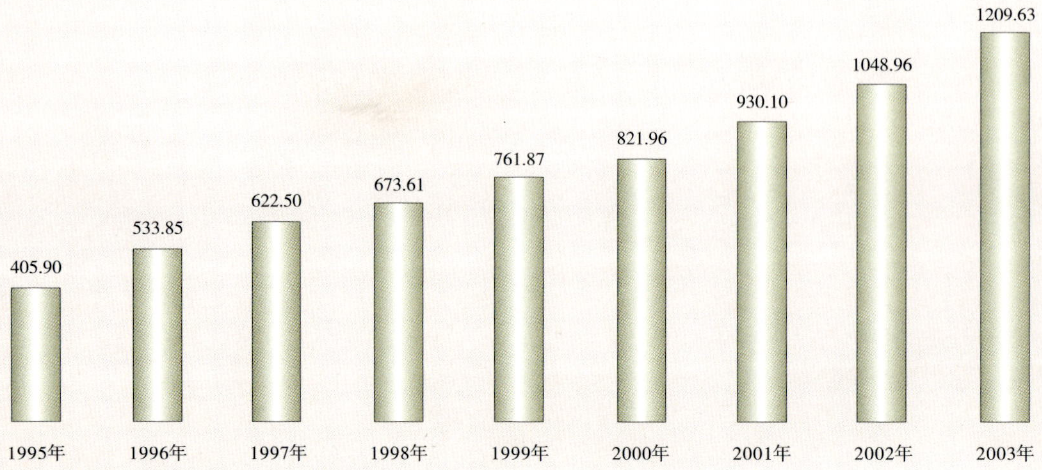

建筑业增加值
Value-added of Construction

亿元
100 mil. Yuan

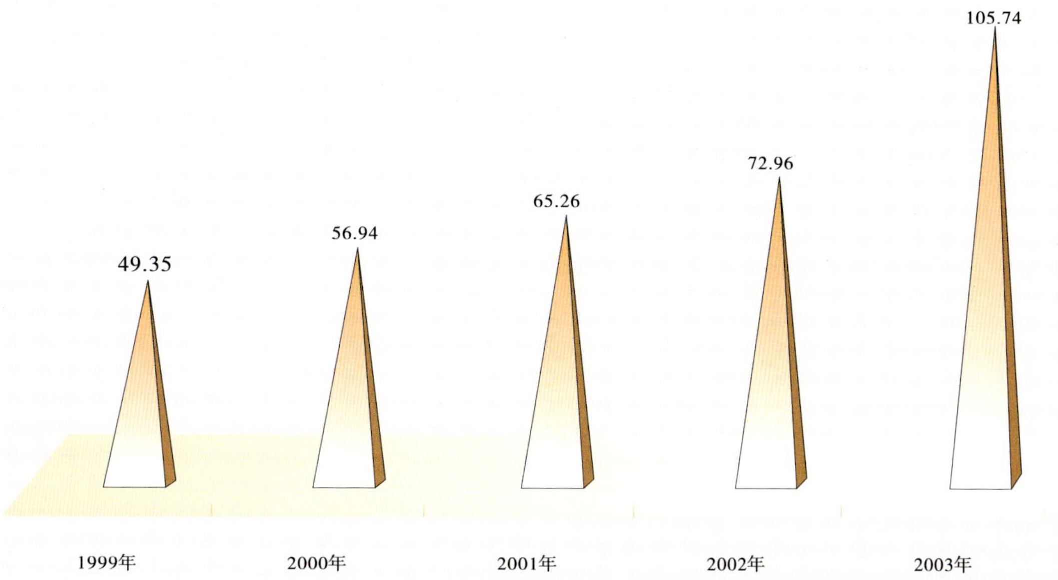

邮电业务总量
Business Volume of Post and Telecommunications

亿元
100 mil. Yuan

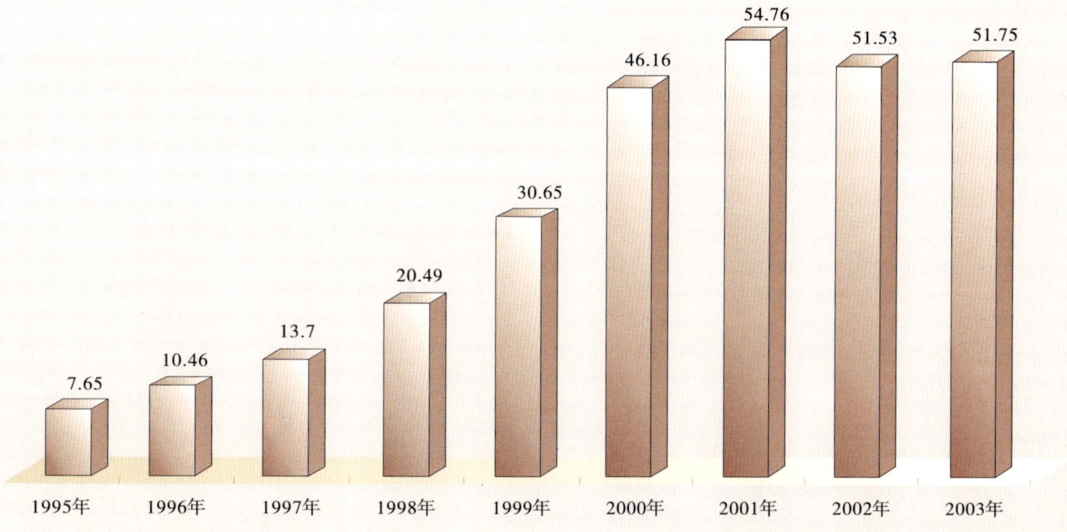

全社会固定资产投资
Investment Fulfilled In Fixed Assets

亿元
100 mil. Yuan

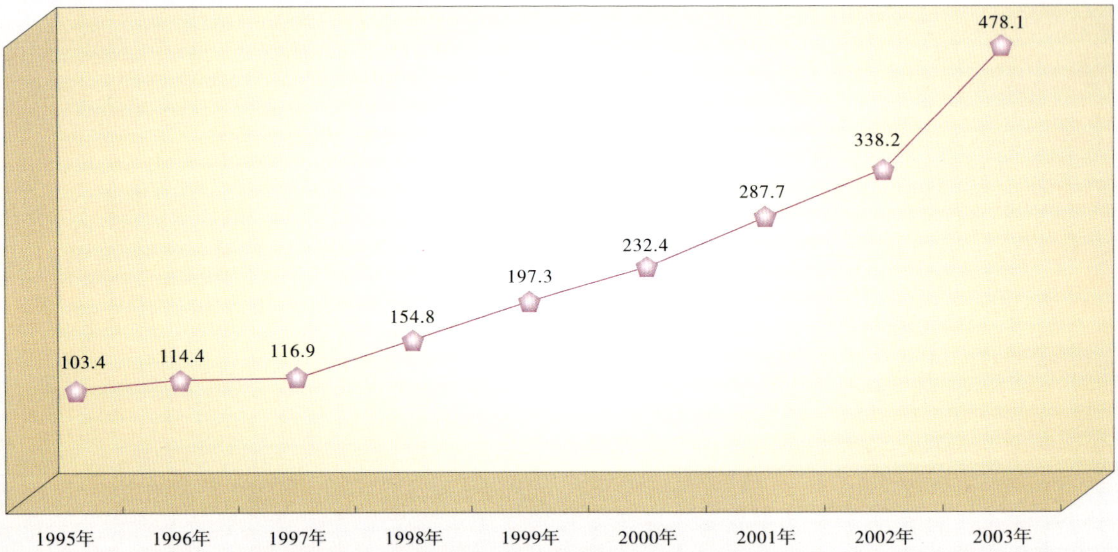

社会消费品零售总额
Total Retail Sales of Consumer Goods

亿元
100 mil. Yuan

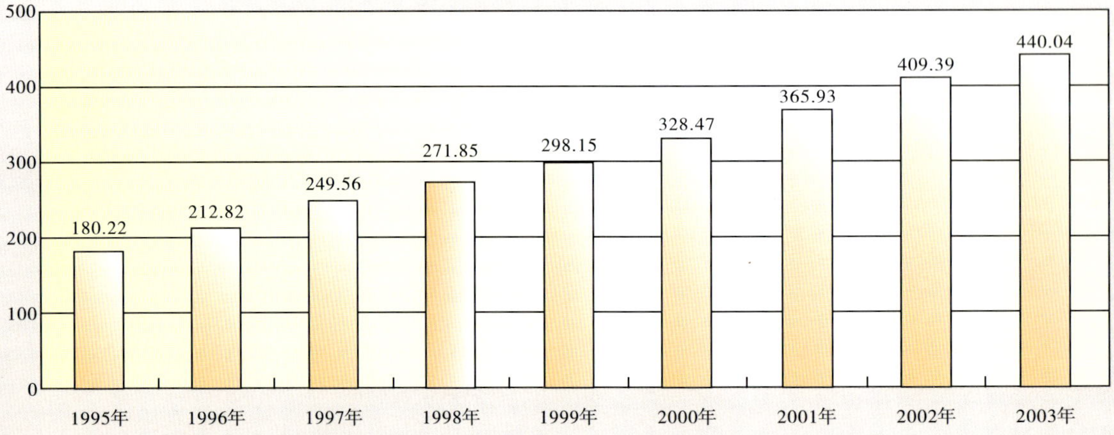

地方财政收入与地方财政支出
Local Government Revenue and Local Government Expenditures

亿元
100 mil. Yuan

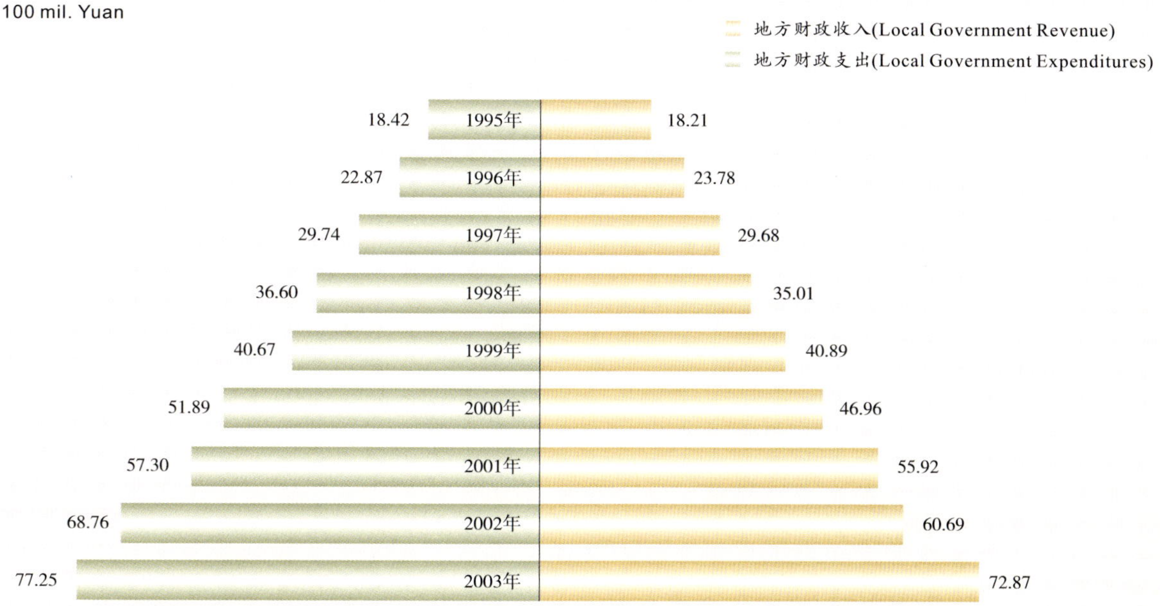

实际利用外商直接投资
Direct Foreign Investment Actually Used

万美元
USD 10 000

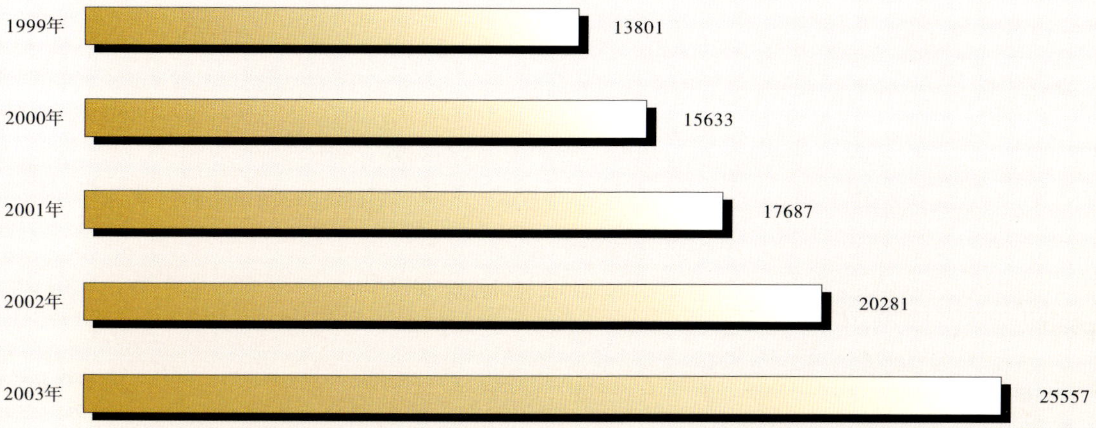

全市进出口总额
Total Imports and Exports

万美元
USD 10 000

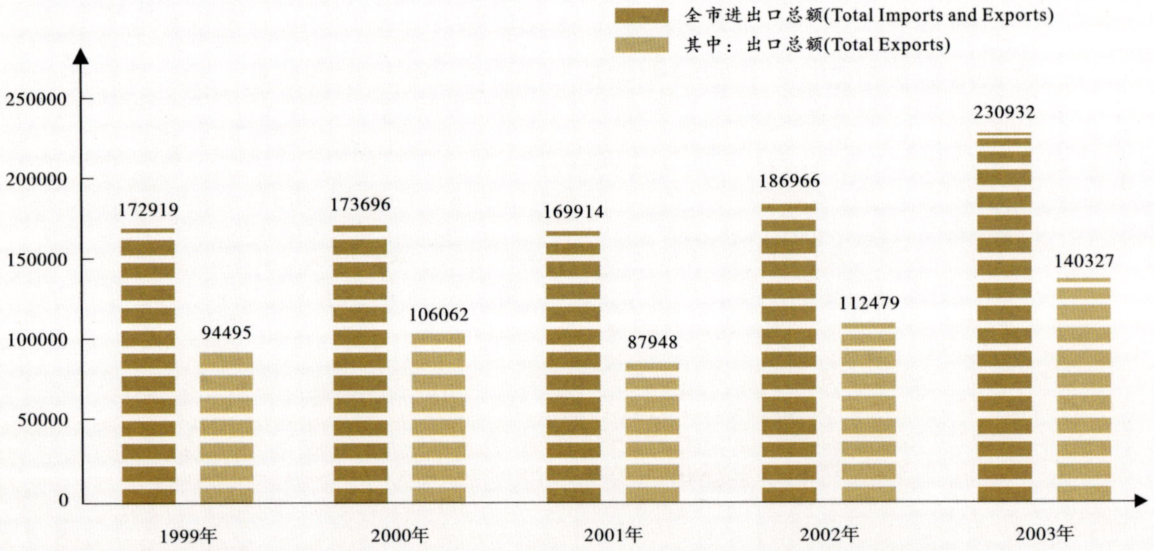

城乡居民储蓄存款年末余额
Total Urban and Rural Savings Deposits

亿元
100 mil. Yuan

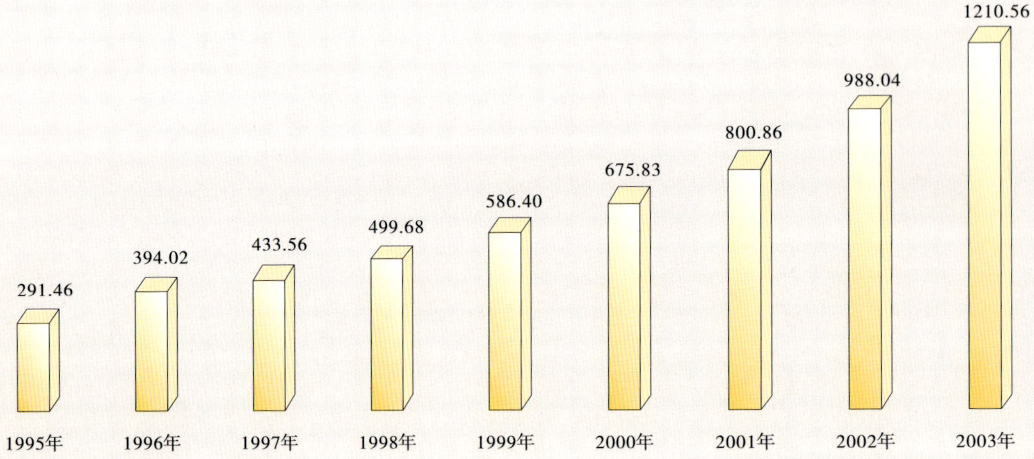

普通高等学校在校学生数
Student Enrollment in Regular Institutions of Higher Education

万人
10 000 Persons

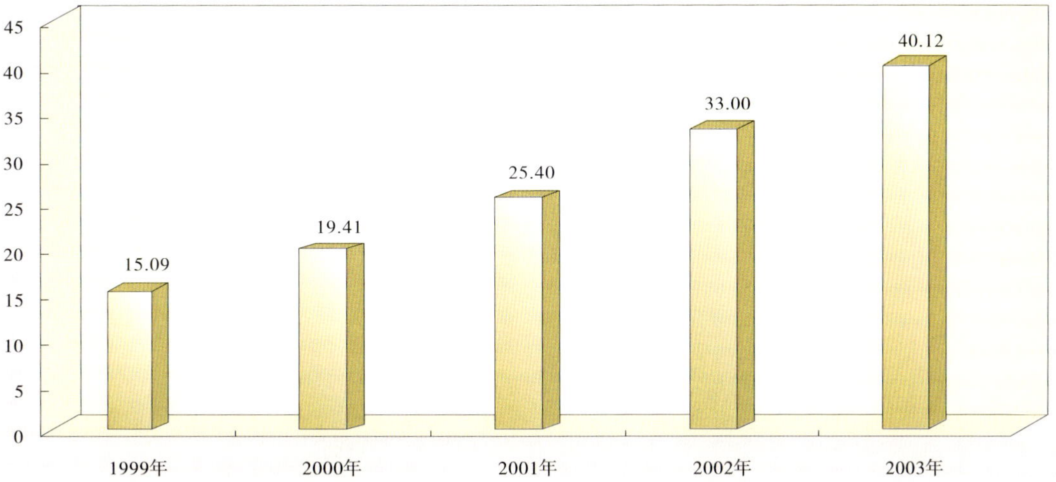

城乡居民收入
Income of Urban and Rural Residents

元
Yuan

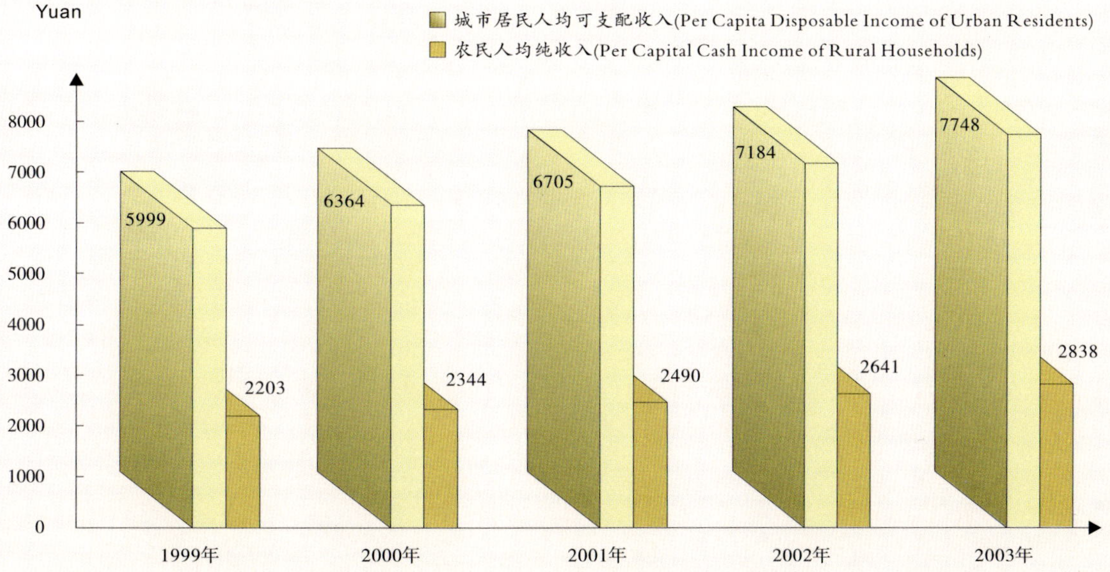

城市道路总长度

Total Length of Roads

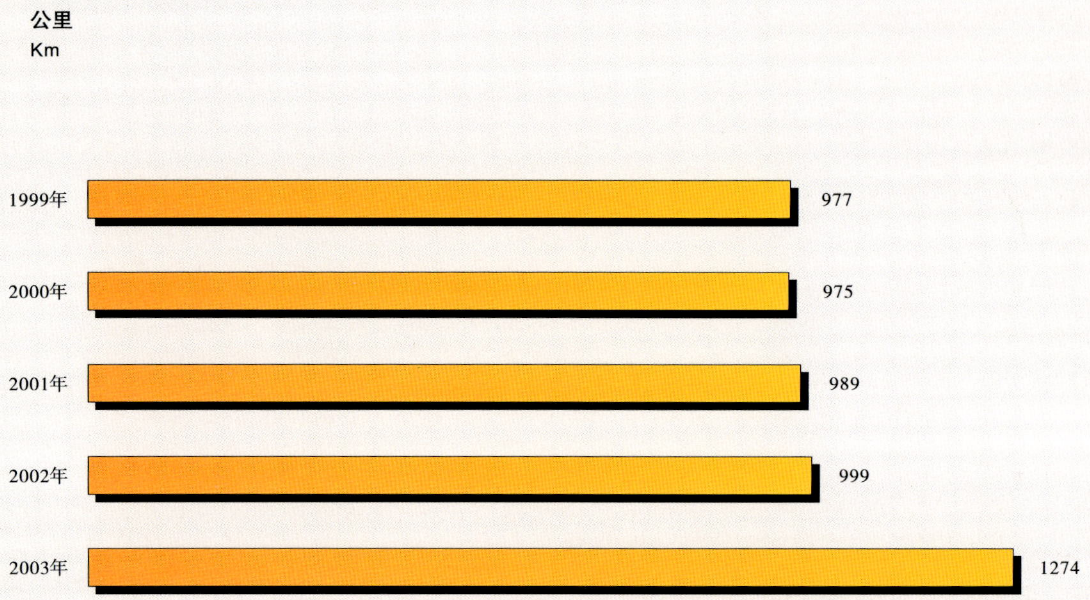

居民消费价格指数

General Consumer Price Index

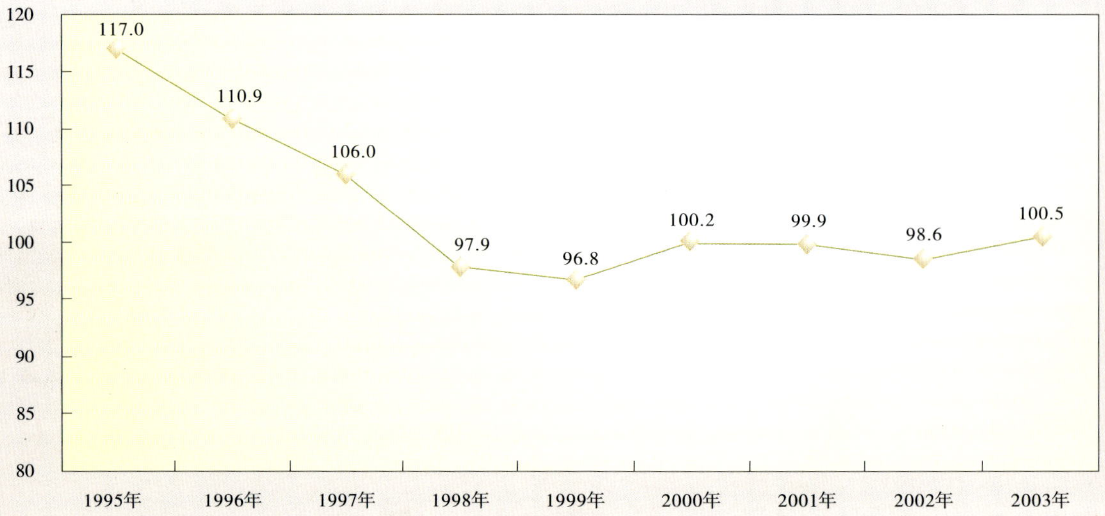

目　录

CONTENTS

西安市2003年国民经济和社会发展统计公报 …………………………………………………………………………（1）
Statistic Communiqu on the 2003 National Economy and Social Development of the City of Xi'an

一、综合

General Survey

1-1　行政区划（2003年）…………………………………………………………………………………（1）
Administrative Division (2003)
1-2　土地面积和人口密度（2003年）……………………………………………………………………（2）
Statistics on Land Area and Population Density (2003)
1-3　自然状况和资源（2003年）…………………………………………………………………………（3）
Nature Conditions and Resources（2003）
1-4　气 象 情 况(2003年)…………………………………………………………………………………（3）
Climate Condition (2003)
1-5　各部门机构数…………………………………………………………………………………………（4）
Grassroots Units in Various Sectors
1-6　平均每天主要社会经济活动…………………………………………………………………………（6）
Selected Indicators on Average Daily Social and Economic Activities
1-7　国民经济和社会发展总量与速度指标………………………………………………………………（8）
Principal Aggregate Indicators on National Economicand Social Development and Their Related Indices and Growth Rates
1-8　国民经济和社会发展结构指标………………………………………………………………………（18）
Structural Indicators on National Economic and Social Development
1-9　国民经济和社会发展比例和效益指标………………………………………………………………（22）
Indicators on Proportions and Efficiency in National Economic and Social Development
1-10　国有土地使用权出让、划拨情况 ……………………………………………………………………（28）
Basic Statistics on Lease and Administrative Allocation of Use Right of State-Owned Land
主要统计指标解释 ………………………………………………………………………………………（29）
Explanatory Notes on Main Statistical Indicators

二、国民经济核算

National Accounts

2-1　主要年份地区生产总值………………………………………………………………………………（37）
Gross Domestic Product In Representative Years
2-2　主要年份地区生产总值指数…………………………………………………………………………（38）
Indices of Gross Domestic Product in Representative Years

2-3 主要年份地区生产总值指数…………………………………………………………………………（39）
Indices of Gross Domestic Product in Representative Years
2-4 主要年份地区生产总值构成…………………………………………………………………………（40）
Composition of In Gross Domestic Product in Respective Years
2-5 总 产 出………………………………………………………………………………………………（41）
Total Output (Calculated at current prices)
2-6 市区四县地区生产总值（2003年）…………………………………………………………………（41）
Gross Domestic Product by Region(2003)
2-7 全市及市区分产业地区生产总值项目构成（2003 年）……………………………………………（41）
Structure of Gross Domestic Product of Whole City and its Urban Districts by Sector(2003)
2-8 分行业地区生产总值及指数…………………………………………………………………………（42）
Gross Domestic Product and Its Indices by Sector
2-9 分行业地区生产总值项目构成（2003年）…………………………………………………………（44）
Composition of Gross Domestic Product by Sector(2003)
2-10 按支出法计算的地区生产总值………………………………………………………………………（46）
Gross Domestic Product by Expenditure Approach
2-11 按行业划分的资本形成总额…………………………………………………………………………（46）
Gross Capital Formation by Sector
2-12 最 终 消 费…………………………………………………………………………………………（47）
Final Consumption Expenditures
2-13 居民总消费水平………………………………………………………………………………………（47）
Consumption of Residents
主要统计指标解释………………………………………………………………………………………（48）
Explanatory Notes on Main Statistical Indicators

三、人口、从业人员与职工工资

Population,Employment and Wages

3-1 主要年份人口、人口密度和人口发展情况……………………………………………………………（55）
Population, Population Density and Population Development in representative
3-2 主要年份人口变动情况…………………………………………………………………………………（56）
Population Changes in Representative Years
3-3 分区县人口和户数(2003年)…………………………………………………………………………（57）
Population and Households by Region(2003)
3-4 分区县人口变动情况(2003年)………………………………………………………………………（57）
Population Changes by Region(2003)
3-5 主要年份社会从业人数…………………………………………………………………………………（58）
Number of Social Laborers in Representative Years
3-6 分行业从业人数（2003年）…………………………………………………………………………（60）
Number Of Employed Persons By Sector(2003)
3-7 劳动力资源总数…………………………………………………………………………………………（62）
Total Number of Labor Resources

3-8 城乡劳动力资源配置情况(2003年)…………(63)
Deployment of Urban and Rural Labor Resources(2003)
3-9 全部单位从业人员情况（2003年）…………(64)
Basic Facts on All Employed Persons(2003)
3-10 国有单位从业人员情况（2003年）…………(66)
Basic Facts on Persons Employed by State-owned Units (2003)
3-11 城镇集体单位从业人员情况（2003年）…………(68)
Basic Facts on Persons Employed by Urban Collective-owned Units (2003)
3-12 其他经济类型单位从业人员情况（2003年）…………(70)
Basic Facts on Persons Employed by Other Units(2003)
3-13 各区县全部从业人员情况(2003年)…………(72)
Basic Facts on All Employed Persons by Region (2003)
3-14 各区县国有单位从业人员情况(2003年)…………(72)
Basic Facts on Persons Employed by State-owned Units By Region (2003)
3-15 各区县城镇集体单位从业人员情况(2003年)…………(74)
Basic Facts on Persons Employed by Collective-owned Units By Region (2003)
3-16 各区县其他经济类型单位从业人员情况(2003年)…………(74)
Basic Facts on Persons Employed by other Units By Region (2003)
3-17 全部单位从业人员劳动报酬（2003年）…………(76)
Remuneration of All Employed Persons(2003)
3-18 国有单位从业人员劳动报酬（2003年）…………(78)
Remuneration of Persons Employed by State-owned Units (2003)
3-19 城镇集体单位从业人员劳动报酬(2003年)…………(80)
Remuneration of Persons Employed by Urban Collective-owned Units in Towns and cities(2003)
3-20 其他经济类型单位从业人员劳动报酬(2003年)…………(82)
Remuneration of Persons Employed by other Units(2003)
3-21 各区县全部从业人员劳动报酬（2003年）…………(84)
Remuneration of All Employed Persons by Region (2003)
3-22 全部单位从业人员平均劳动报酬（2003年）…………(86)
Average Remuneration of Persons Employed by All Units(2003)
3-23 各区县在岗职工平均工资(2003年)…………(87)
Average Salary of Fully Employed Staff and Workers By Region(2003)
3-24 离开本单位仍保留劳动关系职工平均生活费（2003年）…………(88)
Average Living Allowance for Staff and workers off-post but Still Holding Labor Relations (2003)
主要统计指标解释…………(89)
Explanatory Notes on Main Statistical Indicators

四、固定资产投资

Investment in Fixed Assets

4-1 全社会固定资产投资…………(95)
Investment Fulfilled In Fixed Assets
4-2 全市固定资产投资(2003年)…………(96)
Total Investment In Fixed Assets(2003)

4-3 主要年份全市固定资产投资……………………………………………………………………………（100）
Total Investment in Fixed Assets in Representative Years
4-4 国有经济单位固定资产投资……………………………………………………………………………（101）
Investment in Fixed Assets of State-owned Unit
4-5 主要年份城镇集体经济单位固定资产投资…………………………………………………………（103）
Investment in Fixed Assets of Urban Collective Owned Units in Representative Years
4-6 主要年份农村集体固定资产投资……………………………………………………………………（104）
Investment in Fixed Assels of Rural Collective Owned Units in Representative Years
4-7 农村集体固定资产投资(2003年)………………………………………………………………………（106）
Investment in Fixed Assets of Rural Collective Owned Units（2003）
4-8 主要年份市属固定资产投资……………………………………………………………………………（107）
Investment In Fixed Assets of Municipal Units in Representative Years
4-9 市属固定资产投资(2003年)……………………………………………………………………………（108）
Investment in Fixed Assets of Municipal Units（2003）
4-10 市区固定资产投资额(2003年)…………………………………………………………………………（112）
Investments in Fixed Assets of Urban Districts(2003)
4-11 全市固定资产投资效果(2003年)………………………………………………………………………（114）
Achievements of Total Assets Investment of Whole City(2003)
4-12 市属固定资产投资效果(2003年)………………………………………………………………………（114）
Achievement of Fixed Assets Investment of Municipal Units(2003)
4-13 全市固定资产投资资金来源(2003年)…………………………………………………………………（116）
Source of Funds for Total Fixed Assets Investment of Whole City(2003)
4-14 市属固定资产投资资金来源（2003年）………………………………………………………………（116）
Source of Funds for Fixed Estate of Municipal Units(2003)
4-15 四县固定资产投资额(2003年)…………………………………………………………………………（118）
Investments on Fixed Assets of Counties(2003)
4-16 新增生产能力或效益(2003年)…………………………………………………………………………（120）
Newly Increased Production Capacity or Benefit(2003)
4-17 全市按行业分房屋建筑面积(2003年)…………………………………………………………………（124）
Floor Space of Buildings Construction by Sector(2003)
4-18 市属按行业分房屋建筑面积(2003年)…………………………………………………………………（126）
Floors Space of Buildings Construction of Municipal Units by Sector(2003)
4-19 主要年份全市新增固定资产及房屋竣工面积…………………………………………………………（128）
Value of Newly Added Fixed Assets and Floor Spaces Completed of Whole City in Representative Years
4-20 主要年份市属新增固定资产及房屋竣工面积…………………………………………………………（129）
Value of Newly Added Fixed Assets and Floor Spaces Completed of Municipal Units In Representive Years
4-21 全市按行业分施工项目(2003年)………………………………………………………………………（130）
Construction Projects of Whole City by Sector(2003)
4-22 市属按行业分施工项目(2003年)………………………………………………………………………（132）
Construction Projects of Municipal units by Sector(2003)

4-23　城镇和工矿区私人建房……………………………………………………………………（134）
Private Housing in Urban Factory and Mining Zones
4-24　农村私人建房……………………………………………………………………………（136）
Private Buildings Completed in Rural Area
4-25　房地产开发投资主要指标(2003年)……………………………………………………（137）
Main Indicators of Investment in Real Estate Development（2003）
4-26　商品房销售情况(2003年)…………………………………………………………………（138）
Sales of Commercial Houses(2003)
4-27　房地产开发投资资金来源(2003年)……………………………………………………（139）
Source of Funds for Investment in Real Estate Development（2003）
4-28　房地产开发经营情况(2003年)…………………………………………………………（139）
Running of Real Estate Development（2003）
4-29　主要年份房地产开发投资主要指标……………………………………………………（140）
Main Indicators of Investment in Real Estate Development in Representative Years
主要统计指标解释……………………………………………………………………………（142）
Explanatory Notes on Main Statistical Indicators

五、财政

Government Finance

5-1　地方财政收入……………………………………………………………………………（146）
Local Government Revenue
5-2　地方财政支出……………………………………………………………………………（147）
Local Government Expenditures
5-3　分区县地方财政收入(2003年)……………………………………………………………（148）
Financial Revenue of Local Government by Region（2003）
5-4　分区县地方财政支出(2003年)……………………………………………………………（150）
Financial Expenditures of Local Government by Region（2003）
主要统计指标解释……………………………………………………………………………（152）
Explanatory Notes on Main Statistical Indicators

六、物价指数

Price Indices

6-1　各种价格指数(以上年价格为100)………………………………………………………（159）
Price Indices(the price of preceding year=100)
6-2　居民消费价格指数(2003年)………………………………………………………………（160）
Residents Consumer Price Indices(2003)
6-3　商品零售价格指数(2003年)………………………………………………………………（162）
Retail Price Indices(2003)
6-4　工业产品出厂价格指数……………………………………………………………………（164）
Ex-factory Price Indices of Industrial Products
6-5　主要原材料、燃料、动力购进价格指数…………………………………………………（166）
Purchase Price Indices of Major Raw Materials,Fuels and Power

6-6 土地交易价格指数……(167)
Transactions Price Indices of Land
6-7 房屋销售价格指数……(167)
Selling Price Indices of Real Houses
6-8 房屋租赁价格指数……(168)
Renting Price Indices of Real Houses
6-9 固定资产投资价格指数……(168)
Price Indices of Fixed Assets Investment
6-10 建筑安装工程价格指数……(168)
Price Indecies of Construction and Installation Projects
主要统计指标解释……(169)
Explanatory Notes on Main Statistical Indicators

七、人民生活

People's Livelihood

7-1 城市居民家庭基本情况……(172)
Basic Conditions of Urban Households
7-2 城市居民不同收入层次家庭基本情况表(2003年)……(174)
Basic Conditions of Urban Households by Level of Income（2003）
7-3 城市居民不同收入层次每百户耐用消费品拥有量(2003年)……(176)
Basic Conditions of Urban Households by Level of Income（2003）
7-4 城市居民不同收入层次家庭年人均收入情况(2003年)……(178)
Statistics on per Capital Annual Income in Urban Residents by Level of Income（2003）
7-5 城市居民不同收入层次家庭年人均支出情况(2003年)……(180)
Statistics on Per Capital Annual Living Expenditure of Urban Households By Level of Income（2003）
7-6 城市居民不同收入层次家庭年人均消费性支出情况（2003年）……(182)
Statistics on Per Capita Annual Living Expenditure of Residents by Level of Income（2003）
7-7 城市居民家庭年人均购买主要商品数量……(186)
Per Capita Annual Purchases of Principal Goods in Urban Household
7-8 城市居民家庭平均每百户年末拥有主要耐用消费品数量……(187)
Number of Durable Consumer Goods Owned Every 100 Urban Households
7-9 城市居民家庭居住情况……(188)
Conditions of Dwellings of Rural Households
7-10 主要年份农民家庭基本情况……(190)
Bisic Indicators of Rural Households In Representative Years
7-11 农村居民家庭基本情况（2003年）……(192)
Basic Conditions of Rural Households（2003）
7-12 农村居民家庭平均每人总收入和纯收入（2003年）……(194)
Per Capita Annual Total Revenue and Net Income of Rural Households（2003）
7-13 农村居民家庭平均每人全年总支出（2003年）……(194)
Per Capita Annual Total Expenditure of Rural Households（2003）

7-14 农村居民家庭平均每人生活消费支出（2003年）……………………………………………………………（196）
Per Capita Living Expenditure of Rural Households（2003）
7-15 农村居民家庭人均生产情况（2003年）……………………………………………………………………（196）
Output of Major Farm Corps Per Capita by Rural Households（2003）
7-16 农村居民家庭人均出售产品情况（2003年）………………………………………………………………（198）
Per Capita Product Sold by Rural Households（2003）
7-17 农村居民家庭人均粮食收支情况（2003年）………………………………………………………………（198）
Per Capita Annual Income and Expenditure of Grains of Rural Households（2003）
7-18 农村居民家庭平均每人购买消费品（2003年）……………………………………………………………（200）
Per Capita Purichase of Commodities in Rural Households（2003）
7-19 农村居民家庭人均主要食品消费量（2003年）……………………………………………………………（200）
Per Capita Average Food Consumption of Rural Households（2003）
7-20 农村居民家庭每百户耐用消费品年末拥有量（2003年）…………………………………………………（202）
Year-end Possession of Durable Consumer Goods Per 100 Rural Households（2003）
7-21 农村居民家庭人均住房情况（2003年）……………………………………………………………………（202）
Per Capita Housing Conditions of Rural Households（2003）
主要统计指标解释……………………………………………………………………………………………………（204）
Explanatory Notes on Main Statistical Indicators

八、城市公用事业及环境保护

Urban Public Utilities and Environment Protection

8-1 城市供水……（209）
Urban Water Supply
8-2 城市售电……（209）
Urban Consumption of Elecricity
8-3 燃气……（210）
Gas Supply
8-4 城市公共交通……………………………………………………………………………………………………（210）
Urban Public Traffic
8-5 市政设施……（211）
Manicipal Facilities
8-6 城市设施水平……………………………………………………………………………………………………（211）
Urban Manucipal Facilites
8-7 城市设施水平……………………………………………………………………………………………………（212）
Urban Manucipal Facilites
8-8 城市规模及用地情况……………………………………………………………………………………………（212）
City Scale and Land Use
8-9 城市园林绿化……………………………………………………………………………………………………（213）
Urban Park,Gardens and Green Areas in Cities
8-10 城市环境卫生……………………………………………………………………………………………………（213）
Urban Environment Sanitation

8-11 城市环境保护………（214）
Urban Environmental Protection
8-12 城 市 供 热………（214）
Heating in Urban Area
主要统计指标解释……………………………………………………………………………………………………（215）
Explanatory Notes on Main Statistical Indicators

九、农业

Agriculture

9-1 主要年份乡村户数、人口和劳动力………………………………………………………………………………（221）
Rural Household, Population and Labour in Representative Year
9-2 农村基层组织、乡村户数、人口及劳动力情况…………………………………………………………………（221）
Grass-root Organizations, Households, Population and Labor Resources in Rural Area
9-3 各区县农村基层组织、乡村户数及人口（2003年）……………………………………………………………（222）
Grass-root Organizations, Households and Population in Rural Area by Region(2003)
9-4 各区县家庭从业人员数(2003年)…………………………………………………………………………………（222）
Number of Labers in Families by Region（2003）
9-5 主要年份耕地面积………………………………………………………………………………………………（223）
Area of Cultivated Land in Representative Year
9-6 各区县耕地面积(2003年)…………………………………………………………………………………………（224）
Area of Cultivated Land by Region（2003）
9-7 农村非农行业总产值……………………………………………………………………………………………（226）
Gross Output Value of Non-agricultural Trades in Rural Areas
9-8 各区县农村非农行业总产值(2003年)……………………………………………………………………………（227）
Gross Output Value of Non-agricultural Trades in Rural Areas by Region（2003）
9-9 主要年份农林牧渔业总产值及指数………………………………………………………………………………（228）
Gross Output Value of Farming,Forestry,Animal Husbandry and Fishery and Related Indices in Representative Years
9-10 各区县不变价农林牧渔业总产值(2003年)………………………………………………………………………（229）
Gross Output Value of Farming, Forestry, Animal Husbandry and Fishery at Constant Price By Region（2003）
9-11 各区县现价农林牧渔业总产值和构成(2003年)…………………………………………………………………（230）
Gross Output Value and Its Composition of Farming, Forestry, Animal Husbandry and Fishery at Current Price by Region(2003)
9-12 各区县农业物耗占总产值的比重(2003年)………………………………………………………………………（231）
Proportion of Agriculture Material Consumption to Total Output Value（2003）
9-13 农林牧渔业增加值………………………………………………………………………………………………（231）
Value Added of Farming，Forestry，Animal Husbandry and Fishery
9-14 各区县农林牧渔业增加值(2003年)………………………………………………………………………………（232）
Addition Value of Farming, Forestry, Animal Husbandry and Fishing by Region（2003）
9-15 农业机械拥有量…………………………………………………………………………………………………（232）
Possession of Agricultural Machinery

9-16 农业机械、化肥、水利、水电情况……………………………………………………………（233）
Agricultural Machinery,Chemical Fertilizers,Water Conservancy,Hydropower
9-17 主要年份农作物播种面积……………………………………………………………………（234）
Sown Areas of Farm Crops In Representative Years
9-18 各区县主要农作物播种面积(2003年)……………………………………………………………（234）
Sown Areas of Major Farm Crops by Region（2003）
9-19 主要年份农作物产品产量……………………………………………………………………（235）
Yeild of Farm Crops In Representative Years
9-20 各区县主要农作物产品产量（2003年）……………………………………………………（236）
Yeild of Major Farm Crops by Region（2003）
9-21 各区县主要农作物单位面积产量（2003年）…………………………………………………（236）
The Output of Main Crops per Hectare by Region(2003)
9-22 农作物单位面积产量…………………………………………………………………………（238）
Yield of Farm Crops Per Hectare
9-23 林业生产情况…………………………………………………………………………………（238）
Statistcs on Forestry
9-24 各区县林业生产情况（2003年）……………………………………………………………（239）
Statistics On Forestry by Region（2003）
9-25 桑、茶、果生产情况…………………………………………………………………………（239）
Statistics on Mulberry,Tea,Fruits
9-26 各区县桑、果园面积及产量(2003年)……………………………………………………………（240）
Area and Output of Mulberry Yards and Orchards by Region（2003）
9-27 畜牧业生产情况………………………………………………………………………………（240）
Statistics on Livestock Husbandry
9-28 各区县畜牧业生产情况(2003年)…………………………………………………………………（241）
Statistics On Livestock,Animal Husbandry by Region（2003）
9-29 畜产品和水产品产量…………………………………………………………………………（242）
Output of Livestock Products and Aquatic Products
9-30 各区县主要畜产品和水产品产量(2003年)………………………………………………………（242）
Output of Major Livestock Products and Aquatic Products by Region（2003）
9-31 农村经济效益主要指标………………………………………………………………………（244）
Main Index of Rural Economic Benefit
主要统计指标解释………………………………………………………………………………（245）
Explanatory Notes on Main Statistical Indicators

十、工业

Industry

10-1 全市工业总产值(2003年)…………………………………………………………………………（251）
Gross Industrial Output Value Of whole City (2003)
10-2 主要年份全部工业总产值……………………………………………………………………（252）
Gross Output Value of Industry In Representative Years
10-3 规模以上工业企业单位数(按隶属关系分,2003年)………………………………………………（254）
Number of Industrial Enterprises Above Designated Size (Grouped by Ownership,2003)

10-4 规模以上工业企业单位数(2003年)……………………………………………………………………(256)
Number of Industrial Enterprises Above Designated Size (2003)
10-5 市区规模以上工业企业单位数(2003年)………………………………………………………………(258)
Number of Industrial Enterprises Above Designated Size in Urban Districts(2003)
10-6 全部规模以上工业企业职工人数……………………………………………………………………(260)
Number of Staff and Workers of All Indastrial Enterprises Above Designated Size
10-7 全部规模以上工业企业年末职工人数（2003年）……………………………………………………(262)
Number of Staff and Workers at the Year End in All Industrial Enterprises Above Designated Size（2003）
10-8 各区县规模以上工业企业年末职工人数(按登记类型分,2003年)……………………………………(263)
Number of Staff and Workers in All Industrial Enterprise Above Designated Size By Region at the Year End（Grouped by Registion Status）(2003)
10-9 全市规模以上工业总产值（2003年）…………………………………………………………………(266)
Gross Industrial Output Value Of All Enterprises Above Designated Size Whole City (2003)
10-10 全市规模以上工业总产值（2003年）………………………………………………………………(268)
Gorss Industrial Output Value Of All Enterprises Above Designated Size Whole City (2003)
10-11 市属规模以上工业总产值（2003年）………………………………………………………………(270)
Total Gross Output of All Municipal Enterprises Above Designated Size（2003）
10-12 分区县规模以上工业总产值(2003年)………………………………………………………………(272)
Gross Output Value of Industry Industrial Enterprises Above Designated Size by Region (2003)
10-13 规模以上工业企业 主要产品产量……………………………………………………………………(273)
Output of Major Industrial Products Of Enterprises Above Designated size
10-14 全部规模以上工业企业主要经济指标（2003年）……………………………………………………(278)
Main Economic Indicators of All Industrial Enterprises Above Designafed size(2003)
10-15 全部规模以上国有工业企业主要经济指标（2003年）………………………………………………(294)
Economic Indicators of All State-owned Industrial Enterprises Above the Designated Size
10-16 全部规模以上集体工业企业主要经济指标（2003年）………………………………………………(310)
Economic Indicators of All Collective-owned Industrial Enterprises Above Designated Size（2003）
10-17 全部规模以上三资工业企业经济指标(2003年)………………………………………………………(326)
Economic Indicators of Foreign Fund Industrial Enterprises Above Designated Size (2003)
10-18 全部规模以上国有控股工业企业主要经济指标(2003年)……………………………………………(342)
Main Indicators of State-holding Share Industrial Enterprises Above Designated Size (2003)
10-19 全部规模以上股份制工业企业主要 经济指标（2003年）……………………………………………(354)
Main Indicators of Share-holding Corporation Industrial Enterprises Above Designated Size (2003)
10-20 分区县全部规模以上工业企业经济指标(2003年)……………………………………………………(370)
Economic Indicators of Industrial Enterprises Above Designated Size by Region（2003）
10-21 规模以上工业企业主要经济效益指标 (2003年)………………………………………………………(376)
Main Indicators On Economic Beneficial Results of Industrial Enterprises Above Designated Size（2003）
10-22 工业企业能源购进、消费及库存(2003年)……………………………………………………………(380)
Energy Purchases Consumption and Inventory of Industrial Enterprises（2003）

10-23 主要能源按工业行业分组消费量(2003年)……（382）
Majar Energy Consumption by Sector(2003)
10-24 西安名牌产品一览表（2003年）……（384）
A Survey of Products of famous Brand Made in Xi'an(2003)
主要统计指标解释……（387）
Explanatory Notes on Main Statistical Indicators

十一、建筑业

Construction

11-1 全市建筑施工企业基本情况……（397）
Main Indicators on Construction Enterprise of Xi'an
11-2 全市建筑施工企业生产情况（2003年，按经济类型分）……（398）
Main Indicators on Construction Enterprise of Xi'an Grouped by Registion Status（2003）
11-3 全市建筑施工企业生产情况（2003年，按行业类别分）……（400）
Main Indicators on Construction Enterprise of Xi'an Grouped by Sector（2003）
11-4 全市建筑施工企业财务状况（2003年）……（402）
Financial Status of Building Construction Enterprises In Xi'an(2003)
11-5 施工总承包二级以上建筑企业一览表（2003年）……（404）
List of Construction Enterprises of First Class and Second Class（2003）
主要统计指标解释……（408）
Explanatory Notes on Main Statistical Indicators

十二、运输和邮电

Transportation,Post and Telecommunication Services

12-1 各种交通线路里程和桥梁数……（413）
Length of Transportation Routes and Number of Bridges
12-2 全社会车辆数……（414）
Civil Motor Vehicles
12-3 交通运输量及运输周转量……（415）
Passenger Traffic and Kilometers and Freight Traffic and Ton-kilometers
12-4 邮政业务及服务网点……（416）
Posts Service and Branch Post Office
12-5 电信业务情况……（416）
Telecommunication service
主要统计指标解释……（417）
Explanatory Notes on Main Statistical Indicators

十三、国内贸易

Domestic Trade

13-1 主要年份社会消费品零售总额……（423）
Total Retail Sales of Consumer Goods in Representative years

13-2 全市批发零售贸易业基本情况…………………………………………………………………………（424）
Basic Conditions in Wholesale and Retail Trades
13-3 限额以上批发零售贸易业商品购进、销售、库存总额（2003年）……………………………（426）
Total Purchases,Sales and Inventory of Enterprises above Designated Size in Wholesale and Retail Trades(2003)
13-4 限额以上批发零售贸易业商品分类销售额(2003年)…………………………………………（432）
Total Sales of Enterprises Above Designated Size in Wholesale and Retail Trades Grouped by Category of Commodities(2003)
13-5 限额以上批发零售贸易商品销售(2003年)……………………………………………………（433）
Total Sales of Enterprises Above Designated Size in Wholesale and Retail Trades(2003)
13-6 社会消费品零售总额(2003年)…………………………………………………………………（435）
Total Retail Sales of Consumer Goods(2003)
13-7 批发贸易业机构、网点、人员(2003年)………………………………………………………（436）
Organizations, Establishments and Persons Engaged in Whole-sale Trade(2003)
13-8 零售贸易业机构、网点、人员 (2003年)………………………………………………………（438）
Organizations, Establishments and Persons Engaged in Retail Trade(2003)
13-9 餐饮业机构、网点、人员(2003年)……………………………………………………………（440）
Organizations Staff and Branch Shopes of Catering Trade(2003)
13-10 限额以上批发零售贸易企业财务状况 (2003年)………………………………………………（442）
Financial Status of Enterprises Above Designated Size in Wholesale and Retail(2003)
13-11 限额以上餐饮企业财务状况(2003年)…………………………………………………………（454）
Finacial Status of Catering Enterprises Above Designated Size(2003)
13-12 商品交易市场成交量………………………………………………………………………………（458）
Transactions Volume in Commodities Markets
13-13 商品交易市场成交额………………………………………………………………………………（459）
Transactions Value in Commodities Markets
13-14 消费品批发市场情况………………………………………………………………………………（460）
Statistics on Consumer Goods Wholesale Markets
13-15 商品交易市场分类情况……………………………………………………………………………（461）
Statistics on Classification on Commodities Markets
主要统计指标解释……………………………………………………………………………………（462）
Explanatory Notes on Main Statistical Indicators

十四、对外经济贸易和旅游

Foreign Trade and Economic Cooperation,Tourism

14-1 外资、外贸和国际旅游基本情况…………………………………………………………………（466）
Main Indicators on Foreign Investments、International Trading and International Tourism
14-2 外国和港澳台地区在西安直接投资………………………………………………………………（467）
Direct Investments from Foreign Countries and Hong Kong, Macao and Taiwan in Xi'an
14-3 主要商品分大类出口金额…………………………………………………………………………（468）
Export Value of Major Merchandise by Type

14-4 主要商品分大类进口金额……………………………………………………………………（470）
Import Value of Major Merchandise by Type
14-5 外贸商品进出口总额分国别和地区(2003年)………………………………………………（471）
Total Value of Imports and Exports by Country and Region(2003)
14-6 接待国际旅游者人数…………………………………………………………………………（472）
Overseas Tourists Received
14-7 国际旅游收入…………………………………………………………………………………（473）
Earning of International Tourism
14-8 主要涉外星级宾馆接待海外旅游者情况……………………………………………………（474）
Mainly Concerning Oversea Tourists Reception in Star Hotels
主要统计指标解释……………………………………………………………………………（475）
Explanatory Notes on Main Statistical Indicators

十五、金融和保险

Banking and Insurance

15-1 金融机构本外币存款年末余额…………………………………………………………………（481）
Financial institution balance of bisic currency and foreign currency at the end of the year
15-2 金融机构本外币贷款年末余额…………………………………………………………………（481）
Financial institution loan balance of bisic currency and foreign currency at the end of the year
15- 3 金融机构存款年末余额………………………………………………………………………（482）
Year-end Balance of Deposit in Financial Institutions
15- 4 金融机构贷款年末余额………………………………………………………………………（482）
Year-end Balance of Loans in Financial Institutions
15- 5 金融机构现金收入……………………………………………………………………………（483）
Cash Income of Financial Institutions
15- 6 金融机构现金支出……………………………………………………………………………（483）
Cash Expenditure of Financial Institutions
15- 7 保险业务情况…………………………………………………………………………………（484）
Indicators of Insurance Business
15- 8 西安证券期货市场基本情况…………………………………………………………………（485）
Basic Facts on Securities and Futures Markets in Xi'an
15- 9 西安市企业股票股本构成情况………………………………………………………………（485）
Constituent of Subscribed Capital for Xi'an Enterprises
15- 10 西安市股票发行情况一览……………………………………………………………………（486）
List of Security Issued By Xi'an Enterprises
主要统计指标解释……………………………………………………………………………（487）
Explanatory Notes on Main Statistical Indicators

十六、教育和科技

Education,Science and Technology

16-1 主要年份各类普通教育基本情况………………………………………………………………（491）
Basic Statistics on Regular Eduction In Representative Years

16-2 各级普通教育基本情况(2003年)……………………………………………………………………………（492）
Basic Facts on Regular Education by School Type（2003）
16-3 普通高等教育基本情况……………………………………………………………………………………（493）
Basic Statistics on Regular Institutions of Higher Education
16-4 普通高等学校和科研机构研究生…………………………………………………………………………（493）
Post-graduates in Regular Institutions of Higher Education and Scientific Researeh
16-5 普通高等学校分学校研究生(2003年)……………………………………………………………………（494）
Post-graduates in Regular Institutions of Higher Education(2003)
16-6 全市普通高等学校分学校情况(2003年)…………………………………………………………………（495）
Basic Facts on Regular Higher Education by Unit(2003)
16-7 普通中等专业学校基本情况………………………………………………………………………………（497）
Basic Statistics on Specialized Secondary Schools
16-8 中等技术学校分学校基本情况(2003年)…………………………………………………………………（498）
Situation of every secondary technical school (2003)
16-9 普通中学基本情况…………………………………………………………………………………………（499）
Baisc Statistics on Regular Secondary Schools
16-10 各区县普通中学(2003年)………………………………………………………………………………（499）
Regular Secondary Schools by Region (2003)
16-11 职业中学基本情况………………………………………………………………………………………（500）
Basic Statistics on Vocational Secondary Schools
16-12 各区县职业中学(2003年)………………………………………………………………………………（500）
Vocational Secondary Schools by Region (2003)
16-13 小学基本情况……………………………………………………………………………………………（501）
Basic Statistics on Primary Schools
16-14 各区县小学基本情况(2003年)…………………………………………………………………………（501）
Primary Schools by Region (2003)
16-15 幼儿园基本情况…………………………………………………………………………………………（502）
Basic Statistics on Kindergartens
16-16 特殊教育学校基本情况…………………………………………………………………………………（502）
Basic Statistics on Special Education Schools
16-17 小学、初中升学率………………………………………………………………………………………（503）
Rate of Graduates from Junior Schools and Primary Schools Entering Higher Level Schools
16-18 小学学龄儿童入学率……………………………………………………………………………………（504）
Percentage of School-Age Children Enrolled
16-19 平均每万人口在校学生数和大中小学生构成……………………………………………………………（505）
Student Enrollment Per 10000 Populations and Composition of Students Enrolled
16-20 成人教育情况(2003年)…………………………………………………………………………………（506）
Adult Education (2003)
16-21 科学研究机构基本情况…………………………………………………………………………………（508）
Basic Facts on Scientific Research Institutions
16-22 科研院所科技活动情况表………………………………………………………………………………（509）
Scientific and Technological Activities Facts in Scientific Research Institutions

16-23 大专院校科技活动情况表……………………………………………………………………………………(510)
Scientific and Technological Activities Facts in Universities
16-24 大中型工业企业科技活动情况……………………………………………………………………………(511)
Scientific and Technological Activities Facts in Large-size and Medium-size Industrial Enterprises
16-25 企事业单位知识产权情况…………………………………………………………………………………(512)
Intellectual Property Right of Enterprises and Institutions
16-26 西安市高新技术产业开发区情况…………………………………………………………………………(513)
Basic Statistics of Hi-Tech Development Zone of XI'AN
16-27 高新区发展规模(2003年)…………………………………………………………………………………(514)
Development Status of Hi-Tech Zone (2003)
16-28 高新区建设与集资情况……………………………………………………………………………………(514)
Capital Construction and Funds-Raising of Hi-Tech Development Zone
主要统计指标解释………………………………………………………………………………………………(515)
Explanatory Notes on Main Statistical Indicators

十七、文化、体育、卫生、社会福利和其他

Culture, Sports, Public Health , Social Welfare Institutions and Other Social Activities

17-1 文化事业机构和人数(2003年)……………………………………………………………………………(523)
Number of Institutions and Personnel in Culture and Art (2003)
17-2 文化事业发展情况(2003年)………………………………………………………………………………(523)
Basic Statistics on Culture Development(2003)
17-3 群众艺术馆、文化馆(站)活动情况…………………………………………………………………………(524)
Basic Statistics on Activities of Mass Art Centers and Cultural Centers
17-4 文物保护业基本情况(2003年)……………………………………………………………………………(524)
Basic Statistics on Cultural Relics Protection(2003)
17-5 广播电台及节目制作情况…………………………………………………………………………………(525)
Basic Statistics of Broadcasting Stations and Program Production
17-6 电视台及节目制作情况……………………………………………………………………………………(525)
Basic Statistics of TV Stations and Production of TV Program
17-7 各级体育局及各直属单位职工人数(市属)(2003年)…………………………………………………(526)
Number of Staff and Workers in Sports Commissions at All Levels and Their Affiliated Units(Under Municipality) (2003)
17-8 《国家体育锻炼标准》施行情况(市属)………………………………………………………………(526)
Practice of 《State Physical Training Standards》(Under Municipality)
17-9 少年儿童分项业余体校情况(市属)(2003年)…………………………………………………………(527)
Basic Statistics of Youth Part-time Physical Training School (2003)
17-10 卫生机构、床位及人员数(2003年)……………………………………………………………………(528)
Health Institutions,Beds and Peasons (2003)
17-11 各区县卫生机构、床位及人员数(2003年)……………………………………………………………(532)
Health Institutions、Beds And Peasons by Region (2003)

17-12 卫生机构各类人员数…………………………………………………………………………（533）
Number of Employed Personnel in Health Institutions by Type of Occupation
17-13 卫生部门卫生机构各类人员数……………………………………………………………（533）
Number of Employed Personnel in Health Institutions under Heath Department by Type of Occupation
17-14 医院、卫生院诊疗人次及诊疗情况(2003年)………………………………………………（534）
Statistics on Hospital Patients and Diagnosis in Hospital and Health Centers(2003)
17-15 医院、卫生院床位及病人治疗情况(2003年)………………………………………………（536）
Basic Statistics on Beds and Patients Hospital and Health Center（2003）
17-16 县（区）村卫生室基本情况(2003年)……………………………………………………（538）
The Market Circumstance of the Consumer Goods Wholesales(2003)
17-17 社会福利事业单位基本情况(2003年)……………………………………………………（540）
Basic Statistics on Social Welfare Insititutions（2003）
17-18 社会福利事业单位机构、人员数…………………………………………………………（540）
Number of Social Welfare Institutions and Employed Persons
17-19 福利企业单位基本情况(2003年)…………………………………………………………（540）
Base Statistics on Socical Welfare Enterprises（2003）
17-20 各区县优抚对象人员情况(2003年)………………………………………………………（541）
Statistics on Persons Enjoying Favoured Treatment by Region（2003）
17-21 计划生育和婚姻情况(2003年)……………………………………………………………（542）
Conditions of Birth Control and Marriage Registration(2003)
17-22 离休、退休、退职人员情况(2003年)……………………………………………………（543）
Statistics on Retired and Resigned Persons（2003）
17-23 离退休、退职人员保险福利费用构成情况(2003年)………………………………………（543）
Composition of Social Insurance and Welfare Fund of Retires（2003）
17-24 律师、公证及调解基本情况………………………………………………………………（544）
Basic Statisics on Lawyer、Notaries and Mediation
17-25 共青团组织情况……………………………………………………………………………（545）
Basic Facts on Communist Youth League
17-26 各级妇联基本情况…………………………………………………………………………（545）
Basic Statistics on Women's Federation at All Levels
17-27 妇联工作情况………………………………………………………………………………（546）
Basic Facts on Women's Federation
17-28 交通事故情况………………………………………………………………………………（547）
Statistics on Traffic Accidents
17-29 火灾情况……………………………………………………………………………………（547）
Statistics on Fires
17-30 安全生产情况………………………………………………………………………………（548）
Data on safty in production
17-31 公安局刑事案件情况………………………………………………………………………（549）
Data on criminal cases from public security bureau
17-32 公安局治安案件情况………………………………………………………………………（549）
Data on public order cases from public security bureau

17-33 公安局分区县刑事、治安案件情况(2003年)…………(550)
Data on criminal cases and public order cases from public security bureau grouped
By districts and counties(2003)
17-34 西安市人民检察院案件受理情况(2003年)…………(551)
Data on acceptance of cases of Xi'an people's procuratorate(2003)
17-35 西安市中级人民法院案件基本情况（2003年）…………(552)
Xi'an intermediate people's court Basic data of the law cases(2003)
主要统计指标解释…………(554)
Explanatory Notes on Main Statistical Indicators

十八、企业调查

Enterprises Investigation

18-1 年主营业务收入亿元以上企业集团经营情况(2003年)…………(561)
Operation status of Enterprise Groups with over 100 Million Yuan Annual Income of
Majar Business (2003)
18-2 重点企业建立现代企业制度企业主要经济指标(2003年)…………(562)
Major Economic Indicators on Establishing Modern Enterprise System of Key Enterprises(2003)
18-3 企业景气指数(2003年)…………(563)
Business Climate Index(2003)
18-4 企业家信心指数(2003年)…………(564)
Entrepreneur Expectation Indicator(2003)
主要统计指标解释…………(565)
Explanatory Notes on Main Statistical Indicators

十九、附录

Appendix

全国各省、市、自治区国民经济主要指标（2003年）…………(569)
Main Indicators Of National Economy By Province , Municipality And Autonomous Region (2003)
全国重点城市主要经济指标（2003年）…………(573)
Main Economic Indicators in Major City (2003)

西安市2003年国民经济和社会发展统计公报

西安市统计局

2004年3月2日

2003年是西安经济社会发展极不寻常的一年。国民经济经受了“非典”疫情和秋季洪水危害的严峻考验。全市人民在市委、市政府的正确领导下，高举邓小平理论伟大旗帜，努力实践“三个代表”重要思想，认真贯彻党的十六大和十六届三中全会精神，以“建强创佳”为目标，解放思想，与时俱进，特别是面对灾害的挑战，市委、市政府统揽全局、沉着应对，适时采取了“农业增收、工业增速、投资增量、开发区增贡献、三产补欠”的四增一补有力措施，领导全市人民团结奋斗、顽强拼搏，战胜了比预计要大的困难，夺取了比预期要好的成就。国民经济持续发展，社会稳定进步。

一、经济发展

全市经济在持续、协调、快速、健康的轨道上运行，经济总量继续扩大，经济结构得到优化。据初步核算，2003年西安市生产总值（GDP）940.4亿元，按可比价格计算，比上年增长13.5%。其中第一产业增加值49.2亿元，比上年增长1.3%；第二产业增加值447亿元，增长17.4%；第三产业增加值444.2亿元，增长11.3%。全社会固定资产投资479亿元，比上年增长41.7%。全年财政总收入117.3亿元，比上年增长23.8%；其中地方财政收入72.9亿元，比上年增长23.7%。地方财政支出77.4亿元，比上年增长21%。

农林牧渔业

全市农林牧渔业生产在结构调整中稳步发展，各级政府正在把发展农林牧渔业生产做为增加农民收入和全面建设小康社会的重要举措，认真安排部署，切实抓紧抓好。伴随国民经济的持续增长，特别是通过积极培育高新技术产业和优质高效特色农业，推进产业结构优化升级，我市农业经济结构调整也取得了实质性进展。农业产业多元化、商品化、社会化程度明显提高。全年实现农业总产值83.8亿元,比上年增长1.5%。粮食生产受播种面积调整及局部地区干旱气候及洪涝灾害的影响，总产有所下降，经济作物产量有增有减。全市造林面积20.5千公顷，比上年减少8.5%，零星植树1024万株，比上年增长42.7%。猪、羊年末存栏数增加，大牲畜、家禽年末存栏数均有所上升，肉、奶、禽蛋产量均有较大增长。全年水产品养殖面积1654公顷，比上年减少25%。2003年全市主要农林牧渔业产品产量及畜禽存栏情况如下：

产品名称	计量单位	绝对数	比上年增长（%）
粮食	万吨	176.3	-8.3
棉花	万吨	0.2	22.9
油料	万吨	1.1	-7.4
蔬菜	万吨	169.7	持平
水果	万吨	38.4	2.3
肉类	万吨	16.6	3
#猪肉	万吨	12.3	3.5
奶类	万吨	33.6	16.8
#牛奶	万吨	24.5	21
禽蛋	万吨	12.9	4.1
水产品	万吨	1	-16.7
肉猪出栏头数	万头	159.5	4.8
大牲畜年末存栏数	万头	28.5	11.8
猪年末存栏数	万头	139.8	0.6
羊年末存栏数	万只	51.4	7.1
家禽年末存栏数	万只	1651.4	1

农业生产条件继续得到改善。全市拥有农业机械总动力208.1万千瓦，比上年增长1.4%；有效灌溉面积203.4千公顷，下降4.5%；全年农用化肥施用量（按折纯量计算）20万吨，比上年下降0.4%；农村用电量11.6亿千瓦小时，比上年增长6.1%。

工业和建筑业

工业生产保持快速增长。2003年，西安市工业呈现增速加快、结构优化、产销两旺的良好态势，工业对经济的主导作用增强。全市实现工业增加值

347.1亿元，比上年增长13.9%，实现工业总产值1209.4亿元，比上年增长14.4%，其中国有及

年销售收入500万元以上非国有工业企业（以下简称规模以上工业企业）实现总产值779.6亿元，增长17.0%。全年工业用电量46.5亿千瓦小时，增长7.6%。

工业结构继续调整，产销衔接良好。在规模以上工业企业中，国有工业企业继续保持了较快的增长速度，完成工业总产值179.4亿元，增长22.6%；股份合作企业工业总产值6.6亿元，增长19.7%；股份制企业工业总产值453.5亿元，增长18.2%；集体企业工业总产值26.0亿元，增长7.2%；三资企业工业总产值105.9亿元，增长9.3%。2003年在全市规模以上工业总产值中轻工业总产值181.8亿元，增长10.4%；重工业总产值597.8亿元，增长19.2%。

工业运行质量改善，经济效益继续提高。全市规模以上工业企业产品销售率97.6%，比上年提高0.97个百分点。全市规模以上工业企业实现销售收入634.0亿元，增长15.6%；工业产成品资金占用70.3亿元，增长13.0%，低于产品销售收入增幅2.58个百分点；利税总额57.2亿元，其中利润总额29.3亿元，较上年增长16.5%；工业经济效益综合指数114.8，比上年提高6.02个百分点。2003年全市规模以上工业企业主要产品产量情况如下：

产品名称	计量单位	绝对数	比上年增长（%）
发电量	万千瓦小时	204114	7.5
方便主食品	吨	69483	105
乳制品	吨	51625	85.3
饮料酒	万吨	24.62	1.2
#啤酒	万吨	24.55	1.2
纱	吨	71266	2.6
机制纸	吨	85545	36.6
缝纫机	万架	55.8	12.1
化学试剂	吨	1578	17.3
合成洗涤剂	万吨	5.86	0.3
中成药	吨	1059	–3.5
水泥	万吨	135	–7.4
钢	吨	35792	15.6
工业锅炉	蒸发量吨	1178	21.8
汽车	辆	41051	23.7
交流电动机	万千瓦	276.22	57.9
变压器	万千伏安	2017.84	23.7
电力电缆	公里	280	–13
通讯电缆	公里	26534	14.9
彩色显象管	万只	665.89	8.9
电工仪器仪表	台	10124	–35

建筑市场不断规范，工程质量不断提高。建筑业全员劳动生产率102659元/人，比上年增长22%。全市建筑施工企业全年施工项目4859个，竣工项目2119个；施工面积1229.6万平方米，竣工面积428万平方米，与上年基本持平；实现总产值169.6亿元，增长27%；施工工程优良品率65%。

运输邮电业

社会运输能力提高，货运量平稳增长。年末拥有民用车辆50.9万辆，比上年增长12%，其中汽车24.2万辆，增长17.3%。全年完成客运量8792万人次，下降5.5%；旅客周转量239.0亿人公里，下降1.6%；完成货运量8901万吨，增长8.9%；货物周转量499.6亿吨公里，增长9.9%。

邮电获得较快发展，邮电业务收入51.4亿元，比上年增长11.9%。全年发送函件14909万件、特快专递171.5万件，报刊1.21亿份；年末邮政储蓄余额73.8亿元，比上年增长42.1%。电子通信各项业务保持快速增长，新兴业务增长明显加快。西安电话号码顺利实现8位升级；年末市话和农话交换机总容量316.3万门，比上年增长19.5%；市话和农话用户237.5万户，其中住宅电话129.6万户；移动电话用户232.2万户，增长18.2%，城乡话机普及率每百人66.2部。年末电信局计算机互联网用户88.6万户，以ADSL为代表的宽带网用户达10.7万户。

国内贸易

全年实现社会消费品零售总额440.0亿元，增长13.0%。其中城镇消费品零售额416.7亿元，增长13.3%；农村消费品零售额23.3亿元，增长8.1%。批发零售贸易业零售额325.8亿元，比上年增长14.9%；餐饮业零售额102.5亿元，增长7.8%；其他行业零售额11.7亿元，增长9.1%。年末拥有各类贸易市场514个，其中年成交额超亿元的市场有16个。

市场物价

2003年，西安市市场物价运行呈现由降转升态势。全年居民消费价格指数为100.5，较上年上升0.5个百分点。与上年相比，食品、居住两大类价格较上年分别上升4.6%和4%。烟酒及饮料、衣着、家庭设备用品及维修服务、医疗保健和个人用品、交通和通讯、娱乐教育文化用品及服务分别下降0.5%、1.0%、3.3%、2.4%、6.1%和3.1%。商品零售价格总水平与上年持平。

金融、证券、保险业

金融支持力度加大，个人消费贷款大幅增长。年末金融机构各项存款余额2665.9亿元，比年初增长21.4%；各项贷款余额1954.2亿元，增长21.9%。存款中，企业存款余额1041.9亿元，比年初增加153.0亿元。贷款中，短期贷款946.6亿元，增长21.1%；中长期贷款659.7亿元，增长30.8%。全年金融机构现金收入4909.3亿元，增长22.3%；现金支出4690.5亿元，增长23.2%；全年现金净回笼218.8亿元。

证券市场健康发展，营业网点继续增加。年内新设立1家证券营业部，年末全市证券营业部有52个。企业资本运作取得新进展，全市进入上市辅导期的企业49家。在股市不振的情况下，全市证券交易额1749亿元，较上年增长45.8%。

保险业务迅速发展，保费收入大幅增长。2003年又有中华联合和天安保险二家保险机构进驻西安，全市保险主体达到12家，全年保险业务收入36.2亿元，比上年增长26.4%；已决赔款及给付6.5亿元。在保险业务收入中，人寿保险份额加速增长，财产险与人寿险的比例从1：2.9变化为1：3.0。

房地产业

全市房地产市场供销两旺，商品房竣工、销售均出现持续增长的势头。全市房地产开发量1336万平方米，比上年增长13.9%；商品房销售面积250.3万平方米，销售额54.1亿元，与去年基本持平。其中商品住宅销售面积227.9万平方米。个人购房比重持续提高，达到94.1%。

旅游业

2003年全市旅游业因“非典”疫情受到直接影响。国际、国内旅游全面受挫。全年共接待旅游、参观、访问及从事其他活动的海外游客33.7万人次，比上年下降54.6%；接待国内旅游者1614万人次，比上年下降15.5%；旅游总收入105.7亿元，其中国际旅游外汇收入1.46亿美元，分别比上年下降19.3%和54%。全市拥有年接待游客10万人以上的景区30个，国家4A级景区9个；年末全市星级宾馆59家，其中五星级宾馆4家，四星级宾馆8家。

二、改革开放

体制改革

体制改革继续为发展注入新的活力。《进一步深化国有企业改革的实施意见》出台以及13户重点国企改制的基本完成，为在整体上搞活西安国有经济，进一步深化国企改革奠定了基础。行政审批制度改革迈出新步伐，新取消审批项目350项，使总精简率达到69%。建立了投资项目行政审批“绿色通道”制度，简化了办事程序和缩短了审批时限。积极推进国有土地储备制度，对四类经营性用地实行了招、拍、挂的营运管理方法。城镇职工基本医疗保险制度改革、医疗卫生体制改革、药品生产流通体制改革稳步推进。文化体制改革试点工作启动。推行农业特产税改征农业税试点，减负率达58%。全面推行政务公开和行政执法责任制，重视决策的科学化和民主化，试行听证制度。全年提交市人大常委会审议地方性法规11件，修改政府规章、规范性文件68件。非公有制经济发展的政策环境进一步优化。体制改革总体向深层次、宽领域推进。

对外贸易

对外贸易克服了“非典”疫情的影响，特别是实施“走出去”的招商引资战略初见成效，对外贸易再创新高。全年西安地区累计进出口总值23.1亿美元，比上年增长23.6%，其中出口14亿美元，增长24.9%。全市自营进出口总值6.9亿美元，增长24.3%，其中出口4.8亿美元，增长43.8%。提前两年实现市政府要求的跨越目标。外贸出口总值第一次列西部地区省会城市之首。

利用外资

招商引资出现新局面，利用外资稳步增长。2003年全市新批外商投资企业132个，比去年同期减少了8%；合同外资额9.6亿美元，实际利用外资2.6亿美元，分别比上年增长36%和26%。已有56个国家和地区在我市投资设立项目。新批外商投资企业中合资项目50个，占新批项目总数的37.8%；合作项目21个，占新批项目总数的15.9%；独资项目61个，占新批项目总数的46.3%。

外经合作

外经合作取得新进展。我市最大的国际受援项目日本政府无偿援助的总金额13亿日元的垃圾处理项目，已进入实施阶段。国际受援、境外承包工程、劳务输出全面增长，年末在境外劳务人数1729人。全年境外承包营业额达到4208万美元，创历史最好水平。

开发区建设

高新技术开发区和经济技术开发区以“二次创业”为动力，经济发展保持了较快的增长态势。全年高新技术产业开发区完成固定资产投资56亿元，较上年增长50%；合同引进外资额3.0亿美元，增长27%；实际引进外资额1.0亿美元，增长38.4%；财政收入7.3亿元，增长29%。经济技术开发区完成固定资产投资23.5亿元，较上年增长96%；合同引进外资额2.5亿美元，增长19.5%；实际引进外资额0.8亿美元，增长26%；财政收入1.9亿元，增长30.7%。曲江新区建设取得突破性进展，大雁塔北广场建成开放。开发区和曲江新区的发展对全市经济辐射带动和创新示范作用进一步加强。

三、社会事业

科技事业

2003年末，全市拥有各类专业技术人员36.2万人。组织实施科技计划项目411项，投入市级科研经费4000万元。积极争取国家支持，列入科技部各类科技计划和重大专项110项，获资金支持4200万元。实施重点科技成果转化项目30项，技术市场交易额5.3亿元。全市专利申请量2341件，专利授权量1099件。累计专利申请量16762件，专利授权量9030件。高新技术产业化进程加快，新认定高新技术企业184家，累计全市高新技术企业971家。

教育事业

继续实施高标准义务教育，加快普及高中阶段教育，大力发展职业教育和民办高等教育，全面推进素质教育，全市教育整体水平进一步提高。全市小学、初中入学率分别为99.9%和98.5%。全市小学、初中、普通高中、职业高中在校学生分别为66.8万人、38.9万人、17.5万人、4.4万人；普通中等专业学校在校学生5.4万人，毕业生1.7万人；普通高教在校学生40.1万人，毕业生6.5万人。社会力量办学蓬勃发展，全市拥有民办其他高等教育机构25所，民办普通中小学87所，民办职业学校31所。

文化事业

群众文化繁荣活跃，文化产业健康发展。加大了在广播影视方面的投入力度，广播电视覆盖网不断完善和扩大。广播、电视、报刊等宣传媒体围绕市委、市政府重要工作、重大活动、重点工程，开展了形式多样富有成效的新闻宣传。文化出版市场管理和文物管理工作进一步加强，文化、广电等企事业改革进一步深化，为文化市场增添了活力。全市有文艺表演团体22个，群众艺术馆2个、文化馆13个、文化站181个，公共图书馆14个，出版社15家。公开出版报纸33种。

卫生事业

全面实施区域卫生规划，推进城乡联动的社区卫生服务，健全了卫生监督和疾病控制体系。加强卫生防病工作，医疗卫生条件继续改善，服务水平进一步提高。农村社区合作医疗覆盖面达65.6％。年末全市拥有医疗卫生机构2785 个，其中医院、卫生院474个，专业卫生技术人员4.1万人，其中职业医师1.5万人；卫生机构床位3.3万张。

体育事业

体育事业向产业化迈进，群众体育工作有了新发展。2003年全市已有10个全国体育先进社区，23个省级体育先进社区，17个全国体育先进乡镇。全年培训和审定了500名社会体育指导员，共有社会体育指导员1984人。全年各体育协会和体育社团共组织群众性体育竞赛活动150项次，参加人数达10万人次。全民健身广场增至170个。竞技体育取得新成绩，在2003年第五次全国城市运动会上，我市体育代表团获得5枚金牌、11枚银牌、5枚铜牌，取得总分493.5分的好成绩，在西部省区参赛城市中列第二位。

四、城乡建设和管理

固定资产投资

投资力度继续加大，投资结构进一步改善。全年完成全社会固定资产投资479亿元，其中国有单位投资280.3亿元，增长40.1%;城镇集体投资22.3亿元，增长62.9%;非公有制经济投资176.4亿元，增长41.8%。从各类投资看，基本建设投资228.4亿元，增长47.4%；更新改造投资71.5亿元，增长24.4%；房地产开发投资124. 7亿元,增长57.1%；其他投资21.3亿元，增长38.2%。全市建成投产项目483个，项目建成投产率50.3%。

城市建设规划和管理

城市建设的道桥工程、排水工程、绿化美化工程进展顺利。二环路全线贯通，朱雀路至含光路增设立交完工通车，机场高速公路顺利通车，枣园东西路、纬一街、西影路、高新四路、东仪路、五星街、东关正街、太华路北段、友谊路疏导线等十五条道路建设改造全面完工。背街小巷及断头路改造工程中的光华路、解家村路、齿轮厂门前道路、凤城三路、刁家村、永松路南段等道路改造工程已经完工。邓家村污水处理厂改造工程、北石桥污水深度处理回用工程已完工投入运行。纬一街雨水截流干管工程、翠华路排水工程基本完工，西斜三明渠改造工程进展顺利。具有现代化气息的大雁塔北广场竣工开放，大水大绿工程正式启动。城市绿化工程及绿化养护工作完成了钟楼盘道改造、西华门西广场改造、长乐东路行道树补栽、南门广场喷灌、公园南路、新城广场、纬二十九街行道树栽植、兴庆湖综合治理等工程。

城市规划和管理力度加大，城市环境综合整治取得明显成效，市容市貌得到改善。完成了城六区分区规划及城六区详细规划编制。城市重点建设项目规划工作得到强化，编制完成了环山路两侧用地控制规划、背街小巷道路整治及城市断头路打通工程方案设计、城市点亮工程系统规划、城市雕塑体系规划、城中村及旧村改造规划、大明宫御道广场规划、建筑垃圾造景选址规划、城市基础地理空间数据库的建立、三环道路工程项目规划、西安市道路体系规划、西安市绿化体系规划、新建改造公共厕所布点规划。全年市区新增绿地60公顷，绿化覆盖率38.8%，比上年提高7.98个百分点，人均公共绿地面积4.15平方米，比上年增加0.38平方米。

公用事业

2003年全年新建改建道路15公里，30万平方米，修补、翻修沥青路面72万平方米，修补人行道51000平方米，新增雨水管道34公里，污水管道14公里，新增供水管道10431米。天然气改造燃煤锅炉1328台，管道敷设400多公里。新增供热面积30万平方米。城市路灯改造累计完成电缆敷设47公里，立灯杆1794根，新安、改造路灯4471套，改造无灯街巷123条。全年处理污水4847万立方米，全市污水处理能力达到31万吨。各级市容环卫部门负责清扫的道路面积1500万平方米，道路冲洒水面积达440万平方米。全年收集、清运、处理垃圾113.2万吨。年末市区公交营运线路152条，营运车辆3431标台，线路总长度795公里；全年客运总量5.5亿人次；营运出租汽车10430辆。新增公交线路8条，延伸调整19条，新增公交车辆348辆，更新公交车辆115辆。城市管道煤气家庭用户5万户,液化气用户63.4万户,天然气用户38.3万户，城市居民燃气普及率91.2%。自来水日供水能力197.4万吨,供水总量36122万吨,其中居民生活用水12002万吨；集中供热面积2175万平方米。全市全社会用电量102.0亿千瓦时,比上年增长9.2%,其中城乡居民生活用电18.8亿千瓦时,增长10.8%。

环境保护与治理

环境保护、污染治理工作力度加大。围绕创建国家环保模范城市，加强对水环境污染的综合整治，实施对污染物总量的控制，城市环境质量进一步改善。江村沟垃圾填埋厂二期工程的前期工程基本完工。累计拆除燃煤锅炉1883台。全市建立各级环境监测站15个，烟尘控制区9个，面积196.7平方公里；环境噪声达标区6个，面积81平方公里。市区环境空气主要污染物年日均值二氧化硫为0.019毫克/立方米，二氧化氮为0.015毫克/立方米，可吸入颗粒物为0.136毫克/立方米。城区环境空气质量好于国家二级标准(优良)的天数255天,比2002年增加80天,优良天气率提高了22个百分点,其中二氧化硫、二氧化氮双双达到国家二级标准,全年达标率100%，饮用水源水质达标率100%，工业废水排放达标率77.1%。

五、人口与人民生活

人口和就业

全市计划生育工作进一步加强，人口出生率稳定在较低水平上。2003年人口出生率为9.83，人口自然增长率为4.43。年末全市户籍总人口716.6万人，其中农业人口403.7万人，非农业人口312.9万人。年末全市城镇从业人员185.6万人，城镇登记失业率4.5%。

人民生活

2003年，全市在岗职工平均工资13504元，比上年增长11.3%；城镇居民人均可支配收入7748元，农村居民人均纯收入2838元，分别比上年增长7.9%和

7.4%。生活质量进一步提高，城镇居民人均生活消费支出6805元，农民人均生活消费支出1803元，分别增长6.0%和1.2%；食品消费支出占生活消费支出的比重城市居民为34.8%，农村居民为37.6%。年末城乡居民储蓄存款余额1210.6亿元，比年初增加222.5亿元。住房条件进一步改善，城镇居民人均住房使用面积12.06平方米，农村居民人均居住面积33.9平方米。

社会保障

全市社会保障体系逐渐完善，养老、失业、医疗、工伤和生育等保险制度基本建立，社会保障水平进一步提高。

2003年，全市参加养老保险的单位11500户，参保人员95.7万人，共收缴基本养老金17.5亿元，拨付23.5亿元。对全市35.2万离退休人员的养老保险金发放实行了与用人单位脱钩的社会化发放，发放率保持在100%。全市参加失业保险的单位11577户，参保人数127.1万人。全市失业保险基金收入1.8亿元，支出8569.5万元。全市已有4.6万名下岗失业人员领到了《优惠证》，下岗失业人员再就业3.1万人。医疗保险覆盖面不断扩大，全市参加医疗保险单位4300户，参保职工123.4万人，比上年增长15.3%。

社会福利事业不断发展。2003年全市各类可提供食宿的收养性社会福利单位床位2799张，收养各类人员1619人。全市建立各种社区服务设施1734个，其中综合性社区服务中心114个。全年通过销售社会福利彩票筹集社会福利资金1976万元，接收社会捐赠款1027万元。全市共有18.1万人纳入低保范围，其中城镇16.9万人，农村1.2万人。

2003年，全市国民经济和社会发展中存在的突出问题是：国企改革仍然步履维艰；工业产业聚集度低，结构调整缓慢，竞争力不强；城乡居民收入增长缓慢；农业经济增长乏力；就业、再就业压力增大；城市交通状况亟待改善。对此，市委、市政府以党的十六大和十六届三中全会精神为指导，正在用改革和发展的办法逐步予以解决。

注：1、本公报数为初步统计数，地区生产总值为初步核算数；

2、人口数为公安局户籍年报数；

3、地区生产总值、各行业总产值、增加值的绝对数均按现行价格计算，增长速度按可比价格计算；

4、年末固定电话用户数仅为中国电信的用户数，未含其它通讯公司的用户数。

Statistic Communiqu on the 2003 National Economy and Social Development of the City of Xi'an

Xi'an Bureau of Statistics

Mar.2nd, 2004

2003 is an extra-ordinary year for Xi'an city's economic and social development. National economy has endured the severe test of the SARS and the flood in autumn. Under the guidance of the municipal party committee and the municipal government, people of the city held high the great banner of Deng Xiaoping theory, made great efforts to practice Three Represents Thought, carried out the spirit of the 16th CPC National Congress and the Third Plenum of 16th CPC Central Committee earnestly, liberated idea and advanced with time's progress with founding of strength and setting up goodness as the goal, in particular confronting with the challenge of the calamity, municipal party committee and the municipal government toke control of the overall situation, acted composedly, adopted the increasing harvest of agriculture, speeding up development of industry, increasing quantity of investment, increasing contribution of development zone and making up debt of tertiary industry powerful measure, leading people of Xi'an city strive corporately and struggle tough, overcome difficulties more hard than what one can foresee, reached unforeseen achievement. National economy toke a sustained progress and the society lead a stable progress.

1. Economic Development

While gross economy was keeping enlarging and economic structure keeping optimizing, the economy of the city ran on the sustained, harmonious, fast, healthy track. According to preparatory accounting, the city's GDP reaches RMB 94.04 billion, increased 13.5% compared with last year at constant prices. In it, primary industry added value reached RMB 4.92 billion, increased by 1.3% compared with last year, secondary industry added value reached RMB 44.7 billion, increased by 17.4%, and tertiary industry added value reached RMB 44.42 billion, increased by 11.3%. Overall fixed assets investment was RMB 47.9 billion, increased by 41.7% compared with last year. Gross revenue reached RMB 11.73 billion, increased by 23.8% compared with last year. In it, local revenue is RMB 7.29 billion, increased by 23.7% compared with last year. Local expenditure is RMB 77.4 billion, increased by 218% compared with last year.

1.1 Farming, forestry, animal husbandry and fishery

City's farming, forestry, animal husbandry and fishery production progressed steadily under the structural adjusting environment. All levels governments are taking farming, forestry, animal husbandry and fishery production growing as the main measures of boosting farmer's income and building a all round society with a relatively comfortable life, and they are well planned and deployed, done in real earnest. Accompanying national economy sustained increase, in particular with vigorous fostering of hi-tech industry and high quality, high production agriculture, pushing forward industrial structure upgrading and optimization, the city's agriculture structure adjusting has obtained substantial progress. Agricultural industry pluralism, commercializing, the socialized degree improves obviously. The total output of agriculture reached 83. 800 million Yuan in the whole year, increasing by 1.5% compared with the last year. As a result of adjustment of planting area, arid weather of some areas and the big flood in grain-production, the total output of grains reduced, while the growth rate of output of cash crops differs. New plantation of 2003 is 20.5 thousand hectares in Xi'an, reducing by 8.5% compared with the last year. And there are 10,240 thousand trees Planted step by step, increasing by 42.7% than the last year. The year-end amount in hog, sheep on hand increased, as well as the amount of cattle and fowl increased in some sense. The output of meat, milk and egg increased relatively largely. The aquaculture area reduced 25%, to 1654 hectares. The annual output of main agricultural products in 2003 is as following:

Name of Products	Unit	Output	Increase over the last year (%)
Grain	10,000 ton	176.3	-8.3
Cotton	10,000 ton	0.2	22.9
Edible	10,000 ton	1.1	-7.4
Vegetable	10,000 ton	169.7	0
Fruit	10,000 ton	38.4	2.3
Meat	10,000 ton	16.6	3
#Pork	10,000 ton	12.3	3.5
Milk	10,000 ton	33.6	16.8
#Cow milk	10,000 ton	24.5	21
Egg	10,000 ton	12.9	4.1
Aquatic Product	10,000 ton	1	-16.7
Hog sold	10,000 head	159.5	4.8
Year-end Cattle on hand	10,000 head	28.5	11.8
Year-end Pig on hand	10,000 head	139.8	0.6
Year-end Sheep on Hand	10,000 head	51.4	7.1
Year-end Fowl on Hand	10,000 head	1651.4	1

Achievement was also made in construction of basic facilities for farming. The overall motor power of agricultural machines reached 2.081 million kilowatt, an increase of 1.4%; irrigating area 0.2034 million Hectare, an reduction of 4.5%; fertilizer utilized (converted into pure) 0.20 million tons, 0.4% down, and electricity consumption for agricultural use 1.16 billion kilowatt-hour, 6.1% up.

1.2 Industry and Construction

The industry maintained a steady fast growth. In 2003, the industry presented the good situation of increasing, structure optimization, and both production and marketing thrive. It strengthened the leading role of industry to economy.

The industrial added value is 34.71 billion Yuan, 13.9% more than the previous year.

The total output value reached 120.94 billion Yuan, 14.4% more than the previous year, in which, the state-owned enterprises and non-state-owned enterprises with annual sales income more than 5 million Yuan, (enterprises above designated size for short) realized an output value of 77.96 billion Yuan, an increase of 17.0%. The electricity consumed by industry was 4.65 billion Kilowatts-hour, up 7.6%.

The industrial structure continued to being adjusted. The production and marketing linked up well.

Among enterprises above designated size, the output of state-owned enterprise continued keeping the relatively fast growth and totally reached 17.94 billion Yuan, 22.6% up, the joint share-hold enterprises 0.66 billion Yuan, the share-hold enterprises 45.35 billion Yuan, the collective-owned enterprise 2.6 billion Yuan and the enterprises in the three forms 10.59 billion Yuan, increasing 19.7%, 18.2% and 7.2% and 9.3% respectively.

Output of light industry was 18.18 billion Yuan and heavy industry 59.78 billion Yuan, up 10.4% and 19.2% respectively.

The running quality of industry is improved, and the industrial efficiency continued improving.

Among enterprises above designated size in Xi'an, the ratio of sales is 97.6%, up 0.97%.

Increased by 15.6%, the sales income of industrial enterprises above designated size reached 63.40 billion Yuan. The value of products unfinished and unsold numbered 7.03 billion Yuan, increasing by 13.0%, which is 2.85% lower than the growth rate of sales income. The total profits and taxes amounted 5.72 billion Yuan, including 2.93 billion Yuan of profits, up 16.5%. The comprehensive index of industrial efficiency reached 114.8, up 6.02%. The basic statistics of main products of enterprises above designated size in 2003 are as follows:

Item	Unit	Output	Increase over the last year (%)
Electricity	10,000 kilowatt-hour	204114	7.5
Instant staple food	Ton	69483	105
Dairy	Ton	51625	85.3
Beverage Alcohol	10,000 ton	24.62	1.2
#beer	10,000 ton	24.55	1.2
Yarn	Ton	71266	2.6
Machine Made Paper	Ton	85545	36.6
Sewing machine	10,000 unit	55.8	12.1
Chemical reagent	Ton	1578	17.3
Detergent	10,000 ton	5.86	0.3
Finished traditional Chinese medicine	Ton	1059	-3.5
Cement	10,000 ton	135	-7.4
Steel	Ton	35792	15.6
Industrial Boiler	Ton	1178	21.8
Motor Vehicle	Unit	41051	23.7
Ac Motor	10,000 kilowatt	276.22	57.9
Transformer	10,000 volt-ampere	2017.8	23.7
Electric Cable	Km	280	-13
Telecommunication Cable	Km	26534	14.9
Color Kinescope	10,000 piece	665.89	8.9
Meters and Instrument	Unit	10124	-35

With more measures taken to regularize the construction market, the construction quality improved continually. The productivity of labor reached 102,659 Yuan per capita, increasing by 22%. In 2003, 4859 projects started, and 2119 of them completed. Floor space under construction reaches 12.296 million square meters, and floor space completed 4.28 million square meters, almost same to the last year respectively. Construction industry made an output of 16.96 billion Yuan, increasing by 27%. 65% of construction projects are of superior quality.

1.3 Transport, Post and Telecommunication

The social transport capacity and passenger and freight traffic were in a steady growth. The number of civil vehicles reached 0.509 million and 12% more than the last year, among which, the number of motor vehicles was 0.242 million, an increase of 17.3% over the preceding year. The total passenger traffic reached 87.92 million person-times, and 5.5% less than the preceding year. The turnover volume of passenger traffic was 23.90 billion person-kilometers, a decrease of 1.6 % over the last year. The freight traffic was 89.01 million tons, 8.9% more than the previous year. The turnover volume reached 49.96 billion ton-kilometers, an increase of 9.9%.

The year 2003 also saw the boom of post and telecommunication industry. The income of post and telecommunication reached 5.14 billion Yuan, up 11.9% compared with the last year. In the whole year, there are 149.09 million correspondences, 1.715 million express mails, and 0.121 billion the press. At the end of year the saving balance reached 7.38 billion Yuan, up 42.1%. All kinds of telecommunication business kept fast growth, and new developing business growth is obviously accelerated. The telephone number of Xi'an realized smoothly that 8 upgrade.

The number of urban and rural switchboard's capacity increased by 19.5% to 3.163 million. The telephone subscribers in urban and rural areas reached 2.375 million, including 1.296 million private subscribers. The mobile phone users went to 2.322 million, increasing by 18.2%. Among every 100 people there are 66.2 telephones. The Internet users reached 0.886 million. Represented by ADSL, broadband Internet service reached 0.107 million.

1.4 Domestic Trade

The retail sale of consumer goods totaled 44.00 billion Yuan, increasing by 13.0%. Among it, the retail sale in urban area was 41.67 billion Yuan, 13.3% over the preceding year, and the value in rural area 2.33 billion Yuan, 8.1% more than the preceding year.

The total retail sale of wholesale and retail sale trades reached 32.58 billion Yuan, increasing by 14.9%; retail sale of catering trade was 10.25 billion Yuan, increasing by 7.8%; retail sale of other sectors was 1.17 billion Yuan, increasing by 9.1%. 514 trading markets can be found at the year-end, 16 of which has a yearly transaction value of more than 0.1 billion Yuan.

1.5 Market Price

In 2003, the running of market price in Xi'an presented the posture of transferring to rising.

The consumer price index was 100.5, 0.5% more than last year. In comparison with the preceding year, the price of foodstuff, housing decreased by 4.6%, 4%. And the price of tobacco and alcohol, clothing, home appliance and maintaining service, medical care and body care products, transport and telecommunication, and entertainment and education product decreased by 0.5%, 1.0%, 1.8%, 3.3%, 2.4%, 6.1% and 3.1% respectively. The overall retail price index kept at the same level with the last year.

1.6 Banking, security and insurance industry

Along with the increasingly support of the banking system, personal consumer loans increased by great extent. The deposit balance of all financial institutes reached 266.59 billion Yuan at the year-end, or 21.4% more than the beginning of the year; loan balance reached 195.42 billion Yuan, increasing by 21.9%. Among the deposit balance, 104.19 billion was enterprises deposit, or 15.3 billion more than the beginning of the year. Among the loans 94.66 billion Yuan is short-term loans, an increase of 21.1%; 65.97 billion Yuan is long-and-medium-term loans, an increase of 30.8%.

The total cash income of all financial institutions was 490.93 billion Yuan, an increase of 22.3%; the cash expenditure was 469.05 billion Yuan, an increase of 23.2%. The withdrawal of currency in 2003 reached 21.88 billion Yuan.

Stock market grew steadily with more business

branches set up. 1 new securities firm emerged in 2003. In total there were 52 securities business offices in Xi'an at the year-end. 49 enterprises began their preparation period for IPO. In the situation of stagnant stock market, the stock exchange surpassed 174.9 billion Yuan, up 45.8%, in Xi'an.

Insurance industry grew rapidly with premium increasing greatly. In 2003, 2 new insurance companies, Zhonghua and Tianan set up business in Xi'an, which add the total number of insurance companies to 12. The operational income of insurance industry increased by 26.4%, reached 3.62 billion Yuan. Settled claims amounted to 0.65 billion Yuan. The share of life insurance grew fast. The ratio of property insurance and life insurance changed from 1:2.9 to 1:3.0.

1.7 Real Estate

With more individuals evolved in house purchasing, the total sales of real estate kept growing. At the same time, more investment is putting into real estate development.

The total floor space of buildings under construction of the year 2003 increased by 13.9% to 13.36 million m2, the floor space of commercial houses sold are 2.503 million m2 and total sales are 5.41 billion Yuan, keeping at the same level with the last year respectively. Share of commercial houses purchased by individuals increased dramatically to 2.279 million m2, up 92%.

1.8 Tourism

The tourism of the whole city was influenced directly on SARS in 2003. Both international tourism and domestic tourism are all attacked by SARS. Xi'an city accepted 0.337 million overseas guests for sightseeing, visiting or other activities, which is 54.6% less than the preceding year. Only 16.14 million domestic tourists has visited Xi'an, decreasing by 15.5%. The total income from tourism reached 10.57 billion Yuan, including 0.146 billion US dollars from international tourism, decreasing by 19.3% and 54% respectively. There were 30 tourism sites with yearly tourist capacity over 0.1 million, and 9 national 4-A grade tourism sites. 59 star hotels were in use at the year-end and 4 of them are 5-star hotels and 8 are 4-star hotels.

2.Reform and Opening Up

2.1 System Reform

It's much helpful to developing economy of system reform. The suggestion for further reform of state-owned enterprise showed out and 13 units of important state-owned enterprise reforming were finished, which played an important role for developing economy in Xi'an and further reform of state-owned enterprise. Administrative examination system reform has made now progress, 350 projects has been canceled, making the rate of reduce achieved 69%. Established Green Passage system in the administrative examination of investment projects, simplified processing procedure and shortened the duration of the examination. Pushing forward actively the state-owned land reserve system, attraction, auction and linking administrative measure have been put into practice for four types of operational land. City and town employees' basic medical insurance system reform, medical treatment and health system reform, medicine production and distribution system reform were pushed forward steadily. Culture system reform experiment started up. The changing from agricultural specialty tax to agricultural tax experimental work has been pushed forward, farmers' burden has been reduced by 58%. Government affairs and government administrative execution job responsibility system have been pushed forward in an all-round way. Scientific democratic decision making has been attached importance to. Holding court system has been tried out. Eleven local rule of law have been submitted to municipal Standing Committee of the National People's Congress; 68 governmental regulations and standardized documents have been modified. Further steps have been taken to optimize the policy environment for Non-public ownership economy. Over-all system reform has been pushed forward deeply and broadly.

The examination and approval system reform took new paces, and cancel 350 examination and approval projects newly, totally decreasing by 69%. It established a GREEN ROAD that simplified the procedure of handling affairs and shortened the time limit of examining and approving.

2.2 Foreign Trade

Foreign trade overcame the influence of SARS, especially the investment which implements walking out won initial success strategically, foreign trade hit new peak again.

By the end of 2003, the total imports and exports of Xi'an accumulated to 2.31 billion US dollars, which is 23.6% more than the preceding year. Among it 1.4 billion US dollars was from exports, an increase of 24.9%. Total self-support exports and imports reached 0.69 billion US dollars, increasing by 24.3%, including 0.48 billion US dollars from exports, increasing by 43.8%. It is the fist time that the exports of Xi'an surpasses 0.3 billion US dollars. It is two years ahead of time that realized the goal the municipal government required. The total export value of foreign trade was the first of provincial capital of the western region for the first time.

2.3 Foreign Investment

A new great upsurge in foreign investment appeared, and it was developing step by step.

In 2003, 132 contracts, that is, 8% less than the preceding year, were signed with the contract value of 0.96 billion US dollars, an increase of 36%. The investment in position amounted to 0.26 billion US dollars, increasing by 26%. 56 countries and areas has set up projects in Xi'an already. The new international cooperation projects were 50 units, 37.8% of the total new projects. The cooperation projects were 21 units, 15.9 of the total new projects. The foreign projects were 61 units, 46.3% of the total new projects.

2.4 Economic Cooperation

New progress was made in international economic cooperation made progress. It has carried on already that the biggest international aid offered by Japan reached 1.3 billion Yuan. The international assistance, the project abroad, and the labor service cooperation all increased. At the end of 2003, the labors working abroad numbered 1729, which was the best level among all years.

2.5 Building of Hi-tech Developing Zone

Taking Second Pioneering as the motive power, the economic developing of the hi-tech developing zone and the economic-tcch developing zone kept high increasing speed. The value added of fixed asset investment increased by 50% to 5.6 billion Yuan in the hi-tech zone; contract value of foreign investments increased by 27% to 0.3 billion US dollars, and foreign investments in position increased by 3804% to 0.1 billion Yuan; financial income reached 0.73 billion Yuan, up 29%. In the economic developing zone, the value added of fixed asset investment increased by 96% to 2.35 billion Yuan; contract value of foreign investments increased by 19.5% to 0.25 billion US dollars, foreign investments in position increased by 26% to 0.08 million US dollars and financial income reached 0.19 billion Yuan, up 30.7%. The building of New Qujiang Zone achieved breakthrough development. Northern Dayan Pagoda Square has been built and opened. The innovation and demonstration function of the New Qujiang Zone to the whole city's economy has been strengthened.

3. Social Work

The government followed the principle of sustainable development based on science, technology and education. With science functioning to its full potential and education and other social work developing prosperously, the society advanced in harmony with the growth of economy.

3.1 Science and Technology

By the end of 2003, there were 362,000 technician and experts working on various subjects. In total 411 scientific research projects were carried out into which 40 000 000 of scientific research fund at the civic level were launched. By actively striving for national supports, 110 scientific research projects has been listed in scientific research projects and major projects of Department of Science and Technology. Thirty key science and technological achievement transform projects has been implemented, the amount of the deal in the technology market reached 0.53 billion. In 2003, 2341 patents were applied and 1099 patents approved. The amount of the application of patents adds up to 16762 while 9030 of them approved. The industrialization of hi-tech projects accelerated. By the end of 2003, there were 971 hi-tech enterprises with 184 newly added.

3.2 Education

High quality compulsory education was offered. Efforts were taken to speed up the popularization of senior secondary school education and establishment of vocational education and private-running high education. Quality education was still put in an important position and the quality of civic education improved on the whole. in 2003, the enrollment rates of primary school and junior secondary school were 99.9%和98.5% respectively.

There were 66.8,000 primary school students, 389,000 junior secondary school student, 175,000 senior secondary school students, and 44,000 vocational school students. 54,000 students were secondary in specialized middle schools and 17, 000 graduated in 2003; 401,000 students in colleges and universities and 65,000 graduated. More social funds were put into school running. In 2003, there were25 colleges, 87 primary and secondary schools, and 31 vocational schools run by social resources.

3.3 Culture

Mass cultural activities were prosperous and colorful and cultural cause developed healthily. More investments were put into broadcasting to extend cable broadcasting network. Broadcast TV. Cable broadcasting system, newspaper, journals and other media functioned well in popularization of important projects, activities and work of the city communist party committee and city government. Management of publication market and protection of cultural relics were strengthened. Farther Reform was carried out in cultural institutions. At the end of 2003, there were 22 theatrical performance teams, 2 mass art galleries, 13 cultural centers, 181 cultural stations, 14 public libraries and 15 publishing houses. 33 newspapers and journals were published.

3.4 Medical Care

Regional sanitation planning was promoted in both urban and rural areas. Sanitation monitoring and disease control system was reinforced. Services as well as facilities of medical treatment were improved. In rural area, 65.6% of area could enjoy the service offered by rural community medical care co-operations. More people took part in blood donation. All of the clinic use of blood was donations. At the end of 2003, there were2785 medical institutions in Xi'an, including 474 hospitals and heath centers, staffed by 41000 professionals (including 15000 doctors) and equipped with 33000 beds.

3.5 Sports

Industrialization and popularization are the two trends of development of sports. At the end of 2003, 10 advanced communities and 17 advanced towns/townships in sports were designated at national level and 23 advanced communities in sports at provincial level. In 2003, 400 persons joined into the group of community physical education instructors. The total number of the PE instructors reached 1984. More than 100,000 people participated in more than 150 activities concerning different sports. 170 public bodybuilding squares were in service. In 2003, the municipal sports delegation gained the second place for Shanxi Province in the 5th National Sports Game with 5 gold medals,11silver medals and 5 copper medals with the total score of 493.5.

4. Urban and Rural Construction and Management

4.1 Investments on Fixed Assets

More investments were attracted and put into fixed asset and investment structure farther improved In 2003, investments on fixed assets reached 47.9 billion Yuan, including 28.03 billion Yuan from the state-owned units, an increase of 40.1%, 2.23 billion Yuan from collective-owned units, an increase of 62.9% and 17.64billion Yuan from private sources, increasing by 41.8%. Among all the investments, 22.84 billion Yuan were put into capital construction, 47.4% more than the preceding year; 7.15billion Yuan for renovation, increasing by 24.4%; 12.4 7 billion Yuan for real estate, increasing by 57.1% and 2.13 billion Yuan for other projects, increasing by 38.2%. 483 projects of capital construction and renovation were accomplished and put into use accounting for 50.3% of the total.

4.2 Construction, Planning and Management

Second Ring entirely completed, the additional overpass from Zhuque Road to Hanguang Road has been completed, and express way of airport has been open to traffic successfully, Zaoyuan Donglu and Zaoyuan Xilu, Weiyi Street, Xiying Road, Gaoxin Road 4, Dongyi Road, Wuxing Street, Due Dongguan Street, north part of Taihua Road, reliving way of Youyi Road in total 15 roads' construction and reconstruction entirely completed. Alleyway and dead end reconstruction projects of Guanghua Road, Xiejiacun Road, the road run in front of Gear Wheel Factory,

Fengcheng Road 3, Diaojiacun Road, Southern part of Yongsong Road have been completed. Dengjiacun sewage disposal factory reconstruction work, Beishiqiao sewage deep disposal project have been completed and devoted to operation. Weiyi Street rainwater catching pipe work, Cuihua Road drainage basically completed, and Xixie 3 channel reconstruction work is getting along smoothly. Modernization breath possessing Northern Dayan Pagoda Square is finished and open to the public, Plenty of Water and Rich of Greenness project started up in due form. Plant-trees-and-grass-in-the-city project and greenbelt maintaining work of reconstruction of Bell Tower Ring, Reconstruction of Xihuamen West Square, Changle Donglu Road pavement tree filling, Nanmen Square spray irrigation, and Gongyuan Nanlu Road, Xincheng Square, Wei 29 Street pavement tree planting, Xingqing Lake comprehensive tackling project have all been completed.

All the bridge projects, drainage projects and green projects were in progress smoothly. The progress of main projects are as follows: the road at the east and west exits of the city were broadened; the Xidajie Street Broadening project was completed; the reconstruction of Bell Temple circular Road was accomplished in time; broadening of Xiying Road, Zaoyuan Road, Taihua Road, Dongguan Road, Wuxing Road and Hanguang Road has completed. The east section of elevated road was completed and construction of the west section started the construction of Jinhua Road overpass on the 2nd ring road was started; the second phase of Natural Gas Liquefaction Project and the City Central Heating System Project were heading on; Electric Network Reconstruction project was on its way; Black River Water Conservancy Project was finished; the channel connecting Jianzi River and Southern Suburb Water Factory was on the whole approved in the quality check and put into use; the railway connecting Xi'an and Ankang and Xihu Express way was put into use; the south part of round-city express way was about to finish; the express way leading to the airport was started.

With more efforts put into city plan and planning management, distinctive effects shown up about the city's environmental comprehensive improvement, with the appearance of the city greatly improved. Six districts plan and detailed plan have been completed. City's key construction projects plan has been strengthened. The controlling plan of the land at both side of the road around the mountain has been worked out, also worked out are the alleyway renovate and dead end get through project programmatic design, city light-up project systematic plan, city sculpture systematic plan, in-city village and old village reconstruction plan, Daminggong Royal Road Square plan, site pick plan of making construction garbage into view, city's basic geographical and special database building, the Third Ring road project plan, city road system plan, city green system plan, plan of building new public toilet and reconstruct old toilet and site selection plan. Green land increased 60 hectares in this year. The green coverage rate increased by 7.98%, reached 38.8%. Every resident can share 4.15 m^2 of public green land, 0.38 m^2 more than the preceding year.

4.3 Public Utilities

In total 15 km long and 30 0000 m^2 of streets and roads were built. 51 000 m^2 of pavements and 720 000 m^2 of road were renovated in 2003. 34 km of rainwater tunnels, 14 km of drainage tunnels and 10431 m of water supply tunnels were newly added. There are 1328 coal boiler has been reconstructed into gas boiler. More than 400 kilometers gas pipeline is laid. Newly added 300 000 m2 heating area. On the reconstruction of street lamp, 47km cable was laid, 1794 poles were erected, 4471 street lamp has been built or reconstructed, 123 without-lamps streets and lanes has been reconstructed. Totally 4847 m^3 sewage has been disposed. The capacity of the sewage disposal of city went up to 310 000 tons. The area of the road cleared by all levels general sanitation department reached 15000 000 m^2. Area of watered road reached 4400 000 m^2. There are 1 132 000 tons of garbage has been collected, moved and treated.

At the end of 2003, there were 152 lines in the city's public transport system, that is, 795 km long. In 2003, 8 new lines were opened and 19 old ones extended or changed. 348 new buses were put into use and 115 renewed. In total there were 3431 buses and 10,430 taxies were in service, which completed the service task of 550 million people-times. In Xi'an city, coal gas reached 50,000 households through pipelines, natural gas reached 383,000 households. 634,000 families supplied with liquefied gas. In total 91.2% of the urban residents supplied with gas for fuel. Daily Tap-water-producing capacity was 1.974 million tons. In total 36,122 tons of water were supplied induding12 002 were for the daily use. The central heating system covered an area of 21.75 million m2. Total electricity consumed was 10.2 billion kilo-watt-hour, increasing by 9.2%, 1.88 billion kilo-watt-hour of which was for the use of everyday life, increasing by 10.8%.

4.4 Environment Protection and Renovation

With adequate measures taken to control water and other pollution, the environment of XI'an city was further improved. The second phase of Jiangcungou Garbage Deposit Complex Project has finished. In total 1883 coal-burning boilers were removed. There are 15 environment monitoring stations and 9 smoke-and-dust-control zones, covering an area of 196.7 km2. 6 noise-control zones were set up, covering an area of 81 km2, noise was successfully controlled below the standard. The daily content average value of sulfur dioxide, nitrogen dioxide and inhalant particles, three main pollution of air, was 0.019 mg/ m^3, 0.015mg/ m^3 and 0.136 mg/ m^3, respectively over the year. Number of days of urban air quality being better than second grade of State Standard is 255, 80 days more than year 2002, raised by 22 percent. In it, sulfur dioxide and nitrogen dioxide reached second grade of State Standard in pairs, went up to 100%. Drinking water, reached the standard and 77.1% of the industrial wastewater deposited met the standard.

5. Population and people's life

5.1 Populations and employment

Family planning was reinforced with birth rate kept at a low level. In 2002, the birth rate kept at 9.83 and natural growth rate 4.43 . The year-end registered population increased to 7,166,000. Among them 4,037,000 are rural population and 3,129,000 are non-rural population. At the year-end, in total 1.856 million urban people were employed by various units and organizations. The registered unemployment rate was 4.5%.

5.2 People's Life

The disposable income of urban residents reached 7,784 Yuan, and the net income of rural residents 2,838 Yuan, increasing by 7.9% and 7.4% respectively. The people are leading a more wealthy life. The average expenditure on consumer goods of urban people is 6,805 Yuan and the rural people 1,803 Yuan, an increase of 6.0% and 1.2% respectively. The ratio between expenditure on food and expenditure on consumer goods was 34.8% in urban people in contrast to 37.6% in rural people. The year-end deposit balance reached 121.06 billion Yuan, 22.25 billion Yuan more than the beginning of the year. People's housing condition is improved as well. The per capita floor space of urban residential increased to 12.06 m^2.In rural areas, each person has 33.9 m^2 of living space on the average.

5.3 Social Security

The social security system of Xi'an city has been taking shape. A complete social insurance system has been established. The insurances supplied include: old-age insurance, jobless insurance, medical care insurance, industrial injury insurance, childbirth insurance etc.

In total 11500 units and organizations bought endowment insurance for their staff in 2002, which would benefit 957,000 people. All the 352,000 retirees in Xi'an got retirement pension in 2003. 11577 units and organizations bought jobless insurance, covering 1,271 million people and bring by 180 million Yuan to the Jobless Insurance Funds. 25,699 jobless got financial support from the Funds. In total 62.15 million Yuan was distributed. There were 58,781 people enjoying the lowest-income-insurance. 52,223 of them from the enterprises under the municipal government and the rest 6,558 people are from enterprises at the district or county level. In total 153 million Yuan was distributed directly to the laid-off workers to cover their lowest cost of living and another 101 million Yuan was offered to them for social insurance. More units and people in urban area were included into basic medical care system as well. In 2002, the system covered 4500 units and 1.07 million units, 16.94% more than the ceding year.

Social welfare system functioned more effectively. In 2003, the social welfare units in Xi'an city provided

2,799 beds to homeless people for living and food. 1619 people were kept by those units. 1734 facilities for community service were established, including 114 comprehensive community service centers. 197,6 million Yuan of social welfare funds were collected through publication of social welfare lottery and 102,7million Yuan from social donation. In total 181,000 people were included into the lowest-income insurance system, containing 175,000 people from urban area and 18,000 people from rural area.

In 2003, the main problems existing in national economy and social development are as follows:

-most of the state-owned enterprises are still lack the sense and ability of innovation and are not adaptive enough to the open market;

-innovation of structure of Industry is slow and ability of competition is weak

-income of urban residents increase slowly

-urban traffic situation need improving

-the speed of the increase of farmers' income and elevation of agricultural efficiency is relatively slow;

-employment and reemployment is still a big problem;

-social security system did not play its full function, etc.

Under the Guidance of the important decisions made in the 16th CPC National Congress, the Communist Party Committee and the Government of Xi'an City are taking practical measures to solve the existing problems.

Notes: 1. All statistics in the communiqu are preliminary statistics.

2. Population is based on the registered number at the year-end offered by Public Security Bureau.

3. The figures of gross domestic national product, total output value of all industries and value added of all industries are calculated on current price. The growth speed is based on comparable price.

4. Number of telephones at the end of the year only includes the customers of China-telecom; customers of the other communication companies are not included.

2004 統計年鑒

一、综合

GENERAL SURVEY

简 要 说 明

Brief Introduction

本章主要包括西安市行政区划、自然地理、自然资源、气象、国民经济和社会发展综合资料。由市统计局综合处根据专业及有关部门资料进行整理和编辑。

This chapter consists of mainly unified data of administrative divisions, natural geography, natural resources, meteorology, national economy and social development of Xi'an city. It is compiled by Integration Division of Xi'an Bureau of Statistics according to the reported data from other divisions of the Xi'an Bureau of Statistics and other departments of the municipal government.

1-1 行政区划（2003年）

Administrative Division (2003)

单位:个 (unit)

区县名称	Name of District and County	乡级 Township	镇数 Town	乡数 Township	街道办事处 Urban Subdistrict Office	村民委员会 Villagers' Committee	社区居委会 Neighbourhood Committee
西安市	**Xi'an**	**176**	**54**	**52**	**70**	**3164**	**553**
(一)市区	**Urban Districts**	**108**	**30**	**18**	**60**	**1661**	**519**
新城区	Xincheng	9			9	13	90
碑林区	Beilin	8			8	15	103
莲湖区	Lianhu	9			9	35	113
灞桥区	Baqiao	9	4		5	229	30
未央区	Weiyang	10			10	212	41
雁塔区	Yanta	8			8	120	81
阎良区	Yanliang	7	2		5	80	19
临潼区	Lintong	23	10	7	6	285	21
长安区	Chang'an	25	4	11	10	672	21
(二)四县	**Four Counties**	**68**	**34**	**34**		**1503**	**34**
蓝田县	Lantian	22	10	12		519	5
周至县	Zhouzhi	22	9	13		379	10
户　县	Huxian	16	11	5		518	16
高陵县	Gaoling	8	4	4		87	3

1-2　土地面积和人口密度（2003年）

Statistics on Land Area and Population Density (2003)

区县名称	Name of District and County	土地面积 Area 绝对数（平方公里）Absolute Value (sq.km)	比重 (%) Proportion (%)	总人口（人）Total Population (person)	人口密度（人/平方公里）Density of Population (person/ sq.km)
西 安 市	**Xi 'an**	**9983**	**100**	**7165784**	**718**
(一)市区	**Urban Districts**	**3547**	**35.53**	**5102553**	**1439**
新城区	Xincheng	31	0.31	481787	15542
碑林区	Beilin	22	0.22	691110	31414
莲湖区	Lianhu	38	0.38	590160	15531
灞桥区	Baqiao	322	3.23	445826	1385
未央区	Weiyang	261	2.61	401192	1537
雁塔区	Yanta	152	1.52	669352	4404
阎良区	Yanliang	240	2.40	240278	1002
临潼区	Lintong	898	9.00	668600	745
长安区	Chang'an	1583	15.86	914248	578
(二)四县	**Four Counties**	**6436**	**64.47**	**2063231**	321
蓝田县	Lantian	1977	19.81	632520	320
周至县	Zhouzhi	2956	29.61	627836	212
户　县	Huxian	1213	12.15	568625	469
高陵县	Gaoling	290	2.90	234250	808

1–3　自然状况和资源（2003年）

Nature Conditions and Resources（2003）

指　　标	Item　(unit)	2003
一、自然状况	**Nature Conditions**	
土地总面积(平方公里)	Total Land Area (sq.km)	9983
#市区面积	Urban Area	3547
气候（市区）	Climate (Urban Area)	
年平均气温(℃)	Average Annual Temperature (℃)	14.4
年降水量(毫米)	Total Annual Precipitation (mm)	883.2
日照总时数(小时)	Total Sunshine Time (hour)	1657.2
平均风速(米/秒)	Average Wind-speed (m/sec.)	0.9
二、自然资源	**Natural Resources**	
耕地面积(公顷)	Area of Cultivated Land (ha)	275893
林地面积(公顷)	Area of Forestry (ha)	439787
园地面积(公顷)	Area of Orchards (ha)	34930
内陆水域面积(公顷)	Water Area in the Land (ha)	32298
#可养殖面积	Area for Aquatics Breeding	1654
水资源总量(亿立方米)	Total Water Resource (0.1 billion cu.m)	26.7
#天然地表水资源总量	Total Savageness Surface Water Resource	21.8
地下水资源总量(亿立方米)	Total Ground Water Resource (0.1 billion cu.m)	17.3

1–4　气 象 情 况(2003年)

Climate Condition (2003)

区县名称	Name of District and County	平均气温(℃) Average Temperature (℃)	日照时数(小时) Sunshine Time (hour)	降水天数(天) Raining days (day)	年降水量(毫米) Total Annual Precipitation (mm)	平均风速(米/秒) Average Wind-speed (m/second)
市　区	**Urban Districts**	**14.4**	**1657.2**	**122**	**883.2**	**0.9**
临潼区	Lintong	13.3	2048.2	134	954.9	1.5
长安区	Chang'an	13.5	1674.5	129	922.1	0.5
蓝田县	Lantian	12.9	2036.4	113	920.6	1.3
周至县	Zhouzhi	14.2	1732.3	139	886.8	0.8
户　县	Huxian	14.2	1894.5	154	908.5	0.6
高陵县	Gaoling	14.1	1967.0	112	848.5	1.5

1–5 各部门机构数

Grassroots Units in Various Sectors

部门	Sector	机构数 Grassroots Units	
		2002	2003
农村基层单位（个）	**Rural Grassroots Units（unit）**		
乡政府	Township Governments	52	52
镇政府	Town Governments	64	54
村民委员会	Village Committees	3164	3161
乡村户数(万户)	Numbers of Rural Households(10 000 unit)	99.85	101.33
国营农场(个)	**State-owned Farms(unit)**	**1**	**1**
国有及规模以上非国有工业企业(个)	**State-owned and Non-state-owned above Designated Size Industrial Enterprises(units)**	**771**	**735**
内资企业	Domestic Funded Enterprises	684	653
国有企业	State-owned Industry	220	205
集体企业	Collective-owned Industry	170	115
股份合作企业	Cooperative Enterprises	35	33
联营经济企业	Joint Ownership Enterprises	14	14
国有独资公司	State-owned appropriator ship corporation		12
其他有限责任公司	Limited Liability Corporations	112	133
股份有限公司	Share Holding Enterprises	55	47
私营企业	Private Enterprises	77	92
其他内资企业	Other Enterprises	1	2
港澳台商投资企业	Enterprises with Funds from Hong Kong, Macao and Taiwan	36	29
外商投资企业	Foreign Funded Enterprises	51	53
建筑业企业(个)	**Construction Enterprises and Units(unit)**	**223**	**204**
国有企业	Construction Enterprises	44	61
集体企业	Affiliated Construction Units	83	73
其他	Others	96	70
邮政营销网点(个)	**Establishments of Postal and Telecommunication Services(unit)**	326	338
卫生事业(个)	**Health Care (unit)**	**2726**	**2495**
#医院、卫生院	Urban and Township Hospitals	470	473
疗养院	Sanatoriums	5	4
门诊部	Clinics	198	179
专科疾病防治院	Specialized Prevention & Treatment Stations	5	3
疾病控制预防中心	Sanitation and Antiepidemic Stations	17	19
妇幼保健院	Maternity and Childcare Centers	15	15

1-5 各部门机构数(续)

Grassroots Units in Various Sectors(Continued)

部门	Sector	机构数 Grassroots Units	
		2002	2003
社会福利机构(个)	**Social Welfare Establishments(unit)**	**51**	**56**
#社会福利院	Social Welfare Institutions	5	15
社会福利企业	Social Welfare Enterprises	234	298
教育事业	**Education**		
普通高等学校(所)	Regular Institutions of Higher Education(unit)	35	37
普通中等学校(所)	Secondary Schools(units)	654	651
#普通中学	Regular Secondary Schools	467	467
小学(所)	Primary Schools(units)	2137	2084
幼儿园(所)	Kindergartens (units)	378	610
特殊教育(所)	Special Schools(unit)	5	5
艺术事业(个)	**Art Institutions (unit)**	**47**	**58**
#艺术表演团体	Art Performance Troupes	22	22
艺术表演场所	Art Show Centers	24	24
#剧场、影剧院	Theaters	13	13
公共图书馆(个)	**Public Libraries (unit)**	**14**	**14**
群众文化事业(个)	**Mass Cultural Establishments (unit)**	**185**	**191**
文化馆	Cultural Centers	13	13
其它文化产业	Other Cultural Establishments		
博物馆(个)	Museum(unit)	16	14
广播电视台站(座)	Broadcasting and Television Stations (unit)		
广播电台	Radio Stations	2	2
电视台	Television Stations	2	2
县级广播电视台	Number of Wire Broadcasting and Television Stations in County Level	6	6
科学研究机构(个)	**Scientific Research Institutions (unit)**	**569**	**564**
#科研单位	#Units of Scientific Research	130	131
高等院校	Institutions of Higher Education	340	333
大中型工业企业	Large-scale and Medium-scale Industrial Enterprises	99	100

注：广播电台和电视台未包括县级数。

a)Number of broadcasting and television stations excludes that in county level.

1-6 平均每天主要社会经济活动

指　　标		1990
每天创造的财富	**Daily Production**	
地区生产总值(万元)	Gross Domestic Product(10000 yuan)	2833.16
第一产业	Primary Industry	381.92
第二产业	Secondary Industry	1374.04
#工业	Industry	1279.15
建筑业	Construction	94.88
第三产业	Tertiary Industry	1077.13
#交通运输仓储和邮电通信业	Transport, Storage, Post & Telecommunication Services	230.41
批发和零售贸易餐饮业	Wholesale and Retail Trade & Catering Services	179.55
财政收入(万元)	Government Revenue(10000 yuan)	359.45
财政支出(万元)	Government Expenditures(10000 yuan)	254.79
粮食(吨)	Grain(ton)	4724.11
奶类(吨)	Milk(ton)	224.70
蔬菜(吨)	Vegetables(ton)	3269.04
肉类(吨)	Meat(ton)	173.35
水产品(吨)	Aquatic Products(ton)	11.67
布(万米)	Cloth(10 000 m)	79.00
发电量(万千瓦小时)	Electricity(10000 kwh)	523.00
钢(吨)	Steel(ton)	
水 泥(吨)	Cement(ton)	931.51
每天消费量	**Daily National Consumption**	
最终消费(万元)	Final Consumption Expenditure(10000 yuan)	2816.16
居民消费	Resident Consumption	1834.25
农民	Peasants Consumption	572.88
非农业居民	Non-agricultural Residents' Consumption	1261.37
政府消费	Government Consumption Expenditure	457.26
社会消费品零售总额(万元)	Total Retail Sales of Consumer Goods (10000 yuan)	1870.00
每天其他经济活动	**Other Daily Economic Activities**	
资本形成总额(万元)	Gross Capital Formation(10000 yuan)	1471.80
固定资产形成	Fixed Capital Formation	795.30
存货增加	Changes in Stock	676.40
城镇新建住宅面积(平方米)	Residential Buildings Completed in Urban Areas(sq.m)	3042.56
农民新建房屋面积(平方米)	Private Buildings Completed in Rural Areas(sq.m)	6683.84
货运量(吨)	Freight Traffic(ton)	191238.36
客运量(人)	Passenger Traffic(person)	157490.41
邮电业务总量(万元)	Business Volume of Postal and Telecommunications Services(10000 yuan)	21.40
进出口总额(万美元)	Total Value of Imports and Exports (USD 10000)	34.91
出口总额	Total Exports	25.21
进口总额	Total Imports	9.70
实际利用外资额(万美元)	Foreign Capital Actually Used(USD 10000)	3.16
境外旅游人数(人)	Number of Tourists from Abroad(person)	709.00
城乡居民储蓄额(万元)	Outstanding Amount of Savings Deposit (10000 yuan)	2112.19
每天人口变动和婚姻	**Daily Population Changes and Marriages**	
出 生(人)	Births(person)	340
死 亡(人)	Deaths(person)	94
结 婚(对)	Marriages(couple)	143
离 婚(对)	Divorces(couple)	6

Selected Indicators on Average Daily Social and Economic Activities

1995	2000	2002	2003
9050.68	17623.56	22561.60	25797.26
1134.25	1223.29	1309.60	1389.59
3707.67	7756.71	10205.50	11388.49
3082.19	6196.71	8205.48	8491.51
625.48	1560.00	1198.90	2896.99
4208.77	8643.56	11046.60	13019.18
747.95	1695.07	1947.10	2179.18
938.90	2106.85	2651.50	3173.97
498.79	1304.00	1646.60	1996.36
504.66	1274.06	1884.90	2116.52
4801.37	5532.05	5271.50	4831.23
364.13	673.73	789.10	921.37
3660.27	4442.19	4650.40	4648.49
350.18	404.30	371.20	454.52
23.33	31.19	32.90	27.40
83.00	77.00	76.39	76.47
610.00	534.00	520.40	559.18
	85.10	85.10	98.06
1898.90	3050.68	3677.50	3693.70
6876.44	12683.01	15709.60	17522.19
5084.11	9511.78	11531.50	12977.53
1516.23	2489.59	2820.60	3038.36
3567.90	7022.19	8711.00	9939.18
1792.38	3171.23	3729.90	4544.66
4937.53	8999.18	11216.40	12056.04
4201.60	8040.80	10605.80	13498.63
2986.90	6893.20	8439.50	12333.15
1214.80	1147.70	1166.30	1166.58
6927.40	14930.14	13318.57	15837.39
8630.96	14168.22	15151.50	13828.22
262734.25	191760.10	259835.60	257315.07
248465.75	221041.36	343205.50	312684.93
209.60	1264.70	1411.70	1417.72
110.19	475.88	512.20	632.69
82.45	290.58	308.20	384.46
27.74	185.30	204.00	248.23
51.11	42.83	55.60	70.02
1133.82	1781.88	2030.90	922.34
7985.33	18515.96	27069.60	33166.05
211	247	109	165
88	113	105	91
129	129	122	122
12	14	26	29

1-7 国民经济和社会发展总量与速度指标

指 标	Item	总量指标		
		1990	1995	2000
人口与就业	**Population and Employment**			
人口(万人)	**Population(10 000 persons)**			
年底总人口	Population at the Year-end	608.89	648.21	688.01
非农业人口	Non-agricultural Population	226.98	255.71	285.79
农业人口	Agriculturral Population	381.91	392.50	402.22
男性人口	Male	313.60	334.75	355.18
女性人口	Female	295.29	313.46	332.83
就业(万人)	**Employment(10 000 persons)**			
就业人员数	Employment	343.06	372.60	389.10
#在岗职工人数	Number of Employed Staff and Workers	141.53	141.17	135.84
城镇登记失业人数	Registered Unemployed in Urban Areas		5.92	3.85
宏观经济	**Macroeconomic Indicator**			
国民核算(亿元)	**National Accounting(100 million yuan)**			
地区生产总值	Gross Domestic Product	116.51	330.35	643.26
#第一产业	Primary Industry	13.94	41.40	44.65
第二产业	Secondary Industry	50.15	135.33	283.12
第三产业	Tertiary Industry	52.42	153.62	315.49
#最终消费	Total Consumption		250.99	462.93
居民消费	Resident Consumption		185.57	347.18
政府消费	Public Consumption		65.42	115.75
资本形成总额	Total Investment		153.36	293.49
固定资本形成	Fixed Assets		109.02	251.60
存货增加	Stock		44.34	41.89
固定资产投资(万元)	**Investment in Fixed Assets(10 000 yuan)**			
全社会固定资产投资总额	Total Investment in Fixed Assets	263865	1034184	2323676
#国有单位	State-Owned Units	222084	690806	1596002
集体单位	Collective-Owned Units	14422	97778	146519
个体经济	Individuals	27359	111298	243959
财政(万元)	**Public Finance(10 000 yuan)**			
地方财政收入	Local Financial Revenue	131153	182058	469638
地方财政支出	Local Financial Expenditure	92876	184184	518935
物价总指数(上年=100)	**Price Indices(preceding year=100)**			
商品零售价格指数	Retail Price Index	100.9	114.6	98.7
居民消费价格指数	Consumer Price Index	102.5	117.0	100.2
工业品出厂价格指数	Ex-Factory Price Indices of Industrial Products			99.4
利用外资(万美元)	**Utilization of Foreign Capital(USD 10 000)**			
签订利用外资协议额	Amount of Foreign Capital for Utilization Through Signed Contracts or Agreements	415.3	28956.2	54123.0
实际利用外资额	Amount of Foreign Capital Actually Utilized	1154	18653	15633

Principal Aggregate Indicators on National Economic and Social Development and Their Related Indices and Growth Rates

2002	2003	速度指标(%) Indices and Growth Rates							
		指数 Index (2003比以下各年) (2003 as percentage of the following years)				平均增长速度 Average Annual Growth Rate			
		1990	1995	2000	2002	1990-1995	1990-2000	1990-2003	1995-2003
702.59	716.58	117.69	110.55	104.15	101.99	1.26	1.23	1.26	1.26
300.05	312.88	137.84	122.36	109.48	104.28	2.41	2.33	2.50	2.55
402.54	403.70	105.71	102.85	100.37	100.29	0.55	0.52	0.43	0.35
363.08	370.32	118.09	110.63	104.26	101.99	1.31	1.25	1.29	1.27
339.51	346.26	117.26	110.46	104.04	101.99	1.20	1.20	1.23	1.25
397.16	404.92	118.03	108.67	104.07	101.95	1.67	1.27	1.28	1.05
112.69	113.54	80.22	80.43	83.58	100.75	-0.05	-0.41	-1.68	-2.69
4.10	8.56		144.59	222.34	208.78				4.72
823.50	941.60	522.75	274.45	145.44	113.50	13.75	13.65	13.57	13.45
47.77	50.72	201.85	134.50	107.58	101.80	8.46	6.50	5.55	3.77
372.48	415.68	769.24	340.06	157.00	118.20	17.73	17.22	16.99	16.53
403.25	475.20	424.11	246.22	141.11	111.10	11.49	11.63	11.76	11.92
573.40	639.56								
420.90	473.68								
152.50	165.88								
387.11	492.74								
344.54	450.16								
42.57	42.58								
3381503	4781002	1811.91	462.30	205.75	141.39	31.41	24.30	24.96	21.09
2000636	2648283	1192.47	383.36	165.93	132.37	25.48	21.80	21.01	18.29
137032	223265	1548.09	228.34	152.38	162.93	46.64	26.09	23.46	10.87
446806	734346	2684.11	659.80	301.01	164.35	32.40	24.46	28.80	26.60
600694	728670	555.59	400.24	155.16	121.30	6.78	13.61	14.10	18.93
687566	772529	831.79	419.43	148.87	112.36	14.68	18.77	17.70	19.63
98.5	100.0	99.11	87.26	101.32	101.52	2.58	-0.22	-0.07	-1.69
98.6	100.5	98.05	85.90	100.30	101.93	2.68	-0.23	-0.15	-1.88
98.2	101.5			102.08	103.36				
70692.0	96380.0	23207.32	332.85	178.08	136.34	133.71	62.74	52.04	16.22
20281	25557	2214.64	137.01	163.48	126.01	74.47	29.77	26.91	4.01

1–7 国民经济和社会发展总量与速度指标(续1)

指　标	Item	总量指标 1990	1995	2000
产　业	**Industry**			
农业	**Agriculture**			
耕地面积(千公顷)	Cultivated Areas(1 000 hectares)	330.21	309.31	295.58
农林牧渔业劳动力(万人)	Labor Force of Farming, Forestry, Animal Husbandry and Fishery(10 000 persons)	49.69	152.35	146.07
农林牧渔业总产值(万元)	Gross Output Value of Farming Forestry, Animal Husbandry and Fishery(10 000 yuan)	262073	754597	743712
主要农产品产量(万吨)	Output of Major Farm Products(10 000 tons)			
粮　食	Grain	172.43	175.25	201.92
奶　类	Milk	8.2	13.29	24.59
油　料	Oil-bearing Crops	1.26	2.17	1.34
蔬　菜	Vegetables	119.32	133.6	162.14
水　果	Fruits	6.97	24.13	34.36
肉　类	Meat	6.33	12.78	12.38
水产品	Aquatic Products	0.43	0.85	1.14
工业	**Industry**			
主要工业产品产量	Output of Major Industrial Products			
布(万米)	Cloth(10 000 m)	28874	30332	24818
机制纸及纸板(吨)	Machine-Made Paper and Paperboards(tons)	151154	364400	54711
家用电冰箱(台)	Household Refrigerators(unit)		13000	5860
彩色电视机(台)	Color Television Sets(unit)	434400	223300	8487
房间空调器(台)	Room Air-conditioning(unit)			
发电量(亿千瓦小时)	Electricity(100 million kwh)	19.08	22.26	19.24
钢(吨)	Steel(ton)	333258	334100	31061
成品钢材(吨)	Steel Products(ton)	190189	314400	4320
水　泥(万吨)	Cement(10 000 tons)	34	69.31	111.35
规模以上工业企业主要经济指标（万元）	Principal Indicators of Industrial Enterprises of State Ownership and Non-state-owned Above Designated Size(10 000 yuan)			
工业总产值	Gross industrial Output Value	1483450.6	2997423.4	4179736.3
固定资产原价	Original Value of Fixed Assets	1269475.6	3379284.1	4742075.8
固定资产净值年平均余额	Annual Average Balance of Net Value of Fixed Assets	733078.1	1417811.4	2981896.3
利润总额	Profits		-69402.9	161133.6
建筑业	**Construction**			
建筑业企业人数(人)	Number of Employed Persons(person)			136718
建筑业总产值(万元)	Gross Output Value(10 000 yuan)	184368	425514	1059250
施工房屋面积(万平方米)	Floor Space of Buildings under Construction (10 000 sq.m)	388.82	601.74	793.32

Principal Aggregate Indicators on National Economic and Social Development and Their Related Indices and Growth Rates(Continued 1)

2002	2003	速度指标(%) Indices and Growth Rates							
		指数 Index (2003比以下各年) (2003 as percentage of the following years)				平均增长速度 Average Annual Growth Rate			
		1990	1995	2000	2002	1990-1995	1990-2000	1990-2003	1995-2003
282.97	275.89	83.58	89.23	93.38	97.54	-1.30	-1.10	-1.37	-1.41
141.96	145.43	292.67	95.46	99.56	102.44	25.12	11.39	8.61	-0.58
797444	837857	208.48	143.29	112.69	105.10	7.79	6.34	5.81	4.60
192.41	176.34	102.27	100.62	87.33	91.65	0.32	1.59	0.17	0.08
28.80	33.63	410.12	253.05	136.76	116.77	10.14	11.61	11.47	12.31
1.22	1.13	89.68	52.07	84.33	92.62	11.49	0.62	-0.83	-7.83
169.74	169.67	142.20	127.00	104.64	99.96	2.29	3.11	2.75	3.03
37.58	38.43	551.36	159.26	111.85	102.26	28.19	17.30	14.03	5.99
16.11	16.59	262.09	129.81	134.01	102.98	15.09	6.94	7.69	3.32
1.20	1.00	232.56	117.65	87.72	83.33	14.60	10.24	6.71	2.05
27883	27911	96.66	92.02	112.46	100.10	0.99	-1.50	-0.26	-1.03
62635	99786	66.02	27.38	182.39	159.31	19.24	-9.66	-3.14	-14.95
111410	92654		712.72	1581.13	83.16				27.82
750	57274	13.18	25.65	674.84	7636.53	-12.46	-32.53	-14.43	-15.64
18.99	20.41	106.97	91.69	106.08	107.48	3.13	0.08	0.52	-1.08
31048	35792	10.74	10.71	115.23	115.28	0.05	-21.12	-15.77	-24.36
3340	23860	12.55	7.59	552.31	714.37	10.58	-31.51	-14.76	-27.55
134	135	396.53	194.52	121.08	100.44	15.31	12.60	11.18	8.67
6588906.5	7817317.0	462.67	270.54	161.47	118.55	11.33	11.10	12.51	13.25
5341646.9	5674322.0	446.98	167.91	119.66	106.23	21.63	14.09	12.21	6.69
3250676.1	3432078.7	468.17	242.07	115.10	105.58	14.10	15.06	12.61	11.68
254319.0	338169.4			209.87	132.97				
150845	133186			97.42	88.29				
1334713	1771126	960.65	416.23	167.21	132.70	18.21	19.11	19.01	19.51
1012.91	1291.62	332.19	214.65	162.81	127.52	9.13	7.39	9.67	10.02

1–7 国民经济和社会发展总量与速度指标(续2)

指　标	Item	总量指标		
		1990	1995	2000
竣工房屋面积(万平方米)	Floor Space of Buildings Completed(10 000 sq.m)	152.50	177.15	336.80
交通运输	**Transportation**			
货运量(万吨)	Freight Traffic(10 000 tons)	6980	9590	10191
铁 路	Railways	2826	3317	3101
公 路	Highways	4154	6268	7082
空 运	Civil Aviation	0.93	4.77	8.24
客运量(万人)	Passenger Traffic(10 000 persons)	5748	9069	10756
铁 路	Railways	1974	2678	2130
公 路	Highways	3722	6128	8266
空 运	Civil Aviation	52.50	263.00	360.01
邮电通信业	**Post and Telecommunication Services**			
邮电业务总量(万元)	Total Business Revenue(10 000 yuan)	7843	76450	461628
函 件(万件)	Number of Letters Delivered(10 000 pieces)	8481	14647	8230
本地电话局用交换机容量(门)	Capacity of Local Office Telephone Exchanges (line)	55500	582990	2048400
本地电话年末用户(户)	Number of Subscribers of Local Telephone at Year-end(subscriber)	46935	307871	1412836
城市电话用户	Urban Telephone Subscribers	45267	299485	1242637
乡村电话用户	Rural Telephone Subscribers	1668	8386	170199
移动电话用户(户)	Number of Mobile Telephone Subscribers (subscriber)			731000
国际互联网络用户(户)	Number of Subscribers of Internet Services (subscriber)			207064
国内商业	**Domestic Trade**			
社会消费品零售总额(万元)	Total Retail Sales of Consumer Goods (10 000 yuan)	727725	1802190	3284672
对外经济贸易	**Foreign Trade**			
进出口总额(万美元)	Total Exports and Imports(USD 10 000)		137510	173696
出口额	Exports		110163	106062
进口额	Imports		27347	67634
国际旅游	**International Tourism**			
国际旅游人数(人)	Number of International Tourists(persons)	258786	413481	650385
旅游外汇收入(万元)	Foreign Exchange Earnings from Tourism (10 000 yuan)	19628	103818	224100
金融保险	**Finance and Insurance**			
金融机构各项存款(万元)	Deposits of National Banking System (10 000 yuan)	1123704	3595110	13343798
金融机构各项贷款(万元)	Loans of National Banking System (10 000 yuan)	1316715	3345022	9725155

Principal Aggregate Indicators on National Economic and Social Development and Their Related Indices and Growth Rates(Continued 2)

2002	2003	速度指标(%) Indices and Growth Rates 指数 Index (2003比以下各年) (2003 as percentage of the following years) 1990	1995	2000	2002	平均增长速度 Average Annual Growth Rate 1990-1995	1990-2000	1990-2003	1995-2003
436.98	427.22	280.14	241.16	126.85	97.77	3.04	8.25	8.25	11.63
9484	9392	134.55	97.94	92.16	99.03	6.56	3.86	2.31	-0.26
3167	3662	129.60	110.40	118.09	115.63	3.26	0.93	2.01	1.24
6310	5726	137.85	91.35	80.85	90.74	8.58	5.48	2.50	-1.12
5.00	4.00	430.11	83.86	48.54	80.00	38.68	24.38	11.88	-2.18
12527	11413	198.54	125.85	106.11	91.11	9.55	6.47	5.42	2.92
1997	1889	95.67	70.54	88.69	94.59	6.29	0.76	-0.34	-4.27
10124	9252	248.61	150.98	111.93	91.39	10.49	8.31	7.26	5.28
278.00	272.00	518.10	103.42	75.55	97.84	38.03	21.23	13.49	0.42
515259	517468	6597.92	676.87	112.10	100.43	57.68	50.31	38.02	27.00
10383	14814	174.66	101.14	180.00	142.68	11.55	-0.30	4.38	0.14
2647579	3162678	5698.52	542.49	154.40	119.46	60.06	43.45	36.48	23.54
2454033	2953986	6293.78	959.49	209.08	120.37	45.67	40.56	37.52	32.66
2095230	2538393	5607.60	847.59	204.27	121.15	45.92	39.27	36.31	30.62
358803	415593	24915.65	4955.80	244.18	115.83	38.12	58.81	52.88	62.89
1964200	2412392			330.01	122.82				
675181	940643			454.28	139.32				
4093862	4400454	604.69	244.17	133.97	107.49	19.89	16.27	14.85	11.81
186966	230932		167.94	132.95	123.52				6.69
112479	140327		127.38	132.31	124.76				3.07
74487	90605		331.32	133.96	121.64				16.15
741313	336654	130.09	81.42	51.76	45.41	9.83	9.65	2.04	-2.54
260000	121180	617.38	116.72	54.07	46.61	39.53	27.57	15.03	1.95
21914653	26658682	2372.39	741.53	199.78	121.65	26.19	28.07	27.58	28.46
15984225	19541838	1484.14	584.21	200.94	122.26	20.50	22.14	23.06	24.69

1-7 国民经济和社会发展总量与速度指标(续3)

指 标	Item	总量指标		
		1990	1995	2000
保险公司保险金额(万元)	Insurance Coverage of Insurance Companies (10 000 yuan)	3787594	11550053	15866695
保险公司保费(万元)	Insurance Premium of Insurance Companies (10 000 yuan)	17997	49946	135800
保险公司赔款及付给（万元）	Indemnity Expenditure and Payment of Insurance Companies (10 000 yuan)	6367	113088	39600
教育、科技、文化	**Education, Science and Technology and Culture**			
教育	**Education**			
专任教师数(人)	Full-time Teachers(person)	75251	74905	78973
普通高等学校	Institutions of Higher Education	15562	15914	15679
中等学校	Secondary Schools	28427	28721	32923
小 学	Primary Schools	29090	30270	30215
在校学生数(万人)	Students Enrollment(10000 person)	119.65	131.66	156.16
普通高等学校	Institutions of Higher Education	8.02	10.87	19.41
中等学校	Secondary Schools	35.65	41.43	58.75
小 学	Primary Schools	61.87	79.36	77.81
科技	**Science and Technology**			
各类专业技术人员(人)	Different Kinds of Technical Personnel(person)	315100	356100	369735
经认定的高新技术企业(个)	Identified Hitech Enterprises (unit)			632
文化	**Culture**			
图书馆藏书数(千册)	Total Collections in Library (1000 Volume-time)		2830	3214
文化馆、站（个)	Cultural Centers or Stations (unit)	247	188	251
电影放映单位数(个)	Film Projection Units (unit)	633	587	586
电视节目制作时间(小时)	Time for TV Programs Production(hours)		5738	11871
家庭、生活、环境	**Family, People's Livelihood and Environment**			
家庭	**Family**			
家庭总户数 (万户)	Total Number of Households(10 000 households)	155.82	171.25	187.08
城镇居民平均每户家庭人口(人)	Average Household Size in Urban Areas(person)	3.32	3.88	2.99
农村居民平均每户家庭人口(人)	Average Household Size in Rural Areas(person)	4.80	4.60	4.30
婚姻	**Marriages and Divorces**			
结婚登记总数(对)	Register Number of Marriages(couples)	50134	47236	46415
离婚数(对)	Number of Divorces(couples)	2153	4296	5161
居住	**Housing**			
城镇人均住房使用面积(平方米)	Per Capita Net Living Space in Urban Area(sq.m)	11.48	13.05	14.82
农村居民人均居住面积(平方米)	Per Capita Net Floor Space of Rural Residents(sq.m)	16.37	21.77	28.31
生活	**People's Livelihood**			
城镇居民人均可支配收入(元)	Per Capita Annual Disposable Income of Urban Households (yuan)	1518	4153	6364
农村居民人均纯收入(元)	Per Capita Net Income of Rural Residents(yuan)	610	1353	2344

Principal Aggregate Indicators on National Economic and Social Development and Their Related Indices and Growth Rates(Continued 3)

2002	2003	速度指标(%) Indices and Growth Rates 指数 Index (2003比以下各年) (2003 as percentage of the following years) 1990	1995	2000	2002	平均增长速度 Average Annual Growth Rate 1990-1995	1990-2000	1990-2003	1995-2003
16434570	17268354	455.92	149.51	108.83	105.07	24.98	15.40	12.38	5.16
286546	362245	2012.81	725.27	266.75	126.42	22.65	22.40	25.98	28.10
63635	65286	1025.38	57.73	164.86	102.59	77.79	20.05	19.61	-6.64
88102	87852	116.75	117.28	111.24	99.72	-0.09	0.48	1.20	2.01
20561	22145	142.30	139.15	141.24	107.70	0.45	0.07	2.75	4.22
34559	36176	127.26	125.96	109.88	104.68	0.21	1.48	1.87	2.93
29428	29531	101.52	97.56	97.74	100.35	0.80	0.38	0.12	-0.31
123.73	174.23	145.62	132.34	111.57	140.82	1.93	2.70	2.93	3.56
33.00	40.12	500.07	369.19	206.71	121.59	6.26	9.24	13.18	17.74
66.08	67.33	188.86	162.51	114.60	101.89	3.05	5.12	5.01	6.26
70.78	66.78	107.93	84.15	85.83	94.35	5.10	2.32	0.59	-2.13
355970	362066	114.91	101.68	97.93	101.71	2.48	1.61	1.07	0.21
804	971			153.64	120.77				
3242	3350		118.37	104.23	103.33				2.13
183	191	77.33	101.60	76.10	104.37	-5.31	0.16	-1.96	0.20
588	588	92.89	100.17	100.34	100.00	-1.50	-0.77	-0.57	0.02
27339	32510		566.57	273.86	118.91				24.21
191.71	195.32	125.35	114.06	104.40	101.88	1.91	1.85	1.75	1.66
3.01	3.04	91.57	78.35	101.67	101.00	3.17	-1.04	-0.68	-3.00
4.17	4.14	86.25	90.00	96.28	99.28	-0.85	-1.09	-1.13	-1.31
44593	44510	88.78	94.23	95.90	99.81	-1.18	-0.77	-0.91	-0.74
5476	10670	495.59	248.37	206.74	194.85	14.82	9.14	13.10	12.04
15.15	15.14	131.88	116.02	102.16	99.93	2.60	2.59	2.15	1.87
32.54	33.90	207.09	155.72	119.75	104.18	5.87	5.63	5.76	5.69
7184	7748	510.39	186.58	121.75	107.85	22.29	15.41	13.36	8.11
2641	2838	465.51	209.72	121.08	107.44	17.29	14.42	12.56	9.70

1-7 国民经济和社会发展总量与速度指标(续4)

指 标	Item	总量指标		
		1990	1995	2000
城乡储蓄存款余额(万元)	Outstanding Amount of Saving Deposits in Urban and Rural Areas(10 000 yuan)	770948	2914647	6758327
工资	**Wages and Welfare**			
工资总额(万元)	Total Wages(10 000 yuan)	294784	672268	1016779
职工平均工资(元)	Average Wage of Staff and Workers(yuan)	2136	4763	9179
离休、退休、退职费(万元)	Pensions for Retired Staff and Workers (10 000 yuan)	32359	102535	328672
卫生	**Health Care**			
医院、卫生院(个)	Number of Hospitals(unit)	283	368	426
医生（人）	Number of Doctors(person)	18648	18846	18728
医院、卫生院床位数(张)	Number of Hospital Beds(unit)	24358	28265	28697
市政建设	**City Construction**			
自来水供应量(万吨)	Volume of Tap Water Supply(10 000 tons)	24254	27015	30273
供水管道长度(公里)	Length of Water Supply Pipelines(km)	1074	1066	2237
城市煤气和天然气供气量(万立方米)	Volume of Coal Gas and Natural Gas Supply in Urban Areas (10 000 cu.m)	8679	8419	13676
公共汽(电)车总数(辆)	Total Number of Public Buses and Trolley Buses (unit)	875	977	2573
铺装道路长度(公里)	Length of Paved Roads(km)	1069	835	975
绿地面积(公顷)	Areas of Green Land(hectare)	3542	5603	4116
环境、灾害	**Environment and Disaster**			
环境卫生从业人数（人）	Employed personnel in Envionment Sanitation(person)	2980	2774	7632
工业废水排放量(万吨)	Volume of Waste Water up to the Standard for Discharge(10 000 tons)	11230	12479	9145
工业废水排放达标量（万吨）	Volume of Waste Water up to the Standard for Discharge(10 000 tons)	4947	8408	6130
火灾发生数(起)	Number of Fire Disasters(case)	322	426	1040
火灾损失(万元)	Fire Loss(10 000 yuan)	166	742	472
交通事故发生数(起)	Number of Traffic Accidents(case)		3065	4099
交通事故损失(万元)	Loss of Traffic Accidents(10 000 yuan)		1103	1116

Principal Aggregate Indicators on National Economic and Social Development and Their Related Indices and Growth Rates(Continued 4)

		速度指标(%) Indices and Growth Rates							
2002	2003	指数 Index (2003比以下各年) (2003 as percentage of the following years)				平均增长速度 Average Annual Growth Rate			
		1990	1995	2000	2002	1990-1995	1990-2000	1990-2003	1995-2003
9880414	12105607	1570.22	415.34	179.12	122.52	30.47	24.25	23.59	19.48
1366815	1559517	529.04	231.98	153.38	114.10	17.93	13.18	13.67	11.09
12138	13504	632.21	283.52	147.13	111.25	17.40	15.70	15.24	13.91
478403	448313	1385.44	437.23	136.40	93.71	25.94	26.09	22.41	20.25
470	473	167.14	128.53	111.03	100.64	5.39	4.17	4.03	3.19
18914	16674	89.41	88.48	89.03	88.16	0.21	0.04	-0.86	-1.52
28778	30778	126.36	108.89	107.25	106.95	3.02	1.65	1.82	1.07
33776	36122	148.93	133.71	119.32	106.95	2.18	2.24	3.11	3.70
2453	2318	215.83	217.45	103.62	94.50	-0.15	7.61	6.10	10.20
24069	33526	386.29	398.22	245.14	139.29	-0.61	4.65	10.96	18.85
3024	3736	426.97	382.40	145.20	123.54	2.23	11.39	11.81	18.25
999	1274	119.20	152.57	130.67	127.53	-4.82	-0.91	1.36	5.42
4238	4502	127.10	80.35	109.38	106.23	9.61	1.51	1.86	-2.70
9180	10727	359.97	386.70	140.55	116.85	-1.42	9.86	10.35	18.42
10705	11246	100.14	90.12	122.97	105.05	2.13	-2.03	0.01	-1.29
8249	9047	182.88	107.60	147.59	109.67	11.19	2.17	4.75	0.92
1571	1539	477.95	361.27	147.98	97.96	5.76	12.44	12.79	17.42
195	261	157.42	35.17	55.25	133.85	34.95	11.04	3.55	-12.24
4073	4688		132.89	99.37					5.46
1147	1352		103.98	102.78					2.57

1-8 国民经济和社会发展结构指标

Structural Indicators on National Economic and Social Development

单位: % (%)

指　　标	Item	1990	1995	2000	2002	2003
人口与就业	**Population and Employment**					
人口	**Population**					
农业与非农业结构	Structure					
农业	Agriculture	62.72	60.55	58.46	57.29	56.34
非农业	Non-Agriculture	37.28	39.45	41.54	42.71	43.66
性别结构	Sexual Structure					
男	Male	51.50	51.64	51.62	51.68	51.68
女	Female	48.50	48.36	48.38	48.32	48.32
就业	**Employment**					
产业结构	Industrial Structure					
第一产业	Primary Industry	43.62	41.17	37.79	36.02	36.22
第二产业	Secondary Industry	31.11	29.43	27.57	28.10	26.94
第三产业	Tertiary Industry	25.27	29.40	34.65	35.88	36.84
宏观经济	**Macro Economy**					
国民核算	**National Accounting**					
地区生产总值产业结构	Industrial Structure					
第一产业	Primary Industry	11.96	12.53	6.94	5.80	5.39
第二产业	Secondary Industry	43.04	40.97	44.01	45.23	44.15
第三产业	Tertiary Industry	44.99	46.50	49.05	48.97	50.47
地区生产总值支出结构	Structure of Gross Domestic by Expenditures					
#最终消费	Total Consumption		75.98	71.97	69.63	67.93
居民消费	Resident Consumption		56.17	53.97	51.11	50.31
政府消费	Public Consumption		19.80	17.99	18.52	17.62
资本形成总额	Total Investment		46.42	45.63	47.01	52.33
固定资本形成	Fixed Assets		33.00	39.11	29.70	47.80
存货增加	Stock		13.42	6.51	5.17	4.52
货物和服务净出口	Net Export of Goods and Services		-22.40	-17.59	-16.64	-20.25

1–8　国民经济和社会发展结构指标（续 1）

Structural Indicators on National Economic and Social Development(Continued 1)

单位:%　　(%)

指　　标	Item	1990	1995	2000	2002	2003
投资	**Investment**					
全社会固定资产投资结构	Structure of Total Investment in Fixed Assets					
国有单位	State-owned Enterprises Investment	75.68	84.17	66.80	61.02	59.16
集体单位	Collective-owned Enterprises Investment	7.36	5.47	9.45	5.10	4.05
其他单位投资	Other Investment	16.96	94.53	23.75	33.88	36.78
全市固定资产投资结构	Structure of Investment in Fixed Assets					
基本建设	Capital Construction	48.79	36.77	44.06	50.43	51.18
更新改造	Innovation	40.91	34.67	27.01	18.71	16.03
房地产开发	Real Estate Development	4.09	24.46	25.54	25.83	28.00
其他投资	Other Investment	6.21	4.10	3.39	5.03	4.79
财政	**Government Finance**					
财政收入结构	Structure of Government Revenue					
中央	Central Government			31.94	36.56	37.88
地方	Local Governments			68.06	63.44	62.12
产　业	**Industrial**					
农业	**Agriculture**					
农林牧渔业总产值结构	Structure of Gross Output Value of Agriculture					
农业	Farming	72.91	68.03	69.23	67.71	65.81
林业	Forestry	1.20	0.95	1.14	1.43	1.26
牧业	Animal Husbandry	25.12	30.29	28.59	29.94	32.18
渔业	Fishery	0.77	0.72	1.05	0.92	0.75
工业	**Industry**					
工业总产值经济类型结构	Structure of Gross Output Value of Industry by Registion Status					
国有单位	State-owned Enterprises	67.56	51.04	51.33	47.81	49.35
集体单位	Collective-owned Enterprises	30.97	40.98	27.97	24.60	13.58
其他投资	Others	1.46	7.97	20.70	27.59	37.08
工业总产值轻重结构	Structure of Gross Output Value of Industry by Ligth Industry and Heavy Industry					
轻工业	Light Industry	44.48	40.31	41.68	41.86	36.43
重工业	Heavy Industry	55.52	59.94	58.32	58.14	63.57

1-8　国民经济和社会发展结构指标(续 2)

Structural Indicators on National Economic and Social Development(Continued 2)

单位: %　　(%)

指　　标	Item	1990	1995	2000	2002	2003
工业总产值规模结构	Structure of Gross Output Value of Industry by Size of Enterprises					
大型企业	Large Enterprises	40.45	38.80	45.61	43.20	35.90
中型企业	Medium-sized Enterprises	15.76	9.14	4.39	4.24	18.33
小型企业	Small Enterprises	43.79	52.06	50.00	52.56	45.77
建筑业	**Construction**					
建筑业总产值结构	Structure of Gross Output Value of Construction Industry					
土木工程建筑业	Civil Engineering Construction		86.27	88.50	88.18	53.64
线路管理设备安装业	Line and Equipment Installation		12.84	9.28	9.85	3.77
建筑物装修装饰业	Building Decoration		0.89	2.21	1.97	1.58
交通运输业	**Transportation**					
货运量结构	Structure of Freight Traffic					
按运输方式分	By Means of Transportation					
铁　路	Railways	40.48	34.59	44.30	33.39	38.99
公　路	Highways	59.50	65.36	55.58	66.53	60.97
民用航空	Civil Aviation	0.01	0.05	0.12	0.07	0.04
国内商业	**Domestic Trade**					
社会消费品零售总额构成	Composition of Retail Sales of Consumer Goods					
市	Cities	87.06	88.95	87.99	88.76	89.85
县	Counties	6.47	5.61	5.34	5.06	4.85
县以下	Below Counties	6.46	5.45	6.67	6.18	5.30
国际旅游	**International Tourism**					
国际旅游人数结构	Structure of Tourists					
外国人	Foreigners	59.49	89.76	84.03	88.87	75.90
华侨	Overseas Chinese	1.59	0.19	--	--	--
港澳台同胞	Compatriots form Hong Kong, Macao and Taiwan	38.91	10.54	15.97	11.13	24.10

1-8 国民经济和社会发展结构指标(续 3)

Structural Indicators on National Economic and Social Development(Continued 3)

单位: % (%)

指 标	Item	1990	1995	2000	2002	2003
教育文化、卫生、人民生活	**Education and Culture，Health Care，People's Livelihoo**					
教育	**Education**					
在校学生结构	Structure of Student Enrollment					
大学生	College and University Students	7.60	8.26	12.44	19.43	23.03
中学生	Secondary School Students	33.78	31.47	37.67	38.90	38.64
小学生	Primary School Students	58.62	60.28	49.89	41.67	38.33
专任教师结构	Full-time Teachers by Type					
大学	College and Universities	21.29	21.25	19.89	24.32	25.21
中学	Secondary Schools	38.90	38.34	41.77	40.88	41.18
小学	Primary Schools	39.81	40.41	38.34	34.81	33.61
人民生活	**People's Livelihood**					
城镇居民消费结构	Consumption Structure of Urban Residents					
食品类	Food	53.09	44.68	36.46	34.36	34.84
衣着类	Clothing	14.96	12.67	8.13	8.42	8.44
用品及其他	Articles for Daily Use and Others	30.71	36.16	44.18	45.02	45.26
居住	Residence	1.24	6.49	11.23	12.21	11.45
农村居民消费结构	Consumption Structure of Rural Residents					
食品类	Food	49.48	50.31	36.63	31.07	37.56
衣着类	Clothing	8.68	8.39	6.65	6.45	6.28
用品及其他	Articles for Daily Use and Others	24.52	22.77	35.31	37.51	38.75
居住	Residence	17.33	18.53	21.41	24.97	17.42
卫生	**Health Care**					
卫生技术人员结构	Medical Technical Personnel by Types					
#医生	#Doctor		45.42	44.82	41.34	41.55
护理人员	Nursing Personnel		32.68	34.29	32.05	32.41
药剂人员	Pharmaceutical Personnel		8.78	8.31	7.83	7.73
检验人员	Laboratory Personnel		5.21	5.21	5.22	5.51

1-9 国民经济和社会发展比例和效益指标

指标	Item	1990
人口与就业	**Population and Employment**	
人口	**Population**	
出生率(‰)	Birth Rate(‰)	20.55
死亡率(‰)	Death Rate(‰)	5.72
自然增长率(‰)	Natural Growth Rate(‰)	14.84
就业	**Employment**	
就业者负担人口	Dependency Ratio	0.77
三次产业就业者比例(以第一产业为100)	Employment Ratio by Type of Industry (Employment in primary industry=100)	
第一产业	Primary Industry	100
第二产业	Secondary Industry	43.62
第三产业	Tertiary Industry	31.11
城镇失业率(%)	Unemployment Rate in Urban Areas(%)	
宏观经济	**Macro Economy**	
国民核算	**National Accounting**	
三次产业增加值比例(以第一产业为100)	Ratio of Value-added by Type of Industry (Value added in primary industry=100)	
第一产业	Primary Industry	100
第二产业	Secondary Industry	359.76
第三产业	Tertiary Industry	376.04
全社会劳动生产率(元／人)	Overall Labor Productivity(yuan/person)	3396
第一产业	Primary Industry	932
第二产业	Secondary Industry	4698
第三产业	Tertiary Industry	6048
人均地区生产总值(元)	Per Capita GDP(yuan)	1932
固定资产投资	**Investment in Fixed Assets**	
全社会固定资产投资相当于地区生产总值比例(%)	Proportion of Investment in fixed Assets to GDP(%)	22.65
全社会房屋建筑面积竣工率(%)	Rate of Total Floor Space of Buildings Completed in Construction(%)	40.40
基本建设固定资产交付使用率(%)	Rate of Fixed Assets Completed in Capital Construction and Put into Use(%)	78.40
基本建设项目建成投产率(%)	Rate of Projects Completed in Capital Construction and Put into Use(%)	43.90
财政	**Finance**	
地方财政收入相当于地区生产总值比例(%)	Proportion of Local Government Revenue to GDP(%)	11.26
地方财政支出相当于地区生产总值比例(%)	Proportion of Local Government Expenditures to GDP(%)	7.97
利用外资	**Utilization of Foreign Capital**	
实际利用外资额相当于签订利用外资额比例(%)	Proportion of Foreign Capital Actually Used to Total Amount of Foreign Capital for Utilization by Signed Contracts or Agreements (%)	277.87

Indicators on Proportions and Efficiency in National Economic and Social Development

1995	2000	2001	2002	2003
11.95	13.07	7.39	9.91	8.48
4.98	5.96	4.19	5.50	4.68
6.97	7.11	3.20	4.41	3.80
0.74	0.77	0.78	0.77	0.77
100.00	100.00	100.00	100.00	100.00
41.17	37.79	37.27	36.02	36.22
29.4	27.6	28.0	28.1	26.9
3.10	3.40	3.20	3.70	4.50
100.00	100.00	100.00	100.00	100.00
326.88	634.09	711.62	779.74	819.56
371	707	788	844	937
8866	16532	18851	20735	23254
2699	3037	3161	3340	3458
12340	26396	29958	33370	38104
14024	23403	26733	28298	31858
5131	9446	9832	10862	12233
31.31	36.12	39.21	41.06	50.78
33.41	41.99	39.90	32.26	33.80
68.88	75.59	62.66	63.39	64.46
39.70	45.82	36.78	45.74	43.19
5.51	7.30	7.63	7.29	7.74
5.58	8.07	7.79	8.35	8.20
64.42	28.88	29.12	28.69	26.52

1-9 国民经济和社会发展比例和效益指标（续1）

指　标	Item	1990
产　业	**Industries**	
农业	**Agriculture**	
人均耕地面积(公顷)	Per Capita Cultivated Land(hectare)	0.08
农业从业者人均耕地面积(公顷)	Cultivated Land per Agricultural Laborer(hectare)	0.22
每公顷耕地农业机械总动力(千瓦)	Total Power of Agricultural Machinery per Hectare of Cultivated Land(kw)	4.38
每公顷耕地化肥施用量(公斤)	Chemical Fertilizer Consumption per Hectare of Cultivated Land(kg)	352
每公顷耕地生产的农业产值(元)	Agricultural Output Value per Hectare of Cultivated Land(yuan)	7937
每个农林牧渔业劳动力农产品生产量(公斤)	Output of Farm Products per Farming,Forestry,Animal Husbandry and Fishery Laborer (kg)	
粮食	Grain	1162
蔬菜	Vegetables	804
禽蛋	Poultry Eggs	38
肉类	Meat	43
水产品	Aquatic Products	3
每公顷播种面积农产品产量(公斤)	Output of Farm Crops per Hectare of Sown Area(kg)	
粮食	Grain	3540
油料	Oil-bearing Crops	1545
蔬菜	Vegetables	35235
工业企业效益	**Economic Efficiency of Industry**	
综合经济效益指数（%）	Comprehensive Index of Economic Efficiency	
总资产贡献率(%)	Ratio of Total Assets to Industrial Output Value (%)	
资产负债率(%)	Assets-Liability Ratio(%)	
成本费用利润率(%)	Ratio of Profits to Industrial Cost(%)	
流动资产周转次数(次/年)	Number of Times of Annual of Turnover Circulating Funds(times/year)	
全员劳动生产率(元/人.年)(按增加值计算)	Overall Labor Productivity(yuan/person-year) (in terms of value-addedper employee)	
建筑业	**Construction**	
技术装备率(元／人)	Value of Machinery per Laborer(yuan/person)	3797
产值利税率(%)	Ratio of Per-tax Profits to Gross Output Value (%)	
全员劳动生产率(元／人)(按总产值计算)	Overall Labor Productivity(yuan/person) (in terms of gross output value per employee)	
邮电通信业	**Post and Communication Services**	
电话普及率(含移动电话)(部/百人)	Access to Telephones, National(include mobilphone) (set/100 persons)	0.74
移动电话普及率(部/百人)	Access to Mobilphones (set/100 persons)	
国内商业	**Domestic Trade**	
批零和餐饮业人均消费品零售额(元)	Per Capita Retail Sales of Consumer Goods (yuan)	1132

Indicators on Proportions and Efficiency in National Economic and Social Development(Continued 1)

1995	2000	2001	2002	2003
0.08	0.07	0.07	0.07	0.07
0.20	0.20	0.20	0.20	0.19
5.23	6.78	7.02	7.25	7.54
536	664	672	709	725
24396	25161	26669	28181	30357
1150	1382	1368	1355	1213
877	1110	1061	1196	1167
93	95	92	95	89
84	101	109	113	114
6	8	9	8	7
3806	4342	4360	4402	4182
1753	1526	1562	1603	1532
34800	37797	37105	37599	36657
	93.88	98.64	109.03	122.80
	5.70	5.82	6.21	6.97
	64.97	62.39	60.41	61.31
	4.15	4.10	5.10	5.71
	0.98	0.90	1.06	1.10
	30700	38267	46940	58801
5990	6805	8894	8904	9453
3.50	3.42	4.33	4.78	4.06
37689	74347	73191	80200	132981
7.92	31.16	46.75	57.78	69.09
0.48	10.62	18.38	27.96	33.67
2799	4822	5292	5859	6201

1–9 国民经济和社会发展比例和效益指标（续2）

指　　标	Item	1990
对外经济贸易	**Foreign Trade**	
进出口总额相当于地区生产总值比例(%)	Proportion of Total Imports & Exports to GDP(%)	5.23
国际旅游	**International Tourism**	
每一来华游客花费(元)	Expenditure per International Tourist in China(yuan)	758
金融保险	**Finance and Insurance**	
金融机构存款相当于地区生产总值比例(%)	Bank Deposits as Percentage of GDP(%)	96.45
金融机构贷款相当于地区生产总值比例(%)	Bank Loans as Percentage of GDP(%)	113.01
金融机构现金支出相当于收入比例(%)	Proportion of Cash Outlay to Cash Receipt in Bank(%)	109.25
教育、科技、文化	**Education, Science and Technology and Culture**	
教育	**Education**	
学龄儿童入学率(%)	Rate of School-age Children Enrollment(%)	99.11
小学升学率(%)	Rate of Graduates of Primary Schools Entering Junior Secondary Schools(%)	91.50
初中升学率(%)	Rate of Graduates of Junior Secondary Schools Entering Senior Secondary Schools(%)	52.70
学校教师负担系数(%)	Student-teacher Ratio(in percentage)(%)	
高等学校	Colleges and Universities	5.15
中等学校	Secondary Schools	12.54
小学	Primary Schools	21.27
文化(个)	**Culture (unit)**	
每百万人有艺术表演团体	Number of Troupes per Million Persons	3.78
每百万人有公共图书馆	Number of Public Libraries per Million Persons	2.46
家庭、生活、环境	**Family, People's Livelihood and Environment**	
家庭	**Family**	
城市居民家庭	Urban Households	
平均每户就业面（%）	Percentage of Employees Per Household (%)	55.12
每一就业者负担人数(人)	Persons Supported by Each Laborer (person)	1.81
农村居民家庭	Rural Households	
平均每一劳动力赡养人口（人）	Persons Supported by Each Laborer(person)	1.72
卫生	**Health Care**	
每千人医院数(个)	Number of Hospitals per 1000 Persons(unit)	0.05
每千人医生数(人)	Number of Doctors per 1000 Persons(person)	3.06
每千人医院床位数(张)	Number of Hospital Beds per 1000 Persons(unit)	4.00
市政建设	**City Construction**	
城市自来水普及率(%)	Percentage of Households with Access to Tap Water(%)	
城市用气普及率(%)	Percentage of Households with Access to Tap Gas (%)	
人均公共绿地面积(平方米)	Public Green Areas per 10 000 Persons(hectare)	1.67

Indicators on Proportions and Efficiency in National Economic and Social Development(Continued 2)

1995	2000	2001	2002	2003
34.76	22.35	19.16	18.79	20.30
2511	3445	3582	3507	3584
108.83	207.63	222.08	266.08	283.12
101.26	151.19	161.61	194.10	207.54
191.99	397.30	418.30	292.08	521.38
99.69	99.85	99.84	99.85	99.88
94.85	97.21	97.25	97.25	97.26
72.35	80.50	80.56	82.80	80.26
6.83	12.38	14.55	16.05	19.87
14.42	17.84	18.85	19.12	18.52
26.22	25.75	25.45	24.05	22.69
3.39	3.20	3.17	3.13	3.07
2.31	2.18	2.01	1.99	1.95
55.90	45.73	45.56	48.80	48.00
1.79	2.19	2.19	2.05	2.08
1.58	1.57	1.60	1.59	1.56
0.06	0.03	0.03	0.04	0.04
2.91	2.35	2.31	2.08	2.02
4.36	3.83	3.79	3.90	3.94
	98.95	98.59	98.62	99.04
	81.51	85.43	87.52	91.23
3.80	5.12	5.27	5.42	5.35

1-10 国有土地使用权出让、划拨情况

Basic Statistics on Lease and Administrative Allocation of Use Right of State-Owned Land

项　　目	Item	2000	2001	2002	2003
国有土地使用权出让	**Lease of the Use Right of State-owned Land**				
出让地块(宗)	Land leased (item)	202	305	383	388
协议	Agreement	200	300	376	358
招标	Invitation for Bid				1
拍卖	Auction	2	5	7	7
挂牌交易	Listed Transaction				22
出让面积（公顷）	Area of Totally Leased Land (hectare)	3115	1025	1032	1367
土地使用权出让总收入（万元）	**Total Revenue from Leasing of the Use Right (10 000 yuan)**	38428	106035	127535	149571
国有土地使用权划拨	**Administrative Allocation of the Use Right of State-owned Land**				
划拨地块（宗）	Land Allocated (item)	113	43	67	67
划拨面积（公顷）	Area of Land Allocated(hectare)	12543	99	626	353

主要统计指标解释

行政区划 指国家对行政区域的划分。根据宪法规定，我国的行政区域划分如下:⑴全国分为省、自治区、直辖市;⑵省、自治区分为自治州、县、自治县、市;⑶自治州分为县、自治县、市;⑷县、自治县分为乡、民族乡、镇;⑸直辖市和较大的市分为区、县;⑹国家在必要时设立的特别行政区。

自然资源 指人类可以直接从自然界获得，并用于生产和生活的物质资源。自然资源一般可以分成可再生资源和非再生资源两大类。可再生资源指在较短时间内可以再生、可以循环利用的资源，包括土地资源、水资源、气候资源、生物资源和海洋资源等。非再生资源指在使用后不能再生的资源，包括矿产资源和地热能源。

土地资源 土地指陆地的表层部分，它主要由岩石、岩石的风化物和土壤构成。土地资源按利用类型可以分为农用地、建筑用地和未利用地。农用地包括耕地、园地、林地、牧草地和水面。建筑用地包括居民点及工矿用地、交通用地和水利设施用地。未利用地指农用地和建筑用地以外的土地，包括滩涂、荒漠、戈壁、冰川和石山等。

耕地面积 指经过开垦用以种植农作物并经常进行耕耘的土地面积。包括种有作物的土地面积、休闲地、新开荒地和抛荒未满三年的土地面积。

林业用地面积 指生长乔木、竹类、灌木、沿海红树林等林木的土地面积，包括有林地、灌木林、疏林地、未成林造林地、迹地、苗圃等。

草地面积 指牧区和农区用于放牧牲畜或割草，植被盖度在5%以上的草原、草坡、草山等面积。包括天然的和人工种植或改良的草地面积。

水资源 水在自然界中以固体、液体和气态三种聚集状态存在，分布于海洋、陆地（包括土壤）以及大气之中，通过水循环形成水资源。水资源包括经人类控制并直接可供灌溉、发电、给水、航运、养殖等用途的地表水和地下水，以及江河、湖泊、井、泉、潮汐、港湾和养殖水域等。水资源是发展国民经济不可缺少的重要自然资源。

气温 指空气的温度，我国一般以摄氏度（℃）为单位表示。气象观测的温度表是放在离地面约1.5米处通风良好的百叶箱里测量的，因此，通常说的气温指的是离地面1.5米处百叶箱中的温度。其统计计算方法为:

月平均气温是将全月各日的平均气温相加，除以该月的天数而得。

年平均气温是将12个月的月平均气温累加后除以12而得。

降水量 指从天空降落到地面的液态或固态（经融化后）水，未经蒸发、渗透、流失而在地面上积聚的深度。其统计计算方法为:

月降水量是将全月各日的降水量累加而得。

年降水量是将12个月的月降水量累加而得。

日照时数 指太阳实际照射地面的时间。其统计方法与降水量相同。

可比价格 指计算各种总量指标所采用的扣除了价格变动因素的价格，可进行不同时期总量指标的对比。按可比价格计算总量指标有两种方法:一种是直接用产品产量乘某一年的不变价格计算;另一种是用价格指数进行缩减。

不变价格 指以同类产品某年的平均价格作为固定价格，用于计算各年的产品价值。按不变价格计算的产品价值消除了价格变动因素，不同时期对比可以反映生产的发展速度。新中国成立后，随着工农业产品价格水平的变化，国家统计局先后五次制定了全国统一的工业产品不变价格和农业产品不变价格。从1952年到1957年使用1952年工（农）业产品不变价格，从1957年到1970年使用1957年不变价格，从1971年到1980年使用1970年不变价格，从1981年到1990年使用1980年不变价格，从1991年开始使用1990年不变价格。

平均增长速度 我国计算平均增长速度有两种方法:一种是习惯上经常使用的“水平法”，又称几何平均法，是以间隔期最后一年的水平同基期水平对比来计算平均每年增长（或下降）速度;另一种是“累计法”，又称代数平均法或方程法，是以间隔期内各年水平的总和同基期水平对比来计算平均每年增长（或下降）速度。在一般正常情况下，两种方法计算的平均每年增长速度比较接近;但在经济发展不平衡、出现大起大落时，两种方法计算的结果差别较大。

企业（单位）登记注册类型 是以在工商行政管理机关登记注册的各类企业为划分对象，以工商行政管理部门对企业登记注册的类型为依据，将企业登记注册类型分为内资企业、港澳台商投资企业和外商投资企业三大类。内资企业包括国有企业、集体企业、股份合作企业、联营企业、有限责任公司、股份有限公司、私营公司和其他企业;港澳台商投资企业和外商投资企业分别包括合资经营企业、合作经营企业、独资经营企业和股份有限公司。对不在工商行政管理部门进行登记注册的行政机关、事业单位和社会团体，主要按其经费来源和管理方式进行划分。

国有企业 指企业全部资产归国家所有，并按《中华人民共和国企业法人登记管理条例》规定登记注册的非公司制的经济组织。不包括有限责任公司中的国有独资公司。

集体企业 指企业资产归集体所有，并按《中华人民共和国企业法人登记管理条例》规定登记注册的经济组织。

股份合作企业 指以合作制为基础，由企业职工共同出资入股，吸收一定比例的社会资产投资组建，实行自主经营，自负盈亏，共同劳动，民主管理，按劳分配与按股分红相结合的一种集体经济组织。

联营企业 指两个及两个以上相同或不同所有制性质的企业法人或事业单位法人，按自愿、平等、互利的原则，共同投资组成的经济组织。联营企业包括国有联营企业、集体联营企业、国有与集体联营企业和其他联营企业。

有限责任公司 指根据《中华人民共和国公司登记管理条例》规定登记注册，由两个以上、五十个以下的股东共同出资，每个股东以其所认缴的出资额对公司承担有限责任，公司以其全部资产对其债务承担责任的经济组织。有限责任公司包括国有独资公司以及其他有限责任公司。

股份有限公司 指根据《中华人民共和国公司登记管理条例》规定登记注册，其全部注册资本由等额股份构成并通过发行股票筹集资本，股东以其认购的股份对公司承担有限责任，公司以其全部资产对其债务承担责任的经济组织。

私营企业 指由自然人投资设立或由自然人控股，以雇佣劳动为基础的营利性经济组织。包括按照《公司法》、《合伙企业法》、《私营企业暂行条例》规定登记注册的私营有限责任公司、私营股份有限公司、私营合伙企业和私营独资企业。

其他企业 指上述企业之外的其他内资经济组织。

与港澳台商合资经营企业 指港澳台地区投资者与内地企业依照《中华人民共和国中外合资经营企业法》及有关法律的规定，按合同规定的比例投资设立、分享利润和分担风险的企业。

与港澳台商合作经营企业 指港澳台地区投资者与内地企业依照《中华人民共和国中外合作经营企业法》及有关法律的规定，依照合作合同的约定进行投资或提供条件设立、分配利润和分担风险的企业。

港澳台商独资经营企业 指依照《中华人民共和国外资企业法》及有关法律的规定，在内地由港澳台地区投资者全额投资设立的企业。

港澳台商投资股份有限公司 指根据国家有关规定，经外经贸部依法批准设立，其中港、澳、台商的股本占公司注册资本的比例达25% 以上的股份有限公司。凡其中港、澳、台商的股本占公司注册资本的比例小于25%的，属于内资企业中的股份有限公司。

中外合资经营企业 指外国企业或外国人与中国内地企业依照《中华人民共和国中外合资经营企业法》及有关法律的规定，按合同规定的比例投资设立、分享利润和分担风险的企业。

中外合作经营企业 指外国企业或外国人与中国内地企业依照《中华人民共和国中外合作经营企业法》及有关法律的规定，依照合作合同的约定进行投资或提供条件设立、分配利润和分担风险的企业。

外资企业 指依照《中华人民共和国外资企业法》及有关法律的规定，在中国内地由外国投资者全额投资设立的企业。

外商投资股份有限公司 指根据国家有关规定，经外经贸部依法批准设立，其中外资的股本占公司注册资本的比例达25%以上的股份有限公司。凡其中外资股本占公司注册资本的比例小于25%的，属于内资企业中的股份有限公司。

行政机关、事业单位和社会团体 参照企业登记注册类型，主要按其经费来源和管理方式划分。具体规定如下:

（1）行政机关: 包括国家机关和政党机关，原则上均列为“国有”。但有特殊规定的，如供销社等，则列为“集体”。

（2）事业单位: 包括经国家机构编制部门和有关业务主管部门批准成立的各类事业单位，不包括实行企业化管理的事业单位。事业单位的划分办法如下:

①由国家财政预算拨款或列入财政预算外资金管理以及经费主要来源于国有主管部门或国有上级单位的事业单位，列为“国有”。

②经费主要来源于集体单位的事业单位，列为“集体”。

③公民个人（或个人合伙）开办的事业单位，列为“私营”。

④上述以外的其他事业单位，如果其经费来源不明确，按管理方式进行归类。

（3）社会团体: 包括经民政部门批准成立以及未纳入社会团体管理条例范围的工会、妇联等各类社会团体。社会团体的划分办法如下:

①未纳入民政部社会团体管理条例范围的工会、妇联、共青团、青联、工商联、科协、侨联等社会团体，国家拨款设立的基金会或基金管理组织以及经费主要来源于国有业务主管部门或国有上级单位的社会团体，列为“国有”。

②经费主要来源于集体单位的社会团体，列为“集体”。

③公民个人（或个人合伙）开办的社会团体，划为“私营”。

④上述以外的其他社会团体，如果其经费来源不明确，改按管理方式进行归类。

Explanatory Notes on Main Statistical Indicators

Administrative Division refers to the division of administrative areas by the state. The Constitution of the People's Republic of China stipulates that the administrative areas in China are divided as: 1) The whole country is divided into provinces, autonomous regions and municipalities directly under the central government; 2) Provinces and autonomous regions are divided into autonomous prefectures, counties, autonomous counties and cities; 3) Autonomous prefectures are divided into counties, autonomous counties and cities; 4) Counties and autonomous counties are divided into townships, nationality townships and towns; 5) Municipalities and large cities are divided into districts and counties, 6) The state shall, when necessary, establish special administrative regions.

Natural Resources refer to material resources that could be obtained from the nature by human being and used for production and living. Natural resources in general can be classified as renewable resources and non-renewable resources. Renewable resources refer to resources that could be renewed and recycled during a relatively short period of time, including land resource, water resource, climate resource, biology resource and marine resource. Non-renewable resources include resources that could not be renewed, such as minerals and geothermal resource.

Land Resource Land refers to the surface of the earth, consisting of mainly rocks and its whethering and earth. Land resource can be classified, by its utilization, as land for agriculture, land for construction and unused land. Land for agriculture includes cultivated land, plantation land, forestland, grassland and waters. Land for construction includes land for residential purpose, for manufacturing and mining, for transportation and for water-conservancy projects. Unused land refers to land other than land for agriculture and construction, including beaches, deserts, Gobi, glaciers and rock mountains.

Area of Cultivated Land refers to area of land reclaimed for the regular cultivation of various farm crops, including crop-cover land, fallow, newly reclaimed land and land laid idle for less than 3 years.

Area of Afforested Land refer to land for trees bamboo, bushes and mangrove, including forest-cover land, bush-covered land, sparse forest land, land planned for afforestation and nurseries of young trees.

Area of Grassland refers to areas of grassland, grass-slopes and grass-covered hills with a vegetation-covering rate of over 5% that are used for animal husbandry or harvesting of grass. It includes natural, cultivated and improved grassland areas.

Water Resource Water exists in the nature in solid, liquid and gaseous states, is distributed in the ocean, land (including earth) and air, and constitutes the water resource through the circulation of water. Water resource includes the surface water and underground water that is controlled by the human being for irrigation, power-generation, water supply, navigation and cultivation. It also includes rivers, lakes, wells, springs, tides, gulf and water area for cultivation. Water resource as an important natural resource is indispensable for the development of the national economy.

Temperature refers to the air temperature. China uses centigrade as the unit. The thermometry used for weather observation is put in a breezy shutter, which is 1.5 meters high from the ground. Therefore, the commonly used temperature refers to the temperature in the breezy shutter 1.5 meters away from the ground. The calculation method is as follows:

Monthly average temperature is the summation of average daily temperature of one month divided by the actual days of that particular month.

Annual average temperature is the summation of monthly average of a year divided by 12 months.

Volume of Precipitation refers to the deepness of liquid state or solid state (thawed) water falling from the sky to the ground that has not been evaporated, infiltrated or run off. The calculation method is as follows:

Monthly precipitation is the summation of daily precipitation of a month.

Annual precipitation is the summation of 12 months precipitation of a year.

Sunshine Hours refer to the actual hours of sunirradiating the earth. The calculation method is the same as that of the precipitation.

Comparable Prices refer to prices that are used to remove the factors of price change in calculating economic aggregates, so as to facilitate comparison of aggregates over time. Two methods are used for calculating economic aggregates at comparable prices: 1. Multiplying the output of products by their constant prices of certain year; 2. Deflation of data at current prices by relevant price index.

Constant Price refers to the average price of a

given product in certain year, which is used for comparison of output value over time. As the output value at constant prices removes the factor of price changes, it reflects the trend of production development over time. Since 1949, with the changes in general price level, National Bureau of Statistics has issued nationally unified constant prices five times: the 1952 constant prices for 1949-1957; the 1957 constant prices for 1957-1971; the 1970 constant prices for 1971-1981; the 1980 constant prices for 1981-1990; and the 1990 constant prices have been used since 1991.

Average Annual Growth Rate Two methods for calculating average annual growth rate are applied in China, one is often called level approach, or the method of calculating geometric average, which is derived by comparing the level of the last year of the interval with that of the beginning year; the other is called accumulative approach or algebraic average or equation method, which is derived by the summation of the actual figure of each year in the interval divided by the figure in the base year.

Usually the results calculated by the two methods are fairly close, but they differed sharply when uneven economic development occurred with striking fluctuations in growth.

Registration Status of Enterprises Enterprises are classified into 3 categories, namely domestic-funded enterprises, enterprises with investment from Hong Kong, Macau and Taiwan, and enterprises with foreign investment, in the light of the registration status of an enterprise in industrial and commercial administration agencies. Domestic-funded enterprises include state-owned enterprises, collective-owned enterprises, cooperative enterprises, joint ownership enterprises, limited liability corporations, share-holding corporations Ltd., private enterprises and other enterprises. Included in the enterprises with investment from Hong Kong, Macau and Taiwan and enterprises with foreign investment are joint-venture enterprises, cooperative enterprises, sole investment enterprises and share-holding corporations Ltd. For government agencies, institutions and social organizations which are not requested to be registered in industrial and commercial administration agencies, they are classified mainly by their sources of funds and way of management.

State-owned Enterprises refer to non-corporation economic units where the entire assets are owned by the state and which have registered in accordance with the *Regulation of the Peoples Republic of China on the Management of Registration of Corporate Enterprises*. Excluded from this category are sole state-funded corporations in the limited liability corporations.

Collective-owned Enterprises refer to economic units where the assets are owned collectively and which have registered in accordance with the *Regulation of the Peoples Republic of China on the Management of Registration of Corporate Enterprises*.

Cooperative Enterprises refer to a form of collective economic units (enterprises) where capitals come mainly from employees as their shares, with certain proportion of capital from the outside, where production is organized on the basis of independent operation, independent accounting for profits and losses, joint work, democratic management, and a distribution system that integrates remuneration according to work with dividend according to capital share.

Joint Ownership Enterprises refer to economic units established by two or more corporate enterprises or corporate institutions of the same or different ownership, through joint investment on the basis of equality, voluntary participation and mutual benefits. They include state joint ownership enterprises, collective joint ownership enterprises, joint state-collective enterprises, other joint ownership enterprises.

Limited Liability Corporations refer to economic units established with investment from 2-50investors and registered in accordance with the *Regulation of the Peoples Republic of China on the Management of Registration of Corporations*, each investor bearing limited liability to the corporation depending on its share of investment, and the corporation bearing liability to its debt to the maximum of its total assets. Limited liability corporations include exclusive state-funded limited liability corporations and other limited liability corporations.

Share-holding Corporations Ltd. refer to economic units registered in accordance with the*Regulation of the Peoples Republic of China on the Management of Registration of Corporations*, with total registered capitals divided into equal shares and raised through issuing stocks. Each investor bears limited liability to the corporation depending on the holding of shares, and the corporation bears liability to its debt to the maximum of its total assets.

Private Enterprises refer to profit-making economic units invested and established by natural persons, or controlled by natural persons using employed labour. Included in this category are private limited liability corporations, private share-holding corporations Ltd., private partnership enterprises and private-funded enterprises registered in accordance with the *Corporation Law*, *Partnership Enterprises Law* and *Interim Regulations on Private Enterprises* .

Other Domestic-funded Enterprises refer to domestic-funded economic units other than those mentioned above.

Cooperative Enterprises with Funds from Hong Kong Macau and Taiwan established by investors from Hong Kong, Macau and Taiwan with enterprises in the mainland of China in accordance with the *Law of the Peoples Republic of China on Sino-foreign Cooperative Enterprises* and other relevant laws, where the investment or provision of facilities, and the share of profits and risks is stipulated in the cooperative contract.

Enterprises with Sole (exclusive) Investment from Hong Kong, Macau and Taiwan refer to enterprises established in the mainland of China with exclusive investment from investors from Hong Kong, Macau and Taiwan in accordance with the *Law of the Peoples Republic of China on Foreign-Funded Enterprises* and other relevant laws.

Share-holding Corporations Ltd. with Investment from Hong Kong, Macau and Taiwan refer to share-holding corporations Ltd. established with the approval from the Ministry of Foreign Trade and Economic Relations in line with relevant state regulations, where the share of investment from Hong Kong, Macau or Taiwan businessmen exceeds 25% of the total registered capital of the corporation. In case the share of investment from Hong Kong, Macau or Taiwan is less than 25% of the total registered capital, the enterprise is to be classified as domestic-funded share-holding corporation Ltd.

Joint-venture Enterprises with Foreign Investment refer to enterprises jointly established by foreign enterprises or foreigners with enterprises in the mainland of China in accordance with the *Law of the Peoples Republic of China on Sino-foreign Joint Venture Enterprises* and other relevant laws, where the share of investment, profits and risks is stipulated in the contract.

Cooperation Enterprises with Foreign Investment refer to enterprises jointly established by foreign enterprises or foreigners with enterprises in the mainland of China in accordance with the *Law of the Peoples Republic of China on Sino-foreign Cooperative Enterprises* and other relevant laws, where the investment or provision of facilities, and the share of profits and risks is stipulated in the cooperative contract.

Enterprises with Sole (exclusive) Foreign Investment refer to enterprises established in the mainland of China with exclusive investment from foreign investors in accordance with the *Law of the Peoples Republic of China on Foreign-Funded Enterprises* and other relevant laws.

Share-holding Corporations Ltd. with Foreign Investment refer to share-holding corporations Ltd. established with the approval from the Ministry of Foreign Trade and Economic Relations in line with relevant state regulations, where the share of investment from foreign investors exceeds 25% of the total registered capital of the corporation. In case the share of foreign investment is less than 25% of the total registered capital, the enterprise is to be classified as domestic-funded share-holding corporation Ltd.

Government Agencies, Institutions and Social Organizations are classified into following categories by source of funds and way of management taking reference of the registration status of enterprises:

(1) Government agencies: include state and party agencies, classified in principle as state-owned. There are exceptions, such as supply and marketing cooperatives which are classified as collective-owned.

(2) Institutions: include institutions of various types established with the approval by organization and staffing departments of the government, but excludeInstitutions where enterprise management system is introduced. Institutions are further classified as follows:

(a) Institutions whose main budget is listed in the government budget appropriations or extra-budget funds, or allocated from the budget of their competent government agencies. Such institutions are classified as state-owned.

(b) Institutions whose budget mainly comes from collective units. Such institutions are classified as collective-owned.

(c) Institutions other than those mentioned above whose source of budget is not clear. Such institutions are classified by way of management.

(3) Social organizations: include social organizations established with the approval from the Ministry of Civil Affairs, and organizations that are not covered by social organization management regulations such as trade unions, womens federations etc.. Social organizations are further classified as follows:

(a) Social organizations that are not covered by social organization management regulations of the Ministry of Civil Affairs such as trade unions, womens federations, communist youth leagues, youth associations, industrial and commerce associations, scientists associations, overseas Chinese associations, etc., foundations and fund management organizations established with funds from the state, and social organizations whose funds mainly come from the budget of their competent government agencies. Such institutions are classified as state-owned.

(b) Social organizations whose budget mainly comes from collective units. Such institutions are classified as collective-owned.

(c) Social organizations established by individual or a group of citizens, which are classified as private.

二、国民经济核算

NATIONAL ECONOMIC ACCOUNTS

简 要 说 明

Brief Introduction

本章地区生产总值资料包括各年度全年地区生产总值绝对值、构成和指数，市区四县地区生产总值绝对数、构成和指数，由市统计局国民经济核算处提供。2003年GDP核算不含长庆油田资料，新兴“产业”增加值纳入2002年基数。人均GDP从2001年起按常住人口计算。

The data in this chapter consists of gross amount of regional GDPs, their components and indices of consequent years, compiled by National Economic Accounting Division of the Xi'an Bureau of Statistics.GDP of 2003 doesn't include data of Changqing oil field.Added value of developing industry is brought into the base of 2003.From year 2001,GDP per capita calculated on the base of permanent.

2-1 主要年份地区生产总值

Gross Domestic Product In Representative Years

单位：亿元 (100 million yuan)

年 份 Year	地区生产总值 Gross Domestic Product	第一产业 Primary Industry	第二产业 Secondary Industry	第三产业 Tertiary Industry	人均地区生产总值（元/人） Per Capita Gross Domestic Product （yuan/person)
1952	3.37	1.59	0.88	0.90	135
1957	8.02	2.09	3.97	1.96	249
1965	12.76	2.62	7.22	2.92	323
1970	17.76	3.13	10.96	3.67	412
1975	21.33	4.14	12.63	4.56	448
1978	25.35	4.83	14.59	5.93	513
1980	31.66	4.73	18.69	8.24	623
1983	35.89	5.22	20.14	10.53	674
1984	44.14	7.45	24.17	12.52	817
1985	57.58	8.76	30.83	17.99	1049
1986	65.78	9.59	33.86	22.33	1178
1987	80.16	10.73	37.69	31.74	1409
1988	99.22	11.47	46.58	41.17	1711
1989	109.38	12.78	48.91	47.69	1861
1990	116.51	13.94	50.15	52.42	1932
1991	136.14	17.17	57.06	61.91	2224
1992	164.85	18.78	69.22	76.85	2662
1993	229.56	22.58	110.88	96.10	3661
1994	289.82	31.68	128.27	129.87	4564
1995	330.35	41.40	135.33	153.62	5131
1996	406.95	46.94	166.49	193.52	6246
1997	488.82	51.33	197.97	239.52	7424
1998	525.80	51.90	216.28	257.62	7905
1999	576.39	45.53	246.05	284.81	8585
2000	643.26	44.65	283.12	315.49	9446
2001	733.85	45.87	326.42	361.56	9823
2002	823.50	47.77	372.48	403.25	10862
2003	941.60	50.72	415.68	475.20	12233

2-2 主要年份地区生产总值指数

Indices of Gross Domestic Product in Representative Years

（以上年为100）
(preceding year = 100)
单位：%　　(%)

年　份	Year	地区生产总值 Gross Domestic Product	第一产业 Primary Industry	第二产业 Secondary Industry	第三产业 Tertiary Industry
1952		103.63	92.16	137.47	123.69
1957		100.67	93.80	97.05	120.65
1965		126.10	134.12	133.03	106.65
1970		122.01	109.36	139.97	100.10
1975		103.79	92.61	107.12	107.54
1978		101.73	101.64	99.35	108.21
1980		111.52	83.31	119.70	116.48
1985		112.62	107.52	111.83	116.90
1986		111.44	107.74	108.40	118.82
1987		113.58	100.80	109.10	126.58
1988		111.35	81.18	115.54	114.73
1989		106.67	103.00	104.50	110.83
1990		105.24	102.99	102.50	109.63
1991		109.78	118.57	108.56	108.76
1992		115.59	109.40	118.14	114.45
1993		123.88	112.53	142.76	111.52
1994		110.15	98.42	110.26	113.31
1995		110.00	104.46	112.05	109.51
1996		114.89	106.78	118.84	113.16
1997		114.37	109.06	116.47	113.38
1998		113.27	106.50	117.51	110.18
1999		112.20	97.40	115.70	111.40
2000		113.00	103.50	115.10	110.80
2001		113.10	102.50	115.40	112.50
2002		113.30	103.10	115.10	112.90
2003		113.50	101.80	118.20	111.10
平均每年增长	Yearly Average Growth Rates				
"一五"时期	The First Five-Year Plan Period	15.77	5.94	37.71	16.89
"二五"时期	The Second Five-Year Plan Period	1.99	-3.69	2.44	8.37
1963--1965年	Readjust Period	14.17	16.16	23.34	0.30
"三五"时期	The Third Five-Year Plan Period	7.11	0.12	11.68	5.42
"四五"时期	The Fourth Five-Year Plan Period	4.98	3.98	5.34	5.04
"五五"时期	The Fiifth Five-Year Plan Period	5.99	-0.74	6.50	10.06
"六五"时期	The Sixth Five-Year P!an Period	10.72	7.94	10.41	12.90
"七五"时期	The Seventh Five-Year Plan Period	9.61	-1.33	7.92	15.96
"八五"时期	The Eighth Five-Year Plan Period	13.75	8.46	17.79	11.49
"九五"时期	The Ninth Five-Year Plan Period	13.54	4.57	16.71	11.78

2-3 主要年份地区生产总值指数

Indices of Gross Domestic Product in Representative Years

（以1952年为100）
(1952=100)
单位：% (%)

年　份 Year	地区生产总值 Gross Domestic Product	第一产业 Primary Industry	第二产业 Secondary Industry	第三产业 Tertiary Industry
1952	100	100	100	100
1957	207.93	133.42	495.29	218.23
1965	341.56	173.26	1048.34	329.21
1970	481.58	174.32	1821.04	428.62
1975	614.15	211.91	2362.48	547.90
1978	678.70	231.33	2560.76	643.78
1980	821.38	204.18	3237.19	885.15
1985	1366.78	299.12	5310.63	1632.37
1986	1523.14	322.27	5756.72	1928.89
1987	1729.98	324.85	6280.58	2441.59
1988	1926.33	263.71	7256.58	2801.24
1989	2054.82	271.62	7583.13	3104.61
1990	2162.49	279.74	7772.71	3403.58
1991	2373.98	331.69	8438.05	3701.73
1992	2744.08	362.87	9994.03	4236.63
1993	3399.37	408.23	14267.48	4724.69
1994	3744.41	401.78	15731.32	5353.55
1995	4118.85	419.70	17626.94	5862.67
1996	4732.14	448.16	20947.86	6634.20
1997	5412.15	488.76	24397.97	7521.86
1998	6130.34	520.53	28670.05	8287.59
1999	6878.24	507.00	33171.25	9232.38
2000	7772.41	524.75	38180.11	10229.48
2001	8790.60	537.87	44059.85	11508.17
2002	9959.75	554.54	50712.89	12992.72
2003	11304.32	564.52	59942.64	14434.91

2-4　主要年份地区生产总值构成

Composition of In Gross Domestic Product in Respective Years

单位：%　　(%)

年份	Year	地区生产总值 Gross Domestic Product	第一产业 Primary Industry	第二产业 Secondary Industry	第三产业 Tertiary Industry
1952		100	47.18	26.11	26.71
1957		100	26.06	49.50	24.44
1965		100	20.53	56.58	22.89
1970		100	17.62	61.71	20.67
1975		100	19.41	59.21	21.38
1978		100	19.05	57.55	23.40
1980		100	14.94	59.03	26.03
1985		100	15.22	53.54	31.24
1986		100	14.58	51.47	33.95
1987		100	13.38	47.02	39.60
1988		100	11.56	46.95	41.49
1989		100	12.95	49.58	37.47
1990		100	11.96	43.05	44.99
1991		100	12.61	41.91	45.48
1992		100	11.39	41.98	46.63
1993		100	9.83	48.30	41.87
1994		100	10.93	44.26	44.81
1995		100	12.53	40.97	46.50
1996		100	11.50	40.90	47.60
1997		100	10.50	40.50	49.00
1998		100	9.90	41.10	49.00
1999		100	8.00	42.70	49.30
2000		100	6.90	44.00	49.10
2001		100	6.30	44.50	49.20
2002		100	5.80	45.20	49.00
2003		100	5.39	44.15	50.46
平均每年增长	Yearly Average Growth Rates				
"一五"时期	The First Five-Year Plan Period	100	32.88	43.92	23.20
"二五"时期	The Second Five-Year Plan Period	100	18.08	58.63	23.29
1963--1965年	Readjust Period	100	19.36	55.37	25.27
"三五"时期	The Third Five-Year Plan Period	100	18.60	57.33	24.07
"四五"时期	The Fourth Five-Year Plan Period	100	20.46	59.59	19.95
"五五"时期	The Fiifth Five-Year Plan Period	100	18.40	57.69	23.91
"六五"时期	The Sixth Five-Year Plan Period	100	16.03	55.01	28.96
"七五"时期	The Seventh Five-Year Plan Period	100	12.42	46.11	41.47
"八五"时期	The Eighth Five-Year Plan Period	100	11.44	43.52	45.04
"九五"时期	The Ninth Five-Year Plan Period	100	9.36	41.84	48.80

2-5 总 产 出

Total Output (Calculated at Current prices)

(按当年价格计算)
(calculated at current prices)
单位：亿元 (100 million yuan)

指　标	Item	2003	2002	指数（%） Indices (preceding year=100)
总产出	**Total Output**	**2559.73**	**2203.85**	**115.0**
第一产业	Primary Industry	83.79	79.74	100.7
第二产业	Secondary Industry	1458.18	1219.47	117.0
工 业	Industry	1066.56	935.85	112.3
建筑业	Construction	391.62	283.62	133.7
第三产业	Tertiary	1017.76	904.64	113.5
#交通运输和仓储业	Transportation and Storage	166.05	161.98	108.3
邮电通讯业	Post and Telecommunications	51.51	47.59	127.7
批发和零售贸易、餐饮业	Wholesale,Retail and Catering Businesses	292.20	227.69	126.4

2-6 市区四县地区生产总值（2003年）

Gross Domestic Product by Region(2003)

单位：亿元 (100 million yuan)

区县名称	Name of District and County	地区生产总值 Gross Domestic Product	第一产业 Primary Industry	第二产业 Secondary Industry	第三产业 Tertiary Industry
全 市	**Whole City**	**941.60**	**50.72**	**415.68**	**475.20**
（一）市区	Urban Area	858.52	29.64	384.37	444.51
（二）四县	Four Counties	83.08	21.08	31.31	30.69
户县	Huxian	30.14	5.90	16.84	7.40
周至	Zhouzhi	20.00	5.52	3.65	10.83
高陵	Gaoling	12.63	3.92	5.13	3.58
蓝田	Lantian	20.31	5.74	5.69	8.88

2-7 全市及市区分产业地区生产总值项目构成（2003年）

Structure of Gross Domestic Product of Whole City and its Urban Districts by Sector(2003)

单位：亿元 (100 million yuan)

指　标	Item	增加值 Value of Added	劳动者报酬 Payment for Labor	固定资产折旧 Depreciation of Fixed Assets	生产税净额 Net Amount of Production Tax	营业盈余 Business Surplus
全　市	**Total**					
地区生产总值	Gross Domestic Product	941.60	502.64	156.19	138.56	144.21
第一产业	Primary Industry	50.72	42.10	3.10	1.95	3.57
第二产业	Secondary Industry	415.68	199.99	65.93	78.12	71.64
第三产业	Tertiary Industry	475.20	260.55	87.16	58.49	69.00
市　区	**Urban Area**					
地区生产总值	Gross Domestic Product	858.52	453.07	144.26	128.06	133.13
第一产业	Primary Industry	29.64	24.60	1.81	1.13	2.10
第二产业	Secondary Industry	384.37	184.88	61.11	72.26	66.12
第三产业	Tertiary Industry	444.51	243.59	81.34	54.67	64.91

2-8 分行业地区生产总值及指数

指　　标	Item	分行业地区生产总值（亿元）		
		1995	1998	1999
地区生产总值	**Gross Domestic Product**	**330.35**	**525.80**	**576.39**
第一产业	Primary Industry	41.40	51.90	45.53
第二产业	Secondary Industry	135.33	216.28	246.05
工业	Industry	112.50	174.96	196.70
建筑业	Construction	22.83	41.32	49.35
第三产业	Tertiary Industry	153.62	257.62	284.81
农林牧渔服务业	Farming,Forestry,Animal Husbandry and Fishery	0.66	0.81	0.61
地质勘探、水利管理业	Geological Prospecting and Water Conservancy Servieces	3.62	3.79	3.56
交通运输和仓储邮电通讯业	Transportation,Storage,Post and Telecommunications	27.30	48.64	55.35
批发零售贸易、餐饮业	Wholesale,Retail and Catering Services	34.27	64.93	70.27
金融保险业	Banking and Insurance	29.67	32.95	30.37
房地产业	Real Estate	4.90	11.95	14.42
社会服务业	Social Services	10.56	22.87	25.93
卫生体育、社会福利事业	Health Care,Sports and Social Welfare	5.88	12.99	17.38
教育、文艺、广播电影电视业	Education,Culture and Arts,Radio,Film and Television	15.11	20.16	24.05
科学科研和综合技术服务业	Scientific Research and polytechnic Services	9.17	17.01	18.67
国家政党机关和社会团体	Government and Party Agencies,and Socid Organizations	8.17	14.64	16.66
其他	Others	4.31	6.88	7.54

Gross Domestic Product and Its Indices by Sector

Gross Domestic Product By Sector (100 million yuan)				分行业地区生产总值指数（以上年为100） Indices of Gross Domestic Product By Sector (preceding year=100)						
2000	2001	2002	2003	1995	1998	1999	2000	2001	2002	2003
643.26	**733.85**	**823.50**	**941.60**	**110.0**	**113.3**	**112.2**	**113.0**	**113.1**	**113.3**	**113.5**
44.65	45.87	47.77	50.72	104.5	106.5	97.4	103.5	102.5	103.1	101.8
283.12	326.42	372.48	415.68	112.1	117.5	115.7	115.1	115.4	115.1	118.2
226.18	261.16	299.52	309.94	111.9	117.2	115.5	115.7	116.3	116.5	115.2
56.94	65.26	72.96	105.74	113.1	119.7	117.2	111.1	111.8	109.3	128.9
315.49	361.56	403.25	475.20	109.5	110.2	111.4	110.8	112.5	112.9	111.1
1.02	1.22	1.43	1.63	105.0	102.3	76.3	167.5	119.6	118.9	111.7
2.85	2.82	3.64	3.48	100.7	102.4	95.0	79.8	98.9	130.9	93.8
61.87	66.87	71.07	79.54	111.4	115.9	113.9	111.7	112.2	108.4	113.1
76.90	85.01	96.78	115.85	111.7	114.6	112.2	111.1	111.5	115.6	111
32.39	33.62	35.06	38.16	113.1	90.5	93.3	105.4	103.6	104.6	107.4
16.96	21.26	22.43	49.29	108.6	122.0	121.5	116.0	123.5	105.1	108.8
29.11	36.55	40.71	41.34	107.3	124.4	112.9	112.1	115.8	112.2	105.9
17.98	18.94	17.08	18.00	102.6	118.2	135.4	103.2	102.9	91.5	106.3
31.58	37.98	52.68	59.86	107.6	108.9	120.7	131.1	117.3	140.5	115
18.90	25.58	27.82	32.00	102.3	108.6	111.1	101.0	119.4	110.2	120.7
17.98	22.31	24.24	24.72	100.4	109.4	115.2	107.7	112.5	110.0	111.1
7.94	9.40	10.31	11.33	103.1	107.7	111.0	105.1	115.5	111.2	110.6

2-9 分行业地区生产总值项目构成（2003年）

单位：亿元

指 标	Item	增加值 Value of Addition
地区生产总值	**Gross Domestic Product**	**941.60**
第一产业	Primary Industry	50.72
农业	Agriculture	36.17
第二产业	Secondary Industry	415.68
工业	Industry	309.94
规模以上工业	State-owned Units and those with the Income of Sales Over 5 Million Yuan	202.74
其他	Others	107.20
建筑业	Construction	105.74
第三产业	Tertiary Industry	475.20
农林牧渔服务业	Farming,Forestry,Animal Husbandry and Fishery	1.63
地质勘探、水利管理业	Geological Prospecting and Water Conservancy Servieces	3.48
交通运输和仓储邮电通讯业	Transportation,Storage,Post and Telecommunications	79.54
交通运输和仓储业	Transportation and Storage	42.55
邮电通讯业	Post and communication	36.99
批发零售贸易、餐饮业	Wholesale,Retail Trade and Catering services	115.85
批发零售贸易业	Wholesale and Retail Trade	75.85
餐饮业	Catering Businesses	40.00
金融保险业	Banking and Insurance	38.16
金融业	Banking	23.14
保险业	Insurance	4.02
其他	Others	11.00
房地产业	Real Estate	49.29
#房地产开发与经营业	Real Estate Development and Trade	32.15
城市居民自有住房	Housing Owned by Urban Residents	9.93
农村居民自有住房	Housing Owned by Rural Residents	6.88
社会服务业	Social Services	41.34
卫生体育、社会福利事业	Health Care,Sports and Social Welfare	18.00
教育、文艺、广播电影电视业	Educaiton,Culture Radio Film and Television	59.86
科学科研和综合技术服务业	Scientific Research and Polytechnical Services	32.00
国家政党机关和社会团体	Government and Party Agencies,and Social Organizations	24.72
其他行业	Others	11.33

Composition of Gross Domestic Product by Sector(2003)

(100 million yuan)

劳动者报酬 Payment for Labor	固定资产折旧 Depreciation of Fixed Assets	生产税净额 Net Amount of Production Tax	营业盈余 Business Supplus
502.64	**156.19**	**138.56**	**144.21**
42.10	3.10	1.95	3.57
29.84	2.19	1.55	2.59
199.99	65.93	78.12	71.64
135.78	53.57	56.87	63.72
88.82	35.04	37.20	41.68
46.96	18.53	19.67	22.04
64.21	12.36	21.25	7.92
260.55	87.16	58.49	69.00
1.48	0.16	0.03	-0.04
3.09	0.35	0.04	0.00
21.66	16.55	6.16	35.17
18.00	8.92	4.46	11.17
3.66	7.63	1.70	24.00
53.06	19.31	28.98	14.50
36.41	13.40	20.19	5.85
16.65	5.91	8.79	8.65
13.60	4.15	5.91	14.50
11.92	3.95	5.27	2.00
1.68	0.20	0.64	1.50
			11.00
20.79	22.90	8.47	-2.87
20.47	6.08	8.47	-2.87
	9.93		
	6.88		
24.71	6.29	4.73	5.61
16.10	1.83	0.23	-0.16
48.23	10.31	0.91	0.41
24.59	2.97	2.48	1.96
22.26	2.03	0.52	-0.09
10.98	0.31	0.03	0.01

2-10 按支出法计算的地区生产总值

Gross Domestic Product by Expenditure Approach

单位：亿元 (100 million yuan)

指标	Item	2003	2002	指数（以上年为100）Indices (preceding year=100)
地区生产总值	**Gross Domestic Product**	**941.60**	**823.50**	**113.5**
（一）最终消费	Final Consumption Expenditures	639.56	573.40	110.3
1.居民消费	Resident Consumption Expenditures	473.68	420.90	110.4
农村居民	Village Residents	110.90	102.95	106.8
城镇居民	Urban Residents	362.78	317.95	111.6
2.政府消费	Government Consumption Expenditures	165.88	152.50	110.0
（二）资本形成总额	Gross Total Capital Formation	492.74	387.11	125.0
1.固定资本形成总额	Fixed Capital	450.16	344.54	128.0
2.存货增加	chang of Goods in Stock	42.58	42.57	101.0
（三）货物和服务净出口	Net Export of Goods and Services	-190.70	-137.01	132.8

2-11 按行业划分的资本形成总额

Gross Capital Formation by Sector

单位：亿元 (100 million yuan)

指　　标	Item	2003	2002
资本形成总额	Total Investment		
固定资本形成总额	Gross Fixed Capital Formation	450.16	344.54
第一产业	Primary Industry	3.70	6.41
第二产业	Secondary Industy	84.80	76.56
采掘业	Mining	4.40	1.26
制造业	Manufacturing	61.97	50.65
电力煤气及水的生产和供应业	Production and Supply of Electric Power, Gas and Water	12.56	18.24
建筑业	Construction	5.87	6.41
第三产业	Tertiary Industry	361.66	261.57
交通运输仓储及邮电通信业	Transportation,Storage,Post and Telecommunications	25.33	38.08
批发和零售贸易餐饮业	Wholesale, Retail and Catering Businesses	19.60	10.14
金融保险业	Banking and Insurance	1.18	2.22
房地产业	Real Estate	90.49	79.77
其他行业	Others	225.06	131.36
存货增加	Change of Goods in Stock	42.58	42.57
第一产业	Primary Industry	0.93	2.32
第二产业	Secondary Industy	19.72	13.41
工业	Industry	13.47	8.47
建筑业	Construction	6.25	4.94
第三产业	Tertiary Industry	21.94	26.84
交通运输仓储及邮电通信业	Transportation,Storage,Post and Telecommunications	-0.02	0.05
批发和零售贸易餐饮业	Wholesale, Retail and Catering Businesses	8.66	1.49
其他行业	Others	13.30	25.30

2-12　最 终 消 费

Final Consumption Expenditures

单位：亿元　　　　　　　　　　　　　　　　　　　　　　　　　(100 million yuan)

指　　标	Item	2003	2002
最终消费	**Final Consumption Expenditures**	**639.56**	**573.40**
一、居民消费	**Resident Consumption Expenditures**	**473.68**	**420.90**
1.农村居民	Village Residents	110.90	102.95
自给性消费	Self-Sufficient Consumption	8.23	7.17
商品性消费	Commodity Consumption	66.68	64.25
文化生活服务性消费	Cultural-Life Service Consumption	26.59	23.08
住房及水电消费	Housing,Water and Electricity	9.40	8.45
#住 房	Housing,Water and Electricity	7.36	6.73
2.城镇居民	Urban Residents	362.78	317.95
商品性消费	Commodity Consumption	250.85	221.31
文化生活服务性消费	Cultural-Life Service Consumption	91.86	78.63
住房及水电消费	Housing,Water and Electricity	20.07	18.01
#住 房	Housing	11.05	9.37
二、政府消费	**Government Consumption Expenditures**	**165.88**	**152.50**

2-13　居民总消费水平

Consumption of Residents

指　　标	Item	2003	2002	指数（%）Indices (preceding year=100)
一、按当年价格计算	**Calculated at Current Prices**			
全体居民消费水平(元/人)	Per Capita Consumption of All Residents (yuan/person)	6154	5552	110.8
农村居民(元/人)	Farmer (yuan/person)	2751	2559	107.5
城镇居民(元/人)	Non-Farmer (yuan/person)	9896	8937	110.7
二、按可比价格计算	**Calculated at Comparable Prices (yuan/person)**			
全体居民消费水平(元/人)	Per Capita Consumption of All Residents (yuan/Person)	6064	5575	108.8
农村居民(元/人)	Farmer (yuan/person)	2685	2518	106.6
城镇居民(元/人)	Non-Farmer (yuan/person)	9780	9032	108.3
三、居民年平均人口(万人)	**Average Annual Population of Residents (10 000 persons)**	**769.70**	**758.15**	**101.50**
农村居民(万人)	Farmer (10 000 persons)	403.12	402.38	100.2
城镇居民(万人)	Non-Farmer (10 000 persons)	366.58	355.77	103.0

主 要 统 计 指 标 解 释

地区收入总值（GNI） 是按市场价格计算的一个地区（或国家）所有常住单位在一定时期内收入初次分配的最终结果。一国常住单位从事生产活动所创造的增加值在初次分配中主要分配给该国的常住单位，但也有一部分以生产税及进口税（扣除生产和进口补贴）、劳动者报酬和财产收入等形式分配给非常住单位；同时，国外生产所创造的增加值也有一部分以生产税及进口税（扣除生产和进口补贴）、劳动者报酬和财产收入等形式分配给该国的常住单位，从而产生了地区收入总值的概念。它等于地区生产总值加上来自国外的净要素收入。与地区生产总值不同，地区收入总值是个收入概念，而地区生产总值是个生产概念。

地区**生产总值（GDP）** 是按市场价格计算的一个地区（或国家）所有常住单位在一定时期内生产活动的最终成果。地区生产总值有三种表现形态，即价值形态、收入形态和产品形态。从价值形态看，它是所有常住单位在一定时期内生产的全部货物和服务价值超过同期中间投入的全部非固定资产货物和服务价值的差额，即所有常住单位的增加值之和；从收入形态看，它是所有常住单位在一定时期内创造并分配给常住单位和非常住单位的初次收入分配之和；从产品形态看，它是所有常住单位在一定时期内最终使用的货物和服务价值与货物和服务净出口价值之和。在实际核算中，地区生产总值有三种计算方法，即生产法、收入法和支出法。三种方法分别从不同的方面反映地区生产总值及其构成。

三次产业 是根据社会生产活动历史发展的顺序对产业结构的划分，产品直接取自自然界的部门称为第一产业，对初级产品进行再加工的部门称为第二产业，为生产和消费提供各种服务的部门称为第三产业。它是世界上较为通用的产业结构分类，但各国的划分不尽一致。

我国的三次产业划分是：

第一产业：农业（包括农业、林业、畜牧业和渔业）。

第二产业：工业（包括采掘业，制造业，电力、煤气及水的生产和供应业）和建筑业。

第三产业：除第一、第二产业以外的其他各业。

支出法地区生产总值 指一个地区（或国家）所有常住单位在一定时期内用于最终消费、资本形成总额，以及货物和服务的净出口总额，它反映本期生产的地区生产总值的使用及构成。

最终消费 指常住单位在一定时期内对于货物和服务的全部最终消费支出，也就是常住单位为满足物质、文化和精神生活的需要，从本国经济领土和国外购买的货物和服务的支出；不包括非常住单位在本国经济领土内的消费支出。最终消费分为居民消费和政府消费。

居民消费 指常住住户对货物和服务的全部最终消费支出。居民消费按市场价格计算，即按居民支付的购买者价格计算。购买者价格是购买者取得货物所支付的价格，包括购买者支付的运输和商业费用。居民消费除了直接以货币形式购买货物和服务的消费之外，还包括以其他方式获得的货物和服务的消费支出，即所谓的虚拟消费支出。居民虚拟消费支出包括以下几种类型：单位以实物报酬及实物转移的形式提供给劳动者的货物和服务；住户生产并由本住户消费了的货物和服务，其中的服务仅指住户的自有住房服务；金融机构提供的金融媒介服务；保险公司提供的保险服务。

政府消费 指政府部门为全社会提供公共服务的消费支出和免费或以较低价格向住户提供的货物和服务的净支出。前者等于政府服务的产出价值减去政府单位所获得的经营收入的价值，政府服务的产出价值等于它的经常性业务支出加上固定资产折旧；后者等于政府部门免费或以较低价格向住户提供的货物和服务的市场价值减去向住户收取的价值。

资本形成总额 指常住单位在一定时期内获得的减去处置的固定资产加存货的变动，包括固定资本形成总额和存货增加。

固定资本形成总额 指常住单位购置、转入和自产自用的固定资产，扣除固定资产的销售和转出后的价值，分有形固定资产形成总额和无形固定资产形成总额。有形固定资产形成总额包括一定时期内完成的建筑工程、安装工程和设备工器具购置（减处置）价值，以及土地改良、新增役、种、奶、毛、娱乐用牲畜和新增经济林木价值。无形固定资产形成总额包括矿藏的勘探、计算机软件、娱乐和文学艺术品原件等获得减处置。

存货增加 指常住单位存货实物量变动的市场价值，即期末价值减期初价值的差额。存货增加可以是正值，也可以是负值；正值表示存货上升，负值表示存货下降。它包括生产单位购进的原材料、燃料和储备物资等存货，以及生产单位生产的产成品、在制品等存货等。

货物和服务净出口 指货物和服务出口减货物和服

务进口的差额。出口包括常住单位向非常住单位出售或无偿转让的各种货物和服务的价值；进口包括常住单位从非常住单位购买或无偿得到的各种货物和服务的价值。由于服务活动的提供与使用同时发生，因此服务的进出口业务并不发生出入境现象，一般把常住单位从国外得到的服务作为进口，非常住单位从本国得到的服务作为出口。货物的出口和进口都按离岸价格计算。

劳动者报酬 指劳动者因从事生产活动所获得的全部报酬。包括劳动者获得的各种形式的工资、奖金和津贴，既包括货币形式的，也包括实物形式的；还包括劳动者所享受的公费医疗和医药卫生费、上下班交通补贴和单位支付的社会保险费等。对于个体经济来说，其所有者所获得的劳动报酬和经营利润不易区分，这两部分统一作为劳动者报酬处理。

生产税净额 指生产税减生产补贴后的余额。生产税指政府对生产单位生产、销售和从事经营活动以及因从事生产活动使用某些生产要素（如固定资产、土地、劳动力）所征收的各种税、附加费和规费。生产补贴与生产税相反，指政府对生产单位的单方面收入转移，因此视为负生产税，包括政策亏损补贴、粮食系统价格补贴、外贸企业出口退税收入等。

固定资产折旧 指一定时期内为弥补固定资产损耗按照核定的固定资产折旧率提取的固定资产折旧，或按国民经济核算统一规定的折旧率虚拟计算的固定资产折旧。它反映了固定资产在当期生产中的转移价值。各类企业和企业化管理的事业单位的固定资产折旧是指实际计提并计入成本费中的折旧费；不计提折旧的政府机关、非企业化管理的事业单位和居民住房的固定资产折旧是按照统一规定的折旧率和固定资产原值计算的虚拟折旧。原则上，固定资产折旧应按固定资产的重置价值计算，但是目前我国尚不具备对全社会固定资产进行重估价的基础，所以暂时只能采用上述办法。

营业盈余 指常住单位创造的增加值扣除劳动者报酬、生产税净额和固定资产折旧后的余额。它相当于企业的营业利润加上生产补贴，但要扣除从利润中开支的工资和福利等。

Explanatory Notes on Main Statistical Indicators

Gross National Product (GNI) refers to the final result of the primary distribution of the income created by all the resident units of a region during a certain period at market price. The value-added created by the resident units of a country engaged in production activities is mainly distributed to the resident units of that country while a part of it is distributed to the non-resident units in the form of production tax and import duties (minus subsidies to production and import), remuneration for the labourers and property income. At the meantime, a part of the value-added created abroad is distributed to the resident units of the country in the form of production tax and import duties (minus subsidies to production and import), remuneration for the labourers and property income. Thus the concept of gross national income is formed, which equals to gross domestic product plus net factor income from abroad. Unlike gross domestic product which is a concept of production, gross national income is a concept of income.

Gross Domestic Product (GDP) refers to the final products of all resident units in a oregin (or a country) during a certain period at market price. Gross domestic product is expressed in three different forms, i.e. value, income, and products respectively. The form of value refers to the total value of all products and services produced by all resident units during a certain period of time minus total value of intimidate input of materials and services of the nature of non-fixed assets or the summation of the value-added of all resident units; the form of income includes all the income created by all resident units and distributed primarily to all resident and non-resident units; the form of products refers to the value of all final goods and services for final use by all resident units plus the value of net exports of goods and services during a given period of time. In the practice of national accounting, gross domestic product is calculated with three approaches, i.e. production approach, income approach, and expenditure approach, which reflect gross domestic product and its composition from different aspects.

Three Industries Industry structure has been classified according to the historical sequence of development. Primary industry refers to extraction of natural resources; secondary industry involves processing of primary products; and tertiary industry provides services of various kinds for production and consumption. The above classification is universal although it varies to some extent form country to country. Industry in China comprises:

Primary industry: agriculture (including farming, forestry, animal husbandry and fishery).

Secondary industry: industry (including mining and quarrying, manufacturing, production and supply of electricity, water and gas) and construction.

Tertiary industry: all other industries not included in primary or secondary industry.

GDP Calculated with Expenditure Approach refers to total expenditure on final consumption, total capital formation and net export of goods and services by resident units of a country in a certain period of time. It reflects the composition of GDP by its use.

Final Consumption refers to the total expenditure of resident units on final consumption of goods and services in a certain period, namely the expenditure of the resident units for purchases of goods and services from domestic economic territory and abroad to meet the requirements of material, cultural and spiritual life. It excludes the expenditure of non-resident units on consumption in the economic territory of the country. The final consumption is classified into household consumption and government consumption.

Households Consumption refers to the total expenditure of resident households on the final consumption of goods and services. The households consumption is calculated at market prices, namely the purchasers prices which the households pay; the purchasers prices of goods are the prices the households pay when they obtain the goods, including the transport and commercial expenses paid by the households. In addition to the consumption of goods and services bought by the households directly with money, the expenditure on goods and services obtained by the households in other ways, i.e. the so-called imputed expenditure on consumption, is also included in the households consumption. The imputation expenditure of the households on consumption includes the following types: (a) the goods and services provided to the households by the units in the form of payment in kind and transfer in kind; (b) the goods and services produced and consumed by the households themselves, in which the services refer only to the services provided by the residential buildings owned by the households; (c) the services of financial intermediary provided by the financial institutions; (d) theinsurance services provided by the insurance companies.

Government Consumption refers to the expenditure on the consumption of the public services provided by the government to the whole society and the net expenditure on the goods and services provided by the government to the households at free charge or lower prices. The former equals to the output value of the government services minus the value of operating income obtained by the government departments. (The output value of the government services equals to its current operating expenditure plus depreciation of fixed assets). The latter equals to the market value of the goods and services provided by the government free of charge or at low prices to the households minus the value received by the government from the households.

Total Capital Formation refers to the fixed assets acquired minus those disposed and the change in inventory, including the total fixed assets formation and the increase in inventory.

Total Fixed Capital Formation refers to the value of fixed assets purchased, transferred in by the resident units and those produced and used by themselves deducting the value of fixed assets sold and transferred out. It can be classified into total tangible assets formation and total intangible assets formation. The total tangible assets formation include the value of the construction projects, installation projects completed and the equipment, apparatus and instruments purchased as well as the value of land improved, the value of draught animals, breeding stock, milk, wool and recreational animals and the newly increased economic forest in a certain period. The total intangible assets formation includes the prospecting of minerals, the acquisition of computer software, the originals of recreational works and works of literature and arts minus the disposal of them.

Increase in Inventory refers to the market value of the change in inventory, i.e. the difference of value between the beginning and the end of the period. The increase in inventory can be positive or negative. A positive value indicates the increase in inventory while a negative value indicates the decrease in stock. The inventory includes the raw materials, fuels and reserve materials purchased by the production units as well as the inventory of finished products, semi-finished products, work-in-progress, etc.

Net Export of Goods and Services refers to the difference of the exports of goods and services minus the imports of goods and services. The imports include the value of various goods and services sold or gratuitously transferred by the resident units to the non-resident units. The imports include the value of various goods and services purchased or gratuitously acquired by the resident units from the non-resident units. Because the provision of services and the use of them happen simultaneously, the import and export of services do not appear to have the phenomena of crossing the border of the country. The acquisition of services by the resident units from abroad is usually treated as import while the acquisition of services by non-resident units in this country is usually treated as export. The export and import of goods are calculated at FOB.

Labourers Remuneration refers to the whole payment of various forms earned by the labourers from the productive activities they are engaged in. It includes wages, bonuses and allowances the labourers earned in monetary form and in kind. It also includes the free medical services provided to the labourers and the medicine expenses, traffic subsidies and social insurance fee paid by the labourers working units for them. As the individual economy is concerned, since the labourers remuneration is not easily distinguished from the operating profit, both are treated as labourers remuneration.

Net Taxes on Production refers to the residual of the taxes on production minus the subsidies on production. The taxes on production refers to the various taxes, extra charges and fees levied on the production units on theirproduction, sale and business activities as well as on some factors of production, such as fixed assets, land and labour force, used in the production activities they are engaged in. In contrast to the taxes on production, the subsidies on production refer to the unilateral transfer of part of the governments revenue to the production units and is therefore regarded as negative taxes on production. They include subsidies on the loss due to implementation of government policies, price subsidies to the grain institutions, foreign trade corporations receipts from drawback, etc.

Depreciation of Fixed Assets refers to the depreciation of fixed assets of a given period, drawn in accordance with the stipulated depreciation rate for the purpose of compensating the wear loss of the fixed assets or the depreciation of fixed assets calculated in a fictitious way in accordance with the stipulated unified depreciation rate in the national economic accounting system. It reflects the value of transfer of the fixed assets in the production of the current period. The depreciation of fixed assets in various enterprises and institutions managed as enterprisesrefers to the depreciation expenses actually drawn and calculated as part of the cost. In government agencies and institutions not managed as enterprises which do not draw the depreciation expenses, as well as for the houses of residents, the depreciation of fixed assets is the imputed depreciation, which is calculated in accordance with the stipulated unified depreciation rate. In principle, the depreciation of fixed assets should be calculated on the basis of the re-purchased value of the fixed assets. However, there is no actual condition to re-evaluate all the fixed assets in China. Therefore, the above-mentioned methods are temporarily adopted at present.

Operating Surplus refers to the balance of the value added created by the resident units deducting the labourers remuneration, net taxes on production and the depreciation of fixed assets. It is equivalent to the business profit of the enterprises plus subsidies on production, but the wages and welfare expenses paid from the profits should be deducted.

2004

年統
鑒計

三、人口、从业人员与职工工资

POPULATION,EMPLOYMENT AND WAGES

简　要　说　明

Brief Introduction

本章内容主要包括主要年份人口、分区县人口及变动、从业人员及劳动报酬等。人口资料主要数据由市统计局人口与社会科技处提供。人口为公安年报数，1991年以前年份市区数未包括临潼、长安。

This chapter consists of the data about the population of consequent years, population of all the districts and counties and the correspondent changes, the employed and their wages. The population data is provided primarily by Population & Employment Division and Social & Science and Technology.Division of the Xi'an Bureau of Statistics. The population data are from the annual report of the Xi'an Bureau of Public Security, with Lintong, Chang'an not included before 1991.

3-1 主要年份人口、人口密度和人口发展情况

Population, Population Density and Population Development in represontative

单位：人 （person）

年份 Year	总人口 Total population	市区 Urban Area	女性人口数 Number of Female	非农业人口数 Non-Agricultural Population	人口密度（人/平方公里）Density of Population (person/sq.km)	总人口指数(上年为100) Total Population Index (100 for preceding year) 全市 Whole City	市区 Urban Area
1952	2529228	924220	1188059	576090	254	102.6	103.1
1957	3272826	1470085	1505793	1110763	328	103.2	104.6
1965	4000502	1798785	1907240	1363855	401	102.5	103.4
1970	4351197	1881235	2104689	1391166	436	101.9	101.4
1978	4980995	2101455	2418216	1599849	499	101.7	102.7
1980	5119053	2211871	2492612	1728476	513	101.4	102.6
1985	5531132	2457581	2683953	2019043	554	101.6	102.2
1986	5639673	2517950	2732976	2059200	565	101.9	102.5
1987	5744588	2576926	5781213	2102533	575	101.9	102.3
1988	5858479	2649366	2836814	2169917	587	101.9	102.8
1989	5973588	2708002	2894424	2225428	598	102.0	102.2
1990	6088901	2756926	2952879	2269836	610	101.9	154.8
1991	6154777	4192901	2981337	2308534	617	101.1	101.1
1992	6231978	4295360	3019204	2364545	624	101.3	101.3
1993	6309145	4354082	3052996	2408467	632	101.2	101.3
1994	6394544	4423039	3091700	2483546	641	101.4	101.6
1995	6482079	4486542	3134575	2557090	645	101.4	101.4
1996	6548724	4546828	3165968	2612786	653	101.0	101.3
1997	6620578	4611726	3201816	2675156	663	101.1	101.4
1998	6682168	4663139	3231978	2717526	669	100.9	101.1
1999	6744977	4635634	3261177	2761365	676	100.9	99.4
2000	6880111	4831049	3328256	2857913	689	102.0	104.2
2001	6948369	4898783	3360385	2926240	696	101.0	101.4
2002	7025939	4973845	3395060	3000463	704	101.1	101.5
2003	7165784	5102553	3462628	3128810	718	101.9	102.6

注:人口部分均为公安年报数字。1991年以前年份，市区数未包括临潼、长安。

Note: The population data are taken from annual reports of public recurity.The population of urban area before 1991 does include Lintong and Chang'an.

3-2 主要年份人口变动情况

Population Changes in Representative Years

年份 Year	出生 Birth 人数(人) Population (person)	出生率(‰) Birth Rate (‰)	死亡 Death 人数(人) Population (person)	死亡率(‰) Death Rate (‰)	迁入人口(人) Immigrant population (person)	迁出人口(人) Emigrant population (person)	自然增长率(‰) Natural Gorwth Rate (‰)
1952	76754	30.74	22138	8.86	…	…	21.87
1957	122737	38.09	27612	8.57	259926	229226	29.52
1965	115340	29.19	33590	8.50	131109	108302	20.69
1970	120511	27.96	23448	5.44	68775	83854	22.53
1978	78051	19.04	31699	6.66	89840	91562	12.38
1980	65864	12.96	31930	6.28	133560	96364	6.68
1985	89451	16.30	30085	5.48	115957	87364	10.82
1986	101360	18.15	27777	4.97	117893	83933	13.17
1987	97578	17.14	28288	4.97	125790	92551	12.17
1988	94213	16.24	28905	4.98	135421	89708	11.26
1989	117822	19.92	30379	5.13	127270	101451	14.78
1990	123972	20.55	34469	5.72	118160	98604	14.84
1991	87267	14.25	32615	5.33	89788	60935	8.93
1992	89750	14.49	33928	5.48	139397	95444	9.01
1993	92509	14.75	33707	5.38	114950	83262	9.38
1994	80760	12.71	31584	4.97	134042	85854	7.47
1995	76929	11.95	32061	4.98	144054	88468	6.97
1996	72620	11.15	34111	5.24	119435	88757	5.91
1997	68368	10.38	31247	4.75	125751	86225	5.64
1998	63962	9.62	31007	4.66	108865	83567	4.95
1999	61875	9.22	38815	5.78	125834	92265	3.44
2000	89036	13.07	40587	5.96	171217	92341	7.11
2001	51070	7.39	28939	4.19	151636	108282	3.20
2002	53415	7.64	30842	4.41	138978	94146	3.23
2003	60214	8.48	33213	4.68	205994	91482	3.80

3–3 分区县人口和户数(2003年)

Population and Households by Region(2003)

单位：人 (person)

区 县	District and County	总户数(户) Number of Households (household)	总人口(人) Total Population (person)	非农业人口 Non-agriculture	按性别分 Grouped by Sex 男 Male	女 Female	未落常住户口人数 Population without Permanent Residency Card
新城区	Xincheng	152477	481787	469866	247701	234086	98
碑林区	Beilin	181263	691110	679500	370915	320195	
莲湖区	Lianhu	187889	590160	554564	302926	287234	47
灞桥区	Baqiao	128327	445826	172830	225171	220655	24
未央区	Weiyang	122131	401192	191265	202605	198587	120
雁塔区	Yanta	158175	669352	515361	350629	318723	
阎良区	Yanliang	63780	240278	79548	122457	117821	
临潼区	Lintong	172737	668600	109396	338855	329745	528
长安区	Chang'an	248024	914248	116243	464900	449348	3586
蓝田县	Lantian	163196	632520	68174	329817	302703	3234
周至县	Zhouzhi	156996	627836	50344	332492	295344	1125
户 县	Huxian	158495	568625	96446	296112	272513	249
高陵县	Gaoling	59667	234250	25273	118576	115674	190

3–4 分区县人口变动情况(2003年)

Population Changes by Region(2003)

单位：人 (Person)

地区	Region	出生人口 Number of Births	死亡人口 Number of Deaths	迁入人口 Immigeant Population 省内迁入 Immigrants from Other Areas In the Province	省外迁入 immigrants from Other Provinces	迁出人口 Emigrant Population 迁往省内 Emigrants to Other Places in the Province	迁往省外 Emigrants to Other Provinces
新城区	Xincheng	3557	2188	2244	1777	209	1094
碑林区	Beilin	4041	2037	23345	21334	6211	14082
莲湖区	Lianhu	4276	2087	8412	3223	3312	2775
灞桥区	Baqiao	3753	1541	6462	3076	1695	820
未央区	Weiyang	4350	2757	5321	4031	1595	1127
雁塔区	Yanta	4768	1200	40397	42056	9376	16030
阎良区	Yanliang	2145	806	2809	716	1006	843
临潼区	Lintong	5100	5818	3402	1190	3409	1484
长安区	Chang'an	9482	3889	8447	4120	2311	1042
蓝田县	Lantian	6636	3394	6131	1089	5964	687
周至县	Zhouzhi	4892	3578	5858	391	6529	1259
户 县	Huxian	4824	2617	6615	1030	4688	1379
高陵县	Gaoling	2390	1301	2179	339	2045	510

3–5　主要年份社会从业人数

单位：万人

年 份 Year	合 计 Total	一、按城乡分 Grouped by Urban area and Rural area 1.城镇 Urban	国有经济 State-owned Enterprises	集体经济 Collective-owned Enterprises	其他经济 Others	2.乡村 Village
1985	296.80	129.07	96.80	29.07	3.20	167.73
1986	299.45	132.82	101.28	28.43	3.11	166.63
1987	312.16	138.56	104.58	30.72	3.26	173.60
1988	327.76	142.24	106.46	30.73	5.05	185.52
1989	332.65	145.65	108.80	30.44	6.41	187.00
1990	343.06	147.93	110.95	29.78	7.20	195.13
1991	347.65	149.48	111.87	29.80	7.81	198.17
1992	357.51	151.67	113.19	29.97	8.51	205.84
1993	363.70	155.72	112.98	29.77	12.97	207.98
1994	364.56	154.88	113.39	27.97	13.52	209.68
1995	372.60	158.80	113.79	25.58	19.43	213.80
1996	379.29	164.54	113.29	24.82	26.43	214.75
1997	385.14	169.52	112.44	23.52	33.56	215.62
1998	393.95	177.20	106.06	21.50	49.64	216.75
1999	400.43	180.27	105.08	20.50	54.69	220.16
2000	389.10	176.45	103.46	18.40	54.59	212.65
2001	389.30	177.94	100.47	17.10	60.37	211.36
2002	397.16	181.85	100.54	16.90	64.41	215.31
2003	404.92	183.23	94.51	16.78	71.94	221.69

Number of Social Laborers in Representative Years

(10 000 persons)

二、按三次产业分		Grouped by Industry
第一产业 Primary Industry	第二产业 Secondary Indusyry	第三产业 Tertiary Industry
135.89	98.61	62.30
127.46	100.61	71.38
130.36	107.75	74.05
138.87	108.12	80.77
142.21	106.40	84.04
149.64	106.74	86.68
152.24	108.19	87.22
154.75	110.22	92.54
154.02	114.02	95.66
153.51	108.53	102.52
153.39	109.67	109.54
153.43	109.17	116.69
153.23	109.46	122.45
153.00	110.45	130.50
154.64	110.58	135.21
147.03	107.26	134.81
145.09	108.96	135.25
143.04	111.62	142.50
146.67	109.09	149.16

3-6　分行业从业人数（2003年）

单位：万人

行　　业	Sector	合计 Total
总　计	Total	404.92
一、按国民经济行业分组	Grouped by Economic Sector	
(一)农、林、牧、渔业	Farming,Forestry,Animal Husbandry and Fishery	146.67
(二)采矿业	Mining	0.19
(三)制造业	Manufacturing	76.40
(四)电力、燃气及水的生产和供应业	Production & Supply of Power,Gas & Water	2.14
(五)建筑业	Construction	30.36
(六)交通运输、仓储和邮政业	Transport,Storage and Postal Service	22.53
(七)信息传输、计算机服务和软件业	Information Transmission,Computer Service and Software Service	1.20
(八)批发和零售业	Wholesale and Retail Trade	46.64
(九)住宿和餐饮业	Accommodation and Catering Trade	13.92
(十)金融业	Banking	4.40
(十一)房地产业	Real Estate Trade	0.88
(十二)租赁和商务服务业	Commercial Service	5.20
(十三)科学研究、技术服务和地质勘察业	Scientific Research,Technical Services and Geological Prospecting	10.27
(十四)水利、环境和公共设施管理业	Water conservancy, environment and public facilities administration industry	1.01
(十五)居民服务和其他服务业	Resident Services and Other Services	9.63
(十六)教育	Education	13.93
(十七)卫生、社会保障和社会福利业	Sanitation, social insurance and social welfare industry	6.22
(十八)文化、体育和娱乐业	Culture, physical education and entertainment industry	1.72
(十九)公共管理和社会组织	Public administration non-profit institution	11.61
二、按三次产业分	Guroped by Industry	
第一产业	Primary Industry	146.67
第二产业	Secondary Industry	109.09
第三产业	Tertiary Industry	149.16

Number Of Employed Persons By Sector(2003)

(10 000 persons)

国有经济 State-owned Enterprises	集体经济 Collective-owned Enterprises	城镇其他经济 Urban Other Enterprises	城镇私营经济及个体劳动者 Urban Private Enterprises and Individual Labors	乡镇劳动者 Rural and Urban Labourer
94.73	**16.02**	**26.98**	**45.50**	**221.69**
1.17	0.02	0.03	0.02	145.43
0.02	0.06	0.06	0.05	
30.12	6.66	17.05	6.76	15.81
2.12		0.02		
6.37	2.39	0.66	1.66	19.28
8.46	0.51	0.41	3.30	9.85
0.19		1.01		
6.93	3.77	3.39	23.02	9.53
1.89	0.50	1.38	5.08	5.07
2.73	0.17	0.98		0.52
0.49	0.12	0.27		
1.03	0.91	0.09	2.17	1.00
7.34		0.43		2.50
1.01				
0.99	0.44	1.01	3.19	4.00
12.25	0.01	0.17		1.50
3.18	0.29		0.25	2.50
1.69	0.01	0.02		
6.75	0.16			4.70
1.17	0.02	0.03	0.02	145.43
38.63	9.11	17.79	8.47	35.09
54.93	6.89	9.16	37.01	41.17

3–7 劳动力资源总数

Total Number of Labor Resources

单位：万人 (10 000 persons)

年 份 Year	劳动力资源总数 Total Labourers Resource	社会从业人数 Number of Social Employed Persons	占人口数的比例(%) Percentage in Population (%)
1985	344.85	296.80	62.35
1986	352.71	299.45	62.54
1987	367.71	312.16	64.01
1988	378.33	327.76	64.58
1989	388.94	332.65	65.11
1990	395.92	343.06	65.02
1991	400.01	347.65	64.99
1992	410.80	357.51	65.91
1993	413.33	363.70	65.51
1994	451.88	364.58	70.66
1995	455.90	378.52	70.33
1996	458.47	379.29	70.01
1997	466.18	385.14	70.41
1998	480.26	393.95	71.87
1999	484.79	400.43	71.20
2000	479.40	389.10	69.68
2001	495.24	389.30	71.25
2002	503.39	397.16	71.64
2003	546.21	404.92	76.22

3–8 城乡劳动力资源配置情况(2003年)

Deployment of Urban and Rural Labor Resources(2003)

行业	Sector	城乡合计 Total	城镇 Urban Area	乡村 Rural
一、年末劳动力资源总数	**Total Number of Labor Resources at the Year-end**	**546.21**	**293.98**	**252.23**
#当年新增加的劳动力资源	# Newly Emerged Labor Resources	13.95	5.52	8.43
1.年末16岁以上全部人数	Population Over 16 at the Year-end	534.77	282.59	252.18
2.机械变动差额跨地区人数	Balance on Trans-regional Immigration/emigration	11.44	11.39	0.05
二、经济活动人口	**Economically Active Population**	**413.48**	**191.79**	**221.69**
（一）从业人员	Number of Employed Persons	404.92	183.23	221.69
1.按就业身份分组	Grouped by Employees□Status			
（1）全部职工	Total	137.31	137.31	
（2）再就业的离退休人员	Retirees Reemployed	0.42	0.42	
（3）私营业主	Private Owners	8.79	5.66	3.13
（4）个体户主	Self-employed Persons	20.51	8.49	12.02
（5）私营企业和个体从业人员	Employees in Private Enterprises and	58.35	31.35	27.00
（6）农村劳动力	Rural Labor Resources	179.54		179.54
（7）其他	Others			
2.按国民经济类型分组	Grouped by Type			
（1）国有经济	State-owned Enterprises	95.17	95.17	
（2）集体经济	Collective-owned Enterprises	196.33	16.79	179.54
（3）私营经济	Private Enterprises	35.60	21.86	13.74
（4）个体经济	Individual Enterprises	52.05	23.64	28.41
（5）股份合作经济	Share-Holding Cooperatiive Enterprises	2.21	2.21	
（6）联营经济	Joint -owned Enterprises	0.10	0.10	
（7）有限责任公司	Limited Liability corporations	13.45	13.45	
（8）股份有限公司	Share-Holding Corporation ltd	8.27	8.27	
（9）外商投资经济	Foreign-funded Enterprises	1.25	1.25	
（10）港、澳、台投资经济	Enterprises with Investment from Hong Kong,	0.49	0.49	
（11）其他经济	Others			
3.按国民经济行业分组	Grouped by Economic Sector			
（1）农、林、牧、渔业	Farming,Forestry,Animal Husbandry and Fishery	146.67	1.24	145.43
（2）采矿业	Mining	0.19	0.19	
（3）制造业	Manufacturing	76.40	60.59	15.81
（4）电力、燃气及水的生产和供应业	Production & Supply of Power,Gas & Water	2.14	2.14	
（5）建筑业	Construction	30.36	11.08	19.28
（6）交通运输、仓储和邮政业	Transport,Storage and Postal Service	22.53	12.68	9.85
（7）信息传输、计算机服务和软件业	Information Transmission,Computer Service and Software Service	1.20	1.20	
（8）批发和零售业	Wholesale and Retail Trade	46.64	37.11	9.53
（9）住宿和餐饮业	Accommodation and Catering Trade	13.92	8.85	5.07
（10）金融业	Banking	4.40	3.88	0.52
（11）房地产业	Real Estate Trade	0.88	0.88	
（12）租赁和商务服务业	Commercial Service	5.20	4.20	1.00
（13）科学研究、技术服务和地质勘察业	Scientific Research,Technical Services and Geological Prospecting	10.27	7.77	2.50
（14）水利、环境和公共设施管理业	Water conservancy, environment and public facilities administration industry	1.01	1.01	
（15）居民服务和其他服务业	Resident Services and Other Services	9.63	5.63	4.00
（16）教育	Education	13.93	12.43	1.50
（17）卫生、社会保障和社会福利业	Sanitation, social insurance and social welfare industry	6.22	3.72	2.50
（18）文化、体育和娱乐业	Culture, physical education and entertainment industry	1.72	1.72	
（19）公共管理和社会组织	Public administration non-profit institution	11.61	6.91	4.70
（二）失业人员	Unemployed	8.56	8.56	
三、非经济活动人口	**Non-economical Activity Population**	**108.93**	**78.39**	**30.36**
#16岁以上在校学生	# Students Aged 16 and Over	75.81	67.92	7.89

3-9 全部单位从业人员情况（2003年）

单位：人

行　业	Sector	单位从业人员 Employed Persons	女 性 Female
总　计	**Total**	**1166769**	**432115**
一、按企业、事业、机关分组	**Groped by Character of Unit**		
1.企业	Enterprises	843367	301734
2.事业	Institutions	253400	113313
3.机关	Governmental Agencies	70002	17068
二、按国民经济行业分组	**Grouped by Economic Sector**		
(一)农、林、牧、渔业	Farming,Forestry,Animal Husbandry and Fishery	10270	3289
(二)采矿业	Mining	1458	397
(三)制造业	Manufacturing	433486	157981
(四)电力、燃气及水的生产和供应业	Production & Supply of Power,Gas & Water	20166	6769
(五)建筑业	Construction	77093	15887
(六)交通运输、仓储和邮政业	Transport,Storage and Postal Service	82409	23642
(七)信息传输、计算机服务和软件业	Information Transmission,Computer Service and Software Service	12162	3107
(八)批发和零售业	Wholesale and Retail Trade	94540	44409
(九)住宿和餐饮业	Accommodation and Catering Trade	27649	12371
(十)金融业	Banking	37477	10626
(十一)房地产业	Real Estate Trade	8110	2684
(十二)租赁和商务服务业	Commercial Service	16681	8520
(十三)科学研究、技术服务和地质勘察业	Scientific Research,Technical Services and Geological Prospecting	75180	24809
(十四)水利、环境和公共设施管理业	Water conservancy, environment and public facilities administration industry	10143	3134
(十五)居民服务和其他服务业	Resident Services and Other Services	14773	6818
(十六)教育	Education	120876	58416
(十七)卫生、社会保障和社会福利业	Sanitation, social insurance and social welfare industry	35902	18158
(十八)文化、体育和娱乐业	Culture, physical education and entertainment industry	17647	6759
(十九)公共管理和社会组织	Public administration non-profit institution	70747	18939

Basic Facts on All Employed Persons(2003)

(person)

在岗职工合计 Total Fully Employed Staff and Workers	专业技术人员 Scientific and Technical Personnel	女性 Female	其他从业人员 Other Employed Persons	单位从业人员 平均人数 Average Employment	在岗职工 Fully Employed Staff and Workers	其他从业人员 Other Employed Persons
1135439	**362066**	**144812**	**31330**	**1168459**	**1137343**	**31116**
823002	214207	72693	20365	846645	826138	20507
243328	147776	72094	10072	252574	242798	9776
69109	83	25	893	69240	68407	833
9978	2768	1019	292	10411	10117	294
1455	178	52	3	1460	1457	3
425876	108545	32207	7610	433925	426488	7437
20085	5607	672	81	19234	19155	79
75005	17011	5340	2088	80413	77981	2432
78459	18171	7331	3950	81621	77735	3886
12134	4786	1536	28	12108	12087	21
92931	14627	5590	1609	94736	93190	1546
26637	2297	1025	1012	27621	26675	946
36683	15856	7510	794	38443	37726	717
8014	1512	412	96	7909	7821	88
16154	2599	806	527	16605	16164	441
74232	47748	14588	948	75569	74640	929
9949	2009	790	194	10103	9909	194
13661	1991	922	1112	15462	14211	1251
113764	81325	45173	7112	118908	111900	7008
34582	26220	16460	1320	35875	34708	1167
17237	8367	3268	410	17645	17232	413
68603	449	111	2144	70411	68147	2264

3-10 国有单位从业人员情况（2003年）

单位：人

行 业	Item	单位从业人员 Employed Persons	女性 Female
合 计	**Total**	**795785**	**291685**
一、按隶属关系分组	**Grouped by Administrative Relationship**		
1.中央	Central	349151	119957
2.省、自治区、直辖市	Province,Autonomous Region and Municipalities	179193	62143
3.地区	District	108781	40182
4.县及县以下	County and Below	158660	69403
5.其他	Others		
二、按企业、事业、机关分组	**Grouped by Character of the Unit**		
1.企业	Enterprises	479814	164852
①中央	Central	282613	92860
②省、自治区、直辖市	Province,Autonomous Region and Municipalities	100598	34496
③地区	District	63817	23855
④县及县以下	County and Below	32786	13641
2.事业	Institutions	246388	109930
①中央	Central	63218	26736
②省、自治区、直辖市	Province,Autonomous Region and Municipalities	64725	25168
③地区	District	30615	13695
④县及县以下	County and Below	87830	44331
3.机关	Governmental Agencies	69583	16903
①中央	Central	3320	361
②省、自治区、直辖市	Province,Autonomous Region and Municipalities	13870	2479
③地区	District	14349	2632
④县及县以下	County and Below	38044	11431
三、按国民经济行业分组	**Grouped by Economic Sector**		
(一)农、林、牧、渔业	Farming,Forestry,Animal Husbandry and Fishery	9634	3090
(二)采矿业	Mining	163	43
(三)制造业	Manufacturing	219653	78949
(四)电力、燃气及水的生产和供应业	Production & Supply of Power,Gas & Water	19904	6687
(五)建筑业	Construction	47259	9549
(六)交通运输、仓储和邮政业	Transport,Storage and Postal Service	75889	21979
(七)信息传输、计算机服务和软件业	Information Transmission,Computer Service and Software Service	1971	698
(八)批发和零售业	Wholesale and Retail Trade	44150	19940
(九)住宿和餐饮业	Accommodation and Catering Trade	12033	6891
(十)金融业	Banking	25906	12821
(十一)房地产业	Real Estate Trade	4441	1569
(十二)租赁和商务服务业	Commercial Service	7161	1397
(十三)科学研究、技术服务和地质勘察业	Scientific Research,Technical Services and Geological Prospecting	70708	23111
(十四)水利、环境和公共设施管理业	Water conservancy, environment and public facilities administration industry	10130	3127
(十五)居民服务和其他服务业	Resident Services and Other Services	9457	4031
(十六)教育	Education	118475	57028
(十七)卫生、社会保障和社会福利业	Sanitation, social insurance and social welfare industry	33009	16511
(十八)文化、体育和娱乐业	Culture, physical education and entertainment industry	17282	6592
(十九)公共管理和社会组织	Public administration non-profit institution	68560	17672

Basic Facts on Persons Employed by State-owned Units (2003)

(person)

		单位从业人员平均人数		
在岗职工合计 Total Fully Employed Staff	其他从业人员 Other Employed Persons	Average Employment	在岗职工 Fully Employed Staff and Workers	其他从业人员 Other Employed Persons
774538	**21247**	**796482**	**775349**	**21133**
340091	9060	351172	342197	8975
174952	4241	179357	175203	4154
106894	1887	107763	105809	1954
152601	6059	158190	152140	6050
468962	10852	482080	471037	11043
275597	7016	284462	277318	7144
98484	2114	100796	98714	2082
62642	1175	63893	62636	1257
32239	547	32929	32369	560
236886	9502	245586	236329	9257
61188	2030	63313	61496	1817
62684	2041	64499	62513	1986
30017	598	30536	29953	583
82997	4833	87238	82367	4871
68690	893	68816	67983	833
3306	14	3397	3383	14
13784	86	14062	13976	86
14235	114	13334	13220	114
37365	679	38023	37404	619
9353	281	9773	9490	283
163		165	165	
215937	3716	221295	217524	3771
19831	73	18972	18901	71
46757	502	49371	48644	727
72090	3799	75012	71277	3735
1971		1957	1957	
43237	913	44454	43458	996
11610	423	11952	11586	366
25155	751	26921	26247	674
4392	49	4239	4189	50
6873	288	7119	6865	254
69878	830	71003	70194	809
9936	194	10090	9896	194
9132	325	9469	9130	339
111958	6517	116608	110141	6467
31827	1182	32958	31929	1029
16872	410	17322	16909	413
67566	994	67802	66847	955

3-11　城镇集体单位从业人员情况（2003年）

单位：人

行　业	Item	单位从业人员 Employed Persons	女性 Female
合　计	**Total**	**115626**	**57226**
一、按企业、事业、机关分组	**Grouped by Character of the Unit**		
1.企业	Enterprises	111089	54957
2.事业	Institutions	4118	2104
3.机关	Governmental Agencies	419	165
二、按国民经济行业分组	**Grouped by Economic Sector**		
(一)农、林、牧、渔业	Farming,Forestry,Animal Husbandry and Fishery	300	110
(二)采矿业	Mining	665	141
(三)制造业	Manufacturing	43589	20533
(四)电力、燃气及水的生产和供应业	Production & Supply of Power,Gas & Water		
(五)建筑业	Construction	23078	5968
(六)交通运输、仓储和邮政业	Transport,Storage and Postal Service	2361	1029
(七)信息传输、计算机服务和软件业	Information Transmission,Computer Service and Software Service	40	12
(八)批发和零售业	Wholesale and Retail Trade	21647	13764
(九)住宿和餐饮业	Accommodation and Catering Trade	3231	2139
(十)金融业	Banking	1764	826
(十一)房地产业	Real Estate Trade	882	386
(十二)租赁和商务服务业	Commercial Service	8524	6953
(十三)科学研究、技术服务和地质勘察业	Scientific Research,Technical Services and Geological Prospecting	22	4
(十四)水利、环境和公共设施管理业	Water conservancy, environment and public facilities administration industry	13	7
(十五)居民服务和其他服务业	Resident Services and Other Services	4254	2346
(十六)教育	Education	81	65
(十七)卫生、社会保障和社会福利业	Sanitation, social insurance and social welfare industry	2893	1647
(十八)文化、体育和娱乐业	Culture, physical education and entertainment industry	95	29
(十九)公共管理和社会组织	Public administration non-profit institution	2187	1267

Basic Facts on Persons Employed by Urban Collective-owned Units (2003)

(person)

		单位从业人员平均人数		
在岗职工合计 Total Fully Employed Staff and Workers	其他从业人员 Other Employed Persons	Average Employment	在岗职工 Fully Employed Staff and Workers	其他从业人员 Other Employed Persons
108576	**7059**	**117972**	**110546**	**7426**
104124	6965	113408	106076	7332
4024	94	4140	4046	94
419		424	424	
297	3	302	299	3
665		665	665	
41090	2499	43828	41358	2470
21630	1448	24366	22763	1603
2237	124	2465	2341	124
40		40	40	
21217	430	21272	20867	405
2939	292	3233	2940	293
1721	43	1749	1706	43
880	2	882	880	2
8308	216	8485	8304	181
22		22	22	
13		13	13	
3540	714	4948	4093	855
81		81	81	
2755	138	2917	2779	138
95		95	95	
1037	1150	2609	1300	1309

3-12 其他经济类型单位从业人员情况（2003年）

单位：人

行　业	Sector	单位从业人员 Employed Persons	女性 Female
合　计	**Total**	**255358**	**83204**
一、按登记注册类型分组	**Grouped by Registion Status**		
(一)内资	Domestic Investment	237984	77689
1.股份合作	Share-holding Cooperative	18387	7713
2.联营	Joint Ownership	972	277
3.有限责任公司	Limited Liability Corporations	128310	39852
其中:国有独资	# Sole State-funded	47135	30310
4.股份有限公司	Share-holding Corperation Ltd.	73830	25020
(二)港、澳、台商投资	Enterprises with Investment from Hong Kong,	4892	1930
(三)外商投资	Enterprises with Foreign Investment	12482	3585
二、按企业、事业分组	**Grouped by Enterprise and Instilution**		
1.企业	Enterprises	252464	81925
2.事业	Institutions	2894	1279
三、按国民经济行业分组	**Grouped by Economic Sector**		
(一)农、林、牧、渔业	Farming,Forestry,Animal Husbandry and Fishery	336	89
(二)采矿业	Mining	630	213
(三)制造业	Manufacturing	170244	58499
(四)电力、燃气及水的生产和供应业	Production & Supply of Power,Gas & Water	262	82
(五)建筑业	Construction	6756	370
(六)交通运输、仓储和邮政业	Transport,Storage and Postal Service	4159	634
(七)信息传输、计算机服务和软件业	Information Transmission,Computer Service and Software Service	10151	2397
(八)批发和零售业	Wholesale and Retail Trade	28743	10705
(九)住宿和餐饮业	Accommodation and Catering Trade	12385	3341
(十)金融业	Banking	9807	2379
(十一)房地产业	Real Estate Trade	2787	729
(十二)租赁和商务服务业	Commercial Service	996	170
(十三)科学研究、技术服务和地质勘察业	Scientific Research,Technical Services and Geological Prospecting	4450	1694
(十四)水利、环境和公共设施管理业	Water conservancy, environment and public facilities administration industry		
(十五)居民服务和其他服务业	Resident Services and Other Services	1062	441
(十六)教育	Education	2320	1323
(十七)卫生、社会保障和社会福利业	Sanitation, social insurance and social welfare industry		
(十八)文化、体育和娱乐业	Culture, physical education and entertainment industry	270	138
(十九)公共管理和社会组织	Public administration non-profit institution		

Basic Facts on Persons Employed by Other Units(2003)

(person)

		单位从业人员平均人数		
在岗职工合计 Fully Employed Staff and Workers	其他从业人员 Other Employed Persons	Average Employment	在岗职工 Fully Employed Staff and Workers	其他从业人员 Other Employed Persons
252334	**3024**	**254005**	**251448**	**2557**
235073	2911	236517	234066	2451
18206	181	18576	18431	41
788	184	929	792	137
127094	1216	127685	126600	1085
47135		46849	46849	
73125	705	73075	72660	
4859	33	4832	4799	33
12402	80	12656	12583	73
249916	2548	251157	249025	2132
2418	476	2848	2000	425
328	8	336	328	8
627	3	630	627	3
168849	1395	168802	167606	1196
254	8	262	254	8
6618	138	6676	6574	102
4132	27	4144	4117	27
10123	28	10111	10090	21
28477	266	29010	28865	145
12088	297	12436	12149	287
9807		9773	9773	
2742	45	2788	2752	36
973	23	1001	995	6
4332	118	4544	4424	120
989	73	1045	988	57
1725	595	2219	1678	541
270		228	228	

3-13 各区县全部从业人员情况(2003年)

单位：人

分 类	Item	年末人数 Persons at Year-end 单位从业人员 Total Employed	女 性 Female	在岗职工合计 Total Fully Employed Staff and Workers	其它从业人员 Other Employed Persons
新 城	Xincheng	14482	7618	13989	493
碑 林	Beilin	17756	9150	17312	444
莲 湖	Lianhu	14824	7608	14287	546
灞 桥	Baqiao	9037	4170	8962	75
未 央	Weiyang	8385	4086	8298	87
雁 塔	Yanta	9762	4314	9556	206
阎 良	Yanliang	6621	2822	6369	252
临 潼	Lintong	29995	11326	28762	1233
长 安	Chang'an	25434	12669	23909	1525
蓝 田	Lantian	16168	5820	15592	576
周 至	Zhouzhi	21608	7795	20208	1400
户 县	Huxian	24088	8622	23711	377
高 陵	Gaoling	14548	4788	13165	1383

3-14 各区县国有单位从业人员情况(2003年)

单位:人

分 类	Item	年末人数 Persons Year-end 单位从业人员 Total Employed	女 性 Female	在岗职工合计 Total Fully Employed Staff and Workers	其它从业人员 Other Employed Persons
新 城	Xincheng	8220	4063	7923	297
碑 林	Beilin	9517	5108	9392	125
莲 湖	Lianhu	10071	5475	9620	451
灞 桥	Baqiao	7043	3263	6993	50
未 央	Weiyang	7394	3554	7319	75
雁 塔	Yanta	6802	3404	6665	137
阎 良	Yanliang	6125	2674	5876	249
临 潼	Lintong	27588	10520	26399	1189
长 安	Chang'an	19940	10561	19619	321
蓝 田	Lantian	14455	5209	13879	576
周 至	Zhouzhi	17992	7001	16595	1397
户 县	Huxian	19014	7323	18639	375
高 陵	Gaoling	11032	3868	10034	998

Basic Facts on All Employed Persons by Region (2003)

(person)

	平均人数 Average Persons		
离开本单位仍保留劳动关系的职工 Stall and Workers Off-Post but Still Holding Labor Relation	单位从业人员 Employed Persons	在岗职工 Fully Employed Staff and Workers	离开本单位仍保留劳动关系的职工 Stall and Workers Off-Post but Still Holding Labor Relation
8451	14716	14226	8555
6917	17890	17446	7125
2789	14589	14073	2732
613	8981	8905	613
585	8421	8333	593
751	9705	9548	743
1550	7117	6866	1548
5709	29599	28374	5559
3172	25441	23838	3172
2542	16030	15372	2542
5628	21796	20397	5471
6032	23874	23470	5939
113	14428	13059	106

Basic Facts on Persons Employed by State-owned Units By Region (2003)

(person)

	平均人数 Average Persons		
离开本单位仍保留劳动关系的职工 Stall and Workers Off-Post but Still Holding Labor Relation	单位从业人员 Employed Persons	在岗职工 Fully Employed Staff and Workers	离开本单位仍保留劳动关系的职工 Stall and Workers Off-Post but Still Holding Labor Relation
2360	8304	8009	2329
2968	9588	9463	2924
930	9786	9366	929
270	6990	6939	270
358	7430	7354	366
64	6756	6669	61
1085	6081	5833	1083
4650	27263	26082	4602
1611	19876	19552	1611
1923	14317	13659	1923
3945	18074	16678	3895
4543	19053	18678	4442
85	10993	9999	82

3-15 各区县城镇集体单位从业人员情况(2003年)

单位:人

分 类	Item	年末人数 Persons Year-end 单位从业人员 Total Employed	女性 Female	在岗职工合计 Total Fully Employed Staff and Workers	其它从业人员 Other Employed Persons
新 城	Xincheng	5663	3080	5468	195
碑 林	Beilin	2191	1180	2102	89
莲 湖	Lianhu	4674	2109	4582	92
灞 桥	Baqiao	1517	723	1494	23
未 央	Weiyang	991	532	979	12
雁 塔	Yanta	546	294	526	20
阎 良	Yanliang	496	148	493	3
临 潼	Lintong	2215	723	2198	17
长 安	Chang'an	2743	872	1975	768
蓝 田	Lantian	1463	531	1463	
周 至	Zhouzhi	2708	541	2707	1
户 县	Huxian	3688	660	3686	2
高 陵	Gaoling	1201	384	1095	106

3-16 各区县其他经济类型单位从业人员情况(2003年)

单位:人

分 类	Item	年末人数 Persons Year-end 单位从业人员 Total Employed	女性 Female	在岗职工合计 Total Fully Employed Staff and Workers	其它从业人员 Other Employed Persons
新 城	Xincheng	599	475	598	1
碑 林	Beilin	6048	2862	5818	230
莲 湖	Lianhu	79	24	76	3
灞 桥	Baqiao	477	184	475	2
未 央	Weiyang				
雁 塔	Yanta	2414	616	2365	49
阎 良	Yanliang				
临 潼	Lintong	192	83	165	27
长 安	Chang'an	2751	1236	2315	436
蓝 田	Lantian	240	80	240	
周 至	Zhouzhi	908	253	906	2
户 县	Huxian	1386	639	1386	
高 陵	Gaoling	2315	536	2036	279

Basic Facts on Persons Employed by Collective-owned Units By Region (2003)

(person)

	平均人数		Average Persons
离开本单位仍保留劳动关系的职工 Stall and Workers Off-Post but Still Holding Labor Relation	单位从业人员 Employed Persons	在岗职工 Fully Employed Staff and Workers	离开本单位仍保留劳动关系的职工 Stall and Workers Off-Post but Still Holding Labor Relation
6091	5813	5618	6226
3684	2227	2138	3952
1859	4724	4631	1803
343	1514	1491	343
227	991	979	227
374	547	526	369
465	1036	1033	465
1011	2215	2198	909
1417	2850	1971	1417
619	1463	1463	619
1587	2814	2813	1480
865	3408	3406	873
21	1181	1075	21

Basic Facts on Persons Employed by other Units By Region (2003)

(person)

	平均人数		Average Persons
离开本单位仍保留劳动关系的职工 Stall and Workers Off-Post but Still Holding Labor Relation	单位从业人员 Employed Persons	在岗职工 Fully Employed Staff and Workers	离开本单位仍保留劳动关系的职工 Stall and Workers Off-Post but Still Holding Labor Relation
	599	598	
265	6075	5845	249
	79	76	
	477	475	
313	2402	2353	313
48	121	94	48
144	2715	2315	144
	240	240	
96	908	906	96
624	1386	1386	624
7	2254	1985	3

3-17 全部单位从业人员劳动报酬（2003年）

Remuneration of All Employed Persons(2003)

单位:千元 (1 000yuan)

行业	Sector	单位从业人员劳动报酬 Remuneration of Employment	在岗职工工资总额 Total Wages of Employed Staff and Workers
总计	**Total**	**15595166**	**15358961**
一、按企业、事业、机关分组	**Groped by Character of Unit**		
1.企业	Enterprises	10550212	10380795
2.事业	Institutions	3913472	3852223
3.机关	Governmental Agencies	1131482	1125943
二、按国民经济行业分组	**Grouped by Economic Sector**		
(一)农、林、牧、渔业	Farming,Forestry,Animal Husbandry and Fishery	100931	98601
(二)采矿业	Mining	13512	13494
(三)制造业	Manufacturing	4916303	4841619
(四)电力、燃气及水的生产和供应业	Production & Supply of Power,Gas & Water	320362	319683
(五)建筑业	Construction	795046	776323
(六)交通运输、仓储和邮政业	Transport,Storage and Postal Service	1298596	1273361
(七)信息传输、计算机服务和软件业	Information Transmission,Computer Service and Software Service	478273	477876
(八)批发和零售业	Wholesale and Retail Trade	777127	766229
(九)住宿和餐饮业	Accommodation and Catering Trade	236377	230145
(十)金融业	Banking	859195	851564
(十一)房地产业	Real Estate Trade	98359	97425
(十二)租赁和商务服务业	Commercial Service	181042	176619
(十三)科学研究、技术服务和地质勘察业	Scientific Research,Technical Services and Geological Prospecting	1193052	1181297
(十四)水利、环境和公共设施管理业	Water conservancy, environment and public facilities administration industry	128919	127967
(十五)居民服务和其他服务业	Resident Services and Other Services	132063	126129
(十六)教育	Education	2246324	2207974
(十七)卫生、社会保障和社会福利业	Sanitation, social insurance and social welfare industry	462759	456080
(十八)文化、体育和娱乐业	Culture, physical education and entertainment industry	264857	257855
(十九)公共管理和社会组织	Public administration non-profit institution	1092069	1078720

3-17 全部单位从业人员劳动报酬（2003年)（续）

Remuneration of All Employed Persons(2003)(Continued)

单位:千元 (1 000yuan)

行　业	Sector	其他从业人员劳动报酬 Remuneration of Other Employed Persons	在岗职工平均工资（元）Average Wages of Employed Staff and Workers (yuan)
总　计	**Total**	**236205**	**13504**
一、按企业、事业、机关分组	**Groped by Character of Unit**		
1.企业	Enterprises	169417	12565
2.事业	Institutions	61249	15866
3.机关	Governmental Agencies	5539	16459
二、按国民经济行业分组	**Grouped by Economic Sector**		
(一)农、林、牧、渔业	Farming,Forestry,Animal Husbandry and Fishery	2330	9746
(二)采矿业	Mining	18	9261
(三)制造业	Manufacturing	74684	11352
(四)电力、燃气及水的生产和供应业	Production & Supply of Power,Gas & Water	679	16689
(五)建筑业	Construction	18723	9955
(六)交通运输、仓储和邮政业	Transport,Storage and Postal Service	25235	16381
(七)信息传输、计算机服务和软件业	Information Transmission,Computer Service and Software Service	297	39536
(八)批发和零售业	Wholesale and Retail Trade	10898	8222
(九)住宿和餐饮业	Accommodation and Catering Trade	6232	8628
(十)金融业	Banking	7631	22572
(十一)房地产业	Real Estate Trade	934	12457
(十二)租赁和商务服务业	Commercial Service	4423	10927
(十三)科学研究、技术服务和地质勘察业	Scientific Research,Technical Services and Geological Prospecting	11755	15827
(十四)水利、环境和公共设施管理业	Water conservancy, environment and public facilities administration industry	952	12914
(十五)居民服务和其他服务业	Resident Services and Other Services	5934	8875
(十六)教育	Education	38350	19732
(十七)卫生、社会保障和社会福利业	Sanitation, social insurance and social welfare industry	6679	13140
(十八)文化、体育和娱乐业	Culture, physical education and entertainment industry	7002	14964
(十九)公共管理和社会组织	Public administration non-profit institution	13349	15829

3-18 国有单位从业人员劳动报酬（2003年）

Remuneration of Persons Employed by State-owned Units (2003)

单位:千元 (1 000yuan)

行业	Sector	单位从业人员劳动报酬 Remuneration of Employment	在岗职工工资总额 Total Wages of Employed Staff and Workers
合计	**Total**	**11167794**	**11022814**
一、按隶属关系分组	**Grouped by Administrative Relationship**		
1.中央	Central	5673761	5598554
2.省、自治区、直辖市	Provincial	2307720	2268818
3.地区	District	1402001	1391560
4.县及县以下	County and Below	1784312	1763882
二、按企业、事业、机关分组	**Grouped by Character of the Unit**		
1.企业	Enterprises	6200024	6116826
2.事业	Institutions	3843112	3786869
3.机关	Governmental Agencies	1124658	1119119
三、按国民经济行业分组	**Grouped by Economic Sector**		
(一)农、林、牧、渔业	Farming,Forestry,Animal Husbandry and Fishery	93723	92070
(二)采矿业	Mining	1274	1274
(三)制造业	Manufacturing	2440577	2412768
(四)电力、燃气及水的生产和供应业	Production & Supply of Power,Gas & Water	315792	315153
(五)建筑业	Construction	548091	539511
(六)交通运输、仓储和邮政业	Transport,Storage and Postal Service	1216030	1191765
(七)信息传输、计算机服务和软件业	Information Transmission,Computer Service and Software Service	68250	68250
(八)批发和零售业	Wholesale and Retail Trade	401513	394345
(九)住宿和餐饮业	Accommodation and Catering Trade	104898	103260
(十)金融业	Banking	550787	543504
(十一)房地产业	Real Estate Trade	52405	52029
(十二)租赁和商务服务业	Commercial Service	100427	97160
(十三)科学研究、技术服务和地质勘察业	Scientific Research,Technical Services and Geological Prospecting	1091668	1082376
(十四)水利、环境和公共设施管理业	Water conservancy, environment and public facilities administration industry	128836	127884
(十五)居民服务和其他服务业	Resident Services and Other Services	92495	90947
(十六)教育	Education	2192682	2161485
(十七)卫生、社会保障和社会福利业	Sanitation, social insurance and social welfare industry	434541	428672
(十八)文化、体育和娱乐业	Culture, physical education and entertainment industry	261535	254533
(十九)公共管理和社会组织	Public administration non-profit institution	1072270	1065828

3-18 国有单位从业人员劳动报酬（2003年)（续）

Remuneration of Persons Employed by State-owned Units (2003)(Continued)

单位:千元 (1 000yuan)

行业	Sector	其他从业人员劳动报酬 Remuneration of OtherEmployed Persons	在岗职工平均工资（元） Average Wages of Employed Staff and Workers (yuan)
合计	**Total**	**144980**	**14217**
一、按隶属关系分组	**Grouped by Administrative Relationship**		
1.中央	Central	75207	16361
2.省、自治区、直辖市	Provincial	38902	12950
3.地区	District	10441	13152
4.县及县以下	County and Below	20430	11594
二、按企业、事业、机关分组	**Grouped by Character of the Unit**		
1.企业	Enterprises	83198	12986
2.事业	Institutions	56243	16024
3.机关	Governmental Agencies	5539	16462
三、按国民经济行业分组	**Grouped by Economic Sector**		
(一)农、林、牧、渔业	Farming,Forestry,Animal Husbandry and Fishery	1653	9702
(二)采矿业	Mining		7721
(三)制造业	Manufacturing	27809	11092
(四)电力、燃气及水的生产和供应业	Production & Supply of Power,Gas & Water	639	16674
(五)建筑业	Construction	8580	11091
(六)交通运输、仓储和邮政业	Transport,Storage and Postal Service	24265	16720
(七)信息传输、计算机服务和软件业	Information Transmission,Computer Service and Software Service		34875
(八)批发和零售业	Wholesale and Retail Trade	7168	9074
(九)住宿和餐饮业	Accommodation and Catering Trade	1638	8912
(十)金融业	Banking	7283	20707
(十一)房地产业	Real Estate Trade	376	12420
(十二)租赁和商务服务业	Commercial Service	3267	14153
(十三)科学研究、技术服务和地质勘察业	Scientific Research,Technical Services and Geological Prospecting	9292	15420
(十四)水利、环境和公共设施管理业	Water conservancy, environment and public facilities administration industry	952	12923
(十五)居民服务和其他服务业	Resident Services and Other Services	1548	9961
(十六)教育	Education	31197	19625
(十七)卫生、社会保障和社会福利业	Sanitation, social insurance and social welfare industry	5869	13426
(十八)文化、体育和娱乐业	Culture, physical education and entertainment industry	7002	15053
(十九)公共管理和社会组织	Public administration non-profit institution	6442	15944

3-19 城镇集体单位从业人员劳动报酬(2003年)

Remuneration of Persons Employed by Urban Collective-owned Units in Towns and Cities(2003)

单位:千元 (1 000yuan)

行业	Sector	单位从业人员劳动报酬 Remuneration of Employment	在岗职工工资总额 Total Wages of Employed Staff and Workers
总计	**Total**	**802348**	**761875**
一、按企业、事业、机关分组	**Groped by Character of Unit**		
1.企业	Enterprises	757888	718058
2.事业	Institutions	37636	36993
3.机关	Governmental Agencies	6824	6824
二、按国民经济行业分组	**Grouped by Economic Sector**		
(一)农、林、牧、渔业	Farming,Forestry,Animal Husbandry and Fishery	2077	2017
(二)采矿业	Mining	6329	6329
(三)制造业	Manufacturing	286126	272740
(四)电力、燃气及水的生产和供应业	Production & Supply of Power,Gas & Water		
(五)建筑业	Construction	185613	175611
(六)交通运输、仓储和邮政业	Transport,Storage and Postal Service	17814	16992
(七)信息传输、计算机服务和软件业	Information Transmission,Computer Service and Software Service	402	402
(八)批发和零售业	Wholesale and Retail Trade	122976	120683
(九)住宿和餐饮业	Accommodation and Catering Trade	15078	14308
(十)金融业	Banking	19006	18658
(十一)房地产业	Real Estate Trade	5944	5914
(十二)租赁和商务服务业	Commercial Service	66356	65216
(十三)科学研究、技术服务和地质勘察业	Scientific Research,Technical Services and Geological Prospecting	116	116
(十四)水利、环境和公共设施管理业	Water conservancy, environment and public facilities administration industry	83	83
(十五)居民服务和其他服务业	Resident Services and Other Services	25327	21422
(十六)教育	Education	565	565
(十七)卫生、社会保障和社会福利业	Sanitation, social insurance and social welfare industry	28218	27408
(十八)文化、体育和娱乐业	Culture, physical education and entertainment industry	519	519
(十九)公共管理和社会组织	Public administration non-profit institution	19799	12892

3-19 城镇集体单位从业人员劳动报酬(2003年)（续）

Remuneration of Persons Employed by Urban Collective-owned Units in Towns and Cities(2003)(Continued)

单位:千元 (1 000yuan)

行　业	Sector	其他从业人员劳动报酬 Remuneration of Other Employed Persons	在岗职工平均工资（元） Average Wages of Employed Staff and Workers (yuan)
总　计	**Total**	**40473**	**6892**
一、按企业、事业、机关分组	**Groped by Character of Unit**		
1.企业	Enterprises	39830	6769
2.事业	Institutions	643	9143
3.机关	Governmental Agencies		16094
二、按国民经济行业分组	**Grouped by Economic Sector**		
(一)农、林、牧、渔业	Farming,Forestry,Animal Husbandry and Fishery	60	6746
(二)采矿业	Mining		9517
(三)制造业	Manufacturing	13386	6595
(四)电力、燃气及水的生产和供应业	Production & Supply of Power,Gas & Water		
(五)建筑业	Construction	10002	7715
(六)交通运输、仓储和邮政业	Transport,Storage and Postal Service	822	7258
(七)信息传输、计算机服务和软件业	Information Transmission,Computer Service and Software Service		10050
(八)批发和零售业	Wholesale and Retail Trade	2293	5783
(九)住宿和餐饮业	Accommodation and Catering Trade	770	4867
(十)金融业	Banking	348	10937
(十一)房地产业	Real Estate Trade	30	6720
(十二)租赁和商务服务业	Commercial Service	1140	7854
(十三)科学研究、技术服务和地质勘察业	Scientific Research,Technical Services and Geological Prospecting		5273
(十四)水利、环境和公共设施管理业	Water conservancy, environment and public facilities administration industry		6385
(十五)居民服务和其他服务业	Resident Services and Other Services	3905	5234
(十六)教育	Education		6975
(十七)卫生、社会保障和社会福利业	Sanitation, social insurance and social welfare industry	810	9863
(十八)文化、体育和娱乐业	Culture, physical education and entertainment industry		5463
(十九)公共管理和社会组织	Public administration non-profit institution	6907	9917

3-20　其他经济类型单位从业人员劳动报酬（2003年）

Remuneration of Persons Employed by other Units(2003)

单位: 千元　　　　(1 000 yuan)

行　业	Sector	单位从业人员劳动报酬 Remuneration of Employment	在岗职工工资总额 Total Wages of Employed Staff and Workers
合　计	**Total**	**3625024**	**3574272**
一、按登记注册类型分组	**Grouped by Registion Status**		
(一)内资	Domestic Investment	3242575	3199582
1.股份合作	Share-holding Corperative	133886	132663
2.联营	Joint Ownership	11066	9321
3.有限责任公司	Limited Liability Corporations	1728064	1699724
	Sole State-funded Enterprises		
4.股份有限公司	Share-holding Corperation Ltd.	1195157	1192074
(二)港、澳、台商投资	Enterprises with Investment from Hong Kong, Macao and Taiwan	115643	113578
(三)外商投资	Enterprises with Foreign Investment	266806	261112
二、按企业、事业分组	**Grouped by Enterprise and Institution**		
1.企业	Enterprises	3592300	3545911
2.事业	Institutions	32724	28361
三、按国民经济行业分组	**Grouped by Economic Sector**		
(一)农、林、牧、渔业	Farming,Forestry,Animal Husbandry and Fishery	5131	4514
(二)采矿业	Mining	5909	5891
(三)制造业	Manufacturing	2189600	2156111
(四)电力、燃气及水的生产和供应业	Production & Supply of Power,Gas & Water	4570	4530
(五)建筑业	Construction	61342	61201
(六)交通运输、仓储和邮政业	Transport,Storage and Postal Service	64752	64604
(七)信息传输、计算机服务和软件业	Information Transmission,Computer Service and Software Service	409621	409224
(八)批发和零售业	Wholesale and Retail Trade	252638	251201
(九)住宿和餐饮业	Accommodation and Catering Trade	116401	112577
(十)金融业	Banking	289402	289402
(十一)房地产业	Real Estate Trade	40010	39482
(十二)租赁和商务服务业	Commercial Service	14259	14243
(十三)科学研究、技术服务和地质勘察业	Scientific Research,Technical Services and Geological Prospecting	101268	98805
(十四)水利、环境和公共设施管理业	Water conservancy, environment and public facilitiesadministration industry		
(十五)居民服务和其他服务业	Resident Services and Other Services	14241	13760
(十六)教育	Education	53077	45924
(十七)卫生、社会保障和社会福利业	Sanitation, social insurance and social welfare industry		
(十八)文化、体育和娱乐业	Culture, physical education and entertainment industry	2803	2803
(十九)公共管理和社会组织	Public administration non-profit institution		

3-20 其他经济类型单位从业人员劳动报酬（2003年）（续）

Remuneration of Persons Employed by other Units(2003)(Continued)

单位: 千元 (1 000 yuan)

行业	Sector	其他从业人员劳动报酬 Remuneration of Other Employed Persons	在岗职工平均工资（元） Average Wages of Employed Staff and Workers (yuan)
合计	**Total**	**50752**	**14215**
一、按登记注册类型分组	**Grouped by Registion Status**		
(一)内资	Domestic Investment	42993	13670
1.股份合作	Share-holding Corperative	1223	7189
2.联营	Joint Ownership	1745	11769
3.有限责任公司	Limited Liability Corporations	28340	13420
	Sole State-funded Enterprises		
4.股份有限公司	Share-holding Corperation Ltd.	3083	16406
(二)港、澳、台商投资	Enterprises with Investment from Hong Kong, Macao and Taiwan	2065	23667
(三)外商投资	Enterprises with Foreign Investment	5694	20751
二、按企业、事业分组	**Grouped by Enterprise and Institution**		
1.企业	Enterprises	46389	14239
2.事业	Institutions	4363	14181
三、按国民经济行业分组	**Grouped by Economic Sector**		
(一)农、林、牧、渔业	Farming,Forestry,Animal Husbandry and Fishery	617	13762
(二)采矿业	Mining	18	9396
(三)制造业	Manufacturing	33489	12864
(四)电力、燃气及水的生产和供应业	Production & Supply of Power,Gas & Water	40	17835
(五)建筑业	Construction	141	9310
(六)交通运输、仓储和邮政业	Transport,Storage and Postal Service	148	15692
(七)信息传输、计算机服务和软件业	Information Transmission,Computer Service and Software Service	397	40557
(八)批发和零售业	Wholesale and Retail Trade	1437	8703
(九)住宿和餐饮业	Accommodation and Catering Trade	3824	9266
(十)金融业	Banking		29612
(十一)房地产业	Real Estate Trade	528	14347
(十二)租赁和商务服务业	Commercial Service	16	14315
(十三)科学研究、技术服务和地质勘察业	Scientific Research,Technical Services and Geological Prospecting	2463	22334
(十四)水利、环境和公共设施管理业	Water conservancy, environment and public facilitiesadministration industry		
(十五)居民服务和其他服务业	Resident Services and Other Services	481	13927
(十六)教育	Education	7153	27368
(十七)卫生、社会保障和社会福利业	Sanitation, social insurance and social welfare industry		
(十八)文化、体育和娱乐业	Culture, physical education and entertainment industry		12294
(十九)公共管理和社会组织	Public administration non-profit institution		

3–21 各区县全部从业人员劳动报酬（2003年）

单位: 千元

区 县	District and County	单位从业人员劳动报酬 Remuneration of Employment	在岗职工工资总额 Total Wages of Employed Staff and Workers
新 城	Xincheng	163068	160562
碑 林	Beilin	225877	221366
莲 湖	Lianhu	164094	161065
灞 桥	Baqiao	111510	111083
未 央	Weiyang	129473	128919
雁 塔	Yanta	167788	166629
阎 良	Yanliang	91918	90696
临 潼	Lintong	278803	275077
长 安	Chang'an	220382	207978
蓝 田	Lantian	133663	131622
周 至	Zhouzhi	177861	175326
户 县	Huxian	213322	212368
高 陵	Gaoling	119422	115453

3–21 各区县全部从业人员劳动报酬（2003年)（续）

单位: 千元

区 县	District and County	城镇集体单位	Urban Collective Units
		单位从业人员劳动报酬 Remuneration of Employment	在岗职工工资总额 Total Wages of Employed Staff and Workers
新 城	Xincheng	33728	33091
碑 林	Beilin	19324	18479
莲 湖	Lianhu	29843	29387
灞 桥	Baqiao	11214	11015
未 央	Weiyang	7190	7164
雁 塔	Yanta	3473	3268
阎 良	Yanliang	5817	5794
临 潼	Lintong	15871	15804
长 安	Chang'an	21346	14999
蓝 田	Lantian	12050	12050
周 至	Zhouzhi	16347	16297
户 县	Huxian	24071	24062
高 陵	Gaoling	9571	9090

Remuneration of All Employed Persons by Region (2003)

(1 000yuan)

	国有单位 State-Owned Units		
其他从业人员劳动报酬 Remuneration of Other Employed Persons	单位从业人员劳动报酬 Remuneration of Employment	在岗职工工资总额 Total Wages of Employed Staff and Workers	其他从业人员劳动报酬 Remuneration of Other Employed Persons
2506	120485	118626	1859
4511	149008	147826	1182
3029	133135	130604	2531
427	96009	95799	210
554	122283	121755	528
1159	125758	125243	515
1222	86101	84902	1199
3726	262085	258574	3511
12404	172811	170687	2124
2041	119943	117902	2041
2535	153689	151214	2475
954	182999	182054	945
3969	90371	88071	2300

Remuneration of All Employed Persons by Region (2003)(Continued)

(1 000yuan)

	其它经济单位 Others		
其他从业人员劳动报酬 Remuneration of Other Employed Persons	单位从业人员劳动报酬 Remuneration of Employment	在岗职工工资总额 Total Wages of Employed Staff and Workers	其他从业人员劳动报酬 Remuneration of Other Employed Persons
637	8855	8845	10
845	57545	55061	2484
456	1116	1074	42
199	4287	4269	18
26			
205	38557	38118	439
23			
67	847	699	148
6347	26225	22292	3933
	1670	1670	
50	7825	7815	10
9	6252	6252	
481	19480	18292	1188

3-22 全部单位从业人员平均劳动报酬（2003年）

Average Remuneration of Persons Employed by All Units(2003)

单位：元 (yuan)

分 类	Item	合 计 Total	国有经济 State-owned Enterprises	城镇集体经济 Urban Collective-owned Enterprises	其他经济 Other Enterprises
一、按隶属关系分组	**Grouped by Administrative Relationship**	**13347**	**14021**	**6801**	**14271**
二、按企业、事业、机关分组	**Grouped by Character of the Unit**				
1.企业	Enterprises	12461	12861	6683	14303
2.事业	Institutions	15494	15649	9091	11490
3.机关	Governmental Agencies	16341	16343	16094	
三、按国民经济行业分组	**Grouped by Economic Sector**				
(一)农、林、牧、渔业	Farming,Forestry,Animal Husbandry and Fishery	9695	9590	6877	15271
(二)采矿业	Mining	9255	7721	9517	9379
(三)制造业	Manufacturing	11330	11029	6528	12971
(四)电力、燃气及水的生产和供应业	Production & Supply of Power,Gas & Water	16656	16645		17443
(五)建筑业	Construction	9887	11101	7618	9188
(六)交通运输、仓储和邮政业	Transport,Storage and Postal Service	15910	16211	7227	15625
(七)信息传输、计算机服务和软件业	Information Transmission, Computer Service and Software Service	39501	34875	10050	40512
(八)批发和零售业	Wholesale and Retail Trade	8203	9032	5781	8709
(九)住宿和餐饮业	Accommodation and Catering Trade	8558	8777	4664	9360
(十)金融业	Banking	22358	20459	10867	29612
(十一)房地产业	Real Estate Trade	12436	12363	6739	14351
(十二)租赁和商务服务业	Commercial Service	10903	14107	7820	14245
(十三)科学研究、技术服务和地质勘察业	Scientific Research,Technical Services and Geological Prospecting	15788	15375	5273	22286
(十四)水利、环境和公共设施管理业	Water conservancy, environment and public facilities administration industry	12760	12769	6385	
(十五)居民服务和其他服务业	Resident Services and Other Services	8541	9768	5119	13628
(十六)教育	Education	18891	18804	6975	23919
(十七)卫生、社会保障和社会福利业	Sanitation, social insurance and social welfare industry	12899	13185	9674	
(十八)文化、体育和娱乐业	Culture, physical education and entertainment industry	15010	15098	5463	12294
(十九)公共管理和社会组织	Public administration non-profit institution	15510	15815	7589	

3-23 各区县在岗职工平均工资(2003年)

Average Salary of Fully Employed Staff and Workers By Region(2003)

单位: 元 (yuan)

区 县	District and County	合 计 Total	国有经济 State-owned Enterprises	城镇集体经济 Urban Collective-owned Enterprises	其他经济 Other Enterprises
新 城	Xincheng	11287	14812	5890	14791
碑 林	Beilin	12689	15621	8643	9420
莲 湖	Lianhu	11444	13944	6346	14132
灞 桥	Baqiao	12474	13806	7388	8987
未 央	Weiyang	15471	16556	7318	
雁 塔	Yanta	17452	18780	6213	16200
阎 良	Yanliang	13209	14555	5609	
临 潼	Lintong	9695	9914	7190	7436
长 安	Chang'an	8725	8730	7610	9629
蓝 田	Lantian	8562	8632	8237	6958
周 至	Zhouzhi	8596	9067	5793	8626
户 县	Huxian	9048	9747	7065	4511
高 陵	Gaoling	8841	8808	8456	9215

3-24 离开本单位仍保留劳动关系职工平均生活费（2003年）

Average Living Allowance for Staff and workers off-post but Still Holding Labor Relations (2003)

单位: 元 (yuan)

分类	Item	合计 Total	国有经济 State-owned Enterprises	城镇集体经济 Urban Collective-owned Enterprises	其他经济 Other Enterprises
总 计	**Total**	**2694**	**3081**	**1228**	**3264**
一、按企业、事业、机关分组	**Grouped by Character of the Unit**				
企 业	Enterprises	2567	2912	1228	3264
事 业	Institutions	6828	7214	1163	
机 关	Governmental Agencies	9516	9549	1000	
二、按国民经济行业分组	**Grouped by Economic Sector**				
(一)农、林、牧、渔业	Farming,Forestry,Animal Husbandry and Fishery	2340	2385	178	
(二)采矿业	Mining	3273			4645
(三)制造业	Manufacturing	2439	2745	882	3286
(四)电力、燃气及水的生产和供应业	Production & Supply of Power,Gas & Water	7216	7216		
(五)建筑业	Construction	2434	2731	1531	3318
(六)交通运输、仓储和邮政业	Transport,Storage and Postal Service	3526	4205	710	1500
(七)信息传输、计算机服务和软件业	Information Transmission,Computer Service and Software Service	3541	3541		
(八)批发和零售业	Wholesale and Retail Trade	2134	2279	1402	3169
(九)住宿和餐饮业	Accommodation and Catering Trade	3100	3290	2846	3242
(十)金融业	Banking	8472	8456	3185	28125
(十一)房地产业	Real Estate Trade	3249	5079	918	
(十二)租赁和商务服务业	Commercial Service	1912	4718	1388	4864
(十三)科学研究、技术服务和地质勘察业	Scientific Research,Technical Services and Geological Prospecting	7104	7104		
(十四)水利、环境和公共设施管理业	Water conservancy, environment and public facilities administration industry	2635	2635		
(十五)居民服务和其他服务业	Resident Services and Other Services	1793	1610	1949	
(十六)教育	Education	5653	5691	2500	
(十七)卫生、社会保障和社会福利业	Sanitation, social insurance and social welfare industry	10984	11596	2118	
(十八)文化、体育和娱乐业	Culture, physical education and entertainment industry	5163	5163		
(十九)公共管理和社会组织	Public administration non-profit institution	7103	9163	5082	

主要统计指标解释

人口数 指一定时点、一定地区范围内的有生命的个人的总和。

出生率（又称粗出生率） 指在一定时期内（通常为一年）一定地区的出生人数与同期内平均人数（或期中人数）之比。一般用千分率表示。本资料中的出生率指年出生率，其计算公式为:

出生率=出生人数/年平均人数*1000

式中:出生人数指活产婴儿，即胎儿脱离母体时（不管怀孕月数），有过呼吸或其他生命现象。年平均人数指年初、年底人口数的平均数，也可用年中人口数代替。

死亡率（又称粗死亡率） 指在一定时期内（通常为一年）一定地区的死亡人数与同期内平均人数（或期中人数）之比，一般用千分率表示。本资料中的死亡率指年死亡率，其计算公式为:

死亡率=年死亡人数/年平均人数*1000

人口自然增长率 指在一定时期内（通常为一年）人口自然增加数（出生人数减死亡人数）与该时期内平均人数（或期中人数）之比，一般用千分率表示。计算公式为:

人口自然增长率=（本年出生人数-本年死亡人数）/年平均人数*1000

经济活动人口 指在16岁以上，有劳动能力，参加或要求参加社会经济活动的人口;包括就业人员和失业人员。

就业人员 指从事一定社会劳动并取得劳动报酬或经营收入的人员，包括在岗职工、再就业的离退休人员、私营业主、个体户主、私营和个体就业人员、乡镇企业就业人员、农村就业人员、其他就业人员（包括民办教师、宗教职业者、现役军人等）。这一指标反映了一定时期内全部劳动力资源的实际利用情况，是研究我国基本国情国力的重要指标。

各单位的就业人员 指在各级国家机关、政党机关、社会团体及企业、事业单位中工作，取得工资或其他形式的劳动报酬的全部人员。包括在岗职工、再就业的离退休人员、民办教师以及在各单位中工作的外方人员和港澳台方人员、兼职人员、借用的外单位人员和第二职业者。不包括离开本单位仍保留劳动关系的职工。各单位的就业人员反映了各单位实际参加生产或工作的全部劳动力。

城镇私营和个体就业人员 城镇私营就业人员指在工商管理部门注册登记，其经营地址设在县城关镇（含城关镇）以上的私营企业就业人员;包括私营企业投资者和雇工。城镇个体就业人员指在工商管理部门注册登记，并持有城镇户口或在城镇长期居住，经批准从事个体工商经营的就业人员;包括个体经营者和在个体工商户劳动的家庭帮工和雇工。

城镇登记失业人员 指有非农业户口，在一定的劳动年龄内，有劳动能力，无业而要求就业，并在当地就业服务机构进行求职登记的人员。

城镇登记失业率 指城镇登记失业人数同城镇单位就业人数、城镇私营企业及个体就业人数和城镇登记失业人数之和的比。计算公式为:

城镇登记失业率=城镇登记失业人数/(城镇单位就业人数+城镇私营企业及个体就业人数+城镇登记失业人数)*100%

职工 指在国有经济、城镇集体经济、联营经济、股份制经济、外商和港、澳、台投资经济、其他经济单位及其附属机构工作，并由其支付工资的各类人员，不包括返聘的离退休人员、民办教师、在国有经济单位工作的外方人员和港、澳、台人员。

1998年以后的的职工数据均为在岗职工，其他相关指标如职工工资总额，职工平均工资等指标也从1998年按此口径进行了相应调整。

国有单位职工 指在国有经济单位及其附属机构工作，并由其支付工资的各类人员。

城镇集体单位职工 指在城镇集体经济单位及其管理部门工作，并由其支付工资的各类人员。

其他单位职工 指在联营经济、股份制经济、外商投资经济、港、澳、台投资经济单位工作，并由其支付工资的各类人员。

在岗职工 指在本单位工作并由单位支付工资的人员，以及有工作岗位，但由于学习、病伤产假等原因暂未工作，仍由单位支付工资的人员。

职工工资总额 指各单位在一定时期内直接支付给本单位全部职工的劳动报酬总额。工资总额的计算原则应以直接支付给职工的全部劳动报酬为根据。各单位支付给职工的劳动报酬以及其他根据有关规定支付的工资，不论是计入成本的还是不计入成本的，不论是按国家规定列入计征奖金税项目的，还是未列入计征奖金税项目的，不论是以货币形式支付的还是以实物形式支付的，均包括在工资总额内。

职工平均工资 指企业、事业、机关单位的职工在一定时期内平均每人所得的货币工资额。它表明一定时期职工工资收入的高低程度，是反映职工工资水平的主要指标。计算公式为:

职工平均工资=报告期实际支付的全部职工工资总额/报告期全部职工平均人数

Explanatory Notes on Main Statistical Indicators

Total Population refers to the total number of people alive at a certain point of time within a given area.

Birth Rate or (Crude Birth Rate) refers to the ratio of the number of births to the average population (or mid-period population) during a certain period of time (usually a year) which is often expressed in ‰. Birth rate in the chapter refers to annual birth rate. The following formula is used:

Birth Rate = Number of Births/Average Number of Population×1000‰

Number of births refers to live births i.e. the births when babies had showed any vital phenomena regardless of the length of pregnancy.

Annual Average Number of Population is the average of the number of population at the beginning of the year and that at the end of the year. Sometimes it is substituted for with the mid year population.

Death Rate (or Crude Death Rate) refers to the ratio of the number of deaths to the average population (or mid-period population) during a certain period of time (usually a year) which is often expressed in ‰. Death rate in the chapter refers to annual death rate. The following formula is used:

Death Rate= Number of Deaths/Annual Average Number of Population×1000‰

Natural Growth Rate of Population refers to the ratio of natural increase in population (number of births minus number of deaths) in a certain period of time (usually a year) to the average population (or mid-period population) of the same period which is often expressed in ‰. The following formulas are applied:

Natural Growth of Population = (Number of Births-Number of Deaths)/Average Number of Population× 1000‰

Natural Growth Rate of Population = Birth Rate-Death Rate

Economically Active Population refers to the population aged 16 and over who are capable to work, are participating in or willing to participate in economic activities, including employed persons and unemployed persons.

Employed Persons refer to the persons who are engaged in social working and receive remuneration payment or earn business income, including total staff and workers, re-employed retirees, employers of private enterprises, self-employed workers, employees in private enterprises and individual economy, employees in township enterprises, employed persons in the rural areas, and other employed persons (including teachers in the schools run by the local people, people engaged in religious profession and the servicemen, etc.). This indicator reflects the actual utilization of total labour force during a certain period of time and is often used for the research on China's economic situation and national power.

Persons Employed in Various Units refer to all the persons working in government agencies of various levels, political and party organizations, social organizations, enterprises and institutions, and receiving wages or other forms of payment. They include fully-employed staff and workers, re-employed retirees, teachers in schools run by the local people, foreigners and Chinese compatriots from Hong Kong, Macao, and Taiwan working in various units, part-time employees, employees of other units working temporarily at current posts, and employees holding the second job, but exclude staff and workers who have left their working units while keeping their labour contract (employment relation) unchanged. This indicator reflects the total number of laborers actually engaged in production or other operations in various units.

Persons Employed in Private Enterprises and Self-Employed Individuals in Urban Areas Persons employed in private enterprises refer to the persons employed in the private enterprises which have been registered at the departments of industrial and commercial administration and are situated at a county town (i.e. a town where the county government is located) for business operation or at urban areas with the level higher than a county town. The self-employed individuals in urban areas refer to persons who hold the certificates of residence in urban areas or have resided in the urban areas for a long time and have been registered at the departments of industrial and commercial administration and approved to be engaged in individual industrial or commercial business, including self-employed persons as well as helpers and hired labourers who work in the individual households engaged in industrial or commercial business.

Registered Urban Unemployed Persons The registered unemployed persons in urban areas refer to the persons who are registered as permanent residents in the urban areas engaged in non-agricultural activities, aged within the range of working age, capable to labour, unemployed but desirous to be employed and have been

Registered at the local employment service agencies to apply for a job.

Registered Urban Unemployment Rate Registered unemployment rate in urban areas refers to the ratio of the number of the registered unemployed persons to the sum of the number of persons employed in various units and in private enterprises in urban areas, urban self-employed individuals and the registered urban unemployed persons . The formula is as follows:

Registered urban unemployment rate = number of registered urban unemployed persons ÷ (number of persons employed in urban units + number of persons employed in urban private enterprises + and self-employed individuals in urban Areas + number of registered urban unemployed persons) × 100%.

Staff and Workers refer to the persons who work in (and receive payment therefrom) enterprises and institutions of state ownership, collective ownership, joint ownership, share holding, foreign ownership, and ownership by entrepreneurs from Hong Kong, Macao, and Taiwan, and other types of ownership and their affiliated units, excluding the retired persons invited to work in the units again, teachers in the schools run by the local people and foreigners and persons coming from Hong Kong, Macao and Taiwan and working in the state-owned economic units. (Number of staff and workers in this yearbook include only fully employed staff and workers, excluding those who have left their working units while keeping their labour contract/employment relation unchanged).

Staff and Workers in State-owned Economic Units refer to the persons who work in the state-owned economic units or their attached units and are listed in their payrolls.

Staff and Workers of Collective Owned Units in Urban Areas refer to the persons who work in collective owned units in urban areas and their administration departments and receive payment therefrom.

Staff and Workers in Units of Other types of Ownership refer to those who work in (and receive payment therefrom) enterprises and institutions of joint ownership, share holding, foreign ownership, and ownership by entrepreneurs from Hong Kong, Macao, and Taiwan.

Fully Employed Staff and Workers refer to persons who work in, and receive wages from their working units, as well as persons who have their work posts, but are temporarily absent from work for reasons of study or on sick, injury or maternal leave and still receive wages from their working units.

Total Wages of Staff and Workers refer to the total remuneration payment to staff and workers in various units during a certain period of time. The calculation of total wages is based on the total remuneration payment to the staff and workers. Therefore, all the wages and salaries and other payments to staff and workers are included in the total wages regardless of their sources, category, and forms (in kind or cash). (Total wages of staff and workers in this yearbook include only total wages of fully employed staff and workers, excluding the living allowances distributed to those who have left their working units while keeping their labour contract/employment relation unchanged).

Average Wage of Staff and Workers refers to the average wage in money terms per person during a certain period of time for staff and workers in enterprises, institutions, and government agencies, which reflects the general level of wage income during a certain period of time and is calculated as follows:

Average Wage of Staff and Workers = Total Wages of Staff and Workers at the Report/Average Number of Staff and Workers at the Report Period.

Average Wage Indices of Staff and Workers refers to the ratio of average wage of staff and workers in the report period to that in the base period, which reflects the change of wage of staff and workers at the different period. It is calculated as follows:

Average Wage Indices of Staff and Workers = Average Wage of Staff and Workers at the Report Period / Average Wage of Staff and Workers at the Base Period *100%

Average Real Wage Indices of Staff and Workers average real wage of staff and workers refers to the average wage of staff and workers after removing the effects of the price changes and average real wage indices of staff and workers refers to the change of real wage, which reflects the relative increasing or decreasing level of real wage of staff and workers, which is calculated as follows:

Average Real Wage Indices of Staff and Workers = Average Wage Indices of Staff and Workers at the Report Period / Urban Consumer Price Indices at the Report Period *100%

2004

年統
鑒計

四、固定资产投资

INVESTMENT IN FIXED ASSETS

简 要 说 明
Brief Introduction

本章内容主要包括全社会固定资产投资、基本建设投资、更新改造投资、房地产开发投资、城乡集体固定资产投资和城乡私人建房投资以及分区县房地产开发情况，由市统计局固定资产投资处整理提供。

This chapter consists of primarily the data on fixed asset investment, capital construction investment, renewal and reconstruction investment, real estate development investment, urban and rural area collective fixed asset investment, urban and rural area private housing investment and the classified Data of the districts and the counties on real estate development investment, provided by Fixed Asset Investment Division of the Xi'an Bureau of Statistics.

4-1 全社会固定资产投资

Investment Fulfilled In Fixed Assets

单位：万元 (10 000 yuan)

年 份 Year	合 计 Total	国有经济 State-owned	集体经济 Collective-owned	个体经济 Individual	其他经济 Others
1985	184420	139567	13567	31286	--
1986	221543	180451	9694	31398	--
1987	270470	221845	15020	33605	--
1988	291419	237179	18589	35651	--
1989	283015	232230	14589	36196	--
1990	263865	222084	14422	27359	--
1991	307573	244228	22604	40741	--
1992	384826	320390	14469	49967	--
1993	750640	596635	30254	65549	58202
1994	855718	647126	41425	100862	66305
1995	1034184	690806	97778	111298	134302
1996	1143763	806600	87323	125040	124800
1997	1169014	774602	102138	151064	141210
1998	1547958	1130680	78899	105884	232495
1999	1973060	1365036	136206	162234	309584
2000	2323676	1596002	146519	243959	337196
2001	2877233	1755787	146738	385743	588965
2002	3381503	2000636	137032	446806	797029
2003	4781002	2648283	223265	734346	1175108

注：集体经济：包括城镇集体和农村集体。

个体经济：包括私营个体投资及城镇工矿区私人建房和农村私人建房。

Note: Collective-owned: Including Urban Collective-owned and Rural Collective-owned.

Individual: Including Individual Investment Private Building Construction in Urban Industrial and Mining Regions and Rural Areas.

4-2　全市固定资产投资(2003年)

指　标	Item	合计 Total
一、本年完成投资（万元）	**Accomplished Invstment This Year（10 000yuan)**	**4457381**
按登记注册类型分	Grouped by Registion Status	
内资	Domestic Investment Enterprises	4293034
国有	State-owned Enterprises	2418196
集体	Collective-owned Enterprises	90646
股份合作	Share-holding Corperative	51703
国有联营	State Joint Ownership Enterprises	5050
集体联营	Collective Joint Ownership Enterprises	1700
国有与集体联营	State-owned and Collective-owned Joint Enterprises	1990
其他联营	Other Joint Ownership Enterprises	4510
国有独资公司	Sole State-funded Corporations	225037
其他有限责任公司	Other Limited Liability Corporations	740606
股份有限公司	Share-holding Corperation Ltd.	201763
私营个体	Private and Individual	489941
其他	Others	61892
港澳台商投资	Enterprises with Investment from Hong Kong,Macao and Taiwan	58641
合资经营	Joint Venture	52760
合作经营	Cooperation	3478
独资	Sole-Funded	1733
股份有限	Share-Holding Corporations Ltd.	670
外商投资	Enterprises with Foreign Investment	105706
合资经营	Joint Venture	55660
合作经营	Cooperation	5402
独资	Sole-Funded	44644
股份有限	Share-Holding Corporations Ltd.	
按隶属关系分	Grouped by Administrative Relationship	
中央	Central	587374
省属	Provincial	891260
市属	Municipal	2978747
按建设性质分	Grouped by Construction Nature	
新建	Newly Constructed	1294032
扩建	Expansion of Construction	1102914
改建	Transformed Construction	447944
按构成分	Grouped by Use of Funds	
1.建筑工程	Building Projects	2867818
2.安装工程	Installment Projects	199491
3.设备工器具购置	Purchasing of Equipment,Tools and Instruments	577240
4.其他费用	Others	812832
按工程用途分	Grouped by Purpose of Project	
#住宅	Of the Total: Residential Buildings	1265285
按项目规模分	Grouped by Construction Scale	
#基建大中型	Large/Medium-Size Capital Construction	467496
更改限上项目	Projects of Innovation Over Designated Value	33383

Total Investment In Fixed Assets(2003)

基本建设 Capital Construction	更新改造 Innovation	其他投资 Other Investment	房地产开发 Real Estate Development
2281384	**714483**	**213337**	**1248177**
2242865	689421	210266	1150482
1660562	398223	24567	334844
9986	7060	11851	61749
6600	2122	26306	16675
5050			
1700			
510			1480
4500		10	
157651	27818	17924	21644
256139	185613	46372	252482
63738	48843	24650	64532
33156	9972	49737	397076
43273	9770	8849	
1708	480	2422	54031
935	450	2122	49253
			3478
403	30		1300
370		300	
36811	24582	649	43664
6946	7941	500	40273
1085	926		3391
28780	15715	149	
443860	135249		8265
606051	140203	19903	125103
1231473	439031	193434	1114809
1162398	37120	94514	
539495	484036	79383	
280398	155305	12241	
1686393	206992	141665	832768
53508	61293	16822	67868
185636	327194	36763	27647
355847	119004	18087	319894
435806	5298	40313	783868
467496			
	333838		

4-2 全市固定资产投资(2003年)(续)

指　　标	Item	合计 Total
一、按国民经济行业分	**Grouped by Sector**	
农、林、牧、渔业	Farming,Forestry,Animal Husbandry and Fishery	33409
采矿业	Mining	43718
制造业	Manufacturing	615973
电力、燃气及水的生产和供应业	Production & Supply of Power,Gas & Water	124415
建筑业	Construction	48390
交通运输、仓储和邮政业	Transport,Storage and Postal Service	253078
信息传输、计算机服务和软件业	Information Transmission,Computer Service and Software Service	198737
批发和零售业	Wholesale and Retail Trade	156512
住宿和餐饮业	Accommodation and Catering Trade	36678
金融业	Banking	11751
房地产业	Real Estate Trade	1248177
租赁和商务服务业	Commercial Service	211801
科学研究、技术服务和地质勘察业	Scientific Research,Technical Services and Geological Prospecting	150527
水利、环境和公共设施管理业	Water conservancy, environment and public facilities administration industry	400765
居民服务和其他服务业	Resident Services and Other Services	3827
教育	Education	349110
卫生、社会保障和社会福利业	Sanitation, social insurance and social welfare industry	17580
文化、体育和娱乐业	Culture, physical education and entertainment industry	88245
公共管理和社会组织	Public administration non-profit institution	454688
二、构成（%）	**Proportion (%)**	
按登记注册类型分	Grouped by type of registration	
国有经济	State-owned economy	59.41
集体经济	Collective-owned	3.23
按隶属关系分	Grouped by Administrative Relationship	
中央	Central	13.17
省属	Provincial	20
市属	Municipal	66.83
按建设性质分	Grouped by Type of Construction	
新建	New Construction	40.32
扩建	Expansion	34.37
改建	Reconstruction	13.96
按构成分:	Grouped by Use of Funds	
1.建筑工程	Construction Projects	64.34
2.安装工程	Installation Projects	4.48
3.设备工器具购置	Purchasing of the Equipment,Tools and Instruments	12.95
4.其他费用	Others	18.23
按工程用途分	Grouped by Purpose of Project	
#住宅	Of the Total: Residential Buildings	28.39
三、房屋面积(平方米)	**Floor Space (sq.m)**	
本年施工房屋面积	Floor Space of Buildings Under Construction This Year	27161785
#住宅	Of the Total: Residential Buildings	16556357
本年竣工房屋面积	Floor Space of Buildings Completed This Year	9179629
#住宅	Of the Total: Residential Buildings	5780646
四、本年新增固定资产(万元)	**Newly Increase in Fixed Assets(10 000 yuan)**	**2794439**

Total Investment In Fixed Assets(2003)(Continued)

基本建设 Capital Construction	更新改造 Innovation	其他投资 Other Investment	房地产开发 Real Estate Development
29677		3732	
43513		205	
296850	266523	52600	
96436	27679	300	
36501	10660	1229	
236599	14383	2096	
24562	174175		
115718	24601	16193	
22988	2760	10930	
11751			
			1248177
209584	68	2149	
123846	26382	299	
223991	146399	30375	
3296		531	
287245	920	60945	
13105	3258	1217	
84128	2620	1497	
421594	4055	29039	
79.92	59.63	19.92	28.56
0.8	1.29	17.89	6.28
19.45	18.93		0.66
26.57	19.62	9.33	10.02
53.98	61.45	90.67	89.32
50.95	5.2	44.3	
23.65	67.75	37.21	
12.29	21.74	5.74	
73.92	28.97	66.4	66.72
2.34	8.58	7.89	5.44
8.14	45.79	17.23	2.21
15.6	16.66	8.48	25.63
19.1	0.74	18.9	62.8
11773432	619615	1337516	13431222
6466556	26728	626950	9436123
4835342	221453	726113	3396721
2369872	8736	506473	2895565
1470686	**561072**	**141345**	**621336**

4-3 主要年份全市固定资产投资

Total Investment in Fixed Assets in Representative Years

指　　标	Item	1995	2000	2001	2002	2003
一、投资总额(万元)	**Total Investment (10 000 yuan)**	**884994**	**2030122**	**2569496**	**3072442**	**4457381**
1.按资金来源分	Grouped by Funds Source					
国家预算内投资	State Budgetary Funds	69185	160982	256403	355960	365263
国内贷款	Domestic Loans	216565	432282	672379	666146	1219234
债　券	Bonds	873	32460	6753	766	3278
利用外资	Utilization of Foreign Funds	80792	31622	54907	15192	47509
自筹资金	Self-raised Funds	385047	875352	1121502	1392915	1733132
其它资金	Others	132532	497424	457552	641463	1088965
2.按构成分	Grouped by Use of Funds					
建筑安装工程	Building and Installation Projects	527220	1404184	1698777	2119151	3067309
设备、工具、器具购置	Purchasing of Equipment,Tools and Instruments	233730	382495	452602	552251	577240
其它费用	Others	124044	243443	418117	401040	812832
3.按建设性质分	Grouped by Type of Construction					
新　建	New Construction	210926	533058	723957	874392	1294032
扩　建	Expansion	180210	542510	581138	868603	1102914
改　建	Reconstruction	157457	263657	344879	343184	447944
4.按国民经济行业分	Grouped by Sector					
农林牧渔业	Farming,Forestry,Animal Husbandry and Fishery	1390	7577	8586	42934	33409
工业建筑业	Industry and Construction	288044	572124	633142	743377	832496
运输邮电业	Transportation,Post and Telecommunications	134751	361175	474363	379760	431826
二、新增固定资产(万元)	**Newly Increased Fixed Assets This Year (10 000 yuan)**	**625803**	**1501585**	**1677665**	**1989689**	**2794439**
三、房屋建筑面积(平方米)	**Floor Space of Buildings (sq.m)**					
施工面积	Floor Space Under Construction	10705800	17025783	17671256	23968913	27161785
竣工面积	Floor Space Completed	3576600	7148313	6925619	7732772	9179629
#住宅	Residential Building	2528500	5449502	5022617	4861279	5780646

4-4 国有经济单位固定资产投资

Investment in Fixed Assets of State-owned Units

指 标	Item	1985	1990	1995
一、投资总额(万元)	**Total Investment (10 000 yuan)**	**139567**	**222084**	**690806**
1.按资金来源分	Grouped by Funds Source			
国家预算内投资	State Budgetary Funds	45815	48770	67426
国内贷款	Domestic Loans	27102	58602	145108
债 券	Bonds	-	-	-
利用外资	Utilization of Foreign Funds	2244	9970	46811
自筹资金	Self-raised Funds	56758	91527	330333
其它资金	Others	7648	13215	101128
2.按构成分	Grouped by Use of Funds			
建筑安装工程	Building and Installation Projects	83542	130615	405057
设备、工具、器具购置	Purchasing of Equipment,Tools and Instruments	36328	72043	209351
其它费用	Others	19697	19426	76398
3.按建设性质分	Grouped by Type of Construction			
新 建	New Construction	33366	55242	1738081
扩 建	Expansion	55370	60641	162796
改 建	Reconstruction	33505	63253	145783
4.按国民经济行业分	Grouped by Sector			
农林牧渔业	Farming,Forestry,Animal Husbandry and Fishery	1736	1888	1127
工业建筑业	Industry and Construction	61634	101407	240665
运输邮电业	Transportation,Post and Telecommunication	4949	28180	-
二、新增固定资产(万元)	**Newly Increased Fixed Assets This Year (10 000 yuan)**	**83030**	**195429**	**509328**
三、房屋建筑面积(万平方米)	**Floor Space of Buildings (10 000 sq.m)**			
施工面积	Floor Space Under Construction	586.49	508.73	841
竣工面积	Floor Space Completed	213.92	203.12	303.72
#住宅	Residential Building	125.39	107.58	214.01

4-4 国有经济单位固定资产投资（续）

Investment in Fixed Assets of State-owned Units(Continued)

指 标	Item	2000	2001	2002	2003
一、投资总额(万元)	**Total Investment (10 000 yuan)**	**1596002**	**1755787**	**2000636**	**2648283**
1.按资金来源分	Grouped by Funds Source				
国家预算内投资	State Budgetary Funds	165304	255860	351540	268537
国内贷款	Domestic Loans	280585	471506	453958	823374
债 券	Bonds	32886	6865		2310
利用外资	Utilization of Foreign Funds	15276	20815	6617	4846
自筹资金	Self-raised Funds	689732	715351	840082	803648
其它资金	Others	412219	285390	348439	745568
2.按构成分	Grouped by Use of Funds				
建筑安装工程	Building and Installation Projects	1102548	1177790	1449583	1897323
设备、工具、器具购置	Purchasing of Equipment,Tools and Instruments	328432	334174	347647	335454
其它费用	Others	165022	243823	203406	415506
3.按建设性质分	Grouped by Type of Construction				
新 建	New Construction	390119	486585	537537	883859
扩 建	Expansion	460381	436404	672297	726753
改 建	Reconstruction	254860	328685	272499	377060
4.按国民经济行业分	Grouped by Sector				
农林牧渔业	Farming,Forestry,Animal Husbandry and Fishery	4077	3666	24087	25034
工业建筑业	Industry and Construction	408234	361954	358027	427632
运输邮电业	Transportation,Post and Telecommunications	360779	472278	375131	312306
二、新增固定资产(万元)	**Newly Increased Fixed Assets This Year (10 000 yuan)**	**1220632**	**1120240**	**1134623**	**1732895**
三、房屋建筑面积(万平方米)	**Floor Space of Buildings (10 000 sq.m)**				
施工面积	Floor Space Under Construction	1341.75	1154.67	1590.43	1331.27
竣工面积	Floor Space Completed	577.14	491.8	452.44	513.72
#住宅	Residential Building	475.18	392.32	311.31	342.75

4–5 主要年份城镇集体经济单位固定资产投资

Investment in Fixed Assets of Urban Collective Owned Units in Representative Years

指　标	Item	1990	1995	2000	2001	2002	2003
一、投资总额(万元)	**Total Investment (10 000 yuan)**	**8880**	**59886**	**56893**	**64115**	**68422**	**144049**
按资金来源分	Goruped by Funds Resource						
国家预算内投资	State Budgetary Investment	80	36		861		8380
国内贷款	Domestic Loans	3192	18814	14695	8722	15153	54818
债券	Bonds						
利用外资	Utilization of Foreign Funds	1782	315				
自筹资金	Self-Raised Funds	3522	24744	31971	36724	31848	63595
其他资金	Others	304	15977	10227	17808	21421	17256
按构成分:	Grouped by Use of Funds						
建筑安装工程	Building and Installation Projects	5362	37616	43922	52077	51701	107583
设备、工具、器具购置	Purchasing of Equipment,Tools and Instruments	2521	3298	611	2466	3898	12200
其他费用	Others	997	18972	12360	9572	12823	24266
二、新增固定资产(万元)	**Increased Fixed Assets (10 000 yuan)**	**7571**	**32251**	**76764**	**68406**	**46959**	**74644**
三、项目个数（个）	**Number of Projects(unit)**						
施工项目	Projects Under Construction	82	111	43	44	43	86
投产项目	Projects Completed and Put into Use	57	44	32	23	25	28
四、房屋建筑面积(平方米)	**Floor Space of Buildings(sq.m)**						
施工面积	Floor Space Under Construction	162620	770010	783641	743910	752102	1531483
#住宅	Residential Buildings	44600	547620	394720	569672	624268	915297
竣工面积	Floor Space Completed	87510	218120	500374	315085	389335	423804
#住宅	Residential Buildings	34700	159810	218498	203364	325625	298940

4-6　主要年份农村集体固定资产投资

指　　标	Item	1985
一、投资总额(万元)	**Total Investment (10 000 yuan)**	**8582**
1.按资金来源分	Grouped by Founds Source	
国家资金	State Funds	-
国内贷款	Domestic Loans	2120
引进外资	Utilization of Foreign Funds	-
自筹资金	Self-Raised Funds	5653
群众集资	Mass Fund-Raising	-
其他资金	Others	809
2.按行业划分	Grouped by Economic Sector	
农林牧渔业及地质勘查水利管理业	Farming , Forestry, Animal Husbandry, Fishery & Geological Prospecting and Water Conservancy	213
工业	Industry	4371
建筑业	Construction	-
交通运输邮电业	Transport,Storage,Post and Telecommunications	943
批发和零售贸易餐饮业及仓储业	Wholesale and Retail Trade,Catering Services and Storage	-
金融保险业	Banking and Insurance	-
房地产业及社会服务业	Real Estate and Social Services	-
卫生体育社会福利业	Health Care,Sports and Social Welfare	-
教育文化艺术及广播电影电视业	Education,Culture and Arts,Radio,Film and Television	869
科学研究和综合技术服务业	Scientific Research and Polytechnical Services	-
国家机关政党机关和社会团体	Governmental and Party Agencies and Social Organizations	-
其他行业	Others	-
二、竣工房屋建筑面积(万平方米)	**Floor Space of the Building Completed (10 000 sq.m)**	-
#住宅	Residential Buildings	-
三、本年新增固定资产(万元)	**Newly Increase Fixed Assets This Year (10 000 yuan)**	-

Investment in Fixed Assels of Rural Collective Owned Units in Representative Years

1990	1995	2000	2001	2002	2003
5542	**37892**	**89626**	**82623**	**68610**	**79216**
-	1442	9388	994	2369	3198
2620	10925	2977	5596	1818	742
313	5021	5394	70	8973	3887
1281	12220	53338	58911	41183	52946
-	3732	7413	8248	10647	6256
1328	4552	11116	8804	3620	12187
-	170	9075	4452	4358	3632
-	20286	32437	21155	16998	5228
-	2475	12309	8523	5243	10248
-	668	2444	1023	1057	220
-	3749	8444	26611	9273	2760
-	-	10	700		25
-	2338	12519	8260	10286	19315
-	3054	126	107	281	326
-	4642	6110	7973	9713	4831
-	-	500	790		
-	160	635	1859	2654	12630
-	350	5017	1170	8747	20001
-	**16.08**	**83.96**	**41.1**	**43.31**	**48.26**
-	0.92	21.33	10.82	8.35	23.2
3739	**32405**	**89626**	**75732**	**55215**	**72862**

4–7 农村集体固定资产投资(2003年)

Investment in Fixed Assets of Rural Collective Owned Units（2003）

单位：万元 (10 000 yuan)

指标	Item	全市 the Whole City
一、本年完成投资	**Accomplished Investment This Year**	**79216**
建筑工程	Constrution Projects	61194
安装工程	Installment Projects	4470
设备购置	Purchasing of Equipment	6471
其他	Others	7081
二、本年新增固定资产	**Newly Inceased Fixed Assets This Year**	**72862**
三、本年投资资金来源	**Investment Funds Resource This Year**	**79216**
国家资金	State Funds	3198
国内贷款	Domestic Loans	742
引进外资	Utilization of Foreign Funds	3887
自筹资金	Self-Raised Funds	52946
群众集资	Mass Fund-Raising	6256
其他资金	Others	12187
四、房屋建筑面积(平方米)	**Floor Space of Buildings(sq.m)**	
施工面积	Floor Space Under Construction	616015
#住宅	#Residential Buildings	254632
竣工面积	Floor Space Completed	482577
#住宅	#Residential Buildings	232008

4-8 主要年份市属固定资产投资

Investment In Fixed Assets of Municipal Units in Representative Years

单位：万元 (10 000 yuan)

指　　标	Item	1985	1990	1995	2000	2001	2002	2003
一、投资总额	**Total Investment**	**38896**	**80958**	**432451**	**1263023**	**1539717**	**1848833**	**2978747**
1.按经济类型分	Grouped by Type of Enterprises							
国有经济	State-owned Enterprises	34313	72078	258545	890546	894700	1006245	1586057
集体经济	Collective-owned Enterprises	4583	8880	5720	52893	62895	63877	142849
其他经济	Others	-	-	168186	319584	582122	778711	1249841
2.按管理渠道分	Grouped by Management							
基本建设	Capital Construction	19100	34204	138889	470442	600956	705054	1231473
更新改造	Innovation	15213	30335	90715	250495	263640	299013	439031
其他投资	Others	4583	10934	31556	68299	108564	142533	193434
房地产开发	Real Estate Development	-	5485	171291	473787	566557	702233	1114809
二、新增固定资产	**Newly Increased Fixed Assets**	**27872**	**69434**	**273324**	**953173**	**1159980**	**1295389**	**1812099**
三、房屋竣工面积（平方米）	**Floor Space of the Building Completed(sq.m)**	**986197**	**950215**	**2025223**	**5094751**	**5359752**	**5374374**	**6318902**
#住　宅	Of the Total:Residential Buildings	451128	501234	1433005	3735111	3960060	3314467	3878178

4-9　市属固定资产投资(2003年)

分　类	Item	合计 Total
一、本年完成投资（万元）	**Accomplished Invstment This Year(10 000 yuan)**	**2978747**
按登记注册类型分	Grouped by Registion Status	
内资	Domestic Investment Enterprises	2821626
国有	State-owned Enterprises	1517174
集体	Collective-owned Enterprises	88246
股份合作	Share-holding Corperative	51303
国有联营	State Joint Ownership Enterprises	1800
集体联营	Collective Joint Ownership Enterprises	900
国有与集体联营	State-owned and Collective-owned Joint Enterprises	1990
其他联营	Other Joint Ownership Enterprises	4510
国有独资公司	Sole State-funded Corporations	29823
其他有限责任公司	Other Limited Liability Corporations	417636
股份有限公司	Share-holding Corperation Ltd.	177738
私营个体	Private and Individual	473814
其他	Others	56692
港澳台商投资	Enterprises with Investment from Hong Kong, Macao and Taiwan	54499
合资经营	Joint Venture	48618
合作经营	Cooperation	3508
独资	Sole-Funded	1703
股份有限	Share-Holding Corporations Ltd.	670
外商投资	Enterprises with Foreign Investment	102622
合资经营	Joint Venture	52576
合作经营	Cooperation	5402
独资	Sole-Funded	44644
股份有限	Share-Holding Corporations Ltd.	
按建设性质分	Grouped by Construction Nature	
新建	Newly Constructed	858193
扩建	Expansion	490497
改建	Reconstructior	314088
按构成分	Grouped by Use of Funds	
1.建筑工程	Building Projects	1998450
2.安装工程	Znstallation Projects	131390
3.设备工器具购置	Purchasing of Equipment,Tools and Instruments	271063
4.其他费用	Others	577844
按工程用途分	Grouped by Purpose of Project	
#住宅	Of the Total: Residential Buildings	934377
按项目规模分	Grouped by Construction Scale	
#基建大中型	Large/Medium-Sized Capital Construction	80104
更改限上项目	Projects of Innovation Over Designated Value	118670

Investment in Fixed Assets of Municipal Units（2003）

基本建设 Capital Construction	更新改造 Innovation	其他投资 Other Investment	房地产开发 Real Estate Development
1231473	**439031**	**193434**	**1114809**
1195037	415027	190363	1021199
885881	287682	24383	319228
9986	7060	11851	59349
6200	2122	26306	16675
1800			
900			
510			1480
4500		10	
705	11394	17724	
149959	38314	40053	189310
58167	48713	16650	54208
33156	9972	49737	380949
43273	9770	3649	
1651	480	2422	49946
878	450	2122	45168
	30		3478
403			1300
370		300	
34785	23524	649	43664
4920	6883	500	40273
1085	926		3391
28780	15715	149	
739652	24027	94514	
153037	277052	60408	
191603	110988	11497	
963524	157394	125035	752497
31451	25429	15633	58877
57102	158583	35609	19769
179396	97625	17157	283666
180736	5298	38264	710079
80104			
	118670		

4-9 市属固定资产投资(2003年)(续)

分　　类	Item	合计 Total
一、按国民经济行业分	**Grouped by Sector**	
农、林、牧、渔业	Farming,Forestry,Animal Husbandry and Fishery	22209
采矿业	Mining	38913
制造业	Manufacturing	375796
电力、燃气及水的生产和供应业	Production & Supply of Power,Gas & Water	38524
建筑业	Construction	8192
交通运输、仓储和邮政业	Transport,Storage and Postal Service	83665
信息传输、计算机服务和软件业	Information Transmission,Computer Service and Software Service	76235
批发和零售业	Wholesale and Retail Trade	148072
住宿和餐饮业	Accommodation and Catering Trade	31734
金融业	Banking	1526
房地产业	Real Estate Trade	1114809
租赁和商务服务业	Commercial Service	59808
科学研究、技术服务和地质勘察业	Scientific Research,Technical Services and Geological Prospecting	24205
水利、环境和公共设施管理业	Water conservancy, environment and public facilities administration industry	386525
居民服务和其他服务业	Resident Services and Other Services	3827
教育	Education	79188
卫生、社会保障和社会福利业	Sanitation, social insurance and social welfare industry	14748
文化、体育和娱乐业	Culture, physical education and entertainment industry	23135
公共管理和社会组织	Public administration non-profit institution	447636
二、构成(%)	**Composition (%)**	
按登记注册类型分	Grouped by Registion Status	
国有经济	State-owned	51.99
集体经济	Collective-owned	4.72
按建设性质分	Grouped by Type of Construction	
新建	New Construction	46.04
扩建	Expansion	26.32
改建	Reconstruction	16.85
按构成分:	Grouped by Use of Funds	
1.建筑工程	Construction Projects	67.09
2.安装工程	Installation Projects	4.41
3.设备工器具购置	Purchasing of the Equipment,Tools and Instruments	9.1
4.其他费用	Others	19.4
按工程用途分	Grouped by Purpose of Project	
#住宅	Of the Total: Residential Buildings	31.37
三、房屋面积(平方米)	**Floor Space (sq.m)**	
本年施工房屋面积	Floor Space of Buildings Under Construction in This Year	18822524
#住宅	Of the Total: Residential Buildings	11022309
本年竣工房屋面积	Floor Space of Buildings Completed This Year	6318902
#住宅	Of the Total: Residential Buildings	3878178
四、本年新增固定资产(万元)	**Newly Increase(10 000 yuan)**	**1812099**

Investment in Fixed Assets of Municipal Units（2003）(Continued)

基本建设 Capital Construction	更新改造 Innovation	其他投资 Other Investment	房地产开发 Real Estate Development
18677		3532	
38708		205	
149325	173871	52600	
31073	7151	300	
4133	2830	1229	
67826	13743	2096	
19060	57175		
107698	24181	16193	
18788	2760	10186	
1526			
			1114809
57591	68	2149	
23906		299	
209751	146399	30375	
3296		531	
36282	920	41986	
10273	3258	1217	
19018	2620	1497	
414542	4055	29039	
72.14	68.12	21.77	28.64
1.39	2.09	19.73	6.82
60.06	5.47	48.86	
12.43	63.11	31.23	
15.56	25.28	5.94	
78.24	35.85	64.64	67.5
2.55	5.79	8.08	5.28
4.64	36.12	18.41	1.77
14.57	22.24	8.87	25.45
14.68	1.21	19.78	63.7
4983140	536656	1212620	12090108
2024764	26728	608807	8362010
2333905	194201	693417	3097379
784889	8736	488330	2596223
786631	**318835**	**135767**	**570866**

4-10 市区固定资产投资额(2003年)

指 标	Item	合 计 Total
一、本年完成投资(万元)	**Accomplished Invstment This Year (10 000 yuan)**	**4229306**
按登记注册类型分	Grouped by Registion Status	
内资	Domestic Investment Enterprises	4064959
国有	State-owned Enterprises	2284661
集体	Collective-owned Enterprises	86456
股份合作	Share-holding Corperative	47803
国有联营	State Joint Ownership Enterprises	3250
集体联营	Collective Joint Ownership Enterprises	1700
国有与集体联营	State-owned and Collective-owned Joint Enterprises	1480
其他联营	Other Joint Ownership Enterprises	4500
国有独资公司	Sole State-funded Enterprises	224487
其他有限责任公司	Other Limited Liability Corporations	725604
股份有限公司	Share-holding Corperation Ltd.	178993
私营个体	Private and Individual	481705
其他	Others	24320
港澳台商投资	Enterprises with Investment from Hong Kong, Macao and Taiwan	58641
合资经营	Joint Venture	52760
合作经营	Cooperation	3478
独资	Sole-Funded	1733
股份有限	Share-Holding Corporations Ltd.	670
外商投资	Enterprises with Foreign Investment	105706
合资经营	Joint Venture	55660
合作经营	Cooperation	5402
独资	Sole-Funded	44644
股份有限	Share-Holding Corporations Ltd.	
按国民经济行业分	Grouped by Sector	
农、林、牧、渔业	Farming,Forestry,Animal Husbandry and Fishery	15806
采矿业	Mining	4985
制造业	Manufacturing	530326
电力、燃气及水的生产和供应业	Production & Supply of Power,Gas & Water	111462
建筑业	Construction	44580
交通运输、仓储和邮政业	Transport,Storage and Postal Service	248458
信息传输、计算机服务和软件业	Information Transmission,Computer Service and Software Service	194071
批发和零售业	Wholesale and Retail Trade	150485
住宿和餐饮业	Accommodation and Catering Trade	35601
金融业	Banking	10533
房地产业	Real Estate Trade	1248177
租赁和商务服务业	Commercial Service	211801
科学研究、技术服务和地质勘察业	Scientific Research,Technical Services and Geological Prospecting	154667
水利、环境和公共设施管理业	Water conservancy, environment and public facilities administration industry	386290
居民服务和其他服务业	Resident Services and Other Services	3827
教育	Education	344506
卫生、社会保障和社会福利业	Sanitation, social insurance and social welfare industry	17230
文化、体育和娱乐业	Culture, physical education and entertainment industry	84712
公共管理和社会组织	Public administration non-profit institution	431789
二、房屋面积(平方米)	**Floor Space (sq.m)**	
本年施工房屋面积	Floor Space Under Construction This Year	25924291
#住宅	Of the Total: Residential Buildings	15878555
本年竣工房屋面积	Floor Space Completed This Year	8757815
#住宅	Of the Total: Residential Buildings	5724450
三、本年新增固定资产(万元)	**Newly Increase(10 000 yuan)**	**2641315**

Investments in Fixed Assets of Urban Districts(2003)

基本建设 Capital Construction	更新改造 Innovation	其他投资 Other Investment	房地产开发 Real Estate Development
2094480	**687618**	**199031**	**1248177**
2055961	662556	195960	1150482
1544839	381608	23370	334844
7916	7060	9731	61749
4100	1022	26006	16675
3250			
1700			
			1480
4500			
157301	27818	17724	21644
245077	185433	42612	252482
41838	48143	24480	64532
30000	9972	44657	397076
15440	1500	7380	
1708	480	2422	54031
935	450	2122	49253
			3478
403	30		1300
370		300	
36811	24582	649	43664
6946	7941	500	40273
1085	926		3391
28780	15715	149	
13234		2572	
4985			
228695	255078	46553	
88783	22679		
35591	7830	1159	
232869	13493	2096	
21896	172175		
112861	23641	13983	
21911	2760	10930	
10533			
			1248177
209584	68	2149	
117986	36382	299	
215793	143209	27288	
3296		531	
282641	920	60945	
12755	3258	1217	
81822	2620	270	
399245	3505	29039	
10655839	565715	1271515	13431222
5813394	26728	602310	9436123
4484849	211133	666212	3396721
2338316	8736	481833	2895565
1348903	**542056**	**129020**	**621336**

4-11 全市固定资产投资效果(2003年)

指　　标	Item	合 计 Total
一、建设项目投资率(%)	**Rate of Projects Put Into use(%)**	**39.94**
施工项目个数（个）	Number of Constructing Projects (unit)	1337
本年投产项目个数（个）	Number of Projects Put into Use (unit)	534
二、固定资产交付使用率(%)	**Rate Tate of Fixed Assets Put into Use(%)**	**62.69**
本年新增固定资产（万元）	Newly Increased Fixed Assets This Year (10000.yuan)	2794439
本年完成投资（万元）	Accomplished Investment This Year (10000.yuan)	4457381
三、未完工程占用率(%)	**The Rate of Projects Uncompleted (%)**	**95.78**
未完工程累计投资（万元）	Rate of Investment in Projects Uncompleted (10000.yuan)	4269168
本年完成投资（万元）	Accomplished Investment This Year (10000.yuan)	4457381
四、建设周期(年)	**Construction Period (year)**	**3.21**
计划总投资（万元）	Total Planned Investment (10000.yuan)	14312885
本年完成投资（万元）	Accomplished Investment This Year (10000.yuan)	4457381
五、房屋建筑面积竣工率(%)	**Completion Rate of Buildings (%)**	**33.80**
本年施工房屋面积（平方米）	Floor Space of the Constructing Buildings This Year (sq.m)	27161785
本年竣工房屋面积（平方米）	Floor Space of the Building Completed This Year (sq.m)	9179629

4-12 市属固定资产投资效果(2003年)

指　　标	Item	合 计 Total
一、建设项目投资率(%)	**Rate of Projects put into Use (%)**	**42.91**
施工项目个数(个)	Number of Constructing Projects (unit)	1016
本年投产项目个数(个)	Number of Put into Use (unit)	436
二、固定资产交付使用率(%)	**Rate of Fixed Assets Put into Use(%)**	**60.83**
本年新增固定资产（万元）	Newly Increased Fixed Assets This Year (10000.yuan)	1812099
本年完成投资（万元）	Accomplished Investment This Year (10000.yuan)	2978747
三、未完工程占用率(%)	**The Rate of Projects Uncompleted (%)**	**90.11**
未完工程累计投资（万元）	Rate of Investment in Projects Uncompleted (10000.yuan)	2684193
本年完成投资（万元）	Accomplished Investment This Year (10000.yuan)	2978747
四、建设周期(年)	**Construction Period (year)**	**3.08**
计划总投资（万元）	Total Planned Investment (10000.yuan)	9162168
本年完成投资（万元）	Accomplished Investment This Year (10000.yuan)	2978747
五、房屋建筑面积竣工率(%)	**Completion Rate of Buildings (%)**	**33.57**
本年施工房屋面积（平方米）	Floor Space of the Constructing Building This Year（sq.m）	18822524
本年竣工房屋面积（平方米）	Floor Space of the Building Completed This Year（sq.m）	6318902

Achievements of Total Assets Investment of Whole City(2003)

基本建设 Capital Construction	更新改造 Innovation	其他投资 Others Investment	房地产开发 Real Estate Development
43.19	**49.44**	**80.00**	
653	267	150	267
282	132	120	
64.46	**78.53**	**66.25**	**49.78**
1470686	561072	141345	621336
2281384	714483	213337	1248177
101.93	**79.08**	**51.96**	**101.57**
2325502	565029	110860	1267777
2281384	714483	213337	1248177
3.13	**2.49**	**2.15**	**3.96**
7132322	1779587	458134	4942842
2281384	714483	213337	1248177
41.07	**35.74**	**54.29**	**25.29**
11773432	619615	1337516	13431222
4835342	221453	726113	3396721

Achievement of Fixed Assets Investment of Municipal Units(2003)

基本建设 Capital Construction	更新改造 Innovation	其他投资 Others Investment	房地产开发 Real Estate Development
52.32	**60.75**	**59.31**	
453	186	145	232
237	113	86	
63.88	**72.62**	**70.19**	**51.21**
786631	318835	135767	570866
1231473	439031	193434	1114809
106.81	**57.90**	**44.63**	**92.24**
1315353	254193	86335	1028312
1231473	439031	193434	1114809
2.84	**2.16**	**1.98**	**3.89**
3493588	949889	383431	4335260
1231473	439031	193434	1114809
46.84	**36.19**	**57.18**	**25.62**
4983140	536656	1212620	12090108
2333905	194201	693417	3097379

4–13　全市固定资产投资资金来源(2003年)

单位：万元

指　　标	Item	合　计 Total
一、本年资金来源合计	**Total**	**5163498**
1、上年末结余资金	Balance of Last Year	526443
2、本年资金来源小计	Total Funds This Year	4637055
(1) 国家预算内资金	State Budgetary Funds	379986
(2) 国内贷款	Domestic Loans	1268381
(3) 债券	Bonds	3410
(4) 利用外资	Utilization of Foreign Funds	49425
(5) 自筹资金	Self-raised Funds	1802993
#中央及省自筹	#Central and Provincial	90532
市自筹	Manucipality	516323
(6) 其他资金	Others	1132860
二、本年各项应付款合计	**Total Sums of Money to be Paid This Year**	**544527**

4–14　市属固定资产投资资金来源（2003年）

单位：万元

指　　标	Item	合　计 Total
一、本年资金来源合计	**Total**	**3503514**
1、上年末结余资金	Balance of Last Year	329934
2、本年资金来源小计	Total Funds This Year	3173580
(1) 国家预算内资金	State Budgetary Funds	137564
(2) 国内贷款	Domestic Loans	911948
(3) 债券	Bonds	210
(4) 利用外资	Utilization of Foreign Funds	43784
(5) 自筹资金	Self-raised Funds	1213500
(6) 其他资金来源	Others	866574
二、本年各项应付款合计	**Total Sums of Money to be Paid This Year**	**389428**

Source of Funds for Total Fixed Assets Investment of Whole City(2003)

(10 000 yuan)

基本建设 Capital Construction	更新改造 Innovation	其他投资 Others Investment	房地产开发 Real Estate Development
2563038	**828022**	**211785**	**1560653**
239279	84552	2042	200570
2323759	743470	209743	1360083
255706	105612	5318	13350
618511	167527	44729	437614
3230		180	
32811	13201	149	3264
810736	398522	115866	477869
50973	1048		38511
66572	6661	3732	439358
602765	58608	43501	427986
194101	**36775**	**42930**	**270721**

Source of Funds for Fixed Estate of Municipal Units

(10 000 yuan)

基本建设 Capital Construction	更新改造 Innovation	其他投资 Others Investment	房地产开发 Real Estate Development
1390135	**507509**	**197081**	**1408789**
117192	31170	2042	179530
1272943	476339	195039	1229259
72084	46812	5318	13350
336809	138257	42729	394153
30		180	
27238	13133	149	3264
450567	220413	103162	439358
386215	57724	43501	379134
103145	**24966**	**34931**	**226386**

4-15 四县固定资产投资额(2003年)

Investments on Fixed Assets of Counties(2003)

分类	Item	合计 Total	蓝田 Lantian	周至 Zhouzhi	户县 Huxian	高陵 Gaoling
一、本年完成投资（万元）	**Accomplished Invstment This Year (10 000 yuan)**	**228075**	**46901**	**32046**	**73518**	**75610**
按登记注册类型分	Grouped by Registion Status					
国有经济	State-owned Enterprise	135885	17256	30386	40295	47948
集体经济	Collective-owned Enterprise	8090	5590			2500
按报表种类分	Grouped by Types of Reports					
基本建设	Capital Constrution	186904	28045	29836	53413	75610
更新建设	Innovation	26865	4810	1950	20105	
其他投资	Others	14306	14046	260		
房地产开发	Real Estate Development					
按建设性质分	Grouped by Type of Construction					
新建	Newly Constructed	171912	32155	26207	37940	75610
扩建	Expansion	24473	8734	3939	11800	
改建	Reconstruction	26010	3140	1900	20970	
按构成分	Grouped by Use of Funds					
1.建筑工程	construction Projects	164235	19173	32046	37406	75610
2.安装工程	Installation Projects	6315	4508		1807	
3.设备工器具购置	Purchasing of Equipment,Tools and Instruments	43741	11912		31829	
4.其他费用	Others	13784	11308		2476	
按工程用途分	Grouped by Purpose of Project					
#住宅	Of the Total: Residential Buildings	14293	3243		1050	10000
按国民经济行业分	Grouped by Sector					
农、林、牧、渔业	Farming, Forestry, Animal Husbandry and Fishery	17603	7390	7173	1140	1900
采矿业	Mining	38733	933			37800
制造业	Manufacturing	85647	11477	3660	50598	19912
电力、燃气及水的生产和供应业	Production & Supply of Power, Gas & Water	12953	5153		5000	2800

4-15 四县固定资产投资额(2003年)(续)

Investments on Fixed Assets of Counties(2003)(Continued)

分类	Item	合计 Total	蓝田 Lantian	周至 Zhouzhi	户县 Huxian	高陵 Gaoling
建筑业	Construction	3810	3810			
交通运输、仓储和邮政业	Transport, Storage and Postal Service	4620			1420	3200
信息传输、计算机服务和软件业	Information Transmission, Computer Service and Software Service	4666	2666		2000	
批发和零售业	Wholesale and Retail Trade	6027	3367	1600	960	100
住宿和餐饮业	Accommodation and Catering Trade	1077	77	350	650	
金融业	Banking	1218	218		1000	
房地产业	Real Estate Trade					
租赁和商务服务业	Commercial Service					
科学研究、技术服务和地质勘查业	Scientific Research, Technical Services and Geological Prospecting	5860	70	2130	160	3500
水利、环境和公共设施管理业	Water conservancy, environment and public facilities administration industry	14475	5075	2400	7000	
居民服务和其他服务业	Resident Services and Other Services					
教育	Education	4604	1552		2120	932
卫生、社会保障和社会福利业	Sanitation, social insurance and social welfare industry	350				350
文化、体育和娱乐业	Culture, physical education and entertainment industry	3533	3413			120
公共管理和社会组织	Public administration non-profit institution	22899	1700	14733	1470	4996
二、房屋面积(平方米)	**Floor Space of Buildings (sq.m)**					
本年施工房屋面积	Floor Space Under Construction This Year	1237494	162449	26000	290266	758779
#住宅	Of the Total: Residential Buildings	677802	66726		21076	590000
本年竣工房屋面积	Floor Space Completed This Year	420714	107202	26000	203289	84223
#住宅	Of the Total: Residential Buildings	56196	35120		21076	
三、本年新增固定资产(万元)	**Newly Increase(10 000 yuan)**	**153124**	**36416**	**20542**	**46160**	**50006**

4-16　新增生产能力或效益(2003年)

能力（或效益）名称	Item (unit)	全部建设规模 (Accumulated)
天然气管输（公里）	Natural gas pipe (km)	981
天然气管输（亿立方米／年）	Natural gas Pipe Transport(100 million cu.m/year)	0.3
铁矿开采(原矿)（万吨／年）	Iron ore mining (raw ore) (10 000 tons/year)	0.6
冷加工钢材（万吨／年）	Steel cold working (10 000 tons/year)	200
铜材加工（吨／年）	Copper processing (tons/year)	5000
铅锌采矿(原矿)（万吨／年）	Lead and zinc mining (raw ore) (10 000 tons/year)	3000
火力发电（万千瓦）	Thermal power generation (10 000 kw.)	20
化学原料药（吨／年）	Chemical drug (tons/year)	2700
化学农药原药（吨／年）	Raw agricultural chemical (tons/year)	4500
食用植物油（日处理原料：吨）	Edible vegetable oil (daily raw material processed: tons)	300
食用植物油（日精炼油：吨）	Edible vegetable oil (daily refined oil: tons)	36
中成药（吨／年）	Chinese medicine (tons/year)	2328
原 盐（万吨／年）	Raw salt (110 000 tons/year)	600
肉加工品（吨／年）	Product of meet-making (tons/year)	2400
新建公路（公里）	Newly-built highway (km)	56
其中：高速公路（公里）	Init :freeway (km)	45
改建公路（公里）	Rebuild highway (km)	157
二级公路（公里）	Class 2 highway (km)	13
新建独立公路桥梁（延长米）	Newly-built separate highway bridge (meter added)	1171
新建独立公路桥梁（座）	Newly-built separate highway bridge (number of)	1
新(扩)建客、货运站（个）	Newly-built station of transporting people or goods (unit)	1
新(扩)建客、货运站（平方米）	Newly-built station of transporting people or goods (sq.m)	29400
水库容量(总库容)（亿立方米）	Reservoir volume(100 million cu.m)	0.68
有效灌溉面积（万亩）	Valid irrigation area(10 000 mu)	20.8
粮食仓库（万公斤）	Foodstuff depot (10000 kg)	2000
粮食仓库（平方米）	Foodstuff depot (sq.m)	4716
高等院校：学生席位（个）	Colleges and universities: student seat (seat)	91008
建筑面积（平方米）	Building area (sq.m)	1147024
中等学校：学生席位（个）	Middle school: student seat (seat)	31594
建筑面积（平方米）	Building area (sq.m)	420664
小学校：学生席位（个）	Elementary school: student (seat)	1900
建筑面积（平方米）	Building area (sq.m)	6400
其他院校：建筑面积（平方米）	Other school: building area (sq.m)	28280
公共图书馆：藏书量（万册(件)）	Public library (in 10 000)	10

Newly Increased Production Capacity or Benefit(2003)

本年施工规模 (Current year) 合计 Total	其中：本年新开工 inc: started in current year	新增生产能力（或效益） Newly added production capacity/Benefit 自开始建设至本年累计 accumulated from the starting point	其中：本年新增 inc: newly added in current year
94.04	64.04	569.04	64.04
0.3	0.1	0.3	0.1
0.6	0.6	0.6	0.6
200	200	200	200
5000			
3000	3000	3000	3000
10		10	
2700	2600	2700	2700
1000	1000	1000	1000
300	300	300	300
36	36	36	36
2328			
600		600	600
2400	2400		
56		45	45
45		45	45
157	157	13	13
13	13	13	13
1171	1171		
1	1		
1		1	1
16000		16000	16000
0.68	0.4	0.28	
20.8	4	20.8	4
2000		2000	2000
4716		4716	4716
61308	13553	52248	38203
940834	311441	565167	537367
31594	20780	17280	17280
420664	222078	183422	183422
1900	820		
6400	2400		
28280		22580	22580
10	10	10	10

4-16 新增生产能力或效益(2003年）（续）

能力（或效益）名称	Item (unit)	全部建设规模 (Accumulated)
医院病床（张）	Infirmary sickbed (bed)	1490
宾馆、旅馆、招待所客房数（间）	Hotel, Inn, Hostel room (room)	350
宾馆、旅馆、招待所客房数（平方米）	Hotel, Inn, Hostel room (sq.m)	10500
城市自来水供水能力（万吨/日）	Watering ability of tap water in city (10 000 tons/day)	110
城市自来水管道长度（公里）	Pipeline length of tap water in city (km)	252
城市供热能力：蒸汽（吨／小时）	Heat supply in city: steam (tons/hour)	968000
热水（兆瓦／小时）	Hot water (mw./hour)	968000
城市道路扩建长度（公里）	Extended roadway length in city (km)	89.7
城市道路扩建面积（万平方米）	Extended roadway length in city (10 000 sq.m)	183.2
城市排水管道铺设长度（公里）	Length of paved draining pipeline in city (km)	92
城市永久性桥梁（座）	Perpetual bridge in city (number of)	13
城市防洪堤长度（公里）	Length of dam for preventing flood in city (km)	31.2
铜线材（吨／年）	Copper material (tons/year)	5000
注射液（万支/年）	Liquid for injecting (10 000/year)	10000
输液（万瓶/年）	Infusion (10 000 bottles/year)	4500
软饮料（吨／年）	Soft drink (tons/year)	52664
钢材（万吨／年）	Steels (10 000 tons/year)	200
发电机组容量（万千瓦）	Generator set volume (10 000 kw)	20
输电线路长度(11万伏及以上)（公里）	Length of transiting electricity line(110000 votes and above)(km)	120.35
变电设备能力(11万伏及以上)（万千伏安）	Electricity transiting device capacity(110000 votes and above)	82
交流电动机制造（万千瓦／年）	Production of alternating current machine (10 000 kw./year)	280
建筑机械制造（台／年）	Building machine production(number of/year)	10
棉纺锭（锭）	Cotton ingot (ingot)	13020
棉布织机（台）	Broche machine (unit)	135
酒（万吨／年）	Alcohol drinks（10 000 tons/year）	30
啤 酒（万吨／年）	Beer (10 000 tons/year)	30
缝纫机（架／年）	sewing-machine（number of/year）	30000
城市污水处理能力（万吨／日）	Disposing sewage capacity in city (10000 tons/day)	10
片剂（万片/年）	Tablet(10000 tablets/year)	30000
胶囊剂（万粒/年）	Capsule(10000 pills/year)	12000
电力电缆（公里）	Electric power cable (km)	27
光纤通讯电缆(指生产能力)（芯公里）	Optical fiber communication cable (productive capacity)(core□km)	1440
全塑市话电缆（万对公里）	All-plastic in-city telephone cable (10000 pair□km)	3
程控交换机 (指安装能力)（万线／年）	Program controlled switchboard (install capacity) (10000 lines/year)	20.28

Newly Increased Production Capacity or Benefit(2003)(Continued)

本年施工规模 (Current year) 合计 Total	其中：本年新开工 inc: started in current year	新增生产能力（或效益） Newly added production capacity/Benefit 自开始建设至本年累计 accumulated from the starting point	其中：本年新增 inc: newly added in current year
1490	80	130	130
350		300	300
10500		9000	9000
		110	
131	11	175	11
968000	968000		
968000	968000		
53.6	49.6	69.7	43.6
90	57	157	78
43	5	85	42
7		10	4
30.5	30.5	30	30
5000			
10000		10000	10000
4500	4000	4500	4500
52664	52664	52664	52664
200	200	200	200
10		10	
120.35			
82			
280	80	280	80
10		10	5
13020	13020	13020	13020
69	69	63	33
30000		30000	30000
30000	30000		
12000	12000		
27	27	27	27
1440	1440	1440	1440
3	3	3	3
20.28	20.28	20.28	20.28

4-17 全市按行业分房屋建筑面积(2003年)

单位：平方米

行　　业	Item	本年施工房屋面积 Floor Space of Buildings Under Construction This Year	住宅 Residence
合　　计	**Total**	**27161785**	**16556357**
农、林、牧、渔业	Farming, Forestry, Animal Husbandry and Fishery	26624	8990
采矿业	Mining	841679	795917
制造业	Manufacturing	2363242	925250
电力、燃气及水的生产和供应业	Generation and supply of power, production and supply of gas and water	307323	150037
建筑业	Construction	401191	232811
交通运输、仓储和邮政业	Transportation, storage and postal service	65448	23250
信息传输、计算机服务和软件业	Information transmission, computer service and software service	188258	
批发和零售业	Wholesale and retail trade	1123905	118249
住宿和餐饮业	Accommodation and catering trade	127771	45624
金融业	Banking	198045	138955
房地产业	Real estate trade	13431222	9436123
租赁和商务服务业	Tenancy and commercial service	2262036	1860194
科学研究、技术服务和地质勘查业	Scientific research, technical services and ng geological prospecti	783785	402228
水利、环境和公共设施管理业	Water conservancy, environment and public facilities administration industry	51139	44332
居民服务和其他服务业	Resident services and other services	26641	10300
教育	Education	3001279	1256631
卫生、社会保障和社会福利业	Sanitation, social insurance and social welfare industry	172220	33064
文化、体育和娱乐业	Culture, physical education and entertainment industry	186936	2976
公共管理和社会组织	Public administration non-profit institution	1603041	1071426

Floor Space of Buildings Construction by Sector(2003)

(sq.m)

本年竣工房屋面积 Floor Space of Buildings Completed This Year	住宅 Residence	竣工房屋价值（万元）Value of Buildings Completed(10 000yuan)	住宅 Residence
9179629	**5780646**	**1378119**	**797831**
10951	750	1129	84
207512	201750	17517	16685
827777	301028	113250	26732
215121	118231	47696	25487
150399	106111	14014	9645
19898		2129	
51100		6738	
669259	49147	75355	3614
83509	25624	12543	1850
29076	20876	3847	1747
3396721	2895565	547322	440117
751376	620000	72267	37510
237787	113879	33203	18319
35771	31371	2355	2015
18292	10300	2041	850
1305358	511632	181245	48782
68589	22189	12118	2615
42736	2736	3688	280
1058397	749457	229662	161499

4-18 市属按行业分房屋建筑面积(2003年)

单位：平方米

行　　业	Item	本年施工房屋面积 Floor Space of Buildings Under Construction This Year	住宅 Residence
合　　计	**Total**	**18822524**	**11022309**
农、林、牧、渔业	Farming, Forestry, Animal Husbandry and Fishery	26624	8990
采矿业	Mining	634590	593790
制造业	Manufacturing	1452753	238251
电力、燃气及水的生产和供应业	Production & Supply of Power, Gas & Water	37337	27028
建筑业	Construction	41482	9105
交通运输、仓储和邮政业	Transport, Storage and Postal Service	44550	6250
信息传输、计算机服务和软件业	Information Transmission, Computer Service and Software Service	157716	
批发和零售业	Wholesale and Retail Trade	931018	118249
住宿和餐饮业	Accommodation and Catering Trade	117771	45624
金融业	Banking	29076	20876
房地产业	Real Estate Trade	12090108	8362010
租赁和商务服务业	Commercial Service	298934	22092
科学研究、技术服务和地质勘查业	Scientific Research, Technical Services and Geological Prospecting	204027	12050
水利、环境和公共设施管理业	Water conservancy, environment and public facilities administration industry	51139	44332
居民服务和其他服务业	Resident Services and Other Services	26641	10300
教育	Education	941572	463834
卫生、社会保障和社会福利业	Sanitation, social insurance and social welfare industry	141091	28435
文化、体育和娱乐业	Culture, physical education and entertainment industry	107236	2976
公共管理和社会组织	Public administration non-profit institution	1488859	1008117

Floors Space of Buildings Construction of Municipal Units by Sector(2003)

(sq.m)

本年竣工房屋面积 Floor Space of Buildings Completed This Year	住 宅 Residence	竣工房屋价值(万元) Value of Buildings Completed (10 000 yuan)	住 宅 Residence
6318902	**3878178**	**987770**	**594238**
10951	750	1129	84
4590	3790	220	185
533108	61694	71952	5226
37337	27028	3501	2173
12600		1050	
16000		1513	
51000		6730	
656759	49147	71855	3614
83509	25624	12543	1850
29076	20876	3847	1747
3097379	2596223	498852	391647
131376		34757	
21830	12050	1975	700
35771	31371	2355	2015
18292	10300	2041	850
454231	269572	36687	20695
48960	17560	9533	1673
40736	2736	3568	280
1035397	749457	223662	161499

4–19 主要年份全市新增固定资产及房屋竣工面积

Value of Newly Added Fixed Assets and Floor Spaces Completed of Whole City in Representative Years

年份 Year	新增固定资产(万元) Newly Increased Fixed Assets (10 000 yuan)	房屋竣工面积(平方米) Floor Space of Buildings Completed (sq.m)	住宅 Residence
1978	49582	990996	407554
1980	46377	1648691	1001544
1985	86174	2224195	1290728
1986	134037	2729528	1559067
1987	167160	2414751	1192115
1988	168152	2118312	1024255
1989	165811	1784546	877691
1990	203000	2118777	1110535
1991	178572	1853384	958364
1992	223270	2047478	1126628
1993	416963	2578987	1448829
1994	553714	2829057	1844859
1995	625803	3576699	2528435
1996	600353	3321838	2495208
1997	628819	3744631	2865398
1998	802337	3828026	2756265
1999	1189176	6810370	5508336
2000	1501585	7148313	5449502
2001	1677665	6925619	5022617
2002	1989689	7732772	4861279
2003	2794439	9179629	5780646

4-20 主要年份市属新增固定资产及房屋竣工面积

Value of Newly Added Fixed Assets and Floor Spaces Completed of Municipal Units in Representative Years

年 份 Year	新增固定资产 (万元) Newly Increased Fixed Assets (10 000 yuan)	房屋竣工面积 (平方米) Floor Space of Buildings Completed (sq.m)	住 宅 Residence
1978	7529	249793	103060
1980	10664	497472	284022
1985	27872	986197	451128
1986	47827	1077660	690965
1987	56953	937402	417050
1988	50175	717169	351330
1989	69817	713432	315937
1990	69434	950215	501234
1991	67392	788184	377550
1992	108469	981637	417800
1993	181449	1384411	689602
1994	314996	1351075	894704
1995	273324	2025223	1433005
1996	296898	1984330	1487837
1997	374318	2264862	1666509
1998	521350	2383041	1691699
1999	859070	5012547	4074889
2000	953173	5094751	3735111
2001	1159980	5359752	3960060
2002	1295389	5374374	3314467
2003	1812099	6318902	3878178

4-21 全市按行业分施工项目(2003年)

行 业	Item	本年新增固定资产(万元) Increased Fixed Assets This Year(10 000 yuan)
合 · 计	**Total**	**2794439**
农、林、牧、渔业	Farming,Forestry,Animal Husbandry and Fishery	22737
采矿业	Mining	24402
制造业	Manufacturing	376482
电力、燃气及水的生产和供应业	Production and Supply of Electric Power,Gas and Water	155614
建筑业	Construction	24937
交通运输、仓储和邮政业	Transport, Storage and Postal Service	201161
信息传输、计算机服务和软件业	Information Transmission, Computer Service and Software Service	183039
批发和零售业	Wholesale and Retail Trade	122909
住宿和餐饮业	Accommodation and Catering Trade	30833
金融业	Banking	4976
房地产业	Real Estate Trade	621336
租赁和商务服务业	Commercial Service	73959
科学研究、技术服务和地质勘查业	Scientific Research, Technical Services and Geological Prospecting	57924
水利、环境和公共设施管理业	Water conservancy, environment and public facilities administration industry	233763
居民服务和其他服务业	Resident Services and Other Services	2447
教育	Education	238681
卫生、社会保障和社会福利业	Sanitation, social insurance and social welfare industry	19468
文化、体育和娱乐业	Culture, physical education and entertainment industry	14964
公共管理和社会组织	Public administration non-profit institution	384807

Construction Projects of Whole City by Sector(2003)

施工项目个数（个） Number of Constructing Projects（unit）	本年新开工 Newly Started This Year	投产项目个数(个) Projects put into Use (item)
1337	**591**	**500**
30	17	20
9	7	7
316	159	127
28	13	9
22	13	9
38	22	19
34	28	25
79	48	43
21	14	11
6	2	2
267		
14	2	2
69	24	12
100	61	48
8	7	3
123	78	70
19	12	9
33	17	15
121	67	69

4-22 市属按行业分施工项目(2003年)

行 业	Item	本年新增固定资产（万元）Increased Fixed Assets This Year(10 000 yuan)
合 计	**Total**	**1812099**
农、林、牧、渔业	Farming, Forestry, Animal Husbandry and Fishery	22737
采矿业	Mining	7105
制造业	Manufacturing	246296
电力、燃气及水的生产和供应业	Production & Supply of Power, Gas & Water	9590
建筑业	Construction	3690
交通运输、仓储和邮政业	Transport, Storage and Postal Service	22224
信息传输、计算机服务和软件业	Information Transmission, Computer Service and Software Service	60973
批发和零售业	Wholesale and Retail Trade	119409
住宿和餐饮业	Accommodation and Catering Trade	30089
金融业	Banking	4976
房地产业	Real Estate Trade	570866
租赁和商务服务业	Commercial Service	36449
科学研究、技术服务和地质勘查业	Scientific Research, Technical Services and Geological Prospecting	4275
水利、环境和公共设施管理业	Water conservancy, environment and public facilities administration industry	233763
居民服务和其他服务业	Resident Services and Other Services	2447
教育	Education	38737
卫生、社会保障和社会福利业	Sanitation, social insurance and social welfare industry	16831
文化、体育和娱乐业	Culture, physical education and entertainment industry	6835
公共管理和社会组织	Public administration non-profit institution	374807

Construction Projects of Municipal Units by Sector(2003)

施工项目个数（个） Number of Constructing Projects （unit）	本年新开工 Newly Started This Year	投产项目个数(个) Projects put into Use (item)
1016	**509**	**436**
28	16	20
7	6	6
200	125	103
15	7	7
13	11	6
27	18	12
26	23	21
74	47	43
19	13	11
2	0	2
232		
9	1	2
16	11	3
98	61	48
8	7	3
89	73	59
16	10	8
24	15	14
113	65	68

4-23 城镇和工矿区私人建房

年　份	Year	城镇工矿区个数(个) Urban Factory and Mining Zone(unit)	建房户数 (户) Building Construction Households(Household)
1985		10	13441
1986		17	5595
1987		12	7481
1988		12	5561
1989		11	3171
1990		18	5217
1991		14	3220
1992		12	4084
1993		18	9734
1994		32	6210
1995		21	6742
1996		21	4997
1997		26	5706
1998		18	6603
其中: 扣除农业户后的	After Agricultural Households are Deducted	18	1773
1999		19	4945
其中: 扣除农业户后的	After Agricultural Households are Deducted	19	1612
2000		22	4966
其中: 扣除农业户后的	After Agricultural Households are Deducted	7	3488
2001		14	4482
其中: 扣除农业户后的	After Agricultural Households are Deducted	14	1861
2002		27	4910
其中: 扣除农业户后的	After Agricultural Households are Deducted	27	1310
2003		34	4320
其中: 扣除农业户后的	After Agricultural Households are Deducted	34	990

Private Housing in Urban Factory and Mining Zones

竣工房屋面积 (平方米) Floor Space of Buildings Completed (sq.m)	住宅 Residence	竣工房屋价值(万元) Value of Buildings Completed (10 000 yuan)	住宅 Residence
486000	464000	4112	3879
420639	365840	3647	3200
583509	507240	6014	5407
423903	398549	6290	6064
241964	205640	3939	3298
382754	335624	7435	6278
293044	254921	6134	5336
463409	401304	10278	9131
775128	743816	18445	17143
655474	602437	22411	18636
835881	695441	33737	28948
849734	701774	44864	36753
986114	902893	47596	42534
781293	699092	40620	30520
171095	131423	7770	5438
552338	481438	28354	24258
162801	120170	8886	6418
868976	725171	38248	35339
708844	610020	31964	29796
728772	634653	32976	28281
332723	299221	13704	10894
845286	738751	43947	38949
203915	164471	9983	8720
803721	594608	50263	37562
547045	362746	37644	26308

4-24 农村私人建房

Private Buildings Construction in Rural Area

年 份 Year	竣工房屋投资(万元) Investment of Buildings Completed (10 000 yuan)	房屋竣工面积 (万平方米) Floor Space of Buildings Completed(10 000 sq.m)	竣工房屋造价 (元/平方米) Cost of Buildings Completed(yuan/sq.m)
1985	27174	505.66	53.74
1986	27751	421.75	65.8
1987	27591	382.52	72.13
1988	29361	360.90	81.35
1989	32257	313.34	102.95
1990	19924	243.96	81.67
1991	34607	278.38	124.32
1992	39689	283.79	139.85
1993	47104	297.96	158.09
1994	78451	332.76	235.76
1995	77561	315.03	246.23
1996	80176	303.97	264
1997	103468	356.88	289.92
1998	98114	316.03	310.46
1999	131450	457.06	287.6
2000	165680	517.14	320.38
2001	192138	561.36	342.27
2002	196504	553.03	355.32
2003	194142	481.53	403.18

4-25 房地产开发投资主要指标(2003年)

Main Indicators of Investment in Real Estate Development (2003)

单位：万元 (10 000 yuan)

指 标	Item	全市合计 Total	国有 State-owned	市区 Urban Area	市属 Municipal
企业(单位)个数(个)	Number of Enterprises	267	41	267	232
本年完成投资	Accomplished Investment This Year	1248177	356488	1248177	1114809
其中:商品房建设投资额	Of the Total: Investments in Commercial Houses	936450	289835	936450	852123
土地开发投资额	Investments in Land Development	116238	25821	116238	105645
按工程用途分	Grouped by Function				
住宅	Residence	783868	239867	783868	710079
其中:别墅、高档公寓	Of the Total: Villas and Top-Grade Apartments	48434	1202	48434	
经济适用房	Econornic Apartments	76726	12111	76726	66751
办公楼	Office Buildings	129362	51491	129362	124877
商业营业用房	Buidings for Trade and Catering	164846	26736	164846	122908
其他	Others	170101	38394	170101	156945
本年新增固定资产	Incressed Fixed Assets This Year	621336	255961	621336	570866
房屋建筑面积及竣工价值	Floor Space of Buildings and Value of Buildings Completed				
施工房屋面积(平方米)	Floor Space of Buildings Under Construction (sq.m)	13431222	3855324	13431222	1209108
住宅	Residence	9436123	3106309	9436123	8362010
经济适用房	For Sufficiently-used Households	1299866	237232	1299866	1054201
竣工房屋面积(平方米)	Floor Space of Buildings Completed (sq.m)	3396721	1338314	3396721	3097379
住宅	Residence	2895565	1153648	2895565	2596223
经济适用房	Econornic Apartments	553746	97139	553746	468520
竣工房屋价值	Value of Buildings Completed	547322	240128	547322	498852
住宅	Residence	440117	193647	440117	391647
经济适用房	Econornic Apartments	54656	9005	54656	48010
商品房实际销售面积(平方米)	Floor Space of Houses Sales(sq.m)	2527368	1047614	2527368	2123520
商品房实际销售额	Sales Income of Commercial Houses	542851	184181	542851	457022
年平均从业人员数(人)	Annual Average Number of Employed Persons(Persons)	12192	2829	12192	11116
全年从业人员劳动报酬	Total Income of Working Staff Engaged	16282	4584	16282	14763

4–26 商品房销售情况(2003年)

Sales of Commercial Houses(2003)

指 标	Item	全市合计 Total	国有 State Owned	市属 municipal
商品房实际销售面积(平方米)	**Floor Space of Commodity Housing Sales(sq.m)**	**2527368**	**1047614**	**2123520**
其中: 销售给个人	Of the Total: to Individuals	2380614	1041625	1976766
住宅	Residence	2302924	1009795	1938582
其中:别墅、高档公寓	Of the Total:Villas and Top-Grade Apartments	93374		93374
经济适用房	Econornic Apartments	1157931	708397	999194
办公楼	Office Buildings	138679	22557	138509
商业营业用房	Buidings for Trade and Catering	78599	12690	39263
其他	Others	7166	2572	7166
商品房实际销售额(万元)	**Sales Income of Commodity Housing(10 000 yuan)**	**542851**	**184181**	**457022**
其中: 销售给个人	Of the Total: to Individuals	508450	182404	422621
住宅	Residence	442468	169557	369832
其中:别墅、高档公寓	Of the Total:Villas and Top-Grade Apartments	34009		34009
经济适用房	Econornic Apartments	155028	75515	128791
办公楼	Office Buildings	63575	8980	63516
商业营业用房	Buidings for Trade and Catering	35011	5200	21877
其他	Others	1797	444	1797
商品房预售面积(平方米)	**Presell of Commercial Houses(sq.m)**	**523516**	**124834**	**430677**
住宅	Residence	491159	124834	398320
其中:别墅、高档公寓	Of the Total:Villas and Top-Grade Apartments	21022		21022
经济适用房	Econornic Apartments	92001	44374	47627
办公楼	Office Buildings	2800		2800
商业营业用房	Buidings for Trade and Catering	29557		29557
其他	Others			
商品房空置面积(平方米)	**Vacancy of Commercial Houses(sq.m)**	**638528**	**179351**	**557455**
其中：空置一年以上	Of the Total:Being Idle for One Year	282992	133610	235738
空置三年以上	Being Idie for One Year	53262	1452	51810
住宅	Residence	523449	171363	444494
其中:别墅、高档公寓	Of the Total:Villas and Top-Grade Apartments	51846		51846
经济适用房	Econornic Apartments	66062	2578	66062
办公楼	Office Buildings	59352	4183	58709
商业营业用房	Buidings for Trade and Catering	48520	3461	47389
其他	Others	7207	344	6863
商品房出租面积(平方米)	**Floor Space of Commodity Housing Hired(sq.m)**	**105608**	**48566**	**101458**
其中: 个人	Of the Total: to Individuals	7300		7300
住宅	Residence	54250	41950	54250
办公楼	Office Buildings	18090	1600	18090
商业营业用房	Buidings for Trade and Catering	20452	3000	16302
其他	Others	12816	2016	12816

4-27 房地产开发投资资金来源(2003年)

Source of Funds for Investment in Real Estate Development (2003)

单位：万元 (10 000 yuan)

指标	Item	全市合计 Total	国有 State-owned	市属 Municipal
一、本年资金来源合计	**Total**	**156053**	**399550**	**1408789**
1、上年末结余资金	Balance of Last Year	200570	60228	179530
2、本年资金来源小计	Total Funds This Year	1360083	339322	1229259
(1) 国家预算内资金	State Budgetary Funds	13350	3500	13350
(2) 国内贷款	Domestic Loans	437614	111301	394153
(3) 债券	Bonds			
(4) 利用外资	Utilization of Foreign Funds	3264		3264
其中：外商直接投资	Of the Total:Pirect Foreign Funds	3264		3264
对外借款	Loans from Overseas			
其中：统借统还	Of the Total:Unified Loans and Repayment			
(5) 自筹资金	Self-raised Funds	477869	106589	439358
(6) 其他资金	Others	427986	117932	379134
二、本年各项应付款合计	**Total Sums of Money to be Paid This Year**	**270721**	**35264**	**226386**
其中：工程款	Of the Total:Project Fund	202264	31488	170165
设备、器材款	Equipment and Appliance Fund	17638	2804	13528

4-28 房地产开发经营情况(2003年)

Running of Real Estate Development (2003)

单位：万元 (10 000 yuan)

指标	Item	全市合计 Total	国有 State-owned	市属 Municipal
一、实收资本合计	**Total Capital Hold**	**838855**	**217916**	**765889**
二、年末资产负债情况	**Assets and Liability at the Year-end**			
资产总计	Total Assets	3437859	1092690	3086335
固定资产累计折旧	Accumulative Depreciation of Fixed Assets	42486	13674	36380
负债总计	Total Liabilities	2603684	850537	2329369
所有者权益合计	Total Creditor's Equity	834175	242153	756966
三、损益情况	**Total Revenue**			
1.经营收入总计	Total Trade Revenue	488042	153655	423893
（1）土地转让收入	Revenue of Land Transferred	18114	17896	18114
（2）商品房屋销售收入	Revenue of Commercial Houses Sold	442271	120191	379123
其中：销售给个人	Of the Total: Sold to Residence	402464	116668	339316
商品住宅销售收入	Revenue of Commercial Residential Buildings Sold	368985	113850	319851
其中：销售给个人	Of the Total: Sold to Residence	353794	112859	304660
（3）房屋出租收入	Revenue of Houses Leased	3349	419	3104
（4）其他收入	Others	24308	15149	23552
2.经营成本	Business Cost	390736	112482	338730
3.销售费用	Sales Expenditures	27956	10778	24366
4.经营税金及附加	Business Tax and Extra Charge	22396	6156	18688
5.其他业务利润	Other Business Profit	2731	771	2745
6.管理费用及财务费用	Management and Fiscal Expenditures	67524	21405	59355
7.投资收益及营业外收入	Investment Revenue and Non-business Revenue	6391	5535	5359
8.营业外支出	Non-business Expenditures	2062	437	1599
9.利润总额	Total Profits	-13510	8703	-10741

4-29 主要年份房地产开发投资主要指标

单位：万元

指 标	Item	1997
本年完成投资额	Accomplished Investment This Year	246817
其中: 商品房建设投资额	Of the Total:Investments in Commercial Houses	158543
本年施工面积（平方米）	Floor Space of Buildings Under Construction This Year(sq.m)	4514661
其中：住宅	Of the Total:Residential Buildings	3311624
本年竣工面积（平方米）	Floor Space of Buildings Completed This Year(sq.m)	1356154
其中：住宅	Of the Total:Residential Buildings	1203270
竣工价值	Value of Floor Space of Buildings Completed	119557
其中：住宅	Of the Total:Residential Buildings	96347
商品房实际销售面积（平方米）	Floor Space of Commercial Houses sold(sq.m)	784514
其中：住宅	Of the Total:Residential Buildings	726872
商品房实际销售额	Total Sales of Commercial Houses	128058
其中：住宅	Of the Total:Residential Buildings	113917
商品房预售面积（平方米）	Floor Space of Commercial Houses Presold(sq.m)	263531
其中：住宅	Of the Total:Residential Buildings	232660
商品房空置面积（平方米）	Floor Space of Vacant Commercial Houses(sq.m)	587064
其中：住宅	Of the Total:Residential Buildings	502608
商品房出租面积（平方米）	Floor Space of Commercial Houses Recenting(sq.m)	256918
其中：住宅	Of the Total:Residential Buildings	228672
本年新增固定资产	Fixed Assets Added This Year	143616

Main Indicators of Investment in Real Estate Development in Representative Years

(10 000 yuan)

1998	1999	2000	2001	2002	2003
382142	442982	518460	674211	793689	1248177
292274	187767	238644	501776	583664	936450
6788737	7934602	7631791	7437846	11725803	13431222
5523667	6495345	6198502	5804332	9646770	9436123
1561710	3777862	3210975	3162449	3297069	3396721
1333330	3522764	2955463	2696055	2902965	2895565
143620	382245	269408	372040	369347	547322
109982	330190	229708	286154	304553	440117
1171051	2969705	2129156	2253468	2528958	2527368
1086108	2849545	2007741	1921961	2370397	2302824
177389	351861	325193	472204	513468	542851
154614	323482	294562	355310	454597	442468
2520176	302513	2530349	674407	610198	523516
2467716	273431	2530349	651990	557343	491159
325156	623796	364097	508233	571417	638528
228149	523181	240212	341836	446968	523449
10365	18780	11673	91889	157455	105608
120	1461	200	970	11326	54250
199261	430985	383811	507658	484349	621336

主要统计指标解释

全社会固定资产投资 即固定资产投资额是以货币表现的建造和购置固定资产活动的工作量，它是反映固定资产投资规模、速度、比例关系和使用方向的综合性指标。全社会固定资产投资按登记注册类型可分为国有、集体、个体、联营、股份制、外商、港澳台商、其他等。按照管理渠道，全社会固定资产投资总额分为基本建设、更新改造、房地产开发投资和其他固定资产投资四个部分。

基本建设投资 基本建设指企业、事业、行政单位以扩大生产能力或工程效益为主要目的的新建、扩建工程及有关活动。其综合范围为总投资50万元以上（含50万元，下同）的基本建设项目。

更新改造投资 更新改造指企业、事业单位对原有设施进行固定资产更新和技术改造，以及相应配套的工程和有关活动（不包括大修理和维护工程）。其综合范围为总投资50万元以上的更新改造项目。

房地产开发投资 指房地产开发公司、商品房建设公司及其他房地产开发法人单位和附属于其他法人单位实际从事房地产开发或经营的活动单位统一开发的包括统代建、拆迁还建的住宅、厂房、仓库、饭店、宾馆、度假村、写字楼、办公楼等房屋建筑物和配套的服务设施，土地开发工程（如道路、给水、排水、供电、供热、通讯、平整场地等基础设施工程）的投资;不包括单纯的土地交易活动。

其他固定资产投资 指全社会固定资产投资中未列入基本建设、更新改造和房地产开发投资的建造和购置固定资产的活动。

施工项目 指报告期内曾进行建筑或安装工程施工活动的建设项目，包括报告期内新开工项目、报告期以前开工跨入报告期继续施工的项目以及报告期施过工并在报告期内全部建成投产或停缓建的项目。

全部建成投产项目 工业项目是指设计文件规定形成生产能力的主体工程及其相应配套的辅助设施全部建成，经负荷试运转，证明具备生产设计规定合格产品的条件，并经过验收鉴定合格或达到竣工验收标准，与生产性工程配套的生活福利设施可以满足近期正常生产的需要，正式移交生产的建设项目。非工业项目是指设计文件规定的主体工程和相应的配套工程全部建成，能够发挥设计规定的全部效益，经验收鉴定合格或达到竣工验收标准，正式移交使用的建设项目。

新增生产能力 指通过固定资产投资活动而增加的设计能力或工程效益，它是用实物形态表示的固定资产投资的成果。新增生产能力的计算，是以能独立发挥生产能力或工程效益的单项工程（或项目）为对象。当单项工程（或项目）建成，经有关部门鉴定合格，正式移交投入生产，即可计算新增生产能力。

新增生产能力或工程效益有以下几种表现形式:

(1)以建设项目或单项工程建成后的年产能力表示，如煤炭开采、石油开采等。

(2)以建设项目或单项工程建成后处理原料的能力表示，如选矿工程的年处理矿石能力、洗煤厂年洗原煤能力等。

(3)以新增的主要设备数量或容量表示，如棉纺锭锭数、发电机组容量等。

(4)以建筑物容积、容量、面积或长度表示，如水库容量、铁路公路里程等。

新增生产能力的数量一般按设计能力计算。设计能力是指设计文件中规定的在正常情况下能够达到的生产能力，而不论投产后的实际产量如何。以设备数量、建筑物容积、面积、长度等表示的新增生产能力或工程效益，则按建成的实际数量计算。

房屋建筑面积 指从房屋外墙线算起的各层平面面积的总和，包括可供使用的有效面积和房屋结构（如柱、墙）占用的面积。多层建筑按各层（包括地下室）面积总和计算。

住宅建筑面积 指施工和竣工房屋建筑面积中供居住用的施工和竣工房屋建筑面积。

施工面积 指报告期内施工的全部房屋建筑面积。包括本期新开工的面积、上期跨入本期继续施工的房屋面积、上期停缓建在本期恢复施工的房屋面积、本期竣工的房屋面积及本期施工后又停缓建的房屋面积。

竣工面积 指在报告期内房屋建筑按照设计要求已全部完工，达到住人和使用条件，经验收鉴定合格，正式移交使用单位的建筑面积。

房屋建筑面积竣工率 指一定时期内房屋竣工面积占同期房屋施工面积的比率。它是从房屋建筑施工速度的角度反映投资效果和建筑业经济效益的指标。

新增固定资产 指通过投资活动所形成的新的固定资产价值，包括已经建成投入生产或交付使用的工程价值和达到固定资产标准的设备、工具、器具的价值及有关应摊入的费用。它是以价值形式表示的固定资产投资成果的综合性指标，可以综合反映不同时期、不同部门、不同地区的固定资产投资成果。

建设项目投产率 指一定时期内全部建成投入生产项目个数与同期正式施工项目个数的比率。它是从项目建设速度的角度反映投资效果的指标。

固定资产交付使用率 指一定时期新增固定资产与同期完成投资额的比率。它是反映各个时期固定资产动用速度，衡量建设过程中投资效果的一个综合性指标。

Explanatory Notes on Main Statistical Indicators

Total Investment in Fixed Assets in the Whole Country Total investment in fixed assets refers to the volume of activities in construction and purchases of fixed assets in monetary terms. It is a comprehensive indicator which shows the size, pace, proportional relations and use orientation of the investment in fixed assets. Total investment in fixed assets in the whole country includes, by registration type of ownership, the investment by the state-owned units, collective units, individuals, joint ownership units, share-holding units, as well as investment by businessmen from foreign countries and from Hong Kong, Macau and Taiwan, and by other units. According to China's current management system, the investment in fixed assets in the whole country is classified into the following four parts: investment in capital construction, investment in innovation, investment in real estates development and other investment in fixed assets.

Investment in Capital Construction Capital construction refers to the new construction projects or extension projects and the related activities of the enterprises, institutions or administrative units mainly for the purpose of expanding production capacity or improving project efficiency covering only projects each with a total investment of 500,000 RMB yuan and over.

Investment in Innovation Innovation refers to the renewal of fixed assets and technological innovation of the original facilities by the enterprises and institutions as well as the corresponding supplementary projects and the related activities (excluding major overhaul and maintenance projects) covering only projects each with a total investment of 500,000 RMB yuan and over.

Investment in Real Estate Development It includes the investment by the real estate development companies, commercial buildings construction companies and other real estate development units of various types of ownership in the construction of house buildings, such as residential buildings, factory buildings, warehouses, hotels, guesthouses, holiday villages, office buildings, and the complementary service facilities and land development projects, such as roads, water supply, water drainage, power supply, heating, telecommunications, land leveling and other projects of infrastructure. It excludes the activities in simple land transactions.

Other Investment in Fixed Assets refers to the construction and purchases of fixed assets not listed in the investment in capital construction, investment in innovation and investment in real estate development.

Projects under Construction refer to projects having construction and installation activities undertaken in the reference period, including projects started in the reference period, or continued from the previous period, or completed and put into production or suspended in the reference period.

Projects Completed and Put into Use Industrial projects refer to the major projects and accessory facilities completed which result in forming production capacity and have been checked and accepted while the living and welfare facilities have been completed and can ensure normal production and formally put into production. Non-industrial projects refer to the major projects and accessory facilities completed which possess the designed capacity and have been checked, accepted and formally put into production.

Newly Increased Production Capacity refers to the increase of designed capacity and project efficiency through investment in fixed assets, which reflects the accomplishment of investment in fixed assets in kind. The calculation of newly increased production capacity is based on individual project which operates independently and efficiently. When an individual project is completed and checked and accepted and put into production, it is counted as newly increased production capacity.

The newly increased production capacity and project efficiency are usually expressed in one of the following forms:

(1)annual production capacity, such as extraction of coal and petroleum;

(2)raw material processing capacity, such as ore dressing capacity of ore dressing projects, the dressing capacity of a coal washery;

(3)number or capacity of major equipment increased, such as the number of cotton spindles increased and the capacity of generating sets increased;

(4)physical measures of construction, such as volume, capacity, area, and length, for instance, the capacity of reservoirs, the length of railways or highways.

Newly increased production capacity in terms of quantity is calculated in designed capacity in general, which refers to the production capacity of a project under normal conditions designed in construction documents regardless of the actual output.

Floor Space of Buildings under Construction andCompleted refers to total floor space in each story of buildings calculated from the outside line of building walls, including both usable space and the space occupied by constructions like pillars or walls. The floor space of multi-story buildings includes the total floor space of each story (including basement).

Floor Space of Residential Buildings refers to the floor space of the residential buildings under construction and completed among the total space of buildings under construction and completed.

Floor Space under Construction refers to total floor space of all buildings under construction during the reference period, including floor space of newly started buildings during the reference period, floor space of construction extended from the previous period to the current period, floor space of construction suspended during the previous period and resumed in the current period, floor space of construction completed in the current period, and floor space of construction started and then suspended in the current period.

Floor Space of Buildings Completed refers to the floor space of buildings completed in the reference period, which have come up to the designed standards and have been put into use.

Completion Rate of Floor Space of Buildings refers to the ratio of the floor space of buildings completed in certain period of time to the floor space of buildings under construction in the same period which reflects the investment result and economic efficiency of the construction industry from the angle of the speed of project construction.

Newly Increased Fixed Assets refer to the newly increased value of fixed assets through investment, including the value of projects completed and put into production, the value of equipment, tools, and vessels considered as fixed assets, as well as the relevant expenses as investment in fixed assets. This is a comprehensive indicator of investment in fixed assets, reflecting the achievements of investment in fixed assets in different periods, different sectors, and different regions.

Rate of Construction Projects Completed and Put into Use refers to the ratio of the number of construction projects completed and put into use in certain period of time to the number of projects under construction in the same period. This reflects the investment efficiency from the angle of the speed of projects construction.

Rate of Projects of Fixed Assets Completed and Put into Operation refers to the ratio of the newly increased fixed assets to the total investment made in the same period. This is a comprehensive indicator, reflecting the speed of the employment of fixed assets and the investment efficiency.

五、财 政

GOVERNMENT FINANCE

简 要 说 明

Brief Introduction

本章内容主要包括我市地方财政收入、支出情况以及分区县地方财政收入和支出情况。

本资料由市统计局综合处根据市财政局提供资料整理。

This chapter consists primarily of data on regional revenue, expenditure of the municipal government, regional revenue and expenditure of the districts and the counties. The data are provided by the Xi'an Bureau of Finance and are compiled by Integration division of the Xi'an Bureau of Statistics.

5-1 地方财政收入

Local Government Revenue

单位：万元 （10 000 yuan）

指 标	Item	2003
合 计	**Total**	**728670**
一、基金预算	**Fund Budgetary**	**80633**
二、一般预算	**Ordinary Budgetary**	**648037**
1、增值税	Value Added Tax	105138
2、营业税	Business Tax	231348
3、企业所得税	Enterprise Income Tax	35796
4、企业所得税退税	Return for Enterprises'Income Tax	
5、个人所得税	Individual Income Tax	21526
6、资源税	Resources Tax	170
7、固定资产投资方向调节税	Tax on Adjustment of the Orientation of Investment in Fixed Assets	214
8、城市维护建设税	Tax on City Construction and Maintenance	43361
9、房产税	Tax on Real Estates	34591
10、印花税	Stamp Tax	7844
11、城镇土地使用税	Tax on Use of Urban Land	11621
12、土地增值税	Land Value Added Tax	621
13、车船使用和牌照税	Tax on the Use of Vehicles and Ships	1902
14、屠宰税	Slaughter Tax	
15、筵席税	Banquet Tax	
16、农业税	Agriculture Tax	12788
17、农业特产税	Tax on Special Agricultural Products	
18、牧业税	Tax on the Animal Husbandry	
19、耕地占用税	Tax on the Occupancy of Cultivated Land	7670
20、契税	Contract Tax	18166
21、国有资产经营收益	State-downed Assets Profit	10846
22、国有企业计划亏损补	Subsidies to Loss-suffering State-owned Enterprises	-3105
23、行政性收费收入	Income from Adiministrative Fees	48468
24、罚没收入	Penalty and confiscatory income	28945
25、海域场地矿区使用费收入	Sea mining area rental	39
26、专项收入	Special Revenue	25555
27、其他收入	Other Revenue	4533

5-2 地方财政支出

Local Government Expenditures

单位:万元 (10 000 yuan)

指　　标	Item	2003
合　计	**Total**	**772529**
一、基金预算	**Fund Budgetary**	**48806**
二、一般预算	**Ordinary Budgetary**	**723723**
1.基本建设支出	Expenditure for Capital Construction	38205
2.企业挖潜改造资金	Expenditure for Innovation Enterprises	49654
3.地质勘探费	Expenditure for Geological Prospecting	
4.科技三项费用	Expenditure for Science and Technology Promotion	8020
5.农业 支出	Agriculture expenditure	12505
6.林业支出	Forestry expenditure	4465
7.水利和气象支出	Water conservancy and weather expenditure	7006
8.工业交通等部门的事业费	Expenditure for Operating Expenses of Departments of Industry $ Transportation	9303
9.流通部门事业费	Expenditure for Operating Expenses of Department of Commerce	1611
10.文体广播事业费	Expenditure for Operating Expenses of Culture,Sport& Broadcasting	17206
11.教育支出	Expenditure for Operating Expenses of Education	102179
12.科学支出	Expenditure for Operating Expenses of Department of Science	1479
13.医疗卫生支出	Medical treatment and health expenditure	39204
14.其他部门的事业费	Operational expenses of other department	58985
15.抚恤和社会福利救济费	Expenditure for Pensions and Relief Funds for Social Welfare	26246
16.行政事业单位离退休支出	Expenditure for Operating Expenses of Administrative Department	50391
17.社会保障补助支出	Expenditure on Subsidies to Social Security Programs	4615
18.国防支出	National defense expenditure	40
19.行政管理费	Expenditure for Government Administration	84954
20.外交外事支出	Expenditure for Foreign Affairs	
21.武装警察部队支出	Armed police expenditure	291
22.公检法司支出	Public security organs, procuratorial organs, people`s courts and judicial organs expenditure	81168
23.城市维护费	Expenditure for City Maintenance	79004
24.政策性补贴支出	Expenditure for Price Subsidies	4739
25.支援不发达地区支出	Expenditure for Supporting Underdeveloped Regions	2120
26.海域开发建设和场地使用支出	Expenditure for Developing Land and Sea Area	8
27.债务利息支出	Debt interest expenditure	
28.专项支出	Special Expenditure	22238
29.其他支出	Other Expenditure	18087

5-3 分区县地方财政收入(2003年)

单位：万元

区 县	Region	收入合计 Total Revenue	基金预算 Fund Budgetary	一般预算 Ordinary Budgetary	增值税 Value Added Tax
合 计	**Total**	**728670**	**80633**	**648037**	**105138**
市级合计	**Sum of city level**	**383431**	**72429**	**311002**	**75390**
市本级	**City level**	**291308**	**67938**	**223370**	**54682**
高新区	**High-tech zone**	**72792**	**4491**	**68301**	**15761**
经开区	**Economic exploited area**	**19331**		**19331**	**4947**
区、县合计	Region	345239	8204	337035	29748
新城区	Xincheng	53980		53980	3224
碑林区	Beilin	60148		60148	3288
莲湖区	Lianhu	63678	5	63673	5471
雁塔区	Yanta	38208	64	38144	2112
灞桥区	Baqiao	18585	189	18396	1277
未央区	Weiyang	23008		23008	2801
闫良区	Yanliang	13550	450	13100	1964
临潼区	Lintong	16056	1727	14329	3981
长安区	Chang'an	23695	2564	21131	1448
蓝田县	Lantian	8367	827	7540	330
周至县	Zhouzhi	6516	1029	5487	320
户 县	Huxian	12377	426	11951	2561
高陵县	Gaoling	7071	923	6148	971

Financial Revenue of Local Government by Region（2003）

（10 000 yuan）

营业税 Business Tax	企业所得税 Corporation income tax	个人所得税 Individual income tax	城市维护建设税 City maintenance and building tax	房产税 House property tax	城镇土地使用税 Town area rental
231348	**35796**	**21526**	**43361**	**34591**	**11621**
91548	**21735**	**13253**	**11019**	**11258**	**2840**
55067	**15646**	**11188**	**3457**	**7573**	**1009**
28629	**5333**	**1602**	**6231**	**2925**	**1116**
7852	**756**	**463**	**1331**	**760**	**715**
139800	14061	8273	32342	23333	8781
22955	3735	2117	6091	4650	1235
31315	3206	1966	4947	6412	888
23950	3446	1594	7868	4839	2186
16659	901	1002	3306	2651	910
8813	300	252	1749	786	727
7066	829	438	3347	1053	1115
2683	554	245	1394	1301	702
3727	448	209	1943	607	346
11926	173	155	535	195	144
3221	22	38	148	143	32
1756	15	20	140	84	37
3778	185	193	622	420	267
1951	247	44	252	192	192

5-4 分区县地方财政支出(2003年)

单位:万元

区县	Region	合计 Total	基金预算 Fund Budyetary	一般预算 Ordinary Budgetary	基本建设 Expenditure for Capital Construction
合计	**Total**	**772529**	**48806**	**723723**	**38205**
市级合计	**Sum of city level**	**431266**	**45389**	**385877**	**35173**
市本级	**City level**	**379541**	**43157**	**336384**	**35173**
高新区	**High-tech zone**	**42287**	**2232**	**40055**	
经开区	**Economic exploited area**	**9438**		**9438**	
区、县合计	Region	341263	3417	337846	3032
新城区	Xincheng	32951		32951	
碑林区	Beilin	38180		38180	3026
莲湖区	Lianhu	37434	5	37429	
雁塔区	Yanta	31497	85	31412	
灞桥区	Baqiao	22578	189	22389	
未央区	Weiyang	26668	73	26595	
阎良区	Yanliang	16378	450	15928	
临潼区	Lintong	24729	28	24701	2
长安区	Chang'an	35873	80	35793	
蓝田县	Lantian	20195	940	19255	
周至县	Zhouzhi	19761	960	18801	
户　县	Huxian	21602	140	21462	2
高陵县	Gaoling	13417	467	12950	2

Financial Expenditures of Local Government by Region (2003)

(10 000 Yuan)

企业挖潜改造支出 Enterprise potentialities Transformation expenditure	科技三项费用 Three-item fee of science and technology	农业支出 Agriculture expenditure	教育支出 Education expenditure	科技支出 Scientific and technological expenditure	社会保障补助支出 Social insurance insurance	行政管理费 Subsidy expenditure
49654	**8020**	**12505**	**102179**	**1479**	**4615**	**84954**
47939	**6338**	**4921**	**9628**	**1268**	**2200**	**30898**
17576	**4000**	**4921**	**9426**	**1268**	**2121**	**26464**
25284	**2338**		**202**		**67**	**2014**
5079					**12**	**2420**
1715	1682	7584	92551	211	2415	54056
150	300	10	5072	8	113	4122
242	300		6698	8	323	6811
120	145	1	6969	3	102	5746
	250	1657	6239	23	55	4434
51	101	477	7451	5	45	2996
	156	700	6475	28	51	3742
	134	658	3942	7	137	2773
10	46	650	10628	7	700	4339
143	5	1135	12785	17	479	5470
	78	556	7157	3	45	3067
	2	597	7544	6	24	3831
136	150	755	7886	28	41	3188
863	15	388	3705	68	300	3537

主要统计指标解释

财政收入 指国家财政参与社会产品分配所取得的收入，是实现国家职能的财力保证。财政收入所包括的内容几经变化，目前主要包括:

（1）各项税收:包括增值税、营业税、消费税、土地增值税、城市维护建设税、资源税、城市土地使用税、印花税、个人所得税、企业所得税、关税、农牧业税和耕地占用税等。

（2）专项收入:包括征收排污费收入、征收城市水资源费收入、教育费附加收入等。

（3）其他收入:包括基本建设贷款归还收入、基本建设收入、捐赠收入等。

（4）国有企业亏损补贴:这项为负收入，冲减财政收入。

财政支出 国家财政将筹集起来的资金进行分配使用，以满足经济建设和各项事业的需要，主要包括:

（1）基本建设支出:指按国家有关规定，属于基本建设范围内的基本建设有偿使用、拨款、资本金支出以及经国家批准对专项和政策性基建投资贷款，在部门的基建投资额中统筹支付的贴息支出。

（2）企业挖潜改造资金:指国家预算内拨给的用于企业挖潜、革新和改造方面的资金。包括各部门企业挖潜改造资金和企业挖潜改造贷款资金，为农业服务的县办“五小”企业技术改造补助，挖潜改造贷款利息支出。

（3）地质勘探费用:指国家预算用于地质勘探单位的勘探工作费用，包括地质勘探管理机构及其事业单位经费、地质勘探经费。

（4）科技三项费用:指国家预算用于科技支出的费用，包括新产品试制费、中间试验费、重要科学研究补助费。

（5）支援农村生产支出:指国家财政支援农村集体（户）各项生产的支出。包括对农村举办的小型农田水利和打井、喷灌等的补助费，对农村水土保持措施的补助费，对农村举办的小水电站的补助费，特大抗旱的补助费，农村开荒补助费，扶持乡镇企业资金，农村农技推广和植保补助费，农村草场和畜禽保护补助费，农村造林和林木保护补助费，农村水产补助费，发展粮食生产专项资金。

（6）农林水利气象等部门的事业费用:指国家财政用于农垦、农场、农业、畜牧、农机、林业、森工、水利、水产、气象、乡镇企业的技术推广、良种推广（示范）、动植物（畜禽、森林）保护、水质监测、勘探设计、资源调查、干部训练等项费用，园艺特产场补助费，中等专业学校经费，飞播牧草试验补助费，营林机构、气象机构经费，渔政费以及农业管理事业费等。

（7）工业交通商业等部门的事业费:指国家预算支付给工交商各部门用于事业发展的经费，包括勘探设计费、中等专业学校经费、技术学校经费、干部训练费。

（8）文教科学卫生事业费:指国家预算用于文化、出版、文物、教育、卫生、中医、公费医疗、体育、档案、地震、海洋、通讯、电影电视、计划生育、党政群干部训练、自然科学、社会科学、科协等项事业的经费支出和高技术研究专项经费。主要包括工资、补助工资、福利费、离退休费、助学金、公务费、设备购置费、修缮费、业务费、差额补助费。

（9）抚恤和社会福利救济费:指国家预算用于抚恤和社会福利救济事业的经费。包括由民政部门开支的烈士家属和牺牲病残人员家属的一次性、定期抚恤金，革命伤残人员的抚恤金，各种伤残补助费，烈军属、复员退伍军人生活补助费，退伍军人安置费，优抚事业单位经费，烈士纪念建筑物管理、维修费，自然灾害救济事业费和特大自然灾害灾后重建补助费等。

（10）国防支出:指国家预算用于国防建设和保卫国家安全的支出，包括国防费、国防科研事业费、民兵建设以及专项工程支出等。

（11）行政管理费:包括行政管理支出，党派团体补助支出，外交支出，公安安全支出，司法支出，法院支出，检察院支出和公检法办案费用补助。

（12）价格补贴支出:指经国家批准，由国家财政拨给的政策性补贴支出。主要包括粮食加价款，粮、棉、油差价补贴，棉花收购价外奖励款，副食品风险基金，市镇居民的肉食价格补贴，平抑市价肉食、蔬菜差价补贴等以及经国家批准的教材课本、报刊新闻纸等价格补贴。

中央财政收入和地方财政收入 指按财政体制划分的中央本级收入和地方本级收入。1994年分税制财政体制以后，属于中央财政的收入包括关税、海关代征消费税和增值税，消费税，中央企业所得税，地方银行和外资银行及非银行金融企业所得税，铁道、银行总行、保险总公司等集中缴纳的营业税、所得税、利润和城市维护建设税，增值税的75%部分，证券交易税（印花税）50%部分和海洋石油资源税。属于地方财政的收入包括营业税，地方企业所得税，个人所得税，城镇土地使用税，固定资产投资方向调节税，城镇维护建设税，房产税，车船使用税，印花税，屠宰税，农牧业税，农业特产税，耕地占用税，契税，增值税25%部分，证券交易税（印花税）50%部分和除海洋石油资源税以外的其他资源税。

中央财政支出和地方财政支出 指根据政府在经济和社会活动中的不同职责，划分中央和地方政府的责权，按照政府的责权划分确定的支出。中央财政支出包括国防支出，武装警察部队支出，中央级行政管理费和各项事业费，重点建设支出以及中央政府调整国民经济结构、协调地区发展、实施宏观调控的支出。地方财政支出主要包括地方行政管理和各项事业费，地方统筹的基本建设、技术改造支出，支援农村生产支出，城市维护和建设经费，价格补贴支出等。

Explanatory Notes on Main Statistical Indicators

Government Revenue refers to the revenue of the government finance by means of participating in the distribution of the social products, which is the financial resources for ensuring the government to function. The contents of government revenue have been changed several times. Now it includes the following main items:

(1) Various tax revenues, including value added tax, business tax, consumption tax, land value added tax, tax on city maintenance and construction, resources tax, tax on use of urban land, stamp tax, personal income tax, enterprise income tax, tariff, tax on agriculture and animal husbandry and tax on occupancy of cultivated land, etc.

(2) Special revenues, including revenue collected from imposing fee on sewage treatment, revenue collected from imposing fee on urban water resources, and extra-charges for education, etc.

(3) Other revenues, including revenue from the repayment of capital construction loan, revenue from capital construction projects, and donations and grants.

(4) Planned subsidies for the losses of the state-owned enterprises. This is an item of negative revenue, used to eat up part of the government revenue.

Government Expenditure refers to the distribution and use of the funds the government finance has raised, so as to meet the needs of economic construction and various causes. It includes the following main items:

(1) Expenditure for capital construction: It refers to the non-gratuitous use and appropriation of funds for capital construction in the range of capital construction, outlay of capital as well as the loans on capital construction approved by the government for special purpose or policy purpose and the expenditure with discount paid in an overall way within the amount of the funds appropriated to the departments for capital construction.

(2) Innovation funds of the enterprises: They refer to the funds appropriated from the government budget for the enterprises to tap the latent power, upgrade the technology and carry out innovation, including the innovation fund of the departments, loan of the enterprises for innovation, subsidies on the innovation of the small fertilizer plant, small cement plant, small coal mines, small machinery plant and small steel plant, the expenditure of interest for the loan for innovation.

(3) Geological prospecting expenses: They refer to the expenses appropriated from the government budget to the geological prospecting units for the expenditure of the prospecting work, including the expenditures of the administrative agencies for geological prospecting and their institutional units as well as the geological prospecting expenditure.

(4) expenditures for science and technology promotion: They refer to the expenses appropriated from the government budget for the scientific and technological expenditure, including new products development expenditure, expenditure for intermediate trial and subsidies on important scientific researches.

(5) Expenditure for supporting rural production: It refers to the expenditures appropriated from the government budget for supporting the various expenditures of the rural collective units or households for production, including the subsidies to the small water conservancy projects and well drilling, sprinkling irrigation projects run by the villages; subsidies on the rural water and soil conserving measures; subsidies to the small power stations run by the villages; subsidies to the expenditure for fighting against particularly severe draughts; subsidies on the rural waste land exclamation; fund for supporting the township enterprises; subsidies to the expenditure for popularization of the agricultural technologies and plant protection in the rural areas; subsidies to the expenditure for the protection of grasslands and cattle and fowls; subsidies on afforestation and forest protection in rural areas; subsidies on the rural aquatic products industry; special fund for developing grain production.

(6) Operating expenses of the departments of farming, forestry, water conservancy and meteorology etc.: They refer to the expenses appropriated from the government budget for the expenditures of agricultural exclamation, farms, agriculture, animal husbandry, agricultural machinery, forestry, timber industry, water conservancy, aquatic products industry, meteorology, technology popularization in township enterprises, popularization (demonstration) of improved varieties, plant (cattle and fowls, forest) protection, water quality monitoring, prospecting and designing, resources investigation, cadres training, subsidies to horticulture gardens, expenditure of specialized secondary schools, subsidies on the experiments of sowing herbage seeds by flights, expenditures of afforestation agencies and meteorology agencies, expenses for fishery administration and operating expenses for agricultural administration, etc.

(7) Operating expenses of the departments of industry,

Transport and commerce: They refer to the expenses appropriated from the government budget to the departments of industry, transport and commerce for the expenditure of business development, including expenses for prospecting and designing, expenditures of specialized secondary schools, expenditures of the technical training schools and expenditures for cadres training, etc.

(8) Operating expenses of the departments of culture, education, science and public health: They refer to the expenses appropriated from the government budget for the expenditures of the causes of culture, publication, cultural relics, education, public health, traditional Chinese medical science, free medical services, sports, archives, earthquake, ocean, communications, broadcasting, film and television, family planning; expenditure for training of cadres of government, party and mass organization; expenditures for natural sciences, social sciences, associations for science and technology and the special expenditure for the high-tech researches. They include mainly wages, extra wages, welfare funds, pension for the retirees, stipend, expenses for official business, expenses for equipment purchases, expenses for repairs, business expenses and subsidies to the units which are unable to support their expenditures by their own earnings.

(9) Pension for the disabled or for the families of the bereaved and relief funds for social welfare: They refer to the funds appropriated from the government budget for the expenditures of pension for the disabled or for the families of the bereaved and relief funds for social welfare, including the lump-sum or regular pension paid by the departments of civil affairs to the members of martyrs families and families of those who died for the public interest, pension to the revolutionary disabled, subsidies for permanent disability of various kinds, subsidies to the military martyrs dependents and the demobilized servicemen, expenditure for settling down the demobilized servicemen, operating expenses of the consoling institutions, expenses for management and repair of the commemorative buildings for the martyrs, the expenses managed by the departments of civil affairs for the retirees and those who have quitted their work, expenses for social relief in rural and urban areas, operating expenses for providing relief to the areas of natural calamity and subsidies on the reconstruction after the particularly severe natural calamities, etc.

(10) Expenditures for national defence: They refer to the funds appropriated from the government budget for the expenditures for building up national defence and safeguarding national security, including expenses of national defence, expenses of scientific researches on national defence, expenses for building up peoples militia and expenditure for special projects, etc.

(11) Administrative expenses: They include expenditure for administration, subsidies to the parties and mass organizations, diplomatic expenditure, expenditure for public security, judicial expenditure, law court expenditure, procuratorial expenditure and subsidies to the expenses for treating the cases by the public security departments, procuratorial organs and law courts.

(12) Expenditure for price subsidies: It refers to the expenditure appropriated, with the approval of the government, from the government budget for the policy subsidies to price adjustment, including the fund for the increase of grain prices, the subsidies to the difference between the selling prices and purchasing prices of grains, cotton and edible oil, awards in addition to the purchasing prices of cotton, risk fund for non-staple food, subsidies on the prices of meat and meat products, subsidies on the price difference for curbing the high market prices of meat, meat products and vegetables and the subsidies approved by the government on the prices of textbooks and newsprint of newspapers and periodicals.

Revenue of the central government and revenue of the local governments: In accordance with the classification of the structure of the government finance in 1994 on the basis of the classification of channels for collection of tax revenues, the revenue of the central government and the revenue of the local governments have different coverage. The revenue of the central government includes tariff, consumption tax and value added tax levied by the customs, consumption tax, income tax of the enterprises subordinate to the central government, income taxes of the local banks, foreign-funded banks and non-bank financial institutions, business tax, income tax and profits of railways, head offices of banks, head office of insurance company , which are handed over to the government in a centralized way, tax on city maintenance and construction, 75% of the value added tax, tax on ocean petroleum resources, 50% of the tax on stock dealing (stamp tax). The revenue of the local governments includes business tax, income tax of the enterprises subordinate to the local government, personal income tax, tax on the use of urban land, tax on the adjustment of the investment in fixed assets, tax on town maintenance and construction, tax on real estates, tax on the use of vehicles and ships, stamp tax, slaughter tax, tax on agriculture and animalhusbandry, tax on special agricultural products, tax on the occupancy of cultivated land, contract tax, 25% of the husbandry, tax on special agricultural products, tax on the occupancy of cultivated land, contract tax, 25% of the value added tax, 50% of the tax on stock dealing (stamp tax) and tax on resources other than the ocean petroleum resources.

Expenditure of the central government and expenditure of the local governments: according to the different functions of the central government and local governments in the economic and social activities, the rights of affairs administration are classified between the central government and local governments; and the classification of the expenditure between the central government and local governments are made on the basis of the classification of the rights of affairs administration between them. The expenditure of the central government includes the expenditure for national defence, expenditure for armed police forces, the administrative expenses and various operating expenses at the level of central government, expenditure for key projects and the expenditure of the central government for adjusting the national economic structure, coordinating the development among different regions and exercising the macro-economic regulation and control. The expenditure of the local governments includes mainly the administrative expenses and various operating expenses at the level of local governments, the expenditure for capital construction and technological innovation with the funds raised by the local government, expenditure for supporting rural production, expenditure for city maintenance and construction and expenditure for price subsidies, etc.

Extra-budgetary revenue and expenditure Extra-budgetary fund refers to financial fund of various types not covered by the regular government budgetary management, which is collected, allocated or arranged by government agencies, institutions and social organizations while performing duties delegated to them or on behalf of the government in accordance with laws, rules and regulations. It mainly covers following items: administrative and institutional fees, funds and extra charges that are stipulated by laws and regulations; administrative and institutional fees approved by the State Council and provincial governments and their financial and planning (price management) departments; funds and extra charges established by the State Council and the Ministry of Finance; funds turned over to competent departments by their subordinate institutions; self-raised and collected funds by township governments for their own expenditure; and other financial funds that are not covered in budgetary management. Social security funds are treated as extra-budget fund and managed for its exclusive use, given the circumstance that separate government budgetary system for social security is yet to be designed. Special accounts are opened by the financial departments in banks for the management of revenue and expenditure of extra-budgetary fund. Extra-budgetary revenue and expenditure is managed separately, namely, revenue of institutions and departments must enter into the special accounts of the financial departments at the same administrative level, and their extra-budgetary expenditure is arranged in line with the extra-budget plans and appropriated from these accounts.

六、物价指数

PRICE INDICES

简 要 说 明

Brief Introduction

本资料主要包括居民消费、零售、集贸市场农产品成交、工业产品出厂、主要原材料购进、土地交易、房地产销售、租赁以及固定资产投资和建筑安装工程等价格指数。

本资料由市城市社会经济调查队整理提供。

This chapter consists primarily of data on price indices of residents consumption, retail, country fair farm products deal, industrial products dispatching sales, primary raw material purchasing, land deal, real estate selling, leasing, fixed asset investment and construction installation projects. The data classified Data of the districts and the counties on real estate development investment, provided by Fixed Asset Investment Division of the Xi'an Bureau of Statistics.

6-1 各种价格指数(以上年价格为100)

Price Indices(the price of preceding year=100)

年份 Year	商品零售价格总指数 Retail Price Index	居民消费价格总指数 Consumer Price Index	农副产品收购价格总指数 Purchasing price index of agricultural and sideline products	集贸市场农产品成交价格总指数 Farm Productes Purchasing Price Index
1980	109.3	108.7		
1981	102.7	102.4		
1982	101.0	100.9		
1983	102.0	102.6	104.3	110.5
1984	104.8	104.7	104.6	106.7
1985	109.3	109.7	106.3	116.0
1986	107.4	108.5	104.9	108.7
1987	111.4	110.6	120.4	117.5
1988	123.2	122.8		123.3
1989	117.8	118.3	117.9	112.0
1990	100.9	102.5	97.6	99.6
1991	108.3	109.4	101.8	101.7
1992	112.4	112.2	106.8	107.6
1993	112.8	117.2	110.2	104.0
1994	126.2	128.5	146.2	130.4
1995	114.6	117.0	129.0	115.4
1996	107.9	110.9	106.6	110.4
1997	101.5	106.0	96.5	94.1
1998	95.5	97.9	92.4	88.5
1999	97.4	96.8	94.7	93.9
2000	98.7	100.2	97.7	93.2
2001	98.9	99.9	100.8	96.6
2002	98.5	98.6		97.4
2003	100.0	100.5		

6-2 居民消费价格指数(2003年)

Residents Consumer Price Indices(2003)

(以上年价格为100)　　(the price of Preceding year=100)

类　　别	Item	2003年
居民消费价格总指数	**General Residents Consumer Price Index**	**100.5**
非食品价格指数	Non-foodstuff Price Index	98.4
服务项目价格指数	Price Index of Service	98.4
扣除鲜菜鲜果总指数	Price Index With Fresh Vegetables and Fruits Excluded	99.4
消费品价格指数	Price Index of Consumer Goods	101.2
一、食　　品	**Food**	**104.6**
1.粮　食	Grain	104.8
2.淀粉及薯类	Starches and Its Products	102.3
3.干豆类及豆制品	Bean and Its Products	106.2
4.油　脂	Oil or Fat	112.7
5.肉禽及其制品	Meat,Poultry and Their Products	103.1
6.蛋	Eggs	98.0
7.水产品	Aquatic Products	100.8
8.菜	Vegetables	135.9
9.调味品	Fresh Vegetables	98.6
10.糖	Carbohydrate	102.0
11.茶及饮料	Tea and Beverage	102.4
12.干鲜瓜果	Dried and Fresh Melons and Fruits	96.9
13.糕点饼干面包	Cake,Biscuit and Bread	99.2
14.奶及奶制品	Milk and Its Products	100.2
15.在外用膳食品	Foods Consumed not at Home	99.9
16.其它食品及食品加工服务	Other Food and Foods Processing	97.5
二、烟酒及用品	**Cigarette and Related Articles**	**99.5**
1.烟　草	Cigarette	99.4
2.酒	Liquor and Wine	100.3
3.吸烟饮酒用品	Articles for Smoking and Drinking	97.9
三、衣　　着	**Clothing**	**99.0**
1.服　装	Garments	96.6
2.衣着材料	Clothing Material	99.8
3.鞋袜帽	Footwear and Hats	104.2
4.衣着加工服务	Tailoring Service	100.0
四、家庭设备用品及维修服务	**Household facility and their maintaining service**	**96.7**
1.耐用消费品	Durable consumer goods	94.4

6-2 居民消费价格指数(2003年)(续)

Residents Consumer Price Indices(2003) (Continued)

(以上年价格为100)　　　　(the price of Preceding year=100)

类　　别	Item	2003年
2.室内装饰品	Interior Decorations	97.6
3.床上用品	Bed Articles	100.2
4.家庭日用杂品	Daily Use Household Articles	99.6
5.家庭服务及加工维修服务	Household Service and Maintenance	100.3
五、医疗保健和个人用品	**Medical Service and Personal Articles**	**97.6**
1.医疗保健	Medical and Health Service	96.6
(1)医疗器具及用品	Medical Articles	105.5
(2)中药材及中成药	Traditional Chinese Medicine	101.7
(3)西药	Western Medicine	83.3
(4)保健器具及用品	Health Care Appliances and Articine	96.8
(5)医疗保健服务	Health Care Services	115.9
2.个人用品及服务	Personal Articles and Services	102.3
六、交通和通讯	**Transportation and Communication**	**93.9**
1.交　通	Transportation	99.3
(1)交通工具	Transportation Facility	99.2
(2)车用燃料及零配件	Fuels and Parts	103.6
(3)车辆使用及维修	Using and Upkeeping Fare	98.9
(4)市区公共交通	Incity Traffic Fare	99.2
(5)城市间交通	Intercity Traffic Fare	98.8
2.通　信	Communication	90.8
(1)通信工具	Telecommunication Facility	74.1
(2)通信服务	Telecommunication Service	92.6
七、娱乐教育文化用品及服务	**Recreation,Education and Cultural Goods and Service**	**96.9**
1.文娱用耐用消费品及服务	Durable Consumer Goods and Service on Cultural Recreation	90.8
2.教　育	Education	99.4
3.文化娱乐用品	Cultural and Recreational Articles	102.1
4.旅游及外出	Tourism and Travel	87.9
八、居　　住	**Residence**	**104.0**
1.建房及装修材料	Household Construction and Upholstering	99.9
2.房　租	House Rent	100.0
3.自有住房	Own Residence	98.3
4.水、电、燃料	Water, electricity and fuel	109.4

6-3 商品零售价格指数(2003年)

Retail Price Indices(2003)

(以上年价格为100) (the price of Preceding year=100)

类 别	Item	2003年
商品零售价格总指数	**Total Index**	**100.0**
一、食品类	**Food**	**104.7**
1.粮 食	Grain	104.7
2.淀粉及薯类	Flour and Rice	102.3
3.干豆类及豆制品	Coarse Food Grain	106.3
4.油 脂	Oil or Fat	111.6
5.肉禽及其制品	Meat,Poultry and Eggs	103.1
6.蛋	Aquatic Products	98.1
7.水产品	Fresh Vegetables	100.0
8.菜	Dried Vegetables	132.5
9.调味品	Fresh Fruits	100.1
10.糖	Dried Fruits	102.2
11.干鲜瓜果	Other Food	97.3
12.糕点饼干面包	Condiments	99.7
13.奶及奶制品	Sugar	100.2
14.在外用膳食品	Candy	99.2
15.其它食品	Cake	97.5
二、饮料、烟酒	**Milk and Its Products**	**100.0**
1.茶及饮料	Canned Food	100.2
2.烟草	Catering Trade	99.4
3.酒	Taple Food	100.3
三、服装、鞋帽类	**Fried Dishes**	**99.0**
1.服装	Local Snack	96.4
2.鞋袜帽	Beverage,Tobacco and Liquor	104.5
四、纺织品类	**Beverages**	**103.3**
1.衣着材料	Tobacco and Liquor	100.2
2.床上用品	Garments,Shoes and Hats	104.0
五、家用电器及音像器材	**Garments**	**93.2**
1.家庭设备	Shoes	97.1
2.文娱用耐用消费品	Other Clothing	84.5
3.音像器材类	Textiles	100.0
六、文化办公用品	**Stationery**	**98.5**

6-3 商品零售价格指数(2003年)(续)

Retail Price Indices(2003)（Continued）

(以上年价格为100) (the price of Preceding year=100)

类　　别	Item	2003年
七、日用品	**Blend Cloth**	**98.1**
1.日用百货	Chemical Fiber Cloth	98.5
2.日用杂品	Woolen Fabric	105.3
3.洗涤用品	Silk	94.4
4.其它日用品	Other Textiles	98.4
八、体育娱乐用品	**Traditional Chinese and Western Medicines**	**97.8**
1.体育用品	Traditional Chinese Madicine	99.7
2.娱乐用品	Western Medicine	96.8
九、交通、通信用品	**Medical Articles**	**96.0**
1.交通运输机械	Cosmetics	99.3
2.通讯器材类	Newspapers and Magazines	81.0
十、家具	**Cultural and Sports Goods**	**90.4**
十一、化妆品类	**Cultural Goods**	**99.5**
十二、金银珠宝类	**Sports Goods**	**102.4**
十三、中西药品及医疗保健用品类	**Articles for Daily Use**	**91.6**
	Ordinary Articles for Daily Use	
1.医疗器具及用品	Furniture	105.5
2.中药材及中成药	Sundries for Daily Use	101.7
3.西药	Household Appliances	84.0
4.保健器具及用品	Jewelry	95.8
十四、书报杂志及电子出版物类	**Fuels Building Decoration Materials**	**96.5**
1.教材及参考书	Mechanical and Electrical Products	93.1
2.书报杂志	Books, newspapers and magazine	99.1
3.电子音像制品	Electronic audio-video products	99.7
十五、燃料类	**Fuel**	**108.5**
1.煤炭及制品类	Coal and its products	101.5
2.石油及制品类	Oil and its products	109.4
十六、建筑材料及五金电料	**Building material, ironware and electric stuff**	**99.7**
1.建筑装潢材料	Building decoration stuff	99.8
2.五金电料类	Ironware and electric stuff	99.6

6-4 工业产品出厂价格指数

(上年价格=100)

指　　标	Item	1996	1997
全部工业品	**General Industry Products**	**100.71**	**98.63**
按轻重工业分	Grouped by Light Industry and Heavy Industry		
轻工业	Light Industry	100.93	98.17
以农产品为原料	Using Farm Products as Raw Materials	101.60	99.21
以非农产品为原料	Using Non-farm Products as Raw Materials	98.11	96.79
重工业	Heavy Industry	100.20	98.98
采掘工业	Mining and Quarrying	-	-
原料工业	Raw Materials Industry	99.44	100.96
加工工业	Manufacturing Industry	101.49	97.86
按用途分	Grouped by Use		
生产资料	Means of Production	100.35	99.58
采掘工业	Mining & Quarrying Industry	-	-
原料工业	Raw Materials Industry	99.41	100.89
加工工业	Manufacturing Industry	101.94	98.87
生活资料	Consumer Goods	100.89	97.03
(1)食品	Food	107.95	108.21
(2)衣着	Clothing	98.57	92.96
(3)一般日用品	Articles for Daily Use	97.29	91.63
(4)耐用消费品	Durable Consumer Goods	92.59	99.65
按工业部门分	Grouped by Industrial Sector		
1.冶金工业	Metallurgical Industry	98.63	99.17
2.电力工业	Power Industry	-	111.29
3.煤炭及炼焦工业	Coking,Gas and Coal Products	102.09	98.87
4.石油工业	Petroleum Industry	-	-
5.化学工业	Chemical Industry	101.46	91.77
6.机械工业	Machinery Building Industry	99.47	98.76
7.建筑材料工业	Building Materials Industry	94.49	98.19
8.森林工业	Timber Industry	98.94	107.55
9.食品工业	Food Industry	108.47	106.80
10.纺织工业	Textiles Industry	95.68	94.32
11.缝纫工业	Tailoring Industry	-	100.14
12.皮革工业	Leather Industry	133.81	91.18
13.造纸工业	Paper Industry	98.82	-
14.文教艺术用品工业	Cultural,Educational & Handicrafts Articles	100.87	-
15.其它工业	Other Industry	100.00	109.51

Ex-factory Price Indices of Industrial Products

(the price of Preceding year=100)

1998	1999	2000	2001	2002	2003
94.37	**97.49**	**99.43**	**99.30**	**98.20**	**101.45**
91.11	95.87	97.82	99.60	98.40	101.27
89.47	95.19	99.18	99.00	98.40	104.45
93.41	96.97	95.45	100.60	98.60	99.89
97.30	98.92	100.75	99.20	98.20	101.64
104.14	101.52	97.48	94.80	101.30	103.38
100.70	102.27	107.74	101.10	101.30	111.18
95.63	98.00	98.36	98.50	97.70	100.09
96.57	98.28	100.50	99.10	98.00	101.84
104.14	101.52	97.48	94.80	101.30	103.38
100.57	100.20	106.38	101.10	101.00	108.13
94.67	97.59	98.67	98.50	97.40	100.89
91.36	96.46	97.27	99.90	99.10	100.50
97.75	95.79	94.40	99.60	101.20	101.02
83.88	95.19	101.56	99.40	100.80	99.43
95.06	97.62	96.89	101.90	97.90	101.22
95.41	98.02	95.93	97.00	98.10	97.18
97.50	91.20	98.20	97.20	98.70	103.77
111.23	109.33	109.63	102.40	100.00	103.19
98.48	96.30	100.54	110.30	106.70	136.75
-	107.09	134.24	96.60	100.70	118.63
92.93	96.61	96.69	100.50	99.20	100.16
94.59	98.09	98.02	98.30	97.60	99.83
99.30	96.71	98.51	100.60	99.60	99.69
104.47	97.94	98.90	98.10	98.90	100.08
95.27	95.45	94.32	99.80	101.10	102.78
82.58	93.65	103.35	97.50	94.90	117.34
97.29	99.10	103.50	100.00	101.10	100.22
96.78	98.00	99.20	101.00	101.80	98.68
-	95.33	96.68	102.30	95.00	96.91
-	96.65	96.36	101.10	103.40	97.52
109.22	98.89	104.84	107.10	99.40	103.26

6-5 主要原材料、燃料、动力购进价格指数

Purchase Price Indices of Major Raw Materials,Fuels and Power

(上年价格=100) (the price of Preceding year=100)

类　　别	Item	1996	1997	1998	1999
全部原材料	**Total of Raw Materials**	**103.80**	**102.45**	**97.46**	**96.85**
(一)燃料、动力类	Fuels and Power	112.95	112.79	110.33	100.53
(二)黑色金属材料类	Ferrous Metals	96.47	97.95	96.16	96.52
其中：钢材	Steel	94.89	97.74	96.58	95.95
其它	Others	100.97	98.64	94.61	98.79
(三)有色金属材料和电线类	Non-Ferrous Metals and Electric Wires	94.70	104.26	87.37	97.59
(四)化工原料类	Chemical Materials	100.54	95.59	88.79	98.19
(五)木材及纸浆类	Timber and Paper Pulp	103.56	101.40	102.85	100.63
(六)建筑材料及非金属矿类	Building Materials and Non-metal ores	98.14	99.63	99.67	98.57
(七)其它工业原材料及半成品类	Other Industrial Raw Materials and Semi-Products	-	99.15	93.52	96.98
(八)农副产品类	Agricultural and Sideline Products	111.85	95.39	89.07	90.12
(九)纺织原料类	Textile Raw Materials	112.81	95.56	86.29	90.00

6-5 主要原材料、燃料、动力购进价格指数（续）

Purchase Price Indices of Major Raw Materials,Fuels and Power(continued)

(上年价格=100) (the price of Preceding year=100)

类　　别	Item	2000	2001	2002	2003
全部原材料	**Total of Raw Materials**	**102.38**	**101.00**	**98.40**	**105.29**
(一)燃料、动力类	Fuels and Power	105.01	101.80	100.90	105.65
(二)黑色金属材料类	Ferrous Metals	102.69	102.10	98.50	107.43
其中：钢材	Steel	103.35	102.40	97.90	105.97
其它	Others	100.30	100.90	100.70	112.48
(三)有色金属材料和电线类	Non-Ferrous Metals and Electric Wires	105.17	95.50	96.80	105.80
(四)化工原料类	Chemical Materials	104.55	102.50	97.90	102.43
(五)木材及纸浆类	Timber and Paper Pulp	101.21	102.80	99.40	101.19
(六)建筑材料及非金属矿类	Building Materials and Non-metal ores	100.28	99.70	98.60	99.62
(七)其它工业原材料及半成品类	Other Industrial Raw Materials and Semi-Products	98.75	100.80	98.90	102.50
(八)农副产品类	Agricultural and Sideline Products	100.42	102.80	98.20	113.72
(九)纺织原料类	Textile Raw Materials	98.03	96.80	90.60	103.44

6-6 土地交易价格指数

Transactions Price Indices of Land

(上年价格=100) (the price of Preceding year=100)

项　　目	Item	1998	1999	2000	2001	2002	2003
土地交易价格指数	**Transactions Price Indices of Land**	**100.10**	**100.30**	**100.00**	**100.00**	**100.50**	**100.70**
一、居民住宅用地	**Land for Residential Building Use**	**100.20**	**100.40**	**100.00**	**100.00**	**100.70**	**100.60**
1.豪华住宅用地	Luxury Residential Buildings	99.60	102.50	100.00	100.00	102.10	
2.普通住宅用地	Ordinary Residential Buildings	100.40	100.00	100.00	100.00	100.20	100.60
二、工业用地	**Land for Industry Use**	**99.30**	**99.90**	**100.00**	**99.80**	**100.30**	**100.60**
三、商业、旅游、娱乐用地	**Land for Business,Tour and Entertainment**	**101.30**	**100.00**	**100.00**	**99.90**	**100.20**	**100.70**
四、其它用地	**Land for Others**	**100.00**	**100.00**	**100.00**	**100.00**	**100.10**	**100.70**

6-7 房屋销售价格指数

Selling Price Indices of Real Houses

(上年价格=100) (the price of Preceding year=100)

项　　目	Item	1998	1999	2000	2001	2002	2003
房屋销售价格指数	**Selling Price Indices of Real Houses**	**100.50**	**100.40**	**101.30**	**101.90**	**101.10**	**101.40**
一、商品房	**Commercial Houses**	**100.60**	**100.60**	**102.00**	**102.60**	**101.30**	**101.80**
(一)住　宅	Residential Buildings	100.60	100.60	102.20	102.90	101.70	101.90
1.经济适用房	Economical Houses	100.00	99.80	101.60	110.10	101.60	101.80
2.普通住宅	Ordinary Residential Buildings	102.50	101.30	102.90	102.00	101.80	101.90
(1)多层住宅	Multilayer Buildings	102.30	102.40	104.00	102.20	101.60	102.70
(2)高层住宅	High-Rise Buildings	102.00	99.70	101.20	102.00	101.90	101.70
3.豪华住宅	Luxury Residential Buildings	100.10	101.70	100.20	101.10	101.00	103.60
(1)别墅	Villas	100.50	100.00	100.30	100.60	100.30	104.30
(2)高档公寓	High-grade Apartment	99.90	97.50	99.90	101.20	101.00	100.60
(二)非住宅	Non-Residential Buildings	100.60	100.80	100.40	101.10	100.10	101.20
1.写字楼	Office Buildings	100.10	100.10	100.10	101.10	100.00	101.00
2.商业用房	Houses for Business Use	100.80	100.90	101.50	101.50	100.70	101.30
3.其他	Others	100.30	105.30	100.70	101.80	99.10	
二、公房	**State-owned Houses**	**-**	**-**	**-**	**100.00**	**100.00**	**100.00**
#住宅	Residential Buildings	-	-	-	100.00	100.00	100.00
三、私房	**Private-owned Houses**	**98.80**	**100.00**	**100.00**	**100.70**	**101.20**	**100.50**
(一)住宅	Residential Buildings	99.50	100.00	100.00	100.80	101.10	99.50
(二)非住宅	Non-Residential Buildings	96.60	100.00	100.00	100.10	101.20	102.40

6-8 房屋租赁价格指数

Renting Price Indices of Houses

(上年价格=100) (the price of Preceding year=100)

项　　目	Item	1998	1999	2000	2001	2002	2003
房屋租赁价格指数	**Renting Price Indices of Houses**	**102.50**	**100.60**	**101.20**	**100.30**	**100.60**	**98.90**
一、住　宅	**Residential Buildings**	**102.50**	**101.70**	**100.00**	**100.40**	**99.80**	**97.80**
(一)公　房	State-owned Houses	116.30	100.90	100.00	100.00	100.00	100.50
(二)私　房	Private-owned Houses	100.00	102.00	100.00	100.90	99.60	96.60
二、办公用房	**Office Building**	**101.60**	**98.20**	**98.20**	**100.00**	**99.50**	**99.80**
(一)高标准写字楼	High-grade Office Buildings	99.10	94.40	95.10	100.80	99.20	99.50
(二)普通办公用房	Ordinary Office Buildings	103.40	99.90	99.70	99.70	100.10	100.30
三、商业用房	**Houses for Business**	**100.80**	**101.70**	**100.20**	**99.10**	**100.90**	**98.10**
四、厂房仓库	**Workshops and Storehouses**	**101.70**	**101.70**	**100.40**	**102.00**	**103.20**	**102.50**
(一)工业厂房	Industry Workshops	101.70	99.30	102.00	101.90	102.50	100.80
(二)仓　库	Storehouses	101.80	103.60	98.40	102.10	103.60	103.50

6-9 固定资产投资价格指数

Price Indices of Fixed Assets Investment

(上年价格=100) (the price of Preceding year=100)

项　　目	Item	1999	2000	2001	2002	2003
固定资产投资价格指数	**Price Indices of Fixed Assets Investment**	**100.80**	**102.10**	**101.30**	**101.20**	**102.40**
一、按构成分:	**Grouped by Use of Funds**					
建筑安装、装饰工程	Building installation and decoration works	101.80	103.90	102.50	102.30	103.30
设备、工器具购置	Equipment and Instruments	99.20	97.90	99.30	97.10	99.90
其它费用	Others	99.70	100.00	98.60	101.10	101.50

6-10 建筑安装工程价格指数

Price Indecies of Construction and Installation Projects

(上年价格=100) (the price of Preceding year=100)

项　　目	Item	1999	2000	2001	2002	2003
报告期施工产值价格指数	**Price Indecies of Construction Output**	**101.80**	**103.90**	**102.50**	**102.30**	103.30
其中:	Of the Total:					
人工费	Labor-hour Expense	102.70	103.60	104.10	106.60	105.80
材料费	Material Expense	100.50	104.40	102.40	101.80	103.60
机械使用费	Machinery use Expense	102.10	103.90	102.10	101.00	100.80

主 要 统 计 指 标 解 释

商品零售价格指数 是反映一定时期内城乡商品零售价格变动趋势的一种经济指数。零售物价的调整变动直接影响到城乡居民的生活支出和国家的财政收入，影响居民购买力和市场供需平衡，影响消费与积累的比例。因此，计算零售价格指数，可以从一个侧面对上述经济活动进行观察和分析。

居民消费价格指数 是反映一定时期内城乡居民所购买的生活消费品价格和服务项目价格变动趋势和程度的相对数，是对城市居民消费价格指数和农村居民消费价格指数进行综合汇总计算的结果。利用居民消费价格指数，可以观察和分析消费品的零售价格和服务价格变动对城乡居民实际生活费用支出的影响程度。

城市居民消费价格指数 是反映城市居民家庭所购买的生活消费品价格和服务项目价格变动趋势和程度的相对数。城市居民消费价格指数可以观察和分析消费品的零售价格和服务项目价格变动对职工货币工资的影响，作为研究职工生活和确定工资政策的依据。

农村居民消费价格指数 是反映农村居民家庭所购买的生活消费品价格和服务项目价格变动趋势和程度的相对数。农村居民消费价格指数可以观察农村消费品的零售价格和服务项目价格变动对农村居民生活消费支出的影响，直接反映农民生活水平的实际变化情况，为分析和研究农村居民生活问题提供依据。

工业品出厂价格指数 是反映全部工业产品出厂价格总水平的变动趋势和程度的相对数，包括工业企业售给本企业以外所有单位的各种产品和直接售给居民用于生活消费的产品。通过工业品出厂价格指数能观察出厂价格变动对工业总产值的影响。

固定资产投资价格指数 是反映固定资产投资价格变动趋势和程度的相对数。固定资产投资额是由建筑安装工程投资完成额、设备、工器具购置投资完成额和其他费用投资完成额三部分组成的。编制固定资产投资价格指数应首先分别编制上述三部分投资的价格指数，然后采用加权算术平均法求出固定资产投资价格总指数。

编制固定资产投资价格指数可以准确地反映固定资产投资中涉及的各类商品和取费项目价格变动趋势和变动幅度，消除按现价计算的固定资产投资指标中的价格变动因素，真实地反映固定资产投资的规模、速度、结构和效益，为国家科学地制定、检查固定资产投资计划并提高宏观调控水平，为完善国民经济核算体系提供科学的、可靠的依据。

房地产价格指数 包括房屋销售价格指数、房屋租赁价格指数和土地交易价格指数。这三套指数的计算方法相似，均采用由下到上逐级汇总的方法。即由细项到小类，由小类到中类，再由中类到大类，最后由大类汇出总指数。对没有细项或小类的部分，其起始类就是小类或中类。中类以下（含中类）指数采用样本资料作权数的加权调和平均公式计算，大类和总指数采用固定权数加权的算术平均公式计算。

Explanatory Notes on Main Statistical Indicators

Retail Price Index it is an economic index which reflects the trend of commodity retail price changes of urban and rural area in an period of time. The change and adjustment in retail prices directly affect the living expenditure of urban and rural residents, government revenue, purchasing power of residents and the equilibrium of market supply and demand, and the ratio of consumption to accumulation. Therefore, the calculation of retail price index is useful to analyze the changes of the above economic activities.

Consumer Price Index reflects the trend and degree of changes in prices of consumer goods and services purchased by urban and rural residents, and is a composite index derived from the urban consumer price index and the rural consumer price index. Consumer price index can be used to analyze the impact of consumer price change on actual expenditure for living cost of urban and rural residents.

Urban Consumer Price Index reflects the trend and degree of changes in prices of consumer goods and services purchased by urban households. It can be used to observe and analyze the impact of price changes in consumer goods and services on money wages of staff and workers, and provide basis for policy making concerning the living cost and wages of staff and workers.

Rural Consumer Price Index reflects the trend and degree of changes in prices of consumer goods and services purchased by rural households. It can be used to observe the impact of change in retail prices of consumer goods and service prices in rural areas on living expenditure of rural households, and to show the changes in the living standard of peasants. It provides basis for analysis and research on condition of life in rural areas.

Ex-factory Price Index of Industrial Products reflects the trend and degree of changes in general ex-factory prices of all industrial products, including sales of industrial products by an industrial enterprise to all units outside the enterprise, as well as sales of consumer goods to residents. It can be used to analyze the impact of ex-factory prices on gross industrial output value.

Price Index of Investment in Fixed Assets reflects the trend and degree of changes in prices of investment in fixed assets. The investment in fixed assets consists of three components, namely the investment in construction and installation, the investment in purchases of equipment and instrument, and the investment in other items. Price index of investment in fixed assets is calculated as the weighted arithmetic mean of the price indices of the three components of investment in fixed assets. Removing the factor of price change in the aggregates of investment at current prices, this indicator shows the changes in the prices of commodities and fees involved in the investment of fixed assets, and can be used to observe the actual size, growth, structure, and efficiency of investment in fixed assets and provides reliable and scientific data for government planning, management, decision making, and further improving the current national accounting system.

Price Indices for Real Estate include price index for selling houses and buildings, price index for leasing houses and buildings and price index for land transaction. The methods for the compilation of the three sets of indices are similar in that they all use bottom-up approach, under which indices for the item groups are compiled first, and then indices for the major groups, categories, major categories and finally the overall indices are compiles. The indices for item groups, major groups and categories are calculated using the formulae of weighted harmonic mean with sample data as the weights, and the indices for the major categories and the overall indices are calculated using the arithmetic mean with fixed weights.

2004

統計
年鑒

七、人民生活

PEOPLE S LIVELIHOOD

简 要 说 明

Brief Introduction

本章资料反映我市人民生活状况。主要内容包括城乡居民家庭基本情况、主要商品购买数量、耐用消费品拥有数量等。

资料数据来源于城市社会经济调查队、市农村社会经济调查队。

Data in this chapter reflects situation of the people's daily life of Xi'an city. It consists of mainly basic condition of urban and rural households, volume of primary commodity purchasing, possession of endurable goods, and etc.The data come from Urban Economic Survey Crew. Data on rural households come from Rural Social and Economic Survey crew.

7-1 城市居民家庭基本情况

指　　标	Item	1997
一、调查户数(户)	**Households Surveyed (household)**	**300**
二、平均每户家庭人口(人)	**Average Number of Persons Per Household (person)**	**3.12**
三、平均每户就业人口(人)	**Average Number of Employed Per Housedhold (person)**	**1.65**
四、平均每户就业面(%)	**Percentage of Employees Per Household (%)**	**53**
五、平均每一就业者负担人数(人)	**Persons Supported by Each Laborer (person)**	**1.89**
六、年人均实际收入(元)	**Annual Actual Income Per Capita (yuan)**	**5371.56**
#可支配收入	#Disposable Income	5344.14
工薪工资	Wages of Staff in State-owned Units	3739.87
个体经营者的净收益	Net Income of Self-employed Laborers	50.68
财产性收入	Property Income	245.93
转移性收入	Transfer Income	1335.07
七、年人均实际支出(元)	**Annual Actual Expenditure Per Capita (yuan)**	**5318.1**
1.消费性支出	Consumption Expenditure	4752.61
(1)食品	Food	1934.44
(2)衣着	Clothing	525.83
(3)设备用品及服务	Facilities,Articles and Services	517.5
(4)医疗保健	Medicines and Medical Services	217.28
(5)交通和通讯	Traffic and Communication Services (yuan)	304.05
(6)娱乐教育和文化服务	Recreation,Education and Cultural Services	594.73
(7)居住	Residence	449.88
(8)杂项商品和服务	Miscellaneous Commodities and Services	208.9
2.购房与建房支出	Purchase and Construction Expenditure of Houses	227.28
3.转移性支出	Transfer Expenditure	338.13
4.财产性支出	Property Expenditure	-
5.社会保障支出	Social Services Expenditure	-
八、人均期末手存现金(元)	**Cash Reserves at Hand at the end of Year Per Capita (yuan)**	**366.08**

Basic Conditions of Urban Households

1998	1999	2000	2001	2002	2003
300	**300**	**300**	**300**	**300**	**350**
3.04	**2.99**	**2.99**	**3.03**	**3.01**	**3.04**
1.49	**1.38**	**1.37**	**1.38**	**1.47**	**1.46**
48.9	**46.3**	**45.7**	**45.6**	**48.8**	**48**
2.04	**2.16**	**2.19**	**2.19**	**2.05**	**2.08**
5697.03	**6028.09**	**6394.13**	**6743.56**	**7670.67**	**8315.13**
5669.59	5998.78	6364.16	6704.86	7183.54	7748.38
3505.38	3604.6	3678	4288.09	5075.62	5443.21
89.79	72.19	94.84	135.27	159.03	111.82
292.61	277.71	137.08	49.35	60.9	194.17
1808.95	2073.58	2484.21	2270.41	2375.12	2565.92
5723.83	**6168.52**	**6209.59**	**6678.56**	**7819.74**	**8610.43**
4806.6	5360.98	5445.7	5815.66	6419.21	6805.3
1910.93	1945.36	1985.56	2023.91	2205.38	2371.02
449.58	443.58	442.81	485.93	540.52	574.56
546.23	704.59	616.75	628.91	467.36	403.24
287.7	321.77	393.37	406.13	535.52	602.31
264.68	315.04	377.58	453.12	567.96	630.48
585.08	705.12	748.51	908.07	1126.68	1230.6
534.81	646.79	611.49	531.45	783.56	779.33
227.6	278.73	269.64	378.14	192.23	213.77
534.58	441.37	263.79	289.23	415.08	532.19
382.62	366.16	500.1	573.59	567.81	786.7
-	-	-	-	0	0
-	-	-	-	417.64	486.24
383.32	**431.86**	**389**	**550.39**	**587.82**	**810.6**

7-2 城市居民不同收入层次家庭基本情况表(2003年)

单位：元

指 标	Item	合计 Total	最低10% Lowest	更低5% Lower
一、调查户数(户)	**Number of Households Surveyed (Household)**	**349.40**	**34.90**	**17.70**
二、可支配收入(新算法)(元)	**Disposable Income (Yuan)**	**7748.38**	**2149.44**	**1619.15**
服务性消费支出(元)	Consumption on Service	2249.76	1056.73	890.70
三、家庭类型(世代层次)(合计)(%)	**Family Category (%)**	**100.00**	**100.00**	**100.00**
1.单身户	1. Single	0.95	0.00	0.00
2.一对夫妇户	2. A Couple	14.40	4.06	0.94
3.两代人单亲	3. Single Parent with Kids	4.29	4.77	6.13
4.两代人一个小孩	4. A Couple With One Kid	55.35	53.22	50.00
5.两代人两个小孩	5. A Couple With 2 Kids	4.25	6.20	3.77
6.两代人多个小孩	6. A Couple with more than 2 Kids	0.00	0.00	0.00
7.与父母	7.Live with Parents	1.88	2.39	1.42
8.三代人	8.3 Generations	13.12	26.02	32.08
9.其他	9.Others	5.75	3.34	5.66
四、家庭人口数(人/户)	**Number of Family Members (Person/Household)**	**3.04**	**3.28**	**3.34**
(一)有收入者人数	Family Members Earning Income	2.07	1.68	1.61
1.就业人口数	Family Members Employed	1.46	1.18	1.09
(1)国有经济单位职工人数	Employed by State-Owned Enterprises	1.08	0.61	0.57
(2)城镇集体经济单位职工人数	Employed by Urban Collective Enterprises	0.09	0.21	0.19
(3)其他各种经济类型单位职工	Employed by Other Units	0.05	0.09	0.09
(4)城镇个体经营者人员数	Personnel of Urban Individual Business	0.03	0.06	0.07
(5)城镇个体被雇人员数	Employed by Self-Employers	0.11	0.10	0.09
(6)离退休再就业人员数	Re-Employed Resigned and Retired Personnel	0.09	0.01	0.01
(7)其他就业人员数	Others	0.02	0.09	0.07
2.离退休人数	Resigned and Retired (Person/Household)	0.48	0.17	0.15
3.其他有收入者人数	Others	0.13	0.33	0.38
(二)无收入者人数	Family Members Without No Income	0.96	1.60	1.72
五、期末家庭人口数(人/户)	**Family Members at the Year-end(Person/Household)**	**2.99**	**3.31**	**3.38**
六、非家庭人口在家用餐人次数 (人次/户)	**None-Family Members Eating At Home (Person-Times/Household)**	**7.16**	**2.20**	**2.03**
七、家庭人口在外用餐人次数 (人次/户)	**Family Members Eating Outside (Person-Times/Household)**	**39.89**	**34.82**	**30.67**
八、负担系数(人)	**Supporting Coefficient (Person)**	**0.00**	**0.00**	**0.00**
九、家庭折算人口数（人/户）	**Converted Family Members(Person/Household)**	**2.57**	**2.81**	**2.93**

Basic Conditions of Urban Households by Level of Income（2003）

（yuan）

低10% low	较低20% Comparatively low	中间20% medium	较高20% Comparatively high	高10% high	最高10% highest	更高5% higher
34.9	**69.9**	**69.8**	**69.9**	**34.9**	**35**	**17.5**
3654.97	**4928.99**	**6658.46**	**8765.53**	**11805.25**	**21770.23**	**28777.12**
1148.64	1631.53	2140.75	2659.01	2861.51	5112.24	6976.54
100	**100**	**100**	**100**	**100**	**100**	**100**
2.15	0.36	0.24	1.55	2.39	0.71	0.95
5.97	4.77	14.44	18.47	29.59	29.04	30.47
3.1	5.01	2.74	5.96	4.53	3.1	2.86
61.1	57.09	57.28	52.68	50.6	54.53	54.77
8.12	4.41	2.39	5.25	2.62	1.43	0.48
0	0	0	0	0	0	0
0.95	1.67	3.1	2.03	1.19	0.71	0
16.23	17.64	11.45	9.3	5.97	6.19	5.72
2.39	9.06	8.35	4.77	3.1	4.28	4.76
3.18	**3.24**	**3.03**	**2.94**	**2.72**	**2.79**	**2.73**
1.93	2.08	2.14	2.18	2.11	2.21	2.17
1.45	1.48	1.45	1.55	1.37	1.68	1.67
0.92	1.09	1.13	1.2	1.08	1.28	1.31
0.16	0.12	0.06	0.04	0.03	0.06	0.06
0.05	0.04	0.03	0.05	0.05	0.07	0.03
0.04	0.03	0.01	0.02	0.02	0.02	0.03
0.19	0.13	0.15	0.08	0.05	0.05	0.06
0.04	0.05	0.06	0.14	0.13	0.19	0.18
0.06	0.02	0.01	0	0	0.01	0.01
0.33	0.51	0.61	0.54	0.62	0.41	0.36
0.14	0.09	0.09	0.1	0.12	0.12	0.14
1.25	1.16	0.89	0.75	0.62	0.58	0.57
3.03	**3.18**	**3.02**	**2.96**	**2.61**	**2.65**	**2.59**
3.53	**5.33**	**6.93**	**10.01**	**13.05**	**8.22**	**9.79**
30.09	**40.03**	**38.22**	**42.17**	**44.97**	**48.11**	**53.06**
0	**0**	**0**	**0**	**0**	**0**	**0**
2.8	**2.74**	**2.58**	**2.48**	**2.26**	**2.22**	**2.12**

7-3 城市居民不同收入层次每百户耐用消费品拥有量

指　标	Item	合　计	最低10%	
				更低5%
		Total	Lowest	Lower
十、主要消费品拥有量	**Major Consumer Goods Owned**			
1.成套家具(套/百户)	Composite Furniture (set/100 household)	47.87	47.25	47.17
2.摩托车(辆/百户)	Motorcycle (unit/100 household)	10.23	5.97	6.13
3.自行车(辆/百户)	Bicycle (unit/100 household)	146.34	136.27	135.84
4.助力车(辆/百户)	Electric bicycles (every 100 households)	0.43	0.24	0.00
5.家用汽车(辆/百户)	Automobile (unit/100 household)	0.29	0.00	0.00
6.洗衣机(台/百户)	Washing Machine (unit/100 household)	95.68	84.72	90.09
7.电风扇(台/百户)	Electric Fan (unit/100 household)	138.97	129.12	131.14
8.电冰箱(台/百户)	Refrigerator (unit/100 household)	89.20	74.94	69.81
9.冰柜(台/百户)	Freezer (unit/100 household)	2.58	0.95	0.47
10.彩色电视机(台/百户)	Color Television Set (unit/100 household)	126.97	114.32	112.73
11.影碟机(台/百户)	Video Disc Player (unit/100 household)	59.10	39.62	43.87
12.录音机(台/百户)	Tape Recordeer (unit/100 household)	52.61	39.38	39.15
13.录放像机(台/百户)	Video-recorder(unit/100 household)	22.47	5.97	5.19
14.家用电脑(台/百户)	Computer (unit)	23.85	9.30	9.43
15.组合音响(套/百户)	Hi-Fi Stereo Component System (set)	22.85	15.04	15.56
16.摄像机(架/百户)	Pickup Camera (set)	1.72	0.24	0.00
17.照相机(架/百户)	Camera (set)	48.25	17.42	14.15
18.钢琴(架/百户)	Piano (set)	2.03	0.24	0.00
19.其他中高档乐器(件/百户)	Other Medium and High Grade Musical Instrument (unit)	5.89	3.34	2.83
20.微波炉(台/百户)	Oven (unit)	42.16	14.56	9.90
21.空调器(台/百户)	Air Conditioner (unit)	82.42	31.75	34.44
22.取暖器(台/百户)	Warm-keeper (every 100 households)	21.01	14.32	10.85
23.电炊具(台/百户)	Electricity Cooker (unit)	103.74	79.48	74.05
24.淋浴热水器(台/百户)	Shower (unit)	70.04	34.37	29.25
25.排油烟机(台/百户)	Smoke Absorber (unit)	66.16	40.34	41.04
26.消毒碗柜(台/百户)	Disinfecting cupboard(every 100 households)	4.65	0.96	0.94
27.洗碗机(台/百户)	Dishwasher (unit)	0.00	0.00	0.00
28.饮水机(台/百户)	Drinking water machine(every 100 households)	28.81	10.02	7.08
29.吸尘器(台/百户)	Dust Catcher (unit)	9.09	2.15	0.47
30.健身器材(套/百户)	Healthy Equipment (unit)	2.58	0.48	0.94
31.普通电话(部/百户)	Telephone (unit)	87.10	72.08	70.28
32.移动电话(部/百户)	Hand Telephone (unit)	74.43	30.56	24.53
33.传真机(部/百户)	Electrograph (unit)	0.57	0.00	0.00

Basic Conditions of Urban Households by Level of Income（2003）

低10% low	较低20% Comparatively low	中间20% medium	较高20% Comparatively high	高10% high	最高10% highest	更高5% higher
43.91	48.16	45.70	54.71	40.09	50.24	56.68
6.44	9.89	11.34	11.44	10.26	14.29	10.48
137.23	144.10	148.45	150.53	147.49	156.19	155.72
0.71	0.24	0.60	0.24	0.71	0.48	0.48
0.00	0.00	0.00	0.00	0.00	2.86	5.24
86.87	93.33	101.07	98.33	99.28	100.47	100.00
126.24	138.14	140.69	147.20	143.67	138.58	130.48
77.57	87.01	92.96	92.85	96.18	97.62	97.15
1.67	2.74	0.60	3.22	4.06	5.95	5.23
111.46	122.29	128.75	133.25	133.41	141.91	142.87
42.47	52.80	64.32	64.36	69.45	76.42	73.33
37.23	47.08	54.66	64.12	54.17	63.57	61.91
17.42	20.98	21.00	24.43	35.56	32.86	33.81
15.51	20.26	21.24	23.36	30.79	53.09	50.00
15.27	22.41	21.84	23.72	31.26	30.95	35.24
0.00	0.72	1.91	2.03	3.34	4.28	2.38
20.52	40.17	48.57	59.12	66.35	82.38	83.33
0.00	0.60	3.94	4.17	1.43	1.19	0.95
3.82	3.34	6.09	6.55	6.68	13.10	16.67
23.62	33.38	40.81	52.32	59.89	70.48	65.24
48.44	70.57	91.40	89.04	104.29	137.61	147.13
15.75	21.57	25.53	24.08	21.24	16.43	12.87
76.37	96.42	104.78	119.66	122.42	117.38	116.20
54.17	68.89	74.71	77.83	79.23	89.76	88.10
50.12	63.05	66.59	73.18	79.24	86.18	85.71
0.95	3.58	4.89	7.27	6.68	6.43	5.24
0.00	0.00	0.00	0.00	0.00	0.00	0.00
16.71	22.41	31.26	34.68	38.19	46.42	50.47
3.10	5.24	8.83	12.75	13.12	18.81	21.91
0	1.55	2.27	2.74	3.58	8.57	3.81
83.29	86.53	88.78	88.32	93.55	94.76	94.29
48.67	59.23	73.86	93.80	97.38	113.81	113.34
0.00	0.60	0.24	0.36	1.19	2.14	3.33

7-4 城市居民不同收入层次家庭年人均收入情况(2003年)

单位：元

项目	Item	总平均 Total	最低10% lowest	更低5% lower	低10% low
一、家庭总收入	**Total Family Income**	**8315.13**	**2593.69**	**2238.23**	**3998.24**
其中:可支配收入	Disposable Income	7748.38	2149.44	1619.15	3654.97
(一)工薪收入	Wages Income	5443.21	1717.46	1466.40	2918.70
1.工资及补贴收入	Wages and Subsidies	5256.37	1488.64	1343.87	2691.85
2.其他劳动收入	Other Payments to Labor	186.84	228.82	122.53	226.84
(二)经营净收入	Net Income from Business	111.82	80.02	82.23	55.11
(三)财产性收入	Property Income	194.17	72.11	20.18	33.09
1.利息收入	Interest Income	88.50	4.32	6.58	4.61
2.股息与红利收入	Dividend and Bonus	15.64	1.31	0.00	0.00
3.保险收益	Interests Of Insurance	10.73	0.00	0.00	1.80
4.其它投资收入	Income from Other Investments	0.00	0.00	0.00	0.00
5.出租房屋收入	House Rents	79.30	66.48	13.59	26.68
6.知识产权收入	Income from Intellectual Property Rights	0.00	0.00	0.00	0.00
7.其他财产性收入	Other Property Income	0.00	0.00	0.00	0.00
(四)转移性收入	Transfer Income	2565.92	724.09	669.42	991.34
1.养老金或离退休金	Pensions	1702.86	332.23	285.02	679.83
2.社会救济收入	Social Relieve	24.27	103.77	114.97	42.44
3.辞退金	Severance Pay	0.00	0.00	0.00	0.00
4.赔偿收入	Compensation	0.00	0.00	0.00	0.00
5.保险收入	Insurance Proceeds	35.96	83.63	102.11	44.33
其中:失业保险金	Unemployment Insurance	35.55	83.63	102.11	44.33
6.赡养收入	Support Money from Offsprings	235.30	60.26	62.80	29.27
7.捐赠收入	Donations	402.21	17.83	1.70	60.70
8.亲友搭伙费	Payment For Boarding By Relatives and Friends	5.56	0.00	0.00	0.00
9.提取住房公积金	Withdrawal of Housing Funds	16.69	0.00	0.00	0.00
10.记帐补贴	Book-Keeping Allowances	40.89	38.76	40.71	38.30
11.其他转移性收入	Others	102.18	87.61	62.10	96.47
二、出售财物收入	**Income from Sales Of Property**	**4.66**	**6.18**	**0.29**	**3.38**
1.出售住房收入	Sales of Housing	0.00	0.00	0.00	0.00
2.出售其他物品收入	Sales of Other Properties	4.66	6.18	0.29	3.38
三、借贷收入	**Income For Savings and Credit**	**2278.38**	**1151.07**	**1056.15**	**820.23**
1.提取储蓄存款	Withdrawal of Deposits	1774.08	865.67	593.64	645.31
2.借入款	Borrow Money	395.85	272.69	442.90	164.73
3.收回借出款	Funds Lent out Refunded	11.96	0.00	0.00	0.00
4.收回储蓄性保险本金	Corpus of Insurance Withdrawn	0.94	0.00	0.00	0.00
5.兑售有价证券	En-Cash/Sell Securities	0.00	0.00	0.00	0.00
6.收回投资本金	Corpus of Investments Withdrawn	29.44	0.00	0.00	9.00
7.住房贷款	Housing Credit	0.00	0.00	0.00	0.00
8.汽车贷款	Automobile Credit	0.00	0.00	0.00	0.00
9.教育贷款	Education Credit	0.00	0.00	0.00	0.00
10.其他贷款	Other Credit	0.00	0.00	0.00	0.00
11.其他借贷收入	Other Income from Savings and Credit	66.11	12.71	19.61	1.19

Statistics on Per Capital Annual Income of Urban Residents

by Level of Income（2003）

(yuan)

较低20% comparatively low	中间20% medium	较高20% comparative high	高10% High	最高10% highest	更高5% higher
5330.04	**7153.15**	**9418.44**	**12515.28**	**22953.82**	**30018.74**
4928.99	6658.46	8765.53	11805.25	21770.23	28777.12
3593.59	4871.79	6407.92	7593.13	14082.33	16877.13
3395.58	4665.52	6314.23	7419.73	13849.11	16558.92
198.00	206.27	93.69	173.41	233.23	318.21
58.35	40.63	154.10	171.52	344.54	569.40
82.70	93.12	103.20	306.18	1079.71	1809.25
6.81	10.40	22.59	88.13	779.82	1340.75
0.00	0.00	3.65	0.00	160.79	328.27
10.51	2.84	0.00	15.79	68.69	140.23
0.00	0.00	0.00	0.00	0.00	0.00
65.38	79.88	76.96	202.26	70.42	0.00
0.00	0.00	0.00	0.00	0.00	0.00
0.00	0.00	0.00	0.00	0.00	0.00
1595.40	2147.62	2753.22	4444.44	7447.24	10762.96
1299.80	1801.90	2221.55	3164.96	2678.35	2476.66
25.23	12.86	1.17	0.00	5.11	0.00
0.00	0.00	0.00	0.00	0.00	0.00
0.00	0.00	0.00	0.00	0.00	0.00
44.52	33.28	23.57	18.04	0.00	0.00
44.52	33.28	21.46	18.04	0.00	0.00
52.00	78.45	165.85	570.01	1259.36	2023.66
67.29	106.16	225.22	542.07	2893.97	5124.91
1.77	9.46	11.20	10.53	2.05	0.00
0.00	0.00	0.00	11.59	170.08	347.23
41.33	41.61	41.40	42.19	41.44	38.03
63.47	63.91	63.25	85.06	396.88	752.46
2.52	**3.35**	**1.42**	**13.30**	**10.57**	**9.63**
0.00	0.00	0.00	0.00	0.00	0.00
2.52	3.35	1.42	13.30	10.57	9.63
1400.56	**2683.81**	**2587.12**	**2859.91**	**5198.15**	**6354.50**
939.15	2364.40	2079.42	2035.60	3881.95	4843.76
434.86	147.06	343.14	557.12	1204.74	1315.41
0.09	0.00	53.90	13.70	3.08	0.00
0.00	0.00	4.87	0.00	0.00	0.00
0.00	0.00	0.00	0.00	0.00	0.00
0.00	9.44	31.59	210.15	18.40	37.56
0.00	0.00	0.00	0.00	0.00	0.00
0.00	0.00	0.00	0.00	0.00	0.00
0.00	0.00	0.00	0.00	0.00	0.00
0.00	0.00	0.00	0.00	0.00	0.00
26.46	162.91	74.19	43.34	89.99	157.77

7-5 城市居民不同收入层次家庭年人均支出情况(2003年)

单位:元

项目	Item	总平均 Total	最低10% lowest	更低5% lower
一、家庭总支出(元)	**Total Expenditures (Yuan)**	**8610.43**	**3887.34**	**3563.58**
(一)消费支出	Living Expenditures	6805.30	3255.51	2896.62
其中:服务性消费支出	Living Expenditures in Service Trades	2249.76	1056.73	890.70
1.食品	Food	2371.02	1427.71	1310.24
2.衣着	Clothing	574.56	213.09	154.54
3.家庭设备用品及服务	Household Facilities,Articles and Service	403.24	74.04	64.95
4.医疗保健	Medicine and Medical Service	602.31	227.80	285.56
5.交通和通信	Transport,Post and Communication Services	630.48	265.13	209.82
6.教育文化娱乐服务	Education,Receration and Cultural Services	1230.60	592.86	506.76
7.居住	Residence	779.33	379.06	294.34
8.杂项商品和服务	Miscellaneous Commodities and Services	213.77	75.81	70.41
(二)购房与建房支出	Expenditures on House Purchasing/Construction	532.19	153.89	0.00
1.购房	House Purchasing	532.19	153.89	0.00
2.建房	House Construction	0.00	0.00	0.00
(三)转移性支出	Transfer Expenditures	786.70	90.02	120.83
1.交纳的个人收入税	Personal income Taxes	39.61	17.56	32.23
2.捐赠支出	Expenditures on Donations	371.13	33.26	31.04
3.购买彩票	Expenditures on Lottery	4.99	0.94	0.58
4.赡养支出	Expenditures for Maintenance	345.41	21.58	30.91
其中:在外就学子女费用	Expendrtures for Children Studying Away From Home	85.31	10.04	12.72
5.各种非储蓄性保险支出	Expenditures on Non-saving insurances	7.39	0.51	0.00
其中:车辆保险支出	Expenditures on Vehicles insurance	0.00	0.00	0.00
6.其他转移性支出	Other Transfer Expenditures	18.17	16.16	26.07
(四)财产性支出	Property Expenditures	0.00	0.00	0.00
1.非生产性利息支出	Non-Productive interest Payments	0.00	0.00	0.00
2.其他	Others	0.00	0.00	0.00
(五)社会保障支出	Expenditures on Social Security	486.24	387.92	546.13
1.个人交纳的养老基金	Retirement Funds Raised by individuals	236.41	292.00	438.32
2.个人交纳的住房公积金	Housing Funds Raised by individuals	177.43	44.41	46.36
3.个人交纳的医疗基金	Medical Funds Raised by individuals	52.00	42.21	55.11
4.个人交纳的失业基金	Unemployment Funds Raised by individuals	20.40	9.31	6.34
5.其他社会保障支出	Others	0.00	0.00	0.00
二、借贷支出(元)	**Expenditures on Loans and Debts (Yuan)**	**1592.90**	**238.01**	**174.45**
1.存入储蓄款	Depositting to Bank	1239.54	81.12	86.69
2.借出款	Amout of Money Lent	13.98	6.73	13.08
3.归还借款	Paying off Debts	111.69	134.21	65.46
4.储蓄性保险支出	Expenditures for Savings Premium	93.83	15.95	9.23
5.购买有价证券	Purchasing Securities	37.65	0.00	0.00
6.其它投资支出	Other investments	1.11	0.00	0.00
7.归还住房贷款	Refund Housing Loans	9.36	0.00	0.00
8.归还汽车贷款	Refund Automobile Loans	0.00	0.00	0.00
9.归还教育贷款	Refund Education Loans	0.00	0.00	0.00
10.归还其他贷款	Refund Other Loans	4.01	0.00	0.00
11.其他借贷支出	Others	81.71	0.00	0.00

Statistics on Per Capital Annual Living Expenditure of Urban Households by Level of Income（2003）

(yuan)

低10% low	较低20% comparatively low	中间20% medium	较高20% comparative high	高10% high	最高10% highest	更高5% higher
4583.34	**5883.54**	**8547.89**	**9793.21**	**12527.55**	**18879.57**	**23681.91**
4060.44	4907.00	6754.09	8027.01	9436.41	13466.70	17065.59
1148.64	1631.53	2140.75	2659.01	2861.51	5112.24	6976.54
1695.99	1942.65	2386.98	2678.79	3228.50	3720.64	4340.87
279.66	344.21	510.22	710.69	913.95	1390.02	1575.45
235.04	231.30	549.13	450.32	534.03	836.70	1052.85
348.54	449.40	506.87	778.00	745.01	1382.27	1806.25
373.21	403.86	611.10	743.20	1070.31	1253.33	1537.46
487.57	914.73	1139.37	1319.07	1634.88	3172.42	4178.09
532.54	497.85	855.40	1079.61	996.35	1174.08	1880.56
107.88	123.00	195.01	267.34	313.40	537.24	694.06
70.83	377.69	833.53	472.40	952.60	922.22	419.72
70.83	377.69	833.53	472.40	952.60	922.22	419.72
0.00	0.00	0.00	0.00	0.00	0.00	0.00
154.76	245.61	519.85	715.11	1522.89	3587.35	5307.59
7.67	6.48	12.66	32.83	52.20	238.86	314.58
108.05	178.97	370.56	434.52	743.28	1017.30	1352.83
2.52	1.89	7.02	9.81	5.94	4.30	4.64
10.38	45.52	109.35	200.57	686.74	2284.22	3580.68
0.00	2.87	45.92	72.91	113.04	545.90	505.60
6.19	5.03	1.58	19.07	11.59	6.24	8.60
0.00	0.00	0.00	0.00	0.00	0.00	0.00
19.96	7.72	18.69	18.32	23.15	36.43	46.26
0.00	0.00	0.00	0.00	0.00	0.00	0.00
0.00	0.00	0.00	0.00	0.00	0.00	0.00
0.00	0.00	0.00	0.00	0.00	0.00	0.00
297.30	353.25	440.43	578.68	615.65	903.29	889.01
163.83	184.06	224.28	262.11	264.05	320.40	310.59
76.56	106.47	141.10	231.35	260.62	496.75	492.92
41.06	40.89	50.64	62.06	68.93	67.04	65.84
15.85	21.83	24.41	23.16	22.06	19.11	19.67
0.00	0.00	0.00	0.00	0.00	0.00	0.00
225.15	**795.21**	**947.54**	**1947.96**	**2474.31**	**6376.41**	**8140.35**
120.36	609.34	762.00	1379.55	2163.21	5170.20	6556.84
2.70	7.29	9.96	30.95	36.37	2.05	4.19
82.41	57.25	41.19	157.52	182.56	232.02	327.48
16.88	89.93	60.01	107.01	57.93	361.95	441.47
0.00	0.00	0.00	145.82	0.00	102.50	0.00
0.00	0.64	0.00	0.73	7.46	1.83	0.44
0.00	3.66	8.63	13.60	5.20	40.88	0.00
0.00	0.00	0.00	0.00	0.00	0.00	0.00
0.00	0.00	0.00	0.00	0.00	0.00	0.00
0.00	0.75	12.91	5.65	0.00	2.05	4.19
2.80	26.35	52.85	107.14	21.58	462.92	805.76

7-6 城市居民不同收入层次家庭年人均消费性支出情况（2003年）

单位:元

项　目	Item	总平均 Total	最低10% Lowest	更低5% lower
消费支出	**Living Expenditures**	**6805.30**	**3255.51**	**2896.62**
其中:服务性消费支出	Expenditure on services	2249.76	1056.73	890.70
一、食品	**Food**	**2371.02**	**1427.71**	**1310.24**
(一)粮油类	Grains and oil	336.58	316.99	315.14
1.粮食	Grain	206.75	197.17	190.64
2.淀粉及薯类	Starches and Tubers	22.21	22.83	24.46
3.干豆类及豆制品	Bean and Its Products	33.86	29.08	32.05
4.油脂类	Oil or Fat	73.76	67.91	67.98
(二)肉禽蛋水产品类	Meat,Poultry,Egg and Aquatic Products	431.77	254.99	243.52
1.肉类	Meat	237.73	135.71	129.04
2.禽类	Poultry	69.53	41.48	40.11
3.蛋类	Egg	55.58	46.88	46.89
4.水产品类	Aquatic Products	68.94	30.93	27.48
(三)蔬菜类	Vegetables	212.50	165.90	164.10
1.鲜菜	Fresh Vegetables	196.39	158.74	158.07
2.干菜	Dried Vegetables	8.86	3.43	2.66
3.菜制品	Vegetable Products	7.25	3.73	3.37
(四)调味品	Flavouring	37.11	27.28	28.67
(五)糖烟酒饮料类	Sugar,Tobacco,Liquor and Beverage	259.15	128.90	96.52
1.糖类	Sugar	24.04	11.01	7.71
2.烟草类	Tobacco	133.52	76.91	53.34
3.酒类	Liquor	46.53	12.80	9.43
4.饮料	Beverage	55.06	28.20	26.03
(六)干鲜瓜果类	Dried and Fresh Melons &Fruits	175.69	88.67	75.17
(七)糕点、奶及奶制品	Cakes, Milk and Its Products	207.03	99.52	88.02
1.糕点	Cakes	70.15	29.73	29.69
2.奶及奶制品	Milk and Its Products	136.87	69.79	58.34
(八)其他食品	Others	59.10	24.37	22.23
其中：半成品	Semi-finished Goods	12.31	4.34	2.30
(九)饮食服务	Catering Services	652.07	321.08	276.87
1.食品加工服务费	Charge for Food Processing Services	0.25	0.02	0.00
2.在外饮食	Foods Consumed outside	651.82	321.06	276.87
非食品类	Non food	4434.28	1827.80	1586.38
二、衣着	**Clothing**	**574.56**	**213.09**	**154.54**
(一)服装	Garments	402.95	142.86	95.26
1.男士服装	Men's Clothes	171.30	64.67	42.56
2.女士服装	Lady Clothes	208.63	67.68	41.78
3.童装	Children Clothes	23.02	10.51	10.92
(二)衣着材料	Cloth Materials	12.89	5.93	7.98
(三)鞋类	Shoes	128.39	51.35	39.75
(四)其他衣着用品	Others	24.28	11.26	9.22
(五)衣着加工服务费	Tailoring and Laundering	6.04	1.70	2.32
三、家庭设备用品及服务	**Household Facilities,Articles and Services**	**403.24**	**74.04**	**64.95**
(一)耐用消费品	Durable Consumer Goods	212.93	3.51	2.01
1.家具	Furniture	78.02	1.99	1.19
2.家庭设备	Household Facilities	134.91	1.52	0.81
(二)室内装饰品	Interior Decorations	15.68	1.14	1.56
1.纺织装饰品	Textile ornaments	7.04	1.14	1.56
2.装饰灯具	Ornamental lamps	5.24	0.00	0.00
3.其他装饰品	Others	3.40	0.00	0.00
(三)床上用品	Bed Articles	25.80	3.14	3.12
(四)家庭日用杂品	Daily Use Household Articles	129.45	58.69	54.72
(五)家具材料	Furniture Materials	0.06	0.00	0.00
(六)家庭服务	Household Services	19.31	7.56	3.54

Statistics on Per Capita Annual Living Expenditure of Residents by Level of Income（2003）

(yuan)

低10% low	较低20% Comparatively low	中间20% medium	较高20% Comparative high	高10% high	最高10% highest	更高5% higher
4060.44	**4907.00**	**6754.09**	**8027.01**	**9436.41**	**13466.70**	**17065.59**
1148.64	1631.53	2140.75	2659.01	2861.51	5112.24	6976.54
1695.99	**1942.65**	**2386.98**	**2678.79**	**3228.50**	**3720.64**	**4340.87**
336.88	315.01	355.93	346.27	381.60	303.18	308.65
202.82	193.03	218.22	216.64	230.35	185.70	195.78
20.08	19.42	22.07	24.49	25.23	22.96	21.08
30.53	32.69	33.40	37.10	42.15	32.08	26.47
83.45	69.87	82.25	68.04	83.86	62.43	65.32
340.57	360.75	462.65	488.51	575.73	581.06	614.17
204.72	204.18	248.45	264.44	326.52	306.88	321.20
50.30	59.82	75.24	84.35	74.56	98.29	104.20
46.76	48.55	64.04	59.38	67.34	54.33	50.24
38.79	48.19	74.93	80.34	107.31	121.56	138.53
178.99	176.91	224.66	230.97	272.86	263.86	279.08
168.40	164.51	208.36	211.89	245.89	239.60	249.30
4.45	5.98	9.12	11.21	17.62	12.89	16.99
6.14	6.41	7.18	7.88	9.35	11.37	12.78
32.61	35.46	37.81	39.23	45.53	43.40	47.51
166.25	188.73	242.25	275.83	401.70	543.45	728.68
13.64	16.07	22.35	24.41	47.11	50.02	62.14
98.85	102.95	126.99	143.23	193.05	245.88	320.81
23.30	30.82	45.24	40.80	72.16	138.82	205.10
30.45	38.90	47.67	67.38	89.38	108.73	140.63
123.13	137.38	186.96	203.11	246.10	275.66	295.26
155.18	169.93	233.20	243.23	272.17	281.80	300.02
50.27	54.41	73.27	77.12	104.94	121.41	130.90
104.91	115.52	159.93	166.11	167.23	160.40	169.12
32.71	42.14	54.26	71.99	96.09	116.50	114.21
5.09	8.97	10.80	13.65	19.49	31.02	33.63
329.67	516.34	589.25	779.64	936.70	1311.72	1653.30
0.11	0.27	0.34	0.34	0.36	0.14	0.13
329.55	516.08	588.91	779.30	936.34	1311.58	1653.17
2364.45	2964.34	4367.11	5348.23	6207.91	9746.07	12724.72
279.66	**344.21**	**510.22**	**710.69**	**913.95**	**1390.02**	**1575.45**
189.07	222.18	329.45	508.48	639.13	1077.21	1246.13
94.14	81.93	144.18	216.10	279.43	450.37	525.26
79.64	119.78	165.58	264.55	324.71	588.97	683.01
15.29	20.47	19.69	27.82	34.99	37.87	37.86
9.01	14.91	16.17	12.88	15.00	11.67	12.58
64.09	80.03	132.49	157.16	217.99	247.30	259.21
14.52	20.42	24.45	25.84	32.80	47.69	51.11
2.97	6.67	7.66	6.32	9.03	6.15	6.42
235.04	**231.30**	**549.13**	**450.32**	**534.03**	**836.70**	**1052.85**
104.92	93.56	342.35	226.70	263.25	499.76	631.30
28.38	23.83	126.51	73.89	59.40	270.99	337.69
76.53	69.73	215.85	152.81	203.85	228.77	293.61
2.75	8.12	24.42	11.13	27.83	43.76	82.61
1.04	3.38	5.81	3.47	19.76	27.03	52.18
0.00	0.00	16.26	5.15	1.16	9.79	16.86
1.71	4.74	2.35	2.51	6.91	6.95	13.58
12.31	17.42	21.92	42.90	30.20	55.32	70.13
101.84	102.36	138.11	147.93	179.24	200.59	221.63
0.54	0.00	0.00	0.00	0.00	0.00	0.00
12.68	9.84	22.33	21.67	33.51	37.27	47.17

7-6 城市居民不同收入层次家庭年人均消费性支出情况（2003年）(续)

单位:元

项目	Item	总平均 Total	最低10% Lowest	更低5% lower
四、医疗保健	**Medicine and Medical Services**	**602.31**	**227.80**	**285.56**
㈠医疗器具	Medical Appliances and Articles	12.40	0.12	0.24
㈡保健器具	Health Care Articles	5.76	0.32	0.63
㈢药品费	Medicines	381.51	156.21	189.08
㈣滋补保健品	Tonic	23.24	7.45	0.10
㈤医疗费	Medical Care Services	178.29	63.66	95.46
㈥其他	Others	1.11	0.04	0.05
五、交通和通讯	**Transportation ,Post and Telecommumication Services**	**630.48**	**265.13**	**209.82**
㈠交通	Trasportation	203.16	77.52	45.16
1.家庭交通工具	Family vehicles	19.18	1.31	0.00
2.车辆用燃料及零配件	Fuel and accessories	6.20	1.64	1.78
3.交通工具服务支出	Expenditure on maintenance of vehicles	10.20	1.25	1.31
4.交通费	Transport servi	167.59	73.31	42.07
㈡通信	Telecommumication	427.31	187.61	164.65
1.通信工具	Telecommunication tools	67.02	15.53	9.86
2.通信服务	Telecommunication services	360.30	172.08	154.80
六、教育文化娱乐服务	**Recreation,Culture and Education Services**	**1230.60**	**592.86**	**506.76**
㈠文化娱乐用品	Recreating Goods	234.98	72.93	94.53
㈡文化娱乐服务	Recreation and Culture Services	119.48	38.38	30.35
1.参观游览	Travel	19.53	1.88	2.47
2.健身活动	Health care Activities	2.01	1.56	0.17
3.团体旅游	Traveling in a group	33.10	0.00	0.00
4.其它文娱活动	Others	62.86	33.92	26.58
5.文娱用品修理服务费	Repair and Maintenance of Entertainment Tools	1.98	1.01	1.12
㈢教育	Education	876.14	481.56	381.89
1.教材	Textbook	78.67	57.84	57.73
2.教育费用	Fee of education	797.47	423.72	324.16
七、居住	**Residence**	**779.33**	**379.06**	**294.34**
㈠住房	Housing	353.91	91.04	50.39
1.租赁房房租	House renting	41.59	46.20	47.00
2.自有房租金折算	Converted self-owned house rent	0.00	0.00	0.00
3.住房装潢支出	Home decorate expenditure	291.55	40.37	0.00
4.维修用建筑材料	Building material for repair	20.77	4.47	3.39
5.其他	Others	0.00	0.00	0.00
㈡水电燃料及其他	Water,Electricity,Fuel and Others	407.04	278.41	233.92
1.水	Water	40.44	22.31	21.03
2.电	Electricity	175.73	105.52	106.64
3.燃料	Fuel	105.10	99.27	96.74
4.其他	Others	85.77	51.31	9.51
㈢居住服务费	Cost on housing service	18.38	9.61	10.03
1.物业管理费	Housing management	0.00	0.00	0.00
2.维修服务费	Expenditures on house maintenance	2.41	0.49	0.08
3.其它	Others	15.97	9.12	9.95
八、杂项商品和服务	**Miscellaneous Commodities and Services**	**213.77**	**75.81**	**70.41**
㈠杂项商品	Miscellaneous Commodities	125.44	33.24	29.19
1.金银珠宝饰品	Jewel	25.77	0.31	0.60
2.手表	Watches	2.34	0.46	0.90
3.理发美容用具	Hair-care	2.15	0.18	0.00
4.化妆品	Cosmetics	47.61	13.92	14.53
5.其他杂品	Others	47.58	18.37	13.16
㈡服务	Services	88.33	42.57	41.23
1.旅馆住宿费	Rent for hotels	11.06	0.26	0.00
2.理发洗澡费	Hair-cutting and Bathing	38.22	31.17	28.26
3.美容费	Cosmetic	10.09	0.58	0.34
4.其他服务	Others	28.96	10.56	12.62

Statistics on Per Capita Annual Living Expenditure of Residents

by Level of Income（2003）(Continued)

(yuan)

低10%	较低20%	中间20%	较高20%	高10%	最高10%	
	Comparatively		Comparative			更高5%
low	low	medium	high	high	highest	higher
348.54	**449.40**	**506.87**	**778.00**	**745.01**	**1382.27**	**1806.25**
6.55	12.25	4.79	13.07	19.67	41.75	24.81
3.96	2.18	7.70	9.91	11.53	3.95	0.00
232.53	288.32	328.86	442.55	524.88	877.05	1105.20
14.39	7.08	15.85	31.60	74.32	37.95	39.53
91.04	139.03	148.58	278.57	112.74	419.90	635.65
0.07	0.53	1.10	2.31	1.87	1.68	1.07
373.21	**403.86**	**611.10**	**743.20**	**1070.31**	**1253.33**	**1537.46**
89.63	107.60	201.81	242.21	343.98	484.79	692.72
1.71	5.84	48.16	10.25	61.88	5.42	7.32
3.93	8.83	6.15	4.33	8.62	9.67	16.97
4.87	7.21	12.20	8.47	26.96	16.69	30.89
79.13	85.72	135.30	219.16	246.53	453.01	637.54
283.58	296.26	409.29	501.00	726.32	768.54	844.74
26.41	13.05	75.61	71.37	160.44	179.96	207.43
257.17	283.21	333.69	429.63	565.88	588.58	637.31
487.57	**914.73**	**1139.37**	**1319.07**	**1634.88**	**3172.42**	**4178.09**
63.73	155.24	172.68	325.39	423.04	566.00	679.17
33.04	60.92	78.19	171.53	177.73	371.78	550.59
2.59	4.12	7.02	32.96	19.02	94.49	135.14
0.55	1.25	0.47	1.54	8.64	3.89	6.80
0.00	0.00	16.40	58.99	25.91	174.91	307.02
29.61	53.82	53.23	74.31	119.94	96.70	100.77
0.29	1.74	1.06	3.73	4.21	1.79	0.87
390.80	698.56	888.50	822.15	1034.11	2234.65	2948.33
41.18	62.38	76.87	79.82	116.54	148.11	148.90
349.63	636.18	811.63	742.33	917.57	2086.53	2799.43
532.54	**497.85**	**855.40**	**1079.61**	**996.35**	**1174.08**	**1880.56**
207.43	134.98	421.48	581.85	403.71	661.90	1346.85
31.52	37.52	27.64	81.99	39.41	4.45	6.05
0.00	0.00	0.00	0.00	0.00	0.00	0.00
171.02	87.83	373.14	464.29	306.15	641.07	1308.80
4.89	9.62	20.70	35.57	58.15	16.38	32.00
0.00	0.00	0.00	0.00	0.00	0.00	0.00
315.79	341.72	413.94	474.32	571.65	496.30	519.78
29.65	34.51	48.34	46.94	52.22	45.43	48.17
145.99	147.43	186.59	211.81	225.08	210.05	217.28
100.75	90.37	92.89	121.90	137.52	110.61	109.03
39.40	69.41	86.12	93.67	156.83	130.20	145.30
9.32	21.15	19.98	23.44	20.99	15.89	13.93
0.00	0.00	0.00	0.00	0.00	0.00	0.00
0.27	3.01	2.89	2.86	6.23	0.00	0.00
9.05	18.14	17.09	20.57	14.76	15.89	13.93
107.88	**123.00**	**195.01**	**267.34**	**313.40**	**537.24**	**694.06**
63.89	72.37	95.49	167.16	193.22	337.60	432.73
1.90	6.04	8.65	63.49	26.73	85.22	152.13
0.48	1.38	3.24	0.86	8.92	3.61	4.03
3.01	1.29	0.87	0.47	2.70	11.23	4.98
29.48	29.58	41.96	56.23	73.06	118.86	134.43
29.03	34.09	40.77	46.10	81.80	118.68	137.16
43.99	50.63	99.51	100.19	120.18	199.64	261.33
0.00	0.57	7.20	24.69	11.26	40.11	41.17
34.92	34.20	36.89	42.97	47.28	43.59	44.31
2.44	5.43	5.99	15.86	10.93	36.67	50.09
6.63	10.42	49.44	16.67	50.71	79.26	125.76

7-7 城市居民家庭年人均购买主要商品数量

Per Capita Annual Purchases of Principal Goods in Urban Household

商品名称	Name of Commodities (unit)	1997	1998	1999	2000	2001	2002	2003
粮　食（公斤）	Grain (kg)	80.4	82.2	84.4	82.9	78.6	72.9	75.7
植物油（公斤）	Vegetable Oil(kg)	8	8.7	8.6	10	9.1	9.9	9.4
猪　肉（公斤）	Pork (kg)	12.1	13.2	13.5	13.7	12	12.9	13.6
牛　肉（公斤）	Beef (kg)	2.3	2	1.5	1.7	1.6	1.4	1.5
羊　肉（公斤）	Mutton (kg)	0.6	0.6	0.6	0.7	0.5	0.8	1
鸡　（公斤）	Chicken (kg)	3.8	3.8	4.2	4.4	3.6	3.7	4
鲜　蛋（公斤）	Eggs (kg)	13.6	11.3	13.1	12.3	10.8	11.4	11.9
鱼（公斤）	Fish(kg)	2.9	3.1	4.2	3.7	3.8	4.5	5.2
鲜　菜（公斤）	Fresh Vegetable (kg)	109.3	108	112.5	107	104.5	112.3	109.7
干　菜（公斤）	Dry Vegetable(kg)	0.2	0.2	0.2	0.2	0.2	0.2	0.3
白　酒（公斤）	Liquor(kg)	0.8	0.9	0.8	0.9	1	1	1
果　酒（公斤）	Fruit Wine (kg)	0.1	0.2	0.2	0.2	0.3	0.3	0.2
啤　酒（公斤）	Beer (kg)	4.1	4.1	4	3	3.6	4.7	4
干鲜瓜果（公斤）	Dried and Fresh Melons & Fruits(kg)	61.8	65	65.8	58.5	62.5	70.4	65.8
坚果及果仁（公斤）	Nuts and Kemel(kg)	3.4	5	3.7	3.8	3.3	4	4
糕　点（公斤）	Cakes(kg)	4.1	4.3	4.4	4.6	4.2	4.8	5.3
鲜乳品（公斤）	Fresh Dairy Products (kg)	8.7	9.8	10.6	12	12.8	18.9	21.8
奶　粉（公斤）	Milk Powder (kg)	0.4	0.4	0.5	0.6	0.6	0.6	0.7
男士服装（件）	Men Clothes(unit)	2.3	2.2	2.4	2.2	2.3	2.7	2.9
女士服装（件）	Lady Clothes (unit)	2.7	2.9	3.2	2.9	3.3	3.9	3.6
各式童装（件）	Children Clothes(unit)	0.8	0.8	0.8	0.9	1.1	1	0.9
鞋（双）	Shoes(pair)	2.46	2.47	2.35	2.39	2.46	2.56	2.7
水费（吨）	Water(ton)	23.7	23.8	26	25.7	24.5	28.6	28.8
电费（度）	Electricity (degree)	202.8	226.8	268.8	307.5	309.7	390.8	385.3
煤炭（公斤）	Coal (kg)	75.1	61.2	49.8	62	61.7	51.8	45.1
液化石油气（公斤）	Liquified Petroleum Gas (kg)	21	18.5	19.9	17.9	14.5	13.3	12.2
管道煤气（立方米）	Piping Gas (cu.m)	16.2	20.5	19.5	26.1	26.4	35.1	39

7–8 城市居民家庭平均每百户年末拥有主要耐用消费品数量

Number of Durable Consumer Goods Owned Every 100 Urban Households

商品名称	Commodity Names	1997	1998	1999	2000	2001	2002	2003
成套家具（套）	Composite Furniture (set)	43.3	44	45.3	50	55	45.7	47.9
摩托车（辆）	Motorcycle (unit)	2	2.3	4.3	5	6	8.7	10.2
自行车（辆）	Bicycle (unit)	196.3	188.7	178.3	170.7	177	152.3	146.3
家用汽车（辆）	Car (unit)	0	0	0	0	0	0.3	0.3
洗衣机	Washing Machine (unit)	97.7	98.7	96.3	96.7	97.7	97.3	95.7
电风扇（台）	Electric Fan (unit)	186.7	180.3	179.3	175	169	149	139
电冰箱（台）	Refrigerator (unit)	88.7	92.7	91.7	89.3	89.3	93.7	89.2
冰柜（台）	Freezer (unit)	1.7	1	1	1.7	2	2	2.6
彩色电视机（台）	Color TV Set (unit)	110	113.7	120.7	124	123.7	128.3	127
影碟机（台）	VCD (unit)	5	13.7	25	35.7	42	56	59.1
录放像机（台）	Videorecorder (unit)	22.3	27.7	29.7	28	26.3	23	22.5
家用电脑（台）	Computer (unit)	1.3	2.7	5.3	11.7	15.7	19	23.9
组合音响（套）	Hi-Fi System (set)	8	10.7	13.3	16.7	19.3	23	22.9
收录机（台）	Tape Recorder (unit)	67	60.7	60.7	54.3	57	57.7	52.6
摄像机（台）	Pick-up Camera (unit)	0.7	1	1	1	0.3	1	1.7
照相机（架）	Camera (set)	44	46.3	50	46.3	47.3	48	48.3
钢琴（架）	Piano (set)	0.7	1.3	1.7	1.3	0.3	1.7	2
其它中高档乐器（件）	Other High-Grade Musical Instruments (unit)	3.3	3.3	4.3	2.3	3.7	6.7	5.9
微波炉（台）	Oven (unit)	6.3	10.3	12.3	18	27.7	39.3	42.2
空调器（台）	Air Conditioner (unit)	31	39.3	45	51.3	54.3	75	82.4
电炊具（台）	Electric Cooking Tools (unit)	90.3	96	101.7	105.3	107.3	113.7	103.7
淋浴热水器（台）	Shower(unit)	43.7	50.3	55	52.3	52.3	63.7	70
脱排油烟机（台）	Smoke Absorb(unit)	53.3	61	65	65	63.7	65.7	66.2
吸尘器（台）	Dust Catch (unit)	8.3	8.7	11.7	10	10.7	8.3	9.1
健身器材（件）	Health Care Equipment (unit)	1.7	2	4	3.3	3	1.7	2.6
取暖器(台)	Warm-keeper(unit)	—	—	—	—	—	19	21
消毒碗柜(台)	Disinfecting Cupboard(unit)	—	—	—	—	—	1.7	4.7
洗碗机(台)	Dishwasher (unit)	—	—	—	—	—	0	0
饮水机(台)	Drinking Water Machine (unit)	—	—	—	—	—	25.3	28.8
普通电话(部)	Telephone (unit)	62	70	77.7	81.3	86	88	87.1
传真机(部)	Electrograph (unit)	—	—	—	—	—	0.3	0.6
移动电话(部)	Hand Telephone (unit)	—	1.3	1.7	7.6	19.3	48.3	74.4

7-9 城市居民家庭居住情况

Conditions of Dwellings of Urban Households

住房情况	Accommodation data	2003
1.家庭人口（人/户）	Number of Persons Per Household(person/household)	3.04
2.现住房总建筑面积（平方米/人）	Building Area of Living Houses(sq.m/person)	19.95
3.现住房屋总使用面积（平方米/人）	Floor Space of Living Houses(sq.m/person)	15.14
4.房屋产权(合计)（%）	Proportion of Property Right of Houses(%)	100.00
租赁公房	Public Houses Rent	16.15
租赁私房	Private Houses Rent	1.84
原有私房	Originally Self-owned Houses	6.06
房改私房	Present Self-owned Houses	75.41
商品房	Commercial Houses	0.55
其他	Others	0.00
5.住宅建筑式样(合计)（%）	Proportion of Patterns of Residential Building(%)	100.00
单栋住宅	Flats With Complete Facilities (%)	0.00
四居室	4 Rooms	1.86
三居室	3 Rooms	16.98
二居室	2 Rooms	61.39
一居室	1 Rooms	2.12
普通楼房	Ordinary Storeyed Building	16.48
平房及其他	Single-storey Houses and Others	1.17
6.装修状况(合计)（%）	Proportion of Decoration Condition(%)	100.00
有装修	Decorated	51.30
未装修	Undecorated	48.70
如果装修过,最近一次装修花费（元/户）	Expenditure of Latest Decoration(yuan/household)	9329.56
7.现有住房按市场价估计值（元/户）	Estimated Market Price of Present Houses(yuan/household)	66253.20
8.租赁房房租（元/户）	Expenditure of Rent Houses(yuan/household)	8.99
9.自有房房租折算（元/户）	Rent of Self-owned Houses(yuan/household)	31.98
10.购房总金额（元/户）	Total Expenditure on Purchase of Houses(yuan/household)	25926.29
购房实际支出金额（元/户）	Expenditure on Purchase Practice of Houses(yuan/household)	24141.84
11.饮水情况(合计)（%）	Proportion of Water Drinking(%)	100.00
自来水	Tap Water	82.23
矿泉水	Mineral Water	2.43
纯净水	Pure Water	15.33
井、河水	Well Water and River Water	0.00
其他	Others	0.00
12.用水情况(合计)（%）	Proportion of Water Use Condition(%)	100.00

7–9 城市居民家庭居住情况(续)

Conditions of Dwellings of Urban Households（Continued)

住房情况	Accommodation data	2003
独用自来水	Moloply Use of Tap Water	90.58
公用自来水	Public Tap Water	9.42
井、河水	Well Water and River Water	0.00
其他	Others	0.00
13.卫生设备(合计)（%）	Proportion of Sanitary Facilities(%)	100.00
无卫生设备	Without Sanitary Facilities	2.12
有厕所浴室	With Bathroom and Lavatory	63.20
有厕所无浴室	With Lavatory but without Bathroom	20.56
公用	Common-used Sanitary Facilities	14.12
14.取暖设备(合计)（%）	Proportion of Heating Facilities(%)	100.00
无取暖设备	Without Heating Facilities (%)	15.57
空调设备	Air-conditioner	3.74
暖气	Central Heating	56.48
其他	Others	24.21
15.炊用燃料使用情况(合计)（%）	Proportion of Cooking Fuels(%)	100.00
管道煤气	Pipeline Gas	49.77
液化石油气	Liquefied Gas	38.71
煤	Coal	4.53
其他	Others	6.99
16.通信设备使用情况（%）	Proportion of Communication Equipment(%)	
(1)无电话(合计)	Without Telephone	100.00
是	Yes	4.84
否	No	95.16
(2)固定电话（部/百户）	Fixed Telephone(set/100 households)	87.10
(3)移动电话（部/百户）	Mobile Telephone(set/100 households)	74.43
(4)使用互联网（条/百户）	Internet Extension(unit/100 households)	1.94
17.除了现住房，还有几处其他住房（套/户）	Other Living Houses besides Present Living House(unit/household)	0.09
①出租房（套/户）	Houses for Rent(unit/household)	0.03
使用面积（平方米/户）	Floor Space(sq.m/household)	1.35
②偶尔居住房（套/户）	Houses Seldom Living in (unit/household)	0.04
使用面积（平方米/户）	Floor Space(sq.m/household)	1.17
③其它用途房（套/户）	Houses for other Purposes(unit/household)	0.02
使用面积（平方米/户）	Floor Space(sq.m/household)	0.87

7-10 主要年份农民家庭基本情况

项 目	Item	1995
一、调查户数（户）	**Households Surveyed(household)**	**450**
二、调查人口（人）	**Residents Sueveyed(person)**	
1.常住人口	Average Number of Permanent Residents	2070
2.整半劳动力	Average Number Able-bodied and Semi-able-bodied Laborers Per Households	1312
3.平均每个劳动力负担人口	Persons Supported by Each Laborers	1.58
三、平均每人全年收入(元)	**Per Capita Annual Income(yuan)**	
1.总收入	Total Revenue	1931.64
2.纯收入	Net Income	1353.25
3.现金收入	Cash Income	1370.53
4.可支配收入	Disposable Income	
四、按人均纯收入分组（%）	**Grouped by Per Capita Annual Net Income(%)**	
户数占总户数比重	Percentage of Households	
1000元以下	Below 1000 yuan	
1000-2000元	1000-2000 yuan	
2000-3000元	2000-3000 yuan	
3000-4000元	3000-4000 yuan	
4000-5000元	4000-5000 yuan	
5000元以上	Over 5000 yuan	
五、农民家庭房屋情况	**Rural Household Housing Condition**	
1.年末人均住房价值(元)	Average Value of Living House Per Capita of Year-end(yuan)	2429.95
2.年末人均住房面积(m^2)	Average Floor Space of Living House Per Capita at Year-end(sq.m)	21.77
3.年内人均新建房屋面积(m^2)	Percapita Space of Building Newly Built Within the year (sq.m)	1.66
4.年内人均新建房屋价值(元)	Percapita Value of Building Newly Built Within the Year(yuan)	313.18
六、生活消费支出总计（元）	**Living Expenditure Built(yuan)**	**1220.34**
食品消费支出	Food	613.95
衣着	Clothing	102.41
居住	Residence	226.09
家庭设备用品及服务	Household Facilities,Articles and Services	72.27
医疗保健	Medical and Health Care Services	63.08
交通通讯	Transport,Post and Telecommunication Services	21.74
文化娱乐用品及服务	Culture,Educational and Recreational Articles and Services	98.72
其它商品及服务	Other Commodities and Services	22.08

Bisic Indicators of Rural Households In Representative Years

1996	1997	1998	1999	2000	2001	2002	2003
480	**460**	**460**	**460**	**500**	**770**	**770**	**750**
2151	2057	2028	2024	2147	3214	3212	3102
1352	1289	1279	1296	1371	2008	2017	1993
1.59	1.6	1.59	1.56	1.57	1.6	1.59	1.56
2158.15	2393.2	2597.24	2711.55	2929.23	3185.54	3370.82	3571.71
1585.89	1846.43	2052.07	2202.73	2343.76	2490.27	2641.44	2837.83
1580.71	1832.55	2087.96	2288	2513.14	2747	2965.92	3042.02
				2225.13	2357.3	2560.58	2729.88
						11.69	10
						28.57	26.67
						27.92	26
						15.45	16.13
						5.97	10
						10.4	11.2
3198.31	3809.54	4813.5	4850.32	5398.21	6286.53	6883.06	7354.4
23.98	27.38	27.32	26.8	28.31	29.72	32.54	33.9
1.36	1.28	1.33	2.03	1.58	1.81	2.2	0.98
356.39	279.75	308.01	304.4	408.07	475.33	484.18	239.47
1380.99	**1387.92**	**1564.81**	**1492.43**	**1605.36**	**1676.41**	**1782.13**	**1802.76**
689.25	682.47	663.75	584.18	587.97	567.62	553.78	677.03
120.64	113.13	120.76	112.83	106.8	105.53	115.02	113.15
279.55	237.52	327.56	247.45	343.71	409.9	444.92	314.04
84.3	73.33	87.43	97.79	87.89	74.29	83.64	98.59
63.86	64.75	72.72	94.6	111.25	115.92	136.18	128.47
17.19	28.84	51.99	62.45	67.51	88.83	115.14	143.45
109.83	144.87	196.96	230.09	232.61	241.31	275.38	296.8
16.37	43.01	43.64	63.04	67.62	73.02	58.08	31.22

7-11 农村居民家庭基本情况（2003年）

项　目	Item	西安市 Xi'an	灞桥区 Baqiao	未央区 Weiyang	雁塔区 Yanta
一、调查户数（户）	**Number of Households Surveyed (household)**	**750**	**100**	**60**	**60**
二、常住人口（人）	**Permanent Residents(person)**	**3102**	**407**	**246**	**244**
6岁及以下	6 Year-old and Below	139	15	12	8
7–15岁人口	7-15 Year-old	448	52	29	26
16–60岁人口	16-60 Year-old	2223	315	177	188
61岁以上人口	61 Year-old and Above	292	25	28	22
三、整半劳动力（人）	**Able-bodied and Semi-able-bodied Labourer(person)**	**1993**	**296**	**163**	**182**
四、常住人口外出从业人数（人）	**Permanent Residents Employed in Other Places Outside(person)**	**333**	**18**	**14**	**36**
五、劳动力文化程度（人）	**Labourer Literacy(person)**				
1.不识字或识字很少	Illiterates or Semi-illiterates	36	5	2	
2.小学文化程度	Primary Schools	266	10	11	8
3. 初中文化程度	Junior Secondary Schools	1225	203	113	106
4. 高中程度	Senior Secondary Schools	408	64	30	47
5.中专程度	Specialized Secondary Schools	32	7	5	10
6. 大专及以上	Universities and Colleges and Above	26	7	2	11
六、人均耕地经营面积（亩）	**Area of Cultivated Land Managed per Capita(mu)**	**1.02**	**0.58**	**0.61**	**0.37**

Basic Conditions of Rural Households（2003）

	阎良区 Yanliang	长安区 Chang'an	蓝田县 Lantian	临潼区 Lintong	周至县 Zhouzhi	户　县 Huxian	高陵县 Gaoling	新城区 Xincheng	碑林区 Beilin	莲湖区 Lianhu
	60	**70**	**70**	**80**	**90**	**60**	**100**	**30**	**30**	**30**
	236	**301**	**309**	**329**	**374**	**247**	**409**	**118**	**109**	**121**
	9	8	16	26	11	14	20	3	4	5
	39	34	53	50	68	28	69	8	11	10
	171	215	219	223	256	183	276	105	85	92
	17	44	21	30	39	22	44	2	9	14
	143	**202**	**197**	**199**	**202**	**161**	**248**	**98**	**55**	**80**
	9	**60**	**39**	**44**	**41**	**36**	**36**			**1**
	3	2	1	2	14	3	4			2
	23	24	27	40	50	40	33	1		44
	90	131	141	118	82	81	160	38	23	14
	25	42	27	37	53	36	47	50	24	16
	1	3	1	1			4	7	1	3
	1			1	3	1		2	7	
	1.25	**0.84**	**1.80**	**1.51**	**0.75**	**1.24**	**1.23**			

7-12　农村居民家庭平均每人总收入和纯收入（2003年）

单位：元

项　目	Item	西安市 Xi'an	灞桥区 Baqiao	未央区 Weiyang	雁塔区 Yanta
一、全年总收入	**Annual Total Revenue**	**3571.71**	**3716.82**	**5250.02**	**5200.58**
(一)工资性收入	Wages Income	990.37	1227.58	1489.55	1723.21
1．在非企业组织中劳动得到的	Get from Non-enterprise Organizition	171.96	263.00	379.65	475.30
2．在本乡地域内劳动得到的	Income from labor providing inside administrative region	476.39	839.21	933.16	968.13
3．常住人口外出从业得到的	Get from Permanent Residents	342.02	125.37	176.75	279.77
(二)家庭经营收入	Household Business Income	2134.73	2127.10	3164.21	1925.06
其中:农业收入	Farming	1059.50	946.22	608.44	181.96
牧业收入	Animal Husbandry	247.87	70.90	505.16	
(三)财产性收入	Property Income	262.44	206.05	437.81	1430.28
(四)转移性收入	Transfer Income	184.18	156.10	158.45	122.03
二、全年纯收入	**Annual Net Income**	**2837.83**	**3270.14**	**3877.18**	**3949.13**
三、可支配收入	**Disposable Income**	**2729.88**	**3139.92**	**3776.51**	**3839.64**

7-13　农村居民家庭平均每人全年总支出（2003年）

单位：元

项　目	Item	西安市 Xi'an	灞桥区 Baqiao	未央区 Weiyang	雁塔区 Yanta
全年总支出	**Annual Total Expenditure**	**2607.97**	**1897.33**	**4090.07**	**4112.91**
一、家庭经营费用支出	**Expenditure for Household Business**	**553.42**	**210.94**	**1177.93**	**1080.53**
其中：农业支出	Farming	225.57	101.02	119.28	28
牧业支出	Animal Husbandry	125.36	37.88	260.37	1.9
二、购置生产用固定资产支出	**Purchasing Productive Fixed Assets**	**74.86**	**7.02**	**76.36**	**0.7**
三、建造生产性固定资产雇工支出	**Expenditure on labor hiring on building of productive fixed assets**	**1.54**	**4.91**		
四、税费支出	**Expenditure for Tax and Fee**	**46.63**	**22.27**	**20.93**	**5.05**
五、生活消费支出	**Expenditure for Living Consumption**	**1802.76**	**1514.1**	**2695.99**	**2908.51**
六、财产性支出	**Expenditure for Property**	**4.44**	**0.01**	**0.65**	
七、转移性支出	**Expenditure for Transfer**	**124.34**	**138.06**	**118.21**	**118.12**

Per Capita Annual Total Revenue and Net Income of Rural Households（2003）

（yuan)

阎良区 Yanliang	长安区 Chang'an	蓝田县 Lantian	临潼区 Lintong	周至县 Zhouzhi	户　县 Huxian	高陵县 Gaoling	新城区 Xincheng	碑林区 Beilin	莲湖区 Lianhu
4290.39	**3120.22**	**2739.08**	**3396.57**	**2393.57**	**3193.37**	**3208.56**	**5933.18**	**5792.64**	**6299.88**
657.66	1638.86	739.84	759.36	584.01	1137.11	584.68	631.12	1114.23	1305
71.55	91.79	25.37	170.44	144.94	37.57	154.87	285.95	629.94	205.82
345.7	453.46	502.58	211.94	200.59	475.13	227.57	345.17	484.29	1046.29
240.46	1093.61	211.89	376.98	238.49	624.4	202.25			52.89
3367.75	1268.06	1919.08	2217.71	1596.08	1910.12	1667.34	1847.68	157.14	293.22
2339.69	566.52	472.35	1470.31	982.97	879.02	1055.7			
377.16	106.76	282.67	284.54	278.28	298.3	329.71			
57.15	37.37	54.18	26.54	51.78	15.73	663.04	3309.35	4521.09	4605.95
207.84	175.93	25.99	392.96	161.7	130.41	293.51	145.03	0.18	95.71
3023.18	**2830.07**	**2019.66**	**2662.12**	**1867.97**	**2457.85**	**2555.65**	**5930.04**	**5792.45**	**6276.33**
2710.55	**2828.84**	**1959.13**	**2557.26**	**1735.89**	**2329.31**	**2488.8**	**5785.12**	**5667.49**	**5992.23**

Per Capita Annual Total Expenditure of Rural Households（2003）

(yuan)

阎良区 Yanliang	长安区 Chang'an	蓝田县 Lantian	临潼区 Lintong	周至县 Zhouzhi	户　县 Huxian	高陵县 Gaoling	新城区 Xincheng	碑林区 Beilin	莲湖区 Lianhu
3191.85	**2152.04**	**1861.36**	**2456.25**	**2328.55**	**3195.43**	**2234.08**	**1730.29**	**3664.89**	**3620.5**
1037.19	**173.35**	**640.57**	**461.62**	**425.42**	**561.29**	**418.2**			**0.83**
721.55	141.36	190.87	284.81	216.63	272.11	264.12			
289.43	24.05	65.7	138.21	164.2	155.47	150.63			
10.61	**30.69**	**7.48**	**188.65**	**6.04**	**494.06**	**24.43**			**1.06**
4.24			**5.39**						
95.94	**22.84**	**19.78**	**82.46**	**39.83**	**64.42**	**87.8**			
1691.55	**1890.43**	**1132.99**	**1587.42**	**1720.62**	**1944.48**	**1563.21**	**1582.24**	**3539.74**	**3311.79**
0.73			**7.06**	**3.93**		**23.96**			**1.65**
351.59	**34.74**	**60.54**	**123.66**	**132.72**	**131.18**	**116.48**	**148.05**	**125.06**	**305.17**

7-14　农村居民家庭平均每人生活消费支出（2003年）

单位：元

项　目	Item	西安市 Xi'an	灞桥区 Baqiao	未央区 Weiyang	雁塔区 Yanta
生活消费支出总计	**Living Expenditure**	**1802.76**	**1514.10**	**2695.99**	**2908.51**
一、食品消费支出	**Food**	**677.03**	**495.84**	**791.61**	**654.91**
二、衣着	**Clothing**	**113.15**	**129.06**	**166.46**	**232.16**
三、居住	**Residence**	**314.04**	**315.20**	**382.46**	**775.09**
四、家庭设备用品及服务	**Household Facilities,Articles and Service**	**98.59**	**69.31**	**170.98**	**208.20**
五、医疗保健	**Medical and Health Care Services**	**128.47**	**66.34**	**253.42**	**231.17**
六、交通通讯	**Transport,Post and Telecommunication Services**	**143.45**	**101.82**	**500.34**	**269.67**
七、文化娱乐用品及服务	**Culture,Educational and Recreational Articles and Services**	**296.80**	**306.42**	**404.83**	**470.34**
八、其它商品及服务	**Other Commodities and Services**	**31.22**	**30.10**	**25.88**	**66.98**
附：人均生活消费现金支出	Per Capita Cash Expenditure for Living Consumption	1588.71	1466.08	2578.21	2852.37

7-15　农村居民家庭人均生产情况（2003年）

单位：公斤

项　目	Item	西安市 Xi'an	灞桥区 Baqiao	未央区 Weiyang	雁塔区 Yanta
粮食产量	Output of Grain	556.38	133.18	294.36	90.91
其中：1. 小麦	Of the Total:Wheat	287.57	124.52	133.16	46.05
2. 玉米	Corn	266.50	7.40	160.85	44.86
3. 大豆	Soybean	1.07		0.36	
棉花产量	Output of Cotton	2.83			
油料产量	Output of Oil-bearing Crops	0.12			
蔬菜产量	Output of Vegetables	130.52	312.80	250.56	36.48
水果产量	Output of Fruits	108.85	112.96		10.20

Per Capita Living Expenditure of Rural Households（2003）

（yuan)

阎良区 Yanliang	长安区 Chang'an	蓝田县 Lantian	临潼区 Lintong	周至县 Zhouzhi	户 县 Huxian	高陵县 Gaoling	新城区 Xincheng	碑林区 Beilin	莲湖区 Lianhu
1691.55	**1890.43**	**1132.99**	**1587.42**	**1720.62**	**1944.48**	**1563.21**	**1582.24**	**3539.74**	**3311.79**
740.53	**805.28**	**490.39**	**611.29**	**586.08**	**594.53**	**654.49**	**713.52**	**1269.63**	**1044.52**
103.65	**79.29**	**100.07**	**87.59**	**113.92**	**105.26**	**89.63**	**186.77**	**284.03**	**251.06**
95.38	**382.35**	**120.86**	**450.16**	**199.69**	**571.91**	**212.93**	**213.67**	**195.01**	**580.78**
110.2	**106.07**	**73.13**	**63.21**	**103.69**	**82.05**	**75.52**	**84.86**	**88.41**	**313.09**
58.8	**109.66**	**73.47**	**89.83**	**126.57**	**146.92**	**100.95**	**62.67**	**233.38**	**304.83**
157.19	**66.33**	**86.89**	**104.6**	**111.66**	**135.88**	**110.54**	**134.53**	**246.43**	**234.61**
412.28	**320.05**	**173.68**	**167.61**	**330.73**	**270.67**	**278.99**	**172**	**1191.18**	**545.18**
13.53	**21.4**	**14.51**	**13.13**	**50.72**	**37.27**	**40.16**	**14.22**	**31.68**	**37.72**
1410.95	1616.22	962.21	1369.53	1537.72	1763.66	1395.18	1582.24	3539.74	3311.79

Output of Major Farm Crops Per Capita by Rural Households（2003）

（kg)

阎良区 Yanliang	长安区 Chang'an	蓝田县 Lantian	临潼区 Lintong	周至县 Zhouzhi	户 县 Huxian	高陵县 Gaoling	新城区 Xincheng	碑林区 Beilin	莲湖区 Lianhu
961.93	457.06	331.78	1009.73	381.45	795.55	1072.40			
459.37	235.13	228.16	489.91	195.03	417.57	514.49			
499.89	221.93	93.07	516.73	185.76	377.98	554.56			
0.72		8.64	0.23	0.04		0.73			
37.16									
			0.14	0.35	0.77				
554.00	0.22	97.25	70.44	9.71	48.00	18.31			
150.03			8.45	591.24	11.54	66.08			

7-16 农村居民家庭人均出售产品情况（2003年）

单位：公斤

项 目	Item	西安市 Xi'an	灞桥区 Baqiao	未央区 Weiyang	雁塔区 Yanta
粮食	Grain	212.71	32.06	153.54	23.64
棉花	Cotton	1.41			
油料	Oil-bearing Corps	0.03			
蔬菜	Vegetables	89.27	299.99	199.93	21.43
水果	Fruits	69.91	97.83		8.16
肉猪及猪肉	Fattened Hogs & Pork	17	3.23	13.19	
菜牛及牛肉	Beef Cattle & Beef	1.07	2.87		
菜羊及羊肉	Mutton Sheep & Mutton	0.19	0.22	0.6	
蛋类	Poultry Eggs	1.16			
奶类	Milks	44.64	28.57	181.61	

7-17 农村居民家庭人均粮食收支情况（2003年）

单位：公斤

项 目	Item	西安市 Xi'an	灞桥区 Baqiao	未央区 Weiyang	雁塔区 Yanta
一、粮食收入合计	**Total Grain Income**	**595.39**	**169.02**	**373.79**	**125.84**
1. 家庭经营生产	Self-produced	556.38	133.18	294.36	90.91
2. 购入	Purchased	34.98	35.84	79.18	34.93
3. 借入	Borrowed	0.32			
4. 收回借出粮	Grains Taken Back	3.63			
5. 其它粮食收入	Other Grain Income	0.08		0.24	
二、粮食支出合计	**Total Grain Expenditure**	**417.22**	**103.52**	**321.41**	**106.57**
1. 主食用粮	Staple Food	163	66.53	135.6	81.12
2. 其它生活用粮	Other Living Uses				
3. 出售	Sold Out	212.7	32.06	153.53	23.64
4. 种籽	Seeds	6.11	1	2.51	1.02
5. 饲料	Fodder	33.91	3.39	29.77	0.8
6. 借出	Lent Out	1.34			
7. 归还借粮	Grains Returned				
8. 其它粮食支出	Other Grain Expenditure	0.16			
三、年末粮食结存调查数	**Year-end Grain Deposite Balance**	**492.71**	**210.57**	**192.32**	**2.05**

Per Capita Product Sold by Rural Households（2003）

（kg）

阎良区 Yanliang	长安区 Chang'an	蓝田县 Lantian	临潼区 Lintong	周至县 Zhouzhi	户　县 Huxian	高陵县 Gaoling	新城区 Xincheng	碑林区 Beilin	莲湖区 Lianhu
228.77	189.33	54.78	533.41	113.57	292.45	457.16			
18.56									
			0.07		0.26				
169.40	0.28	75.21	65.33	1.38	40.70	16.85			
122.33		0.11	7.82	317.26	12.45	53.41			
11.15	8.60	23.77	5.84	34.67	40.88	27.89			
		5.64	0.55	0.59					
0.42		0.03	0.41		0.26	0.21			
0.01	0.02		0.62	0.29		8.01			
134.01		2.61	94.24			64.11			

Per Capita Annual Income and Expenditure of Grains of Rural Households（2003）

（kg）

阎良区 Yanliang	长安区 Chang'an	蓝田县 Lantian	临潼区 Lintong	周至县 Zhouzhi	户　县 Huxian	高陵县 Gaoling	新城区 Xincheng	碑林区 Beilin	莲湖区 Lianhu
992.87	**481.9**	**365.11**	**1090.41**	**412.56**	**825.46**	**1096.73**	**54.71**	**41.84**	**91.29**
961.93	457.06	331.78	1009.73	381.45	795.55	1072.4			
30.94	24.83	33.33	42.93	31.1	29.8	24.33	54.71	41.84	91.29
			3.04						
			34.19						
			0.52						
480.44	**352.76**	**269.5**	**819.44**	**363.62**	**569.02**	**741.59**	**41.81**	**35.97**	**72.31**
246.05	157.09	196.33	202.51	180.81	181.99	204.23	41.81	35.97	72.31
228.77	189.33	54.77	533.41	113.57	292.44	457.15			
1.47	3.23	3.03	15.7	8.68	18.95	5.83			
4.14	3.11	15.33	55.22	60.57	75.63	73.17			
			12.61						
						1.2			
290.68	**699.58**	**656.02**	**1119.49**	**287.05**	**716.99**	**637.35**			

7-18 农村居民家庭平均每人购买消费品（2003年）

单位：元

商品名称	Commodity Names	西安市 Xi'an	灞桥区 Baqiao	未央区 Weiyang	雁塔区 Yanta
一、食品类	**Food**	**350.83**	**364.03**	**560.36**	**509.36**
二、衣着类	**Clothing**	**111.76**	**128.63**	**165.1**	**227.93**
三、居住类	**Residence**	**199.52**	**242.14**	**231.87**	**512.44**
四、家用设备和日用品	**Household Facilities,Articles and Services**	**93.76**	**66.66**	**164.63**	**202.09**
五、交通、通讯类	**Transport,post and Telecommunication Services**	**52.45**	**36.82**	**129.87**	**81.19**
六、文教类	**Cultural and Edueation**	**51.55**	**36.06**	**27.98**	**102.38**
七、医疗保健类	**Medicines and Medical Services**	**50.8**	**16.56**	**66.34**	**68.48**
八、其他杂项商品	**Other Commodities and Services**	**10.29**	**9.78**	**7.31**	**26.71**

7-19 农村居民家庭人均主要食品消费量（2003年）

单位：公斤

食品名称	Food Names	西安市 Xi'an	灞桥区 Baqiao	未央区 Weiyang	雁塔区 Yanta
一、粮食	**Grain**	**163**	**66.53**	**135.6**	**81.12**
#小麦	Wheet	127.14	49.63	89.7	40.2
二、油脂类	**Oil or Fat**	**7.24**	**6.75**	**9.37**	**7.36**
三、蔬菜及菜制品	**Vegetable and Its Products**	**43.44**	**41.89**	**77.44**	**33.84**
四、瓜果类	**Melons and Fruits**	**5.86**	**3.23**	**8.49**	**3.32**
五、水果类	**Fruits**	**6.9**	**8.58**	**11.63**	**10.23**
六、肉禽及制品	**Meat,Poultry and Their Products**	**5.56**	**6.16**	**10**	**8.47**
七、蛋类及蛋制品	**Eggs and Its Products**	**3.39**	**4.52**	**6**	**4.19**
八、奶和奶制品	**Milk and Dairy Products**	**2.58**	**2.43**	**7.88**	**4.47**
九、酒	**Liquor**	**2.09**	**4.07**	**3.22**	**2.28**

Per Capita Purchase of Commodities in Rural Households（2003）

（yuan)

阎良区 Yanliang	长安区 Chang'an	蓝田县 Lantian	临潼区 Lintong	周至县 Zhouzhi	户　县 Huxian	高陵县 Gaoling	新城区 Xincheng	碑林区 Beilin	莲湖区 Lianhu
353.18	**359.82**	**284.23**	**349.35**	**259.05**	**315.02**	**371.32**	**661.01**	**1089.37**	**828.28**
98.27	**78.36**	**99.97**	**86.89**	**112.51**	**104.56**	**88.89**	**186.52**	**282.82**	**248.41**
50.5	**86.23**	**57.02**	**330.22**	**119.65**	**377.53**	**132.74**	**100.78**	**45.69**	**289.25**
97.44	**104.72**	**69.08**	**61.63**	**99.14**	**78.03**	**67.3**	**80.94**	**74.74**	**287.47**
93.41	**16.76**	**13.22**	**43.36**	**44.07**	**76.47**	**41.4**	**35.51**	**64.12**	**75.9**
52.71	**70.27**	**40.11**	**42.91**	**50.51**	**68.64**	**48.62**	**18.91**	**111.2**	**159.02**
20.91	**31.84**	**50.07**	**70.01**	**97.56**	**101.05**	**16.22**	**1.11**	**77.98**	**105.93**
2.26	**4.82**	**7.78**	**6.47**	**6.03**	**8.39**	**22.92**	**3.33**	**10.14**	**9.09**

Per Capita Average Food Consumption of Rural Households（2003）

（kg)

阎良区 Yanliang	长安区 Chang'an	蓝田县 Lantian	临潼区 Lintong	周至县 Zhouzhi	户　县 Huxian	高陵县 Gaoling	新城区 Xincheng	碑林区 Beilin	莲湖区 Lianhu
246.05	**157.09**	**196.37**	**202.51**	**180.81**	**181.99**	**204.23**	**41.81**	**35.97**	**72.31**
164.77	136.06	159.91	169.9	121.61	163.67	177.15	17.51	8.31	37.41
8.2	**8.33**	**4.71**	**8.54**	**5.14**	**6.95**	**9.04**	**8.21**	**6.54**	**8.94**
65.54	**48.94**	**23.32**	**48.24**	**38.47**	**32.44**	**42.36**	**60.55**	**50.55**	**74.8**
13.01	**4**	**0.93**	**6.18**	**5.1**	**6.39**	**9.48**	**6.41**	**6.44**	**10.77**
6.72	**7.16**	**1.38**	**7.47**	**8.47**	**5.32**	**5.21**	**13.05**	**12.57**	**17.52**
3.6	**6.63**	**2.05**	**4.72**	**7.29**	**7.76**	**3.77**	**10.48**	**10.22**	**15.67**
3.07	**5.06**	**1.35**	**3.45**	**2.42**	**3.61**	**2.27**	**9.14**	**4.38**	**5.83**
3.69	**1.9**	**2.17**	**3.56**	**0.48**	**1.27**	**1.06**	**2.91**	**10.95**	**17.47**
3.23	**1.77**	**1.14**	**2.77**	**0.63**	**1.17**	**1.92**	**4.03**	**1.61**	**4.05**

7-20 农村居民家庭每百户耐用消费品年末拥有量（2003年）

品　名	Item	西安市 Xi'an	灞桥区 Baqiao	未央区 Weiyang	雁塔区 Yanta
大型家具(件)	Large Furnitures (unit)	250	316	283	247
洗衣机(台)	Washing Machine(unit)	77	85	108	105
电风扇(台)	Electric Fan(unit)	155	178	212	205
电冰箱(台)	Refrigerator(unit)	24	38	68	80
自行车(辆)	Bicycle (unit)	169	165	187	177
摩托车(辆)	Motorcycle(unit)	33	40	40	62
电话机(部)	Telephone (unit)	66	61	80	92
寻呼机(台)	BP (unit)	3		3	18
彩色电视机(台)	Color TV Set(unit)	94	110	130	148
黑白电视机(台)	Black-white TV Set(unit)	32	21	18	23
影碟机(台)	Video Disc Player (unit)	33	57	42	55
照相机(架)	Camera(set)	9	22	20	25
家用计算机(台)	Computer(unit)	1			8

7-21 农村居民家庭人均住房情况（2003年）

指　标	Item	西安市 Xi'an	灞桥区 Baqiao	未央区 Weiyang
一、年末住房面积(平方米)	**Floor Space of Houses at the End of Year (sq.m)**	**33.90**	**31.35**	**34.83**
二、住房类型	**Pattern of Houses**			
1. 楼房面积(平方米)	Floor Space of Storied Building (sq.m)	18.11	20.75	33.50
2. 砖瓦平房面积(平方米)	Floor Space of Single-storey Building(sq.m)	13.27	10.60	1.33
3. 其它(平方米)	Others (sq.m)	2.52		
三、年末住房价值(元)	**Value of Houses at the End of Year (yuan)**	**7354.40**	**7614.74**	**10860.98**
四、年内新建（购）房屋面积(平方米)	**Floor Space Of Newly-Built Purchased Houses (sq.m)**	**0.98**	**1.03**	**0.41**
年内新建（购）房屋价值(元)	Value of Houses of Newly-Built Purchased (yuan)	239.47	339.07	97.56

Year-end Possession of Durable Consumer Goods Per 100 Rural Households（2003）

阎良区 Yanliang	长安区 Chang'an	蓝田县 Lantian	临潼区 Lintong	周至县 Zhouzhi	户 县 Huxian	高陵县 Gaoling	新城区 Xincheng	碑林区 Beilin	莲湖区 Lianhu
277	140	307	316	238	235	153	200	130	260
83	67	53	66	50	70	89	113	100	103
160	141	84	176	83	163	166	170	127	157
15	14	9	9	2	7	14	107	100	97
222	120	134	171	140	233	171	153	143	157
52	14	19	28	28	17	39	23		17
80	50	50	65	60	64	66	100	107	103
		9			2				
90	69	83	78	71	73	96	110	110	143
22	43	41	44	34	57	24			
43	17	44	19	11	23	26	107	47	60
2	3	3		4	3	6	30	20	43
2							33	60	20

Per Capita Housing Conditions of Rural Households（2003）

雁塔区 Yanta	阎良区 Yanliang	长安区 Chang'an	蓝田县 Lantian	临潼区 Lintong	周至县 Zhouzhi	户 县 Huxian	高陵县 Gaoling	新城区 Xincheng	碑林区 Beilin	莲湖区 Lianhu
50.98	**29.08**	**28.17**	**27.15**	**33.66**	**29.14**	**37.08**	**40.43**	**31.65**	**21.32**	**38.89**
49.18	4.62	19.64	13.08	5.99	8.72	21.21	14.45	31.65	21.32	38.89
1.80	24.29	7.80	6.82	25.35	13.39	8.60	25.66			
	0.17	0.73	7.25	2.32	7.03	7.27	0.32			
11515.33	**7008.47**	**6186.05**	**5179.94**	**6146.41**	**5836.10**	**6543.10**	**8056.23**	**9961.86**	**8720.18**	**17967.77**
		0.66	**0.78**	**1.69**	**0.08**	**2.67**	**2.05**			**4.23**
		232.56	161.81	341.10	13.37	596.54	479.22			1487.60

主要统计指标解释

城市居民家庭全部收入 指被调查城市居民家庭全部的实际收入，包括经常或固定得到的收入和一次性收入。不包括周转性收入，如提取银行存款、向亲友借款、收回借出款以及其他各种暂收款。

城市居民家庭可支配收入 指被调查的城市居民家庭在支付所得税、记帐补贴、个人交纳的社会保障费后所余下的实际收入。

城市居民家庭消费性支出 指被调查的城市居民家庭用于日常生活的全部支出，包括购买商品支出和文化生活、服务等非商品性支出。不包括罚没、丢失款和缴纳的各种税款（如个人所得税、牌照税、房产税等），也不包括个体劳动者生产经营过程中发生的各项费用。

农村居民家庭纯收入 指农村常住户当年从各个来源得到的总收入相应地扣除所发生的费用后的收入总和。

农村居民家庭生活消费支出 指农村住户用于物质生活和精神生活方面的支出。

Explanatory Notes on Main Statistical Indicators

Total Income of Urban Households refers to the total actual income of the sample households, including regular or fixed income and occasional income. The income of a circulating nature such as withdrawal from bank deposits, loans borrowed from relatives or friends, repayment of loans received and various temporary collection of money is excluded.

Disposable Income of Urban Households refers to the actual income of the sample households which can be used for daily expenses, i.e., total income minus income tax, sample household subsidy and personal social security.

Expenditure for Consumption of Urban Households refers to total expenditure of the sample households for consumption in daily life, including expenditure for various commodities and expenses for non-commodity items such as culture and service, etc. ,but excluding fines and confiscation, loss, tax payments (such as income tax, license tax, real estates tax, etc.) and various expenses by individual laborers for business purposes.

Net income of country household: it refers to sum of income of country households after taking out of the expenditures from all sides of resources of the year.

Living consuming expenditure of country household: it refers to expenditures used for material life and culture life of the country households.

2004

統計年鑒

八、城市公用事业及环境保护

URBAN PUBLIC UTILITIES AND ENVIRONMENT PROTECITION

简 要 说 明

Brief Introduction

本章资料反映我市公用事业及环境保护的基本情况。公用事业资料主要包括城市供水、售电、燃气、公共交通、市政设施、城市设施水平、城市规模及用地状况、园林绿地、环境卫生、环境保护和城市供热等情况。

本章资料由市统计局人口与社会科技处根据有关部门提供的数据资料整理。

Data in this chapter reflects basic condition of urban public utilities and environment protection of Xi'an city. Data on public utilities are consist of primarily urban water supply, electricity sales, gas sales, public transportation, municipal facilities, condition of city utilities, scale of the city, condition of land utilization, parks, greenbelt, environmental sanitation, environment protection and urban heating.

Data in this chapter is compiled by Population & Employment Division and Social & Science and Technology Division of the Xi'an Bureau of Statistics according to the data provided by department concerned of the municipal government.

8-1 城市供水

Urban Water Supply

指 标	Item	2000	2001	2002	2003
年末水厂个数（个）	Number of Water Factory at Year-end (unit)	8	8	8	8
供水综合生产能力（万立方米/日）	Total Volume of Water Supply (10 000 cu.m\day)	140	159	164	197
#地下水	#Groundwater	74	83	45	73
年末供水管道总长度（公里）	Length of Water Supply Pipelines at Year-end (km)	2237	2376	2453	2318
全年供水总量（万立方米）	Total Annual Volume of Water Supply (10 000 cu.m)	30273	32016	33776	36122
#生产运营用水	#For Productive Use	6486	7132	4827	8694
居民家庭用水	For Residential Use	10949	11653	13181	12002
用水人口（万人)	Population with Access to Tap Water (10 000 persons)	256.97	258.97	249.01	362.7

8-2 城市售电

Urban Consumption of Elecricity

单位:万千瓦时 (10000kwh)

指 标	Item	2000	2001	2002	2003
总 计	**Total**	**732373**	**794623**	**879232**	**968632**
一、农、林、牧、渔、水利业	**Farming,Forestry,Animal Husbandry, Fishery and Water Conservancy**	**77579**	**81966**	**87897**	**91900**
#排灌	#Irrigation Operation Waste	59207	60133	60133	66066
二、工业	**Industry**	**345175**	**351579**	**374939**	**410694**
1 .轻工业用电	Light Industrial	152125	152221	156891	167501
2 .重工业用电	Heavy Industrial	193050	199358	218048	243193
三、地质普查和勘探业	**Geological Census and Prospecting**	**892**	**1030**	**940**	**720**
四、建筑业	**Construction**	**9070**	**10454**	**10919**	**14265**
五、交通运输、邮电通讯业	**Transportation,Post & Telecommunication Services**	**22904**	**32303**	**37642**	**39125**
六、商业、公共饮食、物供和仓储业	**Commerce,Catering Services,Materials Supply, Marketing and Storage**	**54092**	**62866**	**72873**	**77705**
七、其他事业	**Others**	**90143**	**105979**	**124738**	**146745**
八、城乡居民生活用电	**Residential Electricity Consumption**	**132518**	**148446**	**169283**	**187478**
1.乡村	#In Rural Areas	31281	32834	37434	39995
2. 城市	In Urban Areas	101237	115612	131849	147483

8-3 燃气

Gas Supply

指　标	Item	2000	2001	2002	2003
一、煤气	**Goal Gas**				
管道长度（公里）	Total Length of Gas Pipelines (km)	179	150	147	147
供气总量（万立方米）	Total Gas Supply (10 000 cu.m)	2163	1670	1332	1258
#家庭用量	#Residential Households	2056	1580	1132	1006
用气人口（万人）	Population with Access to Gas (10 000 persons)	20	19	19	15.2
二、天然气	**Natural Gas**				
管道长度（公里）	Total Length of Gas Pipelines (km)	480	604	767	713
供气总量（万立方米）	Total Gas Supply(10 000 cu.m)	11513	16712	22737	32268
#家庭用量	#Residential Households	2808	3072	4235	6009
用气人口（万人）	Population with Access to Gas (10 000 persons)	79.51	90.10	118.20	127
三、液化石油气	**Liquefied Petroeum Gas**				
供气总量（吨）	Total Gas Supply (ton)	43304	80643	65406	77084
#家庭用量	#Residential Households	43303	80643	65406	76694
用气人口（万人）	Population with Access to Gas (10 000 persons)	101.55	104.60	83.40	191.9

8-4 城市公共交通

Urban Public Traffic

指　标	Item	2000	2001	2002	2003
运营车辆(辆)	Operating Vehicles (unit)	2573	2740	3024	3736
1.汽车	Bus	2488	2658	2945	3661
#小公共	#Small-scale Bus	486	804	834	1522
2.电车	Trolley	85	82	79	75
标准运营车辆（标台）	Standard Vehicles (unit)	2509	2689	2948	3797
运营线路网长度（公里）	Length of Routes (km)	434	434	416	795
客运总量(万人次)	Number of Passengers earried (10 000 persons)	44570	41489	48054	54492
1.汽车	Bus	41940	39364	47845	52811
#小公共	#Small-scale Bus	6613	6285	7955	11120
2.电车	Trolley	2630	2125	2090	1680
出租汽车数（辆）	Number of Taxis (unit)	10277	10430	11045	11028

8–5　市政设施
Manicipal Facilities

指　　标	Item	2000	2001	2002	2003
一、道路长度（公里）	**Length of Roads （km)**	**975**	**989**	**999**	**1274**
二、道路面积（万平方米）	**Area of Roads (10 000 sq.m)**	**1263**	**1910**	**1939**	**2284**
三、人行道面积（万平方米）	**Area of Sidewalks (10 000 sq.m)**	**636**	**660**	**750**	**923**
四、桥梁数（座）	**Number of Bridges (unit)**	**79**	**79**	**90**	**122**
#立交桥	#Crossroads	22	22	22	27
五、路灯盏数（盏）	**Number of Street Lights (unit)**	**27516**	**29093**	**31187**	**40451**
六、排水管道长度（公里）	**Length of Drainage Pipelines (km)**	**835**	**871**	**877**	**1559**
七、污水年排放量（万立方米）	**Annual Discharge Volume of Sewage (10 000 cu.m)**	**23543**	**32016**	**32036**	**30567**
八、污水处理厂处理能力（万立方米/日）	**Daily Disposal Capacity of Sewage (10 000 cu.m/day)**	**29**	**29**	**31**	**38**
九、污水年处理量（万立方米）	**Year Disposal Capacity of Sewage (10 000 cu.m)**	**5441**	**7025**	**11315**	**11315**
十、防洪堤长度（公里）	**Length of Flood control Dikes (km)**	**1.60**	**1.60**	**1.60**	**20**

8–6　城市设施水平
Urban Manicipal Facilities

（非农业人口）　　(Non-agricultural Population)

指　　标	Item	2000	2001	2002	2003
一、人均拥有城市维护建设资金（元）	**Per Capita City Facility Maintenance Fund(yuan)**	**653.66**	**805.00**	**915.00**	**2390**
二、人均使用面积（平方米）	**Gross Living Space Per Capita (sq.m)**	**13.72**	**14.64**	**15.54**	**15.6**
三、人均居住面积（平方米）	**Net Living Space Per Capita (sq.m)**	**10.19**	**10.90**	**11.05**	**11.15**
四、人均日生活用水量（升）	**Per Capita Daily Consumption of Tap Water For Residential Use (liter)**	**241.54**	**214.37**	**252.34**	**172.29**
五、每万人拥有公共交通车辆（标台）	**Number of Public Transport Vehicles Per 10 000 Population (unit)**	**10.17**	**10.73**	**11.68**	**14.59**
六、人均拥有道路面积（平方米）	**Per Captia Area of Roads (sq.m)**	**5.12**	**5.14**	**7.68**	**8.78**
七、排水管道密度（公里/平方公里）	**Density of Drainage Pipelines (km/sq.km)**	**4.47**	**4.66**	**4.69**	**7.65**
八、污水处理率（%）	**Rate of Sewerage Disposal (%)**	**23.11**	**21.94**	**35.32**	**37.02**
九、园林绿化	**Afforestation in Parks and Gardens**				
#人均公共绿地面积（平方米）	#Per Capita Public Green Areas (sq.m)	5.12	5.27	5.42	5.35
建城区绿地率（%）	Rate of Green Areas in Developed Areas (%)	19.67	20.05	20.76	19.41
建城区绿化覆盖率（%）	Coverage Rate of Green Areas in Developed Areas (%)	33.29	34.22	35.06	32.17
十、垃圾无害化处理率（%）	**Rate of No Harm Disposal of Garbage (%)**	**90.89**	**99.24**	**95.80**	**86.89**

8–7 城市设施水平

Urban Manucipal Facilites

指　　标	Item	2001	2002	2003
一、人均拥有城市维护建设资金（元）	**Per Capita City Facility Maintenance Fund (yuan)**	**570.00**	**646.00**	**1698**
二、人均日生活用水量（升）	**Per Capita Daily Consumption of Tap Water For Residential Use (liter)**	**214.37**	**252.34**	**172.29**
三、用水普及率（%）	**Percentage of Population with Access Tap Water (%)**	**69.88**	**69.67**	**99.04**
四、每万人拥有公共交通车辆（标台）	**Number of Public Transport Vehicles Per 10 000 Population (unit)**	**7.61**	**8.25**	**10.37**
五、用气普及率（%）	**Gas-Consuming Popularization (%)**	**60.55**	**61.84**	**91.23**
六、人均拥有道路面积（平方米）	**Per Captia Area of Roads (sq.m)**	**3.64**	**5.43**	**6.24**
七、排水管道密度（公里/平方公里）	**Density of Drainage Pipelines (km/sq.km)**	**4.66**	**4.69**	**7.65**
八、污水处理率（%）	**Rate of Sewerage Disposal (%)**	**21.94**	**35.32**	**37.02**
九、园林绿化	**Afforestation and Parks and Gardens**			
#人均公共绿地面积（平方米）	#Per Capita Public Green Areas (sq.m)	3.74	3.83	3.8
建城区绿地率（%）	Rate of Green Areas in Developed Areas (%)	20.05	20.76	19.41
建城区绿化覆盖率（%）	Coverage Rate of Green Areas in Developed Areas (%)	34.22	35.06	32.17
十、垃圾无害化处理率（%）	**Rate of No Harm Disposal of Garbage (%)**	**99.24**	**95.80**	**86.89**

8–8 城市规模及用地情况

City Scale and Land Use

指　标	Item	2000	2001	2002	2003
城市面积（平方公里）	Area of city(sq.km)	1256	1256	1276	1275.97
城建区面积（平方公里）	Area of the Constructed Regions (sq.km)	186.97	186.97	202.66	203.77
城市建设用地（平方公里）	Land use for Construction (sq.km)	175.27	183.73	199.80	201.91
#工业用地	#Industrial	35.40	35.81	36.85	36.85
仓储用地	Storage	8.39	8.47	7.65	7.65
对外交通用地	External Transportation	10.25	10.67	11.15	11.15
生活居住用地	Residential Area	73.47	76.99	84.78	85.78

8-9 城市园林绿化

Urban Park,Gardens and Green Areas in Cities

指　标	Item	2000	2001	2002	2003
一、公园个数（个）	**Number of Parks (unit)**	**47**	**47**	**45**	**45**
二、公园面积（公顷）	**Area of Parks (hectare)**	**880**	**1150**	**1202**	**1202**
三、园林绿地总面积（公顷）	**Total Area of Parks,Gardens and Green Areas (hectare)**	**4116**	**4238**	**4238**	**4502**
#公共绿地	#Public Green Areas	1263	1320	1367	1391
四、年末绿化覆盖面积（公顷）	**Coverage Space of Green Areas at year-end (hectare)**	**6542**	**6735**	**6873**	**6994**
五、建城区绿化覆盖率（%）	**Coverage of Green Areas in Developed Areas (%)**	**33.29**	**34.22**	**35.06**	**32.17**

8-10 城市环境卫生

Urban Environment Sanitation

指　标	Item	2000	2001	2002	2003
从业人数(人)	Number of Employed Persons (person)	7632	8575	9180	10727
清扫面积(万平方米)	Area Under Cleaning Program (10 000sq.m)	1739.00	1925.00	1925.00	2652
清运生活垃圾（万吨）	Volume of Residential Garbage Disposal (10 000 tons)	98.00	131.60	126.00	147
清运粪便（万吨）	Volume of Excrement and Urine Disposal (10 000 tons)	5.00	4.50	4.50	4
公共厕所（座）	Number of Public Lavatories (unit)	430	410	370	386
市容环卫专用车辆（台）	Special Vehicles of Environmental Sanitation (unit)	330	369	484	581

8-11 城市环境保护

Urban Environmental Protection

指　标	Item	2000	2001	2002	2003
一、工业废水排放量（万吨）	**Volume of Industrial Wastewater Discharged (10 000 tons)**	**9145**	**7487**	**10705**	**11246**
工业废水排放达标量（万吨）	Volume of Industrial Wastewater up to the Discharge Standards	6130	6596	8249	9047
二、工业废气排放量（万标立方米）	**Total Volume of Industrial Waste Gas Emission (10 000 cu.m)**	**2759719**	**2739806**	**3034592**	**3531403**
#燃料燃烧中排放的	#Volume of Waste Gas in the Process of Fuel Burning	1942884	1975417	2275727	2683018
#生产工艺中排放的	#Volume of Waste Gas from the Process of Production	816835	764389	758865	848385
三、工业固体废物产生量（万吨）	**Volume of Industrial Solid Wastes Produced (10 000 tons)**	**107**	**105**	**118**	**126**
工业固体废物处置量	Volume of Industrial Solid Wastes Treated	20	6	7	5
工业固体废物综合利用量	Volume of Industrial Solid Waste Utilized in a Comprehensive Way	63	69	112	103
四、工业锅炉（台/蒸吨）	**Industrial Boilers(unit/ton)**	**691/6258**	**621/5962**	**746/6097**	**708/6484**
#烟尘排放达标的	#Up to the Standards	662/6107	603/5826	718/6014	683/6365

8-12 城 市 供 热

Heating in Urban Area

指　标	Item	2000	2001	2002	2003
供热能力	Heating Capacity				
蒸气（吨/小时）	Steam (ton/hour)	766	1046	1111	1785
热水（兆瓦）	Hot Water (1 billion kw)	405	405	483	763
供热总量	Volume Supplied				
蒸气（万吉焦）	Steam (10 000 gigajoules)	126	251	262	1499
热水（万吉焦）	Hot Water (10 000 gigajoules)	202	321	386	553
管道长度（公里）	Length of Pipelines (km)				
蒸气	Steam	221	235	268	282
热水	Hot Water	133	126	161	176
供热面积（万平方米）	Heated Area (10 000sq.m)	854	991	1176	2175
#住宅	#Residential Buildings	536	630	781	1772

主要统计指标解释

年末自来水生产能力 指年底城建部门管理的自来水厂和自备水源的社会单位取水、净化、送水、出厂输水干管等环节的实际生产能力。

年末供水管道长度 指从送水泵到用户水表之间所有管道的长度。

全年供水总量 指公用自来水厂和自备水源的社会单位全年的供水总量，包括有效供水量及损失水量。

生活用水量 指居民日常生活与公共福利设施的用水量，包括居民、饮食店、旅馆、医院、理发店、浴池、洗衣店、游泳池、商店、学校、机关、部队等单位的用水量。

城市人口用水普及率 指城市用水人口数与城市人口总数之比。计算公式为:

用水普及率＝城市用水人口数/城市人口总数*100%

人工煤气生产能力 指城市煤气厂制气、净化、输送等环节的综合实际生产能力。

输气管道长度 指由压缩机、鼓风机、储气罐的出口到用户煤气表之间的全部管道长度。

全年供气总量 指全年售给各类用户的全部煤气量，包括工业用量、家庭用量和其他用量。

城市用气普及率 指使用煤气（包括人工煤气、液化石油气、天然气）的城市人口数与城市人口总数之比。计算公式为:

城市用气普及率＝城市用气人口数/城市人口总数*100%

城市供热能力 指热电厂、热力公司和达到标准的集中采暖锅炉房向城市输送的供热源的设计能力，即每小时向城市输送蒸汽、热水的能力。

城市供热总量 指热电厂、热力公司和达到标准的集中采暖锅炉房向城市输送的全部蒸汽、热水量。

城市供热管道长度 指热电厂、热力公司和达到标准的集中采暖锅炉房管理的集中供热热源到用户之间的全部供气、供热水的管道长度。

年底实有铺装道路长度 指除土路外，路面经过铺装宽度在3.5米以上的道路，包括高级、次高级道路和普通道路。

城市桥梁 指城市范围内，修建在河道上的桥梁和道路与道路立交、道路跨越铁路的立交桥及人行天桥。包括永久性桥和半永久性桥，不包括临时性桥、铁路桥、涵洞。

城市下水道总长度 指所有排水总管、干管、支管及暗渠、检查井、连接井进出水口等长度之和。

城市污水日处理能力 指污水处理厂每昼夜处理污水量的设计能力。

年末实有公共汽（电）车 指年底可参加营运的全部车辆数，包括营运车辆数和库存查封未参加营运的车辆。不包括非营运车辆，如架线车、油罐车、工程车、货车及其他专用车辆和借入的客运车辆。

城市园林绿地面积 指城市公共绿地、专用绿地、生产绿地、防护绿地、郊区风景名胜区的全部面积。

公共绿地 指供游览休息的各种公园、动物园、植物园、陵园以及花园、游园和供游览休息用的林荫道绿地、广场绿地，不包括一般栽植的行道树及林荫道的面积。

工业废水排放量 指经过企业厂区所有排放口排到企业外部的工业废水量。包括生产废水、外排的直接冷却水、超标排放的矿井地下水和与工业废水混排的厂区生活污水，不包括外排的间接冷却水（清污不分流的间接冷却水应计算在内）。

工业废水排放达标量 指各项指标都达到国家或地方排放标准的外排工业废水量，包括未经处理外排达标和经过处理后外排达标两部分。

工业废水处理量 指报告期内各种水治理设施实际处理的工业废水量，包括处理后外排和处理后回用的工业废水量和虽经处理但未达到国家或地方排放标准的废水量。如车间和厂排放口均有治理设施，并对同一废水分级处理时，不应重复计算工业废水处理量。

工业废气排放量 指企业厂区内燃料燃烧和生产工艺过程中产生的各种排入空气的含有污染物的气体总量，按标准状态〔273K，101325Pa〕计算。

工业二氧化硫排放量 指企业在燃料燃烧和生产工艺过程中排入大气的二氧化硫数量。

烟尘排放量 指企业厂区内燃料燃烧产生的烟气中夹带的颗粒物数量。

工业粉尘排放量 指企业在生产工艺过程中排放的颗粒物重量，如钢铁企业的耐火材料粉尘、焦化企业的筛焦系统粉尘、烧结机的粉尘、石灰窑的粉尘、建材企业的水泥粉尘等。不包括电厂排入大气的烟尘。

工业固体废物产生量 指企业在生产过程中产生的固体状、半固体状和高浓度液体状废弃物的总量，包括危险废物、冶炼废渣、粉煤灰、炉渣、煤矸石、尾矿、放射性废物和其他废物等;不包括矿山开采的剥离废石和掘进废石（煤矸石和呈酸性或碱性的废石除外）。酸性或碱性废石指采掘的废石其流经水、雨淋水的pH值小于4或pH值大于10.5者。

工业固体废物处置量 指将固体废物焚烧或者最终置于符合环境保护规定要求的场所，并不再回取的工业固体废物量（包括当年处置往年的工业固体废物累计贮存量）。处置方法有填埋（其中危险废物应安全填埋）、焚烧、专业贮存场（库）封场处理、深层灌注、回填矿井等。

工业固体废物排放量 指将所产生的固体废物排到固体废物污染防治设施、场所以外的数量，不包括矿山开采的剥离废石和掘进废石（煤矸石和呈酸性或碱性的废石除外）。

"三废"综合利用产品产值 指利用"三废"（废液、废气、废渣）作为主要原料生产的产品价值（现行价）；已经销售或准备销售的应计算产品价值，留作生产自用的不应计算产品价值。

"三废"综合利用产品利润 指利用"三废"（废液、废气、废渣）生产的产品，销售后所得到的利润。

Explanatory Notes on Main Statistical Indicators

Production Capacity of Tap Water at the Year-end refers to the actual comprehensive production capacity of the waterworks administered by the urban construction department and those owned by enterprises or institutions, taking the capacity of the main links, such as water inflow, purification, conveyance and outflow of the trunk pipelines into account.

Length of Water Supply Pipelines at the Year-end refers to the total length of all the pipelines between the water pumps and the users water meters.

Annual Volume of Water Supply refers to the total volume of water supplied by the public water-works and those owned by individual enterprises and institutions during the whole year, including both the effective water supply and loss during the water supply.

Consumption of Water for Residential Use refers to the water consumption of households for daily life and the water consumption of public welfare facilities, including the consumption of restaurants, hotels, hospitals, barber shops, public bathhouses, laundries, swimming pools, shops, schools, institutions, army units and other units.

Percentage of Urban Population with Access to Tap Water refers to the ratio of the urban population with access to tap water to the total urban population. The formula is:

Percentage of Population with Access to Tap Water=(Urban Population with Access to Tap Water) / (Urban Population) 100%

Production Capacity of Gaswork Gas refers to the actual comprehensive production capacity of the urban gasworks in gas generation, purification and delivery.

Length of Gas Pipelines refers to the total length of pipelines between the outlet of the compressor, blower or gas tank and the gas meters of users.

Volume of Gas Supply refers to the total volume of gas sold to users in a year, including the volume for industrial use, residential use and other uses.

Percentage of Urban Population with Access to Gas refers to the ratio of the urban non-agricultural population with access to gas (including gas, liquefied petroleum gas and natural gas) to the urban population . The formula is:

Percentage of Population with Access to Gas =(Urban Population with Access to Gas) / Urban Population)*100%

Heating Capacity in Urban Area refers to the capacity of hourly supply of steam and hot water to cities by thermal power plants, heating corporations and centralized heating boiler rooms which meet certain standard.

Heating Volume in Urban Area refers to the total volume of steam and hot water supplied to cities every year by thermal power plants, heating corporations and centralized heating boiler rooms which meet certain standard.

Length of Heating Pipelines refers to the total length of pipelines for centralized supply of steam and hot water from the thermal power plants, heating corporations and centralized heating boiler rooms which meet certain standard to the users.

Length of Paved Roads at the Year-end refers to the length of roads with a paved surface, and with a width of more than 3-5 meters, including high quality, medium quality and ordinary roads.

Urban Bridges refer to bridges over river courses, great separated junctions and overpasses in urban areas. Permanent bridges and semi-permanent bridges are included. Temporary bridges, railway bridges and culverts are excluded.

Length of Urban Sewage Pipes refers to the total length of general drainage, trunks. branch and blind drainage, inspection wells, connection wells, inlets and outlets, etc.

Daily Disposal Capacity of Urban Sewage refers to the designed 24 hour capacity of sewage disposal at the sewage treatment works.

Number of Public Vehicles (Buses and Trolley buses) at the Year-end refers to the total number of operational buses available at the year-end, including the year-end operational vehicles and vehicles in stock. Non-operational vehicles such as stringing cars, tank cars, machine shop cars, trucks and other special vehicles and the borrowed passenger vehicles are excluded.

Area of Urban Gardens and Green Areas refers to the total area of urban public green land, special green land, production green land, protection green land and suburban scenic spots.

Public Green Area refers to green areas of various parks, zoos, botanical gardens, cemeteries, amusement parks, tree-flanked boulevards greenland squares for tourism and relaxing. Areas with trees planted along-side the streets and boulevards are excluded.

Volume of Industrial Waste Water Dischargedrefers to the volume of industrial waste water discharged, through all outlets, to the outside of industrial enterprises, including waste water produced, direct-cooling water, underground water from mines that does not meet the standard of discharge, and the domestic sewage mixed up with industrial waste water when discharged, but excluding discharged indirect-cooling water.

Volume of Waste Water up to the Standard for Discharge refers to the volume of discharged industrial waste water that, with or without treatment, has come up to the national or local standards for discharge.

Volume of Treated Industrial Waste Water refers to the volume of industrial waste water after being treated and purified through various water treatment facilities in the reference period, including the volume discharged or recovered after being treated. The volume of waste water that fails to meet the national or local standards after treatment is also included. If there are treatment facilities both at the outlets of workshops and at the outlets of the factory, and the same volume of waste water has been treated twice, duplication should be avoided in the calculation of the volume of treated industrial waste water.

Volume of Waste Industrial Gas Emission refers to waste gas emitted from burning of fuels and from production process in the area of the factory, and is measured by 10000 standard cubic meters each year under normal condition.

Volume of Industrial Sulphur Dioxide Discharged refers to the volume of sulphur dioxide discharged to the air in the process of fuel burning or in the production process.

Volume of Industrial Soot Discharged refers to the volume of solid soot in the smoke discharged in the process of fuel burning in the area of the factory.

Industrial Dust Discharged refers to the total weight of solid dust discharged by industrial enterprises in the production process, such as dust of refractory materials from iron plants, dust from coke-screening system or from sintering machines of coking plants, dust from lime kilns, cement dust from building material enterprises, etc., but excluding smoke and dust discharged by power plants.

Volume of Industrial Solid Wastes Produced refers to the total volume of solid, semi-solid or high concentration liquid residue produced by industrial enterprises in their production process, including dangerous wastes, residues from melting, slag, powdered coal ash, gangue, chemical residues, tailings, radioactive residues and other residues, but excluding stripped or dug stones in mining (except gangue and acid or alkali stones which are stones washed or soaked by water with a pH value smaller than 4 or larger than 10.5)

Volume of Industrial Solid Wastes Treated refers to solid wastes disposed of in a non-recoverable place that meet the requirement of environmental protection, such as burying (The dangerous wastes should be buried safely), burning, piling in designated sites, pouring water into the deep strata, filling of old mines, etc. (including treatment of solid wastes piled up in the previous years).

Volume of Industrial Solid Wastes Discharged refers to the volume of industrial solid wastes produced and discharged at the places outside the special facilities or special sites for preventing against pollution, excluding stripped or dug stones in mining (except gangue and acid or alkali waste stones).

Output Value of Products Made from Utilization of Waste Gas, Waste Water and Industrial Solid Wastes refers to the value of products (calculated at current prices) made by industrial enterprises using recovered waste water, waste gas or solid wastes as main raw materials. Only the value of the products which have been sold or are ready to be sold should be included. The value of the products which will be used in the production of the enterprises should not be included.

Profit Obtained from Utilization of Waste Gas, Waste Water and Industrial Solid Wastes refers to profit obtained from selling or own-consumption of products made by industrial enterprises using recovered waste water, waste gas or solid wastes as main raw materials.

九、农 业

AGRICULTURE

简 要 说 明
Brief Introduction

本章资料反映我市农业生产和农村经济的基本情况。内容主要包括农村基本情况、农业生产条件与生产情况、耕地、农林牧渔业产值、主要农产品产量以及各区县农业生产和农村经济效益主要指标。

本资料由市统计局农村处和市农村社会经济调查队等整理提供。

Data in this chapter reflects basic condition of agriculture production of Xi'an city. It is primarily consist of basic condition of rural area, condition of agriculture production, plow land, production value of farming, forestry, animal husbandry and fishery, gross yield of primary produce and primary Indicators of agriculture production and rural area economic performance.

The data are provided and compiled by Rural Area Division of the Xi'an Bureau of Statistics and Rural area social and economic survey crew of the municipal government.

9-1 主要年份乡村户数、人口和劳动力

Rural Household,Population and Labour in Representative Year

单位：万人 (10 000 person)

指 标	Item	1995	2000	2001	2002	2003
一、乡村户数(万户)	**Number of Households (10 000 households)**	**95.45**	**98.77**	**99.25**	**99.85**	**101.33**
二、乡村人口	**Rural Population**	**395.66**	**401.64**	**404.22**	**405.85**	**405.26**
三、乡村从业人员数	**Rural Laborers**	**212.37**	**212.65**	**211.36**	**215.31**	**221.69**
#女性	Female	102.05	99.07	98.87	100.23	102.78
1.农林牧渔业	Farming,Forestry,Animal Husbandry and Fishery	152.35	146.07	144.04	141.96	145.43
#农 业	Farming	134.32	126.48	119.89	124.24	123.3
2.工业	Industry	17.88	15.43	15.74	16.36	15.81
3.建筑业	Construction	14.49	16.45	16.72	17.69	19.28
4.交通运输仓储、邮电业	Transportation,Postal and Telecommunications Services	6.67	7.64	7.5	8.15	8.85
5.批零贸易餐饮业	Trade and Catering	5.59	8.14	8.25	8.5	8.53
6.金融、保险业	Banking and Insurance	0.31	0.45	0.44	0.68	0.52
7.其它	Other	15.08	18.47	18.67	21.97	23.27
#外出临时工、合同工	Contract or Temporary Workers Going Outside	6.84	9.37	10.7	12.27	12.94

9-2 农村基层组织、乡村户数、人口及劳动力情况

Grass-root Organizations, Households, Population and Labor Resources in Rural Area

指 标	Item	2000	2001	2002	2003
一、农村基层组织情况（个）	**Village Units**				
1.乡镇个数（个）	Number of Township and Town(unit)	168	168	119	108
#镇个数（个）	Number of Town(unit)	52	55	60	50
2.村民委员会个数（个）	Number of Villagers' Committees(unit)	3165	3165	3163	3161
3.村民小组个数（个）	Number of Village Group(unit)	16294	16291	16278	16288
4.区乡(镇)村干部总数（人）	Number of Cadres in Township/District/Town(person)	24142	24142	22297	21566
二、农村人口和从业人员情况	**Rural Population and Employment**				
1.乡村户数（万户）	Number of Households (10 000households)	98.77	99.25	99.85	101.33
2.乡村人口数（万人）	Rural Population(10 000 persons)	401.64	404.22	405.85	405.26
3.乡村劳动力资源总数（万人）	Total Number of Rural Labor Source (10 000 persons)	240.76	242.91	243.38	252.18
#劳动年龄内人口（万人）	#Population at Labor Age(10 000 persons)	232.43	232.73	228.28	228.92
4.乡村从业人员数（万人）	Rural Laborers(10 000 persons)	212.65	211.36	215.31	221.69
#女性	Female	99.07	98.87	100.23	102.78
(1)农林牧渔业	Laborers of Farming,Forestry,Animal,Husbandry and Fishery	146.07	144.04	141.96	145.43
#农业	Laborers of Farming	126.48	119.89	124.24	123.3
(2)工业	Laborers of Industry	15.43	15.74	16.36	15.81
(3)建筑业	Laborers of Construction	16.45	16.72	17.69	19.28
(4)交通仓储邮电业	Laborers of Transportation,Postal and Telecommunications Services	7.64	7.5	8.15	8.85
(5)批零贸易、餐饮业	Laborers of Trade and Catering	8.14	8.25	8.5	8.53
(6)金融、保险业	Laborers of Banking and Insurance	0.45	0.44	0.68	0.52
(7)其它	Laborers of Others	18.47	18.67	21.97	23.27
#外出临时工、合同工	Contract or Temporary Workers Going Outside	9.37	10.7	12.27	12.94
三、国有农林牧渔业从业人员数（万人）	**Number of staff and Workers in State-owned farms(10,000 Persons)**	**0.29**	**0.24**	**0.15**	**0.17**
四、自来水受益村数（个）	**Number of Villages Benefited from the Tap Water System(unit)**	**1527**	**1516**	**1569**	**1552**
通汽车村数	Number of Villages Accessible by motor Vehicles	2785	2818	2886	2876
通电话村数	Number of Villages Accessible by Telephone	2885	3029	3044	3062

9-3 各区县农村基层组织、乡村户数及人口（2003）

Grass-root Organizations, Households and Population in Rural Area by Region(2003)

区县	Region	乡镇个数（个）Number of Township and Town (unit)	镇个数 Number of Town	村民委员会个数 Number of Villagers' Committees	村民小组个数 Number of Village Group	乡村户数（万户）Number of Households (10000households)	乡村人口（万人）Number Rural Population (10 000 persons)
合计	**Total**	**108**	**50**	**3161**	**16288**	**101.33**	**405.26**
新城区	Xincheng			13	20	0.39	1.16
碑林区	Beilin			15	12	0.39	1.12
莲湖区	Lianhu			35	77	1.13	3.42
灞桥区	Baqiao	4	4	229	849	6.78	27.33
未央区	Weiyang			212	642	6.03	20.69
雁塔区	Yanta			120	512	4.23	15.05
阎良区	Yanliang	2	2	80	593	4.17	16.37
临潼区	Lintong	17	10	285	2085	13.57	55.77
长安区	Chang'an	15	4	672	3240	20.03	79.76
蓝田县	Lantian	22	10	519	2471	13.99	56.91
周至县	Zhouzhi	21	8	376	2564	13.62	58.39
户县	Huxian	18	9	518	2483	11.86	48.54
高陵县	Gaoling	9	3	87	740	5.14	20.75

9-4 各区县家庭从业人员数(2003年）

Number of Labers in Families by Region（2003）

单位：万人

区县	Region	乡村从业人员数 合计 Rural Laborers Total	女从业人员数 Female	农林牧渔业 Farming,Forestry Animal Husbandry and Fishery	农业 Farming	工业 Industry
合计	**Total**	**221.69**	**102.78**	**145.43**	**123.3**	**15.81**
新城区	Xincheng	0.5	0.29	0.1	0.03	0.04
碑林区	Beilin	0.59	0.29			
莲湖区	Lianhu	1.83	0.72	0.65	0.65	0.05
灞桥区	Baqiao	15.85	7.55	10.5	9.94	1.33
未央区	Weiyang	10.71	4.89	5.34	4.4	1.6
雁塔区	Yanta	7.12	3.45	3.47	2.88	0.71
阎良区	Yanliang	8.66	4.12	5.43	4.29	0.46
临潼区	Lintong	29.57	14.54	21.22	18.25	1.31
长安区	Chang'an	42.84	19.29	25.79	22.15	3.37
蓝田县	Lantian	31.19	14.33	22.1	14.09	1.01
周至县	Zhouzhi	33.71	14.82	25.34	24.3	1.69
户县	Huxian	27.62	12.98	18.21	16.61	3.67
高陵县	Gaoling	11.5	5.51	7.28	5.71	0.57

9-4 各区县家庭从业人员数(2003年)(续)

Number of Labers in Families by Region（2003）（Continued）

单位：万人 (10 000person)

区 县	Region	建筑业 Construction	交通仓储邮电业 Transportation, Postal and Telecommunication Services	批零贸易餐饮业 Trade and Catering	金融、保险业 Banking and Insurance	其他从业人员数 Others	外出临时工、合同工 Contract or Temporary Workers Going Outside
合 计	**Total**	19.28	8.85	8.53	0.52	23.27	12.94
新城区	Xincheng	0.05	0.06	0.05		0.20	0.02
碑林区	Beilin		0.03	0.04		0.52	0.04
莲湖区	Lianhu	0.12	0.07	0.18		0.76	0.02
灞桥区	Baqiao	0.95	0.58	0.45	0.01	2.03	1.44
未央区	Weiyang	0.64	0.72	0.51	0.03	1.87	0.58
雁塔区	Yanta	0.30	0.65	0.69	0.05	1.25	0.65
阎良区	Yanliang	1.16	0.44	0.42	0.03	0.72	0.37
临潼区	Lintong	2.94	0.90	1.07		2.13	0.95
长安区	Chang'an	5.66	2.05	1.42	0.15	4.40	2.61
蓝田县	Lantian	1.55	0.76	1.39	0.06	4.32	3.16
周至县	Zhouzhi	1.76	1.10	1.05	0.08	2.69	1.90
户 县	Huxian	2.45	0.98	0.84	0.09	1.38	0.61
高陵县	Gaoling	1.70	0.51	0.42	0.02	1.00	0.59

9-5 主要年份耕地面积

Area of Cultivated Land in Representative Year

单位：千公顷 (1000 hectares)

年 份 Year	年末实有耕地面积 Cultivated Area Year-end	水田 Paddy Field	水浇地 Irrigable Land	人均占有耕地面积（公顷）Per Capita Cultivated Area (hectares)
1970	369.39	12.13	198.03	0.13
1975	358.90	13.56	232.75	0.11
1978	353.97	11.13	246.97	0.11
1980	350.86	11.63	248.64	0.10
1985	339.25	11.75	218.73	0.09
1990	330.21	11.98	207.94	0.08
1991	328.06	11.35	206.11	0.08
1992	323.53	10.96	198.79	0.08
1993	319.36	9.57	202.99	0.08
1994	314.29	9.32	199.72	0.08
1995	309.31	11.36	185.34	0.08
1996	301.00	9.47	189.17	0.08
1997	304.41	7.93	193.66	0.08
1998	303.43	7.45	188.15	0.08
1999	300.49	7.54	187.97	0.08
2000	295.58	6.84	189.36	0.07
2001	287.79	6.00	183.15	0.07
2002	282.97	5.32	183.97	0.07
2003	275.89	4.43	175.83	0.07

9-6 各区县耕地面积(2003年)

单位：公顷

区　县	Region	年末实有耕地面积 Cultivated Area Year-end	水田 Paddy Field	旱地 Dry Land	水浇地 Irrigable Land	当年增加的耕地面积 Area of Newly Increased Cultivated Land	新开荒地面积 Area of Newly Reclamation of Wasteland
合　计	**Total**	**275893**	**4430**	**271463**	**175826**	**1610**	**222**
新城区	Xincheng	16		16	16		
碑林区	Beilin	5		5	5		
莲湖区	Lianhu	270		270	270		
灞桥区	Baqiao	14505	47	14458	8814	29	1
未央区	Weiyang	8137	42	8095	8095	94	
雁塔区	Yanta	4859		4859	2486		
阎良区	Yanliang	16656		16656	16654	101	55
临潼区	Lintong	51181	2	51179	38466	19	3
长安区	Chang'an	50457	2150	48307	23521	184	8
农工商	FIC CO.	1271	20	1251	1251	25	
蓝田县	Lantian	40101	873	39228	5027	203	50
周至县	Zhouzhi	33977	655	33322	24202	624	86
户　县	Huxian	39326	641	38685	31887	66	10
高陵县	Gaoling	15132		15132	15132	265	9

Area of Cultivated Land by Region（2003）

(hectares)

当年减少的耕地面积 Decrease in Cultivated Area in the Year	国家基建占地 Capital Construction	乡村集体基建占地 Village Collective Construction	农民个人建房占地 Peasant Housing Construction	退耕改果、茶、桑面积 Area for Change into Fruit, Tea and Mulberry	退耕造林面积 Area for Change into Woods
10282	**3191**	**191**	**257**	**1982**	**3526**
33	20	12	1		
1		1			
20	18	1		1	
221	110	4	13	4	22
432	242	43	13	36	14
304	304				
475	32	12	10	111	
685	148	11	42	14	150
1871	1031	53	61	172	419
34				24	
2350	42	12	38	387	1733
1278	118	19	43	213	832
791	338	15	27	71	325
1787	788	8	9	949	31

9-7 农村非农行业总产值

Gross Output Value of Non-agricultural Trades in Rural Areas

单位：亿元 (100 million yuan)

年 份 Year	农村工业总产值 Gross Output Value of Industry	农村建筑业产值 Gross Output Value of Construction	农村运输业产值 Gross Output Value of Transportation	农村批发、零售、贸易餐饮业产值 Gross Output Value of Sale and Catering Trade
1990	34.39	4.93	5.54	4.49
1991	39.04	5.28	6.14	5.26
1992	49.68	6.69	7.26	6.57
1993	59.12	8.36	9.15	8.67
1994	70.94	10.87	11.53	11.36
1995	84.42	14.13	14.76	14.77
1996	103.84	19.08	18.45	19.35
1997	125.65	24.42	23.43	26.12
1998	154.55	32.23	29.29	34.74
1999	186.19	41.90	36.61	44.81
2000	214.12	56.57	45.40	60.05
2001	246.00	73.92	56.25	78.64
2002	286.21	86.02	58.83	79.61
2003	298.61	86.87	58.12	85.43

9-8 各区县农村非农行业总产值(2003年）

Gross Output Value of Non-agricultural Trades in Rural Areas by Region（2003）

单位：万元 (10 000yuan)

区 县	Region	农村工业总产值 Gross Output Value of Industry	农村建筑业产值 Gross Output Value of Construction	农村运输业产值 Gross Output Value of Transportation	农村批发、零售、贸易餐饮业产值 Gross Output Value of Sale and Catering Trade
合 计	**Total**	**2986119**	**868690**	**581181**	**854338**
新城区	Xincheng	21957	–	24722	10849
碑林区	Beilin	646	312	1463	9100
莲湖区	Lianhu	4378	17621	16439	39751
灞桥区	Baqiao	410318	10104	23611	46657
未央区	Weiyang	586628	21765	26599	151499
雁塔区	Yanta	289416	38900	2780	39900
阎良区	Yanliang	114585	77926	56098	52726
临潼区	Lintong	243800	250530	59965	78001
长安区	Chang'an	630169	314339	207305	254867
蓝田县	Lantian	93300	38306	31057	71574
周至县	Zhouzhi	63969	37618	40998	58478
户 县	Huxian	449600	51197	15936	24354
高陵县	Gaoling	77353	10072	74208	16582

9–9 主要年份农林牧渔业总产值及指数

Gross Output Value of Farming,Forestry,Animal Husbandry and Fishery and Related Indices in Representative Years

单位：万元 （10 000yuan）

年份 Year	总产值 Gross Output Value	农业 Farming	林业 Forestry	牧业 Animal Husbandry	渔业 Fishery	指数（上年=100） Indices(preceding year=100)
1970	40617	35965	713	3896	43	111.2
1975	55322	47378	1509	6403	32	93.9
1978	65423	56519	1444	7427	33	104.7
1980	65322	54004	1177	10106	35	85.0
1985	134933	105888	2559	26186	300	106.4
1990	262073	191088	3134	65840	2011	102.5
1991	295620	208324	3362	81070	2864	108.6
1992	321155	219160	4225	94045	3725	108.6
1993	387068	261959	5031	115810	4268	112.8
1994	565056	359609	7819	192140	5488	102.4
1995	754597	513348	7185	228598	5466	106.8
1996	786003	552726	7573	219214	6490	102.1
1997	836201	585973	9226	233623	7379	110.3
1998	853279	625465	8146	212045	7623	107.5
1999	739905	530029	8883	194552	6441	100.7
2000	743712	514845	8482	212612	7773	104.3
2001	767511	527160	8427	223861	8063	103.2
2002	797444	539978	11378	238761	7327	103.9
2003	837857	551398	10550	269610	6299	105.1

9-10 各县区不变价农林牧渔业总产值(2003年)

Gross Output Value of Farming, Forestry, Animal Husbandry and Fishery at Constant Price by Region（2003）

单位：万元　　　　　　　　　　　　　　　　　　　　(10 000yuan)

区　县	Region	总产值 Gross Output Value	农业产值 Gross Output Value of Farming	林业产值 Gross Output Value of Forestry	牧业产值 Gross Output Value of Animal Husbandry	渔业产值 Gross Output Value of Fishery
全　市	**Total**	**506785**	**336944**	**4562**	**160640**	**4639**
新城区	Xincheng	152	38	1	113	–
碑林区	Beilin	1	–	–	1	–
莲湖区	Lianhu	1048	1048	–	–	–
灞桥区	Baqiao	30308	24573	114	5005	616
未央区	Weiyang	13858	10374	35	2360	1089
雁塔区	Yanta	11340	9907	127	1306	–
阎良区	Yanliang	37676	27463	313	9813	87
临潼区	Lintong	81291	38691	288	41966	346
长安区	Chang'an	79378	48701	572	29569	536
农工商	FIC CO.	2810	837	–	1545	428
蓝田县	Lantian	66104	47732	1514	16360	498
周至县	Zhouzhi	80840	67208	1055	12235	342
户　县	Huxian	55591	35899	480	18878	334
高陵县	Gaoling	46388	24473	63	21489	363

9-11　各区县现价农林牧渔业总产值和构成(2003年)

Gross Output Value and Its Composition of Farming, Forestry, Animal Husbandry and Fishery at Current Price by Region(2003)

单位：万元　　　　　　　　　　　　　　　　　　　　　　　　　　　　　　　　　　　　　　　(10 000yuan)

区　县	Region	总产值 Gross Output Value	农业产值 Gross Output Value of Farming	林业产值 Gross Output Value of Forestry	牧业产值 Gross Output Value of Animal Husbandry	渔业产值 Gross Output Value of Fishery
全　市	**Total**	**837857**	**551398**	**10550**	**269610**	**6299**
新城区	Xincheng	394	116	3	275	_
碑林区	Beilin	4	1	_	3	_
莲湖区	Lianhu	2440	2440	_	_	_
灞桥区	Baqiao	50877	40620	263	9075	919
未央区	Weiyang	23665	18084	115	4044	1422
雁塔区	Yanta	23727	21161	266	2300	_
阎良区	Yanliang	70445	52021	712	17586	126
临潼区	Lintong	148832	77946	770	69625	491
长安区	Chang'an	136346	92117	1380	42121	728
农工商	FIC CO.	5688	1268	9	·3830	581
蓝田县	Lantian	108824	74507	3628	30089	600
周至县	Zhouzhi	88449	65193	2147	20628	481
户　县	Huxian	95305	64849	1062	28965	429
高陵县	Gaoling	82861	41075	195	41069	522
全市（%）	**Total（%）**	**100**	**65.7**	**1.3**	**32.2**	**0.8**
新城区	Xincheng	100	29.4	0.8	69.8	_
碑林区	Beilin	100	25	_	75	_
莲湖区	Lianhu	100	100	_	_	_
灞桥区	Baqiao	100	79.8	0.5	17.9	1.8
未央区	Weiyang	100	76.4	0.5	17.1	6
雁塔区	Yanta	100	89.2	1.1	9.7	_
阎良区	Yanliang	100	73.8	1	25	0.2
临潼区	Lintong	100	52.4	0.5	46.8	0.3
长安区	Chang'an	100	67.6	1	30.9	0.5
农工商	FIC CO.	100	22.3	0.2	67.3	10.2
蓝田县	Lantian	100	68.5	3.3	27.6	0.6
周至县	Zhouzhi	100	73.7	2.4	23.4	0.5
户　县	Huxian	100	68	1.1	30.4	0.5
高陵县	Gaoling	100	49.6	0.2	49.6	0.6

9-12 各区县农业物耗占总产值的比重(2003年)

Proportion of Agriculture Material Consumption to Total Output Value(2003)

单位：% (%)

区县	Region	农、林、牧渔业 Farming,Forestry, Animal Husbandry and Fishery	农业 Farming	林业 Forestry	牧业 Animal Husbandry	渔业 Fishery
全市	**Total**	**39.9**	**33.7**	**48.1**	**50.1**	**53.5**
新城区	Xincheng	25.1	18.1		28.4	
碑林区	Beilin	25.0			33.3	
莲湖区	Lianhu	28.7	28.7			
灞桥区	Baqiao	36.9	28.7	54.4	67.3	76.3
未央区	Weiyang	29.7	24.6	54.8	43.7	48.7
雁塔区	Yanta	37.7	36.7	37.6	45.8	
阎良区	Yanliang	29.1	28.0	46.1	31.0	38.1
临潼区	Lintong	43.1	42.8	69.5	43.0	62.3
长安区	Chang'an	38.2	25.3	43.1	60.8	22.1
农工商	FIC CO.	65.0	53.0	100.0	68.4	68.5
蓝田县	Lantian	42.7	38.9	41.0	50.0	52.0
周至县	Zhouzhi	39.5	33.5	54.2	50.8	49.9
户县	Huxian	38.1	32.6	47.6	49.3	41.5
高陵县	Gaoling	48.7	41.0	76.9	54.8	63.8

9-13 农林牧渔业增加值

Value Added of Farming，Forestry，Animal Husbandry and Fishery

单位:万元 (10 000yuan)

指标 Item	1991	1995	2000	2001	2002	2003
农林牧渔业增加值 Value Added of Farming，Forestry，Animal Husbandry and Fishery	**171708**	**413981**	**446481**	**458720**	**477691**	**458378**
1.农业增加值 Value Added of Farming	135821	329662	336777	342427	351358	312849
#种植业 #Planting	123894	305484	293437	291693	300225	
2.林业增加值 Value Added of Forestry	2248	4413	4323	4258	6419	5473
3.牧业增加值 Value Added of Animal Husbandry	31730	76746	101353	108096	116591	137236
4.渔业增加值 Value Added of Fishery	1909	3160	4028	3939	3323	2820

注：从2003年起增加值按新口径计算。

Note: added value is accounted by new caliber from 2003.

9-14 各区县农林牧渔业增加值(2003年)

Addition Value of Farming, Forestry, Animal Husbandry and Fishing by Region (2003)

单位：万元 (10 000yuan)

区县	Region	农、林、牧、渔业 Farming,Forestry Animal Husbandry and Fishery by Region	农业 Farming	林业 Forestry	牧业 Animal Husbandry	渔业 Fishery
全市	**Total**	**458378**	**312849**	**5473**	**137236**	**2820**
新城区	Xincheng	316	108	3	205	
碑林区	Beilin	3	1		2	
莲湖区	Lianhu	1830	1830			
灞桥区	Baqiao	30896	27920	120	2679	177
未央区	Weiyang	16071	12876	53	2382	760
雁塔区	Yanta	14578	12782	186	1610	
阎良区	Yanliang	42612	30058	357	12134	63
临潼区	Lintong	83075	42888	127	39956	104
长安区	Chang'an	76276	57310	833	17552	581
农工商	FIC CO.	1647	453		1019	175
蓝田县	Lantian	54549	36277	2179	15811	282
周至县	Zhouzhi	41262	29871	990	10134	267
户县	Huxian	57246	40887	580	15527	252
高陵县	Gaoling	38017	19588	45	18225	159

注：从2003年起增加值按新口径计算。

Note: added value is accounted by new caliber from 2003.

9-15 农业机械拥有量

Possession of Agricultural Machinery

指标	Item	2000	2001	2002	2003
农业机械总动力(千瓦)	Total Power of Agricultural Machinery(kw)	2004300	2020946	2052088	2080694
大中型拖拉机(台)	Large and Medium Tractors(unit)	7620	7078	7362	7403
(千瓦)	(kw)	252099	230233	243367	243355
小型拖拉机(台)	Mini-tractors(unit)	30307	29458	28721	27330
(千瓦)	(kw)	330687	327531	321317	301528
大中型拖拉机配套农具（部）	Number of Large and Medium Tractor Towing Farm Machinery(unit)	13035	14649	15818	16743
小型拖拉机配套农具（部）	Mini-Tractor Towing Farm Machinery (unit)	53363	51270	51461	46276
农用排灌动力机械(台)	Machinery for Agricultural Drainage and Irrigation(unit)	101676	91099	88585	85173
(千瓦)	(kw)	383838	420989	408365	376878
#柴油机(台)	Diesel Engines(unit)	1708	3025	3195	2084
(千瓦)	(kw)	15800	23414	24471	19884
电动机(台)	Motors(unit)	80499	84503	85390	83089
(千瓦)	(kw)	368038	397623	383894	356994
农用水泵（台）	Agricultural Water Pump(unit)	82539	80345	80336	78601
联合收割机（台）	Combine Harvesters(unit)	3456	3792	3798	3879
(千瓦)	(kw)	109937	122812	113367	131131
机动脱粒机（台）	Motorized Huller (unit)	17814	18099	16983	15291
机动喷雾(粉)机（部）	Electric Sprayer(unit)	5911	6402	6889	6876
(千瓦)	(kw)	8067	9148	9576	9685
饲料粉碎机（台）	Fodder Disintegrator(unit)	4485	4687	4037	4584
农产品加工动力机械(千瓦)	Agricultural Product Processing Machinery(kw)	163211	152257	157782	158026

9-16 农业机械、化肥、水利、水电情况

Agricultural Machinery,Chemical Fertilizers,Water Conservancy,Hydropower

指标	Item	2000	2001	2002	2003
一、农业机械化情况(千公顷)	**Statistics on Agricultural Machinery (1 000 hectares)**				
当年实际机耕地面积	Area Ploughed by Tractors	244.54	248.3	241.74	242.27
当年实际机播面积	Seeded Area by Tractors	321.83	319.23	336.13	273.49
当年实际机械收获面积	Harvest Area by Tractors	181.89	184.17	193.47	179.79
二、农用化肥施用量(吨)	**Use of Agricultural Fertilizers and Insecticides(Ton)**				
1.按实物量计算	Practicality Consumption	697243	687539	694460	696393
氮 肥	Nitrogenous Fertilizer	392366	392086	389180	391280
磷 肥	Phosphate Fertilizer	155480	149786	145790	147416
钾 肥	Potash Fertilizer	31841	30658	31181	32726
复合肥	Compound Fertilizer	78620	87342	96756	99204
2.按折纯量计算	Standard Consumption	196343	193282	200721	200139
氮 肥	Nitrogenous Fertilizer	102982	103943	105152	106611
磷 肥	Phosphate Fertilizer	18658	17973	17494	17679
钾 肥	Potash Fertilizer	15921	15331	15591	16264
复合肥	Compound Fertilizer	39313	43674	48380	49755
三、农用塑料薄膜使用量（公斤）	**Plastic Sheet for Agricultural Use(Kg)**	1622198	1656604	1792763	1721937
四、农用柴油（吨）	**Diesel Oil for Agricultural Use (Ton)**	52706	56308	42105	46113
五、农药使用量（公斤）	**Pesticide (Kg)**	1559333	1972425	1645464	1455942
六、农村办沼气池（个）	**Number of Mash Gas Pond Managed by Village Government(unit)**	10199	9823	12263	10011
七、农村水利化情况（千公顷）	**Irrigation and Water Conservancy (1 000 hectares)**				
有效灌溉面积	Effective Irrigation Area	223.98	223.27	213.09	203.43
旱涝保收面积	Stable-Harvesting Arable Land	196.04	197.52	193.36	188.74
机电排灌面积	Electrical Irrigation Area	166.07	168.66	172.99	160.47
已配套机电井（眼）	Electricity Powered Well(unit)	50289	49844	48329	48040
八、农村电气化情况	**Rural electrization**				
农村用电量（万千瓦小时）	Electricity Consumed in Rural Area(10 000 kwh)	117974	104406	109268	116040
乡村及村以下办水电站（个）	Hydropower Station in Rural Areas(unit)	67	65	63	65
装机容量（千瓦）	Installed Power Generation Capacity (KW)	7236	7786	7861	8601
发 电 量（万千瓦小时）	Generating Capacity (10 000kwh)	1137.95	1197.75	1082.05	1214.05

9-17 主要年份农作物播种面积

Sown Areas of Farm Crops In Representative Years

单位：千公顷 (1 000 hectares)

年份 Year	总播种面积 Total Sown Area	粮食 Grain Crops	小麦 Wheat	玉米 Corn	棉花 Cotton	油料 Oil-bearing Crops	蔬菜 Vegetables
1980	556.95	470.90	216.11	182.09	54.15	6.67	16.01
1985	530.27	469.57	252.13	180.76	14.01	5.34	30.02
1990	544.27	487.61	258.13	188.09	10.01	8.00	34.02
1991	546.94	487.58	259.46	188.76	12.67	8.67	31.35
1992	547.10	477.00	256.40	182.40	17.80	10.80	36.40
1993	547.75	475.66	253.60	182.46	11.77	9.89	42.60
1994	527.66	479.37	250.62	181.65	13.14	9.17	39.91
1995	523.16	460.42	246.94	173.03	7.38	12.38	38.39
1996	520.55	472.56	244.18	191.17	5.06	12.48	36.96
1997	503.85	447.22	245.14	165.86	3.00	10.35	39.57
1998	526.66	470.02	246.78	190.30	2.37	9.79	40.63
1999	528.72	473.30	247.96	196.00	1.90	8.49	40.45
2000	523.29	465.03	246.59	189.13	1.65	8.97	42.90
2001	508.77	452.03	239.46	185.71	1.94	7.91	41.18
2002	500.73	437.06	233.76	181.30	1.75	7.60	45.14
2003	491.37	421.70	224.03	174.59	2.25	7.36	46.29

9-18 各区县主要农作物播种面积(2003年)

Sown Areas of Major Farm Crops by Region（2003）

单位：公顷 (hectare)

区 县	Region	总播种面积 Total Sown Area	粮食 Grain Crops	夏粮 Summer Grain	小麦 Wheat	秋粮 Autumn Grain	稻谷 Rice	玉米 Corn
合 计	**Total**	**491370**	**421697**	**227982**	**224032**	**193715**	**3807**	**174590**
新城区	Xincheng	71	37	27	27	10		10
碑林区	Beilin	1	1	1	1			
莲湖区	Lianhu	836	68	40	40	28		28
灞桥区	Baqiao	23942	18071	11270	11252	6801	46	6357
未央区	Weiyang	11353	8458	4360	4351	4098		3997
雁塔区	Yanta	6583	4732	3213	3213	1519		1471
阎良区	Yanliang	26772	19186	10458	10437	8728		7680
临潼区	Lintong	89546	76116	41932	41656	34184		31293
长安区	Chang'an	93955	81780	44301	43541	37479	2016	34320
农工商	FIC CO.	508	126	95	92	31		7
蓝田县	Lantian	73714	61775	36441	34438	25334	557	17018
周至县	Zhouzhi	64297	60452	29881	29514	30571	664	28921
户 县	Huxian	68182	62352	31509	31090	30843	524	29958
高陵县	Gaoling	31610	28543	14454	14380	14089		13530

9-19 主要年份农作物产品产量

Yeild of Farm Crops In Representative Years

单位：万吨 （10 000 ton）

年 份 Year	粮食总产量 Total Yield of Grain Crops	夏粮 Summer Grain	小麦 Wheat	秋粮 Autumn Grain	稻谷 Rice	玉米 Corn	棉花 Cotton	油料 Oil-bearing Crops	油菜籽 Rapeseeds	蔬菜 Vegetables
1980	114.41	56.62	52.25	57.79	4.73	47.74	1.97	0.54	0.50	40.13
1985	150.09	76.13	74.78	73.96	5.10	65.07	0.49	0.75	0.39	86.44
1990	172.43	91.65	89.67	80.78	5.46	70.35	0.70	1.26	0.94	119.32
1991	178.83	91.10	89.16	87.73	5.03	77.46	0.97	1.20	0.74	117.40
1992	183.41	101.68	99.55	81.73	4.74	72.26	0.74	1.49	0.87	128.12
1993	190.01	101.09	98.99	88.92	4.86	78.60	0.75	1.40	1.00	145.80
1994	157.37	86.90	84.85	70.47	4.54	61.42	0.65	1.08	0.78	135.26
1995	175.25	99.81	97.38	75.45	3.44	67.76	0.29	2.17	1.90	133.60
1996	187.51	80.13	78.40	107.38	3.37	95.60	0.24	1.83	1.55	138.01
1997	190.51	114.25	112.34	76.26	3.47	69.38	0.17	1.86	1.65	142.11
1998	212.70	104.40	103.95	108.30	3.23	99.08	0.14	1.67	1.36	148.87
1999	204.44	95.50	94.39	108.94	2.88	99.65	0.15	1.30	1.00	153.24
2000	201.92	92.58	91.63	109.34	3.05	100.52	0.14	1.34	0.95	162.14
2001	197.09	98.14	97.20	98.94	2.73	91.30	0.17	1.23	0.90	152.80
2002	192.41	94.50	93.53	97.91	2.13	91.62	0.18	1.22	0.84	169.74
2003	176.34	98.18	96.72	78.16	1.61	72.32	0.22	1.13	0.70	169.67

9-20 各区县主要农作物产品产量（2003年）

单位：吨

区县	Region	粮食总产量 Total Yield of Grain Crops	夏粮 Summer Grain	小麦 Wheat	秋粮 Autumn Grain	稻谷 Rice
合计	**Total**	**1763432**	**981848**	**967236**	**781584**	**16093**
新城区	Xincheng	88	61	61	27	
碑林区	Beilin	6	6	6		
莲湖区	Lianhu	242	153	153	89	
灞桥区	Baqiao	67469	42311	42279	25158	124
未央区	Weiyang	43061	23078	23060	19983	
雁塔区	Yanta	18682	12061	12061	6621	
阎良区	Yanliang	96360	56541	56443	39819	
临潼区	Lintong	298817	168063	167042	130754	
长安区	Chang'an	311052	177027	173990	134025	9072
农工商	FIC CO.	536	437	425	99	
蓝田县	Lantian	210510	127744	120722	82766	2298
周至县	Zhouzhi	234365	127428	125862	106937	2632
户县	Huxian	292429	159398	157906	133031	1967
高陵县	Gaoling	189815	87540	87226	102275	

9-21 各区县主要农作物单位面积产量（2003年）

单位：公斤/公顷

区县	Region	粮食作物 Total Yield of Grain Crops	夏粮 Summer Grain	小麦 Wheat
全市	**Total**	**4182**	**4307**	**4317**
新城区	Xincheng	2378	2250	2250
碑林区	Beilin	6000	6000	6000
莲湖区	Lianhu	3559	3825	3825
灞桥区	Baqiao	3734	3754	3757
未央区	Weiyang	5091	5293	5300
雁塔区	Yanta	3948	3754	3754
阎良区	Yanliang	5022	5406	5408
临潼区	Lintong	3926	4008	4010
长安区	Chang'an	3804	3996	3996
农工商	FIC CO.	4254	4600	4620
蓝田县	Liantian	3408	3506	3506
周至县	Zhouzhi	3877	4265	4265
户县	Huxian	4690	5059	5079
高陵县	Gaoling	6650	6056	6066

Yeild of Major Farm Crops By Region（2003）

(ton)

玉米 Corn	棉花 Cotton	油料 Oil-bearing Crops	油菜籽 Rapeseeds	蔬菜 Vegetables
723213	**2244**	**11275**	**6990**	**1696709**
27				980
89				22984
23925	59	570	464	247584
19466		145	87	89427
6549		78	22	86852
36971	1389	623	110	243327
122534	429	3426	2092	300743
122728	22	1561	1469	297140
40	1	19	2	6034
59822	293	2113	600	91277
101166	11	1751	1489	62659
129778	37	666	509	165177
100118	3	323	146	82525

The Output of Main Crops per Hectare by Region(2003)

(kg/hectare)

秋粮 Autumn Grain	稻谷 Rice	玉米 Corn	棉花 Cotton	油料 Oil-bearing Crops	油菜籽 Rapeseeds	蔬菜 Vegetables
4035	**4227**	**4142**	**998**	**1532**	**1650**	**36657**
2700		2700				28824
3179		3179				29927
3699	2696	3764	820	1727	1950	47879
4876		4870	1000	2458	2486	33835
4359		4452		1472	1375	53912
4562		4814	1249	2209	2444	46516
3825		3916	738	1214	1419	38926
3576	4500	3576	759	2084	2250	31500
3193		5714	1000	2111	2000	32095
3267	4126	3515	731	1185	778	22399
3498	3964	3498	611	2029	2010	26663
4313	3754	4332	1321	2458	2597	37328
7259		7400	500	2307	2179	31366

9-22 农作物单位面积产量

Yield of Farm Crops Per Hectare

单位：公斤/公顷 (kg/hectare)

年份 Year	粮食作物 Grain Crops	夏粮 Summer Grain	小麦 Wheat	秋粮 Autumn Grain	稻谷 Rice	玉米 Corn	棉花 Cotton	油料 Oil-bearing Crops	油菜籽 Rapeseeds	蔬菜 Vegetables
1990	3540	3480	3480	3615	5250	3735	690	1545	1515	35235
1991	3675	3435	3435	3960	4815	4110	765	1410	1335	34980
1992	3840	3885	3885	3795	4725	3960	420	1380	1515	35160
1993	3995	3900	3903	4108	4991	4308	634	1416	1610	34226
1994	3283	3387	3385	3163	4849	3381	494	1181	1258	33893
1995	3806	3945	3943	3638	4353	3916	398	1753	1921	34800
1996	3968	3214	3211	4810	5491	5001	473	1295	1497	37342
1997	4260	4575	4583	3861	5575	4183	572	1138	1931	35918
1998	4525	4172	4178	4927	5659	5207	593	1704	1820	36644
1999	4319	3800	3807	4907	5480	5084	787	1533	1583	37884
2000	4342	3710	3716	5075	6008	5315	831	1526	1676	37797
2001	4360	4052	4059	4715	6013	4917	899	1562	1691	37105
2002	4402	3995	4001	4883	5741	5053	1046	1603	1719	37599
2003	4182	4307	4317	4035	4227	4142	998	1532	1650	36657

9-23 林业生产情况

Statistcs on Forestry

指标	Item	2000	2001	2002	2003
一、营林情况	**Afforestation**				
当年造林面积合计(千公顷）	Build Forestry Areas(1 000hectares)	18.31	18.01	22.43	20.48
1.人工造林	Manpower Forestation	9.11	9.29	12.38	11.96
2.飞播造林	Aerial Plantation	9.20	8.72	10.05	8.52
零星四旁植树（万株）	Planting(10 000 plants)	731	792	717	1024
育苗面积（公顷）	Raise Seedlings Areas(hectares)	1365	2360	2559	3462
#本年新育	# New Seedling of Current Year	1125	1458	1661	1662
二、主要林产品产量（吨）	**Main Forestry Product(ton)**				
生漆	Lacquer	11	19	14	7
核桃	Walnuts	997	366	1287	1545
板栗	Chinese Chestnut	744	433	916	1127
花椒	Pepper	140	132	463	279
木耳	Agaric	72	166	164	114
三、村及村以下采伐木材（万立方米）	**Timber Harvested at or below Village Level（10 000 cu.m)**	**1.62**	**1.10**	**0.71**	**0.89**

9-24 各区县林业生产情况（2003年）

Statistics On Forestry By Region（2003）

区县	Region	当年造林面积（千公顷）Build Forestry Areas in The Year (1 000 hectares)	零星植树（万株）Planting (10 000 Plants)	育苗面积（公顷）Raise Seedlings Areas (hectare)	核桃产量（吨）Output of Walnuts (ton)	板栗产量（吨）Output of Chinese Chestnut (ton)	村及村以下木材采伐量（万立方）Timber Harvesting at\under Vallage level (10 000 cu.m)
全市	**Total**	**20.48**	**1024.20**	**3462**	**1545**	**1127**	**0.89**
新城区	Xincheng			2			
碑林区	Beilin						
莲湖区	Lianhu						
灞桥区	Baqiao	0.43	16.54	114	18	6	
未央区	Weiyang	0.04	39.00	36			
雁塔区	Yanta	0.46	1.00	410			
阎良区	Yanliang	1.34	58.00	76			0.24
临潼区	Lintong	1.26	130.00	138	27	4	
长安区	Chang'an	4.67	140.00	553	160	85	0.08
农工商	FIC CO.		0.66				
蓝田县	Lantian	6.73	379.00	200	1032	852	
周至县	Zhouzhi	1.58	120.00	1535	253	130	0.49
户　县	Huxian	3.84	90.00	333	55	50	
高陵县	Gaoling	0.13	50.00	65			0.08

9-25 桑、茶、果生产情况

Statistics on Mulberry,Tea,Fruits

指　标	Item	1999	2000	2001	2002	2003
果园面积(公顷）	**Areas of Orchards (hectare)**	**35245**	**31907**	**31823**	**33324**	**34930**
苹果园	Apple Orchards	10029	8098	5468	4703	4326
梨园	Pears Orchards	4303	3861	3497	2948	2555
葡萄园	Grapes Orchards	1114	1260	1338	1716	1774
桃园	Peach Orchards	2002	2313	2729	4028	4705
猕猴桃园	Chinese Goosebeery Orchards	11111	11223	11348	11090	11098
杏园	Apricot Orchards	528	416	552	674	830
柿子园	Presimmons Orchards	1078	1305	1464	999	1090
水果产量（吨）	**Output of Fruits (ton)**	**355184**	**343551**	**339189**	**375776**	**384262**
苹果	Apple	108386	89416	77906	55233	65845
梨	Pears	62331	65459	66308	70046	63119
葡萄	Grapes	14932	16647	17733	19962	24098
桃	Peach	30832	27010	29018	38393	47046
猕猴桃	Chinese Goosebeery	86552	96640	105064	111858	105784

9–26　各区县桑、果园面积及产量(2003年）

Area and Output of Mulberry Yards and Orchards by Region（2003）

区　县	Region	果园（公顷）Area of Orchards(hectare)	水果产量（吨）Output of Fruits(ton)
全　市	**Total**	**34930**	**384262**
新城区	Xincheng	3	
碑林区	Beilin		
莲湖区	Lianhu		
灞桥区	Baqiao	3063	33642
未央区	Weiyang	1308	21414
雁塔区	Yanta	484	8254
阎良区	Yanliang	2664	32314
临潼区	Lintong	3009	33527
长安区	Chang'an	2179	24575
农工商	FIC CO.	281	3304
蓝田县	Lantian	6727	87500
周至县	Zhouzhi	9726	72821
户　县	Huxian	2831	39888
高陵县	Gaoling	2655	27023

9–27　畜牧业生产情况

Statistics on Livestock Husbandry

指　标	Item	2000	2001	2002	2003
一、大牲畜年末总头数(头）	**Large Animals In Stock at Year-end (heads)**	**260742**	**247312**	**255158**	**287449**
#能繁殖母畜	#Female Animals of Reprductive Ability	137087	126319	136094	158513
#役　畜	#Draught Animals	98130	89830	84903	88886
1.牛	Cattle	256073	243852	252559	285211
#能繁殖母畜	Female Animals of Reprductive Ability	136626	126030	135807	158172
#当年生仔畜	Newborn Livestock in the Year 2002	69015	73143	63980	72126
(1)黄牛	Farm Cattle	207909	191884	192618	212432
(2)良种及改良奶牛	Cows of Fine Breed & Improved Variety	48164	51968	59941	72779
(3)水牛	Water Cattle				
2.马（匹）	Horses	736	570	529	659
3.驴	Donkeys	476	377	218	238
4.骡	Mutes	3457	2513	1852	1341
二、猪年末头数（头）	**Hogs in Stock Year-end (heads)**	**1284592**	**1336218**	**1389569**	**1397462**
#能繁殖母猪	#Female Hogs of Reprductive Ability	93775	108321	119023	106770
三、羊年末只数（只）	**Sheeps and Goats in Stock at Year-end(heads)**	**421103**	**430174**	**479469**	**513498**
1.山羊	Goats	397121	400461	460686	497313
#奶山羊	Milch Goats	266525	289104	339351	353885
2.绵羊	Sheeps	23982	29713	18783	16185
四、家禽年末存栏数（万只）	**Poultry in Stock at Year-end (10 000 heads)**	**1623.81**	**1573.41**	**1635.32**	**1651.42**
五、年末养蜂箱数（箱）	**Honey (boxes)**	**20408**	**19830**	**21606**	**20300**

9-28 各区县畜牧业生产情况(2003年）

Statistics On Livestock,Animal Husbandry By Region（2003）

区 县	Region	大牲畜年末头数（头） Large Animals In Stock at Year-end (heads)	能繁殖母畜 Female Animals of Reprductive Ability	役畜 Draught Animals	牛（头） Cattle (heads)	奶牛 Dairy Cattle	马（匹） Horses (heads)	驴（头） Donkeys (heads)
全 市	**Total**	**287449**	**158513**	**88886**	**285211**	**72779**	**659**	**238**
新城区	Xincheng	224	106		224	224		
碑林区	Beilin							
莲湖区	Lianhu							
灞桥区	Baqiao	9480	6589	1118	9408	6408	42	
未央区	Weiyang	1506	1068	67	1444	1392		
雁塔区	Yanta	543	342	92	494	455	3	3
阎良区	Yanliang	13452	8036	1302	13430	10297	19	1
临潼区	Lintong	50307	31685	13233	50169	29380	29	41
长安区	Chang'an	49000	23859	3871	48500	5000	182	43
农工商	FIC CO.	4229	2825		4229	4229		
蓝田县	Lantian	85664	40979	47000	85516	980	43	26
周至县	Zhouzhi	40991	22462	16396	40640	695	147	12
户 县	Huxian	18021	8751	5522	17403	2255	80	18
高陵县	Gaoling	14032	11811	285	13754	11464	114	94

9-28 各区县畜牧业生产情况(2003年）（续）

Statistics On Livestock,Animal Husbandry By Region（2003）(Continued)

区 县	Region	骡（头） Mutes (heads)	猪（头） Hogs (heads)	能繁殖母猪 Female Hogs of Reprductive Ability	羊（只） Sheeps and Goats (heads)	山羊 Goats	奶山羊 Milch Goats	家禽（万只） Poultry (10 000 heads)	蜂（箱） Honey (boxes)
全 市	**Total**	**1341**	**1397462**	**106770**	**513498**	**497313**	**353885**	**1651.42**	**20300**
新城区	Xincheng		119	2					
碑林区	Beilin								
莲湖区	Lianhu								
灞桥区	Baqiao	30	31490	1944	12586	12157	7589	45.45	667
未央区	Weiyang	62	32138	2277	2237	2082	1153	17.11	240
雁塔区	Yanta	43	19799	942	1479	1479	1479	5.06	74
阎良区	Yanliang	2	54211	4072	41734	41609	41458	91.35	330
临潼区	Lintong	68	284378	20694	145755	144703	115372	439.63	4442
长安区	Chang'an	275	299000	26808	58600	52256	19350	348	2267
农工商	FIC CO.								
蓝田县	Lantian	79	91557	9740	132012	131794	82540	189	2290
周至县	Zhouzhi	192	210298	15858	26644	25141	8668	83.53	5337
户 县	Huxian	520	253424	13909	25204	24832	17493	189.78	4616
高陵县	Gaoling	70	121048	10524	67247	61260	58783	242.51	37

9-29 畜产品和水产品产量

单位：吨

年 份 Year	肉类总产量 Output of Meat	猪肉 Pork	牛肉 Beef	羊肉 Mutton	禽肉 Poultry	奶类总产量 Output of Milk	牛奶 Cow Milk
1990	63273	50646	4667	1931	5885	82017	50528
1991	72268	55086	5623	2162	9062	91006	57700
1992	88994	68134	6468	2460	11290	100080	63586
1993	93420	71274	7249	2220	12174	111070	73897
1994	106691	79433	8298	2350	15681	145412	99025
1995	127815	86513	11251	3731	23948	132909	85753
1996	91468	63750	5402	2578	19324	133372	86103
1997	106597	75381	6672	3468	20596	150964	98078
1998	134152	98974	8788	4710	21424	174099	119719
1999	130124	93859	9827	4147	21963	209144	145191
2000	147571	106137	12066	4766	23760	245913	176155
2001	157277	113353	11900	5153	20540	255437	179977
2002	161092	118634	11516	5394	20515	288009	202826
2003	165860	122759	13241	5180	19682	336296	245407

9-30 各区县主要畜产品和水产品产量(2003年)

单位：吨

区 县	Region	肉类总产量 Output of Meat	猪肉 Pork	牛肉 Beef	羊肉 Mutton	禽肉 Poultry
全 市	**Total**	**165860**	**122759**	**13241**	**5180**	**19682**
新城区	Xincheng	10	3	3		
碑林区	Beilin					
莲湖区	Lianhu					
灞桥区	Baqiao	3586	2686	236	109	539
未央区	Weiyang	3589	3347	43	28	170
雁塔区	Yanta	2174	2060	12	7	92
阎良区	Yanliang	7132	5430	456	370	853
临潼区	Lintong	35717	27304	2267	1452	4650
长安区	Chang'an	34600	22880	1728	668	4650
农工商	FIC CO.	178		178		
蓝田县	Lantian	18354	8905	6022	1415	1856
周至县	Zhouzhi	18994	16459	1268	232	1018
户 县	Huxian	23994	21061	489	193	2216
高陵县	Gaoling	17532	12624	539	706	3638

Output of Livestock Products and Aquatic Products

(ton)

羊毛 Wool	禽蛋 Poultry Eggs	蜂蜜（公斤） Honey(kg)	水产品 Output of Aquatic Products	养殖面积（公顷） Water Raise Areas (hectare)
3	55938	1035392	4259	1698
11	90558	1022797	4949	1754
12	104970	739275	6015	1864
11	125244	662049	7132	1980
82	146503	547808	7900	2067
8	141227	535891	8517	2140
3	138044	613290	8910	2342
1	156066	713918	10054	2308
5	142519	537304	10480	2266
26	135981	541613	11061	2256
24	138305	460598	11384	2235
22	132303	479839	12480	2112
11	134336	497530	12017	2205
19	128833	537805	9967	1654

Output of Major Livestock Products and Aquatic Products By Region（2003）

(ton)

奶类总产量 Output of Milk	牛奶 Cow Milk	禽蛋 Poultry Eggs	蜂蜜（公斤） Honey(kg)	水产品 Output of Aquatic Products	养殖面积（公顷） Water Raise Areas(hectare)
336296	**245407**	**128833**	**537805**	**9967**	**1654**
1515	851				
25721	23710	3182	20033	1400	190
3784	3470	1102	430	2345	214
1950	1684	402	900		1
49125	38099	7711	12600	177	16
122946	92353	33605	274991	770	229
15500	10372	29679	38661	1054	275
19542	19542			906	103
21873	2886	12600	29800	1000	243
4962	2652	6422	28390	800	213
11384	7371	14729	132000	703	87
57994	42417	19401		812	83

9-31 农村经济效益主要指标

Main Index of Rural Economic Benefit

年 份 Year	每一农业劳动力创造的 农林牧渔业总产值（元） Gross Output Value of Farming,Forestry，Animal Husbandry and Fishery (yuan)	粮食（公斤） Grain Crops(kg)	棉花（公斤） Cotton(kg)	油料（公斤） Oil-bearing Crops(kg)
	Average Labor Force Production			
1990	1944.4	1279.3	5.2	9.4
1991	2169.5	1312.4	7.1	8.8
1992	2343.8	1338.6	5.4	10.9
1993	2528.9	1381.8	5.4	10.2
1994	2277.0	1142.0	4.7	7.9
1995	2433.7	1304.7	2.2	16.2
1996	2468.0	1368.9	1.7	13.3
1997	2726.0	1411.9	1.3	13.8
1998	2955.2	1399.9	0.9	11.0
1999	3433.1	1551.8	1.1	9.9
2000	3728.3	1596.5	1.1	10.8
2001	3631.3	1643.9	1.2	8.6
2002	3517.2	1548.7	1.5	9.8
2003	3484.7	1430.2	1.8	9.1

9-31 农村经济效益主要指标（续）

Main Index of Rural Economic Benefit(Continued)

年 份 Year	每亩耕地种植业产值（元） Output of Each Unit of Area Planting(yuan)	每亩粮耕地平均产量（公斤） Output of Each Unit of Area Plantation(kg)	每百元物耗生产的总产值（元） Output per 100-Yuan of Material Consumed(yuan)
1990	343.3	417.4	233.3
1991	380.4	431.2	238.4
1992	404.9	442.0	241.8
1993	493.4	396.6	240.1
1994	376.0	333.5	227.6
1995	412.8	353.8	225.9
1996	452.0	415.3	234.5
1997	479.0	417.3	239.2
1998	548.0	467.3	247.0
1999	514.4	517.6	251.7
2000	580.2	539.4	250.2
2001	607.3	581.3	248.6
2002	632.0	586.9	265.9
2003	659.4	557.6	254.3

注：按不变价计算。

Note:At Constant Prices

主 要 统 计 指 标 解 释

农林牧渔业总产值 指以货币表现的农、林、牧、渔业全部产品的总量，它反映一定时期内农业生产总规模和总成果。农林牧渔业总产值的计算方法通常是按农、林、牧、渔业产品及其副产品的产量分别乘以各自单位产品价格求得；少数生产周期较长，当年没有产品或产品产量不易统计的，则采用间接方法匡算其产值；然后将四业产品产值相加即为农林牧渔业总产值。

粮食产量 指全社会的产量。包括国有经济经营的、集体统一经营的和农民家庭经营的粮食产量，还包括工矿企业办的农场和其他生产单位的产量。粮食除包括稻谷、小麦、玉米、高粱、谷子及其他杂粮外，还包括薯类和豆类。其产量计算方法，豆类按去豆荚后的干豆计算；薯类（包括甘薯和马铃薯，不包括芋头和木薯）1963年以前按每4公斤鲜薯折1公斤粮食计算，从1964年开始改为按5公斤鲜薯折1公斤粮食计算。城市郊区作为蔬菜的薯类（如马铃薯等）按鲜品计算，并且不作粮食统计。其他粮食一律按脱粒后的原粮计算。

棉花产量 指全社会的产量。包括春播棉和夏播棉。产量按皮棉计算。

油料产量 指全部油料作物的生产量。包括花生、油菜籽、芝麻、向日葵籽、胡麻籽（亚麻籽）和其他油料。不包括大豆、木本油料和野生油料。花生以带壳干花生计算。

水产品产量 指人工养殖的水产品和天然生长的水产品的捕捞量。包括海水的鱼类、虾蟹类、贝类和藻类以及内陆水域的鱼类、虾蟹类和贝类，不包括淡水生植物.

猪、牛、羊肉产量 指当年出栏并已屠宰、除去头蹄下水后带骨肉（即胴体重）的重量。

期初（末）畜禽存栏头（只）数 指报告期初（末）农村各种合作经济组织和国营农场、农民个人、机关、团体、学校、工矿企业、部队等单位以及城镇居民饲养的大牲畜、猪、羊、家禽等畜禽的存栏数。

常用耕地 是指耕地总资源中专门种植农作物并经常进行耕种、能够正常收获的土地。包括当年实际耕种的熟地；弃耕、休闲不满三年，随时可以复耕的地；开荒利用三年以上的地。不包括临时种植农作物的坡度在25度以上的陡坡地；在河套、湖畔、库区临时开发的成片或零星土地；也不包括已列为国家和省（区、市）退耕计划但临时耕种的土地。

农作物播种面积 指实际播种或移植有农作物的面积。凡是实际种植有农作物的面积，不论种植在耕地上还是种植在非耕地上，均包括在农作物播种面积中。在播种季节基本结束后，因遭灾而重新改种和补种的农作物面积，也包括在内。

有效灌溉面积 指具有一定的水源，地块比较平整，灌溉工程或设备已经配套，在一般年景下当年能够进行正常灌溉的耕地面积。在一般情况下，有效灌溉面积应等于灌溉工程或设备已经配备，能够进行正常灌溉的水田和水浇地面积之和。

农用化肥施用量 指本年内实际用于农业生产的化肥数量，包括氮肥、磷肥、钾肥和复合肥。化肥施用量要求按折纯量计算数量。折纯量是指把氮肥、磷肥、钾肥分别按含氮、含五氧化二磷、含氧化钾的百分之一百成份进行折算后的数量。复合肥按其所含主要成分折算。

农业机械总动力 指主要用于农、林、牧、渔业的各种动力机械的动力总和。包括耕作机械、排灌机械、收获机械、农用运输机械、植物保护机械、牧业机械、林业机械、渔业机械和其他农业机械〔内燃机按引擎马力折成瓦（特）计算、电动机按功率折成瓦（特）计算〕。不包括专门用于乡、镇、村、组办工业、基本建设、非农业运输、科学试验和教学等非农业生产方面用的动力机械与作业机械。

农林牧渔业劳动力 指全社会直接参加农林牧渔业生产活动的劳动力。

Explanatory Notes on Main Statistical Indicators

Gross Output Value of Farming, Forestry, Animal Husbandry and Fishery refers to the total value of products of farming, forestry, animal husbandry and fishery, which reflects the total scale and result of agricultural production during a given period. Gross output value of agriculture is obtained by first multiplying the output of each product or by product by its price, resulting in the output value of each single item. For a small number of products, annual output of which is not available or difficult to get due to the long production growing process involved, the output value is estimated through an indirect approach. The sum of output value of all products of farming, forestry, animal husbandry, and fishery is then equal to the gross output value of agriculture.

Grain Output refers to the grain production in the whole country including grains produced by state farms, collective units, industrial enterprises and mines. Grain includes rice, wheat, corn, sorghum, millet and other miscellaneous grains as well as tubers and beans. Output of beans refers to dry beans without pods. The output of tubers (sweet potatoes and potatoes, not including taros and cassava) was converted into that of grain at the ratio 4:1, i.e. 4 kilograms of fresh tubers was equivalent to 1 kilogram of grain up to 1963. Since 1964 the ratio for conversion has been 5:1. Tubers supplied as vegetables (such as potatoes) in cities and suburbs are calculated as fresh vegetables and their output is not included in the output of grain. Output of all other grains refers to husked grain.

Cotton Output refers to the cotton production in the whole country including cotton sown in spring and in autumn. Output is measured as the weight of ginned cotton.

Output of Oil-bearing Crops refers to the total production of oil bearing crops of various kinds, including peanuts, (dry, in shell) rapeseeds, sesame, sunflower seeds, flax seeds, and other oil bearing crops. Soybeans, oil-bearing woody plants, and wild oil-bearing crops are not included.

Output of Aquatic Products refers to catches of both artificially cultured and naturally grown aquatic products, including fish, shrimps, crabs and shellfish in sea and inland water as well as seaweed. Freshwater plants are not included.

Output of Pork, Beef, and Mutton refers to the meat of slaughtered hogs, cattle, sheep and goats with head, feet, and offal taken away.

Number of Livestock or Poultry in Stock at Beginning (or End) refers to the total number of large animals, pigs, sheep, fowls, etc. raised by rural cooperative organizations, state farms, rural individuals, government agencies, schools, industrial and mining enterprises, army, and urban residents at the beginning (or end) of the reference period.

Regularly Cultivated Land refers to farmland among the total land resources which is exclusively used for farming and is under regular cultivation with harvest in normal years. Included are currently cultivated land, land that has been abandoned or put in idle for less than 3 years and could be re-used for cultivation at any time, and new-claimed land that has been put into cultivation for more than 3 years. Excluded under this category are steep slope land over 25 degrees under temporary cultivation, land (large or small plots) that is claimed along river bends, lake sides or banks of reservoirs, as well as land that has been designated under the "Green for Grain" programmes of the state and provincial governments but is still temporarily under cultivation.

Sown Area of Crops refers to area of land sown or transplanted with crops regardless of being in cultivated area or non cultivated area. Area of land re-sown due to natural disasters is also included.

Irrigated Area refers to areas that are effectively irrigated, i.e. level land which has water source and complete sets of irrigation facilities to lift and move adequate water for irrigation purpose under normal conditions. Under normal conditions, irrigated area is the sum of watered fields and irrigated fields where irrigation systems or equipment have been installed for regular irrigation purpose.

Consumption of Chemical Fertilizers in Agriculture refers to the quantity of chemical fertilizers applied in agriculture in the year, including nitrogenous fertilizer, phosphate fertilizer, potash fertilizer, and compound fertilizer. The consumption of chemical fertilizers is required in calculation to convert the gross weight into weight containing 100% effective component (e.g. 100% nitrogen content in nitrogenous fertilizer, 100% phosphorous pentoxide contents in phosphate fertilizer, 100% potassium oxide contents in potash fertilizer). Compound fertilizer is converted with its major component.

Total Power of Farm Machinery refers to total mechanical power of machinery used in farming, forestry, animal husbandry, and fishery, including ploughing, irrigation and drainage, harvesting, transport, plant protection, stock breeding, forestry and fishery. The power of internal combustion engines is required to convert horsepower into watts and the power of electric motors is required to be converted into watts. Machinery employed for non agricultural purposes, such as the machines used in township run and village-run industry, construction, non agricultural transport, scientific experiments and teaching, is excluded.

Labour Force Engaged in Farming, Forestry, Animal Husbandry and Fishery refers to the total laborers who are directly engaged in production of farming, forestry, animal husbandry and fishery.

十、工 业

INDUSTRY

简 要 说 明
Brief Introduction

本章资料主要包括工业企业主要指标，国有及规模以上非国有(规模以上非国有指年产品销售收入在500万元以上的非国有企业)工业企业单位数、总产值、主要经济指标和效益指标，大中型工业企业的主要经济指标和效益指标等。

本章资料由市统计局工业交通处整理提供。

Data in this chapter consists of primarily basic indicators for industrial enterprises, state-owned and non-state-owned industrial enterprises above designated size which refers to non-state-owned, annual sales exceed 5 million of RMB Yuan, number of industrial enterprises, gross product, primary economic and performance indicators for industrial enterprises and primary economic and performance indicators for large and medium industrial enterprises.

Data in this chapter are provided and compiled by Industry & Transportation Division of the Xi'an Bureau of Statistics.

10-1 全市工业总产值(2003年)

Gross Industrial Output Value of whole City (2003)

单位：万元 （10 000 yuan）

分　组	Item	按现价计算 at Current Prices	按1990年不变价计算 at 1990 Constant Prices
总　计	**Total**	**12096282.0**	**11534552.5**
在总计中:中央企业	Of the Total: Central Enterprises	3420877.9	2164507.7
省属企业	Provincial Enterprises	1294113.5	1355615.1
市属企业	Municipal Enterprises	7381290.6	8014429.7
在总计中:规模以上企业	Of the Total: Over 5 Million Yuan	7817317.0	7255587.5
规模以下企业	Below 5 Million Yuan	4278965.0	4278965.0
在总计中:轻工业	Of the Total: Light Industry	4406834.9	4253325.2
重工业	Heavy Industry	7689447.1	7281227.3
在总计中:大型企业	Of the Total: Large-size Enterprises	4342510.5	3834958.9
中型企业	Medium-size Enterprises	2217447.2	2133863.5
小型企业	Small-size Enterprises	5536324.3	5565730.1

注:本表规模以上企业包括长庆油田数据。

Note: Including Data of Changqing Oil Field.

10–2　主要年份全部工业总产值

单位：万元

年　份 Year	全部工业总产值 Gross Industrial Output Value	工业总产值指数（上年=100） Index of Gross Industry Output Value (Preceding Year=100)	国有经济 State-owned Enterprises	集体经济 Collective-owned Enterprises
1952	23512	139.58	9917	464
1957	71513	103.33	61624	7572
1962	120833	86.79	102103	17599
1965	200416	132.12	183164	17252
1970	333386	143.45	305303	28083
1975	385509	106.13	332982	52527
1978	483262	116.86	405376	77886
1979	517483	106.59	438850	78633
1980	531755	101.78	440139	91577
1981	524587	98.58	433740	90675
1982	549200	107.14	450308	98516
1983	603507	112.15	493773	108923
1984	674963	112.82	520593	153056
1985	853196	120.42	632702	218893
1986	976326	112.07	706380	267282
1987	1142220	114.19	809186	328701
1988	1429811	115.99	1012268	416217
1989	1653472	106.05	1160877	486754
1990	1771310	107.37	1196777	548605
1991	2002727	110.00	1325242	604495
1992	2300472	112.53	1488541	561369
1993	3045988	121.68	1748145	1071122
1994	3891584	120.63	1960533	1581321
1995	4058952	108.70	2071755	1663536
1996	5338510	133.36	2132140	2836176
1997	6225025	121.81	2057847	2154613
1998	6736100	117.31	2592588	2076618
1999	7618716	117.10	2560408	2189379
2000	8219646	115.30	4219331	2298848
2001	9301000	116.40	4486977	2688610
2002	10489607	115.81	5014720	2580442
2003	12096282	115.11	5968954	1642227

注:国有经济中含国有控股工业企业。

Note:State-owned eaterprises contain the enterprises that state holds majority shares.

Gross Output Value of Industry In Representative Years

（10 000 yuan）

其他经济类型 Enterprises of Other Ownership	轻工业 Ligth Industry	重工业 Heavy Industry	大型工业 Large-size Industry Enterprises	中型工业 Medium-size Industry Enterprlses	小型工业 Small-size Industry Enterprises
13131	20800	2712			
1217	53280	18233			
1131	68221	52618			
	98631	101785			
	124467	208919			
	167285	218224	145262	130592	109655
	220480	262782	168397	121813	193052
	243043	274440	189877	133759	193847
39	283475	248280	193092	130053	208610
172	309199	215388	178130	140810	205639
456	303249	246031	213015	128597	207668
811	315785	287722	245053	127164	231290
1314	321678	353285	241842	143165	289956
1601	401748	451448	333820	147488	371888
2664	458270	518056	401037	150644	424609
4341	516776	625452	472958	171698	497572
1326	699593	730210	615946	210089	603776
5814	712743	940729	696368	258414	698690
25928	787857	983453	716421	279098	775791
72990	897676	1105051	888052	303151	844524
250562	967104	1333368			
226721	1121957	1924031	1258137	384255	1403596
349730	1578875	2312709	1479613	390233	2021738
323661	1636219	2432733	1575030	371156	2112766
370194	2347887	2990623	1693985	358913	3285612
2012565	2900682	3324343	1800000	295310	4129715
2066894	3231662	3504438	1820982	308327	4606791
2868929	3512869	4105847	2174128	340150	5104438
1701467	3425663	4793983	3748731	360512	4110403
2125413	3972714	5328286	3987379	416120	4897501
2894445	4390985	6098622	4531371	444964	5513272
4485101	4406835	7689447	4342511	2217447	5536324

10-3 规模以上工业企业单位数(按隶属关系分,2003年)

单位：个

分组	Item	合计 Total	内资 国有 State-owned	集体 Collective-owned	股份合作 Share-Holding
总 计	**Total**	**735**	**205**	**115**	**33**
中央企业	Central Enterprises	68	49		
省属企业	Provincial Enterprises	66	40		
市属企业	Municipal Enterprises	601	116	115	33
#市直属企业	Municipal Enterprises Directly under Municipdity	220	61	25	18
区 属	under Urban Districts	265	31	74	11
新城区	Xincheng	21	1	10	
碑林区	Beilin	7	1	1	2
莲湖区	Lianhu	13	1	4	1
灞桥区	Baqiao	42		11	3
未央区	Weiyang	68	3	32	1
雁塔区	Yanta	54	8	6	
阎良区	Yanliang	15	3	2	4
临潼区	Lintong	13	6	2	
长安区	Chang'an	32	8	6	
县 属	under Counties	116	24	16	4
蓝田县	Lantian	29	11	8	1
周至县	Zhouzhi	9	2	1	1
户 县	Huxian	44	6	6	1
高陵县	Gaoling	34	5	1	1

注:该表未包括长庆油田。

Note:Not Including Changqing Oil Field .

Number of Industrial Enterprises

Above Designated Size (Grouped by Ownership,2003)

(unit)

Domestic Investment						港澳台商投资	外商投资
联营经济 Joint Owned	国有独资公司 State-owned apprtion-opriator ship corporation	其它有限责任公司 Other limited corporation	股份有限公司 Share holding corporation ltd.	私营 Private	其它 Others	Funded from Hongkong , Macao,&TaiWan	Foreign Funded
14	**12**	**133**	**47**	**92**	**2**	**29**	**53**
	9	6				1	3
1	1	13	5				6
13	2	114	42	92	2	28	44
3	2	42	22	1	1	16	29
							13
8		40	15	62		11	
		6		3		1	
		1	1	1			1
1		2	1	2			3
		14	5	6			5
2		6	5	8		6	4
3		8	3	19		3	
				6			
2		2				1	
		1		17			2
2		32	5	29	1	1	
		4		5			
2		3					1
		9	2	17	1	1	1
		16	3	7			

10-4 规模以上工业企业单位数(2003年)

Number of Industrial Enterprises Above Designated Size (2003)

单位：个 (unit)

分组	Item	合计 Total
总计	**Total**	**735**
在总计中:轻工业	Grouped by :Light Industry and Heavy Industry	291
重工业	Heavy Industry	444
在总计中:大型工业	Grouped by Size of Enterprises:Large size Industry Enterprises	25
中型工业	Medium-size Industry Enterprises	101
小型工业	Small size Industry Enterprises	609
按经济组织类型分	Grouped by economic type of orgnization	
独资公司	Appropratorship	350
合作合伙公司	Partnership	53
股份有限公司	Corporaton	57
有限责任公司	Limited company	275
按工业行业大类分	Grouped by Sector	
煤炭开采和洗选业	Coal mining and coal washing industry	
石油和天然气开采业	Petroleum and Natural Gas Extraction	1
黑色金属矿采选业	Ferrous Metals Mining and Dressing	1
有色金属矿采选业	Nonferrous Metals Mining and Dressing	3
非金属矿采选业	Nonmetal Minerals Mining and Dressing	2
其他采矿业	Other mining industry	
农副食品加工业	Agricultural products and non-stable food processing industry	36
食品制造业	Food production	23
饮料制造业	Beverage Production	12
烟草加工业	Tobacco Processing	1
纺织业	Textile Industry	23
纺织服装、鞋、帽制造业	Textile clothing, footwear and headgear industry	7
皮革、毛皮、羽毛(绒)及其制品业	Leather, fur, feather (eiderdown) and their products industry	2
木材加工及竹、藤、棕、草制品业	Timber Processing,Bamboo,Cane,Palm Fiber and Straw Products	3

10-4 规模以上工业企业单位数(2003年)（续）

Number of Industrial Enterprises Above Designated Size (2003)(Continued)

单位：个 (unit)

分组	Item	合计 Total
家具制造业	Furniture Manufacturing	9
造纸及纸制品业	Papermaking and paper produts	35
印刷业、记录媒介的复制	Printing,Record Medium Reproduction	33
文教体育用品制造业	Cultural,Educational and Sports Goods	2
石油加工、炼焦及核燃料加工业	Petroleum refining, coke making and nuclear fuel processing industry	6
化学原料及化学制品制造业	Raw Chemical Materials and Chemical Products	37
医药制造业	Medical and Pharmaceutical Products	52
化学纤维制造业	Chemical Fiber	1
橡胶制品业	Rubber Products	2
塑料制品业	Plastic Products	17
非金属矿物制品业	Nonmetal Mineral Products	62
黑色金属冶炼及压延加工业	Smelting and Pressing of Ferrous Metals	10
有色金属冶炼及压延加工业	Smelting and Pressing of Nonferrou Metals	17
金属制品业	Metal Products	19
通用设备制造	General equipment manufacturing industry	61
专用设备制造业	Special Purpose Equipment	64
交通运输设备制造业	Transport Equipment	51
电气机械及器材制造业	Electric Equipment and Machinery	65
通信设备、计算机及其他电子设备制造业	Communication equipment, computer and other electronic equipment manufacturing industry	35
仪器仪表及文化办公用机械制造业	Instruments,Meters,Cultural and office Machinery	20
工艺品及其他制造业	Handicraft and other stuff manufacturing industry	8
废弃资源和废旧材料回收加工业	Discarded resources and waste materials salvaging and processing industry	
电力、热力的生产和供应业	Electric power, heating power generating and supplying industry	6
燃气生产和供应业	Gas mining and supplying industry	1
水的生产和供应业	Water processing and supplying industry	8

注:该表未包括长庆油田。

Note:Not Including Changqing Oil Field

10-5 市区规模以上工业企业单位数(2003年)

Number of Industrial Enterprises Above Designated Size in Urban Districts(2003)

单位：个 (unit)

分组	Item	地区 District	区属 Under District
总计	**Total**	**607**	**265**
按行政区划分	Grouped by Adiministrative Division		
新城区	Xingcheng	67	21
碑林区	Beilin	47	7
莲湖区	Lianhu	86	13
灞桥区	Baqiao	68	42
未央区	Weiyang	115	68
雁塔区	Yanta	149	54
阎良区	Yanliang	16	15
临潼区	Lingtong	23	13
长安区	Chang'an	36	32
按轻重工业分	Grouped by Light Industry and Heavy Industry		
轻工业	Light Industry	236	118
重工业	Heavy Industry	371	147
按企业规模分	Grouped by Size of Enterprises		
大型工业	Large-size Industry Enterproses	25	
中型工业	Medium-size Industry Enterprises	92	15
小型工业	Small-size Industry Enterprises	490	250
按经济组织类型分	Grouped by economic type of orgnization		
独资公司	Appropratorship	297	129
合作合伙公司	Partnership	45	21
股份有限公司	Corporation	46	19
有限责任公司	Limited company	219	96
按工业行业大类分	Grouped by Sector		
煤炭开采和洗选业	Coal mining and coal washing industry		
石油和天然气开采业	Petroleum and Natural Gas Extraction		
黑色金属矿采选业	Ferrous Metals Mining and Dressing		
有色金属矿采选业	Nonferrous Metals Mining and Dressing		
非金属矿采选业	Nonmetal Minerals Mining and Dressing	1	1
其他采矿业	Other mining industry		
农副食品加工业	Agricultural products and non-stable food processing industry	25	18
食品制造业	Food production	18	11
饮料制造业	Beverage production	11	4

10–5 市区规模以上工业企业单位数(2003年)（续）

Number of Industrial Enterprises Above Designated Size in Urban Districts(2003)(Continued)

单位：个 (unit)

分 组	Item	地 区 District	区 属 Under District
烟草加工业	Tobacco Processing	1	
纺织业	Textile Industry	20	6
纺织服装、鞋、帽制造业	Textile clothing, footwear and headgear industry	7	5
皮革、毛皮、羽毛(绒)及其制品业	Leather, fur, feather (eiderdown) and their products industry	2	
木材加工及竹、藤、棕、草制品业	Timber Processing,Bamboo,Cane,Palm Fiber and Straw Products	3	1
家具制造业	Furniture Manufacturing	7	6
造纸及纸制品业	Papermaking and paper products	28	27
印刷业、记录媒介的复制	Printing,Record Medium Reproduction	29	7
文教体育用品制造业	Cultural,Educational and Sports Goods	2	2
石油加工及炼焦业	Petroleum Processing and Coking	6	3
化学原料及化学制品制造业	Raw Chemical Materials and Chemical Products	27	13
医药制造业	Medical and Pharmaceutical Products	45	16
化学纤维制造业	Chemical Fiber		
橡胶制品业	Rubber Products	2	2
塑料制品业	Plastic Products	10	5
非金属矿物制品业	Nonmetal Mineral Products	41	26
黑色金属冶炼及压延加工业	Smelting and Pressing of Ferrous Metals	9	3
有色金属冶炼及压延加工业	Smelting and Pressing of Nonferrou Metals	14	9
金属制品业	Metal Products	19	9
通用设备制造	General equipment manufacturing industry	56	26
专用设备制造业	Special Purpose Equipment	57	16
交通运输设备制造业	Transport Equipment	47	14
电气机械及器材制造业	Electric Equipment and Machinery	55	18
通信设备、计算机及其他电子设备制造业	Communication equipment, computer and other electronic equipment manufacturing industry	35	9
仪器仪表及文化办公用机械制造业	Instruments,Meters,Cultural and	18	3
工艺品及其他制造业	Handicraft and other stuff manufacturing industry	4	1
废弃资源和废旧材料回收加工业	Discarded resources and waste materials salvaging and processing industry		
电力、热力的生产和供应业	Electric power, heating power generating and supplying industry	3	1
燃气生产和供应业	Gas mining and supplying industry	1	
水的生产和供应业	Water processing and supplying industry	4	3

注:该表未包括长庆油田。

Note:Not Including Changqing Oil Field.

10–6 全部规模以上工业企业职工人数

Number of Staff and Workers of All Industrial Enterprises Above Designated Size

单位：人 (person)

分　组	Item	2003
总　计	**Total**	**365486**
按隶属关系分	Grouped by Administrative Relationship	
中央企业	Central Enterprises	154631
省属企业	Provincial Enterprises	60383
市属企业	Municipal Enterprises	150472
按登记注册类型分组	Grouped by Administrative Relationship	
内资企业	Domestic Investment Enterprises	350614
国有经济	State-owned Enterprises	144912
集体经济	Collective-owned Enterprises	19417
股份合作企业	Share-holding Corporative Enterprises	6959
联营企业	Joint Ownership Enterprises	2020
国有独资公司	State-owned Appropriator ship Corporation	52049
其他有限责任公司	Other limited corporation	88831
股份有限公司	Share-holding Corporation Ltd.	23286
私营企业	Private Enterprises	12880
其他内资	Other Domestic Investment Enterprises	260
港、澳、台商投资企业	Enterprises with Investment from Hong Kong,Macao and Taiwan	4548
外商投资企业	Enterprises with Foreign Investment	10324
按轻重工业分	Grouped by Ligth Industry and Heavy Industry	
轻工业	Light Industry	103509
重工业	Heavy Industry	261977
按企业规模分	Grouped by Size of Enterprises	
大型工业	Large-size Industry Enterprises	145306
中型工业	Medium-size Industry Enterprises	123786
小型工业	Small Industry Enterprises	96394
按经济组织类型分	Grouped by economic type of orgnization	
独资企业	Appropratorship	169408
合作、合伙企业	Partnership	9750
股份有限公司	Corporation	24462
有限责任公司	Limited company	161866
按工业行业大类分	Grouped by Sector	
煤炭开采和洗选业	Coal mining and coal washing industry	
石油和天然气开采业	Petroleum and Natural Gas Extraction	665
黑色金属矿采选业	Ferrous Metals Mining and Dressing	120
有色金属矿采选业	Nonferrous Metals Mining and Dressing	1131
非金属矿采选业	Nonmetal Minerals Mining and Dressing	110
其他采矿业	Other mining industry	
农副食品加工业	Agricultural products and non-stable food processing industry	5806

10–6 全部规模以上工业企业职工人数（续）

Number of Staff and Workers of AllIndastrial Enterprises Above Designated Size（Continued)

单位：人 (person)

分　　组	Item	2003
食品制造业	Food production	5508
饮料制造业	Beverage production	3717
烟草加工业	Tobacco Processing	166
纺织业	Textile Industry	33057
纺织服装、鞋、帽制造业	Textile clothing, footwear and headgear industry	2589
皮革、毛皮、羽毛(绒)及其制品业	Leather, fur, feather (eiderdown) and their products industry	1358
木材加工及竹、藤、棕、草制品业	Timber Processing,Bamboo,Cane,Palm Fiber and Straw Products	574
家具制造业	Furniture Manufacturing	2108
造纸及纸制品业	Papermaking and paper products	9287
印刷业、记录媒介的复制	Printing,Record Medium Reproduction	8470
文教体育用品制造业	Cultural,Educational and Sports Goods	152
石油加工、炼焦及核燃料加工业	Petroleum refining, coke making and nuclear fuel processing industry	2283
化学原料及化学制品制造业	Raw Chemical Materials and Chemical Products	25911
医药制造业	Medical and Pharmaceutical Products	16023
化学纤维制造业	Chemical Fiber	85
橡胶制品业	Rubber Products	120
塑料制品业	Plastic Products	1340
非金属矿物制品业	Nonmetal Mineral Products	13215
黑色金属冶炼及压延加工业	Smelting and Pressing of Ferrous Metals	5061
有色金属冶炼及压延加工业	Smelting and Pressing of Nonferrou Metals	2857
金属制品业	Metal Products	2072
通用设备制造	General equipment manufacturing industry	16698
专用设备制造业	Special Purpose Equipment	44189
交通运输设备制造业	Transport Equipment	85446
电气机械及器材制造业	Electric Equipment and Machinery	26176
通信设备、计算机及其他电子设备制造业	Communication equipment, computer and other electronic equipment manufacturing industry	21863
仪器仪表及文化办公用机械制造业	Instruments,Meters,Cultural and Office Machinery	11206
工艺品及其他制造业	Handicraft and other stuff manufacturing industry	1823
废弃资源和废旧材料回收加工业	Discarded resources and waste materials salvaging and processing industry	
电力、热力的生产和供应业	Electric power, heating power generating and supplying industry	9258
燃气生产和供应业	Gas mining and supplying industry	1086
水的生产和供应业	Water processing and supplying industry	3956

10-7 全部规模以上工业企业年末职工人数（2003年）

Number of Staff and Workers at the Year End in All Industrial Enterprises Above Designated Size（2003）

单位:人 (person)

区县名称	Name of District and County	全辖区 total	区县属 under Districts and Counties
总　计	**Total**	**365486**	**58149**
新城区	Xincheng	59819	2363
碑林区	Beilin	14114	1177
莲湖区	Lianhu	70509	2111
灞桥区	Baqiao	45316	6664
未央区	Weiyang	51417	10241
雁塔区	Yanta	47706	5529
阎良区	Yanliang	20417	900
临潼区	Lintong	13731	5577
长安区	Chang'an	9102	4688
蓝田县	Lantian	5170	3083
周至县	Zhouzhi	1495	1375
户　县	Huxian	21949	9700
高陵县	Gaoling	4741	4741

注:该表未包括长庆油田。

Note:Not Including Changqing Oil Field .

10-8 各区县规模以上工业企业年末职工人数(按登记类型分,2003年)

Number of Staff and Workers in All Industrial Enterprise Above Designated Size By Region at the Year End（Grouped by Registion Status)(2003)

单位：人 (person)

分组	Name of District and County	国有经济 State-owned Enterprises	集体经济 Collective-owned Enterprises	股份合作 Corporative Enterprises of Share Holding
全辖区：总计	**Total**	**144912**	**19417**	**6959**
新城区	Xincheng	15321	1859	1112
碑林区	Beilin	6803	364	846
莲湖区	Lianhu	34964	2641	1775
灞桥区	Baqiao	25506	1675	951
未央区	Weiyang	22122	4637	511
雁塔区	Yanta	20219	1414	821
阎良区	Yanliang	206	172	211
临潼区	Lintong	7436	2530	
长安区	Chang'an	4555	682	178
蓝田县	Lantian	2796	1365	50
周至县	Zhouzhi	280	68	261
户 县	Huxian	4345	1345	67
高陵县	Gaoling	359	665	176
区县属：合计	Under Districts and Counties in Total	6479	14291	2477
新城区	Xincheng	50	1426	
碑林区	Beilin	156	23	339
莲湖区	Lianhu	181	426	320
灞桥区	Baqiao		1595	791
未央区	Weiyang	567	3947	262
雁塔区	Yanta	867	483	
阎良区	Yanliang	206	172	211
临潼区	Lintong	1498	2350	
长安区	Chang'an	397	682	
蓝田县	Lantian	709	1365	50
周至县	Zhouzhi	160	68	261
户 县	Huxian	1329	1089	67
高陵县	Gaoling	359	665	176

10-8 各区县规模以上工业企业年末职工人数(按登记类型分,2003年)(续 1)

Number of Staff and Workers in All Industrial Enterprise Above Designated Size by Region at the Year End（Grouped by Registion Status)(2003)(continued 1)

单位：人 (person)

区县名称	Name of District and County	联营企业 Jiont Ownership Enterprises	国有独资公司 State-owned appropriator ship corporation	其它有限责任公司 Other limited corporation	股份有限公司 Share-holding Corporations Ltd.
全辖区：总计	**Total**	**2020**	**52049**	**88831**	**23286**
新城区	Xincheng		23288	14239	2037
碑林区	Beilin	150		1821	3367
莲湖区	Lianhu	130	7823	19725	1877
灞桥区	Baqiao	273	12016	2359	1239
未央区	Weiyang	85	1044	16531	824
雁塔区	Yanta	340		7551	10972
阎良区	Yanliang			19517	
临潼区	Lintong	428		321	2036
长安区	Chang'an			123	
蓝田县	Lantian			615	
周至县	Zhouzhi	614		272	
户 县	Huxian		7878	3592	653
高陵县	Gaoling			2165	281
区县属：合计	Under Districts and Counties in Total	1531		10203	4530
新城区	Xincheng			579	
碑林区	Beilin			37	506
莲湖区	Lianhu	130		282	508
灞桥区	Baqiao			1827	1239
未央区	Weiyang	85		635	824
雁塔区	Yanta	274		670	519
阎良区	Yanliang				
临潼区	Lintong	428		321	
长安区	Chang'an			123	
蓝田县	Lantian			615	
周至县	Zhouzhi	614		272	
户 县	Huxian			2677	653
高陵县	Gaoling			2165	281

10-8 各区县规模以上工业企业年末职工人数(按登记类型分,2003年)(续 2)

Number of Staff and Workers in All Industrial Enterprise Above Designated Size by Region at the Year End（Grouped by Registion Status)(2003)(continued 2)

单位：人 (person)

区县名称	Name of District and County	私营企业 Private Enterprises	其它企业 Other Enterprises	港澳台商投资 Investment from Hong Kong, Macao and Taiwan	外商投资 Foreign Investment
全辖区：总计	**Total**	**12880**	**260**	**4548**	**10324**
新城区	Xincheng	183		351	1429
碑林区	Beilin	116		348	299
莲湖区	Lianhu	180		185	1209
灞桥区	Baqiao	982		85	230
未央区	Weiyang	1187		1402	3074
雁塔区	Yanta	1972	50	1074	3293
阎良区	Yanliang	311			
临潼区	Lintong			980	
长安区	Chang'an	3486			78
蓝田县	Lantian	344			
周至县	Zhouzhi				
户　县	Huxian	3120	210	123	616
高陵县	Gaoling	999			96
区县属：合计	Under Districts and Counties in Total	12862	210	2680	2886
新城区	Xincheng	183		125	
碑林区	Beilin	116			
莲湖区	Lianhu	180			84
灞桥区	Baqiao	982			230
未央区	Weiyang	1187		1112	1622
雁塔区	Yanta	1954		340	422
阎良区	Yanliang	311			
临潼区	Lintong			980	
长安区	Chang'an	3486			
蓝田县	Lantian	344			
周至县	Zhouzhi				
户　县	Huxian	3120	210	123	432
高陵县	Gaoling	999			96

注:该表未包括长庆油田。

Note:Not Including Changqing Oil Field .

10-9 全市规模以上工业总产值（2003年）

Gross Industrial Output Value Of All Enterprises Above Designated Size Whole City (2003)

单位：万元 (10 000 yuan)

分组	Item	企业单位数（个）Number of Enterprises (unit)	工业总产值 Gross Industrial Output Value 按现价计算 At Current Prices	按1990年不变价计算 At 1990 Constant Prices
总计	**Total**	**735**	**6386627.0**	**6977334.5**
按隶属关系分	Grouped by Administrative Relationship			
中央企业	Central Enterprises	68	1990187.9	1886254.7
省属企业	Provincial Enterprises	66	1294113.5	1355615.1
市属企业	City Enterprises	601	3102325.6	3735464.7
市直属企业	City Enterprises Straightway	220	2104651.3	2716432.7
区直属企业	County Enterprises Straightway	51	180390.9	177507.7
按登记注册类型分	Grouped by Registion Status			
内资企业	Domestic Investment Enterprises	653	5429842.8	5893876.9
国有经济	State-owned Enterprises	205	1848814.8	1613721.8
集体经济	Collective-owned Enterprises	115	272958.2	266122.5
股份合作	Share-holding Corperative	33	60528.0	51293.6
联营企业	Joint Ownership Enterprises	14	22347.2	18564.5
国有独资公司	State-owned Appropriator Ship Corporation	12	359465.3	352048.8
其他有限责任公司	Other limited corporation	133	1942521.8	2120362.0
股份有限公司	Share-holding Corporation Ltd.	47	732409.8	1281054.1
私营企业	Private Enterprises	92	187664.3	187576.2
其他内资企业	Other Domestic Znvestmont Enterprises	2	3133.4	3133.4
港、澳、台商投资企业	Enterprises with Investment from Hong Kong, Macao and Taiwan	29	131122.8	105099.8
外商投资企业	Enterprises with Foreign Investment	53	825661.4	978357.8
按轻重工业分	Grouped by Ligth Industry and Heavy Industry			
轻工业	Light Industry	291	1839455.9	1685946.2
重工业	Heavy Industry	444	4547171.1	5291388.3
按企业规模分	Grouped by Size of Enterprises			
大型工业	Large	25	2911820.5	3556705.9
中型工业	Medium-sized	101	2217447.2	2133863.5
小型工业	Small	609	1257359.3	1286765.1
按经济组织类型分	Grouped by economic type of orgnization			
独资企业	Appropratorship	350	2292788.7	2117904.3
合作、合伙企业	Partnership	53	95327.3	82071.1
股份有限公司	Corporaton	57	739873.9	1288008.0
有限责任公司	Limited company	275	3258637.1	3489351.1
按工业行业大类分	Grouped by Sector			
煤炭开采和洗选业	Coal mining and coal washing industry			
石油和天然气开采业	Petroleum and Natural Gas Extraction	1	7028.4	6020.3
黑色金属矿采选业	Ferrous Metals Mining and Dressing	1	780.1	370.5
有色金属矿采选业	Nonferrous Metals Mining and Dressing	3	8873.8	5369.4
非金属矿采选业	Nonmetal Minerals Mining and Dressing	2	483.9	483.8
其他矿采选业	Other Mining and Dressing			
农副食品加工业	Agricultural porducts and non-stable food processing industry	36	222377.6	185936.5
食品制造业	Food Manufacturing	23	133289.7	105514.5

10-9 全市规模以上工业总产值（2003年）（续）

Gross Industrial Output Value Of All Enterprises Above Designated Size Whole City (2003)（Continued)

单位：万元 （10 000 yuan）

分 组	Item	企业单位数（个）Number of Enterprises (unit)	工业总产值 Gross Industrial Output Value 按现价计算 At Current Prices	按1990年不变价计算 At 1990 Constant Prices
饮料制造业	Beverage Manufacturing	12	123325.9	96698.7
烟草加工业	Tobacco Processing	1	1066.0	1247.1
纺织业	Textile Industry	23	179155.8	164839.2
纺织服装、鞋、帽制造业	Textile clothing, footwear and headgear industry	7	20770.0	20749.3
皮革、毛皮、羽毛(绒)及其制品业	Leather, fur, feather (eiderdown) and their products industry	2	16377.6	12436.8
木材加工及竹、藤、棕、	Timber Processing,Bamboo,Cane,Palm Fiber and Straw Products	3	3139.0	3405.3
家具制造业	Furniture Manufacturing	9	9259.0	9869.6
造纸及纸制品业	Papermaking and Paper products	35	73132.6	67816.0
印刷业、记录媒介的复制	Printing,Record Medium Reproduction	33	172939.9	166871.9
文教体育用品制造业	Cultural,Educational and Sports Goods	2	932.8	913.8
石油加工、炼焦及核燃料加工业	Petroleum refining, coke making and nuclear fuel processing industry	6	223561.7	48424.6
化学原料及化学制品制造业	Raw Chemical Materials and Chemical Products	37	244307.2	226109.2
医药制造业	Medical and Pharmaceutical Products	52	606692.1	600932.6
化学纤维制造业	Chemical Fiber	1	2263.3	2263.3
橡胶制品业	Rubber Products	2	2562.3	2622.2
塑料制品业	Plastic Products	17	27814.4	29071.0
非金属矿物制品业	Nonmetal Mineral Products	62	109747.6	92254.6
黑色金属冶炼及压延加工业	Smelting and Pressing of Ferrous Metals	10	65000.9	67178.9
有色金属冶炼及压延加工业	Smelting and Pressing of Nonferrou Metals	17	103317.8	105221.0
金属制品业	Metal Products	19	26961.5	26224.1
通用设备制造	General equipment manufacturing industry	61	299331.5	316403.9
专用设备制造业	Special Purpose Equipment	64	528162.4	610037.8
交通运输设备制造业	Transport Equipment	51	1576986.6	1775739.3
电气机械及器材制造业	Electric Equipment and Machinery	65	616300.5	765319.5
通信设备、计算机及其他电子设备制造业	Communication equipment, computer and other electronic equipment manufacturing industry	35	607210.1	1193987.2
仪器仪表及文化办公用	Instruments,Meters,Cultural and Office	20	115700.5	114458.0
工艺品及其他制造业	Handicraft and other stuff manufacturing industry	8	89474.0	88878.0
废弃资源和废旧材料回收加工业	Discarded resources and waste materials salvaging and processing industry			
电力、热力的生产和供应业	Electric power, heating power generating and supplying industry	6	125045.2	54380.8
燃气生产和供应业	Gas mining and supplying industry	1	2774.7	608.1
水的生产和供应业	Water processing and supplying industry	8	40480.6	8677.7

注:该表未包括长庆油田。

Note:Not Including Changqing Oil Field .

10-10 全市规模以上工业总产值（2003年）

Gross Industrial Output Value Of All Enterprises Above Designated Size Whole City (2003)

单位：万元 （10 000 yuan）

分组	Item	企业单位数（个）Number of Enterprises (unit)	工业总产值 Gross Industrial Output Value 按现价计算 At Current Prices	按1990年不变价计算 At 1990 Constant Prices
总计	**Total**	**607**	**6063883.3**	**6690364.4**
按隶属关系分	Grouped by Administrative Relationship			
中央企业	Central Enterprises	60	1874127.3	1802465.9
省属企业	Provincial Enterprises	63	1288097.2	1351292.4
市属企业	City Enterprises	484	2901658.8	3536606.1
市直属企业	City Enterprises Straightway	219	2103805.2	2715773.4
区直属企业	County Enterprises Straightway	51	180390.9	177507.7
按登记注册类型分	Grouped by Registion Status			
内资企业	Domestic Investment Enterprises	529	5136869.6	5636274.6
国有经济	State-owned Enterprises	174	1767605.5	1564884.5
集体经济	Collective-owned Enterprises	98	251176.0	244471.9
股份合作	Share-holding Corperative	29	55740.2	47536.0
联营企业	Joint Ownership Enterprises	12	15824.6	14941.9
国有独资公司	State-owned Appropriator Ship Corporation	11	333241.3	329640.8
其他有限责任公司	Other limited corporation	99	1864782.6	2035695.5
股份有限公司	Share-holding Corperation Ltd.	42	720758.9	1270556.4
私营企业	Private Enterprises	63	125059.8	125866.9
其他内资企业	Other Domestic Znvestmont Enterprises	1	2680.7	2680.7
港、澳、台商投资企业	Enterprises with Investment from Hong Kong, Macao and Taiwan	28	130157.2	104753.1
外商投资企业	Enterprises with Foreign Investment	50	796856.5	949336.7
按轻重工业分	Grouped by Ligth Industry and Heavy Industry			
轻工业	Light Industry	236	1697683.9	1536577.4
重工业	Heavy Industry	371	4366199.4	5153787.0
按企业规模分	Grouped by Size of Enterprises			
大型工业	Large	25	2911820.5	3556705.9
中型工业	Medium-sized	92	2071511.9	2013148.8
小型工业	Small	490	1080550.9	1120509.7
按经济组织类型分	Grouped by economic type of orgnization			
独资企业	Appropratorship	297	2185677.9	2043221.7
合作、合伙企业	Partnership	45	82696.7	73370.7
股份有限公司	Corporaton	46	723377.6	1273255.2
有限责任公司	Limited company	219	3072131.1	3300516.8
按工业行业大类分	Grouped by Sector			
煤炭开采和洗选业	Coal mining and coal washing industry			
石油和天然气开采业	Petroleum and Natural Gas Extraction			
黑色金属矿采选业	Ferrous Metals Mining and Dressing			
有色金属矿采选业	Nonferrous Metals Mining and Dressing			
非金属矿采选业	Nonmetal Minerals Mining and Dressing	1	9.6	9.5
其他矿采选业	Other Mining and Dressing			
农副食品加工业	Agricultural porducts and non-stable food processing industry	25	174677.3	139701.8
食品制造业	Food Manufacturing	18	129518.6	102757.8

10-10 全市规模以上工业总产值（2003年）（续）

Gross Industrial Output Value Of All Enterprises Above Designated Size Whole City (2003)（Continued)

单位：万元 （10 000 yuan）

分组	Item	企业单位数（个）Number of Enterprises (unit)	工业总产值 Gross Industrial Output Value 按现价计算 At Current Prices	按1990年不变价计算 At 1990 Constant Prices
饮料制造业	Beverage Manufacturing	11	120628.0	94000.8
烟草加工业	Tobacco Processing	1	1066.0	1247.1
纺织业	Textile Industry	20	175136.5	161251.9
纺织服装、鞋、帽制造业	Textile clothing, footwear and headgear industry	7	20770.0	20749.3
皮革、毛皮、羽毛(绒)及其制品业	Leather, fur, feather (eiderdown) and their products industry	2	16377.6	12436.8
木材加工及竹、藤、棕、	Timber Processing,Bamboo,Cane,Palm Fiber and Straw Products	3	3139.0	3405.3
家具制造业	Furniture Manufacturing	7	8357.9	9047.0
造纸及纸制品业	Papermaking and Paper products	28	54259.4	52328.3
印刷业、记录媒介的复制	Printing,Record Medium Reproduction	29	170332.2	164494.8
文教体育用品制造业	Cultural,Educational and Sports Goods	2	932.8	913.8
石油加工、炼焦及核燃料加工业	Petroleum refining, coke making and nuclear fuel processing industry	6	223561.7	48424.6
化学原料及化学制品制造业	Raw Chemical Materials and Chemical Products	27	179817.0	166060.4
医药制造业	Medical and Pharmaceutical Products	45	586860.0	566541.3
化学纤维制造业	Chemical Fiber			
橡胶制品业	Rubber Products	2	2562.3	2622.2
塑料制品业	Plastic Products	10	16990.9	18070.0
非金属矿物制品业	Nonmetal Mineral Products	41	85435.9	73374.7
黑色金属冶炼及压延加工业	Smelting and Pressing of Ferrous Metals	9	62979.7	65157.7
有色金属冶炼及压延加工业	Smelting and Pressing of Nonferrou	14	97300.2	99441.0
	Metals	19	26961.5	26224.1
金属制品业	Metal Products			
通用设备制造	General equipment manufacturing industry	56	292242.9	309168.3
专用设备制造业	Special Purpose Equipment	57	518301.3	600196.2
交通运输设备制造业	Transport Equipment			
电气机械及器材制造业	Electric Equipment and Machinery	47	1554939.8	1753055.2
通信设备、计算机及其他	Communication equipment, computer and other	55	607140.0	756068.5
电子设备制造业	electronic equipment manufacturing industry	35	607210.1	1193987.2
仪器仪表及文化办公用	Instruments,Meters,Cultural and Office	18	114671.1	113486.5
工艺品及其他制造业	Handicraft and other stuff manufacturing industry	4	84985.5	84384.6
废弃资源和废旧材料回收加工业	Discarded resources and waste materials salvaging and processing industry			
电力、热力的生产和供应业	Electric power, heating power generating and supplying industry	3	84360.5	42673.6
燃气生产和供应业	Gas mining and supplying industry	1	2774.7	608.1
水的生产和供应业	Water processing and supplying industry	4	39583.3	8476.0

注:该表未包括长庆油田。

Note:Not Including Changqing Oil Field .

10-11 市属规模以上工业总产值（2003年）

Total Gross Output of All Municipal Enterprises Above Designated Size （2003）

单位：万元 （10 000 yuan）

分组	Item	企业单位数（个）Number of Enterprises (unit)	工业总产值 Gross Industrial Output Value 按现价计算 At Current Prices	按1990年不变价计算 At 1990 Constant Prices
总计	**Total**	**601**	**3102325.6**	**3735464.7**
按隶属关系分	Grouped by Administrative Relationship			
市属企业	Municipal Enterprises	601	3102325.6	3735464.7
市直属企业	Enterprises Directly Under the Municipal Government	220	2104651.3	2716432.7
区直属企业	Enterprises Directly Under the District Government	51	180390.9	177507.7
县直属企业	Enterprises Directly Under the County Government	45	69496.1	63082.7
街道企业	Enterprises at Sub-district Level	34	64256.3	55671.5
镇办企业	Enterprises at Town Level	20	65666.8	39018.6
乡办企业	Enterprises at Township Level	26	56035.4	53373.7
居委会	Enterprises Run by Neighbourhood Committee			
村委会	Villagers Committee	33	52568.3	49953.9
其他	Others	172	509260.5	580423.9
按登记注册类型分组	Grouped by Registion Status			
内资企业	Domestic Investment Enterprises	529	2557467.9	3044289.1
国有经济	State-owned Entrprises	116	851993.5	869139.2
集体经济	Collective-owned Enterprises	115	272958.2	266122.5
股份合作	Share-holding Corperative	33	60528.0	51293.6
联营企业	Joint Ownership Enterprises	13	22151.1	18334.0
国有独资公司	State-owned appropriator ship corporation	2	18890.3	36077.5
其他有限责任公司	Other limited corporation	114	494132.1	467053.7
股份有限公司	Share-holding Corperation Ltd.	42	646017.0	1145559.0
私营企业	Private Enterprises	92	187664.3	187576.2
其他内资企业	Other Domestic Funded Enterprises	2	3133.4	3133.4
港、澳、台商投资企业	Enterprises with Investment from Hong Kong,Macao and Taiwan	28	130974.7	104951.7
外商投资企业	Enterprises with Foreign Investment	44	413883.0	586223.9
按轻重工业分	Grouped by Ligth Industry and Heavy Industry			
轻工业	Light Industry	244	975820.1	886691.5
重工业	Heavy Industry	357	2126505.5	2848773.2
按企业规模分	Grouped by Size of Enterprises			
大型工业	Large-size	7	996464.0	1535702.3
中型工业	Medium-sized	55	1044229.7	1076879.8
小型工业	Small-size	539	1061631.9	1122882.6
按经济组织类型分	Grouped by economic type of orgnization			
独资企业	Appropratorship	261	1295967.4	1373321.7
合作、合伙企业	Partnership	52	95131.2	81840.6
股份有限公司	Corporaton	52	653481.1	1152512.9
有限责任公司	Limited company	236	1057745.9	1127789.5
按工业行业大类分	Grouped by Sector			
煤炭开采和洗选业	Coal mining and coal washing industry			
石油和天然气开采业	Petroleum and Natural Gas Extraction	1	7028.4	6020.3
黑色金属矿采选业	Ferrous Metals Mining and Dressing			
有色金属矿采选业	Nonferrous Metals Mining and Dressing	2	6172.0	3253.0
非金属矿采选业	Nonmetal Minerals Mining and Dressing	2	483.9	483.8
其他矿采选业	Other Mining and Dressing			

10–11 市属规模以上工业总产值（2003年）（续）

Total Gross Output of All Municipal Enterprises Above Designated Size（2003）(Continued)

单位：万元　　　　(10 000 yuan)

分　组	Item	企业单位数（个） Number of Enterprises (unit)	工业总产值 Gross Industrial Output Value 按现价计算 At Current Prices	按1990年不变价计算 At 1990 Constant Prices
农副食品加工业	Agricultural porducts and non-stable food processing industry	34	153273.9	143542.9
食品制造业	Food Manufacturing	22	131564.3	104589.7
饮料制造业	Beverage Manufacturing	12	123325.9	96698.7
烟草加工业	Tobacco Processing			
纺织业	Textile Industry	12	19399.5	16770.4
纺织服装、鞋、帽制造业	Textile clothing, footwear and headgear industry	7	20770.0	20749.3
皮革、毛皮、羽毛(绒)及其制品业	Leather, fur, feather (eiderdown) and their products industry	1	9308.6	8259.5
木材加工及竹、藤、棕、	Timber Processing,Bamboo,Cane,Palm Fiber and Straw Products	1	1038.2	1072.8
家具制造业	Furniture Manufacturing	9	9259.0	9869.6
造纸及纸制品业	Papermaking and Paper products	34	72040.9	66940.3
印刷业、记录媒介的复制	Printing,Record Medium Reproduction	24	66957.6	63036.7
文教体育用品制造业	Cultural,Educational and Sports Goods	2	932.8	913.8
石油加工、炼焦及核燃料加工业	Petroleum refining, coke making and nuclear fuel processing industry	5	26711.8	11584.1
化学原料及化学制品制造业	Raw Chemical Materials and Chemical Products	32	166414.7	157491.1
医药制造业	Medical and Pharmaceutical Products	39	120871.6	135126
化学纤维制造业	Chemical Fiber	1	2263.3	2263.3
橡胶制品业	Rubber Products	2	2562.3	2622.2
塑料制品业	Plastic Products	17	27814.4	29071
非金属矿物制品业	Nonmetal Mineral Products	58	93297.7	82750.4
黑色金属冶炼及压延加工业	Smelting and Pressing of Ferrous Metals	7	57420.4	59585.8
有色金属冶炼及压延加工业	Smelting and Pressing of Nonferrou Metals	17	103317.8	105221
金属制品业	Metal Products	17	23573.1	22835.7
通用设备制造	General equipment manufacturing industry	57	288785.0	303343
专用设备制造业	Special Purpose Equipment	38	179428.7	207465.5
交通运输设备制造业	Transport Equipment	27	86110.7	84599.6
电气机械及器材制造业	Electric Equipment and Machinery	63	614034.0	763031.3
通信设备、计算机及其他电子设备制造业	Communication equipment, computer and other electronic equipment manufacturing industry	28	532092.1	1105402.8
仪器仪表及文化办公用	Instruments,Meters,Cultural and Office	12	14872.8	14855.3
工艺品及其他制造业	Handicraft and other stuff manufacturing industry	7	87978.7	87382.7
废弃资源和废旧材料回收加工业	Discarded resources and waste materials salvaging and processing industry			
电力、热力的生产和供应业	Electric power, heating power generating and supplying industry	2	9966.2	9347.3
燃气生产和供应业	Gas mining and supplying industry	1	2774.7	608.1
水的生产和供应业	Water processing and supplying industry	8	40480.6	8677.7

10-12 分区县规模以上工业总产值(2003年)

Gross Output Value of Industry Industrial Enterprises Above Designated Size by Region (2003)

单位：万元 （10 000 yuan）

区县名称	Name of District and County	企业单位数(个) Number of Enterprises (unit)	按现价计算 At Current Prices		按1990年不变价计算 At 1990 Constant Prices	
			全辖区 Total	区县属 under Districts and Counties	全辖区 Total	区县属 under Districts and Counties
总计	**Total**	**735**	**6386627.0**	**997674.3**	**6977334.5**	**1019032.0**
新城区	Xincheng	67	1374583.9	110716.6	1448027.6	111415.8
碑林区	Beilin	47	222164.8	18330.2	223434.6	18212.7
莲湖区	Lianhu	86	1242365.3	24212.7	1403911.4	19761.2
灞桥区	Baqiao	68	288008.8	92522.5	253383.5	83012.2
未央区	Weiyang	115	932320.1	220889.6	716750.3	226393.0
雁塔区	Yanta	149	1139870.8	127773.9	1778181.4	188796.0
阎良区	Yanliang	16	409806.1	13508.4	410888.2	13192.9
临潼区	Lintong	23	346661.7	142462.1	348679.8	117979.0
长安区	Chang'an	36	108101.8	47437.6	107107.6	42069.9
蓝田县	Lantian	32	49956.4	26197.4	46612.8	22860.8
周至县	Zhouzhi	10	14496.4	13716.3	10649.0	10278.5
户 县	Huxian	52	187364.4	88980.5	162025.3	97377.0
高陵县	Gaoling	34	70926.5	70926.5	67683.0	67683.0

10-13 规模以上工业企业主要产品产量

Output of Major Industrial Products Of Enterprises Above Designated size

产品名称	Name of Products	2003	2002	指数（上年=100）Indices(preceding year=100)
铁矿石成品矿(吨)	Iron Ore(ton)	24868	30518	-19.00
发电量（万千瓦小时）	Electricity Generation Volume(10 000 kw.h)	204114	189930	7.47
火电（万千瓦小时）	Thermal power(10000 km.h)	204114	189930	7.47
水电（万千瓦小时）	Hydropower (10000kw.h)			
供电量（万千瓦小时）	Electricity Supply (10000kw.h)	968632	879232	10.20
供热量（万百万千焦）	Heat Supply(10000 million kj)	843.6	724.4	16.50
自来水生产量（万吨）	Tap Water Production (10 000 tons)	26848	26742	0.47
小麦粉（万吨）	Wheat Flour (10 000 tons)	14	16	-12.00
食用植物油（吨）	Edible Vegetable Oil (ton)	54387	34647	57.00
精炼食用植物油（吨）	Refined Edible Vegetable Oil (ton)	96172	77644	23.90
鲜、冻畜肉（吨）	Fresh/Frozen Meat(ton)	1805	1942	-7.10
饲料添加剂（吨）	Feed Additives (ton)	202	282	-28.00
配混合饲料（吨）	Mixed Feed (ton)	185419	171479	8.13
糕点（吨）	Cake (ton)	1089	1178	-7.60
饼干（吨）	Biscuit (ton)			
方便主食品（吨）	Main Intant Food (ton)	69483	33934	105.00
方便面（吨）	Instant Noodle(ton)	61683	23816	159.00
乳制品（吨）	Dairy Products (ton)	51625	27858	85.30
罐头（吨）	Canned Food (ton)	2531	2569	-1.50
酱油（吨）	Soy sauce(ton)	2108	2601	-19.00
食品添加剂（吨）	Food Additives (ton)	17	51	-67.00
淀粉（吨）	Amylum(ton)	116016	102634	13.00
饮料酒（吨）	Beverage Wine (ton)	246229	243322	1.19
白酒（吨）	Liquor (ton)	746	720	3.61
啤酒（吨）	Beer (ton)	245483	242602	1.19
软饮料（吨）	Soft Beverage (ton)	208309	211634	-1.60
碳酸饮料（吨）	Carbonated Beverage(ton)	84566	86839	-2.60
果汁及果汁饮料（吨）	Juice and Fruit Beverage(ton)	83151	75843	9.64
液体乳（吨）	Milk (ton)	1793	3864	-54.00
冷冻饮品（吨）	Chilled Beverage(ton)	725	1003	-28.00
瓶(罐)装饮用水（吨）	Canned Drinking Water(ton)	32517	38448	-15.00
纱（吨）	Yarn (ton)	71266	69445	2.62
布（万米）	Cloth (10 000 m)	27911	27163	2.76
棉布（万米）	Cotton Cloth (10 000 m)	16871	14649	15.20
混纺交织布（万米）	Blend Fabric (10 000m)	9747	11626	-16.00
纯化纤布（万米）	Pure Chemical-Fibre Cloth (10 000 m)	1293	888	45.60
印染布（万米）	Printing and Dyeing Cloth (10 000 m)	2769	2127	30.20

10-13　规模以上工业企业主要产品产量（续1）

Output of Major Industrial Products Of Enterprises Above Designated size(Continued 1)

产品名称	Name of Products	2003	2002	指数（上年=100）Indices(preceding year=100)
丝织品（万米）	Silk Fabric (10 000 m)	34	102	-67.00
针棉织品折用纱线量（吨）	Cotton Knitwear (ton)	3221	3290	-2.10
服装（万件）	Garment (10 000 units)	605	584	3.64
梭织服装（万件）	Shuttle-Woven Garment (10 000 units)	371	376	-1.10
针织服装（万件）	Knitted Garment(10 000 tons)	234	208	12.20
轻革（平方米）	Light Leather(sq.m)	462586	515773	-10.00
皮鞋（万双）	Leather Shoes (10 000 pairs)	69	44	56.5
人造板（立方米）	Artificial Board (cu.m)	6259	6737	-7.1
纤维板（立方米）	Fibre Board (cu.m)	6259	6737	-7.1
生产用木制品（千元）	Woodware for Production (1000yuan)	1609	1121	43.50
家具（件）	Furniture (unit)	63822	63606	0.34
木制家具（件）	Wooden Furniture(unit)	18564	19216	-3.40
软体家具（包括床垫、沙发）（件）	Soft Furniture (inc.: Sofa , Mattress etc.)(unit)	44530	43163	3.17
纸浆（吨）	Paper Pulp(ton)	3751	3995	-6.10
机制纸（吨）	Machine Made Paper(ton)	85545	62635	36.60
新闻纸（吨）	Newsprint Paper(ton)	31921	23396	36.40
凸版纸（吨）	Halfton Paper(ton)	2382	2014	18.30
纸制品（吨）	Paper-Made Products (ton)	3397	1958	73.50
纸箱（吨）	Carton(ton)			
单色印刷品（万令）	Single Color Products(10000 reams)	91.49	93.2	-1.80
多色印刷品（万对开色令）	Colored Printed products(10000 reams)	483.87	408.81	18.40
工艺美术制品（千元）	Arts and Crafts Products(1 000yuan)	628925	617006	1.93
原油加工量（吨）	Crude Oil Processing (ton)	295965	241540	22.50
汽油（吨）	Petrol (ton)	44086	41063	7.36
溶剂油（吨）	Solvent Oil(ton)			
煤油（吨）	Kerosene(ton)	185	737	-75.00
柴油（吨）	Diesel Oil (ton)	64491	46696	38.10
润滑油（吨）	Lubricating Oil (ton)	3525	2891	21.90
液化石油气（吨）	Liquefied Petroleum Gas (ton)	18435.98	16665.71	10.60
焦炭（吨）	Coke (ton)	301957	280800	7.53
煤气（万立方米）	Coal Gas(10 000cu.m)	2361.41	2762.24	-15.00
硫酸（折100%）（吨）	Sulphric Aicd (100%) (ton)	48396	43714	10.70
盐酸（含量31%以上）（吨）	Salt Acid (Content over31%) (ton)	58703	49102	19.60
氢氧化钠（烧碱）（折100%）（吨）	Caustic Soda Lonverted into(ton)	75820	63510	19.40
碳化钙（电石）（折 300升/千克)（吨）	Calcium Carbide Lonverted into(ton)	39344	37485	4.96
商品液氯（吨）	Commercial Liquidized Nitrogen (ton)	21850	14270	53.10

10-13 规模以上工业企业主要产品产量（续2）

Output of Major Industrial Products Of Enterprises Above Designated size(Continued 2)

产品名称	Name of Products	2003	2002	指数（上年=100）Indices(preceding year=100)
合成氨（吨）	Synthetic Ammonia (ton)	13241	14528	-8.90
农用氮、磷、钾化学肥料总计（吨）	Agricultural Chemical Fertilizer (ton)	23512	21434	9.69
氮肥（折含N 100%）（吨）	Nitrogen Fertilizer converted into100% Nitrogen (ton)	9760	10492	-7.00
磷肥（折合P_2O_5 100%）（吨）	Phosphate Fertilizer converted into 100%P_2O_5(ton)	13752	10942	25.70
丙烯（吨）	Propylene(ton)	1024	627	63.30
油漆（吨）	Paint (ton)	7571.57	7997.08	-5.30
建筑涂料（吨）	Construction Paint(ton)	610.56	266.04	129.00
塑料树脂及共聚物（吨）	Plastic,Resin and Copolymer (ton)	36441	32862	10.90
聚氯乙烯树酯（吨）	PVC(ton)	36441	32862	10.90
化学试剂（吨）	Chemical Reagent(ton)	1578	1345	17.30
表面活性剂（吨）	Surface Active Agent(ton)	14925	12369	20.70
粘合剂（吨）	Binding Agent(ton)	4610	4064	13.40
肥皂（吨）	Soap (ton)	13350	8943	49.30
合成洗涤剂（吨）	Synthetic Detergents (ton)	58603	58428	0.30
合成洗衣粉（吨）	Washing Power(ton)	50520	51920	-2.70
牙膏（自然支）（万支）	Toothpaste(10000 Pieces)	867	1039	-17.00
化学原料药（吨）	Chemical Medicine (ton)	91	140	-35.00
中成药（吨）	Chinese patient Medicine (ton)	1059	1110	-4.60
塑料制品（吨）	Plastic Product (ton)	3131	3442	-9.00
塑料棒管材（吨）	Plastic Pipe and Rod(ton)	1223	917	33.40
塑料包装箱及容器（吨）	Plastic Package and container(ton)	1089	1011	7.72
日用塑料制品（吨）	Commodity Plastic Product(ton)	819	1514	-46.00
水泥（万吨）	Cement (10 000 tons)	134.82	145.53	7.40
水泥排水管（吨）	Cement Drainage Pipe(ton)	172071	131370	31.00
水泥压力管（吨）	Cement pressure pipe(ton)	14599	13376	9.14
水泥电杆（吨）	Cement Pole(ton)	29429	38912	-24.00
水泥预制构件（立方米）	Cement Prefabricated Components(cu.m)	14187	8979	58.00
石棉水泥瓦（平方米）	Asbestos Cement Tile(cq.m)	935500	795500	17.60
砖（折标准砖）（万块）	Bricks (Converted into)	2262	2193	3.12
加气混凝土（立方米）	Aerated Concrete (cu.m)	713625	574683	24.20
油毡油纸（卷）	Asphalt Felt and Oilpaper(roll)	118400	61200	93.50
平板玻璃（重量箱）	Plate Glass (wt.cases)	416710	271576	53.40
日用玻璃制品（吨）	Glassware(ton)	12412	28670	-57.00
釉面砖（万平方米）	Glazed Brick(10 000sq.m)	15	125	-88.00

10-13 规模以上工业企业主要产品产量（续3）

Output of Major Industrial Products Of Enterprises Above Designated size(Continued 3)

产品名称	Name of Products	2003	2002	指数（上年=100）Indices(preceding year=100)
墙地砖（万平方米）	Floor and Wall Brick(10 000sq.m)	207	155	33.40
耐火材料制品（吨）	Fireproof Product(ton)	2958	2494	18.60
石棉制品 （吨）	Asbestos Product(ton)	784	720	8.89
钢（吨）	Steel (ton)	35792	30975	15.60
普通碳素钢（吨）	Ordinary Carbon steel(ton)	19827	15966	24.20
普通低合金钢（吨）	Ordinary Low -Alloy Steel (ton)	5	5	
合金钢（吨）	Alloy steel(ton)	1685	2673	-37.00
其它优质钢（吨）	Other Steel of High Quality(ton)	14275	12331	15.80
成品钢材（吨）	Rolled-steel Final Products (ton)	23860	29118	-18.00
优质型钢材（吨）	High Quality Profiled Steel(ton)	69	181	-62.00
线材（吨）	Wire Rod(ton)		6	
钢带（吨）	Metal Strip(ton)	2535	2716	-6.70
无缝钢管（吨）	Seamless Steel Pipe (ton)	31	34	-8.80
焊接钢管（吨）	Welded Steel Pipes(ton)	21102	26181	-19.00
十种有色金属（吨）	Ten sorts of Non-ferrous Metal(ton)	9463	2901	226.00
铜（吨）	Copper(ton)	38	54	-30.00
铝材（吨）	Aluminum Material(ton)	11691	13105	-11.00
黄金（千克）	Gold(kg)	570	638	-11.00
铜加工材（吨）	Copper product (ton)		24	-100.00
金属结构制品（吨）	Metal Parts(ton)	7045	6246	12.80
建筑用金属品（吨）	Metal Parts for Construction(ton)	145	175	-17.00
焊条（吨）	Welding Rod(ton)			
工业锅炉（蒸发量吨）	Industrial Boiler steam(ton)	1178	967	21.80
内燃机（万千瓦）	Internal Combustion Engines (10 000 kw)		–	–
金属切削机床（台）	Metal-cutting Machines (unit)	50	64	-22.00
数控机床（台）	Numberically Controlled Machine Tools (unit)	12	12	–
锻压设备（吨）	Forging-press Equipment (ton)	1338	1173	14.00
起重设备（吨）	Weight Lifting Machine(ton)	567	117	385.00
泵 （台）	Pump(unit)	2053	2055	-0.10
风机（台）	Fan(unit)	2669	2562	4.18
气体压缩机（台）	Gas Compressor(unit)	116	88	31.80
减速机（台）	Moderator(unit)	2307	2252	2.44
轴承 （万套）	Bearing (10 000 sets)	99	110	-10.00
阀门（吨）	Valves (ton)	396	627	-37.00

10-13 规模以上工业企业主要产品产量（续4）

Output of Major Industrial Products Of Enterprises Above Designated size（Continued4)

产品名称	Name of Products	2003	2002	指数（上年=100）Indices(preceding year=100)
液压元件（件）	Hydraulic Element(unit)	19301	19618	-1.60
密封件（万件）	Seal(10 000unit)	2810	2347	19.70
齿轮（吨）	Gear (ton)	12957	7752	67.10
铸件（吨）	Cast(ton)	16730	15086	10.90
锻件（吨）	Forged Piece;(ton)	17525	14566	20.30
矿山设备（吨）	Mining Equipment (ton)	3667	3211	14.20
工矿配件（吨）	Industrial and Minery Components(ton)	2706	2258	19.80
粮食加工机械（台）	Food Processing Machine(unit)	291	238	22.30
烟草加工机械（台、条、组）	Tobacco Processing Machine(unit)	5	3	66.70
缝纫机（架）	Sewing Machines (unit)	558043	497832	12.10
造纸机械（台）	Paper Making Machine(unit)	8	_	_
石油钻采设备（吨）	Petroleum Exploitation Machine(ton)	390	338	15.40
炼油设备（吨）	Oil Refining Machine(ton)	1100	712	54.50
化工设备（吨）	Equipment for Chemical Industry (ton)	2077	989	110.00
水泥设备（吨）	Cement Producing Equipment(ton)	29069	18001	61.50
金属轧制设备（吨）	Metal-rolling Machine(ton)	185	81	128.00
小型拖拉机（台）	Small Tractor(unit)	261	480	-46.00
铲土运输机械（台）	Earth-moving Machine(unit)	2071	1314	57.60
压实机械（台）	Road Pressing Machine(unit)	54	64	-16.00
货车（辆）	Lorry(unit)	3162	3056	3.47
汽车（辆）	Motor Vehicle (unit)	41051	25407	61.60
载货汽车（辆）	Trucks (unit)	20088	7896	154.00
公路客车（辆）	Buses(unit)	883	1011	-13.00
轿车（辆）	Cars (unit)	20080	16500	21.70
改装汽车（辆）	Refit Trucks (unit)	831	877	-5.20
自行车（辆）	Bicycle (unit)	33690	32281	4.36
交流电动机（千瓦）	Alternating Current Motor (kw)	2762224	1749656	57.90
变压器（千伏安）	Transformer (kwa)	20178403	16313764	23.70
互感器（台）	Mutual Inductor(unit)	4563	4501	1.38
高压断路器（台）	High-voltage Switch(unit)	2239	2315	-3.30
高压开关板（面）	High-voltage Switch Panel	3184	2940	8.30
通迅电缆（公里）	Communication cable (kilometers)	26534	23097	14.90
家用电冰箱（台）	Household refrigerator (number of)	92654	173410	-47.00
程控交换机（线）	Program-controlled telephone exchange (number of lines)	905752	1442442	-37.00
数字程控交换机（线）	Digital program-controlled telephone exchange (number of lines)	828264	1190476	-30.00
彩色显象管（只）	Color kinescope (number of)	6658936	4631004	43.80
自动化仪表及系统（台、套）	Automatization meter and system (number of)	133502	161769	-17.00

10–14　全部规模以上工业企业主要经济指标（2003年）

单位：万元

分　组	Item	企业单位数（个）Number of Enterprises (unit)	亏损企业 Loss Making Enterprises
总　　计	**Total**	**735**	**250**
#市　区	Urban Area	607	199
按隶属关系分	Grouped by Administrative Relationship		
中央企业	Central Enterprises	68	20
省属企业	Provincial Enterprises	66	37
市属企业	Municipal Enterprises	601	193
市直属企业	Municipal Enterprises Straightway	220	85
区直属企业	Enterprises Urban District under	51	18
县直属企业	Enterprises County Under	45	21
市属中其中：区属	Among Municipal EnterPrises: Under Urban District	265	63
县属	Under County	116	45
按登记注册类型分组	Grouped by Registion Status		
内资企业	Domestic Investment Enterprises	653	225
国有经济	State-owned Enterprises	205	95
集体经济	Collective-owned Enterprises	115	25
股份合作	Share-holding Corperative	33	13
联营企业	Joint Ownership Enterprises	14	5
国有独资公司	State-owned appropriator ship corporation	12	5
其他有限责任公司	Other limited corporation	133	42
股份有限公司	Share-holding Corperation Ltd.	47	12
私营企业	Private Enterprises	92	28
其他内资企业	Other Domestic Funded Enterprises	2	
港、澳、台商投资企业	Enterprises with Investment from Hong Kong,Macao and Taiwan	29	10
外商投资企业	Enterprises with Foreign Investment	53	15
在总计中:亏损企业	Of the Total: Deficit Enterprises	250	250
在总计中:国有控股企业	Of the total: Enterprises of Controlling Share Hold by the State	303	132
按轻重工业分	Grouped by Ligth Industry and Heavy Industry		
轻工业	Light Industry	291	108
重工业	Heavy Industry	444	142
按企业规模分	Grouped by Size of Enterprises		
大型工业	Large-size	25	3
中型工业	Medium-size	101	27
小型工业	Small-size	609	220
按经济组织类型分	Grouped by economic type of orgnization		
独资企业	Appropratorship	350	127
合作、合伙企业	Partnership	53	18
股份有限公司	Corporaton	57	18
有限责任公司	Limited company	275	87
按工业行业大类分	Grouped by Sector		
煤炭开采和洗选业	Coal mining and coal washing industry		
石油和天然气开采业	Petroleum and Natural Gas Extraction	1	
黑色金属矿采选业	Ferrous Metals Mining and Dressing	1	1

Main Economic Indicators of All Industrial Enterprises Above Designafed size(2003)

（10 000 yuan）

工业总产值（当年价） Gross Industrial Output Value (At Current Prices)	工业总产值（不变价） Gorss Industrial Output Value (At Constant Prices)	工业增加值（生产法） Value-Added of Industry (Value of Industrial Products Sales)	工业销售产值（当年价） Value of Industry Products Sales (At Current Prices)	全部职工年平均人数（人） Annual Average Employers (person)
6386627.0	**6977334.5**	**2027449.5**	**6150080.1**	**365486**
6063883.3	6690364.4	1919408.6	5832956.0	332131
1990187.9	1886254.7	621591.9	1941529.2	154631
1294113.5	1355615.1	433899.9	1247234.2	60383
3102325.6	3735464.7	971957.7	2961316.7	150472
2104651.3	2716432.7	647436.6	2016526.6	92323
180390.9	177507.7	52033.4	169099.6	8237
69496.1	63082.7	19380.5	64897.2	6837
797853.6	820832.7	265542.7	750291.3	39250
199820.7	198199.3	58978.4	194498.8	18899
5429842.8	5893876.9	1626350.2	5222193.1	350614
1848814.8	1613721.8	585316.1	1812430.8	144912
272958.2	266122.5	79418.8	256168.2	19417
60528.0	51293.6	21500.2	58642.6	6959
22347.2	18564.5	7583.9	21597.5	2020
359465.3	352048.8	93232.5	344001.1	52049
1942521.8	2120362.0	566548.9	1832239.3	88831
732409.8	1281054.1	206846.3	717033.4	23286
187664.3	187576.2	64164.9	176156.5	12880
3133.4	3133.4	1738.6	3923.7	260
131122.8	105099.8	43425.8	126557.3	4548
825661.4	978357.8	357673.5	801329.7	10324
794707.5	767155.1	287342.4	755378.5	97878
4538264.3	5055267.5	1363459.6	4372793.2	286641
1839455.9	1685946.2	668329.0	1798261.4	103509
4547171.1	5291388.3	1359120.5	4351818.7	261977
2911820.5	3556705.9	853891.8	2852726.3	145306
2217447.2	2133863.5	731415.2	2111374.9	123786
1257359.3	1286765.1	442142.5	1185978.9	96394
2292788.7	2117904.3	733543.0	2228923.6	169408
95327.3	82071.1	34608.9	93626.1	9750
739873.9	1288008.0	209480.5	724193.8	24462
3258637.1	3489351.1	1049817.1	3103336.6	161866
7028.4	6020.3	999.7	7028.4	665
780.1	370.5	164.7	771.4	120

10-14 全部规模以上工业企业经济指标（2003年）（续1）

单位：万元

分 组	Item	资产合计 Total Assets	流动资产小计 Total Circulating Funds
总 计	**Total**	**11956854.0**	**6370457.3**
#市 区	Urban Area	11411428.7	6126658.0
按隶属关系分	Grouped by Administrative Relationship		
中央企业	Central Enterprises	4736987.2	2479896.8
省属企业	Provincial Enterprises	2013029.9	1149072.4
市属企业	Municipal Enterprises	5206836.9	2741488.1
市直属企业	Municipal Enterprises Straightway	3937422.9	2143988.6
区直属企业	Enterprises Urban District under	359786.7	160281.8
县直属企业	Enterprises County Under	116120.9	45076.9
市属中其中：区属	Among Municipal EnterPrises: Under Urban District	960936.3	455915.4
县属	Under County	308477.7	141584.1
按登记注册类型分组	Grouped by Registion Status		
内资企业	Domestic Investment Enterprises	10914204.3	5642334.2
国有经济	State-owned Enterprises	4235691.2	2041349.3
集体经济	Collective-owned Enterprises	356389.9	192396.3
股份合作	Share-holding Corperative	135361.6	54950.0
联营企业	Joint Ownership Enterprises	37721.7	18321.3
国有独资公司	State-owned appropriator ship corporation	1005457.0	379395.7
其他有限责任公司	Other limited corporation	3504557.3	2093691.8
股份有限公司	Share-holding Corperation Ltd.	1440371.6	754052.6
私营企业	Private Enterprises	197271.2	107118.3
其他内资企业	Other Domestic Funded Enterprises	1382.8	1058.9
港、澳、台商投资企业	Enterprises with Investment from Hong Kong,Macao and Taiwan	164794.5	92709.3
外商投资企业	Enterprises with Foreign Investment	877855.2	635413.8
在总计中:亏损企业	Of the Total: Deficit Enterprises	2883202.7	1257714.2
在总计中:国有控股企业	Of the total: Enterprises of Controlling Share Hold by the State	9378282.0	4915962.7
按轻重工业分	Grouped by Ligth Industry and Heavy Industry		
轻工业	Light Industry	2722580.4	1283731.2
重工业	Heavy Industry	9234273.6	5086726.1
按企业规模分	Grouped by Size of Enterprises		
大型工业	Large-size	6011479.4	3274396.4
中型工业	Medium-size	3813890.5	1909932.3
小型工业	Small-size	2131484.1	1186128.6
按经济组织类型分	Grouped by economic type of orgnization		
独资企业	Appropratorship	4746245.9	2304342.3
合作、合伙企业	Partnership	182373.7	78002.1
股份有限公司	Corporaton	1456386.4	762676.8
有限责任公司	Limited company	5571848.0	3225436.1
按工业行业大类分	Grouped by Sector		
煤炭开采和洗选业	Coal mining and coal washing industry		
石油和天然气开采业	Petroleum and Natural Gas Extraction	12632.8	5331.6
黑色金属矿采选业	Ferrous Metals Mining and Dressing	1929.5	678.8

Main Economic Indicators of All Industrial Enterprises Above Designafed size(2003)(Continued 1)

（10 000 yuan）

流动资产年平均余额 Annual Average Balance of Circulating Funds	固定资产小计 Total Fixed Assets	固定资产原价合计 Origing Value of Fixed Assets	累计折旧 Accumulative Total Depreciation	本年折旧 Depreciation this year	固定资产净值年平均余额 Annual Balance Net Value of Fixed Assets Assets
5856256.1	**4282941.1**	**5674322.0**	**2110153.0**	**282204.8**	**3432078.7**
5626938.3	4035672.5	5346800.6	1990328.3	269539.9	3216204.4
2203074.1	1930608.3	2560555.9	979571.9	117004.3	1518855.0
1076714.2	627931.7	820494.7	292720.2	37268.7	467619.5
2576467.8	1724401.1	2293271.4	837860.9	127931.8	1445604.2
2022647.4	1272372.4	1787229.4	693981.3	94957.3	1082407.5
159653.2	83909.3	73144.3	28213.8	5255.6	47685.2
41505.6	60144.8	74737.8	18358.1	2574.1	56558.6
423562.1	309103.2	333867.5	102330.3	24350.6	240230.5
130258.3	142925.5	172174.5	41549.3	8623.9	122966.2
5153276.8	4020100.6	5250044.3	1929489.3	253240.3	3178859.7
1891889.5	1844609.7	2548879.8	1000101.5	125538.0	1541633.5
174522.3	87588.7	103968.0	34383.8	5922.0	73478.2
52682.7	44742.4	67664.2	27096.3	2562.3	43006.0
18154.3	16138.8	26798.4	11901.7	1954.6	14568.5
336598.3	565186.5	667064.0	214246.0	18670.8	439081.2
1832060.3	944616.9	1237111.5	450186.8	70070.2	677586.4
750219.6	450093.7	526018.5	174989.7	23577.6	335629.4
96048.0	66810.8	72178.8	16485.5	4930.5	53639.7
1101.8	313.1	361.1	98.0	14.3	236.8
81144.8	64376.8	80132.9	32858.7	4109.4	48282.3
621834.5	198463.7	344144.8	147805.0	24855.1	204936.7
1230592.9	1364376.9	1811601.5	626050.0	89466.2	1168734.3
4489217.3	3474739.6	4737105.5	1819116.8	219877.7	2782724.2
1244366.5	1061887.1	1394893.8	535443.1	80312.9	876855.5
4611889.6	3221054.0	4279428.2	1574709.9	201891.9	2555223.2
2907427.4	2144530.5	2953213.8	1133758.1	147416.5	1661011.2
1836615.5	1414506.4	1778675.6	642872.8	87827.0	1156246.8
1112213.2	723904.2	942432.6	333522.1	46961.3	614820.7
2137025.2	2003291.2	2759455.0	1071244.6	141291.2	1683842.7
75536.5	62631.2	98475.1	41407.3	4828.4	59288.8
758374.3	456182.3	533195.2	176545.8	23926.8	341347.6
2885320.1	1760836.4	2283196.7	820955.3	112158.4	1347599.6
5366.7	5622.3	6675.8	1053.5	322.4	3320.5
724.8	1167.5	1332.7	170.0	70.0	1188.4

10-14　全部规模以上工业企业经济指标（2003年）（续2）

单位：万元

分　组	Item	负债合计 Total Liabilites	流动负债小计 Liquid Liabilities
总　计	**Total**	**7330409.3**	**5830604.1**
#市　区	Urban Area	6970584.4	5571914.1
按隶属关系分	Grouped by Administrative Relationship		
中央企业	Central Enterprises	2816295.2	2143432.9
省属企业	Provincial Enterprises	1492534.9	1194589
市属企业	Municipal Enterprises	3021579.2	2492582.2
市直属企业	Municipal Enterprises Straightway	2293449.4	1927168.2
区直属企业	Enterprises Urban District under	172140.6	134469.9
县直属企业	Enterprises County Under	86091.6	74762.3
市属中其中：区属	Among Municipal EnterPrises: Under Urban District	513075.3	401169.9
县属	Under County	215054.5	164244.1
按登记注册类型分组	Grouped by Registion Status		
内资企业	Domestic Investment Enterprises	6768315.9	5345740.1
国有经济	State-owned Enterprises	2859766.8	2214775.6
集体经济	Collective-owned Enterprises	173699.7	150924.7
股份合作	Share-holding Corperative	94567.3	74377.4
联营企业	Joint Ownership Enterprises	23909	18332
国有独资公司	State-owned appropriator ship corporation	591208.7	381806.6
其他有限责任公司	Other limited corporation	2249624.9	1858845.9
股份有限公司	Share-holding Corperation Ltd.	662945.4	553927
私营企业	Private Enterprises	112103	92290.8
其他内资企业	Other Domestic Funded Enterprises	491.1	460.1
港、澳、台商投资企业	Enterprises with Investment from Hong Kong,Macao and Taiwan	105656.1	86441.2
外商投资企业	Enterprises with Foreign Investment	456437.3	398422.8
在总计中:亏损企业	Of the Total: Deficit Enterprises	2025811.1	1578089.4
在总计中:国有控股企业	Of the total: Enterprises of Controlling Share Hold by the State	5918585.2	4666200.5
按轻重工业分	Grouped by Ligth Industry and Heavy Industry		
轻工业	Light Industry	1515011.3	1215208.2
重工业	Heavy Industry	5815398	4615395.9
按企业规模分	Grouped by Size of Enterprises		
大型工业	Large-size	3493059.6	2800042.6
中型工业	Medium-size	2351761.4	1824260.9
小型工业	Small-size	1485588.3	1206300.6
按经济组织类型分	Grouped by economic type of orgnization		
独资企业	Appropratorship	3103951	2410707.7
合作、合伙企业	Partnership	120663.1	94764.7
股份有限公司	Corporaton	673655.7	562068
有限责任公司	Limited company	3432139.5	2763063.7
按工业行业大类分	Grouped by Sector		
煤炭开采和洗选业	Coal mining and coal washing industry		
石油和天然气开采业	Petroleum and Natural Gas Extraction	7645.2	7645.2
黑色金属矿采选业	Ferrous Metals Mining and Dressing	2458.2	1678.2

Main Economic Indicators of All Industrial Enterprises Above Designafed size(2003)(Continued 2)

(10 000 yuan)

	所有者权益		产品				营业利润
长期负债小计 Long-term Liabilities	合计 Total Creditors Equity	实收资本 Total Capital Hold	销售收入 Sales Revenue	产品销售成本 Cost of Sales	产品销售费用 Sales Expense	产品销售税金及附加 Sales Tax and Extra Charges	Operational profit
1434040.2	**4609691.1**	**2641929.2**	**6455259.8**	**4797631.4**	**380474.6**	**38553.7**	**303681.3**
1341125.8	4424090.7	2505075.5	6169889.9	4548215.5	367272.7	37114.8	316490.9
659391.9	1916510.0	965854.6	2328117.4	1695235.7	40781.6	9510.1	56004.3
296731.0	507923.4	449436.9	1256804.2	906374.1	146757.7	5114.1	73460.9
477917.3	2185257.7	1226637.7	2870338.2	2196021.6	192935.3	23929.5	174216.1
330700.9	1643973.5	869624.1	2002723.3	1506080.5	134770.3	16730.2	115854.1
37598.7	187646.1	73909.7	115157.5	85057.3	7194.1	1521.7	15456.6
11095.8	30029.3	33700.0	60694.6	49251.8	2973.4	264.7	981.0
104626.5	447861.0	254284.7	678216.3	533111.5	46464.0	6098.4	56821.0
42589.9	93423.2	102728.9	189398.6	156829.6	11701.0	1100.9	1541.0
1362845.5	4129134.8	2312414.5	5548528.4	4198029.4	239101.0	36886.4	197712.4
643361.5	1362701.0	844036.0	2046538.7	1447672.2	66060.9	13186.0	2460.8
21589.5	182690.2	62175.8	201004.5	163162.1	7355.9	1851.2	21730.1
20101.9	40794.3	20338.6	58473.3	48166.4	2053.7	640.6	-459.9
5033.1	13812.7	17735.3	21325.4	16992.7	734.3	85.7	456.5
196221.2	410718.1	159896.0	358741.3	282377.4	6350.5	1491.4	-2679.2
369393.8	1254932.4	838776.6	1977777.9	1560318.8	99298.6	14818.9	104315.0
87586.4	777426.2	310664.0	712632.6	536818.4	47465.2	3777.8	64436.7
19527.1	85168.2	58379.2	169914.5	140899.9	9665.3	1014.5	7238.8
31.0	891.7	413.0	2120.2	1621.5	116.6	20.3	213.6
17270.4	59138.4	59037.4	117208.7	86995.3	16060.3	408.2	6695.3
53924.3	421417.9	270477.3	789522.7	512606.7	125313.3	1259.1	99273.6
430956.0	844820.0	703529.1	983963.2	647441.9	47172.0	5786.4	-115977.2
1221465.4	3442943.2	2012642.4	4743136.7	3545811.4	190494.9	29478.7	155968.1
286998.3	1207569.1	716831.0	1724204.2	1213407.3	209784.7	15021.2	150534.8
1147041.9	3402122.0	1925098.2	4731055.6	3584224.1	170689.9	23532.5	153146.5
679531.9	2514567.4	1143850.2	3279596.4	2377443.3	116039.5	12517.3	170777.9
505528.2	1449227.9	867294.6	2032429.1	1502770.1	203751.4	17870.8	99468.2
248980.1	645895.8	630784.4	1143234.3	917418.0	60683.7	8165.6	33435.2
686481.3	1629071.5	965858.9	2411973.5	1737554.1	91713.7	15151.0	36704.0
25258.0	61710.6	42169.6	90958.2	74074.6	3370.5	784.8	1082.3
90131.8	782730.7	311879.6	719514.7	542611.5	47643.3	3820.2	64479.3
632169.1	2136178.3	1322021.1	3232813.4	2443391.2	237747.1	18797.7	201415.7
	4987.6	3730.0	8720.3	6465.4	894.8	181.1	711.0
780.0	-528.7	151.6	771.6	467.8	9.3	16.2	-74.0

10-14 全部规模以上工业企业经济指标（2003年）（续3）

单位：万元

分 组	Item	管理费用 Expenses for Management
总　计	**Total**	**593293.7**
#市　区	Urban Area	562583.2
按隶属关系分	Grouped by Administrative Relationship	
中央企业	Central Enterprises	247247.1
省属企业	Provincial Enterprises	94741.2
市属企业	Municipal Enterprises	251305.4
市直属企业	Municipal Enterprises Straightway	199155
区直属企业	Enterprises Urban District under	9095.1
县直属企业	Enterprises County Under	6369.8
市属中其中：区属	Among Municipal EnterPrises: Under Urban District	37096.4
县属	Under County	15054
按登记注册类型分组	Grouped by Registion Status	
内资企业	Domestic Investment Enterprises	544636.3
国有经济	State-owned Enterprises	232803
集体经济	Collective-owned Enterprises	11502.1
股份合作	Share-holding Corperative	7734.8
联营企业	Joint Ownership Enterprises	2454
国有独资公司	State-owned appropriator ship corporation	61464.4
其他有限责任公司	Other limited corporation	173100.1
股份有限公司	Share-holding Corperation Ltd.	46380.3
私营企业	Private Enterprises	9052.1
其他内资企业	Other Domestic Funded Enterprises	145.5
港、澳、台商投资企业	Enterprises with Investment from Hong Kong,Macao and Taiwan	6642.7
外商投资企业	Enterprises with Foreign Investment	42014.7
在总计中:亏损企业	Of the Total: Deficit Enterprises	115459.7
在总计中:国有控股企业	Of the total: Enterprises of Controlling Share Hold by the State	495162.9
按轻重工业分	Grouped by Ligth Industry and Heavy Industry	
轻工业	Light Industry	120123.8
重工业	Heavy Industry	473169.9
按企业规模分	Grouped by Size of Enterprises	
大型工业	Large-size	314408.5
中型工业	Medium-size	170516.2
小型工业	Small-size	108369
按经济组织类型分	Grouped by economic type of orgnization	
独资企业	Appropratorship	250546.8
合作、合伙企业	Partnership	10839.1
股份有限公司	Corporaton	46909.1
有限责任公司	Limited company	284998.7
按工业行业大类分	Grouped by Sector	
煤炭开采和洗选业	Coal mining and coal washing industry	
石油和天然气开采业	Petroleum and Natural Gas Extraction	556.7
黑色金属矿采选业	Ferrous Metals Mining and Dressing	130.5

Main Economic Indicators of All Industrial Enterprises Above Designafed size(2003)(Continued 3)

（10 000 yuan）

利润总额 Total Profits	亏损企业亏损总额 Total Loss of Deficit Enterprises	利税总额 Total Pre-tax Profits	本年应交增值税 Value Added Tax Payable
338169.4	**111993.5**	**649912.5**	**273189.4**
338572.1	97374.4	637607.2	261920.3
88101.6	30412.7	172965.7	75354.0
85842.9	33116.9	161901.1	70944.1
164224.9	48463.9	315045.7	126891.3
121350.3	37274.8	234173.5	96093.0
12091.3	1646.6	21094.3	7481.3
1447.3	2107.8	3696.4	1984.4
40964.6	5201.8	71166.9	24103.9
1910.0	5987.3	9705.3	6694.4
226960.6	95048.2	485972.5	222125.5
8891.6	65913.4	118789.8	96712.2
12053.4	1272.5	21941.1	8036.5
83.7	2125.4	3138.3	2414.0
433.5	813.1	1427.6	908.4
7887.7	2206.3	16191.2	6812.1
117534.3	13870.6	199877.2	67524.0
73538.8	7502.8	112564.2	35247.6
6503.7	1344.1	11754.4	4236.2
33.9		288.7	234.5
4897.1	973.9	9054.1	3748.8
106311.7	15971.4	154885.9	47315.1
-111993.5	111993.5	-69494.4	36712.7
193644.4	94770.4	415872.3	192749.2
157629.1	26504.8	270872.8	98222.5
180540.3	85488.7	379039.7	174966.9
194632.6	7134.1	328731.9	121582.0
123266.8	57910.8	249596.8	108459.2
20270.0	46948.6	71583.8	43148.2
31526.0	68350.7	159526.3	112849.3
1013.5	2938.5	5736.9	3938.6
73503.9	7740.7	112787.0	35462.9
232126.0	32963.6	371862.3	120938.6
718.2		1149.2	249.9
-77.0	77.0	39.8	100.6

10-14 全部规模以上工业企业经济指标（2003年）（续4）

单位：万元

分组	Item	企业单位数（个） Number of Enterprises(unit)	亏损企业 Loss Making Enterprises
有色金属矿采选业	Nonferrous Metals Mining and Dressing	3	
非金属矿采选业	Nonmetal Minerals Mining and Dressing	2	
其他采矿业	Other mining industry		
农副食品加工业	Agricultural porducts and non-stable food processing industry	36	8
食品制造业	Food Manufacturing	23	9
饮料制造业	Beverage Manufacturing	12	5
烟草加工业	Tobacco Processing	1	
纺织业	Textile Industry	23	13
纺织服装、鞋、帽制造业	Textile clothing, footwear and headgear industry	7	4
皮革、毛皮、羽毛(绒)及其制品业	Leather, fur, feather (eiderdown) and their products industry	2	1
木材加工及竹、藤、棕、草制品业	Timber Processing,Bamboo,Cane,Palm Fiber and Straw Products	3	3
家具制造业	Furniture Manufacturing	9	2
造纸及纸制品业	Papermaking and Paper products	35	9
印刷业、记录媒介的复制	Printing,Record Medium Reproduction	33	12
文教体育用品制造业	Cultural,Educational and Sports Goods	2	
石油加工、炼焦及核燃料加工业	Petroleum refining, coke making and nuclear fuel processing industry	6	1
化学原料及化学制品制造业	Raw Chemical Materials and Chemical Products	37	12
医药制造业	Medical and Pharmaceutical Products	52	19
化学纤维制造业	Chemical Fiber	1	1
橡胶制品业	Rubber Products	2	
塑料制品业	Plastic Products	17	2
非金属矿物制品业	Nonmetal Mineral Products	62	28
黑色金属冶炼及压延加工业	Smelting and Pressing of Ferrous Metals	10	6
有色金属冶炼及压延加工业	Smelting and Pressing of Nonferrou Metals	17	8
金属制品业	Metal Products	19	4
通用设备制造	General equipment manufacturing industry	61	17
专用设备制造业	Special Purpose Equipment	64	20
交通运输设备制造业	Transport Equipment	51	12
电气机械及器材制造业	Electric Equipment and Machinery	65	19
通信设备、计算机及其他电子设备制造业	Communication equipment, computer and other electronic equipment manufacturing industry	35	11
仪器仪表及文化办公用	Instruments,Meters,Cultural and Office	20	7
工艺品及其他制造业	Handicraft and other stuff manufacturing industry	8	6
废弃资源和废旧材料回收加工业	Discarded resources and waste materials salvaging and processing industry		
电力、热力的生产和供应业	Electric power, heating power generating and supplying industry	6	4
燃气生产和供应业	Gas mining and supplying industry	1	1
水的生产和供应业	Water processing and supplying industry	8	5

Main Economic Indicators of All Industrial Enterprises

Above Designafed size(2003)(Continued 4)

(10 000 yuan)

工业总产值（当年价） Gross Industrial Output Value (At Current Prices)	工业总产值（不变价） Gorss Industrial Output Value (At Constant Prices)	工业增加值（生产法） Value-Added of Industry (Value of Industrial Products Sales)	工业销售产值（当年价） Value of Industry Products Sales (At Current Prices)	全部职工年平均人数（人） Annual Average Employers (person)
8873.8	5369.4	4303.4	8807.0	1131
483.9	483.8	194.3	478.3	110
222377.6	185936.5	65580.4	219189.0	5806
133289.7	105514.5	45050.2	128837.8	5508
123325.9	96698.7	48605.2	123746.9	3717
1066.0	1247.1	454.4	1881.7	166
179155.8	164839.2	46986.5	178791.7	33057
20770.0	20749.3	7665.9	25802.9	2589
16377.6	12436.8	4070.6	14826.1	1358
3139.0	3405.3	904.7	2722.5	574
9259.0	9869.6	3105.6	9311.6	2108
73132.6	67816.0	23054.3	74222.7	9287
172939.9	166871.9	66773.0	167371.9	8470
932.8	913.8	326.3	902.8	152
223561.7	48424.6	43061.0	228328.4	2283
244307.2	226109.2	70848.2	227075.7	25911
606692.1	600932.6	270721.1	588036.7	16023
2263.3	2263.3	487.3	2096.5	85
2562.3	2622.2	489.4	2520.2	120
27814.4	29071.0	9216.2	25892.1	1340
109747.6	92254.6	33452.9	105856.3	13215
65000.9	67178.9	19308.6	64373.8	5061
103317.8	105221.0	36020.3	87188.8	2857
26961.5	26224.1	12144.7	25842.9	2072
299331.5	316403.9	121582.2	283942.5	16698
528162.4	610037.8	156429.5	505829.5	44189
1576986.6	1775739.3	435156.1	1529514.7	85446
616300.5	765319.5	173407.5	605605.1	26176
607210.1	1193987.2	158836.6	551563.0	21863
115700.5	114458.0	30113.0	102706.1	11206
89474.0	88878.0	20426.9	80739.4	1823
125045.2	54380.8	97298.3	125054.4	9258
2774.7	608.1	216.9	2774.7	1086
40480.6	8677.7	19993.6	40446.6	3956

10-14 全部规模以上工业企业经济指标（2003年）（续5）

单位：万元

分　组	Item	资产合计 Total Assets	流动资产小计 Total Circulating Funds
有色金属矿采选业	Nonferrous Metals Mining and Dressing	8828.5	2806.3
非金属矿采选业	Nonmetal Minerals Mining and Dressing	1031.0	372.6
其他采矿业	Other mining industry		
农副食品加工业	Agricultural porducts and non-stable food processing industry	178702.5	82635.9
食品制造业	Food Manufacturing	102280.3	45609.8
饮料制造业	Beverage Manufacturing	193448.0	66985.2
烟草加工业	Tobacco Processing	3830.0	842.4
纺织业	Textile Industry	287811.5	121896.6
纺织服装、鞋、帽制造业	Textile clothing, footwear and headgear industry	28629.3	18378.5
皮革、毛皮、羽毛(绒)及其制品业	Leather, fur, feather (eiderdown) and their products industry	45140.8	34246.4
木材加工及竹、藤、棕、草制品业	Timber Processing,Bamboo,Cane,Palm Fiber and Straw Products	23097.2	7648.4
家具制造业	Furniture Manufacturing	16802.4	11938.4
造纸及纸制品业	Papermaking and Paper products	87050.9	33448.1
印刷业、记录媒介的复制	Printing,Record Medium Reproduction	332830.8	124403.0
文教体育用品制造业	Cultural,Educational and Sports Goods	1189.2	949.7
石油加工、炼焦及核燃料加工业	Petroleum refining, coke making and nuclear fuel processing industry	123692.2	45000.7
化学原料及化学制品制造业	Raw Chemical Materials and Chemical Products	601319.2	218618.0
医药制造业	Medical and Pharmaceutical Products	880661.3	523839.8
化学纤维制造业	Chemical Fiber	2302.6	390.5
橡胶制品业	Rubber Products	1831.5	1056.2
塑料制品业	Plastic Products	45071.5	18914.8
非金属矿物制品业	Nonmetal Mineral Products	247912.8	94370.6
黑色金属冶炼及压延加工业	Smelting and Pressing of Ferrous Metals	266497.2	152727.5
有色金属冶炼及压延加工业	Smelting and Pressing of Nonferrou Metals	120832.1	46114.8
金属制品业	Metal Products	53865.6	33373.4
通用设备制造	General equipment manufacturing industry	552440.8	397782.0
专用设备制造业	Special Purpose Equipment	1281931.1	629951.1
交通运输设备制造业	Transport Equipment	3117534.5	1964174.8
电气机械及器材制造业	Electric Equipment and Machinery	1050903.5	637336.5
通信设备、计算机及其他电子设备制造业	Communication equipment, computer and other electronic equipment manufacturing industry	1125922.8	667878.7
仪器仪表及文化办公用	Instruments,Meters,Cultural and Office	271265.3	157799.6
工艺品及其他制造业	Handicraft and other stuff manufacturing industry	147179.0	75318.4
废弃资源和废旧材料回收加工业	Discarded resources and waste materials salvaging and processing industry		
电力、热力的生产和供应业	Electric power, heating power generating and supplying industry	568318.6	114846.1
燃气生产和供应业	Gas mining and supplying industry	14816.4	6099.8
水的生产和供应业	Water processing and supplying industry	157321.3	26692.3

Main Economic Indicators of All Industrial Enterprises Above Designafed size (2003)(Continued 5)

(10 000 yuan)

流动资产 年平均余额 Annual Average Balance of Circulating Funds	固定资产 小计 Total Fixed Assets	固定资产 原价合计 Origing Value of Fixed Assets	累计折旧 Accumulative Total Depreciation	本年折旧 Depreciation this year	固定资产净值 年平均余额 Annual Balance Net Value of Fixed Assets Assets
2345.5	4746.2	8246.1	3499.9	1.6	4470.4
327.7	655.3	718.5	72.0	14.7	656.5
68962.7	64569.5	78766.4	27173.4	4090.5	51113.9
44460.0	45534.1	52957.9	21535.9	3491.2	32954.3
75644.8	99722.8	145429.6	48407.8	10232.5	95772.1
841.3	2385.4	2822.4	436.9	8.5	4882.1
108459.5	142892.4	220635.8	93322.8	13193.8	118777.1
17259.1	7132.3	8415.6	2439.5	432.1	6213.3
30699.7	10043.8	20661.8	12106.6	1036.4	9005.9
8080.9	14106.4	15342.4	1775.5	295.3	13814.9
11345.9	4046.8	6068.6	2426.2	399.2	3850.4
32828.1	45468.4	51081.6	8376.3	1211.0	41971.1
127365.5	143635.5	223232.6	90543.0	15336.6	129418.4
950.6	239.5	314.9	75.4	19.6	239.8
41271.3	76860.6	63125.2	20296.2	1457.1	44946.4
199501.3	308930.0	362890.1	138328.2	12893.6	246149.1
510716.5	257292.0	266838.7	84991.6	13778.1	187462.9
411.1	1528.6	1912.1	590.1	332.8	1322.0
857.0	675.3	781.1	106.4	12.4	675.6
14476.6	21534.7	25720.2	5709.8	1460.2	16994.3
89301.1	117624.3	139373.0	49999.4	5303.6	91253.1
144389.8	97949.3	106989.5	26718.3	5445.1	82859.2
38050.5	38213.6	38757.8	9047.1	2732.4	33453.3
22875.8	15811.9	27449.8	13035.0	2010.3	15029.5
328581.7	115977.8	159394.8	66998.8	8062.2	96014.9
612973.7	558196.9	746294.1	265101.5	22510.8	458907.5
1677412.5	850030.2	1125505.5	444877.2	60665.4	567214.7
605685.9	268859.8	413953.4	180697.5	28371.2	227889.0
648265.9	280641.5	419280.8	148882.5	16299.8	252384.9
156260.6	95755.5	142980.3	60578.5	4724.4	81165.6
67661.6	19386.1	10737.4	3743.2	1247.5	7267.8
127056.6	450917.8	614318.1	198950.5	34044.6	414901.8
5766.7	7817.9	10816.2	3175.5	166.5	7699.4
29077.1	106969.1	154501.2	74911.0	10531.4	80838.6

10-14 全部规模以上工业企业经济指标（2003年）（续6）

单位：万元

分　组	Item	负债合计 Total Liabilites	流动负债 小计 Liquid Liabilities
有色金属矿采选业	Nonferrous Metals Mining and Dressing	7123.7	2740.4
非金属矿采选业	Nonmetal Minerals Mining and Dressing	151.9	151.9
其他采矿业	Other mining industry		
农副食品加工业	Agricultural porducts and non-stable food processing industry	128149.4	100900.6
食品制造业	Food Manufacturing	64883.2	47961.7
饮料制造业	Beverage Manufacturing	121118.6	101101.4
烟草加工业	Tobacco Processing	980.4	980.4
纺织业	Textile Industry	187696.0	162013.7
纺织服装、鞋、帽制造业	Textile clothing, footwear and headgear industry	16445.1	14095.6
皮革、毛皮、羽毛(绒)及其制品业	Leather, fur, feather (eiderdown) and their products industry	34730.3	25283.7
木材加工及竹、藤、棕、草制品业	Timber Processing,Bamboo,Cane,Palm Fiber and Straw Products	15290.1	9982.4
家具制造业	Furniture Manufacturing	9854.0	8762.9
造纸及纸制品业	Papermaking and Paper products	59578.1	50606.0
印刷业、记录媒介的复制	Printing,Record Medium Reproduction	149275.1	109591.5
文教体育用品制造业	Cultural,Educational and Sports Goods	223.5	223.5
石油加工、炼焦及核燃料加工业	Petroleum refining, coke making and nuclear fuel processing industry	100740.2	70247.5
化学原料及化学制品制造业	Raw Chemical Materials and Chemical Products	340142.9	226106.2
医药制造业	Medical and Pharmaceutical Products	454105.4	384302.6
化学纤维制造业	Chemical Fiber	1250.1	1250.1
橡胶制品业	Rubber Products	804.1	739.4
塑料制品业	Plastic Products	27422.0	17537.7
非金属矿物制品业	Nonmetal Mineral Products	177423.3	130185.7
黑色金属冶炼及压延加工业	Smelting and Pressing of Ferrous Metals	187168.3	156679.6
有色金属冶炼及压延加工业	Smelting and Pressing of Nonferrou Metals	80310.5	56615.5
金属制品业	Metal Products	29269.0	24268.0
通用设备制造	General equipment manufacturing industry	389612.1	356314.9
专用设备制造业	Special Purpose Equipment	836601.1	623719.4
交通运输设备制造业	Transport Equipment	2078138.3	1686209.8
电气机械及器材制造业	Electric Equipment and Machinery	661617.2	581676.9
通信设备、计算机及其他电子设备制造业	Communication equipment, computer and other electronic equipment manufacturing industry	686096.7	495622.0
仪器仪表及文化办公用	Instruments,Meters,Cultural and Office	180062.0	158680.5
工艺品及其他制造业	Handicraft and other stuff manufacturing industry	48334.1	47658.0
废弃资源和废旧材料回收加工业	Discarded resources and waste materials salvaging and processing industry		
电力、热力的生产和供应业	Electric power, heating power generating and supplying industry	161956.9	136077.0
燃气生产和供应业	Gas mining and supplying industry	8564.3	7101.4
水的生产和供应业	Water processing and supplying industry	75188.0	25892.8

Main Economic Indicators of All Industrial Enterprises Above Designafed size (2003)(Continued 6)

(10 000 yuan)

长期负债小计 Long-term Liabilities	所有者权益合计 Total Creditors Equity	实收资本 Total Capital Hold	产品销售收入 Sales Revenue	产品销售成本 Cost of Sales	产品销售费用 Sales Expense	产品销售税金及附加 Sales Tax and Extra Charges	营业利润 Operational profit
4383.3	1704.8	1255.7	5773.8	4603.2			-191.6
	879.1	215.8	477.9	265.6	69.3	69.5	34.3
26382.2	50553.1	55926.0	213205.5	194845.4	7606.5	468.5	1857.0
16920.6	37397.1	31521.3	125585.9	94133.9	18172.7	454.1	5828.9
16105.5	72329.4	75655.1	131982.9	81026.6	19488.3	6744.2	17495.6
	2849.6	1514.8	2199.7	1556.8	6.6	19.5	212.1
25675.8	100115.5	53855.9	176455.8	156456.4	2624.8	728.7	-483.4
2300.0	12184.2	11143.0	25083.2	18282.4	2556.6	330.1	586.3
9446.5	10410.5	17180.3	15128.0	13236.0	512.6	11.0	-107.4
5307.7	7807.1	3766.9	2691.9	1750.4	185.4	18.7	-1672.8
1080.1	6948.4	5639.3	9295.2	7025.4	720.9	30.0	474.0
8784.1	27472.8	20180.8	69681.7	57675.3	2668.5	629.8	5646.9
39644.7	183555.7	102809.3	172290.2	120178.8	5733.3	1769.2	22563.3
	965.7	368.0	841.5	633.6	9.9	6.1	223.0
30492.7	22952.0	22797.4	228429.3	206570.9	1193.2	3085.7	7554.0
113983.0	261176.3	190578.0	228124.9	173595.9	11999.6	1396.0	7019.9
63885.6	426555.9	196525.0	571969.0	302854.9	138104.1	2658.3	82786.9
	1052.5	1500.0	1699.3	1568.4	91.2	7.4	-35.5
17.3	1027.4	232.6	2047.3	1502.3	104.1	7.4	198.0
3263.6	17649.5	16149.8	25193.8	19425.1	984.7	76.6	2262.5
45293.2	70489.5	60168.6	95786.4	78472.0	3715.3	726.9	1206.1
30166.5	79328.9	81557.9	59111.7	46983.0	6192.9	574.1	-7646.4
23575.2	40521.6	31791.1	89635.6	74321.1	2474.3	249.0	7412.7
4881.0	24596.6	20836.6	26115.5	19642.9	1207.1	104.5	1784.8
19229.6	162828.7	109828.4	277059.8	193462.1	13196.8	2018.0	33795.9
199045.4	445000.4	373359.2	523808.7	400374.9	21576.5	2858.1	17824.7
391490.3	1035543.8	661979.2	1643412.9	1332221.8	42563.5	4781.6	73693.9
75186.0	389286.3	100015.2	593441.2	459002.6	35963.6	3646.7	17431.8
179140.5	427254.5	207093.4	547687.1	417806.0	32156.8	2160.1	25450.1
20265.9	91203.3	56437.8	117998.8	92956.4	5474.5	553.2	-739.7
676.0	98844.9	20383.5	30460.8	23717.9	927.6	138.8	9533.1
25879.8	406361.7	51235.6	389591.3	158755.8	5.8	1608.7	-28342.0
1462.9	6252.1	7436.2	2774.7	2815.6	586.6	16.1	-1553.6
49295.2	82133.3	47109.9	40726.6	32978.8	696.9	409.8	940.9

10–14 全部规模以上工业企业经济指标（2003年）（续7）

单位：万元

分　组	Item	管理费用 Expenses for Management
有色金属矿采选业	Nonferrous Metals Mining and Dressing	1053.8
非金属矿采选业	Nonmetal Minerals Mining and Dressing	32.3
其他采矿业	Other mining industry	
农副食品加工业	Agricultural porducts and non-stable food processing industry	6239.1
食品制造业	Food Manufacturing	5945.7
饮料制造业	Beverage Manufacturing	6838.3
烟草加工业	Tobacco Processing	428.1
纺织业	Textile Industry	14575.1
纺织服装、鞋、帽制造业	Textile clothing, footwear and headgear industry	3225.7
皮革、毛皮、羽毛(绒)及其制品业	Leather, fur, feather (eiderdown) and their products industry	1392.9
木材加工及竹、藤、棕、草制品业	Timber Processing,Bamboo,Cane,Palm Fiber and Straw Products	868.2
家具制造业	Furniture Manufacturing	779.3
造纸及纸制品业	Papermaking and Paper products	3288.3
印刷业、记录媒介的复制	Printing,Record Medium Reproduction	20484.9
文教体育用品制造业	Cultural,Educational and Sports Goods	55.1
石油加工、炼焦及核燃料加工业	Petroleum refining, coke making and nuclear fuel processing industry	4921.0
化学原料及化学制品制造业	Raw Chemical Materials and Chemical Products	30183.2
医药制造业	Medical and Pharmaceutical Products	36277.0
化学纤维制造业	Chemical Fiber	52.1
橡胶制品业	Rubber Products	254.4
塑料制品业	Plastic Products	1942.0
非金属矿物制品业	Nonmetal Mineral Products	9712.7
黑色金属冶炼及压延加工业	Smelting and Pressing of Ferrous Metals	7262.0
有色金属冶炼及压延加工业	Smelting and Pressing of Nonferrou Metals	3645.3
金属制品业	Metal Products	2551.9
通用设备制造	General equipment manufacturing industry	32605.9
专用设备制造业	Special Purpose Equipment	69850.4
交通运输设备制造业	Transport Equipment	167469.8
电气机械及器材制造业	Electric Equipment and Machinery	73734.4
通信设备、计算机及其他电子设备制造业	Communication equipment, computer and other electronic equipment manufacturing industry	51780.9
仪器仪表及文化办公用	Instruments,Meters,Cultural and Office	17993.7
工艺品及其他制造业	Handicraft and other stuff manufacturing industry	846.0
废弃资源和废旧材料回收加工业	Discarded resources and waste materials salvaging and processing industry	
电力、热力的生产和供应业	Electric power, heating power generating and supplying industry	8936.1
燃气生产和供应业	Gas mining and supplying industry	1089.6
水的生产和供应业	Water processing and supplying industry	6291.3

Main Economic Indicators of All Industrial Enterprises

Above Designafed size(2003)(Continued 7)

（10 000 yuan）

利润总额 Total Profits	亏损企业亏损总额 Total Loss of Deficit Enterprises	利税总额 Total Pre-tax Profits	本年应交增值税 Value Added Tax Payable
32.8		32.8	
34.3		118.8	15.0
2666.8	1144.1	4530.3	1395.0
5536.9	1051.7	10537.5	4546.5
16066.8	687.2	33282.3	10471.3
227.2		442.0	195.3
-524.6	4326.6	8120.3	7916.2
568.1	228.8	1691.7	793.5
-71.8	186.9	365.1	425.9
-2956.4	2956.4	-2808.7	129.0
446.7	106.1	996.4	519.7
2612.6	1188.5	5623.4	2381.0
23906.0	1515.4	36851.7	11176.5
223.0		265.7	36.6
6116.2	2.0	18125.1	8923.2
9714.5	2090.0	22596.2	11485.7
99982.6	6054.8	149164.3	46523.4
-35.5	35.5	6.7	34.8
106.3		210.4	96.7
2419.0	336.8	3508.7	1013.1
-657.2	5754.9	5680.3	5610.6
-8166.4	8282.4	-6127.8	1464.5
7952.9	1740.8	9035.2	833.3
1853.6	79.1	3726.0	1767.9
34682.5	2804.5	55064.1	18363.6
18839.1	20223.0	45978.3	24281.1
89886.8	2016.2	136375.1	41706.7
16035.5	5939.8	46090.4	26408.2
22534.1	21285.7	43825.3	19131.1
-862.1	4595.9	1806.3	2115.2
4123.8	291.9	6436.4	2173.8
-16018.0	16100.1	3606.3	18015.6
-648.5	648.5	-471.7	160.7
900.6	242.9	4038.6	2728.2

10-15　全部规模以上国有工业企业主要经济指标(2003年)

单位：万元

分　组	Item	企业单位数（个）Number of Enterprises (unit)	亏损企业 Loss Making Enterprises
总 计	**Total**	**205**	**95**
#市　区	Urban Area	174	80
按隶属关系分	Grouped by Administrative Relationship		
中央企业	Central Enterprises	49	15
省属企业	Provincial Enterprises	40	28
市属企业	Municipal Enterprises	116	52
#市直属企业	Municipal Enterprises	61	30
区直属企业	District owned enterprises	22	9
县直属企业	County owned enterprises	22	12
#市属中其中：区属	City owned: in it: District owned	31	10
县属	County owned	24	12
在总计中:亏损企业	Of the Total: Deficit Enterprises	95	95
按轻重工业分	Grouped by Ligth Industry and Heavy Industry		
轻工业	Light Industry	76	35
重工业	Heavy Industry	129	60
按企业规模分	Grouped by Size of Enterprises		
大型工业	Large-Size	12	2
中型工业	Medium-size	40	15
小型工业	Small-Size	153	78
按工业行业大类分	Grouped by Sector		
煤炭开采和洗选业	Coal mining and coal washing industry		
石油和天然气开采业	Petroleum and Natural Gas Extraction		
黑色金属矿采选业	Ferrous Metals Mining and Dressing	1	1
有色金属矿采选业	Nonferrous Metals Mining and Dressing	2	
非金属矿采选业	Nonmetal Minerals Mining and Dressing		
其他采矿业	Other mining industry		
农副食品加工业	Agricultural products and non-stable food processing industry	6	3
食品制造业	Food Production	7	3
饮料制造业	Beverage Production	3	1

Economic Indicators of All State-owned Industrial Enterprises Above the Designated Size(2003)

(10 000 yuan)

工业总产值（当年价） Gross Industrial Output Value (At Current Prices)	工业总产值（不变价） Gorss Industrial Output Value (At Constant Prices)	工业增加值（生产法） Value-Added of Industry (Value of Industrial Products Sales)	工业销售产值（当年价） Value of Industrial Products Sales (At Current Prices)	全部职工年平均人数（人） Annual Average Employers (person)
1848814.8	**1613721.8**	**585316.1**	**1812430.8**	**144912.0**
1767605.5	1564884.5	548523.2	1732182.7	137132.0
842462.3	582875.5	302995.0	840723.1	66258.0
154359.0	161707.1	40347.1	134770.3	24858.0
851993.5	869139.2	241974.0	836937.4	53796.0
794239.6	816011.7	222964.7	785358.2	47317.0
17731.2	16402.9	5158.5	16763.5	2831.0
15020.6	11547.2	4899.4	14758.2	2498.0
42577.4	41445.0	14052.0	36616.6	3922.0
15176.5	11682.5	4957.3	14962.6	2557.0
361111.1	297022.7	158563.7	341787.8	47445.0
318129.4	261084.1	115317.3	308226.0	38114.0
1530685.4	1352637.7	469998.8	1504204.8	106798.0
984020.0	971861.5	347769.4	977893.2	53792.0
683798.5	475136.8	176807.1	673415.3	57190.0
180996.3	166723.5	60739.6	161122.3	33930.0
780.1	370.5	164.7	771.4	120.0
2961.8	2357.4	2766.4	2895.0	545.0
9196.6	5901.3	2517.4	9293.4	1693.0
5585.8	3538.4	1540.9	4374.9	1094.0
2257.0	1577.9	1102.5	1908.1	1071.0

10-15 全部规模以上国有工业企业主要经济指标(2003年)(续 1)

单位：万元

分　组	Item	资产合计 Total Assets	流动资产小计 Total Circulating Funds
总 计	**Total**	**4235691.2**	**2041349.3**
#市　区	Urban Area	4109322.6	1982703.8
按隶属关系分	Grouped by Administrative Relationship		
中央企业	Central Enterprises	1682390.4	719162.4
省属企业	Provincial Enterprises	618504.9	334491.8
市属企业	Municipal Enterprises	1934795.9	987695.1
#市直属企业	Municipal Enterprises	1804142.0	943458.0
区直属企业	District owned enterprises	60274.3	18918.2
县直属企业	County owned enterprises	53818.9	16400.3
#市属中其中：区属	City owned: in it: District owned	76537.2	27634.1
县属	County owned	54116.7	16603.0
在总计中:亏损企业	Of the Total: Deficit Enterprises	1483824.6	533146.9
按轻重工业分	Grouped by Ligth Industry and Heavy Industry		
轻工业	Light Industry	678480.5	247743.9
重工业	Heavy Industry	3557210.7	1793605.4
按企业规模分	Grouped by Size of Enterprises		
大型工业	Large-Size	2469740.3	1200985.9
中型工业	Medium-size	1152834.7	575952.0
小型工业	Small-Size	613116.2	264411.4
按工业行业大类分	Grouped by Sector		
煤炭开采和洗选业	Coal mining and coal washing industry		
石油和天然气开采业	Petroleum and Natural Gas Extraction		
黑色金属矿采选业	Ferrous Metals Mining and Dressing	1929.5	678.8
有色金属矿采选业	Nonferrous Metals Mining and Dressing	2400.1	1017.9
非金属矿采选业	Nonmetal Minerals Mining and Dressing		
其他采矿业	Other mining industry		
农副食品加工业	Agricultural products and non-stable food processing industry	24700.2	7922.9
食品制造业	Food Production	6840.3	3222.5
饮料制造业	Beverage Production	14703.2	5037.9

Economic Indicators of All State-owned Industrial Enterprises Above the Designated Size(2003)(Continued 1)

(10 000 yuan)

流动资产年平均余额 Annual Average Balance of Circulating Funds	固定资产小计 Fixed Assets	固定资产原价合计 Origing Value of Fixed Assets	累计折旧 Accumulative Total Depreciation	本年折旧 In this year Depreciation	固定资产净值年平均余额 Average Balance Net Value of Fixed Assets
1891889.5	**1844609.7**	**2548879.8**	**1000101.5**	**125538.0**	**1541633.5**
1831963.9	1782144.1	2456860.9	961917.0	122394.0	1480613.7
700341.7	910357.6	1253707.5	478331.2	66304.1	772127.8
304387.9	221723.3	311626.8	121133.8	7900.7	182821.4
887159.9	712528.8	983545.5	400636.5	51333.2	586684.3
844171.1	641136.1	914685.7	384253.0	48056.0	531781.7
17988.3	29693.7	20140.4	7266.6	1347.1	14013.4
16593.7	34218.8	38066.1	5420.6	949.3	33995.6
26192.3	37078.8	30563.3	10827.6	2321.9	20812.5
16796.5	34313.9	38296.5	5555.9	955.3	34090.1
524688.9	850324.8	1141494.3	389214.5	60018.8	740213.7
232435.6	374880.0	544201.4	238748.4	32471.4	314125.3
1659453.9	1469729.7	2004678.4	761353.1	93066.6	1227508.2
1097523.5	1064629.3	1504015.2	579176.6	83627.6	916247.6
543600.8	489803.8	696071.6	308285.1	30163.9	388367.8
250765.2	290176.6	348793.0	112639.8	11746.5	237018.1
724.8	1167.5	1332.7	170.0	70.0	1188.4
845.3	1223.5	1455.8	232.3	1.6	1111.0
7805.9	16483.5	21837.2	6481.7	113.6	14389.8
3152.5	2633.0	3617.0	1075.8	136.0	2605.1
5067.5	9063.4	10544.8	3222.6	111.8	8123.8

10-15 全部规模以上国有工业企业主要经济指标(2003年)（续 2）

单位：万元

分　组	Item	负债合计 Total Liabilites	流动负债小计 Liquid Liabilities
总计	**Total**	**2859766.8**	**2214775.6**
#市　区	Urban Area	2770463.6	2141045.1
按隶属关系分	Grouped by Administrative Relationship		
中央企业	Central Enterprises	854716.2	630966.8
省属企业	Provincial Enterprises	661284.7	458524.7
市属企业	Municipal Enterprises	1343765.9	1125284.1
#市直属企业	Municipal Enterprises	1238036.2	1048145.1
区直属企业	District owned enterprises	51491.1	28529.2
县直属企业	County owned enterprises	42745.8	38484.3
#市属中其中：区属	City owned: in it: District owned	62809.1	38494.8
县属	County owned	42920.6	38644.2
在总计中:亏损企业	Of the Total: Deficit Enterprises	1078840.5	839292.0
按轻重工业分	Grouped by Ligth Industry and Heavy Industry		
轻工业	Light Industry	429999.1	308656.8
重工业	Heavy Industry	2429767.7	1906118.8
按企业规模分	Grouped by Size of Enterprises		
大型工业	Large-Size	1342830.1	1066682.9
中型工业	Medium-size	925219.5	675164.3
小型工业	Small-Size	591717.2	472928.4
按工业行业大类分	Grouped by Sector		
煤炭开采和洗选业	Coal mining and coal washing industry		
石油和天然气开采业	Petroleum and Natural Gas Extraction		
黑色金属矿采选业	Ferrous Metals Mining and Dressing	2458.2	1678.2
有色金属矿采选业	Nonferrous Metals Mining and Dressing	1827.0	88.7
非金属矿采选业	Nonmetal Minerals Mining and Dressing		
其他采矿业	Other mining industry		
农副食品加工业	Agricultural products and non-stable food processing industry	19862.3	18686.2
食品制造业	Food Production	7163.8	6445.5
饮料制造业	Beverage Production	23191.4	18960.7

Economic Indicators of All State-owned Industrial Enterprises Above the Designated Size(2003)(Continued 2)

(10 000 yuan)

长期负债小计 Long-term Liabilities	所有者权益 合计 Total Creditors Equity	实收资本 Total Capital Hold	产品销售收入 Sales Revenue	产品销售成本 Cost of Sales	产品销售费用 Sales Expense	产品销售税金及附加 Sales Tax and Extra Charges	营业利润 Operational profit
643361.5	**1362701.0**	**844036.0**	**2046538.7**	**1447672.2**	**66060.9**	**13186.0**	**2460.8**
627934.5	1325635.6	824198.3	1996965.0	1392916.1	64722.2	12954.2	17721.6
223555.8	827022.4	369870.4	1101122.5	738422.9	12508.0	6351.7	-2129.0
201756.2	-55351.4	123170.9	137915.8	101058.5	4537.5	871.4	-14554.0
218049.5	591030.0	350994.7	807500.4	608190.8	49015.4	5962.9	19143.8
189676.5	566105.8	314463.5	759601.7	571995.1	46909.2	5617.4	15674.7
22889.9	8783.2	8893.9	15578.6	12628.4	558.0	145.2	186.5
4115.8	11073.1	11566.8	12372.5	8690.4	924.7	61.2	274.8
24242.3	13728.1	24837.0	35346.5	27367.1	1177.7	283.1	3194.0
4130.7	11196.1	11694.2	12552.2	8828.6	928.5	62.4	275.1
238433.4	392412.5	314673.6	595805.3	325819.9	16388.4	3170.8	-71000.7
121195.9	248481.4	178511.4	303911.0	229236.7	9473.7	2843.3	18881.3
522165.6	1114219.6	665524.6	1742627.7	1218435.5	56587.2	10342.7	-16420.5
276086.9	1126276.4	393341.1	1273027.1	782891.3	42048.6	6571.8	48748.9
248941.2	215025.6	279897.3	637468.1	560488.9	16624.6	5416.9	-33120.6
118333.4	21399.0	170797.6	136043.5	104292.0	7387.7	1197.3	-13167.5
780.0	-528.7	151.6	771.6	467.8	9.3	16.2	-74.0
1738.3	573.1	255.7	196.4	102.3			45.6
1030.4	4837.9	15382.0	4327.3	2798.1	248.1	129.6	-716.1
718.3	-323.5	1496.1	4068.3	3079.2	176.7	20.6	-96.3
4230.7	-8488.2	2900.8	1949.1	1329.3	95.5	235.3	-42.6

10-15　全部规模以上国有工业企业主要经济指标(2003年)（续 3）

单位：万元

分　组	Item	管理费用 Expenses for Management
总 计	**Total**	**232803.0**
#市　区	Urban Area	224743.4
按隶属关系分	Grouped by Administrative Relationship	
中央企业	Central Enterprises	90550.7
省属企业	Provincial Enterprises	29511.8
市属企业	Municipal Enterprises	112740.5
#市直属企业	Municipal Enterprises	107572.2
区直属企业	District owned enterprises	1954.0
县直属企业	County owned enterprises	2347.3
#市属中其中：区属	City owned: in it: District owned	2787.0
县属	County owned	2381.3
在总计中:亏损企业	Of the Total: Deficit Enterprises	55252.0
按轻重工业分	Grouped by Ligth Industry and Heavy Industry	
轻工业	Light Industry	39147.2
重工业	Heavy Industry	193655.8
按企业规模分	Grouped by Size of Enterprises	
大型工业	Large-Size	133589.2
中型工业	Medium-size	69188.1
小型工业	Small-Size	30025.7
按工业行业大类分	Grouped by Sector	
煤炭开采和洗选业	Coal mining and coal washing industry	
石油和天然气开采业	Petroleum and Natural Gas Extraction	
黑色金属矿采选业	Ferrous Metals Mining and Dressing	130.5
有色金属矿采选业	Nonferrous Metals Mining and Dressing	36.5
非金属矿采选业	Nonmetal Minerals Mining and Dressing	
其他采矿业	Other mining industry	
农副食品加工业	Agricultural products and non-stable food processing industry	1412.4
食品制造业	Food Production	763.7
饮料制造业	Beverage Production	310.9

Economic Indicators of All State-owned Industrial Enterprises

Above the Designated Size(2003)(Continued 3)

（10 000 yuan）

利润总额 Total Profits	亏损企业 亏损总额 Losses of Deficit Enterprises	利税总额 Total Pre-tax Profits	本年应交 增值税 Value Added Tax Payable
8891.6	**65913.4**	**118789.8**	**96712.2**
15491.1	57071.2	122042.9	93597.6
11920.7	28453.0	65787.4	47515.0
-24447.6	24832.1	-18315.6	5260.6
21418.5	12628.3	71318.0	43936.6
19239.1	10326.0	66132.0	41275.5
-609.2	1185.7	386.0	850.0
578.7	1016.6	1584.0	944.1
1600.4	1285.7	3584.5	1701.0
579.0	1016.6	1601.5	960.1
-65913.4	65913.4	-36812.3	25930.3
17181.2	9102.7	38244.0	18219.5
-8289.6	56810.7	80545.8	78492.7
47427.5	6989.7	117786.3	63787.0
-21096.6	34427.5	10596.6	26276.3
-17439.3	24496.2	-9593.1	6648.9
-77.0	77.0	39.8	100.6
3.2		3.2	
-461.6	569.4	-304.6	27.4
-315.0	361.7	-87.9	206.5
-36.5	290.0	400.8	202.0

10-15 全部规模以上国有工业企业主要经济指标(2003年)（续4）

单位：万元

分　组	Item	企业单位数（个） Number of Enterprises (unit)	亏损企业 Loss Making Enterprises
烟草制品业	Tobacco Processing	1	
纺织业	Textile Industry	8	5
纺织服装、鞋、帽制造业	Textile clothing, footwear and headgear industry		
皮革、毛皮、羽毛(绒)及其制品业	Leather, fur, feather (eiderdown) and their products industry	1	
木材加工及竹、藤、棕、草制品业	Timber Processing,Bamboo,Cane,Palm Fiber and Straw Products	2	2
家具制造业	Furniture Manufacturing	1	
造纸及纸制品业	Papermaking and Paper Products	3	1
印刷业、记录媒介的复制	Printing,Record Medium Reproduction	17	6
文教体育用品制造业	Cultural,Educational and Sports Goods	1	
石油加工、炼焦及核燃料加工业	Petroleum refining, coke making and nuclear fuel processing industry	2	
化学原料及化学制品制造业	Raw Chemical Materials and Chemical Products	8	3
医药制造业	Medical and Pharmaceutical Products	9	5
化学纤维制造业	Chemical Fiber		
橡胶制品业	Rubber Products		
塑料制品业	Plastic Products	1	
非金属矿物制品业	Nonmetal Mineral Products	17	10
黑色金属冶炼及压延加工业	Smelting and Pressing of Ferrous Metals	3	2
有色金属冶炼及压延加工业	Smelting and Pressing of Nonferrou Metals	4	3
金属制品业	Metal Products	3	1
通用设备制造	General equipment manufacturing industry	13	6
专用设备制造业	Special Purpose Equipment	31	14
交通运输设备制造业	Transport Equipment	23	6
电气机械及器材制造业	Electric Equipment and Machinery	8	4
通信设备、计算机及其他电子设备制造业	Communication equipment, computer and other electronic equipment manufacturing industry	7	4
仪器仪表及文化办公用机械制造业	Instruments,Meters,Cultural and	9	4
工艺品及其他制造业	Handicraft and other stuff manufacturing industry	3	2
废弃资源和废旧材料回收加工业	Discarded resources and waste materials salvaging and processing industry		
电力、热力的生产和供应业	Electric power, heating power generating and supplying industry	3	3
燃气生产和供应业	Gas mining and supplying industry	1	1
水的生产和供应业	Water processing and supplying industry	7	5

Economic Indicators of All State-owned Industrial Enterprises

Above the Designated Size(2003)(Continued 4)

(10 000 yuan)

工业总产值 （当年价） Gross Industrial Output Value (At Current Prices)	工业总产值 （不变价） Gorss Industrial Output Value (At Constant Prices)	工业增加值 （生产法） Value-Added of Industry (Value of Industrial Products Sales)	工业销售产值 （当年价） Value of Industrial Products Sales (At Current Prices)	全部职工 年平均人数 （人） Annual Average Employers (person)
1066.0	1247.1	454.4	1881.7	166
97029.1	89128.3	26993.7	95360.2	18894
7069.0	4177.3	1836.6	6973.8	1185
2100.8	2332.5	649.8	1858.7	499
299.6	251.9	124.9	302.9	310
2909.6	2311.1	946.1	4702.9	324
121268.6	111481.6	47133.3	116719.0	6103
312.8	312.8	152.8	312.8	82
219923.5	44709.5	41972.4	224639.3	2164
70325.6	62381.6	18922.3	66461.3	6887
18004.2	18931.8	8679.2	13392.5	1841
3188.1	3188.1	1466.0	3188.1	170
33252.1	24538.7	7797.9	29479.5	6148
46120.5	48188.9	14167.8	45404.1	4101
11741.4	12309.3	4203.5	7996.7	324
2433.4	2941.5	1007.4	2144.1	151
157292.1	162864.0	65914.6	151872.0	7561
147887.3	157742.8	41463.2	141577.4	20376
223389.9	196105.4	61939.2	222950.7	21263
423462.6	505495.3	91086.7	424218.9	17026
74659.7	88126.1	22446.2	68658.3	8976
9833.3	9801.5	4671.3	8649.7	2400
350.1	355.0	90.0	363.2	123
112875.4	43443.8	93438.9	112875.4	8408
2774.7	608.1	216.9	2774.7	1086
38464.1	7002.3	19449.1	38430.1	3821

10-15 全部规模以上国有工业企业主要经济指标(2003年)（续5）

单位：万元

分 组	Item	资产合计 Total Assets	流动资产小计 Total Circulating Funds
烟草制品业	Tobacco Processing	3830.0	842.4
纺织业	Textile Industry	166774.5	75485.6
纺织服装、鞋、帽制造业	Textile clothing, footwear and headgear industry		
皮革、毛皮、羽毛(绒)及其制品业	Leather, fur, feather (eiderdown) and their products industry	23196.4	16526.9
木材加工及竹、藤、棕、草制品业	Timber Processing,Bamboo,Cane,Palm Fiber and Straw Products	15974.7	3705.3
家具制造业	Furniture Manufacturing	2683.7	1575.3
造纸及纸制品业	Papermaking and Paper Products	21422.7	5729.4
印刷业、记录媒介的复制	Printing,Record Medium Reproduction	195406.9	76055.2
文教体育用品制造业	Cultural,Educational and Sports Goods	825.1	810.6
石油加工、炼焦及核燃料加工业	Petroleum refining, coke making and nuclear fuel processing industry	120845.4	43105.5
化学原料及化学制品制造业	Raw Chemical Materials and Chemical Products	197648.7	59711.8
医药制造业	Medical and Pharmaceutical Products	27711.2	18476.7
化学纤维制造业	Chemical Fiber		
橡胶制品业	Rubber Products		
塑料制品业	Plastic Products	3744.9	2250.4
非金属矿物制品业	Nonmetal Mineral Products	128382.1	37467.6
黑色金属冶炼及压延加工业	Smelting and Pressing of Ferrous Metals	120951.2	59319.2
有色金属冶炼及压延加工业	Smelting and Pressing of Nonferrou Metals	9044.8	5753.9
金属制品业	Metal Products	3624.9	2022.2
通用设备制造	General equipment manufacturing industry	318265.4	255321.6
专用设备制造业	Special Purpose Equipment	502163.4	271985.7
交通运输设备制造业	Transport Equipment	400489.9	222403.0
电气机械及器材制造业	Electric Equipment and Machinery	829947.2	500533.2
通信设备、计算机及其他电子设备制造业	Communication equipment, computer and other electronic equipment manufacturing industry	318402.4	198904.3
仪器仪表及文化办公用机械制造业	Instruments,Meters,Cultural and	54166.1	31336.2
工艺品及其他制造业	Handicraft and other stuff manufacturing industry	1784.0	421.7
废弃资源和废旧材料回收加工业	Discarded resources and waste materials salvaging and processing industry		
电力、热力的生产和供应业	Electric power, heating power generating and supplying industry	547950.4	103038.4
燃气生产和供应业	Gas mining and supplying industry	14816.4	6099.8
水的生产和供应业	Water processing and supplying industry	155065.5	24587.4

Economic Indicators of All State-owned Industrial Enterprises Above the Designated Size(2003)(Continued 5)

(10 000 yuan)

流动资产年平均余额 Annual Average Balance of Circulating Funds	固定资产小计 Fixed Assets	固定资产原价合计 Origing Value of Fixed Assets	累计折旧 Accumulative Total Depreciation	本年折旧 In this year Depreciation	固定资产净值年平均余额 Average Balance Net Value of Fixed Assets
841.3	2385.4	2822.4	436.9	8.5	4882.1
63744.9	82081.2	128085.8	55195.5	9822.1	62349.6
12592.4	5819.1	8546.5	4216.0	249.0	4431.3
4283.9	11654.3	12501.8	1387.0	100.8	11263.1
1575.3	1108.4	1340.8	279.2	4.2	1061.6
7047.6	15594.9	15949.8	1150.1	48.9	15218.9
76202.8	106969.0	165732.6	69307.8	10670.0	95634.9
810.6	14.5	52.9	38.4	3.2	14.5
39498.0	76341.1	62119.3	19809.8	1378.4	44327.1
51470.4	104421.5	136016.7	63201.2	6061.7	92311.6
15644.2	8820.0	12199.8	4252.3	315.5	8206.4
2200.7	1247.8	1458.2	305.0	142.5	2119.8
35294.3	64823.6	64514.3	22400.1	1382.3	42898.2
58196.9	54098.4	60209.0	14819.5	3464.5	45449.6
5583.2	3119.5	4110.1	1211.4	124.7	2869.7
838.6	1602.6	2881.5	1281.4	311.6	2551.3
192883.7	55004.0	81995.0	36916.3	3902.5	42468.4
262390.8	198760.2	291895.6	122123.4	8133.0	154324.6
213305.5	157179.7	223932.6	96905.4	9722.7	126856.6
472118.2	206916.7	331381.3	157535.7	22965.0	171994.6
182504.9	77331.4	107302.3	36850.3	1086.9	67879.7
26937.8	18495.0	26858.7	9893.1	1403.4	15720.1
399.0	735.1	896.3	222.7	28.6	701.9
115033.0	444879.3	602209.5	191181.2	33112.1	410297.1
5766.7	7817.9	10816.2	3175.5	166.5	7699.4
27128.8	106818.2	154263.3	74823.9	10496.4	80683.3

10-15 全部规模以上国有工业企业主要经济指标(2003年)（续6）

单位：万元

分 组	Item	负债合计 Total Liabilites	流动负债小计 Liquid Liabilities
烟草制品业	Tobacco Processing	980.4	980.4
纺织业	Textile Industry	127287.1	104762.3
纺织服装、鞋、帽制造业	Textile clothing, footwear and headgear industry		
皮革、毛皮、羽毛(绒)及其制品业	Leather, fur, feather (eiderdown) and their products industry	19186	9739.4
木材加工及竹、藤、棕、草制品业	Timber Processing,Bamboo,Cane,Palm Fiber and Straw Products	9554.6	7486.9
家具制造业	Furniture Manufacturing	1873	1353
造纸及纸制品业	Papermaking and Paper Products	21114.2	20717.6
印刷业、记录媒介的复制	Printing,Record Medium Reproduction	91793.2	61178.7
文教体育用品制造业	Cultural,Educational and Sports Goods	64.4	64.4
石油加工、炼焦及核燃料加工业	Petroleum refining, coke making and nuclear fuel processing industry	98660.6	68833.6
化学原料及化学制品制造业	Raw Chemical Materials and Chemical Products	104524.7	83726.6
医药制造业	Medical and Pharmaceutical Products	17831.1	17331.1
化学纤维制造业	Chemical Fiber		
橡胶制品业	Rubber Products		
塑料制品业	Plastic Products	1396.4	1396.4
非金属矿物制品业	Nonmetal Mineral Products	94830.5	67247.8
黑色金属冶炼及压延加工业	Smelting and Pressing of Ferrous Metals	121635.3	95836.1
有色金属冶炼及压延加工业	Smelting and Pressing of Nonferrou Metals	9345	8396.8
金属制品业	Metal Products	3165.5	2103.9
通用设备制造	General equipment manufacturing industry	280659.3	267342.5
专用设备制造业	Special Purpose Equipment	458479.9	328272.6
交通运输设备制造业	Transport Equipment	249101	197825.3
电气机械及器材制造业	Electric Equipment and Machinery	553353.3	490266.6
通信设备、计算机及其他电子设备制造业	Communication equipment, computer and other electronic equipment manufacturing industry	272700.7	149359.8
仪器仪表及文化办公用机械制造业	Instruments,Meters,Cultural and	37529.8	31410.4
工艺品及其他制造业	Handicraft and other stuff manufacturing industry	1088.2	612.2
废弃资源和废旧材料回收加工业	Discarded resources and waste materials salvaging and processing industry		
电力、热力的生产和供应业	Electric power, heating power generating and supplying industry	147462.5	121782.6
燃气生产和供应业	Gas mining and supplying industry	8564.3	7101.4
水的生产和供应业	Water processing and supplying industry	73083.1	23787.9

Economic Indicators of All State-owned Industrial Enterprises
Above the Designated Size(2003)(Continued 6)

(10 000 yuan)

长期负债	所有者权益		产品				营业利润
小计 Long-term Liabilities	合计 Total Creditors Equity	实收资本 Total Capital Hold	销售收入 Sales Revenue	产品销售成本 Cost of Sales	产品销售费用 Sales Expense	产品销售税金及附加 Sales Tax and Extra Charges	Operational profit
	2849.6	1514.8	2199.7	1556.8	6.6	19.5	212.1
22524.3	39487.4	19565.4	96593.3	84998.9	1430.5	498.7	-288.4
9446.5	4010.4	10620.3	7053.6	5492.8	506.2	11.0	101.2
2067.7	6420.1	1666.9	1838.8	1317.2	126.0	13.7	-1651.5
520.0	810.7	837.3	275.6	158.6	80.3	2.1	0.4
396.5	308.5	3532.5	3449.9	2830.5	631.6	7.9	-670.0
30614.5	103613.7	58159.6	120219.4	78243.6	3577.1	1526.3	19535.2
	760.7	200.0	251.5	116.0	1.5	2.7	186.0
29827.0	22184.8	22024.8	224445.6	203093.8	899.0	3078.1	7407.1
20798.1	93124.0	110543.0	67866.2	54994.1	1487.3	511.6	1577.1
500.0	9880.1	8581.1	10807.4	7534.6	1416.7	49.4	84.2
	2348.5	1101.6	3346.1	1224.7	50.1	30.1	1382.9
26522.5	33551.6	19931.7	22865.3	18476.7	1043.3	218.1	-2606.4
25739.0	-684.1	41660.3	42397.2	34464.7	5766.3	333.4	-6563.5
948.2	-300.2	3792.6	7932.3	5950.1	138.7	6.5	1279.2
999.2	459.4	1697.1	1881.4	1564.0	157.4	4.4	-35.2
13213.8	37606.1	38232.4	144160.1	95549.4	6412.7	1254.8	17889.5
130153.7	43665.5	187595.1	142530.8	113919.9	6085.9	622.6	-10425.7
51132.5	150755.1	87034.5	216740.6	172990.7	2383.5	673.5	3394.2
63086.6	276593.9	24739.0	416058.1	319494.2	29571.2	2183.9	4020.5
123340.7	33130.1	67976.5	73802.2	46984.0	1449.6	276.8	-2423.8
6119.0	16636.3	11735.9	10548.8	7659.7	1062.0	29.1	-292.0
476.0	695.8	645.7	274.3	193.0	16.2	2.5	-32.3
25679.9	400487.9	46551.6	376203.0	146900.7		1183.1	-28127.7
1462.9	6252.1	7436.2	2774.7	2815.6	586.6	16.1	-1553.6
49295.2	81982.4	46473.9	38710.1	31371.2	645.0	228.4	944.7

10-15 全部规模以上国有工业企业主要经济指标(2003年)（续 7）

单位：万元

分 组	Item	管理费用 Expenses for Management
烟草制品业	Tobacco Processing	428.1
纺织业	Textile Industry	8422.0
纺织服装、鞋、帽制造业	Textile clothing, footwear and headgear industry	
皮革、毛皮、羽毛(绒)及其制品业	Leather, fur, feather (eiderdown) and their products industry	1038.1
木材加工及竹、藤、棕、草制品业	Timber Processing,Bamboo,Cane,Palm Fiber and Straw Products	753.3
家具制造业	Furniture Manufacturing	40.8
造纸及纸制品业	Papermaking and Paper Products	677.7
印刷业、记录媒介的复制	Printing,Record Medium Reproduction	16456.1
文教体育用品制造业	Cultural,Educational and Sports Goods	36.3
石油加工、炼焦及核燃料加工业	Petroleum refining, coke making and nuclear fuel processing industry	4708.3
化学原料及化学制品制造业	Raw Chemical Materials and Chemical Products	7742.0
医药制造业	Medical and Pharmaceutical Products	1253.1
化学纤维制造业	Chemical Fiber	
橡胶制品业	Rubber Products	
塑料制品业	Plastic Products	645.5
非金属矿物制品业	Nonmetal Mineral Products	4674.4
黑色金属冶炼及压延加工业	Smelting and Pressing of Ferrous Metals	4864.1
有色金属冶炼及压延加工业	Smelting and Pressing of Nonferrou Metals	286.2
金属制品业	Metal Products	124.9
通用设备制造	General equipment manufacturing industry	21829.4
专用设备制造业	Special Purpose Equipment	27189.3
交通运输设备制造业	Transport Equipment	34668.9
电气机械及器材制造业	Electric Equipment and Machinery	57511.1
通信设备、计算机及其他电子设备制造业	Communication equipment, computer and other electronic equipment manufacturing industry	18842.9
仪器仪表及文化办公用机械制造业	Instruments,Meters,Cultural and	3060.5
工艺品及其他制造业	Handicraft and other stuff manufacturing industry	89.2
废弃资源和废旧材料回收加工业	Discarded resources and waste materials salvaging and processing industry	
电力、热力的生产和供应业	Electric power, heating power generating and supplying industry	7616.5
燃气生产和供应业	Gas mining and supplying industry	1089.6
水的生产和供应业	Water processing and supplying industry	6100.7

Economic Indicators of All State-owned Industrial Enterprises Above the Designated Size(2003)(Continued 7)

（10 000 yuan）

利润总额 Total Profits	亏损企业亏损总额 Losses of Deficit Enterprises	利税总额 Total Pre-tax Profits	本年应交增值税 Value Added Tax Payable
227.2		442.0	195.3
-319.3	2992.1	5119.2	4939.8
115.1		237.6	111.5
-2935.1	2935.1	-2802.5	118.9
0.4		28.5	26.0
-661.2	736.9	-589.3	64.0
18198.9	736.7	27941.6	8216.4
186.0		216.3	27.6
5969.3		17874.2	8826.8
380.0	670.4	5143.7	4252.1
-572.8	1480.8	103.5	626.9
1573.7		2113.3	509.5
-2154.4	2265.2	-431.7	1504.6
-7047.2	7067.1	-5847.1	866.7
1273.8	322.5	1363.5	83.2
-47.6	65.0	-8.1	35.1
19408.3	1522.0	32554.0	11890.9
-14750.7	19421.8	-7514.3	6613.8
6301.6	381.2	12547.3	5572.2
5414.2	396.7	25813.3	18215.2
-4687.2	6335.0	-1586.9	2823.5
-457.9	500.8	-131.9	296.9
-25.9	32.9	-14.5	8.9
-15861.7	15861.7	2898.9	17577.5
-648.5	648.5	-471.7	160.7
899.5	242.9	3739.6	2611.7

10-16 全部规模以上集体工业企业主要经济指标（2003年）

单位：万元

分　组	Item	企业单位数(个) Number of Enterprises(unit)	亏损企业 Loss Making Enterprises
总　计	**Total**	**115**	**25**
#市　区	Urban Area	98	17
按隶属关系分	Grouped by Administrative Relationship		
省属企业	Provincial Enterprises		
市属企业	Municipal Enterprises	115	25
#市直属企业	Enterprises Directly Under the City Government	25	10
县、区属企业	Enterprises Under the District and County Government	90	15
#区属企业	Enterprises Under the District Government	74	8
县属企业	Enterprises Under the County Government	16	7
县、区属中:区县直属	Thereinto:Enterprises Directly Under the District and County Government	16	4
街道企业	Urban Subdistrict Enterprises	14	1
镇办企业	Town Enterprises	12	2
乡办企业	Township Enterprises	16	5
居委会	Neighbourhood Committee		
村委会	Villagers Committee	28	2
其他	Other	4	1
在总计中:亏损企业	Of the Total: Deficit Enterprises	25	25
在总计中：轻工业	Of the total:Light Industry	44	8
重工业	Heavy Industry	71	17
在总计中：大型工业	Of the total: Large-Size		
中型工业	Medium-size	5	
小型工业	Small-Size	110	25
按工业行业大类分	Grouped by Sector		
煤炭开采和洗选业	Coal mining and coal washing industry		
石油和天然气开采业	Petroleum and Natural Gas Extraction	1	
黑色金属矿采选业	Ferrous Metals Mining and Dressing		
有色金属矿采选业	Nonferrous Metals Mining and Dressing		
非金属矿采选业	Nonmetal Minerals Mining and Dressing	1	
其他采矿业	Other mining industry		
农副食品加工业	Agricultural products and non-stable food processing industry	3	

Economic Indicators of All Collective-owned Industrial Enterprises Above Designated Size（2003）

(10 000 yuan)

工业总产值（当年价）Gross Industrial Output Value (At Current Prices)	工业总产值（不变价）Gorss Industrial Output Value (At Current Prices)	工业增加值（生产法）Value-Added of Industry (Value of Industrial Products Sales)	工业销售产值（当年价）Value of Industrial Products Sales (At Current Prices)	全部职工年平均人数（人）Annual Average Employers (person)
272958.2	**266122.5**	**79418.8**	**256168.2**	**19417**
251176.0	244471.9	73500.0	234883.2	15974
272958.2	266122.5	79418.8	256168.2	19417
51453.7	55545.8	16417.9	49587.9	5126
221504.5	210576.7	63000.9	206580.3	14291
200568.4	189585.4	57345.7	186142.1	11104
20936.1	20991.3	5655.2	20438.2	3187
99354.9	102948.3	25948.2	89142.5	2461
31476.4	23247.7	9766.0	29996.9	1784
8426.2	7319.4	2278.4	8110.5	1022
24741.4	23061.2	8013.0	23409.3	2470
47718.3	45260.2	14935.4	46449.5	5663
9787.3	8739.9	2059.9	9471.6	891
26354.6	25680.2	8382.9	23741.9	3983
153866.1	156398.6	41361.2	142645.4	8568
119092.1	109723.9	38057.6	113522.8	10849
123097.8	123363.1	26584.4	115008.2	6120
149860.4	142759.4	52834.4	141160.0	13297
7028.4	6020.3	999.7	7028.4	665
9.6	9.5	2.9	9.6	35
1647.1	1271.8	434.4	1635.8	222

10-16 全部规模以上集体工业企业主要经济指标（2003年）（续1）

单位：万元

分　组	Item	资产合计 Total Assets	流动资产小计 Total Circulating Funds
总　计	**Total**	**356389.9**	**192396.3**
#市　区	Urban Area	320137.3	175130.9
按隶属关系分	Grouped by Administrative Relationship		
省属企业	Provincial Enterprises		
市属企业	Municipal Enterprises	356389.9	192396.3
#市直属企业	Enterprises Directly Under the City Government	79926.5	57794.0
县、区属企业	Enterprises Under the District and County Government	276463.4	134602.3
#区属企业	Enterprises Under the District Government	241796.8	118394.3
县属企业	Enterprises Under the County Government	34666.6	16208.0
县、区属中:区县直属	Thereinto:Enterprises Directly Under the District and County Government	167341.9	88879.7
街道企业	Urban Subdistrict Enterprises	21570.9	14527.5
镇办企业	Town Enterprises	8528.1	4149.6
乡办企业	Township Enterprises	30791.2	10475.2
居委会	Neighbourhood Committee		
村委会	Villagers Committee	32665.8	10272.0
其他	Other	15565.5	6298.3
在总计中:亏损企业	Of the Total: Deficit Enterprises	56192.9	29180.7
在总计中：轻工业	Of the total:Light Industry	207829.4	107317.3
重工业	Heavy Industry	148560.5	85079.0
在总计中：大型工业	Of the total: Large-Size		
中型工业	Medium-size	179692.0	89170.7
小型工业	Small-Size	176697.9	103225.6
按工业行业大类分	Grouped by Sector		
煤炭开采和洗选业	Coal mining and coal washing industry		
石油和天然气开采业	Petroleum and Natural Gas Extraction	12632.8	5331.6
黑色金属矿采选业	Ferrous Metals Mining and Dressing		
有色金属矿采选业	Nonferrous Metals Mining and Dressing		
非金属矿采选业	Nonmetal Minerals Mining and Dressing	673.1	140.0
其他采矿业	Other mining industry		
农副食品加工业	Agricultural products and non-stable food processing industry	3816.2	2092.4

Economic Indicators of All Collective-owned Industrial Enterprises Above Designated Size（2003）(Continued 1)

(10 000 yuan)

流动资产年平均余额 Average Balance of Circulating Funds	固定资产小计 Total Fixed Assets	固定资产原价合计 Origing Value of Fixed Assets	累计折旧 Accumulative Total Depreciation	本年折旧 Depreciation In this year	固定资产净值年平均余额 Annual Average Balance Net Value of Fixed Assets
174522.3	**87588.7**	**103968.0**	**34383.8**	**5922.0**	**73478.2**
158086.3	71407.6	80463.1	26014.3	4309.4	60135.9
174522.3	87588.7	103968.0	34383.8	5922.0	73478.2
54377.3	16083.2	25037.9	9895.5	1386.7	14650.8
120145.0	71505.5	78930.1	24488.3	4535.3	58827.4
104752.0	55848.9	55840.3	16335.6	2993.0	45682.8
15393.0	15656.6	23089.8	8152.7	1542.3	13144.6
79968.4	24517.9	16638.5	6503.4	1578.4	10452.1
10038.1	5186.0	7455.3	3091.6	470.6	3445.6
4146.5	4208.9	5401.7	1778.7	459.3	3816.1
9707.5	10303.9	16138.5	6686.9	1022.5	15976.2
9876.6	19800.5	23929.4	4496.3	588.7	19970.1
6407.9	7488.3	9366.7	1931.4	415.8	5167.3
24341.2	20455.2	31542.1	13911.2	1694.1	17083.9
97581.0	44263.8	42033.2	12580.4	2572.7	29761.7
76941.3	43324.9	61934.8	21803.4	3349.3	43716.5
81492.4	36160.9	30416.2	6506.1	1905.4	21716.0
93029.9	51427.8	73551.8	27877.7	4016.6	51762.2
5366.7	5622.3	6675.8	1053.5	322.4	3320.5
130.0	530.0	550.0	28.0	0.7	532.0
2132.3	1684.7	2076.2	396.7	48.1	1564.8

10-16 全部规模以上集体工业企业主要经济指标（2003年）（续2）

单位：万元

分　组	Item	负债合计 Total Liabilites	流动负债小计 Liquid Liabilities
总　计	**Total**	**173699.7**	**150924.7**
#市　区	Urban Area	146724.5	128921.8
按隶属关系分	Grouped by Administrative Relationship		
省属企业	Provincial Enterprises		
市属企业	Municipal Enterprises	173699.7	150924.7
#市直属企业	Enterprises Directly Under the City Government	49490.1	43663.2
县、区属企业	Enterprises Under the District and County Government	124209.6	107261.5
#区属企业	Enterprises Under the District Government	99086.7	86926.2
县属企业	Enterprises Under the County Government	25122.9	20335.3
县、区属中:区县直属	Thereinto:Enterprises Directly Under the District and County Government	60622.7	58606.3
街道企业	Urban Subdistrict Enterprises	12072.1	11330.3
镇办企业	Town Enterprises	5072.1	3111.4
乡办企业	Township Enterprises	23294.6	12156.5
居委会	Neighbourhood Committee		
村委会	Villagers Committee	13721.0	13073.4
其他	Other	9427.1	8983.6
在总计中:亏损企业	Of the Total: Deficit Enterprises	45237.0	32742.8
在总计中：轻工业	Of the total:Light Industry	79266.0	73099.7
重工业	Heavy Industry	94433.7	77825.0
在总计中：大型工业	Of the total: Large-Size		
中型工业	Medium-size	69000.9	66994.3
小型工业	Small-Size	104698.8	83930.4
按工业行业大类分	Grouped by Sector		
煤炭开采和洗选业	Coal mining and coal washing industry		
石油和天然气开采业	Petroleum and Natural Gas Extraction	7645.2	7645.2
黑色金属矿采选业	Ferrous Metals Mining and Dressing		
有色金属矿采选业	Nonferrous Metals Mining and Dressing		
非金属矿采选业	Nonmetal Minerals Mining and Dressing	30.9	30.9
其他采矿业	Other mining industry		
农副食品加工业	Agricultural products and non-stable food processing industry	510.7	510.7

Economic Indicators of All Collective-owned Industrial Enterprises Above Designated Size（2003）(Continued 2)

(10 000 yuan)

长期负债 小计 Long-term Liabilities	所有者权益 合计 Total Creditors Equity	实收资本 Total Capital Hold	产品 销售收入 Sales Revenue	产品 销售成本 Cost of Sales	产品 销售费用 Sales Expense	产品销售 税金及附加 Sales Tax and Extra Charges	营业利润 Operational profit
21589.5	**182690.2**	**62175.8**	**201004.5**	**163162.1**	**7355.9**	**1851.2**	**21730.1**
16617.2	173412.8	52734.5	179372.6	146182.3	5844.2	1545.6	21192.9
21589.5	182690.2	62175.8	201004.5	163162.1	7355.9	1851.2	21730.1
5826.8	30436.4	14795.7	50745.1	44090.5	1750.5	188.1	290.9
15762.7	152253.8	47380.1	150259.4	119071.6	5605.4	1663.1	21439.2
10975.1	142710.1	38421.6	129474.3	102841.1	4101.5	1359.3	20860.4
4787.6	9543.7	8958.5	20785.1	16230.5	1503.9	303.8	578.8
2016.4	106719.2	24930.7	37017.1	27519.2	892.3	211.0	10818.6
428.0	9498.8	2731.6	29187.8	24385.5	713.9	153.2	2010.4
1643.3	3456.0	2067.0	7862.6	6616.3	227.9	129.5	323.2
10983.0	7496.6	3325.9	19102.4	14960.0	1254.8	389.1	1461.7
562.0	18944.8	7302.6	46012.4	37105.8	1598.3	577.2	6008.4
130.0	6138.4	7022.3	11077.1	8484.8	918.2	203.1	816.9
12494.2	10955.9	13273.4	23207.7	20150.8	940.9	129.6	-1073.7
6032.7	128563.4	31853.5	89740.6	70361.2	3146.3	831.6	16493.8
15556.8	54126.8	30322.3	111263.9	92800.9	4209.6	1019.6	5236.3
2006.6	110691.1	23721.0	66438.7	54797.1	1269.1	498.9	12540.3
19582.9	71999.1	38454.8	134565.8	108365.0	6086.8	1352.3	9189.8
	4987.6	3730.0	8720.3	6465.4	894.8	181.1	711.0
	642.2	50.0	9.2	7.0			2.1
	3305.5	860.0	1856.3	1580.5	140.2	10.5	80.6

10-16 全部规模以上集体工业企业主要经济指标（2003年）（续3）

单位：万元

分　组	Item	管理费用 Expenses for Management
总　计	**Total**	**11502.1**
#市　区	Urban Area	9759.8
按隶属关系分	Grouped by Administrative Relationship	
省属企业	Provincial Enterprises	
市属企业	Municipal Enterprises	11502.1
#市直属企业	Enterprises Directly Under the City Government	4096.6
县、区属企业	Enterprises Under the District and County Government	7405.5
#区属企业	Enterprises Under the District Government	5793.2
县属企业	Enterprises Under the County Government	1612.3
县、区属中:区县直属	Thereinto:Enterprises Directly Under the District and County Government	2070.4
街道企业	Urban Subdistrict Enterprises	1762.2
镇办企业	Town Enterprises	359.2
乡办企业	Township Enterprises	760.9
居委会	Neighbourhood Committee	
村委会	Villagers Committee	1730.7
其他	Other	722.1
在总计中:亏损企业	Of the Total: Deficit Enterprises	2254.7
在总计中：轻工业	Of the total:Light Industry	4193.4
重工业	Heavy Industry	7308.7
在总计中：大型工业	Of the total: Large-Size	
中型工业	Medium-size	1996.2
小型工业	Small-Size	9505.9
按工业行业大类分	Grouped by Sector	
煤炭开采和洗选业	Coal mining and coal washing industry	
石油和天然气开采业	Petroleum and Natural Gas Extraction	556.7
黑色金属矿采选业	Ferrous Metals Mining and Dressing	
有色金属矿采选业	Nonferrous Metals Mining and Dressing	
非金属矿采选业	Nonmetal Minerals Mining and Dressing	0.1
其他采矿业	Other mining industry	
农副食品加工业	Agricultural products and non-stable food processing industry	34.0

Economic Indicators of All Collective-owned Industrial Enterprises Above Designated Size（2003）(Continued 3)

（10 000 yuan）

利润总额 Total Profits	亏损企业亏损总额 Total Loss of Deficit Enterprises	利税总额 Total Pre-tax Profits	本年应交增值税 Value Added Tax Payable
12053.4	**1272.5**	**21941.1**	**8036.5**
11434.8	922.9	20018.7	7038.3
12053.4	1272.5	21941.1	8036.5
656.0	789.3	2980.3	2136.2
11397.4	483.2	18960.8	5900.3
10737.2	175.2	17008.4	4911.9
660.2	308.0	1952.4	988.4
5611.9	129.0	8703.7	2880.8
1846.8	3.0	2585.9	585.9
291.1	13.6	587.5	166.9
290.7	249.3	1233.7	553.9
2434.1	86.3	4260.9	1249.6
922.8	2.0	1589.1	463.2
-1272.5	1272.5	-159.1	983.8
7789.6	623.0	13059.6	4438.4
4263.8	649.5	8881.5	3598.1
5924.7		9111.4	2687.8
6128.7	1272.5	12829.7	5348.7
718.2		1149.2	249.9
2.1		2.2	0.1
30.9		59.1	17.7

10-16　全部规模以上集体工业企业主要经济指标（2003年）（续 4）

单位：万元

分　组	Item	企业单位数 (个) Number of Enterprises (unit)	亏损企业 Loss Making Loss Making Enterprises
食品制造业	Food Production	1	
饮料制造业	Beverage Production		
烟草加工业	Tobacco Processing		
纺织业	Textile Industry	5	2
纺织服装、鞋、帽制造业	Textile clothing, footwear and headgear industry	2	1
皮革、毛皮、羽毛(绒)及其制品业	Leather, fur, feather (eiderdown) and their products industry		
木材加工及木、竹、藤、棕、草制品制造	Timber Processing,Bamboo,Cane,Palm Fiber and Straw Products		
家具制造业	Furniture Manufacturing	1	1
造纸及纸制品业	Papermaking and Paper Products	16	
印刷业和记录媒介的复制	Printing,Record Medium Reproduction	2	2
文教体育用品制造业	Cultural,Educational and Sports Goods		
石油加工、炼焦及核燃料加工业	Petroleum refining, coke making and nuclear	1	1
化学原料及化学制品制造业	Raw Chemical Materials and Chemical Products	6	2
医药制造业	Medical and Pharmaceutical Products	6	1
化学纤维制造业	Chemical Fiber		
橡胶制品业	Rubber Products		
塑料制品业	Plastic Products	3	1
非金属矿物制品业	Nonmetal Mineral Products	16	7
黑色金属冶炼及压延加工业	Smelting and Pressing of Ferrous Metals	1	
有色金属冶炼及压延加工业	Smelting and Pressing of Nonferrou Metals	2	
金属制品业	Metal Products	4	1
通用设备制造	General equipment manufacturing industry	15	
专用设备制造业	Special Purpose Equipment	8	2
交通运输设备制造业	Transport Equipment	4	1
电气机械及器材制造业	Electric Equipment and Machinery	10	2
通信设备、计算机及其他电子设备制造业	Communication equipment, computer and other electronic equipment manufacturing industry	3	
仪器仪表及文化、办公用机械制造业	Instruments,Meters,Cultural and Office Machinery	2	
工艺品及其他制造业	Handicraft and other stuff manufacturing industry	2	1
废弃资源和废旧材料回收加工业	Discarded resources and waste materials salvaging and processing industry		
电力、热力的生产和供应业	Electric power, heating power generating and supplying industry		
燃气生产和供应业	Gas mining and supplying industry		
水的生产和供应业	Water processing and supplying industry		

Economic Indicators of All Collective-owned Industrial Enterprises Above Designated Size（2003）(Continued 4)

(10 000 yuan)

工业总产值（当年价） Gross Industrial Output Value (At Current Prices)	工业总产值（不变价） Gorss Industrial Output Value (At Current Prices)	工业增加值（生产法） Value-Added of Industry (Value of Industrial Products Sales)	工业销售产值（当年价） Value of Industrial Products Sales (At Current Prices)	全部职工年平均人数（人） Annual Average Employers (person)
1006.0	521.0	200.8	1006.0	80
2746.6	2288.9	867.7	2452.0	563
1169.8	1149.1	158.6	1108.0	409
601.5	570.7	136.2	522.2	60
37107.7	35674.9	11291.3	36910.5	4910
1661.3	2634.7	223.7	1577.5	209
805.3	785.0	258.5	739.7	31
5354.1	5149.2	1732.4	5206.3	528
10478.2	13456.7	5070.0	9675.8	834
4694.6	4895.2	1334.7	4445.1	279
14575.8	13349.1	5355.0	13328.1	2198
666.0	651.0	173.0	638.0	90
3431.9	3237.8	978.8	3093.2	178
9664.0	9636.0	4726.2	8891.3	332
24723.2	20011.9	9095.7	23399.3	1933
7450.6	7452.8	2498.9	6740.9	701
17412.5	12545.5	5379.5	16878.9	1360
31751.4	34612.3	8341.6	31198.4	2542
3862.4	5736.4	954.7	3483.9	268
1682.8	1636.2	474.4	1619.2	165
83427.4	82826.5	18730.1	74580.1	825

10-16 全部规模以上集体工业企业主要经济指标（2003年）（续5）

单位：万元

分组	Item	资产合计 Total Assets	流动资产小计 Total Circulating Funds
食品制造业	Food Production	1213.2	919.1
饮料制造业	Beverage Production		
烟草加工业	Tobacco Processing		
纺织业	Textile Industry	3242.4	1695.2
纺织服装、鞋、帽制造业	Textile clothing, footwear and headgear industry	1602.1	917.2
皮革、毛皮、羽毛(绒)及其制品业	Leather, fur, feather (eiderdown) and their products industry		
木材加工及木、竹、藤、棕、草制品制造	Timber Processing,Bamboo,Cane,Palm Fiber and Straw Products		
家具制造业	Furniture Manufacturing	1120.7	879.6
造纸及纸制品业	Papermaking and Paper Products	22334.2	5521.2
印刷业和记录媒介的复制	Printing,Record Medium Reproduction	5515.8	2845.7
文教体育用品制造业	Cultural,Educational and Sports Goods		
石油加工、炼焦及核燃料加工业	Petroleum refining, coke making and nuclear	217.2	173.9
化学原料及化学制品制造业	Raw Chemical Materials and Chemical Products	5244.6	3293.1
医药制造业	Medical and Pharmaceutical Products	17114.9	11568.1
化学纤维制造业	Chemical Fiber		
橡胶制品业	Rubber Products		
塑料制品业	Plastic Products	1934.3	1193.9
非金属矿物制品业	Nonmetal Mineral Products	23969.0	8895.8
黑色金属冶炼及压延加工业	Smelting and Pressing of Ferrous Metals	470.3	190.3
有色金属冶炼及压延加工业	Smelting and Pressing of Nonferrou Metals	2506.4	476.2
金属制品业	Metal Products	14145.1	10952.6
通用设备制造	General equipment manufacturing industry	33131.9	18945.1
专用设备制造业	Special Purpose Equipment	7706.7	5086.0
交通运输设备制造业	Transport Equipment	6491.7	3685.5
电气机械及器材制造业	Electric Equipment and Machinery	45247.2	31778.7
通信设备、计算机及其他电子设备制造业	Communication equipment, computer and other electronic equipment manufacturing industry	3391.5	2337.4
仪器仪表及文化、办公用机械制造业	Instruments,Meters,Cultural and Office Machinery	940.1	502.0
工艺品及其他制造业	Handicraft and other stuff manufacturing industry	141728.5	72975.7
废弃资源和废旧材料回收加工业	Discarded resources and waste materials salvaging and processing industry		
电力、热力的生产和供应业	Electric power, heating power generating and supplying industry		
燃气生产和供应业	Gas mining and supplying industry		
水的生产和供应业	Water processing and supplying industry		

Economic Indicators of All Collective-owned Industrial Enterprises Above Designated Size（2003）(Continued 5)

(10 000 yuan)

流动资产年平均余额 Average Balance of Circulating Funds	固定资产小计 Total Fixed Assets	固定资产原价合计 Origing Value of Fixed Assets	累计折旧 Accumulative Total Depreciation	本年折旧 Depreciation In this year	固定资产净值年平均余额 Annual Average Balance Net Value of Fixed Assets
895.4	197.1	486.1	304.7	85.0	195.9
1230.8	1495.0	1601.8	666.7	62.3	893.1
1153.0	439.7	719.1	297.2	23.1	440.5
855.9	241.1	315.1	158.0	96.7	243.5
5490.4	15155.0	17322.9	2453.6	338.9	14773.3
2884.7	2623.7	4178.5	1725.1	144.4	2501.9
161.4	43.3	75.1	31.8	7.3	46.7
3190.5	1758.0	1793.3	670.6	118.1	1146.5
10085.4	3103.9	4112.4	2477.7	414.0	1728.5
1181.8	570.4	1819.6	1249.2	161.1	598.4
8362.3	12481.6	19174.5	7690.1	1011.5	11939.4
190.0	280.0	326.0	46.0	12.0	280.0
454.7	1999.2	3043.0	1043.8	111.6	1738.2
5732.0	1988.7	2825.6	1559.2	197.8	344.0
17707.7	4542.7	6734.9	2557.6	397.5	10668.8
5225.4	1272.2	2381.9	1175.6	160.6	1300.4
2820.2	2123.1	2694.0	688.3	162.8	1735.2
31308.2	10693.2	14749.8	4274.9	733.7	10585.4
2104.0	1051.3	1775.6	724.3	90.1	1137.9
497.1	438.1	561.4	214.6	81.5	437.3
65362.4	17254.4	7975.4	2896.6	1140.8	5326.0

10-16 全部规模以上集体工业企业经济指标（2003年）（续6）

单位：万元

分 组	Item	负债合计 Total Liabilites	流动负债小计 Liquid Liabilities
食品制造业	Food Production	641.5	103.8
饮料制造业	Beverage Production		
烟草加工业	Tobacco Processing		
纺织业	Textile Industry	1791.9	1569.1
纺织服装、鞋、帽制造业	Textile clothing, footwear and headgear industry	834.8	785.3
皮革、毛皮、羽毛(绒)及其制品业	Leather, fur, feather (eiderdown) and their products industry		
木材加工及木、竹、藤、棕、草制品制造	Timber Processing,Bamboo,Cane,Palm Fiber and Straw Products		
家具制造业	Furniture Manufacturing	1056.9	629.6
造纸及纸制品业	Papermaking and Paper Products	9593.6	9075.9
印刷业和记录媒介的复制	Printing,Record Medium Reproduction	5080.8	2715.6
文教体育用品制造业	Cultural,Educational and Sports Goods		
石油加工、炼焦及核燃料加工业	Petroleum refining, coke making and nuclear	172.1	42.1
化学原料及化学制品制造业	Raw Chemical Materials and Chemical Products	4436.5	4152.8
医药制造业	Medical and Pharmaceutical Products	8209.4	6800.7
化学纤维制造业	Chemical Fiber		
橡胶制品业	Rubber Products		
塑料制品业	Plastic Products	1826.7	1302.3
非金属矿物制品业	Nonmetal Mineral Products	24870.0	13976.5
黑色金属冶炼及压延加工业	Smelting and Pressing of Ferrous Metals	259.3	18.9
有色金属冶炼及压延加工业	Smelting and Pressing of Nonferrou Metals	1126.8	718.8
金属制品业	Metal Products	7532.7	7138.7
通用设备制造	General equipment manufacturing industry	18584.3	17618.0
专用设备制造业	Special Purpose Equipment	3912.9	3911.3
交通运输设备制造业	Transport Equipment	3076.5	2610.2
电气机械及器材制造业	Electric Equipment and Machinery	25535.3	22912.7
通信设备、计算机及其他电子设备制造业	Communication equipment, computer and other electronic equipment manufacturing industry	1589.5	1589.4
仪器仪表及文化、办公用机械制造业	Instruments,Meters,Cultural and Office Machinery	198.0	82.8
工艺品及其他制造业	Handicraft and other stuff manufacturing industry	45183.4	44983.4
废弃资源和废旧材料回收加工业	Discarded resources and waste materials salvaging and processing industry		
电力、热力的生产和供应业	Electric power, heating power generating and supplying industry		
燃气生产和供应业	Gas mining and supplying industry		
水的生产和供应业	Water processing and supplying industry		

Economic Indicators of All Collective-owned Industrial Enterprises Above Designated Size（2003）(Continued 6)

(10 000 yuan)

长期负债小计 Long-term Liabilities	所有者权益合计 Total Creditors Equity	实收资本 Total Capital Hold	产品销售收入 Sales Revenue	产品销售成本 Cost of Sales	产品销售费用 Sales Expense	产品销售税金及附加 Sales Tax and Extra Charges	营业利润 Operational profit
537.7	571.7	380.0	694.7	554.0	45.1	24.4	-0.2
216.8	1450.5	1037.0	2347.3	2095.3	54.9	32.9	22.9
	767.3	1474.0	520.3	446.2	17.9	4.2	-85.7
427.3	63.8	74.2	658.4	620.8	18.9	2.2	-6.3
451.5	12740.6	2546.8	36193.7	29524.4	917.6	413.3	4678.9
2365.2	435.0	1166.7	1426.5	1371.2	30.1	5.4	-252.5
130.0	45.1	33.0	685.1	609.2	8.2	1.7	-2.0
276.7	808.1	1024.5	4930.2	3688.4	279.6	21.7	498.6
1403.8	8905.5	4640.1	8411.6	4872.1	956.5	128.6	1581.1
524.4	107.6	366.5	4449.4	3692.8	416.3	13.9	-7.2
10393.2	-901.0	7511.9	11775.0	9583.8	660.0	141.1	258.0
70.0	211.0	168.0	638.0	558.2	3.5	8.0	43.0
408.0	1379.6	924.0	3187.8	2716.7	99.4	40.7	620.6
394.0	6612.4	545.0	9376.0	7808.0	340.7	57.9	343.3
702.0	14547.6	3022.8	19676.5	16021.6	866.0	428.1	1036.9
	3793.8	3583.2	6308.3	5089.5	296.4	40.8	329.4
466.3	3415.2	2521.0	17194.1	14798.3	50.3	38.4	1274.6
2622.6	19711.9	6756.5	32138.4	27962.0	960.8	83.9	625.1
	1802.0	1071.8	3904.4	3299.1	129.8	14.4	40.0
	742.1	679.0	1595.7	1195.2	137.2	22.1	198.6
200.0	96545.1	18009.8	24307.3	18602.4	31.7	135.9	9739.3

10-16 全部规模以上集体工业企业主要经济指标（2003年）（续7）

单位：万元

分 组	Item	管理费用 Expenses for Management
食品制造业	Food Production	43.6
饮料制造业	Beverage Production	
烟草加工业	Tobacco Processing	
纺织业	Textile Industry	160.0
纺织服装、鞋、帽制造业	Textile clothing, footwear and headgear industry	137.0
皮革、毛皮、羽毛(绒)及其制品业	Leather, fur, feather (eiderdown) and their products industry	
木材加工及木、竹、藤、棕、草制品制造	Timber Processing,Bamboo,Cane,Palm Fiber and Straw Products	
家具制造业	Furniture Manufacturing	18.0
造纸及纸制品业	Papermaking and Paper Products	1270.2
印刷业和记录媒介的复制	Printing,Record Medium Reproduction	268.6
文教体育用品制造业	Cultural,Educational and Sports Goods	
石油加工、炼焦及核燃料加工业	Petroleum refining, coke making and nuclear	62.1
化学原料及化学制品制造业	Raw Chemical Materials and Chemical Products	490.0
医药制造业	Medical and Pharmaceutical Products	960.1
化学纤维制造业	Chemical Fiber	
橡胶制品业	Rubber Products	
塑料制品业	Plastic Products	301.4
非金属矿物制品业	Nonmetal Mineral Products	569.4
黑色金属冶炼及压延加工业	Smelting and Pressing of Ferrous Metals	25.5
有色金属冶炼及压延加工业	Smelting and Pressing of Nonferrou Metals	45.6
金属制品业	Metal Products	582.2
通用设备制造	General equipment manufacturing industry	1262.4
专用设备制造业	Special Purpose Equipment	448.5
交通运输设备制造业	Transport Equipment	1019.6
电气机械及器材制造业	Electric Equipment and Machinery	2254.5
通信设备、计算机及其他电子设备制造业	Communication equipment, computer and other electronic equipment manufacturing industry	400.5
仪器仪表及文化、办公用机械制造业	Instruments,Meters,Cultural and Office Machinery	48.3
工艺品及其他制造业	Handicraft and other stuff manufacturing industry	543.8
废弃资源和废旧材料回收加工业	Discarded resources and waste materials salvaging and processing industry	
电力、热力的生产和供应业	Electric power, heating power generating and supplying industry	
燃气生产和供应业	Gas mining and supplying industry	
水的生产和供应业	Water processing and supplying industry	

Economic Indicators of All Collective-owned Industrial Enterprises Above Designated Size（2003）(Continued 7)

（10 000 yuan）

利润总额 Total Profits	亏损企业亏损总额 Total Loss of Deficit Enterprises	利税总额 Total Pre-tax Profits	本年应交增值税 Value Added Tax Payable
0.4		76.6	51.8
-4.8	36.1	73.5	45.4
-70.0	104.5	-52.2	13.6
-10.4	10.4	-4.3	3.9
2030.5		3119.9	676.1
-251.3	251.3	-221.2	24.7
-2.0	2.0	16.6	16.9
75.9	51.4	223.1	125.5
1231.7	138.3	2187.4	827.1
-8.9	24.8	84.2	79.2
111.1	284.4	904.9	652.7
43.0		60.0	9.0
64.2		165.5	60.6
458.9	3.0	1156.3	639.5
806.3		1845.4	611.0
324.6	144.5	703.2	337.8
1328.6	83.4	1745.6	378.6
773.6	56.0	1724.4	866.9
40.0		247.1	192.7
34.5		74.1	17.5
4326.3	82.4	6600.5	2138.3

10-17 全部规模以上三资工业企业经济指标(2003年)

单位：万元

分组	Item	企业单位数(个) Number of Enterprises (unit)	亏损企业 Loss Making Enterprises
总 计	**Total**	**82**	**25**
#市 区	Urban Area	78	25
按隶属关系分	Grouped by Registion Status		
#市属企业	Municipal Enterprises	72	22
按登记注册类型分组	Grouped by Ligth Induotry and Industry Heavy Industry		
港、澳、台商投资企业	Enterprises with Investment from Hong Kong, Macao and Taiwan	29	10
与港、澳、台商合资经营	Co-investment with businessman from Hong Kong,Macao and Taiwan	27	9
与港、澳、台商合作经营	Partnership with businessman from Hong Kong, Macao and Taiwan		
港澳台商独资	Wholly Funded from Hong Kong,Macao and Taiwan	2	1
港澳台商投资股份有限公司	Share-holding Corporation with Funds from Hong Kong,Macao and Taiwan		
外商投资企业	Enterprises with Foreign Investment	53	15
中外合资经营企业	Joint Ownership Operation With overseas	43	13
中外合作经营企业	Co-operation With Overseas	1	
外资企业	Foreign Funded Enterprises	9	2
外商投资股份有限公司	Foreign funded Share-holding Corporations		
在总计中:亏损企业	Of the Total: Deficit Enterprises	25	25
按轻重工业分	Grouped by Ligth Industry and Heavy Industry		
轻工业	Light Industry	38	14
重工业	Heavy Industry	44	11
按企业规模分	Grouped by Size of Enterprises		
大型工业	Large-size		
中型工业	Medium-sized	12	2
小型工业	Small-size	70	23
按工业行业大类分	Grouped by Sector		
煤炭开采和洗选业	Coal mining and coal washing industry		
石油和天然气开采业	Petroleum and Natural Gas Extraction		
黑色金属矿采选业	Ferrous Metals Mining and Dressing		

Economic Indicators of Foreign Fund Industrial Enterprises Above Designated Size (2003)

(10 000 yuan)

工业总产值（当年价）Gross Industrial Output Value (At Current Prices)	工业总产值（不变价）Gorss Industrial Output Value (At Constant Prices)	工业增加值（生产法）Value-Added of Industry (Value of Industrial Products Sales)	工业销售产值（当年价）Value of Industry Products Sales (At Current Prices)	全部职工年平均人数（人）Annual Average Employers (person)
956784.2	**1083457.6**	**401099.3**	**927887.0**	**14872**
927013.7	1054089.8	389365.8	897327.8	14037
544857.7	691175.6	214227.2	521879.9	12067
131122.8	105099.8	43425.8	126557.3	4548
128759.7	102627.9	42693.9	124187.6	4114
2363.1	2471.9	731.9	2369.7	434
825661.4	978357.8	357673.5	801329.7	10324
668521.4	753914.6	291942.4	653980.8	7248
5285.8	5189.8	2325.3	5485.6	207
151854.2	219253.4	63405.8	141863.3	2869
118497.2	163544.0	41918.5	114066.6	3245
622709.9	586808.2	260279.8	612266.1	8521
334074.3	496649.4	140819.5	315620.9	6351
623373.5	673482.6	273712.7	603543.3	7625
333410.7	409975.0	127386.6	324343.7	7247

10-17 全部规模以上三资工业企业经济指标(2003年）（续1）

单位：万元

分　组	Item	资产合计 Total Assets	流动资产小计 Total Circulating Funds
总　计	**Total**	**1042649.7**	**728123.1**
#市　区	Urban Area	995937.1	694300.4
按隶属关系分	Grouped by Registion Status		
#市属企业	Municipal Enterprises	782683.0	509288.7
按登记注册类型分组	Grouped by Ligth Induotry and Industry Heavy Industry		
港、澳、台商投资企业	Enterprises with Investment from Hong Kong, Macao and Taiwan	164794.5	92709.3
与港、澳、台商合资经营	Co-investment with businessman from Hong Kong,Macao and Taiwan	162170.6	91686.4
与港、澳、台商合作经营	Partnership with businessman from Hong Kong, Macao and Taiwan		
港澳台商独资	Wholly Funded from Hong Kong,Macao and Taiwan	2623.9	1022.9
港澳台商投资股份有限公司	Share-holding Corporation with Funds from Hong Kong,Macao and Taiwan		
外商投资企业	Enterprises with Foreign Investment	877855.2	635413.8
中外合资经营企业	Joint Ownership Operation With overseas	739718.3	572950.6
中外合作经营企业	Co-operation With Overseas	3482.4	2393.9
外资企业	Foreign Funded Enterprises	134654.5	60069.3
外商投资股份有限公司	Foreign funded Share-holding Corporations		
在总计中:亏损企业	Of the Total: Deficit Enterprises	347644.0	257269.1
按轻重工业分	Grouped by Ligth Industry and Heavy Industry		
轻工业	Light Industry	562589.0	375180.9
重工业	Heavy Industry	480060.7	352942.2
按企业规模分	Grouped by Size of Enterprises		
大型工业	Large-size		
中型工业	Medium-sized	627650.4	437968.6
小型工业	Small-size	414999.3	290154.5
按工业行业大类分	Grouped by Sector		
煤炭开采和洗选业	Coal mining and coal washing industry		
石油和天然气开采业	Petroleum and Natural Gas Extraction		
黑色金属矿采选业	Ferrous Metals Mining and Dressing		

Economic Indicators of Foreign Fund Industrial Enterprises Above Designated Size (2003)(Continued 1)

(10 000 yuan)

流动资产年平均余额 Average Balance of Circulating Funds	固定资产小计 Total Fixed Assets	固定资产原价合计 Origing Value of Fixed Assets	累计折旧 Accumulative Total Depreciation	本年折旧 Depreciation this year	固定资产净值年平均余额 Annual Average Balance Net Value of Fixed Assets
702979.3	**262840.5**	**424277.7**	**180663.7**	**28964.5**	**253219.0**
672334.5	250226.3	393262.0	161353.0	28701.9	230389.3
498257.4	228683.1	337537.3	124801.5	25237.9	212592.7
81144.8	64376.8	80132.9	32858.7	4109.4	48282.3
80056.6	62775.8	78429.0	32174.8	3994.4	47207.6
1088.2	1601.0	1703.9	683.9	115.0	1074.7
621834.5	198463.7	344144.8	147805.0	24855.1	204936.7
558746.5	135003.7	244127.2	111799.4	15232.6	142995.0
2353.9	955.9	3094.6	2138.7	255.5	1065.6
60734.1	62504.1	96923.0	33866.9	9367.0	60876.1
258850.2	72051.7	115251.3	43351.4	7625.8	73586.0
352713.9	156775.0	252288.8	114694.8	16058.6	148074.9
350265.4	106065.5	171988.9	65968.9	12905.9	105144.1
435105.6	157614.2	238434.2	94651.7	17523.3	142183.8
267873.7	105226.3	185843.5	86012.0	11441.2	111035.2

10-17 全部规模以上三资工业企业经济指标(2003年）（续2）

单位：万元

分组	Item	负债合计 Total Liabilites	流动负债小计 Liquid Liabilities
总 计	**Total**	**562093.4**	**484864.0**
#市 区	Urban Area	553703.2	476673.8
按隶属关系分	Grouped by Registion Status		
#市属企业	Municipal Enterprises	446730.7	369501.4
按登记注册类型分组	Grouped by Ligth Induotry and Industry Heavy Industry		
港、澳、台商投资企业	Enterprises with Investment from Hong Kong, Macao and Taiwan	105656.1	86441.2
与港、澳、台商合资经营	Co-investment with businessman from Hong Kong,Macao and Taiwan	104670.2	85455.3
与港、澳、台商合作经营	Partnership with businessman from Hong Kong, Macao and Taiwan		
港澳台商独资	Wholly Funded from Hong Kong,Macao and Taiwan	985.9	985.9
港澳台商投资股份有限公司	Share-holding Corporation with Funds from Hong Kong,Macao and Taiwan		
外商投资企业	Enterprises with Foreign Investment	456437.3	398422.8
中外合资经营企业	Joint Ownership Operation With overseas	397252.6	361116.3
中外合作经营企业	Co-operation With Overseas	689.2	689.2
外资企业	Foreign Funded Enterprises	58495.5	36617.3
外商投资股份有限公司	Foreign funded Share-holding Corporations		
在总计中:亏损企业	Of the Total: Deficit Enterprises	248081.9	204654.3
按轻重工业分	Grouped by Ligth Industry and Heavy Industry		
轻工业	Light Industry	309201.6	268100.1
重工业	Heavy Industry	252891.8	216763.9
按企业规模分	Grouped by Size of Enterprises		
大型工业	Large-size		
中型工业	Medium-sized	352113.7	309694.2
小型工业	Small-size	209979.7	175169.8
按工业行业大类分	Grouped by Sector		
煤炭开采和洗选业	Coal mining and coal washing industry		
石油和天然气开采业	Petroleum and Natural Gas Extraction		
黑色金属矿采选业	Ferrous Metals Mining and Dressing		

Economic Indicators Foreign Fund Industrial Enterprises Above Designated Size (2003)(Continued 2)

(10 000 yuan)

长期负债小计 Long-term Liabilities	所有者权益合计 Total Creditor Equity	实收资本 Total Capital Hold	产品销售收入 Salas Revenue	产品销售成本 Cost of Sales	产品销售费用 Sales Expense	产品销售税金及附加 Sales Tax and Extra Charges	营业利润 Operational profit
71194.7	**480556.3**	**329514.7**	**906731.4**	**599602.0**	**141373.6**	**1667.3**	**105968.9**
70994.8	442233.9	317016.7	876055.8	576296.8	141145.8	1667.3	100092.8
71194.7	335952.3	276330.6	511777.5	369972.7	56737.9	1602.8	38931.1
17270.4	59138.4	59037.4	117208.7	86995.3	16060.3	408.2	6695.3
17270.4	57500.4	57999.5	114971.0	85077.4	15880.2	408.2	6674.1
	1638.0	1037.9	2237.7	1917.9	180.1		21.2
53924.3	421417.9	270477.3	789522.7	512606.7	125313.3	1259.1	99273.6
35957.9	342465.7	212105.6	634997.7	394545.3	107362.7	1257.5	86973.2
	2793.2	2569.7	5485.8	4798.9	201.5		256.3
17966.4	76159.0	55802.0	149039.2	113262.5	17749.1	1.6	12044.1
43243.9	99562.1	117267.9	89309.9	69737.3	15548.6	362.3	-15119.5
35428.6	253387.4	160109.9	590703.4	370349.7	114936.9	182.2	80263.7
35766.1	227168.9	169404.8	316028.0	229252.3	26436.7	1485.1	25705.2
38324.4	275536.7	165950.3	575652.1	337572.5	122426.2	331.9	81788.3
32870.3	205019.6	163564.4	331079.3	262029.5	18947.4	1335.4	24180.6

10-17 全部规模以上三资工业企业经济指标(2003年）（续3）

单位：万元

分　组	Item	管理费用 Expenses for Management
总　计	**Total**	**48657.4**
#市　区	Urban Area	47134.7
按隶属关系分	Grouped by Registion Status	
#市属企业	Municipal Enterprises	36058.1
按登记注册类型分组	Grouped by Ligth Induotry and Industry Heavy Industry	
港、澳、台商投资企业	Enterprises with Investment from Hong Kong, Macao and Taiwan	6642.7
与港、澳、台商合资经营	Co-investment with businessman from Hong Kong,Macao and Taiwan	6438.5
与港、澳、台商合作经营	Partnership with businessman from Hong Kong, Macao and Taiwan	
港澳台商独资	Wholly Funded from Hong Kong,Macao and Taiwan	204.2
港澳台商投资股份有限公司	Share-holding Corporation with Funds from Hong Kong,Macao and Taiwan	
外商投资企业	Enterprises with Foreign Investment	42014.7
中外合资经营企业	Joint Ownership Operation With overseas	36078.3
中外合作经营企业	Co-operation With Overseas	379.3
外资企业	Foreign Funded Enterprises	5557.1
外商投资股份有限公司	Foreign funded Share-holding Corporations	
在总计中:亏损企业	Of the Total: Deficit Enterprises	12471.2
按轻重工业分	Grouped by Ligth Industry and Heavy Industry	
轻工业	Light Industry	20862.2
重工业	Heavy Industry	27795.2
按企业规模分	Grouped by Size of Enterprises	
大型工业	Large-size	
中型工业	Medium-sized	27170.2
小型工业	Small-size	21487.2
按工业行业大类分	Grouped by Sector	
煤炭开采和洗选业	Coal mining and coal washing industry	
石油和天然气开采业	Petroleum and Natural Gas Extraction	
黑色金属矿采选业	Ferrous Metals Mining and Dressing	

Economic Indicators of Foreign Fund Industrial Enterprises Above Designated Size (2003)(Continued 3)

（10 000 yuan）

利润总额 Total Profits	亏损企业亏损总额 Total Loss of Deficit Enterprises	利税总额 Total Pre-tax Profits	本年应交增值税 Value Added Tax Payable
111208.8	**16945.3**	**163940.0**	**51063.9**
105367.1	16945.3	156542.0	49507.6
34436.0	16577.8	59033.1	22994.3
4897.1	973.9	9054.1	3748.8
4891.1	966.9	9025.8	3726.5
6.0	7.0	28.3	22.3
106311.7	15971.4	154885.9	47315.1
95799.2	14884.5	136399.7	39343.0
253.8		464.7	210.9
10258.7	1086.9	18021.5	7761.2
-16945.3	16945.3	-14745.9	1837.1
87502.3	2645.8	124540.8	36856.3
23706.5	14299.5	39399.2	14207.6
87450.9	11987.5	125359.0	37576.2
23757.9	4957.8	38581.0	13487.7

10-17 全部规模以上三资工业企业经济指标(2003年）（续4）

单位：万元

分 组	Item	企业单位数 (个) Number of Enterprises (unit)	亏损企业 Loss Making Enterprises
有色金属矿采选业	Nonferrous Metals Mining and Dressing		
非金属矿采选业	Nonmetal Minerals Mining and Dressing		
其他采矿业	Other mining industry		
农副食品加工业	Agricultural products and non-stable food processing industry	1	
食品制造业	Food Production	6	2
饮料制造业	Beverage Production	6	3
烟草加工业	Tobacco Processing		
纺织业	Textile Industry	2	1
纺织服装、鞋、帽制造业	Textile clothing, footwear and headgear industry	1	1
皮革、毛皮、羽毛(绒)及其制品业	Leather, fur, feather (eiderdown) and their products industry	1	1
木材加工及竹、藤、棕、草制品业	Timber Processing,Bamboo,Cane,Palm Fiber and Straw Products	1	1
家具制造业	Furniture Manufacturing	2	
造纸及纸制品业	Papermaking and Record Medium Reproducton	1	
印刷业、记录媒介的复制	Printing,Record Medium Reproduction	3	1
文教体育用品制造业	Cultural,Educational and Sports Goods		
石油加工、炼焦及核燃料加工业	Petroleum refining, coke making and nuclear	1	
化学原料及化学制品制造业	Raw Chemical Materials and Chemical Products	3	
医药制造业	Medical and Pharmaceutical Products	7	3
化学纤维制造业	Chemical Fiber		
橡胶制品业	Rubber Products		
塑料制品业	Plastic Products	4	
非金属矿物制品业	Nonmetal Mineral Products	6	2
黑色金属冶炼及压延加工业	Smelting and Pressing of Ferrous Metals	1	
有色金属冶炼及压延加工业	Smelting and Pressing of Nonferrou Metals	2	2
金属制品业	Metal Products	3	
通用设备制造	General equipment manufacturing industry	6	1
专用设备制造业	Special Purpose Equipment	3	1
交通运输设备制造业	Transport Equipment	2	
电气机械及器材制造业	Electric Equipment and Machinery	9	2
通信设备、计算机及其他电子设备制造业	Communication equipment, computer and other electronic equipment manufacturing industry	7	2
仪器仪表及文化办公用机械制造业	Instruments,Meters,Cultural and Office Machinery	2	1
工艺品及其他制造业	Handicraft and other stuff manufacturing industry	1	1
废弃资源和废旧材料回收加工业	Discarded resources and waste materials salvaging and processing industry		
电力、热力的生产和供应业	Electric power, heating power generating and supplying industry	1	
燃气生产和供应业	Gas mining and supplying industry		
水的生产和供应业	Water processing and supplying industry		

Economic Indicators of Foreign Fund Industrial Enterprises Above Designated Size (2003)(Continued 4)

(10 000 yuan)

工业总产值（当年价）Gross Industrial Output Value (At Current Prices)	工业总产值（不变价）Gorss Industrial Output Value (At Constant Prices)	工业增加值（生产法）Value-Added of Industry (Value of Industrial Products Sales)	工业销售产值（当年价）Value of Industry Products Sales (At Current Prices)	全部职工年平均人数（人）Annual Average Employers (person)
68837.4	42183.9	19315.1	68837.4	219
98704.9	77989.0	35098.4	95919.1	2298
60817.9	62235.2	22741.2	61001.9	1742
5161.8	4844.0	522.8	5185.6	82
1383.6	1383.6	415.1	1383.6	250
9308.6	8259.5	2234.0	7852.3	173
1038.2	1072.8	254.9	863.8	75
3118.2	3536.3	1370.7	3240.6	334
1513.3	1729.5	662.5	1568.6	432
16107.2	18845.3	5806.4	15867.8	129
1064.5	1182.5	343.6	1070.0	20
33440.2	33249.5	12753.4	32249.9	469
316379.7	323656.7	156511.8	310881.8	2160
9979.9	10599.7	3772.0	9415.6	192
21205.5	24624.3	8217.1	21563.9	651
4911.6	4911.6	1330.0	6001.5	45
16812.0	18658.0	6389.5	14417.9	141
8268.9	7083.5	4581.2	8484.0	613
56673.5	69577.6	24945.7	54029.6	1066
56625.1	63661.0	20911.1	49358.1	757
16743.0	18298.5	6068.8	16461.4	249
48057.2	109520.4	23805.5	41862.1	853
96804.5	173146.6	41510.7	96159.8	1493
1366.6	1366.6	887.7	1749.8	291
1495.3	1495.3	325.7	1495.3	15
965.6	346.7	324.4	965.6	123

10-17 全部规模以上三资工业企业经济指标(2003年)（续5）

单位：万元

分　组	Item	资产合计 Total Assets	流动资产小计 Circulating Funds
有色金属矿采选业	Nonferrous Metals Mining and Dressing		
非金属矿采选业	Nonmetal Minerals Mining and Dressing		
其他采矿业	Other mining industry		
农副食品加工业	Agricultural products and non-stable food processing industry	21641.8	16866.4
食品制造业	Food Production	77668.0	32103.9
饮料制造业	Beverage Production	118866.7	42779.5
烟草加工业	Tobacco Processing		
纺织业	Textile Industry	4243.8	2793.5
纺织服装、鞋、帽制造业	Textile clothing, footwear and headgear industry	2323.7	825.1
皮革、毛皮、羽毛(绒)及其制品业	Leather, fur, feather (eiderdown) and their products industry	21944.4	17719.5
木材加工及竹、藤、棕、草制品业	Timber Processing,Bamboo,Cane,Palm Fiber and Straw Products	7122.5	3943.1
家具制造业	Furniture Manufacturing	7251.3	5051.4
造纸及纸制品业	Papermaking and Record Medium Reproducton	4074.0	3644.4
印刷业、记录媒介的复制	Printing,Record Medium Reproduction	10545.8	7773.5
文教体育用品制造业	Cultural,Educational and Sports Goods		
石油加工、炼焦及核燃料加工业	Petroleum refining, coke making and nuclear	774.0	250.6
化学原料及化学制品制造业	Raw Chemical Materials and Chemical Products	40676.1	29631.0
医药制造业	Medical and Pharmaceutical Products	237512.7	209359.3
化学纤维制造业	Chemical Fiber		
橡胶制品业	Rubber Products		
塑料制品业	Plastic Products	17178.3	6997.9
非金属矿物制品业	Nonmetal Mineral Products	31720.9	18450.2
黑色金属冶炼及压延加工业	Smelting and Pressing of Ferrous Metals	2961.5	2534.5
有色金属冶炼及压延加工业	Smelting and Pressing of Nonferrou Metals	13154.7	8168.4
金属制品业	Metal Products	20281.9	9448.1
通用设备制造	General equipment manufacturing industry	50855.5	31574.5
专用设备制造业	Special Purpose Equipment	50884.3	31939.3
交通运输设备制造业	Transport Equipment	20299.9	16971.5
电气机械及器材制造业	Electric Equipment and Machinery	32448.6	22702.8
通信设备、计算机及其他电子设备制造业	Communication equipment, computer and other electronic equipment manufacturing industry	234840.1	197425.6
仪器仪表及文化办公用机械制造业	Instruments,Meters,Cultural and Office Machinery	10268.3	7959.3
工艺品及其他制造业	Handicraft and other stuff manufacturing industry	934.4	347.3
废弃资源和废旧材料回收加工业	Discarded resources and waste materials salvaging and processing industry		
电力、热力的生产和供应业	Electric power, heating power generating and supplying industry	2176.5	862.5
燃气生产和供应业	Gas mining and supplying industry		
水的生产和供应业	Water processing and supplying industry		

Economic Indicators of Foreign Fund Industrial Enterprises Above Designated Size (2003)(Continued 5)

(10 000 yuan)

流动资产年平均余额 Average Balance of Circulating Funds	固定资产小计 Total Fixed Assets	固定资产原价合计 Origing Value of Fixed Assets	累计折旧 Accumulative Total Depreciation	本年折旧 Depreciation this year	固定资产净值年平均余额 Annual Average Balance Net Value of Fixed Assets
10970.4	3743.3	9934.9	6191.6	734.6	3806.2
31200.7	37934.3	42793.0	18601.2	2688.1	26066.3
44966.8	64743.2	92175.4	27573.7	7901.8	63299.8
2751.3	1329.2	3127.0	1797.8	81.4	1501.0
889.8	1498.6	1498.6	581.0	92.2	972.3
18107.3	4224.7	12115.3	7890.6	787.4	4574.6
3797.0	2452.1	2840.6	388.5	194.5	2551.8
4692.2	1508.3	2586.4	1248.7	152.4	1355.7
3143.0	364.2	661.1	314.9	61.3	364.2
5747.3	2619.1	4513.5	1894.4	307.1	2702.2
270.2	234.7	463.4	228.7	39.7	238.0
26714.8	10900.6	28227.4	18469.9	83.0	20840.5
196920.6	21517.8	46204.9	27721.1	2649.7	17466.4
7086.2	7462.1	9909.3	2925.0	649.7	5534.4
17953.2	12341.5	19952.1	8819.6	1076.9	10606.4
1894.0	300.5	363.7	63.2	36.7	2617.5
6540.6	4308.8	5934.6	1625.8	577.1	4548.1
6497.8	9801.5	17019.9	7751.3	1261.6	9739.6
31400.3	17336.8	25133.7	8391.1	2093.5	17185.1
29346.5	15051.7	25521.6	11722.7	1700.2	14240.8
15947.0	2990.8	3860.8	1046.3	332.4	345.0
21258.7	7978.1	13001.3	4429.8	1076.5	7845.8
206099.2	28233.1	48570.4	16911.9	3929.7	30864.0
7617.7	2289.4	5321.6	3049.0	300.4	2399.6
356.2	362.1	381.5	174.2	7.6	207.3
810.5	1314.0	2165.7	851.7	149.0	1346.4

10-17 全部规模以上三资工业企业经济指标(2003年）（续6）

单位：万元

分 组	Item	负债合计 Total Liabilites	流动负债小计 Liquid Liabilities
有色金属矿采选业	Nonferrous Metals Mining and Dressing		
非金属矿采选业	Nonmetal Minerals Mining and Dressing		
其他采矿业	Other mining industry		
农副食品加工业	Agricultural products and non-stable food processing industry	15196.5	15196.5
食品制造业	Food Production	46113.5	32600.0
饮料制造业	Beverage Production	77245.6	62348.9
烟草加工业	Tobacco Processing		
纺织业	Textile Industry	6887.7	6887.7
纺织服装、鞋、帽制造业	Textile clothing, footwear and headgear industry	893.2	893.2
皮革、毛皮、羽毛(绒)及其制品业	Leather, fur, feather (eiderdown) and their products industry	15544.3	15544.3
木材加工及竹、藤、棕、草制品业	Timber Processing,Bamboo,Cane,Palm Fiber and Straw Products	5735.5	2495.5
家具制造业	Furniture Manufacturing	3056.5	3056.5
造纸及纸制品业	Papermaking and Record Medium Reproducton	3473.3	3473.3
印刷业、记录媒介的复制	Printing,Record Medium Reproduction	7772.2	6173.2
文教体育用品制造业	Cultural,Educational and Sports Goods		
石油加工、炼焦及核燃料加工业	Petroleum refining, coke making and nuclear	521.6	206.6
化学原料及化学制品制造业	Raw Chemical Materials and Chemical Products	5422.0	5412.0
医药制造业	Medical and Pharmaceutical Products	117005.8	109735.8
化学纤维制造业	Chemical Fiber		
橡胶制品业	Rubber Products		
塑料制品业	Plastic Products	10607.2	6785.0
非金属矿物制品业	Nonmetal Mineral Products	15006.8	12076.0
黑色金属冶炼及压延加工业	Smelting and Pressing of Ferrous Metals	2587.8	2587.8
有色金属冶炼及压延加工业	Smelting and Pressing of Nonferrou Metals	10322.9	5356.4
金属制品业	Metal Products	5530.1	2728.4
通用设备制造	General equipment manufacturing industry	10739.1	10739.1
专用设备制造业	Special Purpose Equipment	12928.6	11734.3
交通运输设备制造业	Transport Equipment	11438.9	11438.9
电气机械及器材制造业	Electric Equipment and Machinery	10616.9	10460.1
通信设备、计算机及其他电子设备制造业	Communication equipment, computer and other electronic equipment manufacturing industry	161072.1	140759.3
仪器仪表及文化办公用机械制造业	Instruments,Meters,Cultural and Office Machinery	4710.4	4710.4
工艺品及其他制造业	Handicraft and other stuff manufacturing industry	807.0	806.9
废弃资源和废旧材料回收加工业	Discarded resources and waste materials salvaging and processing industry		
电力、热力的生产和供应业	Electric power, heating power generating and supplying industry	857.9	657.9
燃气生产和供应业	Gas mining and supplying industry		
水的生产和供应业	Water processing and supplying industry		

Economic Indicators of Foreign Fund Industrial Enterprises Above Designated Size (2003)(Continued 6)

(10 000 yuan)

长期负债 小计 Long-term Liabilities	所有者权益 合计 Total Creditor Equity	实收资本 Total Capital Hold	产品 销售收入 Salas Revenue	产品 销售成本 Cost of Sales	产品 销售费用 Sales Expense	产品销售 税金及附加 Sales Tax and Extra Charges	营业利润 Operational profit
	6445.3	9134.9	69020.0	62836.7	2699.2		2389.3
13513.4	31554.5	24388.2	92523.7	67676.2	15784.2	3.0	5382.9
10985.0	41621.1	46341.4	69654.6	43392.5	13023.3		8790.8
	-2643.9	2216.3	556.6	450.0	9.2		33.5
	1430.5	809.0	1251.6	1167.7	49.9		7.5
	6400.1	6560.0	8074.4	7743.2	6.4		-208.6
3240.0	1387.0	2100.0	853.1	433.2	59.4	5.0	-21.3
	4194.8	2955.0	3361.3	2114.9	506.6	0.5	241.2
	600.7	398.0	1568.6	1290.6	92.5		55.2
1598.9	2773.6	3507.0	16623.0	15393.2	607.2		332.2
315.0	252.4	300.0	1154.1	1038.1	32.1		16.5
10.0	35254.1	9432.0	32240.9	24262.4	512.9	71.1	6318.8
7269.8	120506.9	48471.7	289307.3	138226.1	81382.5		56856.3
2061.5	6571.1	6673.0	8671.3	6900.6	351.4	5.2	825.1
2762.4	16714.1	12417.6	22238.4	17493.2	864.5	14.8	2193.6
	373.7	150.0	6001.5	4899.3	308.5	154.5	42.8
4966.4	2831.8	6740.0	15310.7	13923.3	938.3		-1017.4
2801.7	14751.8	14083.1	8512.3	5216.2	534.4	1.1	1206.2
	40116.4	31372.8	59922.0	42636.3	2399.2	6.1	10729.6
1011.0	37955.7	18096.6	50620.9	36421.8	1898.2	143.0	10315.9
	8861.0	4341.8	15141.1	9521.3	963.6	212.5	2042.6
156.8	21831.7	13775.1	42179.6	31779.1	2077.5	770.1	4860.8
20302.9	73768.0	55842.0	77824.6	53856.4	14206.7	215.9	-5869.4
	5557.9	7949.2	11617.4	8612.5	1931.9	64.5	563.6
	127.4	160.0	1495.3	1396.6	128.2		-63.1
199.9	1318.6	1300.0	1007.1	920.6	5.8		-55.7

10-17 全部规模以上三资工业企业经济指标(2003年）（续7）

单位：万元

分 组	Item	管理费用 Expenses for Management
有色金属矿采选业	Nonferrous Metals Mining and Dressing	
非金属矿采选业	Nonmetal Minerals Mining and Dressing	
其他采矿业	Other mining industry	
农副食品加工业	Agricultural products and non-stable food processing industry	881.5
食品制造业	Food Production	3011.8
饮料制造业	Beverage Production	3521.2
烟草加工业	Tobacco Processing	
纺织业	Textile Industry	120.0
纺织服装、鞋、帽制造业	Textile clothing, footwear and headgear industry	107.9
皮革、毛皮、羽毛(绒)及其制品业	Leather, fur, feather (eiderdown) and their products industry	354.8
木材加工及竹、藤、棕、草制品业	Timber Processing,Bamboo,Cane,Palm Fiber and Straw Products	114.9
家具制造业	Furniture Manufacturing	353.7
造纸及纸制品业	Papermaking and Record Medium Reproducton	183.3
印刷业、记录媒介的复制	Printing,Record Medium Reproduction	223.7
文教体育用品制造业	Cultural,Educational and Sports Goods	
石油加工、炼焦及核燃料加工业	Petroleum refining, coke making and nuclear	47.1
化学原料及化学制品制造业	Raw Chemical Materials and Chemical Products	1203.5
医药制造业	Medical and Pharmaceutical Products	10449.4
化学纤维制造业	Chemical Fiber	
橡胶制品业	Rubber Products	
塑料制品业	Plastic Products	420.3
非金属矿物制品业	Nonmetal Mineral Products	1463.8
黑色金属冶炼及压延加工业	Smelting and Pressing of Ferrous Metals	590.0
有色金属冶炼及压延加工业	Smelting and Pressing of Nonferrou Metals	1235.0
金属制品业	Metal Products	1174.5
通用设备制造	General equipment manufacturing industry	3706.6
专用设备制造业	Special Purpose Equipment	2644.5
交通运输设备制造业	Transport Equipment	2280.1
电气机械及器材制造业	Electric Equipment and Machinery	2720.3
通信设备、计算机及其他电子设备制造业	Communication equipment, computer and other electronic equipment manufacturing industry	11247.3
仪器仪表及文化办公用机械制造业	Instruments,Meters,Cultural and Office Machinery	441.2
工艺品及其他制造业	Handicraft and other stuff manufacturing industry	41.0
废弃资源和废旧材料回收加工业	Discarded resources and waste materials salvaging and processing industry	
电力、热力的生产和供应业	Electric power, heating power generating and supplying industry	120.0
燃气生产和供应业	Gas mining and supplying industry	
水的生产和供应业	Water processing and supplying industry	

Economic Indicators of Foreign Fund Industrial Enterprises Above Designated Size (2003)(Continued 7)

（10 000 yuan）

利润总额 Total Profits	亏损企业亏损总额 Total Loss of Deficit Enterprises	利税总额 Total Pre-tax Profits	本年应交增值税 Value Added Tax Payable
2410.5		3139.4	728.9
5252.2	527.4	8529.6	3274.4
6591.7	287.9	11033.1	4441.4
45.3	53.6	103.5	58.2
-7.0	7.0	-7.0	
-186.9	186.9	127.5	314.4
-21.3	21.3	-6.2	10.1
219.2		538.8	319.1
50.8		274.4	223.6
182.7	188.1	702.1	519.4
16.5		45.7	29.2
6287.6		7888.5	1529.8
66575.6	1289.0	92054.2	25478.6
795.1		968.0	167.7
2167.8	437.5	3486.7	1304.1
42.8		201.1	3.8
-1016.6	1016.6	-1014.1	2.5
1192.0		2101.0	907.9
10640.2	8.2	14211.7	3565.4
8686.5	1.7	10149.6	1320.1
2038.9		3658.8	1407.4
4997.9	276.4	7774.8	2006.8
-6210.9	12464.3	-3135.9	2859.1
518.4	116.4	1097.1	514.2
-63.0	63.0	-36.4	26.6
2.8		54.0	51.2

10-18　全部规模以上国有控股工业企业主要经济指标（2003年）

单位：万元

分　组	Item	企业单位数（个）Number of Enterprises (unit)	亏损企业 Loss Making Enterprises
总 计	**Total**	**303**	**132**
#市　区	Urban Area	258	111
按隶属关系分	Grouped by Administrative Relationship		
中央企业	Central Enterprises	67	20
省属企业	Provincial Enterprises	52	31
市属企业	Municipal Enterprises	184	81
市直属企业	Enterprises Directly Under the City Government	107	49
区、县属企业	Enterprises Under the District and County Government	77	32
区属企业	Enterprises Under the District Government	42	15
县属企业	Enterprises Under the County Government	35	17
其中：区县直属	Thereinto:Enterprises Directly Under the Government District and County	55	25
在总计中:亏损企业	Of the Total: Deficit Enterprises	132	132
按轻重工业分	Grouped by Ligth Industry and Heavy Industry		
轻工业	Light Industry	110	52
重工业	Heavy Industry	193	80
按企业规模分	Grouped by Size of Enterprises		
大型工业	Large-size	25	3
中型工业	Medium-size	64	22
小型工业	Small-size	214	107
按工业行业大类分	Grouped by Sector		
煤炭开采和洗选业	Coal Mining and Dressing		
石油和天然气开采业	Petroleum and Natural Gas Extraction		
黑色金属矿采选业	Ferrous Metals Mining and Dressing	1	1
有色金属矿采选业	Nonferrous Metals Mining and Dressing	3	
非金属矿采选业	Nonmetal Minerals Mining and Dressing		
其他采矿业	Other mining industry		
农副食品加工业	Agricultural products and non-stable food processing industry	7	3

Main Indicators of State-holding Share Industrial Enterprises Above Designated size (2003)

(10 000 yuan)

工业总产值（当年价）Gross Industrial Output Value (At Current Prices)	工业总产值（不变价）Gorss Industrial Output Value (At Constant Prices)	工业增加值（生产法）Value Added of Industry (Value-of Industrial Products Sales)	工业销售产值（当年价）Value of Industrial Products Sales (At Current Prices)	全部职工年平均人数（人）Annual Average Employers (person)	资产合计 Total Assets	流动资产小计 Total Circulating Funds
4538264.3	**5055267.5**	**1363459.6**	**4372793.2**	**286641.0**	**9378282.0**	**4915962.7**
4369512.6	4926663.1	1302022.6	4205748.1	267803.0	9049797.5	4778463.5
1988277.8	1884344.6	620317.8	1939488.4	154555.0	4735608.6	2478745.1
803985.1	861778.4	234235.4	764125.5	53813.0	1431194.2	777245.4
1746001.4	2309144.5	508906.4	1669179.3	78273.0	3211479.2	1659972.2
1610556.2	2182137.7	465329.2	1541268.6	67024.0	2918250.6	1545956.0
135445.2	127006.8	43577.2	127910.7	11249.0	293228.6	114016.2
86566.8	84924.2	29969.1	80431.3	6103.0	196901.8	76553.6
48878.4	42082.6	13608.1	47479.4	5146.0	96326.8	37462.6
86181.0	77419.5	27662.7	82723.3	8634.0	235231.9	83514.4
578040.7	548245.3	220750.7	557320.0	77100.0	2249476.1	904270.8
686328.9	564254.6	250903.6	675458.2	61919.0	1265825.0	490357.0
3851935.4	4491012.9	1112556.0	3697335.0	224722.0	8112457.0	4425605.7
2911820.5	3556705.9	853891.8	2852726.3	145306.0	6011479.4	3274396.4
1266465.5	1157918.4	386629.4	1186052.8	94971.0	2409691.0	1165918.5
359978.3	340643.2	122938.4	334014.1	46364.0	957111.6	475647.8
780.1	370.5	164.7	771.4	120.0	1929.5	678.8
8873.8	5369.4	4303.4	8807.0	1131.0	8828.5	2806.3
17507.0	13005.5	3915.5	16973.4	1813.0	27598.9	9882.2

10-18 全部规模以上国有控股工业企业主要经济指标（2003年）(续1)

单位：万元

分 组	Item	流动资产年平均余额 Annual Average Balance of Circulating Funds	固定资产小计 Fixed Assets
总 计	**Total**	**4489217.3**	**3474739.6**
#市 区	Urban Area	4357998.4	3317622.1
按隶属关系分	Grouped by Administrative Relationship		
中央企业	Central Enterprises	2201892.0	1930381.4
省属企业	Provincial Enterprises	722827.7	464547.4
市属企业	Municipal Enterprises	1564497.6	1079810.8
市直属企业	Enterprises Directly Under the City Government	1452466.0	964646.1
区、县属企业	Enterprises Under the District and County Government	112031.6	115164.7
区属企业	Enterprises Under the District Government	77721.6	60826.1
县属企业	Enterprises Under the County Government	34310.0	54338.6
其中：区县直属	Thereinto:Enterprises Directly Under the Government District and County	84577.8	89722.2
在总计中:亏损企业	Of the Total: Deficit Enterprises	899099.3	1164683.5
按轻重工业分	Grouped by Ligth Industry and Heavy Industry		
轻工业	Light Industry	481425.7	584130.1
重工业	Heavy Industry	4007791.6	2890609.5
按企业规模分	Grouped by Size of Enterprises		
大型工业	Large-size	2907427.4	2144530.5
中型工业	Medium-size	1132401.4	935964.1
小型工业	Small-size	449388.5	394245.0
按工业行业大类分	Grouped by Sector		
煤炭开采和洗选业	Coal Mining and Dressing		
石油和天然气开采业	Petroleum and Natural Gas Extraction		
黑色金属矿采选业	Ferrous Metals Mining and Dressing	724.8	1167.5
有色金属矿采选业	Nonferrous Metals Mining and Dressing	2345.5	4746.2
非金属矿采选业	Nonmetal Minerals Mining and Dressing		
其他采矿业	Other mining industry		
农副食品加工业	Agricultural products and non-stable food processing industry	9577.6	17344.0

Main Indicators of State-holding Share Industrial Enterprises Above Designated size (2003)(Continued 1)

(10 000 yuan)

固定资产原价合计 Origing Value of Fixed Assets	累计折旧 Accumulative Total Depreciation	本年折旧 Depreciation this year	固定资产净值年平均余额 Balance Net Value of Fixed Assets	负债合计 Total Liabilites	流动负债小计 Liquid Liabilities	长期负债小计 Long-term Liabilities
4737105.5	**1819116.8**	**219877.7**	**2782724.2**	**5918585.2**	**4666200.5**	**1221465.4**
4518335.3	1727555.7	214143.7	2639268.9	5702516.7	4513228.1	1161585.1
2559710.1	978953.0	116967.8	1518617.2	2816173.0	2143310.7	659391.9
629664.2	226388.7	22029.3	338003.4	1159505.0	903319.9	254970.3
1547731.2	613775.1	80880.6	926103.6	1942907.2	1619569.9	307103.2
1417048.5	573784.3	74464.3	832241.6	1753050.4	1472165.7	268121.7
130682.7	39990.8	6416.3	93862.0	189856.8	147404.2	38981.5
64095.0	24658.9	4468.4	42258.7	114538.2	85041.9	29241.0
66587.7	15331.9	1947.9	51603.3	75318.6	62362.3	9740.5
98599.0	30195.8	4108.5	71709.1	148941.7	116935.7	31788.2
1555588.4	534575.0	75479.1	1010063.8	1623813.2	1259132.9	353961.5
855618.5	365903.4	47141.5	510574.2	708883.2	546418.2	162259.8
3881487.0	1453213.4	172736.2	2272150.0	5209702.0	4119782.3	1059205.6
2953213.8	1133758.1	147416.5	1661011.2	3493059.6	2800042.6	679531.9
1262845.8	494973.5	52951.3	775982.2	1625574.4	1214993.9	397920.0
521045.9	190385.2	19509.9	345730.8	799951.2	651164.0	144013.5
1332.7	170.0	70.0	1188.4	2458.2	1678.2	780.0
8246.1	3499.9	1.6	4470.4	7123.7	2740.4	4383.3
23466.9	7250.9	197.4	15262.6	21947.0	20770.9	1030.4

10-18 全部规模以上国有控股工业企业主要经济指标（2003年）(续2)

单位：万元

分组	Item	所有者权益合计 Total Creditor's Equity	实收资本 Total Capital Hold
总 计	**Total**	**3442943.2**	**2012642.4**
#市 区	Urban Area	3330527.20	1954304.60
按隶属关系分	Grouped by Administrative Relationship		
中央企业	Central Enterprises	1915253.60	965329.00
省属企业	Provincial Enterprises	259117.60	356044.70
市属企业	Municipal Enterprises	1268572.00	691268.70
市直属企业	Enterprises Directly Under the City Government	1165200.20	600237.50
区、县属企业	Enterprises Under the District and County Government	103371.80	91031.20
区属企业	Enterprises Under the District Government	82363.60	65267.60
县属企业	Enterprises Under the County Government	21008.20	25763.60
其中：区县直属	Thereinto:Enterprises Directly Under the Government District and County	86290.20	59332.80
在总计中:亏损企业	Of the Total: Deficit Enterprises	613091.3	525033
按轻重工业分	Grouped by Ligth Industry and Heavy Industry		
轻工业	Light Industry	556941.80	378175.00
重工业	Heavy Industry	2886001.40	1634467.40
按企业规模分	Grouped by Size of Enterprises		
大型工业	Large-size	2514567.40	1143850.20
中型工业	Medium-size	771215.40	588316.80
小型工业	Small-size	157160.40	280475.40
按工业行业大类分	Grouped by Sector		
煤炭开采和洗选业	Coal Mining and Dressing		
石油和天然气开采业	Petroleum and Natural Gas Extraction		
黑色金属矿采选业	Ferrous Metals Mining and Dressing	-528.70	151.60
有色金属矿采选业	Nonferrous Metals Mining and Dressing	1704.80	1255.70
非金属矿采选业	Nonmetal Minerals Mining and Dressing		
其他采矿业	Other mining industry		
农副食品加工业	Agricultural products and non-stable food processing industry	5651.90	16082.00

Main Indicators of State-holding Share Industrial Enterprises Above Designated size (2003)(Continued 2)

(10 000 yuan)

产品销售收入 Sales Revenue	产品销售成本 Cost of Sales	产品销售费用 Sales Expense	产品销售税金及附加 Sales Tax and Extra Charges	营业利润 Operational profit	管理费用 Expenses for Management	利润总额 Total Profits	亏损企业亏损总额 Total Loss of Deficit Enterprises	利税总额 Total Pre-tax Profits	本年应交增值税 Value Added Tax Payable
4743136.7	**3545811.4**	**190494.9**	**29478.7**	**155968.1**	**495162.9**	**193644.4**	**94770.4**	**415872.3**	**192749.2**
4606321.0	3421430.9	186784.7	29092.1	168892.4	474775.6	193985.3	84503.7	409777.3	186699.9
2326214.2	1694333.1	40695.1	9510.1	55516.9	246811.6	87601.2	30412.7	172217.8	75106.5
779892.7	610401.5	51269.5	3328.5	12348.4	78561.4	12986.3	30606.6	55320.2	39005.4
1637029.8	1241076.8	98530.3	16640.1	88102.8	169789.9	93056.9	33751.1	188334.3	78637.3
1514456.7	1145863.8	93695.1	14668.6	80189.7	158263.8	85107.9	30048.3	173421.6	73645.1
122573.1	95213.0	4835.2	1971.5	7913.1	11526.1	7949.0	3702.8	14912.7	4992.2
77501.3	59566.6	2618.1	1848.5	6766.3	6164.9	6257.2	1787.9	11450.9	3345.2
45071.8	35646.4	2217.1	123.0	1146.8	5361.2	1691.8	1914.9	3461.8	1647
80135.0	63384.3	3271.9	868.3	2638.2	8689.0	5074.3	3000.3	9367.9	3425.3
790667.9	484646.9	33126.6	4707.4	-100914.9	93274.3	-94770.4	94770.4	-60489.2	29573.8
671427.9	480491.1	52594.1	11320.2	48139.0	71361.0	54143.7	18041	109566.7	44102.8
4071708.8	3065320.3	137900.8	18158.5	107829.1	423801.9	139500.7	76729.4	306305.6	148646.4
3279596.4	2377443.3	116039.5	12517.3	170777.9	314408.5	194632.6	7134.1	328731.9	121582
1165877.3	939664.9	57703.2	14107.5	-8550.0	132768.9	9767.7	56102.5	81551.7	57676.5
297663.0	228703.2	16752.2	2853.9	-6259.8	47985.5	-10755.9	31533.8	5588.7	13490.7
771.6	467.8	9.3	16.2	-74.0	130.5	-77.0	77.0	39.8	100.6
5773.8	4603.2			-191.6	1053.8	32.8		32.8	
12198.5	10121.0	488.4	129.6	-646.1	1571.2	-391.9	569.4	-234.9	27.4

10-18 全部规模以上国有控股工业企业主要经济指标（2003年）（续3）

单位：万元

分组	Item	企业单位数（个） Number of Enterprises (unit)	亏损企业 Loss Making Enterprises
食品制造业	Food Production	12	6
饮料制造业	Beverage Production	7	4
烟草加工业	Tobacco Processing	1	
纺织业	Textile Industry	14	9
纺织服装、鞋、帽制造业	Textile clothing, footwear and headgear industry		
皮革、毛皮、羽毛(绒)及其制品业	Leather, fur, feather (eiderdown) and their products industry	1	
木材加工及竹、藤、棕、草制品业	Timber Processing,Bamboo,Cane,Palm Fiber and Straw Products	2	2
家具制造业	Furniture Manufacturing	1	
造纸及纸制品业	Papermaking and Paper Products	4	2
印刷业、记录媒介的复制	Printing,Record Medium Reproduction	21	6
文教体育用品制造业	Cultural,Educational and Sports Goods	1	
石油加工、炼焦及核燃料加工业	Petroleum refining, coke making and nuclear	3	
化学原料及化学制品制造业	Raw Chemical Materials and Chemical Products	13	6
医药制造业	Medical and Pharmaceutical Products	13	5
化学纤维制造业	Chemical Fiber		
橡胶制品业	Rubber Products		
塑料制品业	Plastic Products	3	
非金属矿物制品业	Nonmetal Mineral Products	22	12
黑色金属冶炼及压延加工业	Smelting and Pressing of Ferrous Metals	4	3
有色金属冶炼及压延加工业	Smelting and Pressing of Nonferrou Metals	6	5
金属制品业	Metal Products	6	1
通用设备制造	General equipment manufacturing industry	19	10
专用设备制造业	Special Purpose Equipment	42	17
交通运输设备制造业	Transport Equipment	34	8
电气机械及器材制造业	Electric Equipment and Machinery	18	7
通信设备、计算机及其他电子设备制造业	Communication equipment, computer and other electronic equipment manufacturing industry	16	7
仪器仪表及文化办公用机械制造业	Instruments,Meters,Cultural and Office Machinery	13	7
工艺品及其他制造业	Handicraft and other stuff manufacturing industry	3	2
废弃资源和废旧材料回收加工业	Discarded resources and waste materials salvaging and processing industry		
电力、热力的生产和供应业	Electric power, heating power generating and supplying industry	4	3
燃气生产和供应业	Gas mining and supplying industry	1	1
水的生产和供应业	Water processing and supplying industry	8	5

Main Indicators of State-holding Share Industrial Enterprises Above Designated size (2003)(Continued 3)

(10 000 yuan)

工业总产值（当年价） Gross Industrial Output Value (At Current Prices)	工业总产值（不变价） Gorss Industrial Output Value (At Constant Prices)	工业增加值（生产法） Value-Added of Industry (Value of Industrial Products Sales)	工业销售产值（当年价） Value of Industrial Products Sales (At Current Prices)	全部职工年平均人数（人） Annual Average Employers (person)	资产合计 Total Assets	流动资产小计 Total Circulating Funds
16387.0	10047.9	5334.0	15045.4	2204.0	16813.5	7933.7
64991.3	36913.4	27248.6	66216.3	2081.0	93095.9	34404.9
1066.0	1247.1	454.4	1881.7	166.0	3830.0	842.4
165407.4	152123.5	42856.1	165464.0	30589.0	264402.1	113193.5
7069.0	4177.3	1836.6	6973.8	1185.0	23196.4	16526.9
2100.8	2332.5	649.8	1858.7	499.0	15974.7	3705.3
299.6	251.9	124.9	302.9	310.0	2683.7	1575.3
3157.3	2547.3	1016.8	4940.0	333.0	25042.5	8036.5
148043.9	138682.8	59650.6	143128.6	6770.0	274044.7	101056.2
312.8	312.8	152.8	312.8	82.0	825.1	810.6
220747.7	45512.9	42245.2	225592.6	2207.0	122288.1	44320.1
148189.1	130732.2	43947.2	140275.3	20638.0	459343.6	149317.4
163720.8	136585.7	65747.5	153992.5	7284.0	227051.7	104396.3
6511.7	6511.7	2932.8	6401.3	275.0	11249.9	6004.8
39188.1	31471.5	9381.1	36986.7	7425.0	147821.5	45910.7
46896.5	48964.9	15002.5	45461.6	4374.0	127749.5	61216.6
13059.4	14163.8	4525.4	9340.3	470.0	16723.9	8196.7
8345.4	7947.9	3730.0	7799.5	703.0	19789.9	8433.9
212728.9	234797.9	89883.9	203984.6	9233.0	394687.8	295854.1
482711.9	564143.4	138528.4	461917.1	41535.0	1218218.7	583717.4
1458730.9	1636204.9	406133.0	1414965.3	81421.0	2963296.1	1903639.3
492577.6	576131.1	122494.1	490446.2	20300.0	909229.4	534543.3
541903.2	1092288.1	130947.5	488473.2	19492.0	1017963.7	582581.7
101475.7	100344.4	23948.4	89020.5	10209.0	247742.8	140301.6
350.1	355.0	90.0	363.2	123.0	1784.0	421.7
121876.0	52444.4	96003.9	121876.0	8627.0	562938.2	112862.4
2774.7	608.1	216.9	2774.7	1086.0	14816.4	6099.8
40480.6	8677.7	19993.6	40446.6	3956.0	157321.3	26692.3

10-18 全部规模以上国有控股工业主要经济指标（2003年）（续4）

单位：万元

分 组	Item	流动资产年平均余额 Annual Average Balance of Circulating Funds	固定资产小计 Fixed Assets
食品制造业	Food Production	8112.9	5697.3
饮料制造业	Beverage Production	40167.0	42730.9
烟草加工业	Tobacco Processing	841.3	2385.4
纺织业	Textile Industry	99980.9	133186.8
纺织服装、鞋、帽制造业	Textile clothing, footwear and headgear industry		
皮革、毛皮、羽毛(绒)及其制品业	Leather, fur, feather (eiderdown) and their products industry	12592.4	5819.1
木材加工及竹、藤、棕、草制品业	Timber Processing,Bamboo,Cane,Palm Fiber and Straw Products	4283.9	11654.3
家具制造业	Furniture Manufacturing	1575.3	1108.4
造纸及纸制品业	Papermaking and Paper Products	9354.7	16895.1
印刷业、记录媒介的复制	Printing,Record Medium Reproduction	105809.5	117360.8
文教体育用品制造业	Cultural,Educational and Sports Goods	810.6	14.5
石油加工、炼焦及核燃料加工业	Petroleum refining, coke making and nuclear	40582.8	76566.3
化学原料及化学制品制造业	Raw Chemical Materials and Chemical Products	132862.6	247608.3
医药制造业	Medical and Pharmaceutical Products	97722.8	73560.3
化学纤维制造业	Chemical Fiber		
橡胶制品业	Rubber Products		
塑料制品业	Plastic Products	6013.6	4975.7
非金属矿物制品业	Nonmetal Mineral Products	42845.5	75164.9
黑色金属冶炼及压延加工业	Smelting and Pressing of Ferrous Metals	60029.5	58871.4
有色金属冶炼及压延加工业	Smelting and Pressing of Nonferrou Metals	8003.3	8315.0
金属制品业	Metal Products	6738.0	9233.0
通用设备制造	General equipment manufacturing industry	236626.3	81650.3
专用设备制造业	Special Purpose Equipment	568209.6	550743.5
交通运输设备制造业	Transport Equipment	1618822.2	768082.7
电气机械及器材制造业	Electric Equipment and Machinery	509844.3	238830.1
通信设备、计算机及其他电子设备制造业	Communication equipment, computer and other electronic equipment manufacturing industry	565101.6	265449.9
仪器仪表及文化办公用机械制造业	Instruments,Meters,Cultural and Office Machinery	139257.5	91491.7
工艺品及其他制造业	Handicraft and other stuff manufacturing industry	399.0	735.1
废弃资源和废旧材料回收加工业	Discarded resources and waste materials salvaging and processing industry		
电力、热力的生产和供应业	Electric power, heating power generating and supplying industry	125138.5	448564.1
燃气生产和供应业	Gas mining and supplying industry	5766.7	7817.9
水的生产和供应业	Water processing and supplying industry	29077.1	106969.1

Main Indicators of State-holding Share Industrial Enterprises Above Designated size (2003)(Continued 4)

(10 000 yuan)

固定资产原价合计 Origing Value of Fixed Assets	累计折旧 Accumulative Total Depreciation	本年折旧 Depreciation this year	固定资产净值年平均余额 Balance Net Value of Fixed Assets	负债合计 Total Liabilites	流动负债小计 Liquid Liabilities	长期负债小计 Long-term Liabilities
9160.0	4408.4	739.8	6062.7	13313.5	12595.1	718.3
64473.1	24416.0	3265.6	41242.1	59734.5	48518.8	11215.7
2822.4	436.9	8.5	4882.1	980.4	980.4	
209829.3	91584.2	12821.6	109782.8	177569.5	152818.0	24751.0
8546.5	4216.0	249.0	4431.3	19186.0	9739.4	9446.5
12501.8	1387.0	100.8	11263.1	9554.6	7486.9	2067.7
1340.8	279.2	4.2	1061.6	1873.0	1353.0	520.0
17589.9	1519.0	102.5	16519.1	24404.2	23407.6	996.5
182636.6	75822.1	11598.3	107930.3	113743.2	81529.7	32213.4
52.9	38.4	3.2	14.5	64.4	64.4	
62375.7	19841.0	1390.2	44545.4	99751.8	69924.8	29827.0
297579.8	118976.5	9109.3	208624.3	256323.2	171276.5	85000.1
91115.5	34304.2	5052.3	53120.9	104474.4	83130.6	21331.8
6866.6	2399.9	513.3	4520.1	5409.8	3348.3	2061.5
81934.5	29583.3	1735.1	53274.8	109534.3	79843.3	28630.8
66739.7	16626.1	3713.1	50269.6	124207.4	98206.0	25849.6
11517.7	3423.5	534.4	7997.4	16742.6	12924.4	3818.2
14668.5	5442.1	1345.1	10548.0	12201.9	8288.6	3850.9
116034.4	50338.2	6130.8	63241.3	309016.6	291577.0	17336.6
733951.7	259445.3	21930.4	452630.0	801261.9	589786.8	198057.4
1031527.7	423095.1	50225.2	491633.1	1983337.8	1605083.4	377816.2
371573.7	167284.5	25743.9	200947.4	593506.0	519394.5	69941.4
396846.9	140876.2	14501.3	238319.4	637993.4	454041.9	172641.2
136757.3	57874.3	4353.3	77004.6	169100.6	148834.3	20265.9
896.3	222.7	28.6	701.9	1088.2	612.2	476.0
609403.1	196269.4	33711.0	412697.0	158930.8	133250.9	25679.9
10816.2	3175.5	166.5	7699.4	8564.3	7101.4	1462.9
154501.2	74911.0	10531.4	80838.6	75188.0	25892.8	49295.2

10-18 全部规模以上国有控股工业企业主要经济指标（2003年）（续5）

单位：万元

分 组	Item	所有者权益 合计 Total Creditor's Equity	实收资本 Total Capital Hold
食品制造业	Food Production	3500.0	7301.5
饮料制造业	Beverage Production	33361.4	36178.8
烟草加工业	Tobacco Processing	2849.6	1514.8
纺织业	Textile Industry	86832.6	40843.3
纺织服装、鞋、帽制造业	Textile clothing, footwear and headgear industry		
皮革、毛皮、羽毛(绒)及其制品业	Leather, fur, feather (eiderdown) and their products industry	4010.4	10620.3
木材加工及竹、藤、棕、草制品业	Timber Processing,Bamboo,Cane,Palm Fiber and Straw Products	6420.1	1666.9
家具制造业	Furniture Manufacturing	810.7	837.3
造纸及纸制品业	Papermaking and Paper Products	638.3	4832.5
印刷业、记录媒介的复制	Printing,Record Medium Reproduction	160301.5	84785.4
文教体育用品制造业	Cultural,Educational and Sports Goods	760.7	200.0
石油加工、炼焦及核燃料加工业	Petroleum refining, coke making and nuclear	22536.3	22364.4
化学原料及化学制品制造业	Raw Chemical Materials and Chemical Products	203020.4	146416.7
医药制造业	Medical and Pharmaceutical Products	122577.3	77756.9
化学纤维制造业	Chemical Fiber		
橡胶制品业	Rubber Products		
塑料制品业	Plastic Products	5840.1	5091.1
非金属矿物制品业	Nonmetal Mineral Products	38287.2	28149.4
黑色金属冶炼及压延加工业	Smelting and Pressing of Ferrous Metals	3542.1	48220.3
有色金属冶炼及压延加工业	Smelting and Pressing of Nonferrou Metals	-18.7	8361.7
金属制品业	Metal Products	7588.0	9480.2
通用设备制造	General equipment manufacturing industry	85671.2	73895.2
专用设备制造业	Special Purpose Equipment	416627.2	352345.5
交通运输设备制造业	Transport Equipment	976105.9	642372.7
电气机械及器材制造业	Electric Equipment and Machinery	315723.4	65823.4
通信设备、计算机及其他电子设备制造业	Communication equipment, computer and other electronic equipment manufacturing industry	367398.7	173936.4
仪器仪表及文化办公用机械制造业	Instruments,Meters,Cultural and Office Machinery	78642.2	48098.8
工艺品及其他制造业	Handicraft and other stuff manufacturing industry	695.8	645.7
废弃资源和废旧材料回收加工业	Discarded resources and waste materials salvaging and processing industry		
电力、热力的生产和供应业	Electric power, heating power generating and supplying industry	404007.4	48867.8
燃气生产和供应业	Gas mining and supplying industry	6252.1	7436.2
水的生产和供应业	Water processing and supplying industry	82133.3	47109.9

Main Indicators of State-holding Share Industrial Enterprises Above Designated size (2003)(Continued 5)

(10 000 yuan)

产品销售收入 Sales Revenue	产品销售成本 Cost of Sales	产品销售费用 Sales Expense	产品销售税金及附加 Sales Tax and Extra Charges	营业利润 Operational profit	管理费用 Expenses for Management	利润总额 Total Profits	亏损企业亏损总额 Total Loss of Deficit Enterprises	利税总额 Total Pre-tax Profits	本年应交增值税 Value Added Tax Payable
14683.3	9988.5	2391.0	86.6	-321.0	2555.3	-644.8	940.2	625.4	1183.6
65667.0	40091.4	6767.8	6714.4	8400.6	3889.1	9170.9	542.2	21953.4	6068.1
2199.7	1556.8	6.6	19.5	212.1	428.1	227.2		442.0	195.3
162974.4	144263.1	2381.2	646.5	-591.2	13890.4	-565.7	4207.6	7506.5	7425.7
7053.6	5492.8	506.2	11.0	101.2	1038.1	115.1		237.6	111.5
1838.8	1317.2	126.0	13.7	-1651.5	753.3	-2935.1	2935.1	-2802.5	118.9
275.6	158.6	80.3	2.1	0.4	40.8	0.4		28.5	26.0
3685.8	3022.7	661.7	9.1	-673.8	686.4	-663.6	739.3	-589.2	65.3
147534.8	100717.9	4654.1	1620.5	21467.4	17452.7	22653.1	736.7	33870.5	9596.9
251.5	116.0	1.5	2.7	186.0	36.3	186.0		216.3	27.6
225579.2	203999.4	980.0	3081.5	7532.8	4762.7	6095.0		18028.7	8852.2
142440.5	111378.6	3272.7	700.4	1487.6	23698.7	5335.3	1472.3	13429.6	7393.9
155496.1	85632.2	32429.9	1650.1	18591.5	15159.1	24224.7	1480.8	39313.8	13439.0
6559.3	3676.5	191.4	30.1	1623.1	899.3	1813.9		2495.5	651.5
29239.6	23588.9	1342.1	255.3	-2975.6	5758.8	-2474.4	2876.4	-346.9	1872.2
42503.4	34581.9	5766.3	334.4	-6939.0	5235.2	-7461.7	7481.6	-6160.5	966.8
9286.9	7255.3	176.4	9.0	938.0	516.1	924.5	671.8	1040.3	106.8
7536.8	5656.8	298.5	16.1	234.8	1001.2	220.0	65.0	710.8	474.7
201868.9	136197.3	8550.4	1308.2	27642.3	26320.4	29186.4	2174.3	45990.7	15496.1
477015.1	364341.9	19238.6	2543.5	13479.0	65713.3	14466.9	19991.0	39064.3	22053.9
1530585.7	1238304.8	37411.9	2820.4	70538.6	160275.5	86341.1	546.8	125906.4	36744.9
480193.6	368630.4	31156.4	3319.3	8930.0	64769.7	8487.3	5285.9	33191.7	21385.1
486447.7	374197.6	27482.3	2000.0	20314.5	44762.4	17420.3	20595.1	35657.0	16236.7
94496.3	75733.1	2824.2	174.0	-2954.6	16978.7	-2486.1	4595.9	-883.2	1428.9
274.3	193.0	16.2	2.5	-32.3	89.2	-25.9	32.9	-14.5	8.9
385203.6	154732.3		1536.1	-28048.4	8315.7	-15782.4	15861.7	3555.5	17801.8
2774.7	2815.6	586.6	16.1	-1553.6	1089.6	-648.5	648.5	-471.7	160.7
40726.6	32978.8	696.9	409.8	940.9	6291.3	900.6	242.9	4038.6	2728.2

10-19 全部规模以上股份制工业企业主要经济指标(2003年)

单位：万元

分　组	Item	企业单位数（个） Number of Enterprises (unit)	亏损企业 Loss Making Enterprises
总　计	**Total**	**332**	**105**
#市　区	Urban Area	265	80
按隶属关系分	Grouped by Administrative Relationship		
中央企业	Central Enterprises	19	5
省属企业	Provincial Enterprises	25	8
市属企业	Municipal Enterprises	288	92
市直属企业	Enterprises Directly Under the City Government	110	35
区县属企业	Enterprises Under the District and County Government	178	57
区属企业	Enterprises Under the District Government	115	34
县属企业	Enterprises Under the County Government	63	23
其中：区县直属	Thereinto:Enterprises Directly Under the District and County Government	24	9
在总计中:亏损企业	Of the Total: Deficit Enterprises	105	105
按轻重工业分	Grouped by Ligth Industry and Heavy Industry		
轻工业	Light Industry	132	51
重工业	Heavy Industry	200	54
按企业规模分	Grouped by Size of Enterprises		
大型工业	Large size	13	1
中型工业	Medium-size	50	11
小型工业	Small-size	269	93
按工业行业大类分	Grouped by Sector		
煤炭开采和洗选业	Coal Mining and Dressing		
石油和天然气开采业	Petroleum and Natural Gas Extraction		
黑色金属矿采选业	Ferrous Metals Mining and Dressing		
有色金属矿采选业	Nonferrous Metals Mining and Dressing		
非金属矿采选业	Nonmetal Minerals Mining and Dressing	1	
其他采矿业	Other mining industry		
农副食品加工业	Agricultural products and non-stable food processing industry	18	1
食品制造业	Food Production	11	5
饮料制造业	Beverage Production	6	3

Main Indicators of Share-holding Corporation Industrial Enterprises Above Designated size (2003)

(10 000 yuan)

工业总产值（当年价） Gross Industrial Output Value (At Current Prices)	工业总产值（不变价） Gorss Industrial Output Value (At Constant Prices)	工业增加值（生产法） Value-Added of Industry (Value of Industrial Products Sales)	工业销售产值（当年价） Value of Industrial Products Sales (At Current Prices)	全部职工年平均人数（人） Annual Average Employers (person)
3998511.0	**4777359.1**	**1259297.6**	**3827530.4**	**186328**
3795508.7	4573772.0	1199660.1	3628533.6	166259
1147725.6	1303379.2	318596.9	1100806.1	88373
1139558.4	1193677.5	393468.4	1112295.8	35459
1711227.0	2280302.4	547232.3	1614428.5	62496
1189307.9	1783268.7	381249.7	1116866.3	34209
521919.1	497033.7	165982.6	497562.2	28287
374960.9	344403.3	123308.4	355058.4	17195
146958.2	152630.4	42674.2	142503.8	11092
79239.9	77399.3	24369.5	74645.4	4678
361306.7	404490.3	101067.3	347387.2	40880
1216405.4	1117392.8	455521.3	1196932.0	49362
2782105.6	3659966.3	803776.3	2630598.4	136966
1927800.5	2584844.4	506122.4	1874833.1	91514
1299813.9	1427626.7	483286.0	1211765.0	56650
770896.6	764888.0	269889.2	740932.3	38164
474.3	474.3	191.4	468.7	75
195007.1	168414.1	54068.0	191056.9	2222
65951.5	35577.8	21022.5	63546.9	2738
71192.5	44433.5	28911.5	71788.9	1556

10-19 全部规模以上股份制工业企业主要经济指标(2003年)(续1)

单位：万元

分组	Item	资产合计 Total Assets	流动资产小计 Total Circulating Funds
总 计	**Total**	**7028234.4**	**3988112.9**
#市 区	Urban Area	6666204.0	3830263.1
按隶属关系分	Grouped by Administrative Relationship		
中央企业	Central Enterprises	3054596.8	1760734.4
省属企业	Provincial Enterprises	1393096.4	813550.9
市属企业	Municipal Enterprises	2580541.2	1413827.6
市直属企业	Enterprises Directly Under the City Government	1921196.6	1086989.8
区县属企业	Enterprises Under the District and County Government	659344.6	326837.8
区属企业	Enterprises Under the District Government	460423.9	228103.3
县属企业	Enterprises Under the County Government	198920.7	98734.5
其中：区县直属	Thereinto:Enterprises Directly Under the District and County Government	156385.3	64533.7
在总计中:亏损企业	Of the Total: Deficit Enterprises	1233971.4	655411.3
按轻重工业分	Grouped by Ligth Industry and Heavy Industry		
轻工业	Light Industry	1642154.6	855012.7
重工业	Heavy Industry	5386079.8	3133100.2
按企业规模分	Grouped by Size of Enterprises		
大型工业	Large size	3541739.1	2073410.5
中型工业	Medium-size	2351014.3	1199340.2
小型工业	Small-size	1135481.0	715362.2
按工业行业大类分	Grouped by Sector		
煤炭开采和洗选业	Coal Mining and Dressing		
石油和天然气开采业	Petroleum and Natural Gas Extraction		
黑色金属矿采选业	Ferrous Metals Mining and Dressing		
有色金属矿采选业	Nonferrous Metals Mining and Dressing		
非金属矿采选业	Nonmetal Minerals Mining and Dressing	357.9	232.6
其他采矿业	Other mining industry		
农副食品加工业	Agricultural products and non-stable food processing industry	117830.9	60042.0
食品制造业	Food Production	52443.3	24611.6
饮料制造业	Beverage Production	113306.2	41072.8

Main Indicators of Share-holding Corporation Industrial Enterprises Above Designated size (2003)(Continued 1)

（10 000 yuan）

流动资产年平均余额 Annual Average Balance of Circulating Funds	固定资产小计 Fixed Assets	固定资产原价合计 Origing Value of Fixed Assets	累计折旧 Accumulative Total Depreciation	本年折旧 Depreciation this year	固定资产净值年平均余额 Balance Net Value of Fixed Assets
3643694.4	**2217018.7**	**2816391.9**	**997501.1**	**136085.2**	**1688947.2**
3500002.7	2057087.5	2617575.0	929665.9	128413.9	1555051.5
1502732.4	1020250.7	1306848.4	501240.7	50700.2	746727.2
771212.5	405817.5	508213.5	171317.4	29360.8	284416.3
1369749.5	790950.5	1001330.0	324943.0	56024.2	657803.7
1070607.6	567112.9	765652.9	262871.9	41276.5	489553.5
299141.9	223837.6	235677.1	62071.1	14747.7	168250.2
210337.6	139573.3	138069.6	39665.9	8858.4	100135.2
88804.3	84264.3	97607.5	22405.2	5889.3	68115.0
70483.8	39891.8	50537.8	19582.4	3082.3	31061.2
642555.0	448737.0	568418.3	193907.7	24108.2	368527.2
840177.3	555507.1	676201.7	235054.0	33805.5	449006.6
2803517.1	1661511.6	2140190.2	762447.1	102279.7	1239940.6
1809903.9	1079901.2	1449198.6	554581.5	63788.9	744763.6
1165718.0	825195.9	951740.8	290784.8	47385.7	682907.5
668072.5	311921.6	415452.5	152134.8	24910.6	261276.1
197.7	125.3	168.5	44.0	14.0	124.5
47864.9	37510.1	38504.9	11731.4	3121.4	26011.7
22652.6	23065.4	15908.5	6743.3	903.3	10555.1
47551.0	52018.7	79374.5	28288.4	4028.3	50976.3

10-19 全部规模以上股份制工业企业主要经济指标(2003年)(续2)

单位：万元

分　组	Item	负债合计 Total Liabilites	流动负债小计 Liquid Liabilities
总　计	**Total**	**4105795.2**	**3325131.7**
#市　区	Urban Area	3880273.7	3175219.4
按隶属关系分	Grouped by Administrative Relationship		
中央企业	Central Enterprises	1961579.0	1512466.1
省属企业	Provincial Enterprises	829812.6	734626.7
市属企业	Municipal Enterprises	1314403.6	1078038.9
市直属企业	Enterprises Directly Under the City Government	934487.1	774656.8
区县属企业	Enterprises Under the District and County Government	379916.5	303382.1
区属企业	Enterprises Under the District Government	250930.5	211161.8
县属企业	Enterprises Under the County Government	128986.0	92220.3
其中：区县直属	Thereinto:Enterprises Directly Under the District and County Government	76789.9	65095.1
在总计中:亏损企业	Of the Total: Deficit Enterprises	822333.5	646042.6
按轻重工业分	Grouped by Ligth Industry and Heavy Industry		
轻工业	Light Industry	904476.6	769519.7
重工业	Heavy Industry	3201318.6	2555612.0
按企业规模分	Grouped by Size of Enterprises		
大型工业	Large size	2150229.5	1733359.7
中型工业	Medium-size	1295135.8	1045401.9
小型工业	Small-size	660429.9	546370.1
按工业行业大类分	Grouped by Sector		
煤炭开采和洗选业	Coal Mining and Dressing		
石油和天然气开采业	Petroleum and Natural Gas Extraction		
黑色金属矿采选业	Ferrous Metals Mining and Dressing		
有色金属矿采选业	Nonferrous Metals Mining and Dressing		
非金属矿采选业	Nonmetal Minerals Mining and Dressing	121.0	121.0
其他采矿业	Other mining industry		
农副食品加工业	Agricultural products and non-stable food processing industry	79210.1	64620.8
食品制造业	Food Production	36817.3	32169.9
饮料制造业	Beverage Production	77049.5	69174.7

Main Indicators of Share-holding Corporation Industrial Enterprises Above Designated size (2003)(Continued 2)

（10 000 yuan）

长期负债小计 Long-term Liabilities	所有者权益合计 Total Creditor's Equity	实收资本 Total Capital Hold	产品销售收入 Sales Revenue	产品销售成本 Cost of Sales	产品销售费用 Sales Expense	产品销售税金及附加 Sales Tax and Extra Charges	营业利润 Operational profit
722300.9	**2918909.0**	**1633900.7**	**3952328.1**	**2986002.7**	**285390.4**	**22617.9**	**265895.0**
654678.8	2782400.1	1530396.3	3753484.1	2821324.4	275492.6	21838.0	263775.2
435836.1	1089487.6	595984.2	1226994.9	956812.8	28273.6	3158.4	58133.3
94974.8	563283.8	325861.0	1118176.6	804818.5	142092.4	4238.2	88106.5
191490.0	1266137.6	712055.5	1607156.6	1224371.4	115024.4	15221.3	119655.2
124595.1	986709.5	503675.0	1125021.8	838599.5	78770.5	10773.1	98552.4
66894.9	279428.1	208380.5	482134.8	385771.9	36253.9	4448.2	21102.8
38116.3	209493.4	130374.6	341393.8	267003.1	27439.0	3835.1	20209.9
28778.6	69934.7	78005.9	140741.0	118768.8	8814.9	613.1	892.9
11694.7	79595.4	50792.3	73333.3	54123.0	7160.6	868.0	3708.0
160819.9	411637.9	344112.2	319912.7	261050.1	27667.8	2356.3	-39707.3
126513.6	737678.0	444656.6	1175274.3	797498.4	179226.9	10738.5	102411.5
595787.3	2181231.0	1189244.1	2777053.8	2188504.3	106163.5	11879.4	163483.5
403445.0	1388291.0	750509.1	2006569.3	1594552.0	73990.9	5945.5	122029.0
232787.3	1055566.9	518449.7	1210012.8	803081.1	169270.0	11922.2	107792.5
86068.6	475051.1	364941.9	735746.0	588369.6	42129.5	4750.2	36073.5
	236.9	165.8	468.7	258.6	69.3	69.5	32.2
13903.4	38620.8	34600.0	192025.4	177043.1	6589.8	231.6	3057.4
4646.5	15626.0	13072.9	62548.4	43022.8	13665.1	77.4	1702.1
7874.8	36256.7	43870.9	71355.3	43358.3	7546.6	6508.9	9043.9

10-19 全部规模以上股份制工业企业主要经济指标(2003年)（续 3）

单位：万元

分 组	Item	管理费用 Expenses for Management
总 计	**Total**	**331907.8**
#市 区	Urban Area	312725.4
按隶属关系分	Grouped by Administrative Relationship	
中央企业	Central Enterprises	156696.4
省属企业	Provincial Enterprises	65102.1
市属企业	Municipal Enterprises	110109.3
市直属企业	Enterprises Directly Under the City Government	79801.9
区县属企业	Enterprises Under the District and County Government	30307.4
区属企业	Enterprises Under the District Government	20973.2
县属企业	Enterprises Under the County Government	9334.2
其中：区县直属	Thereinto:Enterprises Directly Under the District and County Government	5997.9
在总计中:亏损企业	Of the Total: Deficit Enterprises	52310.1
按轻重工业分	Grouped by Ligth Industry and Heavy Industry	
轻工业	Light Industry	69643.6
重工业	Heavy Industry	262264.2
按企业规模分	Grouped by Size of Enterprises	
大型工业	Large size	180819.3
中型工业	Medium-size	94534.9
小型工业	Small-size	56553.6
按工业行业大类分	Grouped by Sector	
煤炭开采和洗选业	Coal Mining and Dressing	
石油和天然气开采业	Petroleum and Natural Gas Extraction	
黑色金属矿采选业	Ferrous Metals Mining and Dressing	
有色金属矿采选业	Nonferrous Metals Mining and Dressing	
非金属矿采选业	Nonmetal Minerals Mining and Dressing	32.2
其他采矿业	Other mining industry	
农副食品加工业	Agricultural products and non-stable food processing industry	3608.9
食品制造业	Food Production	3944.4
饮料制造业	Beverage Production	4313.6

Main Indicators of Share-holding Corporation Industrial Enterprises Above Designated size (2003)(Continued 3)

（10 000 yuan）

利润总额 Total Profits	亏损企业 亏损总额 Total Loss of Deficit Enterprises	利税总额 Total Pre-tax Profits	本年应交 增值税 Value Added Tax Payable
305629.9	**40704.3**	**484649.3**	**156401.5**
300122.5	35513.5	471823.7	149863.2
76180.9	1959.7	107178.3	27839.0
110384.5	8190.8	180261.1	65638.4
119064.5	30553.8	197209.9	62924.1
100408.7	23696.3	160205.7	49023.9
18655.8	6857.5	37004.2	13900.2
18055.8	2431.3	31663.2	9772.3
600.0	4426.2	5341.0	4127.9
6213.2	1115.5	10618.1	3536.9
-40704.3	40704.3	-29690.5	8657.5
121884.3	15169.2	199754.2	67131.4
183745.6	25535.1	284895.1	89270.1
147205.1	144.4	210945.6	57795.0
127804.9	23422.4	212322.7	72595.6
30619.9	17137.5	61381.0	26010.9
32.2		116.6	14.9
3465.3	124.5	4921.1	1224.2
1574.6	687.3	3261.6	1609.6
9414.7	252.2	21809.9	5886.3

10-19 全部规模以上股份制工业企业主要经济指标(2003年)（续4）

单位：万元

分　组	Item	企业单位数(个) Number of Enterprises (unit)	亏损企业 Loss Making Enterprises
烟草加工业	Tobacco Processing		
纺织业	Textile Industry	9	6
纺织服装、鞋、帽制造业	Textile clothing, footwear and headgear industry	4	2
皮革、毛皮、羽毛(绒)及其制品业	Leather, fur, feather (eiderdown) and their products industry	1	1
木材加工及竹、藤、棕、草制品业	Timber Processing,Bamboo,Cane,Palm Fiber and Straw Products	1	1
家具制造业	Furniture Manufacturing	6	1
造纸及纸制品业	Papermaking and Paper products	9	6
印刷业、记录媒介的复制	Printing,Record Medium Reproduction	10	3
文教体育用品制造业	Cultural,Educational and Sports Goods	1	
石油加工、炼焦及核燃料加工业	Petroleum refining, coke making and nuclear fuel processing industry	3	
化学原料及化学制品制造业	Raw Chemical Materials and Chemical Products	22	6
医药制造业	Medical and Pharmaceutical Products	33	11
化学纤维制造业	Chemical Fiber	1	1
橡胶制品业	Rubber Products	2	
塑料制品业	Plastic Products	10	1
非金属矿物制品业	Nonmetal Mineral Products	21	9
黑色金属冶炼及压延加工业	Smelting and Pressing of Ferrous Metals	5	3
有色金属冶炼及压延加工业	Smelting and Pressing of Nonferrou Metals	9	4
金属制品业	Metal Products	10	2
通用设备制造	General equipment manufacturing industry	24	5
专用设备制造业	Special Purpose Equipment	21	4
交通运输设备制造业	Transport Equipment	19	3
电气机械及器材制造业	Electric Equipment and Machinery	36	13
通信设备、计算机及其他电子设备制造业	Communication equipment, computer and other electronic equipment manufacturing industry	24	7
仪器仪表及文化办公用	Instruments,Meters,Cultural and Office	8	3
工艺品及其他制造业	Handicraft and other stuff manufacturing industry	3	3
废弃资源和废旧材料回收加工业	Discarded resources and waste materials salvaging and processing industry		
电力、热力的生产和供应业	Electric power, heating power generating and supplying industry	3	1
燃气生产和供应业	Gas mining and supplying industry		
水的生产和供应业	Water processing and supplying industry	1	

Main Indicators of Share-holding Corporation Industrial Enterprises Above Designated size (2003)(Continued 4)

(10 000 yuan)

工业总产值（当年价）Gross Industrial Output Value (At Current Prices)	工业总产值（不变价）Gorss Industrial Output Value (At Constant Prices)	工业增加值（生产法）Value-Added of Industry (Value of Industrial Products Sales)	工业销售产值（当年价）Value of Industrial Products (At Current Prices)	全部职工年平均人数（人）Annual Average Employers (person)
78869.9	72855.0	18878.3	80469.3	13584
18216.6	18216.6	7092.2	23311.3	1930
9308.6	8259.5	2234.0	7852.3	173
1038.2	1072.8	254.9	863.8	75
6629.3	7023.3	2576.5	6723.1	1599
24695.0	21367.3	7888.1	24594.6	2663
42984.8	45968.8	17554.8	42050.2	1593
620.0	601.0	173.5	590.0	70
2832.9	2930.1	830.1	2949.4	88
166748.6	156786.4	49603.2	153843.6	18025
576653.4	566984.6	256456.6	563610.0	13197
2263.3	2263.3	487.3	2096.5	85
2562.3	2622.2	489.4	2520.2	120
18096.2	19147.2	5929.9	16469.2	759
50222.3	45977.9	16879.9	51253.7	3493
17438.4	17563.0	4133.1	18274.2	597
70446.7	70130.1	24234.2	60784.2	2221
13235.3	12039.9	6094.2	13174.1	1395
107335.2	124232.3	42622.8	98424.2	5115
367564.7	439582.4	110667.0	352155.3	22323
1332663.5	1563603.7	367134.8	1286117.1	62257
112529.6	117537.9	50432.3	110513.2	5406
519081.5	1090518.2	131565.4	469814.3	12562
103966.5	102867.0	24881.0	92223.6	8547
5696.5	5696.5	1606.8	5796.1	875
12169.8	10937.0	3859.4	12179.0	850
2016.5	1675.4	544.5	2016.5	135

10-19 全部规模以上股份制工业企业主要经济指标(2003年)(续5)

单位：万元

分　组	Item	资产合计 Total Assets	流动资产小计 Total Circulating Funds
烟草加工业	Tobacco Processing		
纺织业	Textile Industry	116907.0	44279.1
纺织服装、鞋、帽制造业	Textile clothing, footwear and headgear industry	24703.5	16636.2
皮革、毛皮、羽毛(绒)及其制品业	Leather, fur, feather (eiderdown) and their products industry	21944.4	17719.5
木材加工及竹、藤、棕、草制品业	Timber Processing,Bamboo,Cane,Palm Fiber and Straw Products	7122.5	3943.1
家具制造业	Furniture Manufacturing	12123.2	8762.9
造纸及纸制品业	Papermaking and Paper products	30055.0	15911.4
印刷业、记录媒介的复制	Printing,Record Medium Reproduction	109231.6	36402.0
文教体育用品制造业	Cultural,Educational and Sports Goods	364.1	139.1
石油加工、炼焦及核燃料加工业	Petroleum refining, coke making and nuclear fuel processing industry	2629.6	1721.3
化学原料及化学制品制造业	Raw Chemical Materials and Chemical Products	392732.7	154530.5
医药制造业	Medical and Pharmaceutical Products	833181.8	492127.3
化学纤维制造业	Chemical Fiber	2302.6	390.5
橡胶制品业	Rubber Products	1831.5	1056.2
塑料制品业	Plastic Products	38636.6	15174.0
非金属矿物制品业	Nonmetal Mineral Products	70749.4	39333.1
黑色金属冶炼及压延加工业	Smelting and Pressing of Ferrous Metals	138277.4	91320.6
有色金属冶炼及压延加工业	Smelting and Pressing of Nonferrou Metals	97714.8	32480.4
金属制品业	Metal Products	31108.2	16455.8
通用设备制造	General equipment manufacturing industry	169282.9	111203.2
专用设备制造业	Special Purpose Equipment	764903.0	348595.0
交通运输设备制造业	Transport Equipment	2697571.6	1732556.4
电气机械及器材制造业	Electric Equipment and Machinery	147795.7	84089.1
通信设备、计算机及其他电子设备制造业	Communication equipment, computer and other electronic equipment manufacturing industry	793862.1	456685.6
仪器仪表及文化办公用	Instruments,Meters,Cultural and Office	212974.4	124808.0
工艺品及其他制造业	Handicraft and other stuff manufacturing industry	3666.5	1921.0
废弃资源和废旧材料回收加工业	Discarded resources and waste materials salvaging and processing industry		
电力、热力的生产和供应业	Electric power, heating power generating and supplying industry	20368.2	11807.7
燃气生产和供应业	Gas mining and supplying industry		
水的生产和供应业	Water processing and supplying industry	2255.8	2104.9

Main Indicators of Share-holding Corporation Industrial Enterprises Above the Designated Size(2003)(Continued 5)

(10 000 yuan)

流动资产年平均余额 Annual Average Balance of Circulating Funds	固定资产小计 Fixed Assets	固定资产原价合计 Origing Value of Fixed Assets	累计折旧 Accumulative Total Depreciation	本年折旧 In this year Depreciation	固定资产净值年平均余额 Average Balance Net Value of Fixed Assets
841.3	2385.4	2822.4	436.9	8.5	4882.1
63744.9	82081.2	128085.8	55195.5	9822.1	62349.6
12592.4	5819.1	8546.5	4216.0	249.0	4431.3
4283.9	11654.3	12501.8	1387.0	100.8	11263.1
1575.3	1108.4	1340.8	279.2	4.2	1061.6
7047.6	15594.9	15949.8	1150.1	48.9	15218.9
76202.8	106969.0	165732.6	69307.8	10670.0	95634.9
810.6	14.5	52.9	38.4	3.2	14.5
39498.0	76341.1	62119.3	19809.8	1378.4	44327.1
51470.4	104421.5	136016.7	63201.2	6061.7	92311.6
15644.2	8820.0	12199.8	4252.3	315.5	8206.4
2200.7	1247.8	1458.2	305.0	142.5	2119.8
35294.3	64823.6	64514.3	22400.1	1382.3	42898.2
58196.9	54098.4	60209.0	14819.5	3464.5	45449.6
5583.2	3119.5	4110.1	1211.4	124.7	2869.7
838.6	1602.6	2881.5	1281.4	311.6	2551.3
192883.7	55004.0	81995.0	36916.3	3902.5	42468.4
262390.8	198760.2	291895.6	122123.4	8133.0	154324.6
213305.5	157179.7	223932.6	96905.4	9722.7	126856.6
472118.2	206916.7	331381.3	157535.7	22965.0	171994.6
182504.9	77331.4	107302.3	36850.3	1086.9	67879.7
26937.8	18495.0	26858.7	9893.1	1403.4	15720.1
399.0	735.1	896.3	222.7	28.6	701.9
115033.0	444879.3	602209.5	191181.2	33112.1	410297.1
5766.7	7817.9	10816.2	3175.5	166.5	7699.4
27128.8	106818.2	154263.3	74823.9	10496.4	80683.3

10-19 全部规模以上股份制工业企业主要经济指标(2003年)（续6）

单位：万元

分 组	Item	负债合计 Total Liabilites	流动负债小计 Liquid Liabilities
烟草加工业	Tobacco Processing		
纺织业	Textile Industry	58375.4	55440.7
纺织服装、鞋、帽制造业	Textile clothing, footwear and headgear industry	14717.1	12417.1
皮革、毛皮、羽毛(绒)及其制品业	Leather, fur, feather (eiderdown) and their products industry	15544.3	15544.3
木材加工及竹、藤、棕、草制品业	Timber Processing,Bamboo,Cane,Palm Fiber and Straw Products	5735.5	2495.5
家具制造业	Furniture Manufacturing	6563.6	6421.4
造纸及纸制品业	Papermaking and Paper products	20335.4	13731.6
印刷业、记录媒介的复制	Printing,Record Medium Reproduction	38137.6	35570.1
文教体育用品制造业	Cultural,Educational and Sports Goods	159.1	159.1
石油加工、炼焦及核燃料加工业	Petroleum refining, coke making and nuclear fuel processing industry	1907.5	1371.8
化学原料及化学制品制造业	Raw Chemical Materials and Chemical Products	227314.0	134365.2
医药制造业	Medical and Pharmaceutical Products	426103.5	358231.6
化学纤维制造业	Chemical Fiber	1250.1	1250.1
橡胶制品业	Rubber Products	804.1	739.4
塑料制品业	Plastic Products	23567.2	14323.3
非金属矿物制品业	Nonmetal Mineral Products	43851.1	38993.2
黑色金属冶炼及压延加工业	Smelting and Pressing of Ferrous Metals	62701.6	58454.7
有色金属冶炼及压延加工业	Smelting and Pressing of Nonferrou Metals	60062.0	42689.7
金属制品业	Metal Products	12932.0	9622.1
通用设备制造	General equipment manufacturing industry	67511.8	50114.6
专用设备制造业	Special Purpose Equipment	368958.9	287014.3
交通运输设备制造业	Transport Equipment	1821891.9	1481709.4
电气机械及器材制造业	Electric Equipment and Machinery	69223.6	55916.8
通信设备、计算机及其他电子设备制造业	Communication equipment, computer and other electronic equipment manufacturing industry	405394.6	338260.9
仪器仪表及文化办公用	Instruments,Meters,Cultural and Office	140893.6	125746.7
工艺品及其他制造业	Handicraft and other stuff manufacturing industry	2062.5	2062.4
废弃资源和废旧材料回收加工业	Discarded resources and waste materials salvaging and processing industry		
电力、热力的生产和供应业	Electric power, heating power generating and supplying industry	14494.4	14294.4
燃气生产和供应业	Gas mining and supplying industry		
水的生产和供应业	Water processing and supplying industry	2104.9	2104.9

Main Indicators of Share-holding Corporation Industrial Enterprises Above Designated size (2003)（Continued 6）

（10 000 yuan）

长期负债小计 Long-term Liabilities	所有者权益合计 Total Creditor's Equity	实收资本 Total Capital Hold	产品销售收入 Sales Revenue	产品销售成本 Cost of Sales	产品销售费用 Sales Expense	产品销售税金及附加 Sales Tax and Extra Charges	营业利润 Operational profit
2934.7	58531.6	32888.9	77004.9	68975.1	1137.1	197.1	-304.8
2300.0	9986.4	8860.0	23311.3	16668.5	2488.8	325.9	664.5
	6400.1	6560.0	8074.4	7743.2	6.4		-208.6
3240.0	1387.0	2100.0	853.1	433.2	59.4	5.0	-21.3
131.2	5559.6	4289.8	6842.6	4920.7	618.9	18.6	415.0
6578.3	9719.6	11092.0	22380.3	19087.4	709.0	123.6	1033.9
2567.2	71094.0	38790.9	43188.6	34627.8	1769.2	192.7	2989.3
	205.0	168.0	590.0	517.6	8.4	3.4	37.0
535.7	722.1	739.6	3298.6	2867.9	286.0	5.9	148.9
92902.2	165418.7	78743.7	153762.1	113698.0	10175.7	851.3	5007.7
61959.6	407078.3	182035.8	551084.3	289323.7	135523.4	2466.1	81057.9
	1052.5	1500.0	1699.3	1568.4	91.2	7.4	-35.5
17.3	1027.4	232.6	2047.3	1502.3	104.1	7.4	198.0
2623.2	15069.4	14600.7	15679.8	12958.2	495.0	22.2	742.5
4474.0	26898.3	25433.4	49831.0	40917.2	1468.4	292.8	3446.8
4246.9	75575.8	33169.6	15970.3	11842.9	423.1	231.7	-750.4
17252.6	37652.8	22054.1	62319.0	51132.2	1297.9	184.8	6446.9
3252.4	18176.2	17003.7	13228.1	8840.8	703.3	37.1	1449.2
3697.0	101771.1	63642.4	102496.8	73002.1	5344.1	297.5	15456.6
68569.5	395632.5	180776.9	371445.8	278546.9	15118.3	2171.0	27879.5
339887.5	872461.1	571164.0	1405811.7	1141254.2	40038.8	4037.7	69640.0
8560.3	78572.1	61164.6	107472.5	79528.1	4471.2	1276.5	10104.8
55799.8	388467.5	134319.5	460586.6	359985.1	29991.7	1867.3	27700.2
14146.9	72080.8	43812.9	105667.9	83993.2	4252.8	500.1	-646.7
	1604.0	1728.0	5879.2	4922.5	879.7	0.4	-173.9
199.9	5873.8	4684.0	13388.3	11855.1	5.8	425.6	-214.3
	150.9	636.0	2016.5	1607.6	51.9	181.4	-3.8

10-19　全部规模以上股份制工业企业主要经济指标(2003年)（续7）

单位：万元

分　组	Item	管理费用 Expenses for Management
烟草加工业	Tobacco Processing	
纺织业	Textile Industry	5954.9
纺织服装、鞋、帽制造业	Textile clothing, footwear and headgear industry	2980.8
皮革、毛皮、羽毛(绒)及其制品业	Leather, fur, feather (eiderdown) and their products industry	354.8
木材加工及竹、藤、棕、草制品业	Timber Processing,Bamboo,Cane,Palm Fiber and Straw Products	114.9
家具制造业	Furniture Manufacturing	600.6
造纸及纸制品业	Papermaking and Paper products	1018.0
印刷业、记录媒介的复制	Printing,Record Medium Reproduction	2970.2
文教体育用品制造业	Cultural,Educational and Sports Goods	18.8
石油加工、炼焦及核燃料加工业	Petroleum refining, coke making and nuclear fuel processing industry	150.6
化学原料及化学制品制造业	Raw Chemical Materials and Chemical Products	21659.4
医药制造业	Medical and Pharmaceutical Products	33870.0
化学纤维制造业	Chemical Fiber	52.1
橡胶制品业	Rubber Products	254.4
塑料制品业	Plastic Products	970.6
非金属矿物制品业	Nonmetal Mineral Products	3349.4
黑色金属冶炼及压延加工业	Smelting and Pressing of Ferrous Metals	2001.3
有色金属冶炼及压延加工业	Smelting and Pressing of Nonferrou Metals	1950.4
金属制品业	Metal Products	1713.4
通用设备制造	General equipment manufacturing industry	7804.6
专用设备制造业	Special Purpose Equipment	41703.8
交通运输设备制造业	Transport Equipment	130671.8
电气机械及器材制造业	Electric Equipment and Machinery	12028.6
通信设备、计算机及其他电子设备制造业	Communication equipment, computer and other electronic equipment manufacturing industry	31281.0
仪器仪表及文化办公用	Instruments,Meters,Cultural and Office	14811.1
工艺品及其他制造业	Handicraft and other stuff manufacturing industry	213.0
废弃资源和废旧材料回收加工业	Discarded resources and waste materials salvaging and processing industry	
电力、热力的生产和供应业	Electric power, heating power generating and supplying industry	1319.6
燃气生产和供应业	Gas mining and supplying industry	
水的生产和供应业	Water processing and supplying industry	190.6

Main Indicators of Share-holding Corporation Industrial Enterprises Above Designated size (2003)(Continued 7)

(10 000 yuan)

利润总额 Total Profits	亏损企业亏损总额 Total Loss of Deficit Enterprises	利税总额 Total Pre-tax Profits	本年应交增值税 Value Added Tax Payable
-299.4	1298.4	2778.1	2880.4
645.1	117.3	1750.9	779.9
-186.9	186.9	127.5	314.4
-21.3	21.3	-6.2	10.1
391.8	95.7	828.7	418.3
1040.9	419.6	2383.2	1218.7
5507.8	364.8	8178.3	2477.8
37.0		49.4	9.0
148.9		234.3	79.5
9303.8	1323.0	17149.0	6993.9
99370.4	4340.5	146797.4	44960.9
-35.5	35.5	6.7	34.8
106.3		210.4	96.7
709.9	312.0	1134.3	402.2
1312.8	2992.0	4350.1	2744.5
-747.7	800.8	-27.3	488.7
7548.1	476.4	8405.4	672.5
1414.8	11.1	2494.1	1042.2
15064.0	404.0	20627.7	5266.2
33220.5	656.7	52519.8	17128.3
82866.1	836.4	122476.2	35572.4
7433.6	5487.1	15020.9	6310.8
27082.9	14950.7	44351.3	15401.1
-439.0	4095.1	1843.1	1782.0
-176.6	176.6	-149.6	26.6
-156.3	238.4	707.4	438.1
1.1		299.0	116.5

10-20 分区县全部规模以上工业企业经济指标(2003年)

单位：万元

分 组	Item	企业单位数（个）Number of Enterprises (unit)	亏损企业 Loss Making Enterprises	工业总产值（当年价）Gross Industrial Output Value (At Current Prices)	工业总产值（不变价）Gorss Industrial Output Value (At Constant Prices)
新城区	Xingcheng	67	34	1374583.9	1448027.6
区 属	Under District	21	6	110716.6	111415.8
碑林区	Beilin	47	16	222164.8	223434.6
区 属	Under District	7	1	18330.2	18212.7
莲湖区	Lianhu	86	34	1242365.3	1403911.4
区 属	Under District	13	7	24212.7	19761.2
灞桥区	Baqiao	68	19	288008.8	253383.5
区 属	Under District	42	7	92522.5	83012.2
未央区	Weiyang	115	27	932320.1	716750.3
区 属	Under District	68	10	220889.6	226393.0
雁塔区	Yanta	149	49	1139870.8	1778181.4
区 属	Under District	54	18	127773.9	188796.0
阎良区	Yanliang	16	2	409806.1	410888.2
区 属	Under District	15	2	13508.4	13192.9
临潼区	Lintong	23	9	346661.7	348679.8
区 属	Under District	13	3	142462.1	117979.0
长安区	Chang'an	36	9	108101.8	107107.6
区 属	Under District	32	9	47437.6	42069.9
蓝田县	Lantian	32	15	49956.4	46612.8
县 属	Under County	29	15	26197.4	22860.8
周至县	Zhouzhi	10	3	14496.4	10649.0
县 属	Under County	9	2	13716.3	10278.5
户 县	Huxian	52	21	187364.4	162025.3
县 属	Under County	44	16	88980.5	97377.0
高陵县	Gaoling	34	12	70926.5	67683.0
县 属	Under County	34	12	70926.5	67683.0

Economic Indicators of Industrial Enterprises Above Designated Size by Region（2003）

（10 000 yuan）

工业增加值（生产法）Value-Added of Industry (Value of Industrial Products Sales)	工业销售产值（当年价）Value Of Industrial Products Sales (At Current) Prices	全部职工年平均人数（人）Annual Average Employers (person)	资产合计 Total Assets	流动资产小计 Total Circulating Funds	流动资产年平均余额 Annual Average Balance of Circulating Funds	固定资产小计 Fixed Assets
478348.0	1331251.6	59819	2474071.7	1130903.8	1095792.1	1162513.5
26035.7	100303.3	2363	163286.8	86436.1	78361.6	23264.4
77118.9	172570.9	14114	683734.9	303806.1	307040.2	223153.9
4811.1	18102.0	1177	29190.5	12097.9	14509.2	12846.4
381737.9	1209453.6	70509	2403875.7	1301468.8	1177173.5	782988.1
9350.4	23639.3	2111	38264.3	20471.2	19392.9	11193.8
84944.7	274472.0	45316	548597.3	249856.9	231689.3	265282.7
25605.7	85045.8	6664	92126.3	58435.8	51076.0	27284.4
281616.8	905668.6	51417	1415388.5	677936.0	616385.2	532992.2
82538.8	216562.6	10241	258700.4	90563.8	90916.6	98451.0
365171.6	1089582.0	47706	1987279.8	1133949.0	1072588.6	653323.1
57614.3	111122.4	5529	217311.8	107192.1	97830.2	68519.8
93661.9	410792.5	20417	1223778.9	888939.6	757786.6	240236.5
3905.8	13850.0	900	20191.8	11869.8	11353.1	7496.8
124207.9	336487.6	13731	451049.5	316284.9	256265.4	98340.6
43837.9	137578.9	5577	83790.3	41984.2	35523.0	39168.7
32600.9	102677.2	9102	223652.4	123512.9	112217.4	76841.9
11843.0	44087.0	4688	58074.1	26864.5	24599.5	20877.9
15491.0	47921.5	5170	88568.3	43241.5	42083.6	41343.1
6676.1	24043.5	3083	47741.9	18260.3	17275.1	25841.4
3998.8	13816.8	1495	24246.4	8315.7	9063.5	10168.3
3834.1	13045.4	1375	22316.9	7636.9	8338.7	9000.8
69747.9	189091.6	21949	322112.5	141416.9	133234.0	148421.3
29665.0	91115.7	9700	127920.8	64861.7	59707.8	60747.4
18803.2	66294.2	4741	110498.1	50825.2	44936.7	47335.9
18803.2	66294.2	4741	110498.1	50825.2	44936.7	47335.9

10-20 分区县全部规模以上工业企业经济指标(2003年)（续1）

单位：万元

分　组	Item	固定资产原价合计 Origing Value of Fixed Assets	累计折旧 Accumulative Total Depreciation	本年折旧 Depreciation This year	固定资产净值年平均余额 Average Balance Net Value of Fixed Assets	负债合计 Total Liabilites	流动负债小计 Liquid Liabilities
新城区	Xingcheng	1485087.3	449257.4	67434.5	984459.5	1309963.9	1062472.8
区 属	Under District	16889.3	5879.0	1430.2	11500.3	59704.6	57785.2
碑林区	Beilin	218364.2	53994.0	11028.7	192103.7	371032.8	275470.2
区 属	Under District	11465.2	4228.4	768.8	7270.2	21237.2	12791.9
莲湖区	Lianhu	1153833.2	530958.2	64687.6	619214.9	1470159.7	1153850.4
区 属	Under District	12504.1	4232.6	654.5	9099.9	23727.7	19594.8
灞桥区	Baqiao	372243.7	147591.8	19911.4	226862.1	335770.3	257911.3
区 属	Under District	34641.9	11431.8	3345.6	26326.4	59184.3	50697.1
未央区	Weiyang	738568.6	281023.6	36780.3	430249.2	986670.9	791509.4
区 属	Under District	131171.6	40540.3	11181.5	95539.9	108756.6	78658.3
雁塔区	Yanta	865322.0	306309.7	43235.8	507129.5	1155301.5	893572.6
区 属	Under District	61524.4	20058.7	3696.9	35462.1	138658.5	103355.6
阎良区	Yanliang	295523.3	133006.3	15907.5	126035.8	883278.0	742582.9
区 属	Under District	8699.4	2095.7	401.9	6147.6	10608.1	9699.9
临潼区	Lintong	130504.8	55537.7	6046.5	71562.8	308571.3	280327.1
区 属	Under District	33333.9	8062.6	1879.8	24679.3	61192.9	47050.0
长安区	Chang'an	87353.5	32649.6	4507.6	58586.9	149836.0	114217.4
区 属	Under District	23637.7	5801.2	991.4	24204.8	30005.4	21537.1
蓝田县	Lantian	58171.1	24490.9	2876.1	36474.5	62669.6	42171.4
县 属	Under County	34515.8	10533.7	2657.9	24615.3	40751.6	30186.0
周至县	Zhouzhi	16101.4	6068.2	252.3	9146.2	16223.9	10783.8
县 属	Under County	14768.7	5898.2	182.3	7957.8	13765.7	9105.6
户 县	Huxian	204460.9	81497.3	7199.9	137941.9	210809.5	160853.3
县 属	Under County	74102.0	17349.1	3447.1	58081.4	90415.3	80071.0
高陵县	Gaoling	48788.0	7768.3	2336.6	32311.7	70121.9	44881.5
县 属	Under County	48788.0	7768.3	2336.6	32311.7	70121.9	44881.5

Economic Indicators of Industrial Enterprises Above Designated Size by Region（2003）(Continued 1)

（10 000 yuan）

长期负债小计 Long-term Liabilities	所有者权益合计 Total Creditor's Equity	实收资本 Total Capital Hold	产品销售收入 Sales Revenue	产品销售成本 Cost of Sales	产品销售费用 Sales Expense	产品销售税金及附加 Sales Tax and Extra Charges
233858.6	1163796.2	461494.3	1561173.2	1006798.3	107487.4	5216.1
1869.9	103582.2	24423.5	45834.3	36569.0	1066.2	383.0
77641.8	312702.1	103179.8	218990.8	149336.9	23802.9	1478.7
8373.3	7953.3	5618.9	17251.7	8808.0	4726.5	177.3
316157.2	930497.4	517739.2	1240977.7	901633.9	82532.4	7363.7
4132.9	14536.6	10511.7	20139.4	17201.0	819.3	84.2
76359.5	212827.0	99421.6	270572.7	232575.2	5471.7	3678.2
8079.3	32942.0	28293.8	84593.4	67414.3	1951.3	2796.8
187800.0	428717.6	431548.8	905458.6	726452.7	42335.6	12101.9
24647.5	149943.8	108305.6	211828.2	159929.1	17943.4	1451.1
245195.6	819388.7	590097.0	1048030.9	801927.1	68587.6	4675.9
34448.5	78653.3	45239.2	107285.7	81142.5	5930.1	445.7
140659.4	340500.9	205197.0	485945.8	400053.8	11870.3	262.1
872.5	9583.7	3514.1	12427.1	10992.0	206.4	46.9
27837.6	142478.2	70032.1	342332.0	254085.7	22951.9	1666.3
13736.8	22597.4	15567.0	136200.6	114284.9	12451.4	123.7
35616.1	73182.6	26365.7	96408.2	75351.9	2232.9	671.9
8465.8	28068.7	12810.9	42655.9	36770.7	1369.4	589.7
20498.2	25898.7	20292.3	42708.8	34513.2	1066.6	350.4
10565.6	6990.3	14877.8	21680.8	18326.9	904.3	331.5
5440.1	8022.5	7846.9	13117.2	10223.0	495.4	62.6
4660.1	8551.2	7695.3	12345.6	9755.2	486.1	46.4
49955.9	111303.0	67982.1	162848.8	150839.7	8190.9	737.0
10344.0	37505.5	39423.4	88677.1	74907.5	6861.6	434.1
17020.2	40376.2	40732.4	66695.1	53840.0	3449.0	288.9
17020.2	40376.2	40732.4	66695.1	53840.0	3449.0	288.9

10-20 分区县全部规模以上工业企业经济指标(2003年）（续2）

单位：万元

分 组	Item	营业利润 Operational profit	管理费用 Expenses for Management
新城区	Xingcheng	72322.2	107291.0
区 属	Under District	10372.1	2322.4
碑林区	Beilin	17748.5	20588.6
区 属	Under District	1385.1	2097.2
莲湖区	Lianhu	85268.9	144938.2
区 属	Under District	-70.8	2091.8
灞桥区	Baqiao	-7398.6	33524.2
区 属	Under District	2073.2	8770.8
未央区	Weiyang	48111.4	64724.2
区 属	Under District	25990.9	7547.1
雁塔区	Yanta	54321.8	91926.8
区 属	Under District	11541.7	7312.9
阎良区	Yanliang	7930.9	59103.3
区 属	Under District	389.9	548.8
临潼区	Lintong	32802.0	29674.3
区 属	Under District	3389.8	4457.9
长安区	Chang'an	5383.8	10812.6
区 属	Under District	1749.1	1947.5
蓝田县	Lantian	-218.6	6309.2
县 属	Under County	-239.1	1701.6
周至县	Zhouzhi	-138.8	1742.4
县 属	Under County	-64.8	1611.9
户 县	Huxian	-15344.9	16993.4
县 属	Under County	-1047.8	6075.0
高陵县	Gaoling	2892.7	5665.5
县 属	Under County	2892.7	5665.5

Economic Indicators of Industrial Enterprises

Above Designated Size by Region（2003）(Continued 2)

（10 000 yuan）

利润总额 Total Profits	亏损企业亏损总额 Total Loss of Deficit Enterprises	利税总额 Total Pre-tax Profits	本年应交增值税 Value Added Tax Payable
77384.5	19120.7	153182.7	70582.1
5129.6	283.0	8337.8	2825.2
20789.2	2646.0	31992.8	9724.9
1422.7	29.1	3363.6	1763.6
102853.6	13423.4	174794.2	64576.9
-117.2	467.9	836.3	869.3
-3483.5	10354.5	11410.2	11215.5
2036.0	816.6	7059.3	2226.5
35567.4	14985.1	84028.1	36358.8
17028.4	1706.4	27749.7	9270.2
53817.7	34745.2	102289.3	43795.7
10327.8	1268.6	14812.3	4038.8
9847.0	5.9	17522.8	7413.7
401.2	5.9	762.4	314.3
36242.3	1796.6	54453.4	16544.8
3180.5	327.3	5051.2	1747.0
5553.9	297.0	7933.7	1707.9
1555.6	297.0	3194.3	1049.0
89.1	799.6	1373.2	933.7
-537.9	799.6	667.7	874.1
46.4	227.5	432.4	323.4
123.4	150.5	392.6	222.8
-3766.2	11840.6	5335.2	8364.4
-903.5	3285.8	3480.5	3949.9
3228.0	1751.4	5164.5	1647.6
3228.0	1751.4	5164.5	1647.6

10-21 规模以上工业企业主要经济效益指标（2003年）

单位：%

分 组	Item	工业增加值率 Ratio of Value Added of Industry to Gross Industrial Output Value	资产负债率 Ratio of Total Liabilities to Total Assets
总 计	**Total**	**27.82**	**61.31**
#市 区	Urban Area	27.71	61.08
按隶属关系分	Grouped by Administrative Relationship		
中央企业	Central Enterprises	28.14	59.45
省属企业	Provincial Enterprises	28.67	74.14
市属企业	Municipal Enterprises	27.26	58.03
按登记注册类型分组	Grouped by Registion Status		
内资企业	Domestic Investment Enterprises	26.22	62.01
国有经济	State-owned Enterprises	27.70	67.52
集体经济	Collective-owned Enterprises	25.44	48.74
股份合作	Share-holding Corperative	31.11	69.86
联营企业	Joint Ownership Enterprises	29.94	63.38
国有独资公司	State-owned appropriator ship corporation	24.13	58.80
其他有限责任公司	Other limited corporation	25.61	64.19
股份有限公司	Share-holding Corporation Ltd.	23.74	46.03
私营企业	Private Enterprises		
港、澳、台商投资企业	Enterprises With Investment From Hong kang, Macao and Taiwan	29.59	64.11
外商投资企业	Enterprises with Foreign Investment	38.12	51.99
在总计中:亏损企业	Of the Total: Deficit Enterprises	31.98	70.26
在总计中:国有控股企业	Of the Total: Enterprises of Controlling Share Hold by the State	26.29	63.11
按轻重工业分	Grouped by Ligth Industry and Heavy Industry		
轻工业	Light Industry	31.80	55.65
重工业	Heavy Industry	26.20	62.98
按企业规模分	Grouped by Size of Enterprises		
大型工业	Large-size	25.51	58.11
中型工业	Medium-size	29.01	61.66
小型工业	Small-size	31.13	69.70
按经济组织类型分	Grouped by Administrative Relationship		
独资企业	Appropratorship	28.01	65.40
合作、合伙企业	Partnership	31.84	66.16
股份有限公司	Share-holding Corporation Ltd.	23.82	46.26
有限责任公司	Limited corporation	28.52	61.60
按工业行业大类分	Grouped by Sector		
煤炭开采和洗选业	Coal mining and coal washing industry		
石油和天然气开采业	Petroleum and Natural Gas Extraction	12.82	60.52
黑色金属矿采选业	Ferrous Metals Mining and Dressing	19.17	127.40

注:该表未包括长庆油田。企业规模、行业、轻重工业划分执行新标准。

Note:Not Including Changqing Oil Field . Size of Enterprises, Industry, the Classification of Light and Heavy Industry Practice New Standards.

Main Indicators on Economic Beneficial Results of Industrial Enterprises Above Designated Size(2003)

(%)

总资产贡献率 Ratio of total Assets to Industrial Output	成本费用利润率 Ratio of Profit to Industrial Cost	流动资产周转率（次） Number of Times of Turnover of Funds(times)	资本保值增值率 Ratio of value-added To Total Assets	全员劳动生产率（元/人） Overall Labor Productivity (yuan/person)	工业产品销售率 Ratio of Sales Value of Industrial Products to Output Value
6.97	**5.71**	**1.10**	**111.97**	**58801**	**96.30**
7.14	6.02	1.10	111.96	61258	96.19
5.04	4.33	1.06	111.36	42610	97.56
10.43	7.23	1.17	134.26	76169	96.38
7.41	6.08	1.11	108.31	68470	95.45
5.97	4.43	1.08	114.61	49169	96.18
4.26	0.49	1.08	116.23	42815	98.03
8.37	6.46	1.15	182.74	43356	93.85
2.83	0.14	1.11	63.22	32749	96.89
3.90	2.08	1.17	72.92	39797	96.65
1.65	2.18	1.07	47.97	18987	95.70
10.01	6.28	1.08	215.22	67605	94.32
8.90	11.35	0.95	108.17	94158	97.90
4.33	4.38	1.44	30.04	101212	96.52
21.97	15.38	1.27	132.80	367235	97.05
-1.35	-12.95	0.80		31119	95.05
5.90	4.45	1.06	111.59	50421	96.35
11.02	10.01	1.39	104.55	68441	97.76
5.72	4.15	1.03	114.86	54992	95.70
7.15	6.78	1.13	120.98	62291	97.97
8.20	6.38	1.11	107.87	62632	95.22
4.46	1.81	1.03	92.95	48620	94.32
4.86	1.47	1.13	122.55	45898	97.21
3.40	1.12	1.20	61.38	37626	98.22
8.77	11.22	0.95	106.21	90773	97.88
8.49	7.65	1.12	109.54	68749	95.23
18.92	9.02	1.62		15935	100.00
13.10	-9.28	1.06	118.22	14549	98.88

10-21 规模以上工业企业主要经济效益指标（2003年）(续1)

单位：%

分　组	Item	工业增加值率 Ratio of Value Added of Industry to Gross Industrial Output Value	资产负债率 Ratio of Total Liabilities to Total Assets
有色金属矿采选业	Nonferrous Metals Mining and Dressing	48.50	80.69
非金属矿采选业	Nonmetal Minerals Mining and Dressing	40.11	14.73
其他采矿业	Other mining industry		
农副食品加工业	Agricultural products and non-stable food processing industry	26.68	71.71
食品制造业	Food Production	29.83	63.44
饮料制造业	Beverage Production	31.57	62.61
烟草制品业	Tobacco Processing	31.52	25.60
纺织业	Textile Industry	23.06	65.21
纺织服装、鞋、帽制造业	Textile clothing, footwear and headgear industry	30.50	57.44
皮革、毛皮、羽毛(绒)及其制品业	Leather, fur, feather (eiderdown) and their products industry	22.45	76.94
木材加工及木、竹、藤、棕、草制品制造业	Timber Processing,Bamboo,Cane,Palm Fiber and Straw Products	25.77	66.20
家具制造业	Furniture Manufacturing	29.27	58.65
造纸及纸制品业	Papermaking and Paper Products	27.72	68.44
印刷业和记录媒介的复制	Printing,Record Medium Reproduction	33.51	44.85
文教体育用品制造业	Cultural,Educational and Sports Goods	31.55	18.79
石油加工、炼焦及核燃料加工业	Petroleum refining, coke making and nuclear	16.39	81.44
化学原料及化学制品制造业	Raw Chemical Materials and Chemical Products	25.30	56.57
医药制造业	Medical and Pharmaceutical Products	38.77	51.56
化学纤维制造业	Chemical Fiber	18.99	54.29
橡胶制品业	Rubber Products	16.84	43.90
塑料制品业	Plastic Products	29.17	60.84
非金属矿物制品业	Nonmetal Mineral Products	26.70	71.57
黑色金属冶炼及压延加工业	Smelting and Pressing of Ferrous Metals	26.39	70.23
有色金属冶炼及压延加工业	Smelting and Pressing of Nonferrou Metals	32.67	66.46
金属制品业	Metal Products	38.65	54.34
通用设备制造	General equipment manufacturing industry	35.92	70.53
专用设备制造业	Special Purpose Equipment	26.69	65.26
交通运输设备制造业	Transport Equipment	24.49	66.66
电气机械及器材制造业	Electric Equipment and Machinery	24.27	62.96
通信设备、计算机及其他电子设备制造业	Communication equipment, computer and other electronic equipment manufacturing industry	21.75	60.94
仪器仪表及文化、办公用机械制造	Instruments,Meters,Cultural and Office Machinery	24.36	66.38
工艺品及其他制造业	Handicraft and other stuff manufacturing industry	21.35	32.84
废弃资源和废旧材料回收加工业	Discarded resources and waste materials salvaging and processing industry		
电力、热力的生产和供应业	Electric power, heating power generating and processing industry	66.97	28.50
燃气生产和供应业	Gas mining and supplying industry	6.71	57.80
水的生产和供应业	Water processing and supplying industry	48.79	47.79

Main Indicators on Economic Beneficial Results of Industrial Enterprises Above Designated Size(2003)(Continued 1)

(%)

总资产贡献率 Ratio of total Assets to Industrial Output	成本费用利润率 Ratio of Profit to Industrial Cost	流动资产周转率（次） Number of Times of Turnover of Funds(times)	资本保值增值率 Ratio of value-added To Total Assets	全员劳动生产率（元/人） Overall Labor Productivity (yuan/person)	工业产品销售率 Ratio of Sales Value of Industrial Products to Output Value
0.40	0.55	2.46	74.78	40332	99.25
17.54	9.17	1.46	311.96	18723	98.84
4.32	1.26	3.09	135.94	119730	98.57
11.52	4.63	2.82	82.91	86698	96.66
17.27	14.81	1.74	73.90	138610	100.34
11.12	11.39	2.61	106.23	29016	176.52
3.76	-0.30	1.63	96.18	15067	99.80
5.91	2.34	1.45	-108.48	31386	124.23
2.52	-0.45	0.49	111.56	31773	90.53
-11.66	-62.25	0.33	69.96	16707	86.73
6.37	5.08	0.82	52.50	15616	100.57
8.22	4.01	2.12	96.80	26314	101.49
12.06	16.02	1.35	110.24	83565	96.78
23.83	31.75	0.89	117.32	22755	96.78
18.40	2.85	5.53	173.68	199933	102.13
4.98	4.37	1.14	101.12	28983	92.95
18.26	20.47	1.12	110.25	179095	96.93
1.07	-2.05	4.13	71.74	60769	92.63
3.77	5.60	2.39	-7.44	43230	98.36
11.82	10.50	1.74	213.69	72904	93.09
3.58	-0.69	1.07	110.58	26833	96.45
-0.22	-12.29	0.41	88.62	40441	99.04
10.99	9.63	2.36	135.91	133642	84.39
8.31	7.68	1.14	120.54	62130	95.85
12.30	14.26	0.84	130.65	77181	94.86
5.31	3.67	0.85	106.88	37524	95.77
6.11	5.70	0.98	117.34	53983	96.99
5.57	2.77	0.98	129.97	70222	98.26
5.70	4.31	0.84	115.30	77010	90.84
1.94	-0.72	0.76	98.50	28485	88.77
5.65	15.16	0.45	100.61	118774	90.24
1.78	-9.21	3.07	106.59	111402	100.01
-3.07	-14.36	0.48	90.83	2117	100.00
2.69	2.24	1.40	103.47	53572	99.92

10-22 工业企业能源购进、消费及库存(2003年)

能源名称	Name(Unit)	年初库存 Stock (year-beginning)	购进量
			实物量 Quantity
原煤(吨)	Raw Coal（Ton）	361827	3290442
洗精煤(吨)	Washing Coal(Ton)	67747	386337
其他洗煤(吨)	Other Washed Coals(Ton)	4	121
型煤(吨)	Briquettes(Ton)	186	5487
焦炭(吨)	Coke(Ton)	15637	63923
其他焦化产品(吨)	Other Coking Products(Ton)		467
其他煤气(万立方米)	Other Gases(10 000cu.m)		
天然气(万立方米)	Natural Gas(10 000cu.m)		2708
原油(吨)	Crude Oil(Ton)	352	1093658
汽油(吨)	Gasoline(Ton)	735	14361
煤油(吨)	Kerosene(Ton)	136	11096
柴油(吨)	Diesel Oil(Ton)	1749	23171
燃料油(吨)	Fuel Oil(Ton)	2232	3083
液化石油气(吨)	LPG(Ton)	1	649
其他石油制品(吨)	Other Petroleum Products(Ton)	5	35
热力(百万千焦)	Heat (1 million kilo-joule)		7986444
电力(万千瓦时)	Electricity(10 000kwh)		288538
能源合计(吨标准煤)	Total Energy(ton of SCE)	312137	5796523

Energy Purchases Consumption and Inventory of Industrial Enterprises（2003）

Purchases	消费量 Consumption				年末库存
金额（万元）Sum(10 000 yuan)	合计 Total	工业生产消费 Industrial Production Consume	用于原材料 as raw Material	非工业生产消费 Non-industrial Production Consume	Stock year-end
53567.8	3326213	3172880	437595	153333	293018
14034.0	437633	436913		720	16438
3.0	110	78		32	15
180.8	5489	2223	1500	3266	185
2276.5	66350	66175	10467	175	13167
17.8	467	380		87	
4190.9	2701	2679	9	22	
177050.1	1079799	1079787	3578	12	14220
4997.8	14615	9062	251	5553	685
3483.5	10969	10822	329	147	201
7599.7	24030	21875	772	2155	960
557.2	8737	8722		15	1600
179.7	650	640		10	
15.4	36	36			4
14808.7	9955659	8359390	24	1596269	
125317.6	310141	288825	5196	21316	
439893.2	5977385	5716775	93239	260610	288376

10-23 主要能源按工业行业分组消费量(2003年)

		原煤（吨）Raw Coal (ton)	焦炭（吨）Coke (ton)
总　计	**Total**	**3326213**	**66350**
按工业行业大类分列	Grouped by Sector		
煤炭开采和洗选业	Coal Mining and Dressing		
石油和天然气开采业	Petroleum and Natural Gas Extraction		
黑色金属矿采选业	Ferrous Metals Mining and Dressing		
有色金属矿采选业	Nonferrous Metals Mining and Dressing	860	
非金属矿采选业	Nonmetal Minerals Mining and Dressing		
其他采矿业	Other mining industry		
农副食品加工业	Agricultural products and non-stable food processing industry	62334	
食品制造业	Food Production	17013	11640
饮料制造业	Beverage Production	38514	
烟草制品业	Tobacco Processing		
纺织业	Textile Industry	53512	21
纺织服装、鞋、帽制造业	Textile clothing, footwear and headgear industry	1349	
皮革、毛皮、羽毛(绒)及其制品业	Leather, fur, feather (eiderdown) and their products industry	18226	
木材加工及木、竹、藤、棕、草制品制造	Timber Processing,Bamboo,Cane,Palm Fiber and Straw Products	2044	
家具制造业	Furniture Manufacturing	389	
造纸及纸制品业	Papermaking and Paper products	146253	
印刷业和记录媒介的复制	Printing,Record Medium Reproduction	8109	
文教体育用品制造业	Cultural,Educational and Sports Goods		
石油加工、炼焦及核燃料加工业	Petroleum refining, coke making and nuclear fuel processing industry	28243	
化学原料及化学制品制造业	Raw Chemical Materials and Chemical Products	479902	30340
医药制造业	Medical and Pharmaceutical Products	83239	
化学纤维制造业	Chemical Fiber		
橡胶制品业	Rubber Products		
塑料制品业	Plastic Products	500	
非金属矿物制品业	Nonmetal Mineral Products	200852	524
黑色金属冶炼及压延加工业	Smelting and Pressing of Ferrous Metals	20798	195
有色金属冶炼及压延加工业	Smelting and Pressing of Nonferrou Metals	56703	1692
金属制品业	Metal Products	2015	347
通用设备制造	General equipment manufacturing industry	26110	8044
专用设备制造业	Special Purpose Equipment	96181	5367
交通运输设备制造业	Transport Equipment	335025	1699
电气机械及器材制造业	Electric Equipment and Machinery	65602	421
通信设备、计算机及其他电子设备制造业	Communication equipment, computer and other electronic equipment manufacturing industry	10707	
仪器仪表及文化办公用机械制造业	Instruments,Meters,Cultural and Office	24812	
工艺品及其他制造业	Handicraft and other stuff manufacturing industry	35	1454
废弃资源和废旧材料回收加工业	Discarded resources and waste materials salvaging and processing industry		
电力、热力的生产和供应业	Electric power, heating power generating and supplying industry	1543089	4606
燃气生产和供应业	Gas mining and supplying industry		
水的生产和供应业	Water processing and supplying industry	3797	

Majar Energy Consumption by Sector(2003)

天然气(万立方米) Natural Gas(10 000cu.m)	原油(吨) Crude Oil (ton)	汽油（吨） Gasoline (ton)	煤油（吨） Kerosene (ton)	柴油（吨） Diesel Oil (ton)	热能（百万千焦） Heat (million kilo-joule)	电力（万千瓦时） Electricity (10 000kwh)
2701	**1079799**	**14615**	**10969**	**24030**	**9955659**	**310141**
2		165		308		11
		10		78		75
		24		36		494
		163		312	25	6473
9		250		317	200000	2282
89		163	8	150	85016	6248
						35
		345	29	91	594052	39906
		46		7		225
		15		10		483
		13				282
		70		5		301
		1284		203		11587
179		352	10	69	62075	11224
		6				18
	1079591	85	5	45	418	4516
		608	45	1246	3016205	51238
30		700	1	324	575523	10289
						90
		76		55		1369
259		648	341	4168	77307	12528
		250	2	839		2309
47		86		628		1954
		129		233		1748
207		980	165	603		6867
62	11	1315	48	1878	689448	20606
237		3459	10136	7017	2931407	50740
416		1193	38	111	747977	15260
1165		1253	138	340	788492	19032
		353	1	33	27554	2808
	1	203		60		225
	187	163	2	4793	149028	21361
						85
		208		71	11133	7470

10-24 西安名牌产品一览表（2003年）

A Survey of Products of famous Brand Made in Xi'an(2003)

单位：千元 （1 000yuan）

产品名称 Name of Product	企业名称 Name of Enterprises	工业总产值 Gross Output Value	产品销售收入 Revenne Salas
"唐城"牌工业用合成盐酸	西安化工厂(1)	27897	23596
"唐城"牌工业用氢氧化钠	西安化工厂(2)	114094	112899
"西安"牌利君沙片	西安制药厂(1)	567737	544853
"西安"牌红霉素片	西安制药厂(2)	66676	67171
"大唐"牌SP30超级数字程控交换机	西安大唐电信有限公司	333364	218189
"彩桥"牌防爆胶带	彩桥电子材料有限公司	27670	25247
"晴雨"牌帆布	西安帆布厂	44728	43289
"西沃"牌豪华大客车	西飞集团西沃客车有限公司	406930	387013
"西飞"牌建筑铝型材	西飞集团西安飞机工业铝业公司	188705	190020
"西飞"牌家用空调器变频模糊控制器	西飞集团西飞清华电子有限公司	22200	20123
"西飞"牌铝合金门窗	西安飞机工业装饰工程股份公司	94580	124338
"西飞"牌覆膜金属板	西安飞机国际航空制造股份公司	44689	41948
"XAC"牌客车乘客座椅	西安飞机工业顺达座椅股份公司	6845	8271
"东方"牌旋转式冰箱压缩机	西安东方机械厂	5318	10300
"冰峰"牌汽水	西安市食品厂	13052	13232
"H"牌 DW系列电弧炉短网	西安华兴电炉公司	82956	81550
"碑林"牌金嗓灵系列药品	西安碑林药业股份有限公司	59967	60606
"碑林"牌补肾康乐胶囊	西安碑林药业股份有限公司	2869	3139
"高新"牌3.6-12KV高压限流熔断器	西安熔断器厂	22360	21310
"XD"牌制冷压缩机电机	西安微电机厂	38884	33424
"青竹"牌彩电用回扫变压器	西安无线电二厂(1)	66160	58367
"青竹"牌氧化锌压敏电阻器	西安无线电二厂(2)	48049	30547
"恒通"牌交流调频,调压,调速电梯	西安电梯厂	12426	10821
"西航"牌高速线材精轧机	西安航空发动机公司1	48074	43425
"西航"牌建筑铝型材	西安航空发动机公司2	52305	51119
"西航"牌GA731剑杆织机	西安航空发动机公司3	20837	18477
"西航"牌玻璃、金属建筑幕墙	西安航空发动机公司4	51045	51269
"雁塔"牌硅酸盐水泥	西安雁塔水泥公司	65444	65962
"汉斯"牌啤酒	青岛啤酒西安有限公司	567926	575512
"秦俑"牌复明片	西安更新中药厂	17923	18997
"银泉"牌铝箔衬纸	西安银泉纸业有限公司	30381	32900
"荣氏"牌系列饮品	西安海星饮品有限公司	49193	37585
"华联"牌软牛革	西安华联制皮公司	93086	80744
"陕鼓"牌AV系列轴流E型离心压缩机	陕西鼓风机有限公司1	1005015	834840
"金金博士"牌沙发	西安光明沙发厂	51318	49266
"XD"牌电化学用硅整流装置	西安电力整流器厂	58180	58180
"三宝双喜"牌荣发养颜宝胶囊	西安三宝双喜制药集团	7093	7288

10-24 西安名牌产品一览表（2003年）（续1）

A Survey of Products of famous Brand Made in Xi'an(2003)(Continued 1)

单位：千元 （1 000yuan）

产品名称 Name of Product	企业名称 Name of Enterprises	工业总产值 Gross Output Value	产品销售收入 Revenne Salas
"TST"牌碎石桥梁弹性接缝	西安自力化学工业公司	12208	12208
"秦俑"牌全脂甜牛奶粉	西安银桥乳制品公司	368419	324861
" 维奥欣"牌维奥欣片剂	西安东盛药业集团	108123	87906
"宇航"牌转子式空调压缩机	庆安集团有限公司	719090	862309
"龙首原"牌钢筋混凝土排水管	西安市水泥制管厂	49354	42523
"标准"牌工业缝纫机	中国标准缝纫机集团	613130	740046
"西玛"牌三相异步电机	西安电机厂	365486	366271
"友谊"牌市内通信电缆	西安友谊电缆有限公司	13550	13550
"XD"牌长途对称市内通信通信电缆	西安电缆厂	119452	102453
"福乐"牌弹簧软床垫	福乐家具有限公司	23009	27644
"友谊"牌棒形支柱绝缘子	西安高压电瓷厂(1)	25641	22705
"友谊"牌油纸电容式套管	西安高压电瓷厂(2)	36655	31698
"友谊"牌氧化锌避雷器	西安高压电瓷厂(3)	76820	66343
"汉港"牌VAE系列白乳胶	西安汉港化工公司	55150	40700
"巧媳妇"牌高效自动绞肉压面机	西安市和源电器厂	17745	19702
"魔妮"牌卫生巾	西安魔妮纸品股份公司	21647	18938
" XD"牌户外高压SF6断路器	西安高压开关厂(1)	465950	375148
"XD"牌GIS SF6封闭式组合电器	西安高压开关厂(2)	647250	521170
"XD"牌LW25-126SF6高压断路器	西安高压开关厂（3）	208830	168177
"翠宝"牌镶嵌首饰	西安翠宝实业集团公司	308625	264590
"唐都"牌 特制一等粉	西安市人民面粉厂	26239	18281
"陕汽"牌sx2190越野汽车	陕西汽车制造总厂	608409	591504
陕汽--"斯达·斯太尔"牌载货汽车	陕西汽车制造总厂	1813705	1875031
"秦康"牌大输液	西安京西双鹤药业有限公司	69397	72790
"秦康"牌针剂	西安京西双鹤药业有限公司	12278	12469
"爱菊"牌特制一等粉	西安群众面粉厂	64635	77399
"西矿-鲁奇"牌电收尘器	西安矿山机械厂	159990	192376
"秦川"牌输液瓶	陕西秦宝公司玻璃制瓶厂	11943	14853
"古城"牌火灾自动报警控制器系统	中核久安科技股份公司		
"XD"牌电力变压器	西安变压器厂	320678	255537
"巡洋舰"牌皮鞋	解放军3513工厂		
"开米"牌涤王中性多功能洗衣液	西安开米股份有限公司	92229	82707
"sf"牌单模松套层绞式通信光缆	西古光纤光缆有限公司	124320	134329
"三五"牌毛巾系列产品	解放军3511工厂	88428	104214
"三环"牌工业纯铝圆铸锭	西安远通铝业有限公司	130080	99258
"中华"牌加香洗衣皂(1)	西安南风日化有限公司	10024	10484
"安"牌硫酸钠(AES)(2)	西安南风日化有限公司	38703	27177

10-24 西安名牌产品一览表（2003年）（续2）

A Survey of Products of famous Brand Made in Xi'an(2003)(Continued 2)

单位：千元　　　　（1 000yuan）

产品名称 Name of Product	企业名称 Name of Enterprises	工业总产值 Gross Output Value	产品销售收入 Revenne Salas
"阿房宫"牌结肠炎丸	西安中药厂	37892	30390
"金周"牌SC8/SCB8干式变压器	西安恒利变压器公司		
"一枝刘"牌洁身液	西安一枝刘制药公司	12056	10599
"阿香婆"牌香辣酱	西安太阳食品集团公司	50172	49694
"秦骊"牌多米诺组合式开关柜	西安秦骊成套电器厂	2370	1526
"德联"牌电热锅炉	西安德联电力设备公司	11844	11844
"秦"牌聚酯漆包线	西安电器线材厂	3876	3577
"QD"牌FZW28-12自动负荷开关	西安前进电器实业公司	21487	18354
"QINBANG"牌铝、钢塑复合带	西安秦邦电信材料厂	46082	50260
"秦岭"牌聚氯乙烯绝缘电线	陕西省户县电线厂		
"彩虹"牌彩色显像管	彩虹显示器件股份公司	1535230	1404168
"金花"牌转移因子口服液	金花企业股份有限公司	131348	131378
"TYPICAL BROTHER"牌DB2系列平缝机	西安兄弟标准工业公司	156981	156398
"通视"牌信息卡	西安通视数据有限公司	2873	5501
"渭河"牌普通硅酸盐水泥(425R)	陕西省户县水泥厂	7000	3800
"N"牌射频同轴连接器	西安科耐特科技公司	36969	40525
"HTDL"牌聚氯乙烯护套电力电缆	西安塑力电缆厂	42009	39728
"河山"牌胸腺肽	西安迪赛生物药业公司	120539	102350
"致康"牌致康胶囊	西安千禾药业有限公司	185000	190000
"西岳"牌单级单吸化工离心泵阀	西安泵阀总厂	31102	31332
"米旗"牌食品	西安米旗食品有限公司	31289	43350
"秦老大"牌挂面	西安秦老大食品公司	25000	24570
"秦龙"牌工艺旅游纪念品	西安金都工艺美术集团	1500	168
"班博"牌系列服饰	陕西兰维服饰有限公司	14676	14676
"方欣"牌生鲜猪肉及肉制品	西安方欣食品有限公司	69197	53946
"吗丁啉"牌吗丁啉（片、液）	西安杨森制药有限公司	710231	679224
"达克宁"牌达克宁（乳膏、栓、散）	西安杨森制药有限公司	609701	551008
"斯皮仁诺"牌斯皮仁诺胶囊	西安杨森制药有限公司	244110	188778
"西比灵"牌西比灵胶囊	西安杨森制药有限公司	240148	217215
"息斯敏"牌息斯敏片	西安杨森制药有限公司	171183	166202
"IRICO"牌偏转线圈	西安彩虹资讯有限公司	410793	337060
"伟志"牌服装	陕西伟志集团股份有限公司	85236	101242
"RM"牌沥青混合料搅拌设备	西安筑路机械有限公司	188137	154902
"RM"牌沥青混合料摊铺机	西安筑路机械有限公司	61200	42943
"东方"牌灭菌牛奶	西安市东方乳品厂	104700	104700
"西骏"牌希土金属、稀土氧化物	西安市西骏稀土实业有限责任公司	180000	180000
"华泰"牌汽车驾驶员座椅	西安华泰汽车座椅有限责任公司	54536	50524

主要统计指标解释

工业 指从事自然资源的开采，对采掘品和农产品进行加工和再加工的物质生产部门。具体包括:（1）对自然资源的开采，如采矿、晒盐等（但不包括禽兽捕猎和水产捕捞）;（2）对农副产品的加工、再加工，如粮油加工、食品加工、轧花、缫丝、纺织、制革等;（3）对采掘品的加工、再加工，如炼铁、炼钢、化工生产、石油加工、机器制造、木材加工等，以及电力、自来水、煤气的生产和供应等;（4）对工业品的修理、翻新，如机器设备的修理、交通运输工具（包括小卧车）的修理等。

1984年以前农村的村及村以下办工业归属农业，1984年以后划归工业。

工业统计调查单位 工业统计调查单位分为两类:独立核算法人工业企业和工业活动单位。

（1）独立核算法人工业企业 是指从事工业生产经营活动的单位。独立核算法人工业企业应同时具备以下条件:①依法成立，有自己的名称、组织机构和场所，能够承担民事责任;②独立拥有和使用资产，承担负债，有权与其他单位签订合同;③独立核算盈亏，并能够编制资产负债表。

（2）工业活动单位 是指在一个场所从事一种或主要从事一种工业生产活动的经济单位。它包括独立核算工业企业按主营业务活动（即工业生产活动）划分的主营业务活动单位和非工业企业所属的工业生产活动单位（即原非独立核算工业生产单位）。工业活动单位，一般应同时具备以下三个条件:①具有一个场所，从事一种或主要从事一种工业活动;②单独组织工业生产、经营或业务活动;③单独核算收入和支出。

本年鉴中涉及的企业登记注册类型:

（1）国有及国有控股企业 指国有企业加上国有控股企业。国有企业（即过去的全民所有制工业或国营工业）是指企业全部资产归国家所有，并按《中华人民共和国企业法人登记管理条例》规定登记注册的非公司制的经济组织。包括国有企业、国有独资公司和国有联营企业。1957年以前的公私合营和私营工业，后均改造为国营工业，1992年改为国有工业，这部分工业的资料不单独分列时，均包括在国有企业内。国有控股企业是对混合所有制经济的企业进行的“国有控股”分类。它是指这些企业的全部资产中国有资产（股份）相对其他所有者中的任何一个所有者占资（股）最多的企业。该分组反映了国有经济控股情况。

（2）集体企业 指企业资产归集体所有，并按《中华人民共和国企业法人登记管理条例》规定登记注册的经济组织。是社会主义公有制经济的组成部分。包括城乡所有使用集体投资举办的企业，以及部分个人通过集资自愿放弃所有权并依法经工商行政管理机关认定为集体所有制的企业。

（3）股份合作企业 指以合作制为基础，由企业职工共同出资入股，吸收一定比例的社会资产投资组建，实行自主经营，自负盈亏，共同劳动，民主管理，按劳分配与按股分红相结合的一种集体经济组织。

（4）联营企业 指两个及两个以上相同或不同所有制性质的企业法人或事业单位法人，按自愿、平等、互利的原则，共同投资组成的经济组织。联营企业包括:

国有联营企业指国有企业与国有企业间的联营;

集体联营企业指集体企业与集体企业间的联营;

国有与集体联营企业指国有企业与集体企业间的联营。

（5）有限责任公司 指根据《中华人民共和国公司登记管理条例》规定登记注册，由两个以上，五十个以下的股东共同出资，每个股东以其所认缴的出资额对公司承担有限责任，公司以其全部资产对其债务承担责任的经济组织。

有限责任公司包括国有独资公司以及其他有限责任公司。

（6）股份有限公司 指根据《中华人民共和国企业法人登记管理条例》规定登记注册，其全部注册资本由等额股份构成并通过发行股票筹集资本，股东以其认购的股份对公司承担有限责任，公司以其全部资产对其债务承担责任的经济组织。

（7）私营企业 指由自然人投资设立或由自然人控股，以雇佣劳动为基础的营利性经济组织。包括按照《公司法》、《合伙企业法》、《私营企业暂行条例》规定登记注册的私营有限责任公司、私营股份有限公司、私营合伙企业和私营独资企业。

（8）港、澳、台商投资企业 指企业注册登记类型中的港、澳、台资合资、合作、独资经营企业和股份有限公司之和。

（9）外商投资企业 指企业注册登记类型中的中外合资、合作经营企业、外资企业和外商投资股份有限公司之和。

“三资”企业系指港、澳、台商投资企业和外资企业的简称。

轻工业 指主要提供生活消费品和制作手工工具的工业。按其所使用的原料不同，可分为两大类:（1）以农产品为原料的轻工业，是指直接或间接以农产品为基本原料的轻工业。主要包括食品制造、饮料制造、烟草加工、纺织、缝纫、皮革和毛皮制作、造纸以及印刷等工业;（2）以非农产品为原料的轻工业，是指以工业品为原料的轻工业。主要包括文教体育用品、化学药品制造、合成纤维制造、日用化学制品、日用玻璃制品、日用金属制品、手工工具制造、医疗器械制造、文化和办公用机械制造等工业。

重工业 是指为国民经济各部门提供物质技术基础的主要生产资料的工业。按其生产性质和产品用途，可以分为下列三类:（1）采掘（伐）工业，是指对自然资源的开采，包括石油开采、煤炭开采、金属矿开采、非金属矿开采和木材采伐等工业;（2）原材料工业，指向国民经济各部门提供基本材料、动力和燃料的工业。包括金属冶炼及加工、炼焦及焦炭、化学、化工原料、水泥、人造板以及电力、石油和煤炭加工等工业;（3）加工工业，是指对工业原材料进行再加工制造的工业。包括装备国民经济各部门的机械设备制造工业、金属结构、水泥制品等工业，以及为农业提供的生产资料如化肥、农药等工业。

根据上述划分原则，修理业中以重工业产品为修理作业对象的划为重工业，反之划为轻工业。

工业总产值 是以货币表现的工业企业在一定时期内生产的已出售或可供出售工业产品总量，它反映一定时间内工业生产的总规模和总水平。它包括:在本企业内不再进行加工，经检验、包装入库（规定不需包装的产品除外）的成品价值，对外加工费收入，自制半成品、在产品期末初差额价值。工业总产值采用“工厂法”计算，即以工业企业作为一个整体，按企业工业生产活动的最终成果来计算，企业内部不允许重复计算，不能把企业内部各个车间（分厂）生产的成果相加。但在企业之间、行业之间、地区之间存在着重复计算。

轻重工业总产值的划分是按“工厂法”计算的，即一个工业企业生产的主要产品性质属于轻工业，则该企业的全部总产值作为轻工业总产值; 如它的主要产品性质属于重工业，则该企业的全部总产值作为重工业总产值。

工业增加值 是指工业行业在报告期内以货币表现的工业生产活动的最终成果。

实收资本 指企业实际收到的投资人投入的资本。按投资主体可分为国家资本、集体资本、法人资本、个人资本、港澳台资本和外商资本等。

资产合计 指企业拥有或控制的能以货币计量的经济资源。包括各种财产、债权和其他权利。资产按其流动性划分为流动资产、长期投资、固定资产、无形及递延资产和其他资产。

（1）流动资产　指企业可以在一年内或者超过一年的一个生产周期内变现或耗用的资产合计。包括现金及各种存款、短期投资、应收及预付款项、存货等。

（2）固定资产　指企业固定资产净值、固定资产清理、在建工程、待处理固定资产损失所占用的资金合计。

（3）无形资产　指企业长期使用而没有实物形态的资产。包括专利权、非专利技术、商标权、著作权、土地使用权、商誉等。

负债合计 指企业承担的能以货币计量，将以资产或劳务偿付的债务。负债一般按偿还期长短分为流动负债和长期负债、递延税项等。

（1）流动负债　指企业在一年内或者超过一年的一个营业周期内需要偿还的债务合计，其中包括短期借款、应付及预收款项、应付工资、应交税金和应交利润等。

（2）长期负债　指企业在一年以上或者超过一年的一个营业周期以上需要偿还的债务合计，其中包括长期借款、应付债务、长期应付款项等。

所有者权益 指企业投资人对企业净资产的所有权。企业净资产等于企业全部资产减去全部负债后的余额，其中包括投资者对企业的最初投入，以及资本公积金、盈余公积金和未分配利润，对股份制企业即为股东权益。

固定资产原价 指企业在建造、购置、安装、改建、扩建、技术改造某项固定资产时所支出的全部货币总额。它一般包括买价、包装费、运杂费和安装费等。

固定资产净值 是指固定资产原价减去历年已提折旧额后的净额。

流动资产 是指可以在一年或者超过一年的一个营业周期内变现或者耗用的资产，包括现金及各种存款、短期投资、应收及预付货款、存货等。

产品销售收入 指企业销售产品和提供劳务等主要经营业务取得的收入总额。

产品销售成本 指企业销售产品和提供劳务等主要经营业务的实际成本。

产品销售税金及附加 指企业销售产品和提供工业性劳务等主要经营业务应负担的城市维护建设税、消费税、资源税和教育费附加。

利润总额 指企业实现的利润。

应交增值税 指企业在报告期内应交纳的增值税额。

总资产贡献率 反映企业全部资产的获利能力，是企业经营业绩和管理水平的集中体现，是评价和考核企业盈利能力的核心指标。计算公式为：

总资产贡献率=(利润总额+税金总额+利息支出)/平均资产总额*100%

资产负债率 该指标既反映企业经营风险的大小，也反映企业利用债权人提供的资金从事经营活动的能力。计算公式为：

资产负债率=负债总额/资产总额*100%

工业成本费用利润率 指在一定时期内实现的利润与成本费用之比，是反映工业生产成本及费用投入的经济效益指标，同时也是反映降低成本的经济效益的指标。计算公式为：

工业成本费用利润率(%)=利润总额/成本及费用总额*100%

工业增加值率 指在一定时期内工业增加值占同期工业总产值的比重，反映降低中间消耗的经济效益。计算公式为：

工业增加值率(%)=工业增加值(现价)/工业总产值*100%

流动资产周转次数 指在一定时期内流动资产完成的周转次数，反映流动资产的周转速度。计算公式为：

流动资产周转次数=产品销售收入/全部流动资产平均余额

产品销售率 指报告期工业销售产值与同期全部工业总产值之比，是反映工业产品已实现销售的程度，分析工业产销衔接情况，研究工业产品满足社会需求程度的指标。计算公式为：

产品销售率(%)=工业销售产值/工业总产值(现价)*100%

全员劳动生产率 指根据产品的价值量指标计算的平均每一个就业人员在单位时间内的产品生产量。是考核企业经济活动的重要指标，是企业生产技术水平、经营管理水平、职工技术熟练程度和劳动积极性的综合表现。目前我国的全员劳动生产率是将工业企业的工业增加值除以同一时期全部就业人员的平均人数来计算的。计算公式为：

全员劳动生产率(%)=工业增加值/全部就业人员平均人数*100%

Explanatory Notes on Main Statistical Indicators

Industry refers to the material production sector which is engaged in extraction of natural resources and processing and reprocessing of minerals and agricultural products, including (1) extraction of natural resources, such as mining, salt production, (but not including hunting and fishing); (2) processing and reprocessing of farm and sideline produces, such as rice husking, flour milling, wine making, oil pressing, cotton ginning, silk reeling, spinning and weaving, and leather making; (3) manufacture of industrial products, such as steel making, iron smelting, chemicals manufacturing, petroleum processing, machine building, timber processing; water and gas production and electricity generation and supply; (4)repairing of industrial products such as the repairing of machinery and means of transport (including cars).

Prior to 1984, the rural industry run by villages and cooperative organizations under village was classified into agriculture. Since 1984, it has been grouped into industry.

Units of Industrial Statistics and Inquiry: They are classified into two categories (1) corporate industrial enterprises with independent accounting system (2) industrial establishments.

(1) Corporate industrial enterprises with independent accounting system refer to enterprises engaging in industrial production activities, which meet the following requirements: ① They are established legally, having their own names, organizations, location, able to take civil liability; ② They possess and use their assets independently, assume liabilities, and are entitled to sign contracts with other units; ③ They are financially independent and compile their own balance sheets.

(2)Industrial establishments refer to economic units which located in one single place and engaged entirely or primarily in one kind of industrial activity, including financially independent industrial enterprises and units engaged in industrial activities under the non industrial enterprises (or financially dependent). Industrial establishments generally meet the following requirements: ① They have each one location and are engaged in one kind of industrial activity each; ② They operate and manage their industrial production activities separately;③ They have accounts of income and expenditures separately.

(1) State-owned Enterprises refer to industrial enterprises where the means of production or income are owned by the state. Joint state-private industries and private industries, which existed before 1957, have been transformed into state industries. Statistics on these enterprises has been included in the state-owned industries since 1957 when separation of data was no longer necessary.

(2) Collective-owned Enterprises refer to industrial enterprises where the means of production are owned collectively, including urban and rural enterprises invested by collectives and some enterprises which were formerly owned privately but have been registered in industrial and commercial administration agency as collective units through raising fund from the public.

(3) Share-holding Cooperative Enterprises refer to economic units set up on cooperative basis, with funding partly from members of the enterprise and partly from outside investment, where the operation and management is decided by the members who also participate in the production, and the distribution of income is based both on work (labour input) and on shares (capital input).

(4) Joint-operation enterprises refer to economic units that are established by joint investment by two or more corporate enterprises or institutions of the same or different types of ownership on voluntary, equal and mutual-beneficial basis. They include:

a) state-owned joint-operation enterprises (joint operation between state-owned enterprises);

b) collective joint-operation enterprises (joint operation between collective enterprises; and

c) state-collective joint-operation enterprises (joint operation between state and collective enterprises).

(5) Limited Liability Corporations refer to economic units registered in accordance with the Regulation of the People's Republic of China on the Management of Registration of Corporations, with capitals from 2 to 49 investors, each investor bears limited liability to the corporation depending on his/her holding of shares, and the corporation bears liability to its debt to the maximum of its total assets.

(6) Share-holding Corporations Ltd. refer to economic units registered in accordance with the Regulation of the People's Republic of China on the Management of Registration of Corporate Enterprises, with total registered capitals divided into equal shares and raised through issuing stocks. Each investor bears limited liability to the corporation depending on the holding of shares, and the corporation bears liability to its debt to the maximum of its total assets.

(7) Private Enterprises refer to economic units

invested or controlled (by holding the majority of the shares) by natural persons who hire labours for profit-making activities. Included in this category are private limited liability corporations, private share-holding corporations Ltd., private partnership enterprises and private sole investment enterprises registered in accordance with the Corporation Law, Partnership Enterprise Law and Tentative Regulation on Private Enterprises.

(8) Enterprises with Funds form Hong Kong, Macao and Taiwan refers to all industrial enterprises registered as the joint-venture, cooperative, sole (exclusive) investment industrial enterprises and limited liability corporations with funds from Hong Kong, Macao and Taiwan.

(9) Foreign Funded Enterprises refers to all industrial enterprises registered as the joint-venture, cooperative, sole (exclusive) investment industrial enterprises and limited liability corporations with foreign funds.

Light Industry refers to the industry that produces consumer goods and hand tools. It consists of two categories, depending on the materials used:

(1)Industries using farm products as raw materials. These are branches of light industry which directly or indirectly use farm products as basic raw materials, including the manufacture of food and beverages, tobacco processing, textile, clothing, fur and leather manufacturing, paper making, printing, etc.

(2)Industries using non farm products as raw materials. These are branches of light industry which use manufactured goods as raw materials, including the manufacture of cultural, educational articles and sports goods, chemicals, synthetic fiber, chemical products for daily use, glass products for daily use, metal products for daily use, hand tools, medical apparatus and instruments, and the manufacture of cultural and clerical machinery.

Heavy Industry refers to the industry which produces capital goods, and provides various sectors of the national economy with necessary material and technical basis. It consists of the following three branches according to the purpose of production or the use of products:

(1)Mining, quarrying and logging industry refers to the industry that extracts natural resources, including extraction of petroleum, coal, metal and non-metal ores and logging.

(2)Raw materials industry refers to the industry that provides various sectors of the national economy with raw materials, fuels and power. It includes smelting and processing of metals, coking and coke chemistry, chemical materials and building materials such as cement, plywood, and power, petroleum refining and coal dressing.

(3)Manufacturing industry refers to the industry that processes raw materials. It includes machine building industry which equips sectors of the national economy, industries of metal structure and cement products, industries producing means of agricultural production, such as chemical fertilizers and pesticides. According to the above principle of classification, the repairing trades which are engaged primarily in repairing products of heavy industry are classified into heavy industry while these engaged in repairing products of light industry are classified into light industry.

Gross Industrial Output Value is the total volume of industrial products sold or available for sale in value terms which reflects the total achievements and overall scale of industrial production during a given period. It includes the value of the finished products, which are not to be further processed in the enterprises and have been inspected, packed and put in storage, the value of industrial services rendered to other units, and the changes in the value of the semi-finished products and products in process between the beginning and closing of the period. The gross industrial output value is calculated with "factory method". No double calculations are to be made within the same enterprise. However, double counting does occur among different enterprises.

Output value of light and heavy industries is based on the "factory" method. If the major products of an industrial enterprise are classified as light industry products, the entire gross output value of that enterprise is classified into the light industry; the same principle applies to heavy industry.

Value-added of Industry refers to the final results of industrial production of the industrial trade in money terms during the reference period.

Capital Obtained refers to capital actually received by the enterprise from investors. It can be further classified by investors as state capital, collective capital, corporate capital, individual capital, capital from Hong Kong, Macau and Taiwan and foreign capital.

Total Assets refer to all economic resources, owned or controlled by enterprises, that could be measured in monetary terms, including properties, creditors equity and other economic rights of all forms. Classified by the degree of equitability, total assets include circulating assets, long term investment, fixed assets, intangible assets anddeferred assets, and other assets.

(1)Circulating assets (working capital) refer to assets which can be cashed in or spent or consumed in an operating cycle of one year or over one year, including cash, all kinds of deposits, short term investment, receivables, advance payment, stock, etc.

(2)Fixed assets refer to the net value of fixed assets, clearance of fixed assets, project under construction, fixed assets losses in suspense. These are corporations□ fund holdings.

(3)Intangible assets refer to the assets without material form used by enterprises over a long time, such as patents, non-patent technologies, trade marks, copyright, land use right, business reputation, etc.

Total Liabilities refer to the debts, measured in monetary terms, that enterprises are responsible for repayment in the form of cash, assets or labour. Classified by terms of repayment, liability include liquid liabilities and long-term liabilities.

(1)Liquid liabilities (also called quick liabilities or immediate liabilities) refer to enterprises' total debt payable within an operating cycle of one year or over one year, including short term loans, payable and advance payments, wages payable, taxes payable and profit payable, etc.

(2)Long term liabilities refers to total debt payable within an operating cycle of one year or over one year, including long-term loans, payable liabilities, long-term payable, etc.

Creditors' Equity refers to investors ownership of net assets of the enterprise. It is equal to the total assets of the enterprise minus its total liabilities, including the primary input from investors, capital accumulation fund, surplus accumulation fund and undistributed profit. It is the shareholder's equity in share-holding companies.

Original Value of Fixed Assets refers to the original value of all fixed assets owned by industrial enterprises, calculated at the cost paid at the time of purchase, installation, reconstruction, expansion, and technical innovation and transformation of the said assets, which includes expenses on purchase, package, transportation, and installation, etc.

Net Value of Fixed Assets is obtained by deducting depreciation over years from the original value of fixed assets.

Working Capital (Circulating Assets) refers to assets which can be cashed in or spent or consumed in an operating cycle of one year or over one year, which includes cash, various deposits, short term investment, and receivable payments, and advance payments, stock, etc.

Sales Revenue of Industrial Products refers to the revenue from the sales of products by industrial enterprises and the revenue from services provided and etc.

Sales Cost of Industrial Products refers to the actual cost of products of industrial enterprises and industrial services provided, etc.

Tax and Extra Charges on Sales of Products refer to the tax on city maintenance and construction, consumption tax, resources tax and extra charges for education, which should be borne by the enterprises in selling products and providing industrial services.

Total Profits refer to the profits gained by the enterprises.

Value-added Tax Payable refers to the amount of the value added tax which should be paid by the enterprises in the reporting period.

Ratio of Profits, Taxes and Interests to Average Assets reflects the profit-making capability of all assets of the enterprise and is a key indicator manifesting the performance and management and evaluating the profit-making potential of the enterprise. It is calculated as follows:

Ratio of profits, taxes and interests to average assets (%) = [(Total profits+total Taxes+interest payment) / average assets]×100%

Ratio of Debts to Assets reflect both the operation risk and the capability of the enterprise in making use of the capital from the creditors. It is calculated as follows:

Ratio of debts to assets (%) = (Total debts / total assets)×100%

Ratio of Profits to Total Industrial Costs refers to the ratio of profits realized in a given period to the total costs in the same period, which reflects the economic efficiency of input cost and is calculated as follows:

Ratio of Profits to Total Industrial Cost(%)=(Total Profits/ Total Costs)×100%

Value-added Rate of Industry refers to the ratio of value added of industry in a given period to the gross output value in the same period, which reflects the economic efficiency of cutting down the intermediate input and is calculated as follows:

Value-added Rate of Industry(%)=[Value-added of Industry (at current prices)] / [Gross Output Value (at Current Prices)]×100%

Turnover of Working Capital refers to the number of times of turnover of working capital in a given period of time, which reflects the speed of the turnover of working capital and is calculated as follows:

Turnover of Working Capital(%)=(Sales Revenue ofProducts) / (Average Balance of Total Working Capital)×100%

Ratio of Sales to Gross Output Value refers to the sales of industrial products to the gross industrial output value during the reference period, and is important in reflecting the linkage between production and sales and the extent of the needs of the society that has been met by the supply of industrial products. It is calculated as follows:

Ratio of Sales to Gross Output Value=[Industrial sales / Gross industrial output value (at current prices)] ×100%

Overall Labour Productivity of Industrial Enterprises refers to the average output per employed person in industrial enterprises in value terms. At present, the value added and the average number of staff and workers of an industrial enterprises in a given period are used to calculate the overall labour productivity. The formula used is:

Overall Labour Productivity=(Value Added of Industry) / (Average Number of Staff and Workers)

2004

年統
鑒計

十一、建筑业

CONSTRUCTION

简 要 说 明
Brief Introduction

本章资料主要包括我市建筑业基本情况，建筑业施工企业生产情况和财务状况。由市统计局固定资产投资处提供资料。

Data in this chapter consists of basic situation of the construction industry, production situation and financial situation of the construction enterprises, number of construction projects and area of the buildings, provided by Fixed Asset Investment Division of the Xi'an Bureau of Statistics.

11-1 全市建筑施工企业基本情况

Main Indicators on Construction Enterprise of Xi'an

指　　标	Item	2003
企业个数(个)	Number of Enterprises (unit)	204
二级以上企业（施工总承包）	First and Second Class Enterprise(Overall Cortractor For Construction)	61
国有及国有控股	State-owned Or State Holding Majority Shares	51
平均人数(人)	Average Employed Persons (person)	156300
二级以上企业（施工总承包）	First and Second Class Enterprise (Overall Cortractor For Construction)	114746
国有及国有控股	State-owned Or State Holding Majority Shares	102548
建筑业总产值(万元)	Total Output Value (10 000 yuan)	1771126
二级以上企业（施工总承包）	First and Second Class Enterprise (Overall Cortractor For Construction)	1523068
国有及国有控股	State-owned Or State Holding Majority Shares	1466160
增加值(万元)	Value-added (10 000 yuan)	276990
二级以上企业（施工总承包）	First and Second Class Enterprise (Overall Cortractor For Construction)	231372
国有及国有控股	State-owned Or State Holding Majority Shares	221852
全员劳动生产率(元/人)	Overall Labor Productivity (yuan/person)	
按总产值计算	Calculated by Total Output Value	113316
按增加值计算	Calculated by Value-added	17722

11-2 全市建筑施工企业生产情况（2003年，按经济类型分）

指　　标	Item	签定的合同额（万元） Contract Value (10 000 yuan)
总　　计	**Total**	**3528235**
其中：国有及国有控股	Of the Total:State-Owned and State Holding Majority Shares	3031375
一、按登记注册类型分	**Grouped by Registion Status**	
内资	Domestic Investment Enterprises	3528235
国有企业	State-owned Enterprises	2493156
集体企业	Collective-owned Enterprises	223646
股份合作企业	Share-holding Corperative Enterprises	2763
联营企业	Joint Ownership Enterprises	51612
有限责任公司	Limited Liability Corporations	646836
股份有限公司	Share-holding Corperation Ltd	39269
私营企业	Private Enterprises	70931
港、澳、台商投资企业	Enterprises with Investment from Hongkong,Macao and Taiwan	
外商投资企业	Enterprises with Foreign Investment	
二、按国民经济行业分	**Grouped by Sector**	
土木工程建筑业	Civil Engineering Construction	2180130
房屋工程建筑		1184759
装修装饰业	Fitting and Decoration	30803
三、按隶属关系分	**Grouped by Administrative Relationship**	
中　央	Central	2282628
省　属	Provincial	532860
市　属	Municipal	712747
四、按企业资质等级分	**Grouped by Class of Enterprises**	
1.施工总承包	Overall Contractor for Construction	3346521
其中:一级	Of the Total:First Class	2740736
二级	Second Class	389111
2.专业承包	Special Contractor	181714
其中:一级以上	Of the Total: First Class	81443

Main Indicators on Construction Enterprise of Xi'an Grouped by Registion Status（2003）

建筑业总产值（万元）Total Output Value of Constrution (10 000 yuan)	建筑工程产值 Output Value of Constrution	安装工程产值 Output Value of Installation	其他产值 Others	计算劳动生产率的平均人数（人）Average Number of Employed Persons in Calculation of Labour Productivity(person)	期末从业人数（人）Number of Employment at Year-end (person)	工程技术人员 Technical Personnel	企业总产值（万元）Total Output Value of Enterprises (10 000 yuan)	对内销售产值 Domestic Sales out put
1771126	**1581122**	**163643**	**26361**	**156300**	**133186**	**24598**	**1833198**	**19727**
1466160	1331302	119201	15657	102548	81501	16298	1520993	16214
1771126	1581122	163643	26361	156300	133186	24598	1833198	19727
1199911	1075386	109059	15466	77597	56993	12667	1240874	8530
134010	123522	8356	2132	29271	28897	4593	134870	482
2446	1734	22	690	595	622	140	2446	
18433	18433			3723	3385	449	18433	
340968	304664	35637	667	37052	36869	5180	357952	10715
28016	21213	4614	2189	2651	1637	470	31043	
47309	36170	5955	5184	5403	4775	1093	47547	
950078	873407	68480	8191	47014	46252	10434	997736	18464
702761	658943	40313	3505	96761	76930	12467	711300	1041
28026	23844	390	3792	2087	1894	388	28264	
994984	905053	83902	6029	59929	45597	9696	1035002	9759
318213	284398	24195	9620	27372	20846	3946	323455	579
457929	391671	55546	10712	68999	66743	10956	474741	9389
1655905	1508185	129862	17858	142070	121394	22435	1714229	19505
1279703	1188277	76072	15354	73634	64596	13765	1333669	16214
243365	217156	24807	1402	41112	31228	4920	243917	
115221	72937	33781	8503	14230	11792	2163	118969	222
42196	23521	18621	54	4669	3026	514	42677	222

11-3 全市建筑施工企业生产情况（2003年，按行业类别分）

指　　标	Item	单位工程施工个数（个）Number of Projects under Constrution	本年新开工 Beginning Projects in this Year
总计	**Total**	**4427**	**2357**
其中：国有及国有控股	Of the Total:State-owned or State Holding Majority Shares	2809	1339
一、按登记注册类型分	**Grouped by Registion Status**		
内资	Domestic Investment Enterprises	4425	2357
国有企业	State-owned Enterprises	2173	1132
集体企业	Collective-owned Enterprises	950	644
股份合作企业	Share-holding Corperative Enterprises	44	33
联营企业	Joint Ownership Enterprises	10	6
有限责任公司	Limited Liability Corporations	948	350
股份有限公司	Share-holding Corperation Ltd	64	49
私营企业	Private Enterprises	236	143
港、澳、台商投资企业	Enterprises with Investment from Hongkong, Macao and Taiwan		
外商投资企业	Enterprises with Foreign Investment	2	
二、按国民经济行业分	**Grouped by Sector**		
土木工程建筑业	Civil Engineering Construction	3304	1874
线路、管道和设备安装业	Electric Line,Pipe and Equipment Instllation	1123	483
装修装饰业	Fitting and Decoration		
三、按隶属关系分	**Grouped by Administrative Relationship**		
中　央	Central	1884	803
省　属	Provincial	712	441
市　属	Municipal	1831	1113
四、按企业资质等级分	**Grouped by Class of Enterprises**		
1.施工总承包	Overall Contractor for Construction	3597	1835
其中:一级	Of the Total:First Class	2134	810
二级	Second Class	626	487
2.专业承包	Special Contractor	597	343
其中:一级以上	Of the Total: First Class	192	163

Main Indicators on Construction Enterprise of Xi'an Grouped by Sector（2003）

房屋建筑竣工面积(平方米) Floor Space of Buildings under Construction (sq.m)	自有机械设备年末净值(万元) Net Value of Mechanical Equipment owned by Constructions Enterprises at Year-end(10 000yuan)	自有机械设备年末总台数(台) Number of Mechanical Equipment Owend By Construction Enterprises at Year-end(unit)	自有机械设备年末总功率(万千瓦) Total Power of Mechanical Equipment Owned by Construction Enterprises at Year-end(10000kw)	施工机械总功率 Total Power of Construct Mechinery
12916215	**147755**	**46424**	**778994**	**521607**
7621060	103690	20647	530171	318916
12916215	147755	46424	778994	521607
6934866	78478	14272	422521	276816
2798632	25743	16928	173496	138207
30042	1758	509	7388	4961
389256	2308	1928	8999	8050
165117	32667	9544	141944	73035
357541	2190	1074	5115	4785
753761	4611	2169	19531	15753
203259	73851	10166	356293	241334
62541	59998	6272	261769	205142
	2896	759	9335	8592
3119905	67941	9402	336838	219870
3398159	23304	8016	94905	52182
6398151	56510	29006	347251	249555
11763922	136272	43090	725142	484286
5515434	85018	15851	433439	267657
4308874	27989	14135	157948	104499
1152293	11483	3334	53852	37321
14963	4518	970	24991	13708

11-4　全市建筑施工企业财务状况（2003年）

单位: 万元

项　目	Item	总　计 Total
流动资产小计	Circulating Assets	1357940
其中: 存货	Of the Total:Stocks	286408
其中: 在建工程	Of the Total:Projects Under Construction	16989
长期投资	Long-term Investment	63928
固定资产合计	Fixed Assets	425515
固定资产原价	Original Value of Fixed Assets	593958
其中: 生产经营用	Of the Total:Using for Production and Management	437025
累计折旧	Accumulative Total Depreciation	195991
其中: 本年折旧	Of the Total:Depreciation Within the Year	31024
无形及递延资产合计	Intangible and Deferred Assets	25256
其中: 无形资产	Of the Total:Intangible Assets	15760
资产合计	Total Assets	1901076
流动负债小计	Liquid Liabilities	1218984
长期负债小计	Long-term Liabilities	102725
负债合计	Total Liabilities	1321709
所有者权益合计	Owner Rights and Interests	579367
其中: 实收资本	Of the Total:Actual Capital Hold	414663
1.国家资本	State Capital	97962
2.集体资本	Collective Capital	55972
3.法人资本	Corporation Capital	214568
4.个人资本	Individual Capital	46161
5.港澳台资本	Capital from HongKong,Macao and Taiwan	
6.外商资本	Foreign Capital	
工程结算收入	Revenue of Project Settlement Accounts	1975516
工程结算成本	Costs of Project Settlement Accounts	1806932
工程结算税金及附加	Taxs and Extra Charges on Project Settlement Accounts	51438
工程结算利润	Profits of Projet Settlement Accounts	117146
其他业务利润	Other Profits from Business	14228
管理费用	Management Expenses	99713
其中: 税金	Of the Total:Tax Revenue	1899
财产保险费	Expense of Property and Insurance	519
劳动、待业保险费	Expense of Insurance for Laboring、Employment	15405
财务费用	Financial Expenditures	11790
营业利润	Operating Surplus	19871
利润总额	Total Profits	18587
其中: 应交所得税	Of the Total:Income taxes Payable	4789
应付利润	Profits Payable	3482
本年应付工资总额	Total Wages Payable this Year	132281
本年应付福利费总额	Total Welfare Expense Payable in this Year	25072
年末拖欠工程款	In Arrears With Project Funds at Year-end	266242
亏损企业个数（个）	Number of Loss-making Enterpriese(unit)	28
亏损额	Total loss	828

Financial Status of Building Construction Enterprises In Xi'an(2003)

(10 000yuan)

国有及国有控股 State-Owned and State Holding Majority Shares Enterprises	中央企业 Enterprises Central	省属企业 Province Enterprises	市属企业 Municipal Enterprises
1111226	634152	322054	401734
218140	122516	74779	89113
11640	6270	3883	6836
54804	52947	2371	8610
335725	185888	100639	138988
485045	296261	129033	168664
352050	260344	54179	122502
170591	123492	33441	39058
27402	20147	4891	5986
13674	9348	3625	12283
5867	3739	1757	10264
1529682	884681	431302	585093
1035723	604601	287759	326624
85067	41161	35454	26110
1120790	645762	323213	352734
408892	238919	108089	232359
279830	154280	73636	186747
97834	28022	25542	44398
3552		4460	51512
176808	126258	41404	46906
1636		2230	43931
			0
			0
1718707	1305302	257044	413170
1582590	1211866	225620	369446
43395	29857	8572	13009
92722	63579	22852	30715
11515	7593	1087	5548
79906	55575	19366	24772
1354	723	300	876
394	216	5	298
14516	9891	3537	1977
9596	6025	2122	3643
14735	9572	2451	7848
13438	8641	3185	6761
3048	1791	285	2713
1590	801	207	2474
99486	60934	25050	46297
20964	13152	6398	5522
205360	69910	84068	112264
7	2	4	22
549	119	104	605

11-5 施工总承包二级以上建筑企业一览表（2003年）

企业名称 Name of Enterprises	施工产值（万元） Output Value Under Construction (10 000 yuan)	从业人员平均数（人） Average Employed persons (person)	全员劳动生产率（元/人） Overall Labor Productivity (yuan/person)
西安市第一住宅建筑公司	3001	817	36732
陕西电力建设总公司	20659	848	248007
路桥集团第二公路工程局	426315	7368	496697
陕西省第八建筑工程公司	30534	1683	72700
陕西省第五建筑工程公司	40116	1870	208287
陕西省第三建筑工程公司	38070	1103	146311
陕西省设备安装工程公司	39542	2955	119174
陕西省新安建筑工程处	2000	103	105263
陕西省机械施工公司	32233	1555	194175
中国水利水电第三工程局	107263	8155	130363
陕西省第一建筑工程公司	37901	1492	117304
陕西航天建筑工程公司	75200	1400	64109
陕西省路桥工程公司	41196	2872	133450
陕西铁路工程承包公司	100139	10727	96352
西安铁路工程有限责任公司	42537	1818	171728
铁道部第一工程部建筑安装工程总公司	6928	1865	52247
陕西联合建筑工程公司	1310	223	58744
陕西省市政建筑工程公司	10280	1986	41120
西安飞机工业建筑安装工程公司	1714	472	73879
西安市水利建设工程总公司	35096	1741	181562
陕西送变电工程公司	43037	3044	135124
西北电力建筑第四工程公司	27741	1551	180253
西安市第一市政工程公司	13101	922	127194
西安市第四建筑工程公司	11512	1740	66161
西安市第二建筑工程公司	28430	1403	230950
西安市第二市政工程公司	12068	1600	70573
西安市第一建筑工程公司	5601	1954	28753
西安市第五建筑工程公司	1732	1330	13023
西安市第二住宅建筑公司	160	54	29630

List of Construction Enterprises of First Class and Second Class（2003）

实收资本合计（万元） Total Actual Capitals Hold (10 000yuan)	工资总额（万元） Total Amount of Wages (10 000 yuan)	利润总额（万元） Total Profits (10 000 yuan)	房屋建筑施工面积（平方米) Floor Space of Buildings Under Construction (sq.m)
2100	607	-81	60800
35639	1539	293	59590
34583	11776	6320	
5251	2065	101	491683
5197	'3022	85	636022
5043	2213	85	811253
6068	3460	286	
30	170		18000
6386	1807	26	
14333	9952	-104	13976
5895	2041	76	856118
5000	4782	461	1544926
6743	4135	1984	
10380	9998	269	54534
5841	2562	259	682919
2025	811	12	181966
1647	236	-14	18300
2500	1312	19	92405
2010	225	-272	
7289	3524	184	2951
10368	5248	17	295422
4604	2105	761	
5100	900	2	305806
7612	349	2	210621
4325	2123	207	
5100	343	3	260466
5660	1301	2	139348
2004	268		10
2004	130	3	40524

11-5　施工总承包二级以上建筑企业一览表（2003年）（续）

企业名称 Name of Enterprises	施工产值 (万元) Output Value Under Construction (10 000 yuan)	从业人员平均数 (人) Average Employed persons (person)	全员劳动生产率 (元/人) Overall Labor Productivity (yuan/person)
西安市建筑工程总公司西京建筑工	160	54	29630
核工业西北工程建设总公司	7460	413	204945
西安经纬建筑工程有限公司	3142	632	42005
陕西省第六建筑工程公司西安工程	100	20	100000
陕西省第一建筑工程公司第四工程	1500	320	57252
西安航空发动机公司建筑安装工程	2702	1259	21444
西安雁塔建设工程有限公司	27002	1240	216362
陕西华油建筑工程有限公司	4918	1602	30950
西安市阎良区第三建筑工程公司	8009	985	148315
西安市长安区水利建筑工程总公司	1510	160	65652
西安市长安建筑开发集团公司	6120	1760	30800
西安市临潼区建筑工程联合公司	2494	526	47414
西安市临潼区建筑工程公司	8155	920	88641
西安筑邦建筑工程公司	6730	2035	31000
户县建筑公司	8538	2318	41751
西安秦户建司	2831	2342	14623
高陵县建筑工程公司	11365	126	249232
陕西深蓝工程总承包有限责任公司	1964	682	97711
西安中煤建筑工程公司	8236	649	125167
西安多国建筑艺术装潢公司	1000	240	41667
西安秦大建设公司	1982	565	37396
陕西省第三建筑工程公司第四分公	4200	128	136808
秦海国际工程总公司	76437	4734	186295
西安航空发动机集团天鼎有限公司	9956	560	102218
陕西安达建设有限责任公司	2823	35	188200
陕西华山环境保护工程有限公司责	14151	1386	112220
陕西华达建筑工程有限公司	15366	301	128586
西安市红庙坡建筑工程有限公司	3735	721	51660
西安仁和建筑工程有限公司	13256	750	194941
陕西省宝天建筑工程有限公司	6900		1600
陕西宏远通信科技有线公司	1858		258
西安市政道桥建设有限公司	19087		1193
陕西秦地建设有限公司	4125		713

List of Construction Enterprises of First Class and Second Class（2003）(Continued)

实收资本合计（万元）Total Actual Capitals Hold (10 000yuan)	工资总额（万元）Total Amount of Wages (10 000 yuan)	利润总额（万元）Total Profits (10 000 yuan)	房屋建筑施工面积（平方米) Floor Space of Buildings Under Construction (sq.m)
618	12	-22	2330
3138	210	48	
2055	280	39	46415
780	3		1610
600	273	20	25206
2180	471	88	42959
5236	2000		335177
5016	401	188	128620
2092	580	64	168651
2000	118	85	8020
2442	1176	277	128790
2010	470	50	44043
2655	1729	3	106916
2688	1105	358	90349
2344	1563	4	235286
1932	1104	40	70700
2904	100	5	185615
5000	42		
2106	1031	196	164216
132	135	10	
2460	391	99	21214
145	93		89309
10717	5496	369	32174
3275	762	85	126829
2000	40	128	31340
5000	1177	170	198251
5000	250	-10	323434
2000	172	45	51800
2007	138	12	217070
5000	1134	8	98000
1500	443	335	
4020	2478	365	
3087	1314	12	112868

主要统计指标解释

建筑业统计单位 指从事房屋、构筑物建造和设备安装活动的法人企业。建筑业法人企业应同时具备的条件是:①依法成立，有自己的名称、组织机构和场所，能够承担民事责任;②独立拥有和使用资产，承担负债，有权与其他单位签订合同;③独立核算盈亏，能够编制资产负债表。

建筑业总产值（即自行完成施工产值） 是以货币表现的建筑安装企业在一定时期内生产的建筑业产品的总和。建筑业总产值包括:

（1）建筑工程产值:指列入建筑工程预算内的各种工程价值。

（2）设备安装工程产值:指设备安装工程价值，不包括被安装设备本身价值。

（3）房屋、构筑物修理产值:指房屋、构筑物修理所完成的价值，但不包括被修理房屋、构筑物本身的价值和生产设备的修理价值。

（4）非标准设备制造产值:指加工制造没有定型的、非标准的生产设备的加工费和原材料价值，以及附属加工厂为本企业承建工程制作的非标准设备的价值。

建筑业增加值 指建筑业企业在报告期内以货币表现的建筑业生产经营活动的最终成果。目前建筑业增加值采用分配法（收入法）计算，即从收入的角度出发，根据生产要素在生产过程中应得的收入份额计算。具体计算公式为:

建筑业增加值＝本年提取的固定资产折旧+应付工资+应付福利费+管理费用中的劳动待业保险金、税金+工程结算税金及附加+工程结算利润

房屋建筑施工面积 指在报告期内施工的全部房屋建筑面积，包括本期新开工的房屋面积、上期施工跨入本期继续施工的房屋面积、上期停缓建在本期恢复施工的房屋面积、本期竣工的房屋面积及本期施工后又停缓建的房屋面积。

房屋建筑竣工面积 指在报告期内房屋建筑按照设计要求全部完工，达到了住人和使用条件，经验收鉴定合格，正式移交使用单位的房屋建筑面积。

自有机械设备年末总台数 指归本企业所有，属于本企业固定资产的生产性机械设备年末总台数。包括施工机械、生产设备、运输设备以及其他设备。

自有机械设备年末总功率 指本企业自有施工机械、生产设备、运输设备以及其他设备等列为在册固定资产的生产性机械设备年末总功率，按设定能力或查定能力计算。包括机械本身的动力和为该机械服务的单独动力设备，如电动机等。计算单位用千瓦，动力换算可按1马力＝0.735千瓦折合成千瓦数。电焊机、变压器、锅炉不计算动力。

工程结算收入 指企业承包工程实现的工程价款结算收入，以及向发包单位收取的除工程价款以外的按规定列作营业收入的各种款项，如临时设施费、劳动保险费、施工机械调迁费等以及向发包单位收取的各种索赔款。

工程结算利润 指已结算工程实现的利润，如亏损以“－”号表示。计算公式为:

工程结算利润＝工程结算收入－工程结算成本－工程结算税金及附加

企业总收入 指与企业生产经营直接有关的各项收入，包括工程结算收入和其他业务收入。计算公式为:

企业总收入＝工程结算收入＋其他业务收入

Explanatory Notes on Main Statistical Indicators

Statistical Unit in Construction refers to corporate enterprise engaged in the construction of buildings and structures and in the installation of equipment. A corporate construction enterprise should meet the following 3 requirements:①being set up in line with relevant legal basis, having its full name, organization and location, and capable of taking civil liabilities;② independently possessing and using its assets and assuming its liabilities, and entitled to sign contracts with other institutions; and ③ making independent accounts of its profits and losses, and capable of compiling its own balance sheet.

Gross Output Value of Construction (Output Value of Projects Under Construction) refers to total of construction products, expressed in money terms, completed by construction and installation enterprises during a given period of time. It includes:

(1)Output value of construction projects, that is the value of projects covered by the project budgets;

(2)Output value of installation projects, that is the value of the installation of equipment, (excluding the value of the equipment to be installed);

(3)Output value of repair of buildings and structures, that is the value created through the repairs of buildings or structures, but does not include the value of buildings or structures being repaired and the value of the repair of production equipment;

(4)Output value of manufactured non-standard equipment, that is the value of non-standard production equipment (including raw materials and manufacturing cost) made for the construction project, and the equipment manufactured by subsidiary workshops.

Value-added of Construction refers to the final result of the activities of production and management of construction in monetary terms in the reference period. At present, the value-added of construction is calculated with the income approach. In other words, it is the sum of income of various production factors in the production process. The formula is as follows:

Value-added of construction=depreciation of fixed assets in the year+wages payable+welfare expenses payable+insurance premium and tax for waiting for employment in the administrative expenses +taxes and surcharges on project settlement+profit gained from project settlement.

Floor Space of Buildings Under Construction refers to floor space of buildings under construction during the reference period, including newly started buildings, buildings started earlier and continued during the reference period, and buildings suspended earlier but restarted during the reference period, buildings completed during the reference period, and buildings under construction and then suspended during the reference period.

Floor Space of Buildings Completed refers to the floor space of buildings that are completed in the reference period in accordance with the requirements of the design, up to the standard for putting them into use, and have been checked and accepted by concerned departments as qualified ones.

Total Number of Machinery and Equipment Owned by the End of Year refers to the number of machines and equipment owned by the enterprises, and listed as the fixed assets of the enterprises by the end of the year, including machinery and equipment for construction, production and transportation.

Total Power of Machinery and Equipment Owned by the End of Year refers to the total power of machinery and equipment owned by the enterprises, and listed as the fixed assets of the enterprises by the end of the year, including machinery and equipment for construction, production and transportation. The power of the machinery is calculated on basis of the designed or verified capacity, covering the power of the machinery/equipment and the separate power equipment serving the machinery/equipment (such as electric motors), but excluding welders, transformers and boilers. The unit used for the calculation of power is kilowatt, with horsepower converted to kilowatt by 1 horsepower=0.735 kilowatt.

Income from Settlement of Projects refers to the income received by the construction enterprise from the contracted project through settlement procedures, and other charges to the contractoree as operational costs in addition to the value of the project, such as temporary facility fee, labour insurance premium, moving cost of construction equipment, as well as various types of claimsto the contractee.

Profit from Settlement of Projects refers to profit realized through settled projects. It is calculated with the following formula:

Profit from Settlement of Projects=Income from Settlement of Projects-Settled Cost-Settled Taxes and Other Cost

Total Revenue of Enterprises refers to the sum of income from production and operation of enterprises, including income from settlement of projects and other operational income, namely:

Total Revenue of Enterprises=Income from Settlement of Projects+Other Operational Income

2004 年鉴 統計

十二、运输和邮电

TRANSPORATION AND POSTAL SERVICE

简 要 说 明
Brief Introduction

本章资料主要包括我市交通运输业和邮电通信业的基本情况、交通运输工具、货物和旅客运输量、邮电业务基本情况、邮政局所及服务点等。

本章资料由市统计局工业交通处整理提供。

Data in this chapter consists of primarily basic data of communication, transportation and postal service industry, transportation facility, amount of goods and passenger transportation, basic data of postal service, post offices and service establishments of Xi'an City.

Data in this chapter is compiled and provided by Industry & Transportation Division of the Xi'an Bureau of Statistics.

12-1 各种交通线路里程和桥梁数

Length of Transportation Routes and Number of Bridges

项目	Item	2003	2002	2003年比2002年增长（%）Increase Rate in 2003 over 2002(%)
铁路正线延展里程 (公里)	Extendtion Length of the Trunk Lines(km)	2089	1968	6.15
营业里程	Length in Operation	1522	1543	-1.36
电气化营业里程	Length of Electrified Railways in Operation	823	1009	-18.43
复线里程	Double-Tracking Length	543	394	37.82
公路里程 (公里)	Length of Highways (km)	8360	7862	6.33
#晴雨通车里程	#Length of Highways in All Weathers	3853	3355	14.84
等级公路	Expressways and Class Ⅰ to Ⅳ Highways	3853	3355	14.84
高速	Expressways	251	192	30.73
一级	First Class	121	81	49.38
二级	Second Class	781	680	14.85
三级	Third Class	1223	925	32.22
四级	Forth Class	1477	1477	0.00
等外公路	Highways below Class Ⅳ	4507	4507	0.00
桥梁	Bridges			
座 (座)	Seat (seat)	629	629	0.00
长度 (米)	Length (m)	29799	29799	0.00
永久式桥梁	Permanent			
座 (座)	Seat (seat)	629	629	0.00
长度 (米)	Length (m)	29799	29799	0.00
半永久式桥梁	Semi Permanent			
座 (座)	Seat (seat)			
长度 (米)	Length (m)			
民航通航里程 (公里)	Length of Total Civil Aviation Routes(km)	381800	211000	80.95

12-2 全社会车辆数

Civil Motor Vehicles

项目	Item	2003	2002
合 计 (辆)	**Total (unit)**	**516719**	**454998**
民用汽车 (辆)	Civil Motor Vehicles(unit)	242599	206653
载客汽车 (辆)	Number of Passenger Vehicles (unit)	163872	134527
#大型	#Large	6245	5760
小轿车	Small Saloon Car	90098	72755
载客汽车载客量 (客位)	Number of Seats of Passenger Vehciles(set)		1021242
#大型	#Large		209123
普通载货汽车 (辆)	Ordinary Trucks (unit)	70781	64623
#大型	#Large	31037	28393
普通载货汽车载重量 (吨位)	Capacity of Ordinary Truck (unit)		184131
#大型	#Large		150292
专用载货汽车 (辆)	Trucks for Special Use (unit)		
专用载货汽车载重量(吨位)	Capacity of Trucks for Special Use (unit)		
其他汽车 (辆)	Others (unit)	7946	7503
特种汽车	Special--model Vehicles	479	204
农用运输车 (辆)	Vehicles for Agricultural Purposes(unit)	47110	35019
1.三轮	Three Wheelers	38348	30946
2.四轮	Four Wheelers	8762	4073
拖拉机 (台)	Tractors(unit)	34733	36083
1.大型	Large -sized	7403	7362
2.小型	Small-sized	27330	28721
摩托车 (辆)	Motorcycle (unit)	191834	176960
普通摩托车	#Bicycle Motor	146434	132538
挂车 (辆)	Articulated Trailers (unit)	285	121
其他类型车 (辆)	Others (unit)		

12-3　交通运输量及运输周转量

Passenger Traffic and Kilometers and Freight Traffic and Ton-kilometers

指　标	Item	2003	2002	2003年比2002年增长(%) Increase Rate in 2003 over 2002(%)
一、客运量（万人次）	**Passenger Traffic(10 000 person-times)**	**11413**	**12399**	**-7.95**
铁路	Railway	1889	1997	-5.41
公路	Highway	9252	10124	-8.61
民用航空	Civil Aviation	272	278	-2.16
二、旅客周转量（万人公里）	**Passenger-Km (10 000 person-Km)**	**2596402**	**2524444**	**2.85**
铁路	Railway	1652456	1590403	3.90
公路	Highway	602572	575653	4.68
民用航空	Civil Aviation	341374	358388	-4.75
三、货运量（万吨）	**Freight Traffic(10 000 tons)**	**9392**	**9482**	**-0.95**
铁路	Railway	3662	3167	15.63
公路	Highway	5726	6310	-9.25
民用航空	Civil Aviation	4	5	-20.00
四、货物周转量（万吨公里）	**Freight Ton-Km (10 000 ton-Km)**	**5037684**	**4544040**	**10.86**
铁路	Railway	4427166	4073220	8.69
公路	Highway	604755	462961	30.63
民用航空	Civil Aviation	5763	7859	-26.67

12-4 邮政业务及服务网点

Postal service and branch post office

指 标	Item	2003	2002	2003年比2002年增长(%) Increase Rate in 2003 over 2002(%)
一、邮政业务总量（万元）	Amount of post service (10 000 Yuan)	50270	44767	12.29
二、邮政业务总收入（万元）	Gross income of post service (10 000 Yuan)	47392	44975	5.37
三、函件（万件）	Letters (10 000 pcs)	14814	10383	42.67
四、包件（万件）	Parcels (10 000 pcs)	112	141	-20.57
五、汇票（万张）	Money order (10 000 pcs)	168	156	7.69
六、报纸订销累计份数（万份）	Accumulated newspaper prescribing and sales volume (10 000 pcs)	11165	10914	2.30
七、杂志订销累计份数（万份）	Accumulated magazine prescribing and sales volume (10 000 pcs)	782	781	0.13
八、特快专递类业务（万件）	Express mail service volume (10 000 pcs)	1068	165	547.27
九、集邮业务量（万枚）	Philately volume (10 000 pcs)	2399	2444	-1.84
十、邮政储蓄余额（万元）	Postal savings deposit balance (10 000 Yuan)	716914	519483	38.01
十一、邮政营销网点（处）	Number of post office branch establishments (unit)	338	326	3.68
#设在农村的局所	number of post offices in rural area	113	117	-3.42
十二、邮政信筒信箱（个）	Number of mailboxes(unit)	1160	1130	2.65

12-5 电信业务情况

Telecommunication service

指 标	Item	2003	2002	2003年比2002年增长(%) Increase Rate in 2003 over 2002(%)
一、电信业务总量（万元）	**Amount of telecommunicationService (10 000 Yuan)**	607634	470492	29.15
二、电信业务总收入（万元）	Gross income of of telecommunicationService (10 000 Yuan)	467198	411221	13.61
三、固定电话年末户数（户）	Number of immobile telephone at the end of the year (subscriber)	2538393	2095230	21.15
四、农村电话年末户数（户）	Number of telephone in rural areas at the end of the year (subscriber)	415593	358803	15.83
五、长途电话通话总数（万次）	Number of long-distance telephone call (10 000 times)	21955	23343	-5.95
六、电话交换机容量（门）	Capacity (number) of telephone switchboard (line)	3162678	2647579	19.46
七、移动电话用户年末数（户）	Number of mobile phone at the end of the year (subscriber)	2412392	1964200	22.82
八、互联网年末户数（户）	Number of internet users (subscriber)	940643	710411	32.41
#宽带网户数	number of broad band net user	160900	35230	356.71
窄带网户数	Number of narrow band net user	779743	675181	15.49

主要统计指标解释

铁路营业里程 又称营业长度（包括正式营业和临时营业里程），指办理客货运输业务的铁路正线总长度。凡是全线或部分建成双线及以上的线路，以第一线的实际长度计算；复线、站线、段管线、岔线和特殊用途线以及不计算运费的联络线都不计算营业里程。铁路营业里程是反映铁路运输业基础设施发展水平的重要指标，也是计算客货周转量、运输密度和机车车辆运用效率等指标的基础资料。

铁路正线延展里程 指正线第一线、第二线、第三线和其他正线建筑里程之和，不包括站线、段管线、岔线及特殊用途线的延展里程。它是作为计算铁路线上钢轨、枕木及路基砂石需要量的主要依据。

公路里程 指在一定时期内实际达到《公路工程[WTBZ]技术标准JTJ01-88》规定的等级公路，并经公路主管部门正式验收交付使用的公路里程数。包括大中城市的郊区公路以及通过小城镇街道部分的公路里程和桥梁、隧道渡口的长度，不包括大中城市的街道、厂矿、林区生产用道和农业生产用道的里程。两条或多条公路共同经由同一路段，只计算一次，不得重复计算里程长度。它是反映公路建设发展规模的重要指标，也是计算运输网密度等指标的基础资料。

民用航空航线里程 指民航运输定期班机飞行的航线长度的总和。航线长度按机场之间的距离计算，通常有两种计算方法：一是将每条航线长度相加称为重复计算航线里程；一是将两线或两条以上航线经过同一区段里程，只计算一次航线长度称为不重复计算航线里程。一般常用的是后者，它能确切反映民航运输网的规模，是表明民航事业为国民经济服务和方便人民生活程度的主要指标。

货（客）运量 指在一定时期内，各种运输工具实际运送的货物（旅客）数量。它是反映运输业为国民经济和人民生活服务的数量指标，也是制定和检查运输生产计划、研究运输发展规模和速度的重要指标。货运按吨计算，客运按人计算。货物不论运输距离长短、货物类别，均按实际重量统计。旅客不论行程远近或票价多少，均按一人一次客运量统计；半价票、小孩票也按一人统计。

货物（旅客）周转量 指在一定时期内，由各种运输工具运送的货物（旅客）数量与其相应运输距离的乘积之总和。它是反映运输业生产总成果的重要指标，也是编制和检查运输生产计划，计算运输效率、劳动生产率以及核算运输单位成本的主要基础资料。计算货物周转量通常按发出站与到达站之间的最短距离，也就是计费距离计算。计算公式为：

货物（旅客）周转量 = ∑货物（旅客）运输量 × 运输距离

邮电业务总量 指以价值量形式表现的邮电通信企业为社会提供各类邮电通信服务的总数量。邮电业务量按专业分类包括函件、包件、汇票、报刊发行、邮政快件、特快专递、邮政储蓄、集邮、公众电报、用户电报、传真、长途电话、出租电路、无线寻呼、移动电话、分组交换数据通信、出租代维等。计算方法为各类产品乘以相应的平均单价（不变价）之和，再加上出租电路和设备、代用户维护电话交换机和线路等的服务收入。它综合反映了一定时期邮电业务发展的总成果，是研究邮电业务量构成和发展趋势的重要指标。计算公式为：

邮电业务总量 = ∑（各类邮电业务量 × 不变单价）+ 出租代维及其他业务收入

无线寻呼用户 无线寻呼是指电话用户通过无线寻呼中心，在规定范围内向携带小型寻呼机的用户发出声音、数字或文字显示信息。在寻呼台办理登记手续携带小型寻呼机的用户，称为无线寻呼用户。

移动电话用户 是指通过移动电话交换机进入移动电话网、占用移动电话号码的电话用户。用户数量以报告期末在移动电话营业部门实际办理登记手续进入移动电话网的户数进行计算，一部移动电话统计为一户。

电话用户 指接入国家公众固定电话网，并按固定电话业务进行经营管理的电话用户。1997年以前，电话用户分为市内电话用户和农村电话用户。“市内电话用户”是指接入县城及县以上城市的电话网上的电话用户；“农村电话用户”是指接入县邮电局农话台及县以下农村电话交换点，以县城为中心（除市话用户外）联通县、乡（镇）、行政村、村民小组的用户。从1997年起，电话用户数分组调整为以用户所在区域划分为“城市电话用户”和“乡村电话用户”，与过去的按市内电话和农村电话划分方法不同。而电话用户总数、电话机总部数统计范围不变。

城市电话用户 指直辖市、省辖市、地级市、县级市的市区、市郊区及县城（包括县人民政府所在地的县城关区或行政建制相当于县人民政府所在地的镇）范围内接入局用交换机的电话用户数，包括分布在农村地区的独立工矿区、林区、驻军等接入局用交换机的电话用户数。

乡村电话用户 指县城关区以下的集镇和农村接入局用交换机的电话用户数。

住宅电话用户 是指安装在居民住宅或农民家里并按照住宅电话用户登记注册和收费的电话用户。包括私人付费、单位付费和按规定免费安装的住宅电话用户。

局用交换机容量 是指安装在本地电信运营商内用于接续本地固定电话的电话交换机容量，有倍增设备按倍增后的数量计数。包括现用和备用的人工或自动交换机的全部容量。

Explanatory Notes on Main Statistical Indicators

Length of Railways in Operation refers to the total length of the trunk line under passenger and freight transportation (including both full operation and temporary operation). The calculation is based on the actual length of the first line even if this line has a full or partial double track or more tracks, excluding double tracks, station sidings, tracks under the charge of stations, branch lines, special-purpose lines and the non-payable connecting lines. The length of railways in operation is an important indicator to show the development of the infrastructure for the railway transport, and also the essential data to calculate volume of passenger freight transport, traffic density and utilization efficiency of the locomotives and carriages.

Extenuation Length of Trunk Lines refers to the sum of the first, the second, the third lines and other constructed length of the trunk railways, excluding the extenuation length of the station lines, lines under the jurisdiction of depots, sidings and lines for special purpose. It provides important information for the calculation of the needs for rails, sleepers, sand and stone for the construction of railways.

Length of Highways refers to the length of highways which are built in conformity with the grades specified by the highway engineering standard formulated by the Ministry of Communications, and have been formally checked and accepted by the departments of highways and put into use. The length of highways includes that of the suburb highways at large and medium-sized cities, highways passing through streets at small cities and towns, and also the length of bridges、 tunnel and ferries. It does not include the length of streets in big and medium-sized cities and highways built for the production purpose at factories, mines, forest areas and agricultural areas. If two or more highways go the same section of the way, the length of the section is only calculated for once and no duplication is allowed. The length of highways is an important indicator to show the development of the highway construction and to provide essential information to calculate the transport network density.

Length of Civil Aviation Routes refers to the length of all routes for regular civil aviation flights. There are usually two ways to calculate the distance between airports connected by the route length: One is to put the length of all air routes together, called duplicated calculation of the length of the routes; the other is not to allow the duplication in calculation when two or more routes passing the same section of aviation routes. The latter is usually used, as it can precisely show the size of the civil aviation network and indicate the extent of civil aviation serving the national economy and the people.

Freight (Passenger) Traffic refers to the volume of freight (passenger) transported with various means. Freight transport is calculated in tons and passenger traffic is calculated in the number of persons. Despite the type of freight and travelling distance, the freight transport is calculated in the actual weight of the goods: and despite the travelling distance and ticket price, the passenger traffic is calculated by the principle that one person can be counted only once in one travel. The passenger who travel with a half price ticket or a child ticket is also calculated as one person. The freight (passenger) traffic provides a quantitative measure to show how the transport industry serves the national economy and people, and is also an important indicator for planning the transport industry and for studying the development scale and speed of the transport industry.

Freight Ton-kilometers (Passenger-kilometers) refer to the sum of the products of the volume of transported cargo (passengers) multiplying by the transport distance, usually using ton-kilometer and passenger-kilometer as units for measurement. Normally, the shortest distance between the departure station and the destination station (i.e., the payable distance) is the basis to calculate the freight ton-kilometers. This is an important indicator to show the total results of the transport industry, to prepare and examine the transport plan and to measure the efficiency, the labour productivity and the unit cost of transport.

The formula is as follows:

Freight Ton-kilometers (Passenger-kilometers) =Σ {Freight (Passenger) Traffic x Distance of Transportation}

Measuring unit: ton-kilometer (person-kilometer)

Business Volume of Post and Telecommunications refers to the total amount of post and telecommunications services, expressed in value terms, provided by the post and telecommunications departments for the society. Post and telecommunication services can be classified as letters, parcels, remittance, issue of newspapers and magazines, fast mail service, express mail service, savings deposits, stamps for collection, public and individual telegraph service, facsimiles, long-distance telephone service,leasing of telephone lines, urban paging service, mobile telephone service, data transfer and transmission, etc. The accounting approach is to multiply the service products of all types with their average unit price (constant price) to get sum of business value, plus income from other services such as leasing of telephone lines and equipment, maintenance of telephone switchboards and lines on behalf of customers. This indicator reflects the overall results of post and telecommunications service during a given period, and is important to study the composition of business service and the development of post and telecommunications service.

The formula is as follows:

Business Volume of Post and Telecommunications=Σ (Transaction of Post and Telecommunication Service x Constant Price) + Income from Leasing, Maintenance and other Services

Subscribers of Wireless Paging Services Wireless paging service refers the service by which telephone users send audio, digital or character signals to persons carrying small-size pagers within the designated areas through wireless paging centers. The page carriers who have registered in paging centers are counted as paging subscribers.

Mobile Telephone Subscribers refer to the persons who own mobile telephone numbers and are connected with the mobile telephone communication network through the mobile telephone switchboards. The number of subscribers is calculated by the subscribers who have completed registration at mobile communication business centers and entered into the mobile telephone network. One mobile telephone is taken as a subscriber.

Telephone Subscribers refer to subscribers that are connected to the public line telephone network provided with telephone services. Before 1997, telephone subscribers were classified as city subscribers and village subscribers. City subscribers referred to those connected to city telephone networks in county towns and cities, while village subscribers referred to those connected to village telephone stations at and below counties. Since 1997, the classification of telephone subscribers was modified on the basis of physical location of the subscribers as Urban telephone subscribers and rural telephone subscribers , which is different from the previous classification of categorizing local telephones and rural telephones , while the definition of total subscribers and total number of telephones remain unchanged.

Urban Telephone Subscribers refer to subscribers telephone subscribers, located at municipalities, cities under the jurisdiction of province, cities at prefectural level, downtown and suburb of city at county level town and county towns (including country towns where county government located, and towns of county level according to the administrative organizational system), that are connected to the public line telephone network, including rural mineral area, forest area, military area.

Rural Telephone Subscribers refer to telephone subscribers, located at towns under county town and country, that are connected to the public line telephone network.

Household Telephone Subscribers refer to telephone sets installed in the dwelling units of urban or rural residents, and registered as residence subscribers for payment, including 3 types of payment for the service: private payment, public payment and free service.

Capacity of Office Telephone Exchanges refers to the capacity (measured in gate) of telephone exchanges installed in the offices of local telecommunication service providers for communication between fixed telephones. It includes the capacity of both manual and automatic exchanges in use and for stand-by purpose. Equipment with expansion function is to be counted by the expanded capacity.

2004

統計年鑒

十三、国内贸易

DOMESTIC TRADE

简 要 说 明
Brief Introduction

本章资料主要内容有社会消费品零售总额，批发零售贸易业商品购、销等情况，限额以上批发零售贸易业主要商品销售情况，限额以上批发零售贸易和餐馆企业财务状况、经济效益，以及交易市场情况。

本章资料由市统计局贸易外经处整理提供。

Content of this chapter consists of total amount of retailing social consumer goods, sails data on commodity purchasing and sails of wholesale and retail trade, sales data on primary goods exceeds quotation, financial, economic performance and market data on wholesale and retail trade and food services industry exceeds quotation.

Data in this chapter is compiled and provided by Trade and Foreign Economy Division of the Xi'an Bureau of Statistics.

13-1 主要年份社会消费品零售总额

Total Retail Sales of Consumer Goods in Representative Year

单位:亿元 (100 million yuan)

年份、时期	Year,Period	总计 Total	批发零售业 Wholesale、Retail Trades	餐饮业 Catering Services	制造业 Manufacturing	其他行业 Other Sectors	农民对非农业居民的零售额 Retail Sales of Peasants Urban Residence
1952		2.35	1.86	0.06	0.40		0.03
1957		4.88	3.96	0.24	0.57		0.11
1962		5.98	4.73	0.50	0.22	0.07	0.46
1965		5.89	5.10	0.30	0.35	0.10	0.04
1970		7.43	6.88	0.25	0.13	0.13	0.04
1975		10.33	9.15	0.46	0.40	0.23	0.09
1978		12.70	11.01	0.53	0.79	0.21	0.16
1980		15.88	13.05	0.80	1.52	0.20	0.31
1985		32.92	25.04	1.69	3.74	0.48	1.97
1990		72.77	57.46	3.79	5.09	0.90	5.53
1995		180.22	109.68	11.37	15.98	9.13	34.06
1996		212.82	135.93	14.84	19.79	1.41	40.85
1997		249.56	155.89	20.39	24.03	3.98	45.27
1998		271.85	166.66	28.14	25.81	4.27	46.97
1999		298.15	186.35	31.17	26.52	4.85	49.26
2000		328.47	205.77	36.60	28.81	5.43	51.86
2001		365.93	231.24	42.60	31.95	5.86	54.28
2002		409.39	260.75	49.66	35.94	6.45	56.59
2003		440.05	325.79	102.57		11.69	
1950-1952	Economic Rehabilitatin Period	6.21	4.83	0.16	1.13		0.09
"一五"时期	The First Five-Year Plan Period	19.87	16.17	0.77	2.54		0.39
"二五"时期	The Second Five-Year Plan Period	28.89	24.29	1.65	1.91	0.10	1.03
1963-1965	Readjust Period	17.23	14.56	0.94	1.07	0.20	0.46
"三五"时期	The Third Five-Year Plan Period	33.58	30.71	1.39	0.91	0.52	0.05
"四五"时期	The Fourth Five-Year Plan Period	46.89	41.79	2.10	1.51	1.18	0.31
"五五"时期	The Fiifth Five-Year Plan Period	64.35	55.40	2.88	4.14	0.97	0.96
"六五"时期	The Sixth Five-Year Plan Period	114.56	91.02	5.69	11.67	1.72	4.46
"七五"时期	The Seventh Five-Year Plan Period	281.83	218.91	14.21	25.31	3.57	19.83
"八五"时期	The Eighth Five-Year Plan Period	622.12	407.67	38.54	53.88	18.83	103.20
"九五"时期	The Ninth Five-Year Plan Period	1360.85	850.60	131.14	124.96	19.94	234.21
1979-2003		3624.54	2410.91	385.81	286.23	68.47	473.12

13-2 全市批发零售贸易业基本情况

指　　标	Item	1995	1996
一、批发零售贸易业网点数(个)	**Number of Wholesale and Retail Trades (unit)**	**76187**	**84836**
#国有经济	State-owned	5354	5373
集体经济	Collective-owned	25020	26113
二、批发零售贸易业人员数(人)	**Number of Employed Persons in wholesale and Retail Trades (person)**	**427767**	**505495**
#国有经济	State-owned	82243	84838
集体经济	Collective-owned	236476	241875
三、餐饮业网点数(个)	**Number of Catering Services (unit)**	**15485**	**15668**
四、餐饮业人员数(人)	**Number of Employed Persons in Catering Services (person)**	**68782**	**78313**
五、社会消费品零售总额(亿元)	**Total Retail sales of Consuming Goods (100 billion yuan)**	**180.22**	**212.82**
#国有经济零售额	#Retail Sales of State-owned	60.93	54.92
集体经济零售额	Retail Sales of Collective-owned	38.98	41.87
#市的零售额	#Retail Sales of City	160.30	189.20
# 批发零售贸易业零售额	#Retail Sales of Wholesale and Retail Trades	109.68	135.93
农民对城镇居民零售	Retail Sales af Peasants to Urban Residence	34.06	40.85

Basic Conditions in Wholesale and Retail Trades

1997	1998	1999	2000	2001	2002	2003
88793	**105836**	**107381**	**104321**	**105948**	**109035**	**113038**
5800	5968	5722	4961	4680	3537	3378
27225	28983	28317	25754	22329	16035	16405
539998	**601143**	**602793**	**573602**	**575733**	**572672**	**607909**
89212	90969	85837	80204	76390	66366	64725
254336	265483	228878	202825	185488	144125	144528
20259	**22500**	**24977**	**27531**	**28219**	**29219**	**32899**
82917	**100862**	**118442**	**124988**	**128738**	**140623**	**150883**
249.56	**271.85**	**298.15**	**328.47**	**365.93**	**409.39**	**440.05**
59.80	59.38	60.17	62.95	42.29	49.50	50.16
49.45	50.17	51.19	53.28	47.56	52.30	47.82
224.74	240.08	261.22	289.01	323.37	363.37	395.37
155.89	166.66	186.35	205.77	231.24	260.75	325.79
45.27	46.97	49.26	51.87	54.29	56.59	

13-3 限额以上批发零售贸易业商品购进、销售、库存总额（2003年）

单位：万元

指标	Item	购进总额 Total Purchases	进口 Import
总计	**Total**	**3316144.1**	**10086.5**
一、批发业	**Wholesale Trade**	**2517872.9**	**10086.5**
其中：国有及国有控股	Of the total State-owned and State Holding Majority Shares	1957074.0	9549.9
1.按登记注册类型分组	Grouped by Registration Status		
内资企业	Domestic Funded Enterprises	2389160.4	10086.5
国有企业	State-owned Enterprises	1501003.2	5411.5
集体企业	Collective-owned Enterprises	24993.8	
股份合作企业	Share-Holding Cooperative Enterprises		
联营企业	Joint Ownership Enterprises	22913.1	
国有联营企业	State Joint Ownership Enterprises	22913.1	
集体联营企业	Collective Joint Ownership Enterprises		
国有与集体联营企业	Joint State-collective Enterprises		
其他联营企业	Other JointOwnership Enterprises		
有限责任公司	Limited Liability Corporations	630093.4	2473.2
国有独资企业	State Sole Funded Corporations		
其他有限责任公司	Other Limited Liability Corporations	630093.4	2473.2
股份有限公司	Share-holding Corporations Ltd.	178800.7	2201.8
私营企业	Private Enterprises	31356.2	
私营独资企业	Private-funded Enterprises		
私营合伙企业	Private Partnership Enterprises		
私营有限责任公司	Private Limited Liability Corporations	31356.2	
私营股份有限公司	Private Share-holding Corporations ltd.		
其他企业	Other Enterprises		
港、澳、台商投资企业	Enterprises with Investment from Hong Kong, Macao and Taiwan		
合资经营企业	Joint-venture Enterprises		
合作经营企业	Cooperative Enterprises		
独资经营企业	Enterprises with Sole Funds		
投资股份有限公司	Share-holding Corporations Ltd.with the Funds		
外商投资企业	Foreign Funded Enterprises	128712.5	
中外合资经营企业	Joint-venture Enterprises	112844.7	
中外合作经营企业	Cooperation Enterprises		
外资企业	Enterprise with Sole Foreign Funds	15867.8	
外商投资股份有限公司	Share-holding Corporations Ltd. With Foreign funds		
2.按国民经济行业分组	Grouped By Sector		
农畜产品批发业	Farm produce and livestock products wholesale trade	13880.5	
食品、饮料及烟草制品批发业	Foodstuff, beverage and tobacco wholesale trade	495333.0	
米、面制品及食用油批发业	Rice, wheat flour products and edible oil wholesale trade	892.7	
烟草制品批发业	Tobacco wholesale trade	483862.2	
纺织、服装及日用品批发业	Textile, costume and commodity wholesale trade	162746.9	482.4
服装批发业	Costume wholesale trade	37416.5	239.8
文化、体育用品及器材批发业	Stationery, sports goods wholesale trade	79349.5	
医药及医疗器材批发业	Medicine and medical apparatus and instruments wholesale trade	268261.3	

Total Purchases,Sales and Inventory of Enterprises above Designated Size in Wholesale and Retail Trades(2003)

(10 000 Yuan)

销售总额 Total Sales	批 发 Wholesale Trade	出口 Export	零售 Retail Trade	年末库存总额 Inventory (year-end)
3535590.9	**2604093.2**	**394825.4**	**931497.7**	**291938.3**
2713883.1	**2544835.5**	**394825.4**	**169047.6**	**172752.9**
2130202.9	1990214.3	394825.4	139988.6	155466.5
2577683.1	2408635.5	394825.4	169047.6	172048.6
1581239.9	1534190.7	288334.8	47049.2	97729.6
26281.4	26091.8		189.6	4414.6
23564.0	23564.0	3925.8		994.0
23564.0	23564.0	3925.8		994.0
716789.2	643289.3	97521.8	73499.9	35221.6
716789.2	643289.3	97521.8	73499.9	35221.6
199055.6	162068.8	5043.0	36986.8	31274.1
30753.0	19430.9		11322.1	2414.7
30753.0	19430.9		11322.1	2414.7
136200.0	136200.0			704.3
119948.8	119948.8			
16251.2	16251.2			704.3
15022.4	15022.4	3263.0		3415.8
527560.8	522173.4		5387.4	8932.0
552.0	552.0			352.4
512626.3	511047.8		1578.5	6746.9
170866.4	170348.0	106158.1	518.4	16962.6
37297.7	37297.7	37057.9		5422.0
96334.4	92415.4		3919.0	8148.8
286041.3	209732.0	1646.3	76309.3	25452.8

13-3 限额以上批发零售贸易业商品购进、销售、库存总额（2003年）（续1）

单位：万元

指标	Item	购进总额 Total Purchases	进口 Import
矿产品、建材及化工产品批发业	Ore products, building materials and chemical products wholesale trade	806514.5	3228.4
煤炭及制品批发业	Coal and coal products wholesale trade	349.0	
石油及制品批发业	Oil and oil products wholesale trade	426916.1	
金属及金属矿批发业	Metal and metal ore wholesale trade	350930.2	3228.4
建材批发业	Building materials wholesale trade		
化肥批发业	Fertilizer wholesale trade	14373.2	
机械设备、五金交电及电子产品批发业	Machinery, ironware, transportation, wiring and electronic products wholesale trade	684491.3	6375.7
汽车、摩托车及零配件批发业	Motorcars, motorcycles, spare parts and fittings of motorcars and motorcycles wholesale trade	229086.9	
家用电器批发业	Electrical household appliances wholesale trade	21604.8	
计算机、软件及辅助设备批发业	Computers, computer software and auxiliary equipment wholesale trade	123589.8	536.6
贸易经纪与代理	Trade broker and agent		
其他批发业	Other whole trade	7295.9	
二、零售业	**Retail**	**798271.2**	
其中：国有及国有控股	Of the total State-owned and State Holding Majority Shares	222444.1	
1. 按登记注册类型分组	Grouped by Registration Status		
内资企业	Domestic Funded Enterprises	795504.3	
国有企业	State-owned Enterprises	112374.2	
集体企业	Collective-owned Enterprises	3471.4	
股份合作企业	Share-Holding Cooperative Enterprises	33187.9	
联营企业	Joint Ownership Enterprises		
国有联营企业	State Joint Ownership Enterprises		
集体联营企业	Collective Joint Ownership Enterprises		
国有与集体联营企业	Joint State-collective Enterprises		
其他联营企业	Other Joint Ownership Enterprises		
有限责任公司	Limited Liability Corporations	360966.0	
国有独资企业	State Sole Funded Corporations		
其他有限责任公司	Other Limited Liability Corporations	360966.0	
股份有限公司	Share-holding Corporations Ltd.	116918.2	
私营企业	Private Enterprises	168586.6	
私营独资企业	Private-funded Enterprises	45169.9	
私营合伙企业	Private Partnership Enterprises		
私营有限责任公司	Private Limited Liability Corporations	117909.5	
私营股份有限公司	Private Share-holding Corporations ltd.	5507.2	
其他企业	Other Enterprises		
港、澳、台商投资企业	Enterprises with Funds From Hong Kong, Macao and Taiwan	2766.9	
合资经营企业	Joint-venture Enterprises	2766.9	
合作经营企业	Cooperative Enterprises		
独资经营企业	Enterprises With Sole Funds		
投资股份有限公司	Share Holding Corporations Ltd		
外商投资企业	Foreign Funded Enterprises		
中外合资经营企业	Joint-venture Enterprises		
中外合作经营企业	Cooperation Enterprises		
外资企业	Enterprise with Sole Foreign Funds		

Total Purchases,Sales and Inventory of Enterprises above Designated Size in Wholesale and Retail Trades(2003)(Continued 1)

(10 000 Yuan)

销售总额 Total Sales	批 发 Wholesale Trade	出口 Export	零售 Retail Trade	年末库存总额 Inventory (year-end)
835006.7	813525.9	27795.2	21480.8	67369.8
479.7	418.1		61.6	239.2
440467.2	421943.3		18523.9	29333.4
364834.6	362015.1	27795.2	2819.5	33204.5
14172.8	14097		75.8	1790.6
775537.8	714105.1	255962.8	61432.7	42153.8
217985.2	162447.7		55537.5	13587.8
21301.8	16778.5		4523.3	3873
131232.5	129860.6		1371.9	437
7513.3	7513.3			317.3
821707.8	**59257.7**		**762450.1**	**119185.4**
243744.3	47681.9		196062.4	26589.5
818940.9	59257.7		759683.2	118913.7
104762	47102.5		57659.5	18197.2
3904	463.3		3440.7	278.2
43544.9	579.4		42965.5	1240.6
409046.3	10523.5		398522.8	72114.3
409046.3	10523.5		398522.8	72114.3
137917.2			137917.2	6540.8
119766.5	589		119177.5	20542.6
54136.4			54136.4	6801.4
60931.6	589		60342.6	13741.2
4698.5			4698.5	
2766.9			2766.9	271.7
2766.9			2766.9	271.7

13-3 限额以上批发零售贸易业商品购进、销售、库存总额（2003年）（续2）

单位：万元

指标	Item	购进总额 Total Purchases	进口 Import
2．按国民经济行业分组	Grouped by Sector		
综合零售业	Comprehensive retail trade	645404.9	
百货零售业	General merchandise retail trade	391129.1	
超级市场零售业	Supermarket retail trade	254275.8	
食品、饮料及烟草制品专门零售业	Foodstuff, beverage and tobacco special retail trade	2652.4	
纺织、服装及日用品专门零售业	Textile, costume and commodity special retail trade	14865.3	
服装零售业	Costume retail trade	6368.6	
文化、体育用品及器材专门零售业	Stationery, sports goods special retail trade	29703.3	
体育用品零售业	Sports goods retail trade	4363.1	
图书零售业	Book retail trade	24917.5	
医药及医疗器材专门零售业	Medicine and medical apparatus and instruments special retail trade	1595.8	
药品零售业	Medical drugs retail trade	1595.8	
汽车、摩托车、燃料及零配件专门零售业	Motorcars, motorcycles, fuel, spare parts and fittings of motorcars and motorcycles special retail trade	365.7	
汽车零售业	Motorcars retail trade		
机动车燃料零售业	Motor vehicle fuel retail trade		
家用电器及电子产品专门零售业	Electrical household appliances and electronic products special retail trade	98159.3	
家用电器零售业	Electrical household appliances retail trade	98159.3	
计算机、软件及辅助设备零售业	Computers, computer software and auxiliary equipment retail trade		
通讯设备零售业	Communication equipment retail trade		
五金、家具及室内装修材料专门零售业	Ironware, furniture and room fitting stuff special retail trade	5524.5	
无店铺及其他零售业	Shopless retail trade and other retail trades		
邮购及电子销售业	Mail order and electronic distribution trade		

Total Purchases,Sales and Inventory of Enterprises above Designated Size in Wholesale and Retail Trades(2003)(Continued 2)

(10 000 Yuan)

销售总额 Total Sales	批 发 Wholesale Trade	出口 Export	零售 Retail Trade	年末库存总额 Inventory (year-end)
664558.7	38931.9		625626.8	49852.5
459779.9	38931.9		420848.0	20814.8
204778.8			204778.8	29037.7
2729.0	426.4		2302.6	1648.5
18277.1	118.0		18159.1	3617.7
10106.3			10106.3	688.0
31396.8	8668.9		22727.9	9660.4
5445.8			5445.8	2114.2
25406.1	8668.9		16737.2	7385.2
1509.6			1509.6	503.0
1509.6			1509.6	503.0
1089.2	589.0		500.2	288.6
97343.9	10523.5		86820.4	53469.3
97343.9	10523.5		86820.4	53469.3
4803.5			4803.5	145.4

13-4 限额以上批发零售贸易业商品分类销售额(2003年)

Total Sales of Enterprises Above Designated Size in Wholesale and Retail Trades Grouped by Category of Commodities(2003)

单位：万元 (10 000 yuan)

指　标	Item	商品销售额 Total sace of Commodtg 合计 Total	批发 Wholesale Trade	零售 Retail Trade
合　计	**Total**	**3085384.1**	**2166665.5**	**918718.6**
食品类、饮料、烟酒类	Food,Beverages,Tobacco and Liquor	705213.1	534451.6	170761.5
肉禽蛋类	Meat,Poultry and Eggs	19435.8	2445.3	16990.5
其它食品类	Other Food	130274.3	30072.2	100202.1
饮料类	Beverages	32098.2	8706.8	23391.4
烟酒类	Tobacco and Liquor	523404.8	493227.3	30177.5
服装鞋帽、针、纺织品类	Garments,Shoes,Hats and Textiles	272511.1	64182.8	208328.3
服装类	Garments	156397.4	25225.2	131172.2
鞋帽类	Shoes and Hats	55626.7	6050.2	49576.5
针纺织类	Knitwear and Textiles	60487.0	32907.4	27579.6
化妆品类	Cosmetics	42609.6	10788.2	31821.4
金银珠宝类	Gold,Silver and Jewelry	27406.5	1793.0	25613.5
日用品类	Articles for Daily Use	131937.3	64529.2	67408.1
洗涤用品类	Washing Articles	46620.0	19565.8	27054.2
儿童玩具类	Children Toys	4679.9	1147.2	3532.7
五金、电料类	Hardware and Electrical Materials	68215.2	64616.5	3598.7
体育、娱乐用品类	Sports and Recreation Articles	20725.1	6892.6	13832.5
书报、杂志类	Newspapers and Magazines	96065.2	77072.1	18993.1
电子出版及音像制品类	E-journal and Video Products	6898.5	4098.2	2800.3
家用电器和音像器材类	Household Electric Appliances and Video Appliances	164912.3	19657.1	145255.2
中西药品类	Traditional Chinese and Western Medicines	268665.4	190258.5	78406.9
西药	Western Medicines	195972.9	134971.3	61001.6
中草药及中成药	Traditional Chinese Medicines	68043.8	52182.9	15860.9
文化办公用品类	Cultural and Official Goods	44481.6	27367.3	17114.3
家俱类	Furniture	1978.9	306.0	1672.9
通讯器材类	Communication Appliances	115422.8	62634.4	52788.4
煤炭及制品类	Coal and Related Products	6286.1	6226.6	59.5
木材及制品类	Timber and Wooden Products	2481.5	1142.2	1339.3
石油及制品类	Petroleum and Related Products	405729.6	386973.4	18756.2
化工材料及制品类	Chemical Materials and products	62508.8	62508.8	
化肥类	Chemical Fertilizer	14024.8	14024.8	
金属材料类	Metal Materials	176267.4	176267.4	
建筑及装潢材料类	Building and Decoration Materials	23185.6	8208.6	14977.0
机电产品及设备类	Mechanical and Electrical Products	420193.0	377114.2	43078.8
农机类	Agricultural Machinery	4590.2	4590.2	
汽车类	Motor Vehicles	208763.2	171129.2	37634.0
种子饲料类	Seed and Feedstuff			
棉麻类	Cotton,Hemp	11632.8	11632.8	
其它类	Others	10056.7	7944.0	2112.7

13-5 限额以上批发零售贸易商品销售(2003年）

Total Sales of Enterprises Above Designated Size in Wholesale and Retail Trades (2003)

指　标	Item	商品销售量 Total Sace Yolame of Commodtg		
		合 计 Total	批 发 Wholesale Trade	零 售 Retail Trade
粮食(吨)	Grain(ton)	72113	46184	25929
食用植物油（公斤）	Edible Vegetable Oil (kg)	7532032		7532032
食糖（公斤）	Sugar (kg)	5354552	3706879	1647673
卷烟 （万支）	Cigarettes (10 000 pcs)	4052158	4017899	34259
酒 （公斤）	Alcohol drinks（kg）	13675149	261680	13413469
#白酒（公斤）	distilled spirit (kg)	4876153	226513	4649640
啤酒（公斤）	Beer (kg)	2056215		2056215
棉花（公斤）	Cotton (kg)	8334235	8332995	1240
布（百米）	Cloth (100 meters)	233835	229783	4052
各种服装（百件）	Clothing (100 pcs)	138407	60661	77746
#童装（百件）	Children's (100 pcs)	26481	18070	8411
鞋（百双）	Shoes(100 pairs)	56243	9331	46912
照相机（台）	Camera (pcs)	19981	271	19710
#数码照相机（台）	Digital camera (pcs)	2780		2780
彩色电视机（台）	Television (unit)	170292	15822	154470
组合音响（台）	Hi-Fi Stereo (unit)	10367	727	9640
摄像机（台）	Pickup Camera (unit)	3848	511	3337
影碟机（台）	Video Disc Player (unit)	94632	12812	81820
家用电冰箱（台）	Houshold Refrigerator (unit)	62133	7460	54673
家用洗衣机（台）	Household Washing Machine (unit)	69331	6786	62545
房间空调器（台）	Room Air Conditioner (unit)	89411	15859	73552

13-5 限额以上批发零售贸易商品销售(2003年）(续)

Total Sales of Enterprises Above Designated Size in Wholesale and Retail Trades(2003) (continued)

指标	Item	商品销售量 Total Sace Yolame of Commodtg		
		合计 Total	批发 Wholesale Trade	零售 Retail Trade
微波炉（台）	Micro-over (unit)	84668	15190	69478
微型计算机(台)	Personal Computer (unit)	16839	2470	14369
普通电话机（部）	Telephone (unit)	164866	129371	35495
移动电话机（部）	Hand Telephone (unit)	791996	434415	357581
化学肥料（吨）	Chemical Fertilizer (ton)	126676	126676	
化学农药 (吨)	Chemical Pesticide(ton)	274	274	
农用塑料薄膜 (吨)	Plastic Film For Agriculture(ton)	16	16	
煤炭 (吨)	Coal(ton)	22299	17081	5218
木材 (立方米)	Timber(cu.m)	6726	2664	4062
汽油 (吨)	Gasoline(ton)	172413	146551	25862
煤油 (吨)	Kerosene(ton)	127875	127782	93
柴油 (吨）	Diesel Oil(ton)	932807	932807	
钢材 (吨)	Rolled-Steel(ton)	322882	322882	
铜(吨）	Copper(ton)	4110	4110	
铝 (吨）	Alluminium(ton)	253	253	
水泥 (吨）	Cement(ton)	54292	54292	
汽车 (辆）	Motor Vehicles(unit)	22327	18037	4290
其中：轿车(辆)	Automobile（unit)	10224	8157	2067
摩托车（辆）	Motorcycles(unit）	9091	4908	4183
拖拉机 (台）	Tractors(unit)	180	180	

13–6 社会消费品零售总额(2003年)

Total Retail Sales of Consumer Goods(2003)

单位:万元 (10 000 yuan)

分 类	Classify	金 额 Sum
社会消费品零售总额	**Total Retail Sales of Consumer Goods**	**4400454**
(一)按销售地区分:	Grouped by Region	
(1)市的零售额	Retail Sales of Urban Area	3953660
(2)县的零售额	Retail Sales of County	213531
(3)县以下的零售额	Retail Sales Under County Level	233263
(二)按行业和登记注册类型分:	Grouped by Sector and Registration Status	
(1)批发、零售贸易业	Wholesale、Retail Trades	3257915
内资企业	Domestic Funded Enterprises	2297115
国有企业	State-owned Enterprises	411766
集体企业	Collective-owned Enterprises	420160
股份合作企业	Share-Holding Cooperative Enterprises	157739
联营企业	Joint Ownership Enterprises	10564
有限责任公司	Limited Liability Corporations	499398
股份有限公司	Share-holding Corporations Ltd.	206254
私营企业	Private Enterprises	589970
其他企业	Other Enterprises	1264
港澳台商投资企业	Enterprises Funded by Enterpreneurs from Hong Kong, Macao &Taiwan	46039
外商投资企业	Foreign- Funded Enterprises	9164
个体经济	Individuals	905597
(2)餐饮业	Catering Services	1025716
内资企业	Domestic Funded Enterprises	513348
国有企业	State-owned Enterprises	83263
集体企业	Collective-owned Enterprises	58011
股份合作企业	Share-Holding Cooperative Enterprises	17707
联营企业	Joint Ownership Enterprises	2947
有限责任公司	Limited Liability Corporations	109053
股份有限公司	Share-holding Corporations Ltd.	118994
私营企业	Private Enterprises	122496
其他企业	Other Enterprises	877
港澳台商投资企业	Enterprises Funded by Enterpreneurs from Hong Kong, Macao &Taiwan	84981
外商投资企业	Foreign- Funded Enterprises	26730
个体经济	Individuals	400657
(3)其他行业	Other Sectors	116823

13-7 批发贸易业机构、网点、人员(2003年)

单位:个、人

分类	Classify	合计 Total 法人单位 Constitutional Unit	活动单位 Movemental Unit	网点 Branch Shop	人员 Personnel
总计	**Total**	**1724**	**2283**	**13274**	**117740**
一、按登记注册类型分组	**Grouped by Type of Registration**				
内资企业	Domestic Funded Enterprises	1693	2216	6243	95360
国有企业	State-owned Enterprises	253	478	1078	34216
集体企业	Collective-owned Enterprises	317	426	1179	12124
股份合作企业	Share-Holding Cooperative Enterprises	42	55	1229	12706
联营企业	Joint Ownership Enterprises	13	15	36	403
有限责任公司	Limited Liability Corporations	334	405	891	14271
股份有限公司	Share-holding Corporations Ltd.	77	101	271	6290
私营企业	Private Enterprises	647	726	1463	14959
其他企业	Other Enterprises	10	10	96	391
港澳台商投资企业	Enterprises Funded by Entrepreneurs from Hong Kong，Macao &Taiwan	19	29	29	1232
外商投资企业	Foreign- Funded Enterprises	12	38	38	501
个体经济	Individuals			6964	20647
二、按国民经济行业分组	**Grouped by Sector**				
食品、饮料、烟草和家庭用品批发业	Wholesale of Food, Beverages, Tobaccos and Things of Household	835	1018	8863	52575
食品、饮料、烟草批发业	Wholesale Trade of Food、Beverage and Tobacco	361	436	2144	16256
棉、麻、土畜产品批发业	Wholesale Trade of Cotton, Hemp and Animal Products	28	33	279	754
纺织品、服装和鞋帽批发业	Wholesale Trade of Textile, Garments, Shoes and Hat	99	116	3046	3638
日用百货批发业	Wholesale Trade of Articles For Daily Use	95	128	1504	4364
日用杂品批发业	WholeSale Trade of Household Commodities	82	92	389	775
五金、交电、化工批发业	Wholesale Trade of Hardwares、Electrical Appliances and Chemicals	76	86	686	12688
药品及医疗器械批发业	Wholesale Track of Medicine and Medical Appliances	94	127	815	14100
能源、材料和机械电子设备批发业	Wholesale Trade of Energy，Materials，Mechanical and Electrial Products	724	846	3680	50057
能源批发业	Wholesale Trade of Energy	48	85	393	9300
化工材料批发业	Wholesale Trade of Chemical Materials	91	91	385	3611
木材批发业	Wholesale Trade of Timber	45	47	171	1074
建筑材料批发业	Wholesale Trade of Building Materials	86	89	610	4906
矿产品批发业	Wholesale Trade of Ore Products	8	8	55	755
金属材料批发业	Wholesale Trade of Metal Materials	120	163	552	8722
机械、电子设备批发业	Wholesale Trade of Machinery and Electrical Prodcuts	228	258	1108	17332
汽车、摩托车及零配件批发业	Wholesale Trade of Motor Vehicle and Motorcycle Products	72	74	241	3097
再生物资回收批发业	Wholesale Trade of Recycled of Materials	26	31	165	1260
其他批发业	Other Wholesale Trades	165	419	731	15108
工艺美术品批发业	Wholesale Trade of Handicraft Articles	18	18	48	3276
图书报刊批发业	Wholesale Trade of Books and Newspapers and Magazines	64	176	303	2567
农业生产资料批发业	Wholesale Trade of Agricultural Production Goods	56	65	216	5851
其他类未包括的批发业	Wholesale Trade of Others	27	160	164	3414

Organizations, Establishments and Persons Engaged in Whole-sale Trade(2003)

（unit,person）

市 City				县 County				县以下 Under County Level			
法人单位 Constitutional Unit	活动单位 Movemental Unit	网点 Branch Shop	人员 Personnel	法人单位 Constitutional Unit	活动单位 Movemental Unit	网点 Branch Shop	人员 Personnel	法人单位 Constitutional Unit	活动单位 Movemental Unit	网点 Branch Shop	人员 Personnel
1473	**1905**	**12138**	**107259**	**123**	**190**	**554**	**5151**	**128**	**188**	**582**	**5330**
1442	1838	5444	86612	123	190	375	4133	128	188	424	4615
111	241	588	27669	79	122	242	2603	63	115	248	3944
259	347	932	10713	31	52	117	1144	27	27	130	267
39	52	1226	12633	3	3	3	73				
13	15	36	403								
333	404	890	14241	1	1	1	30				
71	84	254	5945	5	8	8	262	1	9	9	83
606	685	1422	14617	4	4	4	21	37	37	37	321
10	10	96	391								
19	29	29	1232								
12	38	38	501								
		6627	18914			179	1018			158	715
660	749	8093	44065	83	134	449	3959	92	135	321	4551
253	283	1698	10142	41	58	237	2362	67	95	209	3752
16	18	238	388	8	11	27	241	4	4	14	125
92	107	3009	3374	7	9	35	260			2	4
81	110	1452	4041	10	14	46	263	4	4	6	60
72	78	349	447	4	8	34	286	6	6	6	42
66	73	649	12437	4	7	30	206	6	6	7	45
80	80	698	13236	9	27	40	341	5	20	77	523
685	778	3526	48814	26	38	74	792	13	30	80	451
31	42	315	8629	14	23	32	365	3	20	46	306
90	90	381	3581	1	1	2	20			2	10
38	39	155	914	5	6	12	139	2	2	4	21
81	84	586	4746	2	2	19	136	3	3	5	24
8	8	55	755								
116	159	544	8665	1	1	3	22	3	3	5	35
228	258	1107	17329							1	3
71	73	230	3042	1	1	2	29			9	26
22	25	153	1153	2	4	4	81	2	2	8	26
128	378	519	14380	14	18	31	400	23	23	181	328
18	18	26	3223							22	53
63	175	297	2530	1	1	2	22			4	15
22	28	36	5235	11	14	25	356	23	23	155	260
25	157	160	3392	2	3	4	22				

13-8 零售贸易业机构、网点、人员(2003年)

单位：个、人

分类	Classify	合计 法人单位 Constitutional Unit	活动单位 Movemental Unit	网点 Branch Shop	Total 人员 Personnel
总计	**Total**	**6081**	**7263**	**99764**	**490169**
一、按登记注册类型分组	**Grouped by Type of Registration**				
内资企业	Domestic Funded Enterprises	6057	7181	28938	302077
国有企业	State-owned Enterprises	594	838	2300	30509
集体企业	Collective-owned Enterprises	1165	1496	15226	132404
股份合作企业	Share-Holding Cooperative Enterprises	148	160	162	6987
联营企业	Joint Ownership Enterprises	56	59	60	973
有限责任公司	Limited Liability Corporations	1248	1267	1472	17589
股份有限公司	Share-holding Corporations Ltd.	24	35	75	13951
私营企业	Private Enterprises	2812	3315	9291	98883
其他企业	Other Enterprises	11	11	352	781
港澳台商投资企业	Enterprises Funded by Enterpreneurs from Hong Kong，Macao &Taiwan	12	34	34	3565
外商投资企业	Foreign- Funded Enterprises	12	48	48	945
个体经济	Individuals			70744	183582
二、按国民经济行业分组	**Grouped by Sector**				
食品、饮料和烟草零售业	Retail of Food,Beverages and Tobaccos	712	990	26570	112266
日用百货零售业	Retail of Daily Consumer Goods	1332	1765	18484	160678
纺织品、服装和鞋帽零售业	Reail of Textiles,Garments,Shoes and Hats	751	786	22124	74716
日用杂品零售业	Retail of Daily Sundry Articles	102	123	10097	32057
五金、交电、化工零售业	Retail of Hardware,Transport,Electric and Chemical Products	1051	1308	10913	53629
药品及医疗器械零售业	Retail of Medicines and Medical Appliances	341	436	1608	4532
图书报刊零售业	Retail of Books,Newspapers and Magazines	145	181	894	8724
其他零售业	Other Retail Trade	1647	1674	9074	53567

Organizations, Establishments and Persons Engaged in Retail Trade(2003)

（unit,person）

市 City				县 County				县以下 Under County Level			
法人单位 Constitutional Unit	活动单位 Movemental Unit	网点 Branch Shop	人员 Personnel	法人单位 Constitutional Unit	活动单位 Movemental Unit	网点 Branch Shop	人员 Personnel	法人单位 Constitutional Unit	活动单位 Movemental Unit	网点 Branch Shop	人员 Personnel
5411	**6375**	**67446**	**411829**	**133**	**186**	**8809**	**25122**	**537**	**702**	**23509**	**53218**
5387	6293	26030	289163	133	186	549	4142	537	702	2359	8772
556	726	1804	28142	18	39	236	1419	20	73	260	948
1013	1212	13311	126607	13	35	199	936	139	249	1716	4861
142	154	154	6337	5	5	7	537	1	1	1	113
56	59	60	973								
1222	1240	1442	17334	1	2	2	89	25	25	28	166
21	33	73	13742	1	1	1	73	1	1	1	136
2366	2858	8834	95247	95	104	104	1088	351	353	353	2548
11	11	352	781								
12	34	34	3565								
12	48	48	945								
		41334	118156			8260	20980			21150	44446
533	766	19631	96598	25	34	1729	5008	154	190	5210	10660
1184	1586	12838	146773	44	47	1259	4212	104	132	4387	9693
692	706	10632	45375	25	31	4857	11676	34	49	6635	17665
33	40	8946	27626	21	27	218	1226	48	56	933	3205
997	1250	10185	50556	6	8	173	910	48	50	555	2163
317	369	1273	3493	2	24	72	261	22	43	263	778
131	134	537	7644	5	6	91	374	9	41	266	706
1524	1524	3404	33764	5	9	410	1455	118	141	5260	8348

13-9 餐饮业机构、网点、人员(2003年)

单位:个、人

分　类	Classify	合　计 Total			
		法人单位 Constitutional Unit	活动单位 Movemental Unit	网点 Branch Shop	人员 Personnel
总计	**Total**	**1120**	**1507**	**32899**	**150883**
一、按登记注册类型分组	**Grouped by Type of Registration**				
内资企业	Domestic Funded Enterprises	1098	1454	2663	37254
国有企业	State-owned Enterprises	63	152	178	6710
集体企业	Collective-owned Enterprises	109	124	282	3582
股份合作企业	Share-Holding Cooperative Enterprises	26	37	44	475
联营企业	Joint Ownership Enterprises	6	6	6	145
有限责任公司	Limited Liability Corporations	165	208	340	6146
股份有限公司	Share-holding Corporations Ltd.	24	24	44	6074
私营企业	Private Enterprises	692	860	1669	13550
其他企业	Other Enterprises	13	43	100	572
港澳台商投资企业	Enterprises Funded by Enterpreneurs from Hong Kong，Macao &Taiwan	13	41	41	2690
外商投资企业	Foreign- Funded Enterprises	9	12	12	1214
个体经济	Individuals			30183	109725
二、按餐饮业行业分组	**Grouped by Sector of Catering Trade**				
正　餐	Dinner	769	949	7174	49974
快　餐	Fast Food	108	237	3497	29728
其他餐饮业	Others	243	321	22228	71181

Organizations Staff and Branch Shopes of Catering Trade(2003)

(unit,person)

市 City				县 County				县以下 Under County Level			
法人单位 Constitutional Unit	活动单位 Movemental Unit	网点 Branch Shop	人员 Personnel	法人单位 Constitutional Unit	活动单位 Movemental Unit	网点 Branch Shop	人员 Personnel	法人单位 Constitutional Unit	活动单位 Movemental Unit	网点 Branch Shop	人员 Personnel
1065	**1424**	**26672**	**132936**	**23**	**38**	**1204**	**4966**	**32**	**45**	**5023**	**12981**
1043	1371	2485	35246	23	38	107	1271	32	45	71	737
57	135	160	6526	6	16	17	174		1	1	10
102	104	251	3414	6	8	10	96	1	12	21	72
24	32	36	205	2	5	8	270				
6	6	6	145								
164	207	339	6081					1	1	1	65
23	23	43	5956					1	1	1	118
654	821	1550	12347	9	9	72	731	29	30	47	472
13	43	100	572								
13	41	41	2690								
9	12	12	1214								
		24134	93786			1097	3695			4952	12244
725	898	7009	48694	21	24	56	671	23	27	109	609
108	237	3464	29626			33	102				
232	289	16199	54616	2	14	1115	4193	9	18	4914	12372

13-10 限额以上批发零售贸易企业财务状况(2003年)

单位：万元

指标	Item	流动资产小计 Circulating Funds	存货 Inventories	固定资产小计 Total Fixed Assets
批发、零售贸易企业总计	**Total Wholesale and Retail Trades Enterprises**	**1388410.0**	**247740.4**	**429648.8**
一、批发企业	**Wholesale Enterprises**	**1030556.5**	**178063.9**	**178228.0**
其中：国有及国有控股	State-owned and State-holding Majority Shares	789414.4	161554.5	158201.7
(一)按登记注册类型分组	Grouped by Type of Registration			
内资企业	Domestic Funded Enterprises	1009595.2	177359.6	178045.2
国有企业	State-owned Enterprises	577100.6	116250.9	131715.3
集体企业	Collective-owned Enterprises	64563.4	4264.8	6762.4
股份合作企业	Share-Holding Cooperative Enterprises			
联营企业	Joint Ownership Enterprises	4704.1	994.0	70.6
国有联营企业	State Joint Ownership Enterprises	4704.1	994.0	70.6
集体联营企业	Collective Joint Ownership Enterprises			
国有与集体联营企业	Joint State-collective Enterprises			
其他联营企业	Other Joint Ownership Enterprises			
有限责任公司	Limited Liability Corporrations	258512.1	33214.7	18496.5
国有独资企业	State Sole Funded Corporations			
其他有限责任公司	Other Limited Liability Corporrations	258512.1	33214.7	18496.5
股份有限公司	Share-holding Corporations Ltd.	90537.7	20511.3	19787.1
私营企业	Private Enterprises	14177.3	2123.9	1213.3
私营独资企业	Private-funded Enterprises			
私营合伙企业	Private Partnership Enterprises			
私营有限责任公司	Private Limited Liability Corporations	14177.3	2123.9	1213.3
私营股份有限公司	Private Share-holding Corporations Ltd.			
其他企业	Other Enterprises			
港、澳、台商投资企业	Enterprises Funded by Entrepreneurs from Hong Kong，Macao &Taiwan			
合资经营企业	Joint-venture Enterprises			
合作经营企业	Cooperative enterprises			
独资经营企业	Enterprise with Sole Investment			
投资股份有限公司	Share-holding Corporations Ltd. With the Investment			
外商投资企业	Foreign Funded Enterprises	20961.3	704.3	182.8
中外合资经营企业	Joint-venture Enterprises	16789.8		158.1
中外合作经营企业	Cooperation Enterprises			
外资企业	Foreign Funded Enterprises	4171.5	704.3	24.7
外商投资股份有限公司	Share-holding Corporations Ltd. With Foreign funds			
(二)按国民经济行业分组	Grouped by Sector			
农畜产品批发业	Farm produce and livestock products wholesale trade	34614.3	2876.4	5174.4
食品、饮料及烟草制品批发业	Foodstuff, beverage and tobacco wholesale trade	47641.1	17484.5	25391.1
米、面制品及食用油批发业	Rice, wheat flour products and edible oil wholesale trade	548.5	360.7	325.1
烟草制品批发业	Tobacco wholesale trade	29499.5	15445.9	20421.8
纺织、服装及日用品批发业	Textile, costume and commodity wholesale trade	141796.7	13646.0	38298.6
服装批发业	Costume wholesale trade	47362.4	5152.5	12726.3
文化、体育用品及器材批发业	Stationery, sports goods wholesale trade	28115.8	8158.8	14571.0
医药及医疗器材批发业	Medicine and medical apparatus and instruments wholesale trade	98723.0	23700.0	14461.4
矿产品、建材及化工产品批发业	Ore products, building materials and chemical products wholesale trade	303198.2	40462.6	46803.7
煤炭及制品批发业	Coal and coal products wholesale trade	2415.2	314.2	13695.5

Financial Status of Enterprises Above Designated Size in Wholesale and Retail(2003)

(10 000 yuan)

固定资产原价 Fixed Assets Original Value	累计折旧 Accumulate Depreciation	资产总计 Total Assets	负债合计 Total Liabilities	所有者权益合计 Creditors'Equity	实收资本 Total Capital Hold	商品销售收入净额 Retained Profit of Sales Revenue
478535.5	**131183.2**	**2031754.7**	**1753267.1**	**278487.6**	**413126.9**	**3132234.6**
199083.2	**46431.9**	**1333986.7**	**1264586.6**	**69400.1**	**265006.7**	**2323149.9**
179459.8	41023.2	1027035.9	983414.2	43621.7	220053.3	1516008.4
198598.7	46130.2	1312839.2	1245877.4	66961.8	259866.7	2191326.7
145979.6	33123.4	749564.5	683537.5	66027.0	113720.5	1116815.3
9222.9	3722.6	98421.3	100440.5	-2019.2	9770.4	25770.0
185.7	115.1	4779.8	4302.8	477.0	91.3	23625.1
185.7	115.1	4779.8	4302.8	477.0	91.3	23625.1
16727.5	3517.4	310531.9	258030.8	52501.1	37280.0	915353.0
16727.5	3517.4	310531.9	258030.8	52501.1	37280.0	915353.0
25172.6	5554.6	134651.3	188022.8	-53371.5	95544.5	81616.6
1310.4	97.1	14890.4	11543.0	3347.4	3460.0	28146.7
1310.4	97.1	14890.4	11543.0	3347.4	3460.0	28146.7
484.5	301.7	21147.5	18709.2	2438.3	5140.0	131823.2
450.7	292.6	16951.3	18617.9	-1666.6	1000.0	115572.0
33.8	9.1	4196.2	91.3	4104.9	4140.0	16251.2
7872.7	2710.0	69463.4	85733.8	-16270.4	7763.1	24695.3
27182.4	4412.9	76326.6	53424.8	22901.8	6984.4	176317.2
353.3	47.3	873.7	1153.7	-280.0	303.9	552.0
20678.1	2634.6	51336.4	27712.8	23623.6	2329.5	163654.8
36020.6	8581.3	217293.5	245806.3	-28512.8	57121.3	151309.3
11129.6	3407.4	71534.4	77758.2	-6223.8	12938.8	40798.6
17320.9	2945.2	44088.5	24679.4	19409.1	10782.0	76610.7
19052.6	4829.7	130605.8	124798.5	5807.3	22063.5	253226.8
49626.2	10766.0	369980.7	327428.2	42552.5	119879.3	643014.6
13646.1	1354.8	16431.6	11962.7	4468.9	11417.8	479.7

13-10 限额以上批发零售贸易企业财务状况(2003年)(续1)

单位：万元

指　　标	Item	商品销售成本 Cost of Sales	经营费用 Expenses for Business Operation
批发、零售贸易企业总计	**Total Wholesale and Retail Trades Enterprises**	**2905298.9**	**118204.1**
一、批发企业	**Wholesale Enterprises**	**2206469.0**	**58539.6**
其中：国有及国有控股	State-owned and State-holding Majority Shares	1420081.2	46847.7
(一)按登记注册类型分组	Grouped by Type of Registration		
内资企业	Domestic Funded Enterprises	2077756.5	53760.1
国有企业	State-owned Enterprises	1043046.8	33511.8
集体企业	Collective-owned Enterprises	24613.6	442.3
股份合作企业	Share-Holding Cooperative Enterprises		
联营企业	Joint Ownership Enterprises	23047.3	398.7
国有联营企业	State Joint Ownership Enterprises	23047.3	398.7
集体联营企业	Collective Joint Ownership Enterprises		
国有与集体联营企业	Joint State-collective Enterprises		
其他联营企业	Other Joint Ownership Enterprises		
有限责任公司	Limited Liability Corporrations	886258.9	13739.2
国有独资企业	State Sole Funded Corporations		
其他有限责任公司	Other Limited Liability Corporrations	886258.9	13739.2
股份有限公司	Share-holding Corporations Ltd.	74110.8	4926.4
私营企业	Private Enterprises	26679.1	741.7
私营独资企业	Private-funded Enterprises		
私营合伙企业	Private Partnership Enterprises		
私营有限责任公司	Private Limited Liability Corporations	26679.1	741.7
私营股份有限公司	Private Share-holding Corporations Ltd.		
其他企业	Other Enterprises		
港、澳、台商投资企业	Enterprises Funded by Entrepreneurs from Hong Kong，Macao &Taiwan		
合资经营企业	Joint-venture Enterprises		
合作经营企业	Cooperative enterprises		
独资经营企业	Enterprise with Sole Investment		
投资股份有限公司	Share-holding Corporations Ltd. With the Investment		
外商投资企业	Foreign Funded Enterprises	128712.5	4779.5
中外合资经营企业	Joint-venture Enterprises	112844.7	4592.4
中外合作经营企业	Cooperation Enterprises		
外资企业	Foreign Funded Enterprises	15867.8	187.1
外商投资股份有限公司	Share-holding Corporations Ltd. With Foreign funds		
(二)按国民经济行业分组	Grouped by Sector		
农畜产品批发业	Farm produce and livestock products wholesale trade	23501.0	386.1
食品、饮料及烟草制品批发业	Foodstuff, beverage and tobacco wholesale trade	151106.9	4986.7
米、面制品及食用油批发业	Rice, wheat flour products and edible oil wholesale trade	540.3	3.5
烟草制品批发业	Tobacco wholesale trade	141154.6	3217.0
纺织、服装及日用品批发业	Textile, costume and commodity wholesale trade	139995.4	8811.3
服装批发业	Costume wholesale trade	39076.1	896.8
文化、体育用品及器材批发业	Stationery, sports goods wholesale trade	70458.5	3241.4
医药及医疗器材批发业	Medicine and medical apparatus and instruments wholesale trade	240151.9	6480.0
矿产品、建材及化工产品批发业	Ore products, building materials and chemical products wholesale trade	623515.8	9371.9
煤炭及制品批发业	Coal and coal products wholesale trade	480.2	48.7

Financial Status of Enterprises Above Designated Size in Wholesale and Retail(2003)(Continued 1)

(10 000 Yuan)

商品销售税金及附加 Sales Tax and Surcharge	代购代销收入 Buy And Sell Income On SB□Behalf	主营业务利润 Profits from Main Operation	管理费用 Managerial Expenditures	营业利润 Operation Profit	利润总额 Total Profits	本年应付工资总额 Payment
5000.5	**1806.3**	**105537.4**	**151718.4**	**-28454.6**	**-28681.4**	**45938.7**
1851.8	**1794.8**	**58084.3**	**101076.3**	**-39281.4**	**-42167.4**	**21802.6**
1370.0	1794.8	49504.3	91134.4	-36420.8	-42979.9	17283.6
1847.7	1794.8	59757.2	100943.0	-37487.1	-40388.8	20795.7
842.0	1545.0	40959.7	35955.0	14629.7	13593.6	12487.0
17.1		697.0	1710.0	-693.1	-170.9	662.7
11.7	51.1	218.5	250.2	47.6	50.0	66.9
11.7	51.1	218.5	250.2	47.6	50.0	66.9
884.8	132.6	14602.7	12202.7	521.9	2805.3	5049.0
884.8	132.6	14602.7	12202.7	521.9	2805.3	5049.0
77.3	66.1	2568.2	50386.5	-52065.7	-56724.9	2214.8
14.8		711.1	438.6	72.5	58.1	315.3
14.8		711.1	438.6	72.5	58.1	315.3
4.1		-1672.9	133.3	-1794.3	-1778.6	1006.9
4.1		-1869.2		-1861.9	-1844.7	936.3
		196.3	133.3	67.6	66.1	70.6
2.5	21.4	827.1	1627.4	-2150.3	-1828.7	540.3
427.8		19795.8	8853.7	11367.3	10911.4	3249.9
		8.2	41.6	-92.5	-67.7	11.5
391.6		18891.6	7534.5	11024.0	11500.6	2572.1
100.4	274.6	2676.8	54059.0	-46441.6	-51520.3	2180.4
0.2	107.9	933.4	3705.0	5510.8	5627.1	541.1
68.1		2842.7	2795.4	18.3	68.4	1352.7
80.5		6514.4	5764.9	-537.4	-489.9	3579.4
233.5	489.3	10382.7	8364.9	136.4	2822.7	3460.1
2.5		-51.7	648.4	-680.0	-641.4	248.4

13-10 限额以上批发零售贸易企业财务状况(2003年）（续2）

单位：万元

指　标	Item	流动资产小计 Circulating Funds	存货 Inventories	固定资产小计 Total Fixed Assets
石油及制品批发业	Oil and oil products wholesale trade	76006.6	3725.1	3337.8
金属及金属矿批发业	Metal and metal ore wholesale trade	178101.6	31975.9	24815.5
建材批发业	Building materials wholesale trade			
化肥批发业	Fertilizer wholesale trade	38492.6	1920.6	2961.1
机械设备、五金交电及电子产品批发业	Machinery, ironware, transportation, wiring and electronic products wholesale trade	373467.3	71511.5	29421.2
汽车、摩托车及零配件批发业	Motorcars, motorcycles, spare parts and fittings of motorcars and motorcycles wholesale trade	67617.4	10411.0	5825.8
家用电器批发业	Electrical household appliances wholesale trade	18536.5	4936.3	644.9
计算机、软件及辅助设备批发业	Computers, computer software and auxiliary equipment wholesale trade	61604.5	1124.8	179.8
贸易经纪与代理	Trade broker and agent			
其他批发业	Other whole trade	3000.1	224.1	4106.6
二、零售企业	**Retail**	**357853.5**	**69676.5**	**251420.8**
其中：国有及国有控股	Of the Totd State-owned and State Holding Majority Shares	100988.7	22379.1	110524.8
(一)按登记注册类型分组	Grouped by Registration Status			
内资企业	Domestic Funded Enterprises	355899.2	68851.8	251346.4
国有企业	State-owned Enterprises	52439.6	15676.9	32756.9
集体企业	Collective-owned Enterprises	2399.0	265.8	1171.4
股份合作企业	Share-Holding Cooperative Enterprises	6509.7	1048.7	12615.3
联营企业	Joint Ownership Enterprises			
国有联营企业	State Joint Ownership Enterprises			
集体联营企业	Collective Joint Ownership Enterprises			
国有与集体联营企业	Joint State-collective Enterprises			
其他联营企业	Other Joint Ownership Enterprises			
有限责任公司	Limited Liability Corporations	153654.9	26736.9	87160.5
国有独资企业	State Sole Funded Corporations			
其他有限责任公司	Other Limited Liability Corporations	153654.9	26736.9	87160.5
股份有限公司	Share-holding Corporations Ltd.	84034.0	5754.8	83662.0
私营企业	Private Enterprises	56862.0	19368.7	33980.3
私营独资企业	Private-funded Enterprises	14451.3	6784.6	2484.3
私营合伙企业	Private Partnership Enterprises			
私营有限责任公司	Private Limited Liability Corporations	42004.3	12584.1	28693.2
私营股份有限公司	Private Share-holding Corporations ltd.	406.4		2802.8
其他企业	Other Enterprises			
港、澳、台商投资企业	Enterprises with Funds From Hong Kong, Macao and Taiwan	1954.3	824.7	74.4
合资经营企业	Joint-venture Enterprises	1954.3	824.7	74.4
合作经营企业	Cooperative Enterprises			
独资经营企业	Enterprises With Sole Funds			
投资股份有限公司	Share Holding Corporations Ltd			

Financial Status of Enterprises Above Designated Size in Wholesale and Retail(2003)(Continued 2)

(10 000 yuan)

固定资产原价 Fixed Assets Original Value	累计折旧 Accumulate Depreciation	资产总计 Total Assets	负债合计 Total Liabilities	所有者权益合计 Creditors'Equity	实收资本 Total Capital Hold	商品销售收入净额 Retained Profit of Sales Revenue
4940.2	1607.1	79569.1	71566.4	8002.7	6857.5	245855.9
25384.7	5716.5	221544.1	196184.1	25360.0	94743.5	369455.4
3047.5	1390.4	41896.1	38645.3	3250.8	4614.5	13848.2
36984.3	11200.4	418716.5	391583.2	27133.3	38220.1	991508.8
6709.4	1801.7	82895.9	89730.6	-6834.7	13628.3	142994.9
320.6	75.7	18809.3	17431.4	1377.9	1400.0	20160.7
494.2	314.4	61787.7	52814.6	8973.1	1600.0	415424.0
5023.5	986.4	7511.7	11132.4	-3620.7	2193.0	6467.2
279452.3	**84751.3**	**697768.0**	**488680.5**	**209087.5**	**148120.2**	**809084.7**
125975.3	33164.7	263888.1	180827.4	83060.7	54803.3	217242.1
279297.7	84671.1	692563.0	483604.7	208958.3	145120.2	806719.8
29585.3	7430.5	97150.5	82627.2	14523.3	18453.0	97712.5
1411.3	239.9	3586.6	2978.4	608.2	584.3	3632.7
8059.6	2310.9	13572.0	11475.4	2096.6	1147.4	37228.7
91717.1	16178.5	267609.7	186997.8	80611.9	45171.5	396712.0
91717.1	16178.5	267609.7	186997.8	80611.9	45171.5	396712.0
109153.1	25736.6	215284.3	129238.2	86046.1	58864.0	117698.5
39371.3	32774.7	95359.9	70287.7	25072.2	20900.0	153735.4
3641.4	1187.0	18166.3	13694.8	4471.5	3000.0	42676.2
32719.8	31380.4	73787.4	53284.0	20503.4	17400.0	106360.7
3010.1	207.3	3406.2	3308.9	97.3	500.0	4698.5
154.6	80.2	5205.0	5075.8	129.2	3000.0	2364.9
154.6	80.2	5205.0	5075.8	129.2	3000.0	2364.9

13-10 限额以上批发零售贸易企业财务状况(2003年)（续3）

单位：万元

指　标	Item	商品销售成本 Cost of Sales	经营费用 Expenses for Business Operation
石油及制品批发业	Oil and oil products wholesale trade	239877.7	3136.0
金属及金属矿批发业	Metal and metal ore wholesale trade	357432.1	5199.8
建材批发业	Building materials wholesale trade		
化肥批发业	Fertilizer wholesale trade	13268.4	353.7
机械设备、五金交电及电子产品批发业	Machinery, ironware, transportation, wiring and electronic products wholesale trade	951485.8	25209.8
汽车、摩托车及零配件批发业	Motorcars, motorcycles, spare parts and fittings of motorcars and motorcycles wholesale trade	139308.8	1922.9
家用电器批发业	Electrical household appliances wholesale trade	19197.2	1060.1
计算机、软件及辅助设备批发业	Computers, computer software and auxiliary equipment wholesale trade	406481.3	5962.4
贸易经纪与代理	Trade broker and agent		
其他批发业	Other whole trade	6253.7	52.4
二、零售企业	**Retail**	**698829.9**	**59664.5**
其中：国有及国有控股	Of the Totd State-owned and State Holding Majority Shares	186190.8	7789.0
(一)按登记注册类型分组	Grouped by Registration Status		
内资企业	Domestic Funded Enterprises	697425.1	59603.3
国有企业	State-owned Enterprises	84588.1	5863.0
集体企业	Collective-owned Enterprises	3318.7	134.8
股份合作企业	Share-Holding Cooperative Enterprises	35015.9	700.0
联营企业	Joint Ownership Enterprises		
国有联营企业	State Joint Ownership Enterprises		
集体联营企业	Collective Joint Ownership Enterprises		
国有与集体联营企业	Joint State-collective Enterprises		
其他联营企业	Other Joint Ownership Enterprises		
有限责任公司	Limited Liability Corporations	348571.5	26137.8
国有独资企业	State Sole Funded Corporations		
其他有限责任公司	Other Limited Liability Corporations	348571.5	26137.8
股份有限公司	Share-holding Corporations Ltd.	94593.5	7993.9
私营企业	Private Enterprises	131337.4	18773.8
私营独资企业	Private-funded Enterprises	38467.8	5723.8
私营合伙企业	Private Partnership Enterprises		
私营有限责任公司	Private Limited Liability Corporations	88832.7	12749.5
私营股份有限公司	Private Share-holding Corporations ltd.	4036.9	300.5
其他企业	Other Enterprises		
港、澳、台商投资企业	Enterprises with Funds From Hong Kong, Macao and Taiwan	1404.8	61.2
合资经营企业	Joint-venture Enterprises	1404.8	61.2
合作经营企业	Cooperative Enterprises		
独资经营企业	Enterprises With Sole Funds		
投资股份有限公司	Share Holding Corporations Ltd		

Financial Status of Enterprises Above Designated Size in Wholesale and Retail(2003)(Continued 3)

(10 000 Yuan)

商品销售税金及附加 Sales Tax and Surcharge	代购代销收入 Buy And Sell Income On SB□Behalf	主营业务利润 Profits from Main Operation	管理费用 Managerial Expenditures	营业利润 Operation Profit	利润总额 Total Profits	本年应付工资总额 Payment
76.8		2765.4	1675.0	762.9	393.4	835.9
134.7	489.3	7178.1	4812.7	603.2	3441.9	1763.4
4.7		221.4	570.4	-415.8	-215.2	194.2
932.7	1009.5	14890.0	19269.2	-1387.0	-1848.4	7328.6
21.9		1741.3	2420.4	-1434.9	-782.1	601.0
17.6		-114.2	74.8	-405.6	-603.4	175.0
337.7		2642.6	6291.2	-1543.6	-1709.1	2643.4
6.3		154.8	341.8	-287.1	-282.6	111.2
3148.7	**11.5**	**47453.1**	**50642.1**	**10826.8**	**13486.0**	**24136.1**
864.8	11.5	22409.0	22920.7	1444.4	3386.4	9223.6
3148.7	11.5	46554.2	50063.9	10794.6	13457.5	24136.1
298.3	11.5	6974.6	6984.4	-65.2	604.3	3446.9
9.4		169.8	205.7	7.6	-2.9	114.1
30.0		1482.8	1472.5	154.7	142.2	726.0
1724.6		20278.1	17163.9	11041.1	11733.4	8698.5
1724.6		20278.1	17163.9	11041.1	11733.4	8698.5
770.5		14340.6	16982.6	540.9	1494.8	6546.8
315.9		3308.3	7254.8	-884.5	-514.3	4603.8
119.9		-1635.3	695.0	-1007.7	-1016.8	1670.5
174.4		4604.1	6222.3	121.0	501.2	2863.7
21.6		339.5	337.5	2.2	1.3	69.6
		898.9	578.2	32.2	28.5	
		898.9	578.2	32.2	28.5	

13-10 限额以上批发零售贸易企业财务状况(2003年)（续4）

单位：万元

指 标	Item	流动资产小计 Circulating Funds	存 货 Inventories	固定资产小计 Total Fixed Assets
外商投资企业	Foreign Funded Enterprises			
中外合资经营企业	Joint-venture Enterprises			
中外合作经营企业	Sino-foreign Joint Ventures Enterprises			
外资企业	Foreign Funded Enterprises			
外商投资股份有限公司	Foreign- Funded Corporations Ltd			
（二）按国民经济行业分组	Grouped by Sector			
综合零售业	Comprehensive retail trade	273275.9	48843.3	227414.0
百货零售业	General merchandise retail trade	156081.5	19090.1	183303.2
超级市场零售业	Supermarket retail trade	117194.4	29753.2	44110.8
食品、饮料及烟草制品专门零售业	Foodstuff, beverage and tobacco special retail trade	7547.4	1653.7	9408.3
纺织、服装及日用品专门零售业	Textile, costume and commodity special retail trade	24356.2	2548.8	7394.8
服装零售业	Costume retail trade	19834.8	688.0	6616.5
文化、体育用品及器材专门零售业	Stationery, sports goods special retail trade	13686.7	7759.9	3025.0
体育用品零售业	Sports goods retail trade	2036.9	1807.0	382.4
图书零售业	Book retail trade	11113.1	5791.9	2471.8
医药及医疗器材专门零售业	Medicine and medical apparatus and instruments special retail trade	846.5	443.4	229.8
药品零售业	Medical drugs retail trade	846.5	443.4	229.8
汽车、摩托车、燃料及零配件专门零售业	Motorcars, motorcycles, fuel, spare parts and fittings of motorcars and motorcycles special retail trade	1275.3	365.7	645.9
汽车零售业	Motorcars retail trade			
机动车燃料零售业	Motor vehicle fuel retail trade			
家用电器及电子产品专门零售业	Electrical household appliances and electronic products special retail trade	33806.0	7912.3	491.7
家用电器零售业	Electrical household appliances retail trade	33806.0	7912.3	491.7
计算机、软件及辅助设备零售业	Computers, computer software and auxiliary equipment retail trade			
通讯设备零售业	Communication equipment retail trade			
五金、家具及室内装修材料专门零售业	Ironware, furniture and room fitting stuff special retail trade	3059.5	149.4	2811.3
无店铺及其他零售业	Shopless retail trade and other retail trades			
邮购及电子销售业	Mail order and electronic distribution trade			
（三）按业态分组	Grouped by trade form			
百货商店	Department Store	160939.9	22289.4	183573.5
超级市场	Super Market	144043.4	33493.7	53490.4
专业（专卖）商店	Specialty store	46768.1	11928.8	13182.7
其他	Others	6102.1	1964.6	1174.2

Financial Status of Enterprises Above Designated Size in Wholesale and Retail(2003)(Continued 4)

(10 000 yuan)

固定资产原价 Fixed Assets Original Value	累计折旧 Accumulate Depreciation	资产总计 Total Assets	负债合计 Total Liabilities	所有者权益合计 Creditors'Equity	实收资本 Total Capital Hold	商品销售收入净额 Retained Profit of Sales Revenue
251199.1	78428.6	584898.9	393852.6	191046.3	126719.1	666339.0
196454.8	40416.8	412008.4	257994.0	154014.4	94667.9	400731.7
54744.3	38011.8	172890.5	135858.6	37031.9	32051.2	265607.3
11117.6	1932.6	20421.3	19137.1	1284.2	8327.0	2694.1
7671.2	1506.1	31230.6	24114.9	7115.7	8003.3	13372.7
6616.5	1227.6	25660.8	19276.2	6384.6	7700.0	10106.3
4707.2	2248.1	17232.1	14954.7	2277.4	1000.9	27419.4
432.6	50.2	2467.9	2179.3	288.6	300.0	4654.5
3955.7	2049.8	13636.7	11819.6	1817.1	567.8	22288.3
239.9	54.6	1097.9	909.7	188.2	169.9	1299.0
239.9	54.6	1097.9	909.7	188.2	169.9	1299.0
816.7	178.9	1921.3	1438.4	482.9	1000.0	1099.9
651.9	165.0	34781.7	30597.3	4184.4	2300.0	92061.1
651.9	165.0	34781.7	30597.3	4184.4	2300.0	92061.1
3048.7	237.4	6184.2	3675.8	2508.4	600.0	4799.5
197383.0	41074.7	414860.0	263833.6	151026.4	91370.1	424909.6
65448.1	39499.0	215582.3	171455.3	44127.0	44025.2	303577.9
15067.3	3795.8	59806.9	47544.7	12262.2	12066.4	49867.1
1553.9	381.8	7518.8	5846.9	1671.9	658.5	30730.1

13-10 限额以上批发零售贸易企业财务状况(2003年）（续5）

单位：万元

指 标	Item	商品销售成本 Cost of Sales	经营费用 Expenses for Business Operation
外商投资企业	Foreign Funded Enterprises		
中外合资经营企业	Joint-venture Enterprises		
中外合作经营企业	Sino-foreign Joint Ventures Enterprises		
外资企业	Foreign Funded Enterprises		
外商投资股份有限公司	Foreign- Funded Corporations Ltd		
（二）按国民经济行业分组	Grouped by Sector		
综合零售业	Comprehensive retail trade	572923.7	49814.7
百货零售业	General merchandise retail trade	346061.3	15099.8
超级市场零售业	Supermarket retail trade	226862.4	34714.9
食品、饮料及烟草制品专门零售业	Foodstuff, beverage and tobacco special retail trade	2766.2	231.3
纺织、服装及日用品专门零售业	Textile, costume and commodity special retail trade	8832.4	1434.9
服装零售业	Costume retail trade	6368.6	651.8
文化、体育用品及器材专门零售业	Stationery, sports goods special retail trade	21381.3	3051.8
体育用品零售业	Sports goods retail trade	3806.5	892.7
图书零售业	Book retail trade	17281.3	2129.3
医药及医疗器材专门零售业	Medicine and medical apparatus and instruments special retail trade	1043.1	194.5
药品零售业	Medical drugs retail trade	1043.1	194.5
汽车、摩托车、燃料及零配件专门零售业	Motorcars, motorcycles, fuel, spare parts and fittings of motorcars and motorcycles special retail trade	977.5	49.6
汽车零售业	Motorcars retail trade		
机动车燃料零售业	Motor vehicle fuel retail trade		
家用电器及电子产品专门零售业	Electrical household appliances and electronic products special retail trade	86780.2	4535.4
家用电器零售业	Electrical household appliances retail trade	86780.2	4535.4
计算机、软件及辅助设备零售业	Computers, computer software and auxiliary equipment retail trade		
通讯设备零售业	Communication equipment retail trade		
五金、家具及室内装修材料专门零售业	Ironware, furniture and room fitting stuff special retail trade	4125.5	352.3
无店铺及其他零售业	Shopless retail trade and other retail trades		
邮购及电子销售业	Mail order and electronic distribution trade		
（三）按业态分组	Grouped by trade form		
百货商店	Department Store	368439.2	17528.9
超级市场	Super Market	263308.3	34728.4
专业（专卖）商店	Specialty store	39371.1	5064.4
其他	Others	27711.3	2342.8

Financial Status of Enterprises Above Designated Size in Wholesale and Retail(2003)(Continued 5)

(10 000 Yuan)

商品销售税金及附加 Sales Tax and Surcharge	代购代销收入 Buy And Sell Income On SB Behalf	主营业务利润 Profits from Main Operation	管理费用 Managerial Expenditures	营业利润 Operation Profit	利润总额 Total Profits	本年应付工资总额 Payment
2477.1		41123.5	42211.3	9090.3	10605.6	20997.7
1788.2		37782.4	32066.1	9729.8	10771.4	12325.1
688.9		3341.1	10145.2	-639.5	-165.8	8672.6
2.2		-305.6	591.4	-783.0	-190.1	474.6
357.2		2748.2	2953.0	117.1	1.5	485.2
335.3		2750.6	2455.5		-87.0	368.2
96.1	11.5	2901.7	2477.0	399.8	896.4	709.6
16.8		-61.5	369.9	20.9	20.9	100.3
77.4	11.5	2811.8	2010.9	356.9	853.5	531.7
2.0		59.4	97.8	-15.3	-15.3	161.4
2.0		59.4	97.8	-15.3	-15.3	161.4
1.3		71.5	73.8	5.8	8.0	27.3
190.8		554.7	1844.5	2105.5	2274.2	1180.5
190.8		554.7	1844.5	2105.5	2274.2	1180.5
22.0		299.7	393.3	-93.4	-94.3	99.8
1813.9		37127.6	32333.9	8981.0	10022.8	12876.8
820.0		4721.2	11965.1	1664.7	2890.5	9288.9
451.4	11.5	4991.7	5377.0	-394.4	-75.8	1447.0
63.4		612.6	966.1	575.5	648.5	523.4

13-11 限额以上餐饮企业财务状况(2003年)

单位：万元

指　标	Item	年末资产负债			
		流动资产小计 Circulating Funds	存　货 Inventories	长期投资 Long-Term Investment	固定资产小计 Total Fixed Assets
总　计	**Total**	**64057.9**	**4433.8**	**10758.2**	**62940.4**
其中：国有及国有控股	Of the total State-owned and State-holding Majority Shares	34027.4	1718.9	8731.2	53066.7
一、按登记注册类型分组	**Grouped by Type of Registration**				
内资企业	Domestic Funded Enterprises	42095.7	2342.3	8695.2	53771.9
国有企业	State-owned Enterprises	2125.3	127.3	262.6	4343.2
集体企业	Collective-owned Enterprises				
股份合作企业	Share-Holding Cooperative Enterprises	14.2			14.4
联营企业	Joint Ownership Enterprises				
国有联营企业	State Joint Ownership Enterprises				
集体联营企业	Collective Joint Ownership Enterprises				
国有与集体联营企业	Joint State-collective Enterprises				
其他联营企业	Other Joint Ownership Enterprises				
有限责任公司	Limited Liability Corporrations	1945.3	357.2	0.0	1923.1
国有独资企业	State Sole Funded Corporations				
其他有限责任公司	Other Limited Liability Corporrations	1945.3	357.2	0.0	1923.1
股份有限公司	Share-holding Corporations Ltd.	29263.1	1408.5	8432.6	46096.3
私营企业	Private Enterprises	8747.8	449.3	0.0	1394.9
私营独资企业	Private-funded Enterprises	290.6	83.2	0.0	103.6
私营合伙企业	Private Partnership Enterprises				
私营有限责任公司	Private Limited Liability Corporations	8321.1	358.0	0.0	1281.6
私营股份有限公司	Private Share-holding Corporations Ltd.	136.1	8.1	0.0	9.7
其他企业	Other Enterprises				
港、澳、台商投资企业	Enterprises Funded by Entrepreneurs from Hong Kong，Macao &Taiwan	10773.4	1772.6	236.0	8085.8
合资经营企业	Joint-venture Enterprises	2426.4	753.3	200.0	1896.8
合作经营企业	Cooperative enterprises	3050.6	378.6	36.0	3306.4
独资经营企业	Enterprise with Sole Investment	5296.4	640.7	0.0	2882.6
投资股份有限公司	Share-holding Corporations Ltd. With their Investment				
外商投资企业	Foreign Funded Enterprises	11188.8	318.9	1827.0	1082.7
中外合资经营企业	Joint-venture Enterprises	3046.3	70.7	1827.0	551.1
中外合作经营企业	Cooperation Enterprises	7572.8	188.8	0.0	95.8
外资企业	Foreign Funded Enterprises	569.7	59.4	0.0	435.8
外商投资股份有限公司	Share-holding Corporations Ltd. With Foreign funds				
二、按餐饮业行业分组	**Grouped by Sector of Catering Trade**				
正餐	Dinner	57832.9	3554.3	10758.2	58996.2
快餐	Fast Food	6225.0	879.5	0.0	3944.2
其他餐饮业	Others				

Finacial Status of Catering Enterprises Above Designated Size（2003）

（10 000 yuan)

Assets Liabilities (year-end)						
固定资产原价	累计折旧		资产合计	负债合计	所有者权益合计	
Original Value of Fixed Assets	Accumulated Depreciation	本年折旧 In The Year	Total Assets	Total Liabilities	Owners Equity	实收资本 Paid in Capital
54395.8	**20215.1**	**3325.6**	**156227.2**	**103455.0**	**52772.2**	**40324.0**
36994.9	11612.9	1726.3	104420.2	71820.0	32600.2	23389.8
37038.3	10958.5	1853.4	115780.0	79251.8	36528.2	26302.0
5139.1	842.6	242.1	7383.6	6674.5	709.1	480.0
74.1	59.7	8.0	99.1	14.2	84.9	78.0
2630.3	714.5	185.2	4053.6	3373.8	679.8	1155.6
2630.3	714.5	185.2	4053.6	3373.8	679.8	1155.6
26301.9	7843.6	1047.7	90004.1	61108.1	28896.0	18405.4
2892.9	1498.1	370.4	14239.6	8081.2	6158.4	6183.0
144.6	41.0	6.2	394.1	366.2	27.9	40.0
2694.8	1413.2	357.6	13699.7	7665.6	6034.1	6063.0
53.5	43.9	6.6	145.8	49.4	96.4	80.0
14311.9	7260.5	1255.8	24770.9	9385.7	15385.2	11782.8
1427.1	563.8	75.0	4523.2	2942.1	1581.1	1500.0
6376.9	3071.4	481.2	8771.2	3699.9	5071.3	6369.3
6507.9	3625.3	699.6	11476.5	2743.7	8732.8	3913.5
3045.6	1996.1	216.4	15676.3	14817.5	858.8	2239.2
1745.4	1194.4	130.5	6820.7	5984.9	835.8	1312.0
145.9	50.1	10.3	7847.0	7561.0	286.0	513.3
1154.3	751.6	75.6	1008.6	1271.6	-263.0	413.9
45973.7	15703.2	2515.4	142109.5	99885.6	42223.9	34258.5
8422.1	4511.9	810.2	14117.7	3569.4	10548.3	6065.5

13-11 限额以上餐饮企业财务状况（2003年）（续）

单位：万元

指　标	Item	损益及分配			
		营业收入 Sales	营业成本 Cost of Sales	营业费用 Operation Expenses	营业税金及附加 Sales Tax and Extra Charges
总　计	**Total**	**102316.6**	**48781.4**	**33343.8**	**4134.5**
其中：国有及国有控股	Of the total State-owned and State-holding Majority Shares	38961.4	16969.4	13986.9	1536.5
一、按登记注册类型分组	**Grouped by Type of Registration**				
内资企业	Domestic Funded Enterprises	63046.3	31871.4	20314.0	2651.0
国有企业	State-owned Enterprises	2797.8	980.5	1313.0	122.3
集体企业	Collective-owned Enterprises				
股份合作企业	Share-Holding Cooperative Enterprises	262.8	86.2		11.9
联营企业	Joint Ownership Enterprises				
国有联营企业	State Joint Ownership Enterprises				
集体联营企业	Collective Joint Ownership Enterprises				
国有与集体联营企业	Joint State-collective Enterprises				
其他联营企业	Other Joint Ownership Enterprises				
有限责任公司	Limited Liability Corporrations	10059.6	6437.4	2153.3	449.2
国有独资企业	State Sole Funded Corporations				
其他有限责任公司	Other Limited Liability Corporrations	10059.6	6437.4	2153.3	449.2
股份有限公司	Share-holding Corporations Ltd.	34777.3	15640.9	12083.6	1379.9
私营企业	Private Enterprises	15148.8	8726.4	4764.1	687.7
私营独资企业	Private-funded Enterprises	753.9	507.6	129.6	26.1
私营合伙企业	Private Partnership Enterprises				
私营有限责任公司	Private Limited Liability Corporations	13871.7	7901.2	4483.2	636.1
私营股份有限公司	Private Share-holding Corporations Ltd.	523.2	317.6	151.3	25.5
其他企业	Other Enterprises				
港、澳、台商投资企业	Enterprises Funded by Entrepreneurs from Hong Kong，Macao &Taiwan	32840.9	14358.9	11112.3	1218.7
合资经营企业	Joint-venture Enterprises	8646.3	4611.7	2452.4	334.9
合作经营企业	Cooperative enterprises	4712.8	2222.8	1290.8	177.8
独资经营企业	Enterprise with Sole Investment	19481.8	7524.4	7369.1	706.0
投资股份有限公司	Share-holding Corporations Ltd. With their Investment				
外商投资企业	Foreign Funded Enterprises	6429.4	2551.1	1917.5	264.8
中外合资经营企业	Joint-venture Enterprises	1065.4	541.9	454.2	51.9
中外合作经营企业	Cooperation Enterprises	4148.4	1746.0	945.6	161.9
外资企业	Foreign Funded Enterprises	1215.6	263.2	517.7	51.0
外商投资股份有限公司	Share-holding Corporations Ltd. With Foreign funds				
二、按餐饮业行业分组	**Grouped by Sector of Catering Trade**				
正餐	Dinner	79026.4	39615.0	24930.2	3273.5
快餐	Fast Food	23290.2	9166.4	8413.6	861.0
其他餐饮业	Others				

Finacial Status of Catering Enterprises Above Designated Size（2003）(Continued)

（10 000 yuan)

	Profit and Loss&Distribute				本年应付工资总额	本年应付福利费总额
经营利润 Management Profit	管理费用 Managenment Expenses	财务费用 Financial Expenses	营业利润 Business Profits	利润总额 Total Profit	Total Salary payable	Total Welfare Payable
16056.9	**8961.0**	**2240.3**	**4855.6**	**5655.2**	**8318.6**	**823.4**
6468.6	3654.3	1507.9	1306.4	1906.1	3452.0	494.7
8209.9	4515.7	1502.2	2192.0	2877.5	5463.8	660.1
382.0	510.8	111.7	-240.5	-239.8	434.9	26.0
164.7	160.7		4.0	4.0	49.8	7.0
1019.7	1125.9	19.2	-125.4	-143.0	728.8	107.0
1019.7	1125.9	19.2	-125.4	-143.0	728.8	107.0
5672.9	1896.4	1213.0	2563.5	3166.7	2591.2	383.0
970.6	821.9	158.3	-9.6	89.6	1659.1	137.1
90.6	89.7	0.3	0.6	0.0	69.4	0.0
851.2	710.6	158.0	-17.4	82.4	1511.0	137.1
28.8	21.6		7.2	7.2	78.7	0.0
6151.0	2705.0	304.4	3141.6	3250.2	2133.9	85.7
1247.3	578.7	136.3	532.3	534.9	77.3	0.0
1021.4	1542.3	193.0	-713.9	-718.9	701.0	85.7
3882.3	584.0	-24.9	3323.2	3434.2	1355.6	0.0
1696.0	1740.3	433.7	-478.0	-472.5	720.9	77.6
17.4	216.4	420.1	-619.1	-612.9	119.3	14.6
1294.9	1291.4	15.2	-11.7	-10.9	533.2	63.0
383.7	232.5	-1.6	152.8	151.3	68.4	0.0
11207.7	7877.5	2257.0	1073.2	1768.3	6704.3	823.4
4849.2	1083.5	-16.7	3782.4	3886.9	1614.3	0.0

13-12 商品交易市场成交量

Transactions Volume in Commodities Markets

单位：吨 (ton)

商品名称	Commodity Names	2002 全市 Total	2002 城市 Urban	2002 农村 Rural	2003 全市 Total	2003 城市 Urban	2003 农村 Rural
消费品类	**Consumer Goods**						
粮食类	Grain	573901	480179	93722	490919	390025	100894
#大米	Rice	269435	251551	17884	241352	227009	14343
小麦	Wheat	149556	124593	24963	127427	96859	300568
油脂油料类	Oil or Fat	122667	111765	10902	72493	62612	9881
棉烟麻类	Cotton,Tobacco and Fiber	656	5	651	1202	573	629
肉食禽蛋类	Meat,Poultry and Eggs	288550	264021	24529	274879	249774	25105
#猪肉	# Pork	106051	93356	12695	103981	90632	13349
牛肉	Beef	43743	42225	1518	50021	48118	1903
羊肉	Mutton	20271	19633	638	24461	23613	848
鲜蛋	Eggs	80485	74749	5736	65265	59426	5839
家禽	Fowls	29436	27888	1548	27985	25328	2657
水产品类	Aquatic Products	148454	145324	3130	132066	128335	3731
蔬菜类	Vegetables	1405915	1253478	152437	768471	610423	158048
干鲜果类	Dried and Fresh Melons and Fruits	655346	589942	65404	439179	385317	53862
大牲畜类（头）	Large Livestock(head)	7985		7985	7178		7178
家畜幼禽类	Livestock and Young Fowls	7633		7633	7864		7864
生产资料类	**Production Means**						
机动车（辆）	Vehicle(unit)	15265	15180	85	4774	4774	
#汽车	Motor Vehicles	15202	15155	47	4774	4774	
钢材（吨）	Steels(ton)				187910	187910	
木材（立方米）	Timber(m^3)	41080	23120	17960	154394	144994	9400

13-13　商品交易市场成交额

Transactions Value in Commodities Markets

单位：万元　　　　　　　　　　　　　　　　　　　　　　　　　　　　　　　　　　　　　　（10 000 yuan）

项　　目	Item	2002 全市 Total	2002 城市 Urban	2002 农村 Rural	2003 全市 Total	2003 城市 Urban	2003 农村 Rural
总计	**Total**	**2556751**	**2430934**	**125817**	**2161340**	**2043770**	**117570**
按市场类型分	Grouped by Type of Markets						
消费品市场	Consumer Goods Markets	2223466	2099326	124140	1863848	1747288	116560
综合市场	Comprehensive Markets	585078	516997	68081	446252	377369	68883
农副产品市场	Agricultural Products and By-products Markets	709875	679252	30623	707103	671814	35289
工业消费品市场	Industrial Consumer Goods Markets	781069	761160	19909	593137	585391	7746
其他	Others	147444	141917	5527	117356	112714	4642
生产资料市场	Production Means Markets	333285	331608	1677	297492	296482	1010
综合市场	Comprehensive Markets	56550	56550		57230	57230	
农业生产资料市场	Agricultural Production Means Markets						
工业生产资料市场	Industrial Production Means Markets	213722	212154	1568	154466	153666	800
其他	Others	63013	62904	109	85796	85586	210
按商品类别分	Grouped by Type of Commodities						
消费品市场	Consumer Goods	2223466	2099326	124140	1863848	1747288	116560
粮食类	Grain	140555	128458	12097	125658	113005	12653
油脂油料类	Oil or Fat	141177	133884	7293	94961	87498	7463
棉烟麻类	Cotton,Tobacco and Fiber	711	5	706	695	5	690
肉食禽蛋类	Meat,Poultry and Eggs	264018	241114	22904	299945	278061	21884
水产品类	Aquatic Products	175872	173068	2804	190184	187046	3138
蔬菜类	Vegetables	271302	245207	26095	232949	208905	24044
干鲜果类	Dried and Fresh Melons and Fruits	200445	185738	14707	196358	181274	15084
大牲畜类	Large Livestock	1169		1169	1180		1180
家畜幼禽类	Livestock and Young Fowls	4365		4365	4176		4176
工业品类	Industrial Products	776850	750766	26084	541570	519754	21816
其他	Others	247002	241086	5916	176172	171740	4432
生产资料类	Production Means	333285	331608	1677	297492	296482	1010
机动车	Vehicle	136224	136181	43	119112	119112	
#汽车	Motor Vehicles	136177	136177		119112	119112	
钢材	Steels				10000	10000	
木材	Timber	32216	31313	903	30232	29432	800
其他	Others	50214	50214		114856	114646	210

13-14 消费品批发市场情况

Statistics on Consumer Goods Wholesale Markets

项　目	Item	批发市场（个）Wholesale Markets(unit)	城 市 City
合　计	**Total**	**66**	**55**
综合批发市场	Comprehensive Wholesale Markets	12	12
工业消费品批发市场	Industrial Consumer Goods Wholesale Markets	27	26
农副产品批发市场	Agricultural Products and By-products Wholesale Markets	27	17
蔬菜市场	Vegetables	9	3
干鲜果市场	Dried and Fresh Melons and Fruits	5	4
水产品市场	Aquatic Products	2	2
肉食禽蛋市场	Meat,Poultry and Eggs	2	2
粮食市场	Grains	6	3
其他市场	Others	3	3

13-14 消费品批发市场情况（续）

Statistics on Consumer Goods Wholesale Markets(Continued)

项　目	Item	成交额（万元）Transactions Value(10000 Yuan)	城 市 City	成交量（吨）Transactions Volume(Ton)	城 市 City
合　计	**Total**	**644989**	**632669**		
综合批发市场	Comprehensive Wholesale Markets	87447	87447		
工业消费品批发市场	Industrial Consumer Goods Wholesale Markets	313208	312235		
农副产品批发市场	Agricultural Products and By-products Wholesale Markets	244334	232987		
蔬菜市场	Vegetables	65700	59521	248780	192860
干鲜果市场	Dried and Fresh Melons and Fruits	44694	44634	40410	40210
水产品市场	Aquatic Products	22184	22184	6340	6340
肉食禽蛋市场	Meat,Poultry and Eggs	27381	27381	31393	31393
粮食市场	Grains	37569	32461	47498	1550
其他市场	Others	46806	46806		

13-15 商品交易市场分类情况

Statistics on Classification on Commodities Markets

单位：个 (unit)

项目	Item	2001 全市 Total	2001 城市 Urban	2001 农村 Rural	2002 全市 Total	2002 城市 Urban	2002 农村 Rural	2003 全市 Total	2003 城市 Urban	2003 农村 Rural
消费品市场	**Consumer Goods**	**312**	**210**	**102**	**444**	**278**	**166**	**433**	**268**	**165**
消费品综合市场	Consumer Comprehensive Markets	114	56	58	179	81	98	167	69	98
农副产品市场	Agricultural Products and By-products Markets	43	24	19	134	101	33	108	78	30
农副产品综合市场	Agricultural Products and By-products Comprehensive Markets	15	12	3	85	64	21	76	56	20
农副产品专业市场	Agricultural Products and By-products Speciality Markets	28	12	16	49	37	12	32	22	10
工业消费品市场	Industrial Consumer Goods Markets	104	88	16	93	75	18	128	109	19
工业消费品综合市场	Industrial Consumer Goods Market Comprehensive Markets	16	15	1	14	13	1	52	51	1
工业消费品专业市场	Industrial Consumer Goods Market Speciality Markets	88	73	15	79	62	17	76	58	18
其他市场	Others	51	42	9	38	21	17	30	12	18
生产资料市场	**Production Means Markets**	**87**	**77**	**10**	**44**	**40**	**4**	**70**	**68**	**2**
生产资料综合市场	Production Means Comprehensive Markets	16	15	1	13	13		13	13	
农业生产资料市场	Agricultural Production Means Markets	3	2	1						
农业生产资料综合市场	Agricultural Production Means Comprehensive Markets									
农业生产资料专业市场	Agricultural Production Means Speciality Markets	3	2	1						
工业生产资料市场	Industrial Production Means Markets	53	50	3	21	17	4	34	33	1
工业生产资料综合市场	Industrial Production Means Comprehensive Markets									
工业生产资料专业市场	Industrial ProductionMeans Speciality Markets									
其他市场	Others	15	10	5	10	10		23	22	1

主要统计指标解释

社会消费品零售额 指各种经济类型的批发零售贸易业、餐饮业和其他行业对城乡居民和社会集团的消费品零售额总和。这个指标反映通过各种商品流通渠道向居民和社会集团供应的生活消费品来满足他们生活需要，是研究人民生活、社会消费品购买力，货币流通等问题的重要指标。对居民的消费品零售额：指售给城乡居民用于生活消费的商品。对社会集团的消费品零售额：指售给机关、团体、部队、学校、企业、事业单位和城市街道居民委员会，农村村民委员会用公款购买的用作非生产、非经营使用的消费品。

社会消费品零售额包括：

售给社会集团的办公用品、纸张、账册、文印用品和纺织品、针织品；学校用的教学用具；文体用品；非专用的劳动保护用品，如工作服、套袖、围群、手套、毛巾、肥皂等；日用百货和杂品，包括职工食堂用的餐具、炊具、设备和清洁卫生工具等；家具、设备、日用电器、电讯设备、电影器材和照相器材等；取暖用的设备和燃料，防署、降温的饮料；非生产经营用的交能工具如小轿车、面包车、工具车、卡车和油料；零星修理用的各种零配件、材料、工具、建筑材料等；举办各种招待会、茶话会、宴会用的烟酒茶和各种食品及馈赠的礼品；从公费医疗经费中开支的中、西药品、中药材和医疗器材以及其他非生产性设备和用品。

批发零售贸易业商品购、销、存总额 指各种登记注册类型的批发、零售贸易业企业（单位）以本企业（单位）为总体的商品购进、销售、库存总额。

商品购进总额 指从本企业（单位）以外的单位和个人购进（包括从境外直接进口）作为转卖或加工后转卖的商品总额。它反映批发零售贸易业从国内、国外市场上购进商品的总量。商品购进总额包括:（1）从工农业生产者购进的商品;（2）从出版社、报社的出版发行部门购进的图书、杂志和报纸;（3）从各种登记注册类型的批发零售贸易企业（单位）购进的商品;（4）从其他单位购进的商品，如从机关、团体、企业等单位购进的剩余物资，从餐饮业、服务业购进的商品，从海关、市场管理部门购进的缉私和没收的商品，从居民手中收购的废旧商品等;（5）从国（境）外直接进口的商品。不包括企业（单位）为自身经营用和未通过买卖行为而收入的商品以及销售退回、商品升溢等。

商品销售总额 指对本企业（单位）以外的单位和个人出售（包括对境外直接出口）的商品总额。它反映批发零售贸易业在国内市场上销售商品以及出口商品的总量。商品销售总额包括:（1）售给城乡居民和社会集团消费用的商品;（2）售给工业、农业、建筑业、运输邮电业、批发零售贸易业、餐饮业、服务业等作为生产、经营使用的商品;（3）售给批发零售贸易业作为转卖或加工后转卖的商品;（4）对国（境）外直接出口的商品。不包括出售本企业（单位）自用的废旧包装用品;未通过买卖行为付出的商品;经本单位介绍，由买卖双方直接结算，本单位只收取手续费的业务;购货退出的商品以及商品损耗和损失等。

批发零售贸易业库存 指报告期末各种登记注册类型的批发零售贸易企业（单位）已取得所有权的商品。它反映批发零售贸易企业（单位）的商品库存情况和对市场商品供应的保证程度。期末库存包括:（1）存放在批发零售贸易业经营单位（如门市部、批发站、经营处）仓库、货场、货柜和货架中的商品;（2）挑选、整理、包装中的商品;（3）已记入购进而尚未运到本单位的商品，即发货单或银行承兑凭证已到而货未到的部分;（4）寄放他处的商品，如因购货方拒绝承付而暂时存放在购货方的商品和已办完加工成品收回手续而未提回的商品;（5）委托其他单位代销（未作销售或调出）尚未售出的商品;（6）代其他单位购进尚未交付的商品。不包括所有权不属于本单位的商品、拨付除批发零售贸易业以外的其他行业所属独立核算加工厂等加工生产尚未收回成品的商品、代国家物资储备部门保管的商品等。

库存总额采用的计算价格是:农副产品采购单位按购进价计算;批发单位按进货价计算;零售单位按核算价格计算，即按什么价格核算就按什么价格计算。

消费品市场成交额 指从事消费品交易的商品市场的全部商品成交金额。消费品市场包括农副产品市场和工业消费品市场。

Explanatory Notes on Main Statistical Indicators

Total Retail Sales of Consumer Goods it refers to sum of retail amount of consumer goods sold by wholesale and retail trade in all kinds of economic type, accommodation trade and other industry sold to urban and countryside citizens and social groups. This indicator reflects all living consumer goods supplied by all kinds of commodity channel to residents and social group to meet the needs of their life, and it is an important indicator to study people's life, social consumer goods purchasing power and circulation of currency and so on. Volume of retail sales of consumer goods to residents: it refers to commodities sold to residents of urban and rural area used for daily consuming. Volume of retail sales of consumer goods to social groups: it refers to the amount of consumer goods bought by government functionary office, groups, army, schools, enterprises, institutions, residents committees in urban area and villagers committees in rural area using public money, used for non-productive, non-operational purposes.

Volume of retail sales of social consumer goods consists of items sold to social groups such as stationery, papers, account books, printing articles, computing instruments, books, newspapers, magazines and awards; public facilities, dry goods and hosiery; teaching instruments for schools; recreation and sports facilities; non-special labor safety articles, such as work clothes, over sleeves, apron, gloves, towels, soaps etc.; articles for everyday use, commodities and sundry goods, include table wares, cooking utensils, equipment and cleaning and sanitary facilities for staff eateries; furniture, equipment, electrical appliances of daily use, telecommunication equipment, film equipment, photo equipment etc.; equipment and fuel for heating, drinks for sunstroke prevention and lowering the temperature; non-productive and operational vehicles such as sedans, vans, tool cars, trucks and fuels; various parts, fittings, materials, tools, building materials for fragmentary repairing; cigarettes, alcoholic drinks and tea leafs for various receptions, tea parties and banquets and all kinds of foods and gifts for present; Chinese traditional medicine, Western medicine, Chinese traditional medicinal materials, medical treatment equipment paid by public health service outlays and other non-productive equipment and facilities.

Purchase, Sales and Stock of Commodities by Wholesale and Retail Trade refer to the purchase, sales and stock of commodities by wholesale and retail establishments of different status of registration (excluding individual sellers).

Total Purchases of Commodities refer to the total value of purchases of commodities by the establishments from other establishments or individuals (including direct import from abroad) for the purpose of re-selling, either with or without further processing of the commodities purchased. This indicator is used to show the total value of purchases of commodities by wholesale and retail establishments from domestic and overseas markets. The total purchases include: (1) agricultural and industrial products purchased from producers; (2) books, magazines and newspapers purchased from distribution departments of the publishers; (3) commodities purchased from wholesale and retail establishments of different status of registration; (4) commodities purchased from other units, such as surplus materials purchased from government agencies, enterprises or institutions, commodities purchased from catering and service establishments, confiscated goods purchased from customs authorities or market management agencies, second-hand goods and wastes purchased from residents; and (5) commodities directly imported from abroad. Excluded are commodities purchased by establishments (units) for use in their own business operation, commodities obtained without buying or selling procedures, rejected commodities, etc.

Total Sales of Commodities refer to value of commodities sold by the establishments to other establishments and individuals (including direct export). This indicator is used to show the total value of sales of commodities at domestic markets and export. The total sales include: (1) commodities sold to urban and rural residents and social groups for their consumption; (2) commodities sold to establishments in industry, agriculture, construction, transportation, post and telecommunications, wholesale and retail trades, catering trade and public utility for their production and operation; (3) commodities sold to wholesale and retail establishments for re selling, with or without further processing; and (4)commodities for direct export to other countries. Excluded are selling of waste packaging materials used by the establishments (units) themselves, commodities transferred without buying or selling procedures, commission income from brokerage in transactions whose settlement is directly handled by buyers and sellers, rejected commodities in the purchase, loss in commodities, etc.

Commodity Stock of Wholesale and RetailEnterprises refers to total commodities possessed by Wholesale and retail enterprises (units) of various types of registration status at the end of the reference period, which reflects the commodity stock level of various wholesale and retail enterprises and the potential for market supply. It includes: (1) commodities located in storage, garages, counters, and shelves of operating units (such as sale stores, wholesale centers, and operating offices) of wholesale and retail enterprises; (2) commodities in the process of selecting, sorting, and packing; (3)commodities not arrived but recorded as purchase in the account, i.e. commodities not arrived but payment receipts for the commodities from the sellers or the banks arrived; (4) commodities deposited in other places rather than places mentioned above, for instance: commodities in the hold of purchasers temporarily due to the refusal of payment and commodities not taken back after going through the formalities; (5) commodities entrusted to other units to sell but not sold yet; (6) commodities purchased for other units but not delivered yet. Commodities not included as stock are those not owned by the enterprises (units), those allocated to financially independent factories rather than wholesale and retail enterprises for processing but not taken back yet, and finally those put in stock by wholesale and retail enterprises on behalf of the state material reserves units.

For the calculation of the value of commodities stock, the value is calculated at purchasing prices in agricultural goods purchasing units and wholesale units, and at the accounting prices in retail units.

Volume of Transaction at Free Markets for Consumer Goods refers to the value of transaction of all goods at the free trade markets for consumer goods, where markets include both free markets for farm and sideline products and for manufactured consumer goods.

十四、对外经济贸易和旅游

FOREIGN TRADE AND ECONOMIC COOPERATION, TOURISM

简要说明
Brief Introduction

本章资料包括我市对外贸易、利用外资以及旅游方面的资料。对外经济贸易、国外友好城市交流和旅游资料由市统计局外经处根据市外经贸易局、海关、市政府对外办公室和市旅游局资料整理提供。

Data in this chapter consists of data on foreign trade, using of foreign capital and fund and tourism. Data on foreign economy and trade, intercommunion to foreign cities of friendship and tourism are compiled and provided by Foreign Economy Division of the Xi'an Bureau of Statistics according to the data from Xi'an Bureau of Foreign Economy and Trade, Xi'an Custom Office, Foreign Affairs Office of the Xi'an Municipal Government and Xi'an Bureau of Tourism.

14-1 外资、外贸和国际旅游基本情况

Main Indicators on Foreign Investments,International Trading and International Tourism

指 标	Item	1990	1995	1998	1999
一、利用外资签订协议项目(个)	**Number of Projects of Foreign Capital Used through the Signed Agreements and Contracts**	**11**	**184**	**112**	**98**
利用外资签订协议金额(万美元)	Value of Foreign Capital Used through the Signed Agreements and Contracts(USD10 000)	415.3	28956.2	40034	40390
实际利用外资额(万美元)	Total Amount of Foreign Capital Actually Used (USD10 000)	1154	18653	22286	13801
年末已建成投产企业数(个)	Number of Enterprises Completed and put into use at Year-end(unit)	-	-	600	754
二、进出口总额(万美元)	**Total Imports and Exports (USD10 000)**		**137510**	**180590**	**172919**
#进口总额	#Total Imports		27347	80098	78424
出口总额	Total Exports		110163	100492	94495
进出口差额	Balance of Imports and Exports		82816	20394	16071
三、国际旅游人数总计(人)	**Total Number of International Tourists (person)**	**258786**	**413481**	**479836**	**554016**
#外国人	#Foreigners	153964	371127	379324	454666
港澳台同胞	Compatriot From Hong Kong,Macao and Taiwan	100706	41564	95146	94585
旅游外汇收入总额(万元)	Total Foreign Exchange Earnings (10 000 yuan)	19628	103818	160244	186282
#商品性收入	#Income from Commodity	4441	25686	48073	59610
劳务性收入	Income from Labour Service	15187	78132	112171	126672
旅游者在西安人均停留天数(天)	Number of Days of Average Tourists Staying in Xi'an (day)	2.13	2.04	2.58	2.50
旅游者在西安人均消费(元)	Consumption of Average Tourists in xi'an (yuan)	758.46	2510.83	3393.84	3362.39

14-1 外资、外贸和国际旅游基本情况（续）

Main Indicators on Foreign Investments,International Trading and International Tourism(Continued)

指 标	Item	2000	2001	2002	2003
一、利用外资签订协议项目(个)	**Number of Projects of Foreign Capital Used Through the Signed Agreements and Contracts**	**135**	**129**	**144**	**132**
利用外资签订协议金额(万美元)	Value of Foreign Capital Used through the Signed Agreements and Contracts(USD10 000)	54123	60736	70692	96380
实际利用外资额(万美元)	Total Amount of Foreign Capital Actually Used (USD10 000)	15633	17687	20281	25557
年末已建成投产企业数(个)	Number of Enterprises Completed and put into use at Year-end(unit)	808	795		
二、进出口总额(万美元)	**Total Imports and Exports (USD10 000)**	**173696**	**169914**	**186966**	**230932**
#进口总额	#Total Imports	67634	81966	74487	90605
出口总额	Total Exports	106062	87948	112479	140327
进出口差额	Balance of Imports and Exports	38428	5982	37992	49722
三、国际旅游人数总计(人)	**Total Number of International Tourists (person)**	**650385**	**672015**	**741313**	**336654**
#外国人	#Foreigners	546544	587547	658775	255537
港澳台同胞	Compatriot From Hong Kong,Macao and Taiwan	103841	84468	82538	81117
旅游外汇收入总额(万元)	Total Foreign Exchange Earnings (10 000 yuan)	224100	240700	260000	121180
#商品性收入	#Income from Commodity	77000	84004	104520	48713
劳务性收入	Income from Labour Service	147000	156712	155480	72467
旅游者在西安人均停留天数(天)	Number of Days of Average Tourists Staying in Xi'an (day)	2.50	2.40	2.20	2.45
旅游者在西安人均消费(元)	Consumption of Average Tourists in xi'an (yuan)	3444.50	3582.01	3507.29	3584.04

14-2 外国和港澳台地区在西安直接投资

Direct Investments from Foreign Countries and Hong Kong, Macao and Taiwan in Xi'an

分类	Classity	新签协议情况 New-signed Agreement Circumstances		客商实际投资（万美元）
		合同数(个) Number of Constracts	客商投资额(万美元) Value of Foreign Investment (USD10 000)	Value of Foreign Actual Investment (USD10 000)
合计	**Total**	**132**	**96380**	**25557**
一、按投资方式分	**Grouped by Investment Mode**			
1.中外合资经营企业	Joint-venture Enterprises	50	22071	10595
2.中外合作经营企业	Cooperation Enterprises	21	36933	6094
3.外资企业	Enterprises with Sole Foreign Investment	61	37286	8778
4.外资企业再投资	Re-investment from Foreign-funded Enterprises		90	90
二、按国民经济行业分组	**Grouped by Trade**			
1.农林牧渔业	Farming,Forestry,Animal, Husbandy and Fishery	6	3242.2	–
2.制造业	Manufacturing	93	50145.6	–
3.电力、煤气及水的生产和供应业	Power,gas and Water Production and Supply			–
4.建筑业	Construction			–
5.交通运输、仓储及邮电通信业	Transporation,Storage,Postal and Telecommunications			–
6.批发和零售贸易、餐饮业	Wholesale, Retail and Catering Businesses		6	–
7.房地产业	Real Estate	4	18674.4	–
8.社会服务业	Social Services	14	8872	–
9.其他行业	Others	15	15439.3	–
三、按投资国别、地区分组	**Grouped by Different Countries and Regions**			
香港	Hong Kong	38	41522	–
澳门	Macao	1	102.6	–
台湾	Taiwan	12	1935.5	–
日本	Japan	9	3857.5	–
泰国	Tailand	1	1000	–
马来西亚	Malaysia	1	6	
新加坡	Singapore	12	3215.6	–
韩国	Republic of Korea	3	608.7	–
德国	Germany	1	99.6	–
比利时	Belgium	2	201.8	–
法国	France	2	282.1	
英国	United Kingdom	4	231.6	–
俄罗斯	Russia	1	500	–
加拿大	Canada	4	16202.7	–
美国	Unite States	28	18029.4	–
澳大利亚	Australia	2	1074.5	–
维尔京群岛	Virgin Islands	8	3101.5	–
其它	Others	3	4408.4	

注:年末实有三资企业1975家。

Note:A total of 1975 enterprises with foreign investment at the Year-end.

14-3 主要商品分大类出口金额

单位：万美元

商品分类	Merchandise	1998
食用蔬菜、根及块茎	Edible Vegetables, roots amd tubers	1666
蔬菜、水果、坚果或植物其它部分的制品	vegetables, fruits, muts, or products made of other parts of plants	1597
矿砂、矿渣及矿灰	ores slags and calxes	1573
无机化学品；贵金属、稀土金属、放射性元素及其同位素的有机及无机化合物	Inorganic chemicals, noble melals, rare Earth Metals Radiactive Elements and their Organic and Inorganic compounds	6475
有机化学品	Organic chemicals	2898
羊毛、动物细毛或粗毛、马毛纱线及其机织物	Wod ,Fine and coarse Animal wod,Horse woolen yarn and the woven Goods	908
棉花	Cotton	4235
化学纤维短纤	Short staple chemicd fibers	4939
针织或钩编的服装及衣着附件	Crochet and Knit G and Accessorles	10632
非针织或非钩编的服装及衣着附件	wom-crochet or knit Garment and Accessories	12019
其它纺织制成品；成套物品；旧衣着及旧纺织品	Other Textile products;suit products; second-hand clothing and textiles	1380
鞋靴、护腿和类似品及其零件	Shoes,Gaiter and similar products and their parts	1300
玻璃及其制品	Glass and Glasswares	3079
钢铁	Sted and Iron	3523
钢铁制品	Sted and Iron Products	3866
铅及制品	Lead and Its products	749
锌及制品	Zinc and Its Products	1064
其它贱金属、金属陶瓷及其制品	Other cheap metals,metal-ceramic and their Goods	2783
贱金属工具、器具、利口器、餐匙、餐叉及其零件	Cheap meld tods,appliances,spoons, Forks and Their Parts	2739
核反应堆、锅炉、机器、机械器具及其零件	Nuclear Reactors Boilers Machines Mechanical Appliances and Their Parts	8854
电机、电气设备及其零件；录音机及放声机、电视图像、声音的录制和重放设备及其零件、附件	Electric Motors and Equipment and their parts,Tape-recorders Microphones,Video-Audio Recording and Broadcasting Equipment and parts and Accessories	4336
光学、照相、电影、计量、检验、医疗或外科用仪器及设备、精密仪器及设备；上述物品的零件、附件	Optic,camera,Film,Metering,Checking,Medical and Surgerical Instruments and Appliances; Precision Instrument and Equipment and Their Parts and Accessories	2821
家具、寝具、褥垫、弹簧床垫、软床垫及类似的填充制品；未列名灯具及照明装置；发光标志、发光名牌及类似品；活动房屋	Furnitures,Beddings,beddings and clsions,Sofa cusions,Spring cusions and similar Goods;Lamps and Lighting Installations;Luminous Marks and plates and similar Articles; Movable Houses	684

Export Value of Major Merchandise by Type

(USD10 000)

1999	2000	2001	2002	2003
1450	1095	1957	1275	1379
2692	2076	2684	3470	4490
2677	4083	4649	8714	11224
3447	3714	4141	4141	5814
2830	2367	3279	4883	4757
1621	810	829	1313	1600
3714	3197	2734	3826	3984
5029	5061	3612	2512	2120
7752	6753	1632	2660	341
6818	7269	3319	3629	4981
1408	1649	1002	1432	2203
1564	1347	279	296	585
3440	3376	3838	5542	6667
2087	3534	1197	2167	2779
5128	5535	6401	7414	8474
1369	1371	1363	444	232
3001	4031	1945	1895	2200
1734	1066	1704	1546	3150
2605	2933	2669	2613	3232
7620	10915	11979	16140	21281
8103	8339	8696	8962	15106
2197	2020	2818	5395	3339
1435	2587	2150	2715	3994

14-4 主要商品分大类进口金额

Import Value of Major Merchandise by Type

单位:万美元 (USD 10 000)

商品分类	Merchandise	1999	2000
无机化学品；贵金属、稀土金属、放射性元素及其同位素的有机及无机化合物	Inorganic Chemicals,Noble Metals,Rare-earth metals,Radioactive Elements and Their organic and Inorganic Compounds	1066	1467
有机化学品	Organic Chemicals	7222	7257
塑料及其制品	Plastic and Their Goods	3061	2559
钢铁	Steel and Iron	2674	2467
铜及制品	Copper and Its produce	3928	2367
铝及制品	Aluminium and Its Plastic	3666	2652
核反应堆、锅炉、机器、机械器具及其零件	Nuclear Responses,Boilers,Machines, Mechanical Appliances and Their Parts	16902	12990
电机、电气设备及其零件；录音机及放声机、电视图像、声音的录制和重放设备及其零件、附件	Electrode Motors and Equipment and Their Parts;Tape-recorder and Microphones Voice-Audio Recording and Broadcating Equipment and Their Parts and Accessories	5448	5911
车辆及其零件、附件，铁道及电车道车辆除外	Vehicles and Related part and Accessories not Including Railway and Trolley Vehicles	1754	1530
航空器、航天器及其零件	Aeroplanes and spaceflight and Their Parts	22263	10443
光学、照相、电影、计量、检验、医疗或外科用仪器及设备、精密仪器及设备；上述物品的零件、附件	optic,camera,Film,Metering,checking,Medical or surgerical Intrument and Appliances;precision Instruments and Equipment;and Their Parts and Accessories	3207	3673

14-4 主要商品分大类进口金额（续）

Import Value of Major Merchandise by Type（Continued）

单位:万美元 (USD 10 000)

商品分类	Merchandise	2001	2002	2003
无机化学品；贵金属、稀土金属、放射性元素及其同位素的有机及无机化合物	Inorganic Chemicals,Noble Metals,Rare-earth metals,Radioactive Elements and Their organic and Inorganic Compounds	1806	548	4082
有机化学品	Organic Chemicals	6020	9237	11852
塑料及其制品	Plastic and Their Goods	2639	2104	2358
钢铁	Steel and Iron	2528	1335	2086
铜及制品	Copper and Its produce	4936	2804	1487
铝及制品	Aluminium and Its Plastic	2561	1341	1194
核反应堆、锅炉、机器、机械器具及其零件	Nuclear Responses,Boilers,Machines, Mechanical Appliances and Their Parts	26534	22893	31100
电机、电气设备及其零件；录音机及放声机、电视图像、声音的录制和重放设备及其零件、附件	Electrode Motors and Equipment and Their Parts;Tape-recorder and Microphones Voice-Audio Recording and Broadcating Equipment and Their Parts and Accessories	9974	11571	12200
车辆及其零件、附件，铁道及电车道车辆除外	Vehicles and Related part and Accessories not Including Railway and Trolley Vehicles	1881	2494	2759
航空器、航天器及其零件	Aeroplanes and spaceflight and Their Parts	3111	1681	768
光学、照相、电影、计量、检验、医疗或外科用仪器及设备、精密仪器及设备；上述物品的零件、附件	optic,camera,Film,Metering,checking,Medical or surgerical Intrument and Appliances;precision Instruments and Equipment;and Their Parts and Accessories	8587	6980	8111

14-5 外贸商品进出口总额分国别和地区(2003年)

Total Value of Imports and Exports by Country and Region(2003)

单位：万美元 (USD10 000)

国别和地区	Country and Region	进出口总额 Total Imports and Exports	出口 Exports
亚洲	Asia	77671	54418
#香港	Hong kong	7195	6655
台湾	Taiwan	4279	2782
日本	Japan	25688	10685
菲律宾	Phiilippines	1236	1161
马来西亚	Malaysia	1954	1386
韩国	Republic of Korea	8583	6097
非洲	Africa	8723	7021
#埃及	Egypt	676	656
突尼斯	Tunisia	187	187
埃塞俄比亚	Ethiopia	130	130
博茨瓦那	Botswana	7	7
南非	South Africal	2822	2822
欧洲	Europe	85419	39708
#德国	Germany	20014	6573
法国	France	4121	1177
意大利	Italy	7939	4371
荷兰	Netherland	10918	10507
英国	United Kingdom	6976	5493
瑞士	Switzerland	2323	60
西班牙	Spain	2270	2130
俄罗斯联邦	Russia	1756	1357
拉丁美洲	Latin America	12205	8885
#哥伦比亚	Colombia	323	323
巴西	Brazil	1443	708
阿根廷	Argentina	557	313
北美洲	North America	40983	27441
#加拿大	Canada	3231	2480
美国	United States	37752	24960
大洋洲及太平洋岛屿	Oceanic and Pacific Islands	5917	2840
#澳大利亚	Australia	5074	2057
新西兰	New Zealand	667	607

14-6　接待国际旅游者人数

Overseas Tourists Received

项　目	Item	2000		2001	
		人数(人) Number of persons(person)	人天数(人天) Number of Day Per Person(person/day)	人数(人) Number of persons(person)	人天数(人天) Number of Day Per Person(person/day)
合　计	**Total**	**650385**	**1625963**	**672015**	**1481699**
1.外 国 人	Foreigners	546544	1314440	587547	1269296
2.华　侨	Overseas Chinese	...	...	...	...
3.港澳台同胞	Compatriots from HongKong , Macao,Taiwan	103841	311523	84468	212403

14-6　接待国际旅游者人数（续）

Overseas Tourists Received(Continued)

项　目	Item	2002		2003	
		人数(人) Number of persons(person)	人天数(人天) Number of Day Per Person(person/day)	人数(人) Number of persons(person)	人天数(人天) Number of Day Per Person(person/day)
合　计	**Total**	**741313**	**1638301**	**336654**	**824802**
1.外 国 人	Foreigners	658775	1422954	255537	626066
2.华　侨	Overseas Chinese	...	...		
3.港澳台同胞	Compatriots from HongKong , Macao,Taiwan	82538	215347	81117	198736

14–7 国际旅游收入

Earning of International Tourism

单位:万美元 （USD10 000）

项　目	Item	1999	2000	2001	2002	2003
合　计	Total	22525	27000	29002	32000	14600
一、长途交通费	**Long Distance Transportation**	**7003**	**7047**	**7946**	**6816**	**3109**
1.飞机	Airplane	5418	6011	7395	5536	2526
2.火车	Train	901	273	203	288	131
3.汽车	Highway	684	763	348	992	452
二、游览	**Visiting**	**1135**	**1296**	**1276**	**1120**	**511**
三、住宿	**Accommodation**	**3430**	**3051**	**3684**	**4480**	**2044**
四、餐饮	**Food and Beverage**	**2170**	**2673**	**3074**	**3264**	**1489**
五、娱乐	**Entertainment**	**823**	**1512**	**1074**	**896**	**409**
六、购物	**Shopping**	**5038**	**6615**	**7047**	**9600**	**4380**
七、邮电通讯	**Post and Communication Services**	**1126**	**1350**	**899**	**1120**	**512**
八、市内交通	**Local Transportation**	**928**	**1566**	**899**	**768**	**350**
九、其它	**Others**	**870**	**1890**	**3103**	**3936**	**1796**

注：此表根据国家旅游局抽样调查资料取得。

Note:The data in the list is taken from the sample survey Information of National Tourism Bureau.

14-8 主要涉外星级宾馆接待海外旅游者情况

Mainly Concerning Oversea Tourists Reception in Star Hotels

项　目	Item	2002	2003
人数合计（人次）	**Total Number of Tourists(person-time)**		
海外旅游者	International Tourists	741313	336654
外国人	Foreigners	658775	255537
#日本	Japan	167570	51418
菲律宾	Philippines	2135	375
新加坡	Singapore	4690	2134
美国	United States	106591	32927
加拿大	Canada	16531	6385
英国	Britain	47154	21122
法国	France	39567	8131
德国	Germany	55442	15966
意大利	Italy	13447	3290
瑞士	Switzerland	2240	656
澳大利亚	Australia	15012	7801
新西兰	New Zealand	1618	1336
华侨	Overseas Chinese		
港澳和台湾同胞	Chinese from Hong Kong, Macao and Taiwan	82538	81117
#台湾同胞	# Taiwan		46751

主要统计指标解释

进出口总额 海关进出口总额指实际进出我国国境的货物总金额。包括对外贸易实际进出口货物，来料加工装配进出口货物，国家间、联合国及国际组织无偿援助物资和赠送品，华侨、港澳台同胞和外籍华人捐赠品，租赁期满归承租人所有的租赁货物，进料加工进出口货物，边境地方贸易及边境地区小额贸易进出口货物（边民互市贸易除外），中外合资企业、中外合作经营企业、外商独资经营企业进出口货物和公用物品，到、离岸价格在规定限额以上的进出口货样和广告品（无商业价值、无使用价值和免费提供出口的除外），从保税仓库提取在中国境内销售的进口货物，以及其他进出口货物。进出口总额用以观察一个国家在对外贸易方面的总规模。我国规定出口货物按离岸价格统计，进口货物按到岸价格统计。

利用外资 指我国各级政府、部门、企业和其他经济组织通过对外借款、吸收外商直接投资以及用其他方式筹措的境外现汇、设备、技术等。

对外借款 是我国利用外资的重要部分。指通过对外正式签订借款协议，从境外筹措的资金，包括外国政府贷款、国际金融组织贷款、外国银行商业贷款、出口信贷以及对外发行债券等。1996年及以前还包括对外发行股票。

外商直接投资 指外国企业和经济组织或个人（包括华侨、港澳台胞以及我国在境外注册的企业）按我国有关政策、法规，用现汇、实物、技术等在我国境内开办外商独资企业、与我国境内的企业或经济组织共同举办中外合资经营企业、合作经营企业或合作开发资源的投资（包括外商投资收益的再投资），以及经政府有关部门批准的项目投资总额内企业从境外借入的资金。

外商其他投资 指除对外借款和外商直接投资以外的各种利用外资的形式。包括企业在境内外股票市场公开发行的以外币计价的股票（目前主要是在香港证券市场发行的H股和在境内证券市场发行的B股）发行价总额，国际租赁进口设备的应付款，补偿贸易中外商提供的进口设备、技术、物料的价款，加工装配贸易中外商提供的进口设备、物料的价款。

对外承包工程 指各对外承包公司以招标议标承包方式承揽的下列业务：（1）承包国外工程建设项目，（2）承包我国对外经援项目，（3）承包我国驻外机构的工程建设项目，（4）承包我国境内利用外资进行建设的工程项目，（5）与外国承包公司合营或联合承包工程项目时我国公司分包部分，（6）对外承包兼营的房屋开发业务。对外承包工程的营业额是以货币表现的本期内完成的对外承包工程的工作量，包括以前年度签订的合同和本年度新签订的合同在报告期内完成的工作量。

对外劳务合作 指以收取工资的形式向业主或承包商提供技术和劳动服务的活动。我国对外承包公司在境外开办的合营企业，中国公司同时又提供劳务的，其劳务部分也纳入劳务合作统计。劳务合作营业额按报告期内向雇主提交的结算数（包括工资、加班费和奖金等）统计。

旅游者人数

（1）入境国际旅游者人数：指来中国参观、访问、旅行、探亲、访友、休养、考察、参加会议和从事经济、科技、文化、教育、宗教等活动的外国人、华侨、港澳同胞和台湾同胞的人数。不包括外国在我国的常驻机构，如使领馆、通讯社、企业办事处的工作人员；来我国常住的外国专家、留学生以及在岸逗留不过夜人员。

（2）出境居民人数：指大陆居民因公务活动或私人事务短期出境的人数。公务活动出境居民人数包括在国际交通工具上的中国服务员工，因私出境居民人数不包括在国际交通工具上的中国服务员工。

（3）国内旅游者人数：指我国大陆居民和在我国常住1年以上的外国人、华侨、港澳台同胞离开常住地在境内其他地方的旅游设施内至少停留一夜，最长不超过6个月的人数。

国际旅游（外汇）收入 指入境旅游的外国人、华侨、港澳同胞和台湾同胞在中国大陆旅游过程中发生的一切旅游支出，对于国家来说就是国际旅游（外汇）收入。

国际旅行社 指经营对外招徕并接待外国人、华侨、港澳同胞和台湾同胞来中国、归国或回内地旅游业务的旅行社。

国内旅行社 指负责经营招徕、组团、接待国内旅客的旅游业务，以及不对外招徕，负责经营接待国际旅行社或其它涉外部门组织的外国人、华侨、港澳同胞和台湾同胞来中国、归国或回内地的旅游业务的旅行社。

涉外饭店 指经有关部门批准，允许接待外国人、华侨、港澳同胞和台湾同胞的饭店。

Explanatory Notes on Main Statistical Indicators

Total Imports and Exports at Customs refer to the value of commodities imported into and exported from the boundary of China. They include the actual imports and exports through foreign trade, imported and exported goods under the processing and assembling trades and materials, supplies and gifts as aid given gratis between governments and by the United Nations and other international organizations, and contributions donated by overseas Chinese, compatriots in Hong Kong and Macao and Chinese with foreign citizenship, leasing commodities owned by tenant at the expiration of leasing period, the imported and exported commodities processed with imported materials, commodities trading in border areas (excluding mutual exchange goods), the imported and exported commodities and articles for public use of the Sino-foreign joint ventures, cooperative enterprises and ventures exclusively with foreign own investment. Also included are import or export of samples and advertising goods for whose CIF or FOB value are beyond the permitted ceiling (excluding goods of no trading or use value and free commodities for export), imported goods sold in China from bonded warehouses and other imported or exported goods. The indicator of the total imports and exports at customs can be used to observe the total size of external trade in a country. In accordance with the stipulation of the Chinese government, imports are calculated at CIF, while exports are calculated at FOB

Utilization of Foreign Capital refers to remittance, equipment and technology financed from abroad, by loans, foreign direct investment and other forms undertaken by the Chinese governments at all levels, by various departments, enterprises and other economic units.

Foreign Borrowings an important part of Chinas utilization of foreign capital, it refer to funds borrowed from abroad through formal signing of borrowing agreements with foreign institutions, including loans of foreign governments, loans of international financial institutions, commercial loans of foreign banks, export credit, and funds raised by Chinese bonds (and shares before 1996) issued abroad.

Direct Investment by Foreign Entrepreneurs refers to the investments inside China by foreign enterprises and economic organizations or individuals (including overseas Chinese, compatriots from Hong Kong and Macao, and Chinese enterprises registered abroad), following the relevant policies and laws of China, for the establishment of ventures exclusively with foreign own investment, Sino-foreign joint ventures and cooperative enterprises or for co-operative exploration of resources with enterprises or economic organizations in China. It includes the re investment of the foreign entrepreneurs with the profits gained from the investment and the funds that enterprises borrow from abroad in the total investment of projects which are approved by the relevant department of the government.

Other Investment by Foreign Entrepreneurs refers to all forms of utilization of foreign capitals other than foreign borrowings and foreign direct investment. It includes the total value of stock shares in foreign currencies issued by enterprises at domestic or foreign stock exchanges (now mainly consisting of H shares issued at Hong Kong Security Market and B shares issued at domestic security markets), rent payable for the imported equipment through international leasing arrangement, cost of imported equipment, technology and materials provided by foreign counterparts in compensation trade and processing and assembly trade.

Contracted Projects with Foreign Countries refer to projects undertaken by Chinese contractors (project contracting companies) through bidding process. They include: (1)overseas civil engineering construction projects financed by foreign investors; (2)overseas projects financed by the Chinese government through its foreign aid programs; (3)construction projects of Chinese diplomatic missions, trade offices and other institutions stationed abroad; (4)construction projects in China financed by foreign investment; (5)sub-contracted projects to be taken by Chinese contractors through a joint umbrella project with foreign contractor(s); (6)housing development projects. The business income from international contracted projects is the work volume of contracted projects completed during the reference period, expressed in monetary terms, including completed work on projects signed in previous years.

Service Cooperation with Foreign Countries refers to the activities of providing technology and labour services to employers or contractors in the forms of receiving salaries and wages. Labour services providing by contractual joint ventures of Chinese international contracting corporations should be included in the statistics of service co-operation with foreign countries. The business income of labour service co operation is theincome in the form of wages and salaries, overtime pay, bonuses and other remuneration received from the employers during the reference period.

Number of Tourists

(1) International tourists refer to foreigners, overseas Chinese, Chinese compatriots from Hong Kong, Macao and Taiwan coming to China for sight-seeing, visits, tours, family reunions, vacations, study tours, conferences and other activities of a business, scientific and technological, cultural, educational and religious nature. It does not include representatives and employees of resident institutions of foreign countries in China such as embassies, consulates, news agencies and offices of foreign companies and organizations, nor does it include long-term foreign experts or students residing in China, or persons in transition without spending a night in China.

(2) Chinese residents going abroad refer to Chinese residents going abroad for short terms for either public business or private purposes. Chinese employees working on international transport carriers are included in those going abroad for public business purpose, not in those for private purpose.

(3) Domestic tourists refer to residents of the mainland of China who stay for one night at least but no more than 6 months at tourist facilities in other places than their permanent residence within the territory of the mainland China, including foreigners, overseas Chinese and Chinese compatriots from Hong Kong, Macao and Taiwan who have resided in China for over one year.

Foreign Exchange Earnings from International Tourism refer to the total expenditures of foreigners, overseas Chinese, Chinese compatriots from Hong Kong, Macao and Taiwan during their stay in the mainland of China, which are earnings of foreign exchange from international tourism from the point of view from China.

International Travel Agencies refer to travel agencies engaged in the promotion, solicitation, organization and reception of tours to the mainland of China by foreigners, overseas Chinese, Chinese compatriots from Hong Kong, Macao and Taiwan.

Domestic Travel Agencies refer to travel agencies engaged in the promotion, solicitation, organization and reception of domestic tourists, and in the reception of foreigners, overseas Chinese, Chinese compatriots from Hong Kong, Macao and Taiwan organized by international travel agencies or other departments concerned, without their own promotion and solicitation programmes.

Tourist Hotels refer to hotels that are able, with the approval of departments concerned, to accommodate foreigners, overseas Chinese, Chinese compatriots from Hong Kong, Macao and Taiwan Province.

十五、金融和保险

BANKING AND INSURANCE

简 要 说 明
Brief Introduction

本章资料包括我市金融、证券和保险业情况，由市统计局综合处根据有关部门资料整理编辑。

Data in this chapter consists of data of financial, negotiable securities and insurance industry of Xi'an city, compiled by Integration Division of the Xi'an Bureau of Statistics, according to data from other departments concerned of Xi'an Municipal Government.

15-1 金融机构本外币存款年末余额

Financial institution balance of bisic currency and foreign currency at the end of the year

单位：万元　　10 000yuan
(汇率：8.2767)　　(Exchange rate:8.2767)

指　　标	Item	2003年	比上年增加 Increase over Preceding Year
合　计	**Total**	**27908323**	**4656543**
一、企事业单位存款	**Enterprise and institution deposit**	**10792413**	**1514686**
1.活期存款	Demand deposit	8156606	1036716
2.定期存款	Time deposit	2635808	477970
二、储蓄存款	**Savings deposit**	**12912271**	**2177681**
1.活期储蓄	Current saving	3938886	674746
2.定期储蓄	Time saving	8973385	1502935
三、信托存款	**Trust deposit**	**3438**	**-5681**
四、委托存款	**Consignment deposit**	**905412**	**80317**
五、其他存款	**Other deposits**	**3294789**	**889540**

15-2 金融机构本外币贷款年末余额

Financial institution loan balance of bisic currency and foreign currency at the end of the year

单位：万元　　10 000yuan
(汇率：8.2767)　　(Exchange rate: 8.2767)

指　　标	Item	2003年	比上年增加 Increase over Preceding Year
合　计	**Total**	**20291823**	**3751995**
一、短期贷款	**Short term loan**	**9911938**	**1870521**
二、中长期贷款	**Intermidiate and long term loan**	**7522061**	**1346036**
三、信托贷款	**Trust loan**	**48955**	**13415**
四、委托贷款	**Consignment loan**	**811314**	**92078**
五、其它贷款	**Other loans**	**191622**	**21166**
六、票据融资	**Instrument financing**	**1698549**	**413186**
七、各项垫款	**Sum of money advance**	**107384**	**-4407**

15–3 金融机构存款年末余额

Year-end Balance of Deposit in Financial Institutions

单位:万元 (10 000yuan)

指　　标	Item	2003	比上年增加 Increase over Preceding Year
合　计	**Total**	**26658682**	**4703624**
一、企业存款	**Deposits of Enterprses**	**10414342**	**1530076**
1 .活期存款	Current Deposits	7996021	990284
2 .定期存款	Fixed Deposits	2418321	539792
二、财政存款	**Treasury Deposits**	**167292**	**-67205**
三、机关团体存款	**Deposits of Government Agencies and Organizations**	**724542**	**269382**
四、储蓄存款	**Savings Deposits**	**12105607**	**2224730**
# 定期储蓄	Fixed Savings	8259950	1582532
五、农业存款	**Agricultural Deposits**	**508297**	**99043**
六、信托存款	**Credit Deposits**	**3438**	**-5640**
七、委托存款	**Trusted Deposits**	**905412**	**80317**
八、其他存款	**Other Deposits**	**1829752**	**572921**

15–4 金融机构贷款年末余额

Year-end Balance of Loans in Financial Institutions

单位:万元 (10 000 yuan)

指　　标	Item	2003	比上年增加 Increase Over Preceding Year
合　计	**Total**	**19541838**	**3509673**
一、短期贷款	**Short-term Loans**	**9466080**	**1649111**
1 .工业贷款	Industrial Loans	3015145	572961
2. 商业贷款	Commercial Loans	1384328	232404
3.建筑业贷款	Construction Loans	220441	22311
4.农业贷款	Agricultural Loans	574347	63820
5.乡镇企业贷款	Loans to Township Enterprises	638509	49182
6.三资企业贷款	Loans to Sino-foreige Joint Venture and Cooperative Enterprises and Foreign-funded Enterprises	64261	-12006
7.私营企业及个体贷款	Loans to Private Enterprises and Individuals	86173	16641
8.其他短期贷款	Other Short-term Loans	3482876	703798
二、中期流动资金贷款	**Medium-term Circulating Funds Loans**	**840508**	**-198684**
三、中长期贷款	**Medium-term &Long-term Loans**	**6596692**	**1553202**
1 .基本建设贷款	Loans to Capital Construction	2544707	459064
2. 技术改造贷款	Loans to Technical Innovation	635721	165808
3 .其他中长期贷款	Other Medium-term&Long-term Loans	3416264	928330
四、信托贷款	**Credit Loans**	**48955**	**13415**
五、融资租赁	**Financial Leasing**	**3418**	**-275**
六、委托贷款	**Trusted Loans**	**811314**	**92078**
七、票据融资	**Bill Financing**	**1698367**	**413227**
八、各项垫资	**Various Advance Funds**	**76504**	**-12401**

15-5 金融机构现金收入

Cash Income of Financial Institutions

单位:万元 (10 000yuan)

收入项目	Income of Item	2003	指数（上年=100）Indices (preceding year=100)
合　计	**Total**	**49093031**	**22.30**
一、商品销售收入	**Income from Commodity Sales**	**7165657**	**9.97**
二、服务业收入	**Income from Service Trade**	**1937765**	**7.22**
三、税款收入	**Income from Taxes**	**269781**	**3.20**
四、城乡个体经营收入	**Income from Urban and Rural Individual Business**	**2464405**	**36.72**
五、储蓄存款收入	**Income from Savings Deposits**	**30859460**	**24.07**
六、其它金融机构收入	**Income from Other Financial Institutions**	**677078**	**17.96**
七、居民归还贷款收入	**Income from Repayment of Loans by Residents**	**384659**	**57.13**
八、汇兑收入	**Income from Remittances**	**752841**	**2.72**
九、有价证券收入	**Income from Securities**	**158202**	**6.85**
十、其他收入	**Other Income**	**4423183**	**38.99**

15-6 金融机构现金支出

Cash Expenditure of Financial Institutions

单位:万元 (10000 Yuan)

支出项目	Expenditure of Item	2003	指数（上年=100）Indices (preceding year=100)
合　计	**Total**	**46905195**	**23.22**
一、工资性支出	**Wages**	**2993129**	**18.28**
#国家工资及奖金支出	Government Wages and Bonus Expenditure	1693550	13.71
国家对个人其他支出	Other Government Expenditure to Employees	406122	-7.15
二、农副产品采购支出	**Purchases of Agricultural and Sideline Products**	**1071189**	**31.97**
三、工矿及其他产品采购支出	**Expenditure for Purchases of Individual Business**	**1015693**	**48.37**
四、行政企事业管理费支出	**Governmennt and Enterprises Overhead**	**3607171**	**6.43**
五、城乡个体经营支出	**Expenditure for Individual Business**	**3127798**	**49.93**
六、储蓄存款支出	**Expenditure for Savings Deposits**	**29007970**	**22.60**
七、其他金融机构支出	**Expenditure for Other Financial Institutions**	**551919**	**12.27**
八、居民提取贷款支出	**Expenditure for Loans by Residents**	**385607**	**36.25**
九、汇兑支出	**Expenditure for Remittances**	**428453**	**11.11**
十、有价证券支出	**Expenditure for Securities**	**509668**	**304.32**
十一、其他支出	**Other Expenditure**	**4206598**	**16.34**

15-7 保险业务情况

Indicators of Insurance Business

单位：万元 (10 000 Yuan)

指　　标	Item	2002	2003
保险金额	**Amount Insured**	**16434570**	**17268354**
保费收入	**Premiums**	**286546.17**	**362244.67**
一、财产险	**Property Insurance**	**73542.19**	**90314.06**
（一）财产保险	Property Insurance	70282.84	86745.47
1.机动车辆及第三者责任	Motor Vehicle and Outside Person Liability	46405.30	53880.46
2.企业财产险	Enterprise Property Insurance	11871.45	13126.47
3.货物运输保险	Freight Transport Insurance	2956.42	2873.99
4.家庭财产保险	Family Property Insurance	837.46	4055.98
5.建工及安工保险及其责任险	Construction and Installation Projects Insurance and Related Libility Insurance	1145.86	951.00
6.其他	Others	7066.35	11857.57
（二）责任保险	Liability Insurance	2028.12	2125.99
（三）信用保险	Credit Insurance	435.00	25.58
（四）保证保险	Guarantee Insurance	741.33	1317.22
（五）农业保险	Farm Insurance	54.90	99.80
二、人身险	**Personnel Insurance**	**213003.98**	**271930.61**
（一）人寿保险	Life Insurance	198332.97	247480.04
1.非分红保险	Non-Dividend Insurance	81939.37	88310.40
2.分红保险	Dividend Insurance	97220.29	153600.35
3.投资连接保险	Insurance Connection Insurance	5342.60	4979.59
4.万能保险	Universal Insurance	13830.70	589.70
（二）意外伤害保险	Unforeseen Injury Insurance	6450.34	6512.18
（三）健康保险	Health Insurance	8220.67	17938.39
赔款支出和各项给付	**Indemnity and Other Expenditure**	**63634.96**	**65285.79**
一、财产险	**Property Insurance**	**38013.24**	**39371.78**
（一）财产保险	Property Insurance	34763.42	37126.90
1.机动车辆及第三者责任	Motor Vehicle and Outside Person Liability	25635.33	28682.60
2.企业财产险	Enterprise Property Insurance	7424.48	5590.56
3.家庭财产保险	Freight Transport Insurance	772.14	116.69
4.货物运输保险	Family Property Insurance	121.09	1315.89
5.建工及安工保险及其责任险	Construction and Installation Projects Insurance and Related Libility Insurance	564.61	957.44
6.其他	Others	245.77	463.72
（二）责任保险	Liability Insurance	1796.72	1222.91
（三）信用保险	Credit Insurance	0.00	1.50
（四）保证保险	Guarantee Insurance	1404.00	954.87
（五）农业保险	Farm Insurance	49.10	65.60
二、人身险	**Personnel Insurance**	**25621.72**	**25914.01**
（一）人寿保险	Life Insurance	20877.62	19837.76
1.非分红保险	Non-Dividend Insurance	20643.53	17994.67
2.分红保险	Dividend Insurance	109.27	1711.68
3.投资连接保险	Insurance Connection Insurance	117.61	117.51
4.万能保险	Universal Insurance	7.20	13.90
（二）意外伤害保险	Unforeseen Injury Insurance	1668.15	2375.88
（三）健康保险	Health Insurance	3075.95	3700.37
退保金	**Withdrawal**		
人身险	Personnel Insurance	8257.42	14604.11
（一）人寿保险	Life Insurance	8247.81	14397.66
1.非分红保险	Non-Dividend Insurance	7119.62	9389.39
2.分红保险	Dividend Insurance	1013.85	4387.80
3.投资连接保险	Insurance Connection Insurance	41.84	242.47
4.万能保险	Universal Insurance	72.50	378.00
（二）意外伤害保险	Unforeseen Injury Insurance	0.32	1.21
（三）健康保险	Health Insurance	9.29	205.25

15–8 西安证券期货市场基本情况

Basic Facts on Securities and Futures Markets in Xi'an

指标名称	Item	2003
一、上市证券公司情况	**Listed Securities Companies**	
拥有上市股份公司（个）	Number of Listed Share-holding Companies(unit)	18
占全国比重（%）	percentage to National Total(%)	1.4
上市股份公司总股本（亿股）	Total Capital of Listed Share-holding Companies(100 millon shares)	41.6
#流通股（亿股）	Negotiable shares(100million shares)	17.1
总市值（亿元）	Total Market Capitalization(100million yuan)	296.9
累计证券市场筹措资金（亿元）	Accumulated Capital Raised by Securities Markets(100millon yuan)	67
二、证券经营机构情况	**Securities Trading Organizations**	
拥有证券公司（个）	Number of Securities Companies(unit)	4
#证券营业部（个）	Number of Securities Business Departments(unit)	52
占全省比重（%）	Percentage in Shaanxi Province(%)	80
投资者开户数（万户）	Number of Investors Who have Opened an Account(10000 accounts)	75.5
证券交易总额（亿元）	Total Turnover(100 million yuan)	1749
三、期货市场情况	**Futures Market**	
拥有期货经纪公司（个）	Number of Futures Business Management Companies(unit)	3
期货营业部（个）	Number of Futures Business Departments(unit)	2
期货代理交易额（亿元）	Total Transaction Value in Futures Commissioning(100million yuan)	119
每个经纪公司平均拥有注册资金（万元）	Average Registered Capital of Each Business Management Company(10000yuan)	3000

15–9 西安市企业股票股本构成情况

Constituent of Subscribed Capital for Xi'an Enterprises

单位：万股 (10 000 shares)

股票名称 Name	总股本 Total Share	国家股 Government Share	法人股 Cooperation Share	流通股 Current Share
总　计	**416539.87**	**138368.98**	**106964.41**	**171200.60**
陕解放A	13037.83	2804.63	5887.75	4345.45
陕国投A	31418.70	16036.05	2746.66	12636.00
西安民生	20200.70	5180.52	1352.18	13663.90
西安旅游	16759.79	6355.79	5100.00	5304.00
西安饮食	17162.27	5250.00	5711.09	6199.40
西飞国际	39150.00	21450.00		17700.00
陕西金叶	23700.77	8701.77	3974.35	11024.64
金花股份	23083.52		13099.52	9984.00
精密股份	26119.62	7665.30	5144.40	13309.92
海星科技	21780.00		14300.00	7480.00
秦丰农业	12882.00	7257.00	825.00	4800.00
标准股份	31900.98	19606.27	3294.71	9000.00
航天动力	18500.00		12000.00	6500.00
数码测绘	29089.80	6129.01	7391.67	15569.13
长安信息	8733.34	1404.98	3578.37	3750.00
彩虹股份	42114.88	24016.00	3734.40	14364.48
达 尔 曼	28663.94		18192.44	10471.50
广电网络	12241.72	6511.67	631.87	5098.18

15-10 西安市股票发行情况一览表

List of Security Issued By Xi'an Enterprises

股票名称 Name	发行时间 Issued Time	发行价 (元) Issue Price (yuan)	发行量(万股) Issue Value (10 000 shares)	筹资额 (万元) Raised Capital(10 000 yuan)
陕解放A	1993年8月9日	2.50	1307	3267
陕国投A	1994年1月10日	2.00	5000	10000
西安民生	1994年1月10日	2.50	3596	8990
西安旅游	1996年9月26日	3.80	2236	8497
西安饮食	1997年4月30日	3.15	4000	12600
西飞国际	1997年6月26日	6.15	6000	36900
陕西金叶	1998年6月23日	5.26	3000	15780
金花股份	1997年6月12日	6.16	3000	18480
精密股份	1997年6月26日	3.00	4000	12000
海星科技	1999年6月11日	4.68	6800	31824
标准股份	2000年12月13日	9.07	4500	40815
航天动力	2003年4月8日	3.68	6500	23920
数码测绘	1996年4月30日	1.50	1981	2971
长安信息	1996年5月16日	1.50	1356	2034
彩虹股份	1996年5月20日	1.50	9208	13812
达 尔 曼	1996年12月30日	7.30	2100	15330
广电网络	1994年2月24日	4.00	3090	12359
秦丰农业	2000年6月22日	7.68	4800	35808

主 要 统 计 指 标 解 释

信贷资金 指金融机构以信用方式积聚和分配的货币资金。金融机构信贷资金的来源有各项存款、对国际金融机构负债、流通中货币、银行自有资金及当年结益等；信贷资金的运用有各项贷款、黄金占款、外汇占款、财政借款及在国际金融机构中的资产等。

存款 指企业、机关、团体或居民根据资金必须收回的原则，把货币资金存入银行或其他信用机构保管并取得一定利息的一种信用活动形式。根据存款对象的不同可划分为企业存款、财政存款、机关团体存款、基本建设存款、城镇储蓄存款、农村存款等科目。它是银行信贷资金的主要来源。

贷款 指银行或其他信用机构根据资金必须归还的原则，按一定利率，为企业、个人等提供资金的一种信用活动形式。我国银行贷款分为流动资金贷款、固定资产贷款、城乡个体工商户贷款以及农业贷款等科目。

保险金额 指保险人承担赔偿或者给付保险金责任的最高限额。

保费 指投保人为取得保险人在约定范围内所承担赔偿责任而支付给保险人的费用。

赔款 指保险人根据保险合同的规定，向被保险人支付的赔偿保险责任损失的金额。

给付 包括死伤医疗给付和满期给付。死伤医疗给付是指保险人根据人寿保险及长期健康保险合同的规定，因被保险人在保险期内发生保险责任范围内的保险事故支付给被保险人（或受益人）的金额。满期给付是指被保险人生存期满，保险人按人寿保险合同规定支付给被保险人的满期保险金额。

Explanatory Notes on Main Statistical Indicators

Credit Funds refer to the funds issued as loans by banking institutions. The sources of credit funds of the banking institutions included deposits, liabilities to international financial institutions, currency in circulation, self-owned funds and current retained profits, etc. The credit funds can be used in forms of loans, gold, foreign exchange, government debt and assets in the international financial institutions.

Deposit is a form of credit by which enterprises, institutions, organizations or households can put money into banks and other credit institutions for safekeeping and interest earning under the principle of free withdrawal. According to different depositors, deposits are divided into enterprise deposits, treasury deposits, deposits of government agencies and organizations, capital construction deposits, urban savings deposits, rural deposits and other deposits. Deposits are major sources of the credit funds of banks.

Loan is a form of credit by which banks and other credit institutions provide funds at certain interest rate to enterprises and individuals in the light of the principle of unconditional repayment. Loans from Chinese banks include circulating capital loans, fixed assets loans, loans to urban and rural individuals engaged in industrial and commercial business and agricultural loans.

Amount Insured refers to the maximum that the insurant will get for the claim of the case insured.

Premium is the fee paid by the insurant to the insurer to obtain the obligation of compensation from the insurance within the agreed terms.

Settled Claim is the compensation paid by the insurer to the insurant in accordance with the insurance contract.

Payment includes payment for death, injury or medical treatment and mature payment. Payment for death, injury or medical treatment refers to the money paid to the insurant (or the beneficiary) in accordance with the life or health insurance contract when the insurant encounters accidents within the insured period covered in the contract. Mature payment refers to the mature payment to the insurant in accordance with the life insurance contract at the end of the insured period.

2004

統計年鑒

十六、教育和科技

EDUCATION,SCIENCE AND TECHNOLOGY

简 要 说 明
Brief Introduction

本章资料包括我市教育事业、科技活动基本情况，由市统计局人口与社会科技处根据有关部门资料整理。

教育部分包括高等、中等、初等、幼儿、特殊教育和成人教育，科学技术部分主要包括科技机构、大中型工业企业和高等院校的科技活动以及高新区基本情况。

Data in this chapter consists of primarily data of educational undertakings, science and technologyActivities of Xi'an city, compiled by Population and Employment division and Society and Science and Technology Division, according to data from Xi'an Municipal Government Departments concerned.

Education section consists of higher education, secondary education, elementary education, preschool education, special education, and adult education. Science and technology section consists of primarily science and technology institution, science and technology activities of large, medium industrial enterprises and high-tech zone.

16-1 主要年份各类普通教育基本情况

Basic Statistics on Regular Eduction In Representative Years

指 标	Item	1990	1995	2000	2001	2002	2003
学校数(所)	Number of Schools (unit)						
普通高等教育	Regular Institutions of Higher Education	31	32	25	32	35	37
中等学校	Secondary Schools	689	666	671	665	654	651
#专业学校	#Specialized Secondary Schools	44	46	47	47	46	34
普通中学	Regular Secondary Schools	518	485	466	470	467	467
小学	Primary Schools	2343	2360	2323	2277	2137	2084
幼儿园	Kindergartens	256	257	367	366	378	610
毕业生数(万人)	Graduates (10 000 persons)						
普通高等教育	Regular Institutions of Higher Education	2.17	3.04	3.03	3.69	4.23	6.49
中等学校	Secondary Schools	10.78	10.55	15.09	16.99	18.62	19.86
#专业学校	#Specialized Secondary Schools	0.56	0.97	1.63	1.7	1.6	1.6
普通中学	Regular Secondary Schools	9.11	8.13	12.01	13.85	15.76	16.76
小学	Primary Schools	8.68	9.93	13.83	14.2	13.9	12.97
招生数(万人)	New Student Enrollment (10 000 persons)						
普通高等教育	Regular Institutions of Higher Education	2.15	3.4	7.49	9.24	11.88	13.65
中等学校	Secondary Schools	12.52	15.62	21.58	22.52	23.49	22.72
#专业学校	#Specialized Secondary Schools	0.68	1.37	1.9	1.58	1.69	1.8
普通中学	Regular Secondary Schools	10.49	12.04	17.88	18.98	19.68	18.78
小学	Primary Schools	10.85	14.09	11.51	11.07	10.13	9.28
幼儿园	Kindergartens	...	11.18	8.71	7.83	7.21	7.06
在校学生(万人)	Student Enrollment (10 000 persons)						
普通高等教育	Regular Institutions of Higher Education	8.02	10.87	19.41	25.49	33	40.12
中等学校	Secondary Schools	35.65	41.43	58.75	62.77	66.08	67.33
#专业学校	#Specialized Secondary Schools	2.09	3.74	6.02	5.63	5.57	5.28
普通中学	Regular Secondary Schools	30.03	32.32	48.31	52.5	55.36	56.44
小学	Primary Schools	61.87	79.36	77.81	74.51	70.78	66.78
幼儿园	Kindergartens	14.04	16.4	12.85	11.97	11.53	12.39
教职工（人）	Staff and teachers (person)						
普通高等教育	Regular Institutions of Higher Education	41551	42074	38067	42977	46708	49219
中等学校	Secondary Schools	40592	44465	48194	47749	48878	50389
#专业学校	#Specialized Secondary Schools	7136	5903	6964	5252	5170	4562
普通中学	Regular Secondary Schools	30739	30423	34385	35442	36706	38252
小学	Primary Schools	37788	35568	35336	34257	34143	34080
幼儿园	Kindergartens	6123	6173	6346	6224	6541	8959
专任教师(人)	Number of Full-time Teachers (person)						
普通高等教育	Regular Institutions of Higher Education	15562	15914	15679	17523	20561	22145
中等学校	Secondary Schools	28427	28721	32923	33292	34559	36176
#专业学校	#Specialized Secondary Schools	2891	2533	3172	2467	2508	2302
普通中学	Regular Secondary Schools	22386	21984	26230	27190	28335	29887
小学	Primary Schools	29090	30270	30215	29281	29428	29531
幼儿园	Kindergartens	2058	2659	2995	3069	3397	4853

16-2 各级普通教育基本情况(2003年)

Basic Facts on Regular Education by School Type（2003）

指　标	Item	学校数（所）Number of schools (unit)	毕业生数(人) Number of Graduates (person)	招生数(人) New student enrollment (person)
一、研究生	**Postgraduates**		**11353**	**14322**
1.普通高校	Regular Institutions of Higher Education		11026	13882
2.科研机构	Scientific Research Institution		327	440
二、普通高等学校	**Regular Institutions of Higher Education**	**37**	**84234**	**122142**
三、普通中等学校	**Regular Institutions of Secondary Schools**	**651**	**213734**	**227182**
1.中等专业学校	Specialized Secondary Schools	34	16038	17990
2.普通中学	Regular Secondary Schools	467	181324	187857
3.技工学校	Technical Schools	62	4000	4000
4.职业中学	Vocational Schools	87	12372	17310
5.工读学校	Reformatory Schools	1		25
四、小学	**Primary Schools**	**2084**	**122459**	**92753**
五、特殊教育学校	**Special Education Schools**	**5**		**161**
六、幼儿园及学前班	**Kindergartens**	**610**		**70649**

16-2 各级普通教育基本情况(2003年)(续)

Basic Facts on Regular Education by School Type（2003）（Continued）

指　标	Item	在校学生数(人) Student Enrollment (Person)	教职工数(人) Number of Staff and Teachers(person)	专任教师(人) Full-time Teachers(person)
一、研究生	**Postgraduates**	**36936**		
1.普通高校	Regular Institutions of Higher Education	35790		
2.科研机构	Scientific Research Institution	1146		
二、普通高等学校	**Regular Institutions of Higher Education**	**364244**	**49219**	**22145**
三、普通中等学校	**Regular Institutions of Secondary Schools**	**673333**	**50389**	**36176**
1.中等专业学校	Specialized Secondary Schools	52831	4562	2302
2.普通中学	Regular Secondary Schools	564378	38252	29887
3.技工学校	Technical Schools	12000	3500	1500
4.职业中学	Vocational Schools	44033	4036	2458
5.工读学校	Reformatory Schools	91	39	29
四、小学	**Primary Schools**	**667804**	**34080**	**29531**
五、特殊教育学校	**Special Education Schools**	**1380**	**237**	**166**
六、幼儿园及学前班	**Kindergartens**	**123863**	**8959**	**4853**

16-3 普通高等教育基本情况

Basic Statistics on Regular Institutions of Higher Education

年 份 Year	学校数(所) Number of Schools (unit)	毕业生数(万人) Number of Graduates (10 000 persons)	招生数(万人) New Student Enrollment (10 000 persons)	在校学生数(万人) Student Enrollment (10 000 persons)	教职工数(万人) Number of Staff and Teachers (10 000 persons)	专任教师（万人） Full-time Teachers (10 000 persons)
1978	21			2.88		0.87
1980	25			4.17		0.97
1985	28			6.49		1.28
1990	31	2.17	2.15	8.02	4.15	1.56
1995	32	3.04	3.40	10.87	4.21	1.59
1996	29	2.91	3.54	11.59	4.06	1.55
1997	29	3.04	3.54	11.89	4.00	1.51
1998	29	2.84	3.69	12.66	3.91	1.50
1999	29	3.13	5.62	15.09	3.95	1.52
2000	25	3.03	7.49	19.41	3.80	1.57
2001	32	3.69	9.24	25.49	4.30	1.75
2002	35	4.23	11.88	33.00	4.67	2.06
2003	37	6.49	13.65	40.12	4.92	2.21

16-4 普通高等学校和科研机构研究生

Post-graduates in Regular Institutions of Higher Education and Scientific Researeh

单位：人 (person)

年 份 Year	毕业生数 Graduates	高等学校 Institution of Higher Education	招生数 New Student Enrollment	高等学校 Institution of Higher Education	在校人数 Student Enrollment	高等学校 Institution of Higher Education
1978						
1980					651	651
1985					4799	4799
1990	2051	2051	1662	1662	5275	5275
1995	1769	1769	2712	2712	7974	7974
1996	2172	2172	3003	3003	8647	8647
1997	2619	2619	3423	3423	9393	9393
1998	2316	2316	3888	3888	10833	10833
1999	2903	2903	5020	5020	12986	12986
2000	3236	3236	6924	6924	16620	16620
2001	3881	3770	9274	8966	22564	21855
2002	4103	3952	11282	10882	28446	27471
2003	5971	5765	14322	13882	36936	35790

注：2000年以前资料内不含科研机构培养的研究生。

Note:Graduate students educated in scientific research institutions are not included in the data before 2000.

16–5　普通高等学校分学校研究生(2003年)

Post-graduates in Regular Institutions of Higher Education(2003)

单位：人　　　　　　　　　　　　　　　　　　　　　　　　（person）

校名 Name of Schools	毕业生 Graduates	招生 New Student Enrollment	在校学生 Student Enrollment	博士 Doctor	硕士 Master	毕业班学生数 Number of Students in Graduate-class
合计	**5765**	**13882**	**35790**	**7714**	**27765**	**11026**
1.西安交通大学	1754	3686	10714	3302	7412	3749
2.陕西师范大学	281	827	1769	145	1624	416
3.西北工业大学	975	2437	6547	2078	4469	2167
4.西安理工大学	354	950	2465	295	1859	856
5.西安电子科技大学	562	1812	4631	901	3730	1346
6.西安工业学院	45	141	319		319	67
7.西安建筑科技大学	336	860	2016	299	1717	551
8.西安科技大学	120	377	819	55	764	180
9.西安石油大学	44	148	331		331	77
10.长安大学	413	875	1961	299	1662	477
11.西安工程科技学院	60	150	342		342	87
12.西北政法学院	307	386	1001		1001	345
13.西安体育学院	28	65	150		150	40
14.西北大学	404	993	2248	340	1908	556
15.西安外国语学院	51	140	301		301	71
16.西安音乐学院	14	35	80		80	20
17.西安美术学院	17		96		96	21

16–6　全市普通高等学校分学校情况(2003年)

Basic Facts on Regular Higher Education by Unit(2003)

单位：人　　　　　　　　　　　　　　　　　　　　　　　　　　　　　　　　　　　（person）

校 名 Name of Schools	在校学生数 Student Enrollment 合计 Total	本科 Regular College	专科 Junior College	教职工 Staff and Teachers 合计 Total	其中专任教师 Full-time Teachers
合　计	**364244**	**224965**	**139279**	**49219**	**22145**
一、国家部委直属院校	**94877**	**81565**	**13312**	**18361**	**8261**
西安交通大学	22052	20278	1774	6755	3255
西北工业大学	22183	15823	6360	3177	1456
西安电子科技大学	17271	15376	1895	2640	1064
长安大学	20870	18755	2115	3373	1387
陕西师范大学	12501	11333	1168	2416	1099
二、陕西省属院校	**236896**	**135263**	**101633**	**30158**	**13535**
西北大学	14769	11922	2847	2128	1059
西安理工大学	17544	15216	2328	2275	1049
西安工业学院	13210	11253	1957	1343	872
西安建筑科技大学	16818	13529	3289	2040	933
西安科技大学	11871	10844	1027	1510	775
西安石油大学	16578	12889	3689	1384	827
西安工程科技学院	15188	13131	2057	1440	770
西安外国语学院	8216	6145	2071	1077	585
西北政法学院	11599	9561	2038	1038	538
西安体育学院	5475	5256	219	643	294
西安音乐学院	3425	3425		465	247
西安美术学院	4184	3568	616	479	286
西安财经学院	18296	10332	7964	1295	686
西安邮电学院	10316	7818	2498	809	483
西安航空技术高等专科学校	5210		5210	611	179
西安电力高等专科学校	796		796	400	109
陕西医学高等专科学校	3969		3969	409	177
西安欧亚职业学院	9255		9255	1392	1209
西安外事职业学院	11820		11820	1752	526
西安翻译职业学院	8019		8019	1412	167
西京职业学院	6254		6254	1045	251
陕西国防工业职业技术学院	2889		2889	401	196
西安航空职业技术学院	3065		3065	454	146

注:军校只包括地方招生计划招收的部分。其他学校属成人学校，只统计按普通高校招生计划招收的部分。

Note: Military school includes only that recruited under local recruiting plan. Other schools mean adult schools, only that recruited under ordinary colleges and universities' recruiting plan are taken into account.

16-6 全市普通高等学校分学校情况(2003年)（续）

Basic Facts on Regular Higher Education by Unit(2003)(Continued)

单位：人 （person）

校 名 Name of Schools	在校学生数 Student Enrollment 合计 Total	本科 Regular College	专科 Junior College	教职工 Staff and Teachers 合计 Total	其中专任教师 Full-time Teachers
陕西省交通职业技术学院	4167		4167	280	93
西安科技商贸职业学院	153		153	328	85
陕西电子信息职业技术学院	117		117	186	78
西安培华学院	5331	374	4957	553	348
陕西职业技术学院	3541		3541	466	230
西安思源职业学院	2249		2249	849	139
西安高新科技职业学院	2250		2250	943	138
西安三资职业学院	322		322	211	60
三、西安市直属院校	**7327**	**2129**	**5198**	**700**	**349**
西安文理学院	6680	2129	4551	700	349
西安市广播电视大学	507		507		
西安师范学院大专班	98		98		
西安市职工大学	42		42		
四、其它院校	**25144**	**6008**	**19136**		
武警工程学院	290	290			
空军工程大学	3201	2958	243		
西安政治学院	227	227			
西安通信学院	1458	984	501		
第四军医大学	3129	356	2773		
第二炮兵工程学院	1090	706	384		
西安陆军学院	804	487	317		
铁路运输职工大学	922		922		
陕西航天职工大学	1100		1100		
西安铁路工程职工大学	672		672		
陕西省建筑职工大学	450		450		
陕西省政法管理干部学院	2499		2499		
陕西省广播电视大学	5258		5258		
陕西教育学院	1054		1054		
西安航空职工大学	772		772		
西安飞机工业公司职工学院	577		577		
陕西省经济管理干部学院	1062		1062		
陕西青年管理干部学院	361		361		
陕西兵器工业职工大学	32		32		
西安外贸职工大学	86		86		
陕西工运学院	73		73		

16-7 普通中等专业学校基本情况

Basic Statistics on Specialized Secondary Schools

年份 Year	学校数(所) Number of Schools (unit)	毕业生数(万人) Number of Graduates (10 000 persons)	招生数(万人) New Student Enrollment (10 000 persons)	在校学生数(万人) Stument Enrollment (10 000 persons)	教职工数(人) Number of Staff and Teachers (person)	专任教师（人） Full-time Teachers(person)
1978	19			0.87		1110
1980	33			1.50		1474
1985	37			1.70		2363
1990	44	0.56	0.68	2.09	7136	2891
1995	46	0.97	1.37	3.74	5903	2533
1996	47	1.15	1.61	4.18	5940	2573
1997	47	1.20	1.65	4.63	6124	2731
1998	47	1.26	1.62	5.08	6181	2840
1999	46	1.42	2.11	5.75	6385	2865
2000	47	1.63	1.90	6.02	6964	3172
2001	47	1.70	1.58	5.63	5252	2467
2002	46	1.60	1.69	5.57	5170	2508
2003	34	1.62	1.80	5.28	4562	2302

16-8 中等技术学校分学校基本情况（2003年）

Situation of every secondary technical school（2003）

单位:人　　(person)

校名	毕业生数 Number of graduates	招生数 Number of recruiting students	在校学生数 Number of faculty	教职工数 Number of faculty	其中：专任教师 Init :full time teachers
总　计	**15126**	**16399**	**48317**	**3937**	**1930**
一、中央部门属学校	**1852**	**2305**	**8192**	**853**	**372**
1.西安航天工业学校	600	584	2126	228	108
2.西安铁路运输学校	1030	1661	5861	451	192
3.西安交通大学附设卫生学校	87		73	60	23
4.西安铁路人民警察学校	135	60	132	114	49
二、陕西省属学校	**5279**	**9003**	**22926**	**2112**	**1115**
1.陕西省城乡建设学校	320	198	882	74	40
2.陕西省对外贸易学校	566	334	1467	106	54
3.陕西省体育运动学校	289	408	1357	86	46
4.陕西省艺术学校	451	650	2614	153	90
5.陕西省电影电视学校	134	147	449	59	37
6.陕西省旅游学校	280	287	880	78	44
7.陕西省人民武装学校	210	138	338	126	50
8.西安电力工业学校		130	161	351	130
9.陕西省电子信息学校	331	1992	3645	116	80
10.陕西省城市经济学校	146	109	676	84	50
11.陕西省理工学校	510	1565	2842	145	90
12.西安音乐学院附属中专	67	98	305	20	12
13.西安美术学院附属中专	37	211	553	33	27
14.陕西省石油化工学校	520	1081	2490	258	135
15.陕西省经贸学校	689	754	1893	114	65
16.陕西银行学校	242	406	989	90	51
17.陕西省商贸学校	274	87	520	110	62
18.陕西省建材工业学校	213	408	865	109	52
三、西安市属学校	**2164**	**2212**	**7411**	**972**	**443**
1.西安市艺术学校	192	194	800	119	70
2.西安市卫生学校	496	732	1934	156	88
3.西安市财政会计学校	244	229	558	77	41
4.西安市体育运动学校	145	88	315	107	45
5.西安市经济贸易学校	442	288	1370	128	74
6.西安市工业学校	259	603	1734	280	76
7.西安市农业学校	386	78	700	105	49
8.西安市人民警察学校					
四、其他机构	**5831**	**2879**	**9788**		
1.陕西交通职业技术学院	770		33		
2.陕西医学高等专科学校	301	440	1310		
3.西安体育学院附属竞技体校	50	79	272		
4.西安体育学院附属体校	100	100	300		
5.西安仪表工业学校	567	188	1236		
6.陕西省轻工业学校	361		364		
7.陕西警官职业学院	486	499	499		
8.西北税务学校	619				
9.西安航空职业技术学院	1286	284	1563		
10.西安煤炭卫生学校	688		536		
11.陕西职业技术学院	27	850	1280		
12.陕西国防工业职业技术学院	576	439	2395		

16-9　普通中学基本情况

Baisc Statistics on Regular Secondary Schools

年 份 Year	学校数(所) Number of Schools (unit)	毕业生数(万人) Number of Graduates (10 000 person)	招生数(万人) New Student Enrollment (10 000 person)	在校学生数(万人) Student Enrollment (10 000 person)	教职工数(人) Number of Staff and Teachers(person)	专任教师（人） Full-time Teachers(person)
1978	962	□	□	44.16	□	20660
1980	1002	12.33	14.03	44.08	29867	22530
1985	563	10.72	13.05	38.24	30063	22050
1990	518	9.11	10.49	30.03	30739	22386
1995	485	8.13	12.40	32.32	30423	21984
1996	462	8.67	13.03	35.25	30902	22478
1997	466	9.96	13.83	37.16	31682	23129
1998	467	10.64	15.00	39.79	32371	23884
1999	469	11.21	16.58	43.49	33387	25114
2000	466	12.01	17.88	48.31	34385	26230
2001	470	13.85	18.98	52.50	35442	27190
2002	467	15.76	19.68	55.36	36706	28335
2003	467	16.76	18.78	56.44	38252	29887

16-10　各区县普通中学(2003年)

Regular Secondary Schools by Region (2003)

单位：所、人　　　　(unit,person)

区 县	Region	学校数 Number of Schools	毕业生数 Number of Graduates	高中 Senior	招生数 New Student Enrollment	高中 Senior	在校学生数 Student Enrollment	高中 Senior	教职工数 Number of Staff and Teachers	专任教师 Full-time Teachers
合　计	**Total**	**467**	**167629**	**42493**	**187857**	**62159**	**564378**	**175385**	**38252**	**29887**
新城区	Xincheng	34	12228	3994	14495	6122	43285	16746	2998	2170
碑林区	Beilin	45	12151	4426	14465	7116	42630	18670	3214	2268
莲湖区	Lianhu	27	10910	2733	11877	4390	35939	12490	2808	2017
灞桥区	Baqiao	35	10897	2663	11402	3868	34956	10898	2663	2064
未央区	Weiyang	33	9335	2412	10146	3570	30731	9944	2657	1938
雁塔区	Yanta	46	12033	3259	13879	5745	41428	14993	3545	2574
阎良区	Yanliang	13	6063	1443	7202	2256	21469	6204	1304	1095
临潼区	Lintong	42	17351	3492	19625	4689	59250	14204	3462	2880
长安区	Chang'an	57	22432	5085	24243	7509	73729	21244	4712	3826
蓝田县	Lantian	47	12976	2589	16304	4088	46317	10984	2896	2315
周至县	Zhouzhi	37	17115	4002	20091	4621	60543	15070	3266	2693
户　县	Huxian	36	17275	4921	17373	6005	52625	17911	3306	2847
高陵县	Gaoling	15	6863	1474	6755	2180	21476	6027	1421	1200

16-11 职业中学基本情况

Basic Statistics on Vocational Secondary Schools

年 份 Year	学校数(所） Number of Schools (unit)	毕业生数（人） Number of Graduates (person)	招生数（人） New Student Enrollment (person)	在校学生数（人） Student Enrollment (person)	教职工数（人） Number of Teachers and Staff (person)	专任教师（人） Full-time Teachers(person)
1978						
1980						
1985	40	1661	8346	17621	1375	868
1990	58	5936	8095	20151	2674	1574
1995	71	8976	12490	32673	2394	1877
1996	67	9235	10563	25955	3098	1735
1997	73	8756	13390	29068	2993	1709
1998	89	7753	13949	31264	3152	1823
1999	91	8480	13062	31973	3217	1908
2000	95	9949	13903	32188	3311	1997
2001	85	10300	15591	34336	3517	2113
2002	78	8659	17231	39428	3461	2192
2003	87	10755	17310	44033	4036	2458

16-12 各区县职业中学(2003年)

Vocational Secondary Schools by Region (2003)

区 县	Region	学校数(所） Number of Schools (unit)	毕业生数（人） Number of Graduates (person)	招生数（人） New Student Enrollment (person)	在校学生数（人） Student Enrollment (person)	教职工数（人） Number of Teachers and Staff (person)	专任教师（人） Full-time Teachers(person)
合 计	**Total**	**87**	**10755**	**17310**	**44033**	**4036**	**2458**
新城区	Xincheng	7	847	1627	3941	391	248
碑林区	Beilin	19	2786	3384	10547	830	510
莲湖区	Lianhu	8	1219	1700	4558	511	304
灞桥区	Baqiao	3	78	924	1727	212	113
未央区	Weiyang	6	697	1061	2851	497	228
雁塔区	Yanta	15	1138	1502	4243	477	235
阎良区	Yanliang	1	607	576	1907	115	91
临潼区	Lintong	5	600	787	2545	176	132
长安区	Chang'an	8	508	2078	3950	260	189
蓝田县	Lantian	2	346	740	1818	55	38
周至县	Zhouzhi	5	439	1035	2059	172	115
户 县	Huxian	7	1304	1657	3347	268	211
高陵县	Gaoling	1	186	239	540	72	44

16-13 小学基本情况

Basic Statistics on Primary Schools

年 份 Year	学校数(所) Number of Schools (unit)	毕业生数（万人） Number of Graduates (10 000 person)	招生数（万人） New Student Enrollment (10 000 person)	在校学生数（万人） Student Enrollment (10 000 person)	教职工数（人） Number of Teachers and Staff (person)	专任教师（人） Full-time Teachers(person)
1978	2667			74.03		26428
1980	2337	11.91	12.57	73.36	31770	28360
1985	2337	11.21	9.57	62.16	31075	26430
1990	2343	8.67	10.85	61.87	37788	29090
1995	2360	9.93	14.09	79.36	35568	30270
1996	2362	10.48	13.63	81.81	35821	30267
1997	2368	10.98	12.48	82.67	35767	30117
1998	2361	12.18	11.88	82.03	35576	30089
1999	2354	13.65	11.61	79.81	35639	30196
2000	2323	13.83	11.51	77.81	35336	30215
2001	2277	14.20	11.07	74.51	34257	29281
2002	2137	13.89	10.13	70.78	34143	29428
2003	2084	12.97	9.28	66.78	34080	29531

16-14 各区县小学基本情况(2003年)

Basic Statistics on Primary Schools by Region (2003)

区 县	Region	学校数(所) Number of Schools (unit)	毕业生数（人） Number of Graduates (person)	招生数（人） New Student Enrollment (person)	在校学生数（人） Student Enrollment (person)	教职工数（人） Number of Teachers and Staff (person)	专任教师（人） Full-time Teachers(person)
合 计	**Total**	**2084**	**129652**	**92753**	**667804**	**34080**	**29531**
新城区	Xincheng	41	7384	6706	42636	2167	1825
碑林区	Beilin	52	6882	6502	39788	2322	1830
莲湖区	Lianhu	50	7497	6827	43499	2565	2180
灞桥区	Baqiao	110	7789	5159	38073	2607	2172
未央区	Weiyang	78	6898	5928	38276	2663	2239
雁塔区	Yanta	62	7988	8143	48733	2953	2366
阎良区	Yanliang	82	5004	2665	21989	1220	1045
临潼区	Lintong	288	16447	10133	75197	3278	2937
长安区	Chang'an	349	18248	10954	85757	3963	3339
蓝田县	Lantian	372	13211	10296	72594	3371	3269
周至县	Zhouzhi	286	15952	9617	81775	3352	3009
户 县	Huxian	223	11338	7196	56080	2811	2651
高陵县	Gaoling	91	5014	2627	23407	808	669

16-15　幼儿园基本情况

Basic Statistics on Kindergartens

年 份 Year	园 数(所) Number of Kindergartens (unit)	班 数(个) Number of Class (unit)	在园幼儿数(万人) Student Enrollment (10000 person)	教职工数(人) Number of Staff and Teachers (person)	专任教师(人) Full-time Teachers(person)
1978	363		4		1315
1980	186		10	5525	2657
1985	310	3135	10	6887	2770
1990	256	3816	14	6123	2058
1995	257	4464	16	6173	2659
1996	244	4313	15	5918	2661
1997	228	4243	15	6065	2748
1998	235	4195	13	6272	2910
1999	234	4222	13	6329	2982
2000	367	4142	13	6346	2995
2001	366	4306	12	6224	3069
2002	378	4186	12	6541	3397
2003	610	4470	12	8959	4853

注:幼儿园中包括学前班。

Note:"Kindergartens" here including units providing pre-school education.

16-16　特殊教育学校基本情况

Basic Statistics on Special Education Schools

年 份 Year	学校数(所) Number of Schools (unit)	毕业生数（人） Number of Graduates (person)	招生数（人） New Student Enrollment (person)	在校学生数（人） Student Enrollment (person)	教职工数（人） Number of Teachers and Staff (person)	专任教师（人） Full-time Teachers(person)
1978						
1980	1	48	64	315	66	43
1985	2	14	36	318	94	59
1990	5	35	111	451	142	96
1995	5	27	147	1363	204	141
1996	5	60	164	1520	210	150
1997	5	153	164	1655	210	148
1998	5	266	140	2145	232	157
1999	5	349	115	1912	235	160
2000	5	269	145	1880	230	156
2001	5	237	209	1915	238	162
2002	5	216	148	1661	232	157
2003	5			1380	237	166

注:包括盲、聋、哑、弱智儿童教育在内。

Note:Including schools providing education for blind, deaf and dumb children and children with weak intelligence .

16–17　小学、初中升学率

Rate of Graduates from Junior Schools and Primary Schools Entering Higher Level Schools

年 份 Year	小学 Primary Schools 小学毕结业生数（万人） Graduates of Primary Schools (10 000 person)	升学人数（万人） Number of Graduates from Primary Schools (10 000 persons)	升学率 (%) Percentage of Graduates from Primary Schools Entering Junior Secondary Schools (%)
1978			
1980	11.91	10.43	87.60
1985	11.21	9.56	85.30
1990	8.68	8.09	91.50
1995	10.02	9.50	94.85
1996	10.62	10.15	95.62
1997	11.04	10.56	95.65
1998	12.25	11.76	96.02
1999	13.77	13.23	96.04
2000	13.83	13.44	97.21
2001	14.22	13.83	97.25
2002	13.92	13.54	97.25
2003	12.97	12.61	97.26

16–17　小学、初中升学率（续）

Rate of Graduates from Junior Schools and Primary Schools Entering Higher Level Schools(Continued)

年 份 Year	初中 JunionSchools 初中毕结 业 生 数(万人) Graduates from Junior Secondary Schools (10 000 persons)	升学人数（万人） Number of Graduates from Junior Secondary （10 000persons）	升学率 (%) Percentage of Graduates from Junior Secondary Schools Entering Senior Secondary Schools (%)
1978			
1980			60.71
1985	8.36	4.63	55.30
1990	6.86	2.39	52.70
1995	6.35	4.60	72.35
1996	6.66	5.39	81.00
1997	7.98	6.14	76.93
1998	8.53	6.56	76.90
1999	9.19	7.08	77.00
2000	9.35	7.53	80.50
2001	10.88	8.77	80.56
2002	12.31	10.19	82.80
2003	12.66	10.16	80.26

16-18 小学学龄儿童入学率

Percentage of School-Age Children Enrolled

年 份 Year	学龄儿童总数 (万人) Total School-Age Children (10000 persons)	农村 Rural Areas	入学儿童总数 (万人) Total School-Age Children (10000 persons)	农村 Rural Areas	入学率（%） Enrollment Rate (%)	农村 Rural Areas
1978						
1980					98.42	
1985	63.02	32.57	62.16	31.95	98.62	98.10
1990	62.42	34.35	61.87	33.88	99.11	98.66
1995	77.86	29.12	77.62	28.98	99.69	99.49
1996	81.40	27.69	81.19	27.58	99.75	99.61
1997	82.45	24.30	82.24	24.21	99.74	99.65
1998	81.69	22.52	81.54	22.44	99.82	99.66
1999	79.66	21.67	79.55	21.61	99.86	99.75
2000	77.68	20.44	77.56	20.37	99.85	99.68
2001	69.69	41.31	69.58	41.22	99.84	99.77
2002	65.76	36.59	65.66	36.50	99.85	99.75
2003	62.44	33.78	62.37	33.72	99.88	99.81

16-19 平均每万人口在校学生数和大中小学生构成

Student Enrollment Per 10000 Populations and Composition of Students Enrolled

年 份 Year	占全市人口 Percentage of Population of Whole City	平均每万人口中 Students Per 10000 P opulation		
		大学生（人） University and College Students(person)	中学生（人） Secondary School Students(person)	小学生（人） Primary School Students(person)
1978	25.37	58	886	1486
1980	25.92	84	906	1434
1985	22.24	117	692	1124
1990	19.84	123	493	1016
1995	22.86	168	639	1224
1996	23.37	177	672	1249
1997	23.54	180	701	1249
1998	23.62	189	740	1228
1999	24.06	224	798	1183
2000	24.56	282	854	1131
2001	25.17	366	903	1072
2002	25.84	470	940	1007
2003	26.06	560	939	932

16-19 平均每万人口在校学生数和大中小学生构成（续）

Student Enrollment Per 10000 Populations and Composition of Students Enrolled(Continued)

年 份 Year	大中小学生各占学生总数% Students of Different Level as Percentage of Total Students (%)		
	大学生 University and College Students	中学生 Secondary School Students	小学生 Primary School Students
1978	2.28	34.94	58.57
1980	3.14	33.21	55.27
1985	5.32	31.34	50.93
1990	6.71	25.10	51.71
1995	7.33	27.96	53.55
1996	7.57	24.73	53.46
1997	7.63	29.77	53.05
1998	8.01	31.34	52.01
1999	10.14	36.20	53.66
2000	12.44	37.67	49.89
2001	14.57	35.88	42.59
2002	18.17	36.40	38.99
2003	21.48	36.05	35.76

16-20 成人教育情况(2003年)

		学校数(所) Number of Schools (unit)	毕业生数(人) Graduates (person)
合　计	**Total**	**2055**	**284185**
一、成人高等学校	**Adult Higher Education Institution**	**19**	**19110**
1.广播电视大学	Radio and TV Universities	2	9724
2.职工高等学校	Schools of Higher Education for Staff and Workers	11	3392
3.管理干部学院	Colleges for Management Cadres	5	2196
4.教育学院	Pedagogical Colleges	1	3798
二、普通高校成教学院	**Adult Education Units in Regular Institutions**	**(24)**	**31384**
1.函授部	Correspondence Divisions	(18)	18916
2.夜大学	Evening Schools	(14)	3354
3.成人脱产班	Short-cycle Courses for Adults	(21)	9114
三、成人中等学校	**Adult middle school**	**1985**	**232219**
1.成人中等专业学校	Specialized Secondary Schools for Adults	26	8413
(1)广播电视中专	Radio and TV Specialized Secondary School	5	6171
(2)职工.干部.函授中专	Specialized Correspondence Secondary Schools for	8	1687
(3)教师进校	Teacher Training Schools	13	
(4)其他机构	Other institutions	6	555
2.成人中学	Adult middle school	4	756
3.成人技术培训学校	Adult technology training school	1955	223050
四、成人初等学校	**Adult elementary school**	**51**	**1472**

注:1.本表是西安市行政辖区内各级各类成人学校的全口径数据(不含党校)

2.( )内数因与普通高校重复,不加入总计数。

Adult Education (2003)

招生数（人） New Student Enrollment (person)	在校学生数（人） Student Enrollment (person)	教职工数（人） Teachers and Staff (person)	专任教师 Full-time Teachers
65220	**405285**	**11801**	**6089**
16200	**43693**	**6548**	**3184**
5803	20082	2833	1451
4366	11885	1879	963
2467	4356	1293	493
3564	7370	543	277
41008	**118780**		
23703	77754		
3775	11051		
13530	29975		
8012	**241523**	**5206**	**2872**
8012	20582	2387	1280
5726	13383	1155	517
1584	5262	780	513
		452	250
702	1937		
	756	40	39
	220185	2779	1553
	1289	**47**	**33**

a): First,The table Shows the Data of All the Adult Education Schools in Xi'an Administrative Region (Party Schools not included).

b): Number in brackets overlapped over that of Regular Schools for higher education, so it is not excluded from the total.

16-21 科学研究机构基本情况

Basic Facts on Scientific Research Institutions

指　标	Item	2000	2001	2002	2003
一、科技机构数(个)	**Number of Scientific and Technological Institutions (unit)**	**732**	**735**	**569**	**564**
#科研单位	#Units of Scientific Research	219	216	130	131
高等院校	Institutions of Higher Education	393	396	340	333
大中型工业企业	Large-scale and Medium-scale Industrial Enterprises	120	123	99	100
二、科技活动人员数（人）	**Number of Persons Engaged in Scientific and Technological Activities (person)**	**106803**	**85210**	**80243**	**89316**
#科研单位	Units of Scientific Research	36911	27253	28827	31997
高等院校	Institutions of Higher Education	23790	22366	22006	24565
大中型工业企业	Large-scale and Medium-scale Industrial Enterprises	46102	35591	29410	32754
三、科技活动经费筹集总额（万元）	**Total Funding for Scientific and Technological Activities (10 000 yuan)**	**459873**	**522394**	**625653**	**736342**
#科研单位	Units of Scientific Research	241020	282711	332824	399388
高等院校	Institutions of Higher Education	90841	60262	127113	160111
大中型工业企业	Large-scale and Medium-scale Industrial Enterprises	128012	179421	165716	176843
四、科技活动经费使用总额（万元）	**Total Expenditures on Scientific and Technical Activities (10 000 yuan)**	**416907**	**551456**	**603435**	**729237**
#科研单位	Units of Scientific Research	213828	291548	325750	390900
高等院校	Institutions of Higher Education	73068	120016	123425	149260
大中型工业企业	Large-scale and Medium-scale Industrial Enterprises	130011	139892	154260	189077
五、科技成果与著作情况	**Basic Facts on Scientific and Technical Research Achievements and Works**				
1.科技论文（篇）	Scientific and Technical Thesis (piece)	17010	16195	19009	22299
2.出版科技著作（种）	Scientific and Technical Works Published (book)	709	683	705	794

16–22　科研院所科技活动情况表

Scientific and Technological Activities Facts in Scientific Research Institutions

指标名称	Item	2000	2001	2002	2003
一、基本情况					
单位数（个）	Number of Unit	130	130	130	131
#有科技活动的单位数	#:Number of Units with Scientific and Technical Activities		110	116	118
单位从业人员数（人）	Number of Emplogment (person)	53882	40094	42062	42220
从事科技活动人员（人）	Number of Personnel Engaged in Scientific Research (person)	36911	27253	28827	31997
#科学家和工程师	#Scientists and Engineers	20220	16208	14324	15756
二、科技活动经费筹集与使用	**Raising and Use of Funds for Scientific and Technical Activities**				
当年科技活动经费筹集总额（万元）	Total Funds for Scientific and Technical Activities (10000 yuan)	241020	282711	332824	399388
1.政府资金	Government Funds	113690	205368	236098	283317
2.企业资金	Enterprise Funds	32502	27871	34531	41437
3.事业单位资金	Enterprises Unit Funds	32000	26314	36467	43760
4.金融机构资金	Finance Institution Funds	11879	10536	9516	11419
5.外国资金	Foreign Funds				
6.其他资金	Others	50949	12622	16212	19455
当年科技活动经费支出总额（万元）	Total Expenditures on Scientific and Technical Activities(10000 yuan)	213828	291548	325750	390900
内部支出	Interior Expenditure		271577	271467	325760
#1.经常费支出	Regularity Expenditure		219407	217864	261436
#人员劳务费	# Labor Expenses		51035	61307	63994
2.科研基建支出	Scientific Research and Capital Construction Expenditure		49358	53603	64324
#固定资产购建	Purchase of Fixed Assets		38943	32593	39111
#设备购置	#Purchase of Equipment		30990	28354	34024
三、研究与实验发展情况	**Research and Experiment Development**				
有R&D活动的单位数（个）	Number of Units with R&D Activities (unit)			106	118
R&D人员折合全时人员（人年）	Number of R&D Personnel Converted into Full-time Employees (person-year)		17667	14891	15006
#a.基础研究	#Fundamental Research		1991	921	1800
b.应用研究	Applied Research		5508	3420	4020
c.试验发展	Experimental Development		10168	10510	9186
R&D经费支出	R&D Expenditures		200685	160180	192216
内部支出（万元）	Interior Expenditure (10000yuan)	160228	197164	150048	180057
四、科技成果情况	**Scientific and Technical Research Achievements**				
1.申请专利数（件）	Number of Patent Applications (item)	79	86	145	159
#发明专利数	#Number of Invent Patent		38	68	74
2.拥有发明专利数	Patent Owned	58	106	202	222
3.发表科技论文（篇）	Scientific and Technical Thesis (piece)	2810	2338	2306	2536
4.出版科技著作（种）	Scientific and Technical Works Published (book)	127	125	121	133
五、科技项目（课题）情况	**Scientific and Technnical Projects**				
1.项目（课题）数（项）	Number of Projects (item)		3292	3081	3389
2.项目（课题）参加人员折合全时当量（人年）	Number of Personnel Converted into Full-time Employees (person-year)		14507	16091	17700
3.项目（课题）实际经费支出（万元）	Expenditures for Projects (10000 yuan)		142481	169062	185968

16-23 大专院校科技活动情况表

Scientific and Technological Activities Facts in Universities

指标名称	Item	2000	2001	2002	2003
一、基本情况					
单位数（个）	Number of Unit	25	32	35	37
#有科技活动的单位数	#:Number of Units with Scientific and Technical Activities			21	24
单位从业人员数（人）	Number of Emplogment (person)	53689	48596	46708	45924
从事科技活动人员（人）	Number of Personnel Engaged in Scientific Research (person)	23790	22366	22006	24565
#科学家和工程师	#Scientists and Engineers	17580	19756	16607	18401
二、科技活动经费筹集与使用	**Raising and Use of Funds for Scientific and Technical Activities**				
当年科技活动经费筹集总额（万元）	Total Funds for Scientific and Technical Activities (10000 yuan)	90841	60262	127113	160111
1.政府资金	Government Funds	42100	27689	66153	78548
2.企业资金	Enterprise Funds		16630	26016	36552
3.事业单位资金	Enterprises Unit Funds	3781	6460	16524	13202
4.金融机构资金	Finance Institution Funds			760	2100
5.外国资金	Foreign Funds		40	697	679
6.其他资金	Others	44960	9443	16963	29030
当年科技活动经费支出总额（万元）	Total Expenditures on Scientific and Technical Activities(10000 yuan)	73068	120016	123425	149260
内部支出	Interior Expenditure		116929	115223	144823
#1.经常费支出	Regularity Expenditure		89999	85143	121534
#人员劳务费	# Labor Expenses		19396	20515	48472
2.科研基建支出	Scientific Research and Capital Construction Expenditure		26930	30080	23289
#固定资产购建	Purchase of Fixed Assets		14049	18843	16255
#设备购置	#Purchase of Equipment		12688	17301	14462
三、研究与实验发展情况	**Research and Experiment Development**				
有R&D活动的单位数（个）	Number of Units with R&D Activities (unit)			21	24
R&D人员折合全时人员（人年）	Number of R&D Personnel Converted into Full-time Employees (person-year)		4629	4646	4699
#a.基础研究	#Fundamental Research		896	1199	1163
b.应用研究	Applied Research		1988	2170	2251
c.试验发展	Experimental Development		1745	1277	1285
R&D经费支出	R&D Expenditures		44973	54496	63509
内部支出（万元）	Interior Expenditure (10000yuan)	29428	44454	53752	62742
四、科技成果情况	**Scientific and Technical Research Achievements**				
1.申请专利数（件）	Number of Patent Applications (item)	85	126	254	380
#发明专利数	#Number of Invent Patent		74	167	297
2.拥有发明专利数	Patent Owned	70	86	380	351
3.发表科技论文（篇）	Scientific and Technical Thesis (piece)	14200	13857	16703	19763
4.出版科技著作（种）	Scientific and Technical Works Published (book)	582	558	584	661
五、科技项目（课题）情况	**Scientific and Technnical Projects**				
1.项目（课题）数（项）	Number of Projects (item)		5488	7193	8464
2.项目（课题）参加人员折合全时当量（人年）	Number of Personnel Converted into Full-time Employees (person-year)		5857	5296	5740
3.项目（课题）实际经费支出（万元）	Expenditures for Projects (10000 yuan)		59129	65765	85874

16-24 大中型工业企业科技活动情况

Scientific and Technological Activities Facts in Large-size and Medium-size Industrial Enterprises

指标名称	Item	2000	2001	2002	2003
一、企业基本情况	**Basic Statistics of Enterprises**				
企业数（个）	Number of Enterprise (unit)	149	150	133	125
#有科技活动的企业数	#Number of Enterprises with Sicentific and Technical Activities		70	66	72
从业人员年平均人数（人）	Annual Average Number of Employment (person)	392866	286793	265260	260546
工程技术人员（人）	Technical Personnel (person)		36925	39238	35304
二、科技活动情况	**Research and Experiment Development**				
（一）科技活动人员（人）	Personnel Eagaged in Scientific and Technical Activities (person)	46102	35591	29410	32754
1.全时人员	Full-time Personnel		20562	22167	22726
2.非全时人员	Part-time Personnel		15029	7243	10028
合计中：研究与试验发展人员	Among the Total Number: Personnel for Research Experimeat and Development		19796	21210	21164
（二）科技活动经费筹资总额（万元）	Total Funds for Scientific and Technical Activities (10000 yuan)	128011	179421	165715	176843
1.企业资金	Enterprise Funds	58892	102323	64824	101324
2.金融机构资金	Finance Institution Funds	4177	19025	9419	7960
3.来自政府部门的资金	Funds from Government	42891	27322	69198	45158
4.来自事业单位的资金	Funds from Enterprises Unit		764	776	1317
5.来自国外的资金	Foreign Funds				
6.其他资金	Others	22051	29986	21498	21084
（三）科技活动经费支出总额（万元）	Total Expenditures for Scientific and Technical Activitics (10000yuan)	130011	139892	154260	189077
1.内部支出（万元）	Interior Expenditure		117567	135714	168796
#劳务费	# Labor Expenses	45607	33808	44563	49144
R&D经费支出	#Research and Development Development	76399	88834	106458	108502
新产品开发经费支出	#New product Development Expenditure		84098	94754	79349
2.外部支出	Extenal Expenditure		22324	18546	20281
三、科技项目情况	**Scientific and Technical Projects**				
1.全部项目数（项）	Total Number of Projects (item)		1436	1571	1835
2.全部科技项目参加人员（人）	Total Number Participating in Scientific and Technical Projects (person)		23832	15471	16625
3.全部科技项目经费内部支出（万元）	Total Interier Expenditures for Scientific and Technical Projects (10000yuan)		117567	129115	120527
四、专利情况	**Scientific and Technical Research Achievements**				
1.专利申请数（件）	Number of Patent Applications (item)		93	72	159
#发明专利	#Number of Invent Patent		14	13	50
2.拥有发明专利（件）	Patent Owned (item)		99	58	95

16-25 企事业单位知识产权情况

Intellectual Property Right of Enterprises and Institutions

指标名称	Name of Item	2002	2003
一、单位基本情况	**Basic facts**		
1.创造知识产权人数（人）	Number of people creating IPR(person)	49367	58253
2.知识产权管理机构数（个）	Number of IPR management units(unit)	138	143
二、科技活动情况	**Science and technology activities**		
1.科技活动人员合计（人）	People involved into activities(person)	114200	127594
2.科技活动经费支出总额（万元）	Total expenditure on activities(10000 yuan)	694474.8	809975.0
3.科技活动机构数（个）	Units involved into activities(unit)	782	786
4.科技活动项目（课题）数（项）	Number of activity projects(item)	12555	13811
三、知识产权拥有量情况	**Number of IPR**		
1.专利情况（件）	Patents(item)		
（1）累计申请专利	Accumulated patent applications	14421	16762
#发明专利	Invention patents	3585	4167
当年申请专利	Patent applictions in 2002	1702	2341
#发明专利	Invention patents	497	684
（2）累计授权专利	Accumulated patents awarded	7931	9030
#发明专利	Invention patents	2179	2481
当年授权专利	Patents awarded in 2002	1002	1099
#发明专利	Invention patents	261	286
2.商标情况	Trade marks		
（1）累计注册商标申请	Accumulated trade mark registration claimed	12406	16136
#当年注册商标申请	Trade mark registration claimed in 2002	2074	3730
（2）累计注册商标	Accumulated trade mark registrations	11537	13899
#当年注册商标	Trade mark registrations in 2002	1908	2362
3.版权情况	Copyright		
累计版权登记	Accumulated copyright registered	486	606
#当年版权登记	Copyright registered in 2002	89	120
4.计算机软件情况	Computer software		
累计计算机软件登记	Accumulated software registered	139	214
#当年计算机软件登记	Software registered in 2002	95	75
5.集成电路布图设计情况	Integrated circuit designs		
累计集成电路布图设计	Accumulated integrated circuit designs	1	2
#当年集成电路布图设计	Integrated circuit designs in 2002	1	1
四、知识产权纠纷（件）	**IPR controversy(item)**		
1.专利纠纷	Patent controversies	30	26
2.商标纠纷	Trade mark controversies	5	4
3.版权纠纷	Copyright controversies	24	30
4.计算机软件纠纷	Computer software controversies	1	
5.集成电路布图设计纠纷	Integrated circuit design controversies		

16-26 西安市高新技术产业开发区情况

Basic Statistics of Hi-Tech Development Zone of XI'AN

指　　标	Item	2000	2001	2002	2003
1.开发区企业数(个)	Number of Enterprises in Development Zone (unit)	3025	4000	4991	5828
高新技术企业数(个)	Number of High-tech Enterprises (unit)	632	717	755	894
2.年末从业人员(人)	Number of Persons Employed at year-end (person)	97738	130963	146436	209000
大专以上学历人数(人)	Population with More Than 3 Year Formal College Education (person)	49579	61010	68937	98500
从事技术开发人数（人）	Number of Persons Engaged in Technology Development(person)	17335	17979	18036	18726
3.技术开发经费筹集额（万元）	Funds for Technology Development (10 000 yuan)	164571	143900	99530	115080
4.技术开发经费支出总额（万元）	Expenditures on Technology Development (10 000 yuan)	134285	105000	83958	94909
研究与发展支出（万元）	Expenditures on Research and Development (10 000 yuan)	16109	36914	30267	44212
5.利润总额（万元）	Total Profits (10 000 yuan)	158360	162500	213933	253572
6.上缴税费总额（万元）	Sum of tax (10000yuan)	107454	149800	181227	270066
7.出口创汇总额（千美元）	Foreign Exchange Earnings of Exports (USD 1000)	104079	175000	209850	334000

注：此表数据来源于西安市高新技术开发区。

Date on this bable is from Hi-Tech Development Zone of XI'AN.

16-27 高新区发展规模(2003年)

Development Status of Hi-Tech Zone（2003）

指标	Item	合计 Total	政策区 Zone	新建区 Newlyconstructed Zone
累计已开发面积（平方公里）	Accumulated Areas Developed (sq.km)	34.32	19.15	15.17
高新区工商注册（个）	Registered Enterprises in Hi-tech Zones (unit)	5828	2000	3828
#工业型技术开发技术服务型企业数（个）	#Number of industrial technology developing enterprises (nuit)	3015	815	2200
#三资企业数（个）	#Enterprises of Joiut Venture,Cooperation and Foreign-funded (unit)	252	90	162
已认定的高新技术企业数（个）	Hi-tech Enterprises Designated (unit)	894	300	594

注：此表数据来源于西安市高新技术开发区。

Date on this bable is from Hi-Tech Development Zone of XI'AN.

16-28 高新区建设与集资情况

Capital Construction and Funds-Raising of Hi-Tech Development Zone

指标	Item	2002	2003
一、基建投资	**Investment on Capital Construction**		
本年基建投资（千元）	Investment on Capital Construction of 2002 (1 000yuan)	3754600	6517400
1.生产业务用房（千元）	#Building for Production	2030401	3258092
2.住　宅（千元）	Residential Buildings (1 000 yuan)	1099779	1685220
3.公用设施（千元）	Public Installations (1 000 yuan)	468000	674088
4.基础设施（千元）	Fundamental Facilities (1 000yuan)	156420	400000
5.征地拆迁（千元）	Resettlement (1 000yuan)		500000
二、开发面积	**Area Developed**		
新建区累计开发土地面积（平方公里）	Accumulated Area Developed in Newly Constructed Zone (sq.km)	15.70	15.17
#当年新开发土地面积（平方公里）	#Area Developed in 2002 (sq.km)	4.30	
累计竣工建筑面积（平方米）	Accumulated Floor Space Completed (sq.m)	5688000	7502674
#当年竣工建筑面积（平方米）	#Floor Space Completed in 2002 (sq.m)	1176700	1876732
三、当年内资金筹集情况	**Funds Raised in 2002**		
当年内资金筹集总额（千元）	Total Funds Raised in 2002 (1 000yuan)	6366600	8047523
#政府拨款（千元）	Allocations from the Government (1 000yuan)	158860	173070
贷　款（千元）	Loans (1 000yuan)	3754600	1909453
四、吸引外资	**Foreign Investment**		
年末累计境外客商协议投资额（千美元）	Contracted Foreign Investment Accumulated at Year-end (USD 1 000)	1170429	1467889
年末累计境外客商实际投资额（千美元）	Actual Foreign Investment Accumulated at Year-end (USD 1 000)	464848	570808
#当年实际投资额（千美元）	#Actual Investmen in 2002 (USD 1 000)	237945	105960

注：此表数据来源于西安市高新技术开发区。

Date on this bable is from Hi-Tech Development Zone of XI'AN.

主要统计指标解释

普通高等学校 指按照国家规定的设置标准和审批程序批准举办，通过国家统一招生考试，招收高中毕业生为主要培养对象，实施高等教育的全日制大学、独立设置的学院和高等专科学校、短期职业大学。

成人高等学校 指按照国家有关规定审批，招收通过全国成人高教统一招生考试的具有高中毕业或同等学历的在职从业人员，利用脱产、半脱产、业余或函授等多种形式对其实施高等学历教育，培养高等教育专科或本科毕业水平的专门人才，修业年限、课程设置和总学时数均按高等学历教育要求付诸实施的学校。包括广播电视大学、职工高等学校、农民高等学校、管理干部学院、教育学院、独立设置的函授学院等。

小学学龄儿童入学率 指调查范围内已入小学学习的学龄儿童占校内外学龄儿童总数（包括弱智儿童，不包括盲聋哑儿童）的比重。计算公式为:

小学学龄儿童入学率＝已入学的小学学龄儿童数/校内外小学学龄儿童总数*100%

科技活动 指在自然科学、农业科学、医药科学、工程与技术科学、人文与社会科学领域（简称科学技术领域）中，与科技知识的产生、发展、传播和应用密切相关的有组织的活动。可分为研究与试验发展（R&D）、研究与试验发展成果应用及相关的科技服务三类活动。

科技活动人员 指直接从事科技活动、以及专门从事科技活动管理和为科技活动提供直接服务的人员。累计从事科技活动的实际工作时间占全年制度工作时间10%及以上的人员。（1）直接从事科技活动的人员包括:在独立核算的科学研究与技术开发机构、高等学校、各类企业及其他事业单位内设的研究室、实验室、技术开发中心及中试车间（基地）等机构中从事科技活动的研究人员、工程技术人员、技术工人及其它人员;虽不在上述机构工作，但编入科技活动项目（课题）组的人员;科技信息与文献机构中的专业技术人员;从事论文设计的研究生等。（2）专门从事科技活动管理和为科技活动提供直接服务的人员包括:独立核算的科学研究与技术开发机构、科技信息与文献机构、高等学校、各类企业及其他事业单位主管科技工作的负责人，专门从事科技活动的计划、行政、人事、财务、物资供应、设备维护、图书资料管理等工作的各类人员，但不包括保卫、医疗保健人员、司机、食堂人员、茶炉工、水暖工、清洁工等为科技活动提供间接服务的人员。

科学家与工程师 指科技活动人员中具有高、中级技术职称（职务）的人员和不具有高、中级技术职称（职务）的大学本科及以上学历人员。

研究与试验发展（R&D） 指在科学技术领域，为增加知识总量、以及运用这些知识去创造新的应用而进行的系统的创造性的活动，包括基础研究、应用研究、试验发展三类活动。

基础研究 指为了获得关于现象和可观察事实的基本原理的新知识（揭示客观事物的本质、运动规律，获得新发现、新学说）而进行的实验性或理论性研究，它不以任何专门或特定的应用或使用为目的。其成果以科学论文和科学著作为主要形式。

应用研究 指为获得新知识而进行的创造性研究，主要针对某一特定的目的或目标。应用研究是为了确定基础研究成果可能的用途，或是为达到预定的目标探索应采取的新方法（原理性）或新途径。其成果形式以科学论文、专著、原理性模型或发明专利为主。

试验发展 指利用从基础研究、应用研究和实际经验所获得的现有知识，为产生新的产品、材料和装置，建立新的工艺、系统和服务，以及对已产生和建立的上述各项作实质性的改进而进行的系统性工作。其成果形式主要是专利、专有技术、具有新产品基本特征的产品原型或具有新装置基本特征的原始样机等。在社会科学领域，试验发展是指把通过基础研究、应用研究获得的知识转变成可以实施的计划（包括为进行检验和评估实施示范项目）的过程。人文科学领域没有对应的试验发展活动。

研究与试验发展人员 指参与研究与试验发展项目研究、管理和辅助工作的人员，包括项目（课题）组人员，企业科技行政管理人员和直接为项目（课题）活动提供服务的辅助人员。

研究与试验发展人员全时当量 指全时人员数加非全时人员按工作量折算为全时人员数的总和。例如:有两个全时人员和三个非全时人员（工作时间分别为20%、30%和70%），则全时当量为2+0.2+0.3+0.7=3.2人年。

专业技术人员 指从事专业技术工作和专业技术管理工作的人员，即企事业单位中已经聘任专业技术职务从事专业技术工作和专业技术管理工作的人员，以及未聘任专业技术职务，现在专业技术岗位上工作的人员。包括工程技术人员、农业技术人员、科学研究人员、卫生技术人员、教学人员、经济人员、会计人员、统计人员、翻译人员、图书资料、档案、文博人员、新闻出版人员、律师、公证人员、广播电视播音人员、工艺美术人员、体育人员、艺术人员及企业政治思想工作人员，共十七个专业技术职务类别。

科技活动经费筹集 指从各种渠道筹集到的计划用于科技活动的经费，包括政府资金、企业资金、事业单位资金、金融机构贷款、国外资金和其他资金等。

政府资金 指从各级政府部门获得的计划用于科技活动的经费，包括科学事业费、科技三项费、科研基建费、科学基金、教育等部门事业费中计划用于科技活动的经费以及政府部门预算外资金中计划用于科技活动的经费等。

企业资金 指从自有资金中提取或接受其他企业委托的、科研院所和高校等事业单位接受企业委托获得的，计划用于科研和技术开发的经费。不包括来自政府、金融机构及国外的计划用于科技活动的资金。

金融机构贷款 指从各类金融机构获得的用于科技活动的贷款。

科技活动经费内部支出 指报告年内用于科技活动的实际支出包括劳务费、科研业务费、科研管理费，非基建投资购建的固定资产、科研基建支出以及其他用于科技活动的支出。不包括生产性活动支出、归还贷款支出及转拨外单位支出。

劳务费 指以货币或实物形式直接或间接支付给从事科技活动人员的劳动报酬及各种费用。包括各种形式的工资、津贴、奖金、奖金、福利、离退休人员费用、人民助学金等。

固定资产购建费 指报告年内使用非基建投资购建的固定资产和用于科研基建投资的实际支出额，即固定资产实际支出和科研基建投资实际完成额之和。固定资产是指长期使用而不改变原有实物形态的主要物资设备、图书资料、实验材料和标本以及其他设备和家具、房屋、建筑物。

新产品 指采用新技术原理、新设计构思研制、生产的全新产品，或在结构、材质、工艺等某一方面比原有产品有明显改进，从而显著提高了产品性能或扩大了使用功能的产品。既包括政府有关部门认定并在有效期内的新产品，也包括企业自行研制开发，未经政府有关部门认定，从投产之日起一年之内的新产品。

专利 是专利权的简称，是对发明人的发明创造经审查合格后，由专利局依据专利法授予发明人和设计人对该项发明创造享有的专有权。包括发明、实用新型和外观设计。

发明 指对产品、方法或者其改进所提出的新的技术方案。

实用新型 指对产品的形状、构造或者其结合所提出的适于实用的新的技术方案。

外观设计 指对产品的形状、图案、色彩或者其结合所作出的富有美感并适于工业上应用的新设计。

Explanatory Notes on Main Statistical Indicators

Regular Institutions of Higher Learning refer to educational establishments set up according to the government evaluation and approval procedures, enrolling graduates from senior secondary schools and providing higher education courses and training for senior professionals. They include full-time universities, colleges, high professional schools and short-term professional universities.

Institutions of Higher Learning for Adults refer to educational establishments, set up in line with relevant rules approved by the government, enrolling staff and workers with senior secondary school or equivalent education ,and providing higher education courses in many forms of full time, part time, spare time, or correspondence for adults. Professionals thus trained receive a qualification equivalent to graduates studying regular courses at regular universities, colleges and professional colleges. Institutions of higher learning for adults include Radio and TV universities, schools of high education for staff and workers and peasants, colleges for management cadres, pedagogical colleges, independent correspondence colleges.

Enrollment Rate of Primary School Age Children refers to the proportion of school age children enrolled at schools to the total number of school age children both in and outside schools (including retarded children ,but excluding blind, deaf and mute children). The formula is:

Enrollment Rate of Primary School-age Children = (Total Primary School-age Children at Schools) (Total Primary School age Children Both at and Outside Schools) 100%

Scientific and Technological Activities (S&T Activities) refer to organized activities which are closely related with the creation, development, dissemination and application of the scientific and technical knowledge in the fields of natural sciences, agricultural science, medical science, engineering and technological science, humanities and social sciences (referred to as scientific and technological fields). S&T activities can be classified in to 3 categories: research and development (R&D) activities, application of R&D results, and related S&T services.

Personnel Engaged in S&T Activities refer to personnel directly engaged in S&T activities, in the management of S&T activities, and in providing direct service to S&T activities, who spend over 10% of the total working hours in a year in S&T activities. (1) Personnel directly engaged in S&T activities include researchers, engineers, technicians and other related personnel engaged in S&T activities in independent-accounting R&D institutions, institutions of higher learning, and in research institutes, laboratories, technology development centers and central experiment workshops under enterprises and institutions. Also included are people working in S&T research project teams, professional and technical personnel working in S&T information archiving institutes, and graduate students working on the design of their thesis. (2) Personnel engaged in the management of S&T activities and in providing direct service to S&T activities include senior management people responsible for S&T activities in independent-accounting R&D institutions, S&T information archiving institutes, institutions of higher learning, and in enterprises and institutions where S&T activities are undertaken. Also included are people responsible for the planning, administration, personnel management, financial management, logistics supply, equipment maintenance, information and library management that are related with S&T activities. People providing indirect services are excluded, such as security, medical service, drivers, plumbers, cleaners and those providing catering and related service.

Scientists and Engineers refer to persons engaged in S&T activities who have obtained titles of senior and middle level professional positions, and those without such position but have completed university or higher education.

Research and Development (R&D) refers to systematic and creative activities in the field of science and technology aiming at increasing the knowledge and using the knowledge for new application. R&D includes 3 categories of activities: basic research, applied research and experiments and development.

Basic Research refers to empirical or theoretical research aiming at obtaining new knowledge on the fundamental principles of phenomena of observable facts to reveal the nature and law of movement of objects and to acquire new discoveries or new theories. Basic research takes no specific or designated application as the aim of the research. Results of basic research are mainly released or disseminated in the form of scientific papers or monographs.

Applied research refers to creative research aimingat obtaining new knowledge on a specific objective or target. Purpose of the applied research is to identify the possible use of results from basic research, or to explore new (fundamental) methods or new approaches. Results of applied research are expressed in the form of scientific papers, monographs, fundamental models or invention patents.

Experiments and Development refer to systematic activities aiming at using the knowledge from basic and applied researches or from practical experience to develop new products, materials and equipment, to establish new production process, systems and services, or to make substantial improvement on the existing products, process or services. Results of experiment and development activities are embodied in patents, exclusive technology, monotype of new products or equipment. In social sciences, experiment and development activities refer to the process of converting the knowledge from basic or applied researches into feasible programmes (including conduct of demonstration projects for assessment and evaluation). There is no experiment and development activities in the science of humanities.

R&D Personnel refer to persons engaged in research, management and supporting activities of R&D, including persons in the project teams, persons engaged in the management of S&T activities of enterprises and supporting staff providing direct service to the research projects.

Full-time Equivalent of R&D Personnel refers to the sum of the full-time persons and the full-time equivalent of part-time persons converted by workload. For instance, if there are 2 full-time persons and 3 part-time workers (20%, 30% and 70% of working hours respectively on R&D activities), the full-time equivalent is 2+0.2+0.3+0.7=3.2 person-years.

Professional and Technical Personnel refer to person engaged in professional and technical work or in the management of professional and technical activities, i.e., people with professional or technical positions who are engaged in professional and technical work or in the management of professional and technical activities, and people without professional or technical positions but are working on professional or technical posts. They include professionals and technicians working in 17 categories of technical occupations including engineering, agriculture, scientific researches, medical service, teaching, economic research and application, accounting, statistics, translation, libraries, archives, cultural and museum service, journalism and publication, lawyers, notarization service, radio and television broadcasting, handicraft and fine arts, sports, performing art, and political workers in enterprises.

Funding for S&T Activities refers to funds obtained from various sources for S&T activities, including government funds, self-raised funds by enterprises, self-raised funds by institutions, loans from financial institutions, foreign funds and other funds.

Government Funds refer to funds obtained from government agencies at all levels to be used for S&T activities, including fund for scientific undertakings, 3 kinds of fund for S&T activities, fund for capital construction for scientific researches, science fund, funds from education expenditures by education departments for S&T activities, and extra-budget fund from government agencies for S&T activities.

Self-raised Funds by Enterprises refers to self-raised funds by enterprises from their own expenditure or from other enterprises and funds received by universities or research institutions from enterprises for scientific research or technical development projects. Excluded in this category are funds from government agencies, financial institutions or from foreign institutions.

Loans from Financial Institutions refer to loans from various financial institutions for S&T activities.

Internal Expenditures on S&T activities refer to the actual expenditures on S&T activities during the reference year, including service fees, expenditure on research activities, expenditure on research management, purchase or construction of fixed assets not included in the investment for capital construction, expenditure on capital construction for scientific researches, and other expenditures on S&T activities. Not included are expenditure on production activities, repayment of loans and transfer expenditure.

Service Fees refer to direct or indirect payment, in cash or in kind, made to personnel engaged in S&T activities as remuneration and other fees. They include, in various forms, salaries, subsidies, bonus, benefits, retirement pension, stipend, etc.

Purchase or Construction of Fixed Assets refers to the fixed assets purchased or constructed using funds other than the investment in capital construction, and the actual expenditure on capital construction for scientific researches. In other words, it is the sum of the actual expenditure on fixed assets and the accomplished investment in capital construction for scientific researches. Fixed assets refer to main materials and equipment, literatures and documents in libraries, materials for experiments, specimen, instruments, furniture, buildingsand constructions that can be used for a long time without changing the form and shape of those articles or constructions.

New Products refer to new products produced with new technology and new design, or products that representnoticeable improvement in terms of structure, material, or production process so as to improve significantly the character or function of the older versions. They include new products certified by relevant government agencies within the period of certification, as well as new products designed and produced by enterprises within a year without certification by government agencies.

Patent is an abbreviation for the patent right and refers to the exclusive right of ownership by the inventors or designers for the creation or inventions, given from the patent offices after due process of assessment and approval in accordance with the Patent Law. Patents are granted for inventions, utility models and designs.

Inventions refer to the new technical proposals to the products or methods or their modifications.

Utility Models refer to the practical and new technical proposals on the shape and structure of the product or the combination of both.

Designs refer to the aesthetics and industrially applicable new designs for the shape, pattern and color of the product, or their combinations.

十七、文化、体育、卫生、社会福利和其他

CULTURE,SPORTS,PUBLIC HEALTH,SOCIAL WELFARE INSTITUTIONS AND OTHER SOCIAL ACTIVITIES

简　要　说　明
Brief Introduction

本章资料主要包括文化、卫生、民政、劳动保障、体育、计划生育、共青团、妇联以及公、检、法等内容。由市统计局人口与社会科技处和综合处根据有关部门资料整理提供。

Data in this chapter consists of primarily data of culture, sanitation, civil administration, labor ensure, physical education, family planning, Communist Youth League, the Women's Federation, public security organs, procuratorial organs and people's court, compiled and provided by Population and Employment Division and Integration Division of Xi'an Municipal Government, according to data from Xi'an Municipal Government Department concerned.

17-1　文化事业机构和人数(2003年)

Number of Institutions and Personnel in Culture and Art（2003）

项　目	Item	机 构(个) Institutions (unit)	人员数（人） Number of Personnel (person)
一、电影事业	**Career of Film**		
制片厂	Studio	1	
发行放映管理机构	Number of Film Projection and Publication Administrating Institutions	1	
电影放映单位	Unit of Film shows	588	
#电影院	#Cinema	26	
影剧院	Theaters	13	
放映队	Film Projection Team	393	
二、艺术事业	**Art**	**58**	**3178**
表演团体	Performance Troupes	22	2736
表演场所	Artcenters	24	321
三、图书馆事业	**Libraries**	**14**	**333**
四、群众文化事业	**Mass Culture**	**191**	**889**
#文化馆	#Cultural Centers	13	210
文化站	Culture Stations	176	558
五、教育事业	**Educations**	**5**	**350**

17-2　文化事业发展情况（2003年)

Basic Statistics on Culture Development(2003)

指　标	Item	2002	2003
电影放映场数 (千场)	Number of Film shows (1 000 shows)	43	34
观众人数(千人次)	Number of Spectators (1 000 person-times)	6785	4595
艺术表演团体演出场次(国内)(千场)	Number of Art Performance Troupes Performers(1 000 shows)	5	3
观众人数(千人次)	Number of Spectators (1 000 person-times)	10498	8560
图书馆藏书数(千册)	Number of Collections in libraries(1 000 volumes)	3242	3350
书刊文献外借人次(千人次)	Books, Journals and Documents Borrowing (1 000 Person-times)	294	801
书刊文献外借册次(千册)	Books, Journals and Documents Borrowing (1 000 Volume-time)	647	455

17-3 群众艺术馆、文化馆(站)活动情况

Basic Statistics on Activities of Mass Art Centers and Cultural Centers

指　　标	Item	2002	2003
机构数(个)	Number of Insititutions (unit)	185	191
举办展览个数(个)	Number of Exhibitions (unit)	403	370
组织文艺活动次数(次)	Art Performances and Story-telling Sessions (times)	1199	1035
举办训练班班次(个)	Number of Training Courses (unit)	698	925
举办训练班结业人次(千人次)	Number of Persons Completing Courses (1 000 persons-time)	42	27
藏　　书(千册)	Collections (1 000 volumes)	206	267
本年收入(千元)	Income of this year (1 000 yuan)	10706	10955
本年支出(千元)	Expenditure of this year (1 000 yuan)	10643	10926

17-4 文物保护业基本情况(2003年)

Basic Statistics on Cultural Relics Protection(2003)

指 标	Item	机构（个） Insititution (unit)	人员（个） Personnel (unit)	文物藏品 实际数量（件） Factual Number of Collections(piece)	一级品 Grade One	参观人员（千人次） Number of Visitors (1000 person-times)
总 计	**Total**	**49**	**2412**	**628944**	**2808**	**3311**
文物保护管理机构	Protection and Management Agencies	27	711	15373	29	1103
其他文物机构	Other Agencies	2	48			
博物馆	Museums	14	1318	471223	2526	2208
文物商店	Cultural Relics Agencies	1	61			
文物科研机构	Scientific Research of Historical Relics Preservation	4	274	142348	253	

17–5 广播电台及节目制作情况

Basic Statistics of Broadcasting Stations and Program Production

指　标	Item	2000	2001	2002	2003
省、地广播电台(座)	Broadcasting Stations at the Province and District Level (set)	2	2	2	2
县级广播电视台(座)	Number of Wire Broadcast Stations and TV Relaying Stations (set)	4	2	6	6
中短波、调频发射台及转播台(座)	Medium/Short Wave and FM Broadcast Transmission Stations and Relaying Stations (set)	234	237	266	280
进广播的乡(个)	Townships Covered by Broadcasting System(unit)	195	168	116	116
进电视的乡(个)	Townships with TV Program Available(unit)	195	169	116	116
进广播的村(个)	Villages with TV Program Available(unit)	3150	3146	3146	3146
进电视的村(个)	Villages with TV Program Available(unit)	3156	3165	3164	3164
节目(套)	Number of Programs (set)	13	13	13	14
平均每日播出时间(时:分)	Brocasting Hours per Day (hour:minute)	182:15	182:20	188:25	387:56
广播人口覆盖率(%)	Listener Rating (%)	98:69	98:75	98:79	98:85
制作广播节目(时:分)	Prduction of Broadcasting (hour:minute)	43729:00	42704:00	52181:00	72796:00
#新闻节目(时:分)	#News Programs (hour:minute)	4226:00	3765:00	4414:00	4862:00
专题节目(时:分)	Special Subject Programs (hour:minute)	10495:00	6988:00	12090:00	18644:00
教育节目(时:分)	Educational Programs (hour:minute)	905:00	1200:00	1704:00	2334:00
文艺节目(时:分)	Entertainment Programs (hour:minute)	13747:00	14402:00	16912:00	26413:00
服务节目(时:分)	Service Programs (hour:minute)	10617:00	7632:00	9654:00	14083:00

注:地、市以上级称广播电台，县级称广播电视台，故从1998年起资料分组。

Note:Data has been grouped from year of 1998,as we call broadcasting station at the district and city level,and broadcaststations and TV relaying stations at the County level.

17–6 电视台及节目制作情况

Basic Statistics of TV Stations and Production of TV Program

指　标	Item	2000	2001	2002	2003
电视台(座)	Number of Televisions Stations (set)	2	2	2	2
发射台及转播台(座)	Number of Televisions Transmissions Stations and Relaying Stations (set)	237	236	297	297
无线电视节目(套)	Programs Production of Non-cable Televisions Stations (set)	6	6	6	6
有线电视节目(套)	Programs Production of cable Televisions Stations (set)	-	8	8	8
平均每周播出时间 (时:分)	Average Brocasting Hours per Week (hour:minute)	522:42	1370:00	1420:30	1537:35
电视人口覆盖率(%)	Viewer Rating (%)	95:08	96.36	96.7	97.07
卫星电视地面站(座)	Earth Stations of Satellite TV（2002）	148	1002	1122	1319
制作电视节目 (时:分)	Prduction of TV Programs (hour:minute)	11871:00	28046:00	27339:00	32510:00
#新闻节目 (时:分)	#News Programs (hour:minute)	1508:00	2982:00	3311:00	4038:00
专题节目 (时:分)	Special Subject Programs (hour:minute)	1478:00	4666:00	4509:00	5660:00
教育节目 (时:分)	Educational Programs (hour:minute)	920:00	594:00	683:00	776:00
文艺节目 (时:分)	Entertainment Programs (hour:minute)	1945:00	4385:00	4613:00	4969:00
服务节目 (时:分)	Service Programs (hour:minute)	897:00	2717:00	3048:00	4093:00
有线电视用户(万户)	User of cable Televisions Stations (10 000 households)	82.09	83.12	83.3	87.73

注:有线电视并入无线电视,2001年起数据含有线及无线电视节目。

Cable and Non-cable TV Program has been combined. The datd contains both cable and Non-cable TV programs from 2001.

17–7 各级体育局及各直属单位职工人数(市属)(2003年)

Number of Staff and Workers in Sports Commissions at All Levels and Their Affiliated Units(Under Municipality)（2003）

单位：人 (person)

指　标	Item	合计 Total	公务员 Public Official	专职教练员 Full-time Coaches	运动员 Athletes	医务人员 Medical Personnel	文化教师 Full-time Teachers	管理人员 Manager	其他人员 Other Personnel
总　计	**Total**	**624**	**74**	**103**	**28**	**6**	**37**	**219**	**157**
体育行政机关	P.E. administration organ	79	74					1	4
体育运动学校	Sports school	108		26	17	3	16	29	17
业余体校	Spare-time P.E. school	236		64	11	1	21	79	60
体育场馆	Gymnasium	186		13		2		98	73
其他事业单位	Other institutions	15						12	3

17–8 《国家体育锻炼标准》施行情况(市属)

Practice of 《State Physical Training Standards》(Under Municipality)

单位：人、所 (person、unit)

指　标	Items	2002	2003
学校总数	Total Number of Schools	2682	2533
在校学生总数	Total Student Enrollment	1300872	1276215
施行锻炼标准学校数	Number of Schools Practicing Physical Traiming Standard	2624	2517
施行锻炼标准学校的学生人数	Studeat Number of Schools Practicing Physical Training Standard	1016937	
实际参加达标活动的学生人数	Number of Students Actually Taking Part in the Activity	913709	979614
达标人数	Number of Students up to the Standards	911433	880599
#及格级	#Pass	521167	496133
良好级	Good	270905	255772
优秀级	Excellent	119361	128694

17-9　少年儿童分项业余体校情况(市属)(2003年)

Basic Statistics of Youth Part-time Physical Training School（2003）

单位：人　　　　　　　　　　　　　　　　　　　　　　　　　　(person)

指　标	Items	2003
一、在读学生数	**Student Enrollment**	
总　计	**Total**	**2777**
田　径	Track and Field	623
游　泳	Swimming	170
体　操	Gymnastics	41
举　重	Weightlifting	103
国际式摔跤	Wrestling	25
柔　道	Judo	75
射　击	Shooting	385
射　箭	Archery	85
足　球	Football	331
蓝　球	Basketball	280
排　球	Volleyball	83
乒乓球	Table Tennis	200
拳　击	Box	15
武　术	Wu Shu	307
跆拳道	Kickboxing	54
二、职工数	**Number of Staff and Workers**	**236**

17-10 卫生机构、床位及人员数(2003年)

卫生机构名称	Name of Medical Institution	机构数(个) Number of Institutions (unit)	床位数(张) Number of Beds (unit)
总计	**Tltal**	**2495**	**33518**
一、医院	**Hospitals**	**282**	**28251**
综合医院	General Hospitals	215	22980
县医院	County Hospitals	5	982
其他医院	Other Hospitals	210	21998
中医医院	Hospitals of Chinese Medicine	36	2105
中西医结合医院	Hospitals Integrating Traditional Chinese Therapeutics with Western Therapeutics in Practice	3	144
民族医院	Nationalities Hospitals		
专科医院	Specialized Hospitals	28	3022
口腔医院	Stomatological Hospitals	5	96
眼科医院	Ophthalmological Hospitals	3	119
耳鼻喉科医院	Ear-Nose-Throat Hospitals	1	32
肿瘤医院	Tumor Hospitals	1	400
心血管病医院	Cardiovascular Hospitals		
胸科医院	Thoracic Hospitals		
血液病医院	Hematonosis Hospitals	1	30
妇产（科）医院	Gynaecological and Obstetrical Hospitals	1	20
儿童医院	Children's Hospitals	1	405
精神病医院	Mental Hospitals	3	560
传染病医院	Infections Disease Hospitals	1	292
皮肤病医院	Dermatological Hospitals		
结核病医院	Tuberculosis Hospitals	1	315
麻风病医院	Leprosarium		
职业病医院	Occupational Disease Hospitals		
骨科医院	Orthopaedics Hospitals	3	355
康复医院	Rehabilitation Hospitals	3	240

Health Institutions,Beds and Peasons(2003)

人员合计(人) Number of Medical Personnel (Person)	卫生技术人员 Total Number of Medical Technical Personnel	其他技术人员 Other Technical Personnel	管理人员 Management Personnel	工勤人员 Logistics Workers
50423	**40129**	**1122**	**4933**	**4239**
34726	**27038**	**674**	**3890**	**3124**
28970	22728	583	3128	2531
1640	1311	11	148	179
27330	21417	572	2980	2361
2726	2156	49	276	245
68	50	3	8	7
2962	2104	39	478	341
347	241	1	52	53
103	73	1	9	20
33	25	3	3	2
367	267	8	59	33
26	16	2	3	5
12	12			
759	560	12	118	69
407	287		79	41
302	184	7	68	43
319	220	1	61	37
121	87	2	10	22
64	52		8	4

17-10 卫生机构、床位及人员数(2003年)（续）

卫生机构名称	Name of Medical Institution	机构数(个) Number of Institutions (unit)	床位数(张) Number of Beds (unit)
整形外科医院	Plastic Surgery Hospitals		
美容医院	Beauty Hospitals		
其他专科医院	Other Specialized Hospitals	4	158
护理院	Nursmg Centets		
二、疗养院	**Sanitary**	**4**	**1028**
三、社区卫生服务中心	**Commuting health care service centre**		
四、卫生院	**Small hospital**	**191**	**2527**
街道卫生院	Urban Township Health Centers	25	677
乡镇卫生院	Rural Twnship Heatth Centers	166	1850
五、门诊部	**Policlinic**	**179**	**164**
六、急救中心（站）	**Emergency centre (station)**	**2**	
七、采供血机构	**Blood collect and supply institution**	**2**	
八、妇幼保健院（所、站）	**Health center for women and children (institute, station)**	**15**	**570**
九、专科疾病防治院（所、站）	**Special disease prevention and cure hospital (institute, station)**	**3**	**328**
十、疾病预防控制中心（防疫站）	**Disease prevention and control centre (epidemic prevention station)**	**19**	
十一、卫生监督所	**Hygiene supervision centre**	**2**	
十二、卫生监督检验（监测）所、站	**Hygiene supervision and verification (monitoring) institute, station**		
十三、医学科学研究机构	**Medicine science research institution**	**4**	
十四、医学在职培训机构	**Medicine incumbency training institution**	**8**	
十五、健康教育所（站、中心）	**Health education centre**	**2**	
十六、其他卫生机构	**Other hygiene institution**	**10**	**650**
十七、诊所	**Clinic**	**1308**	
十八、卫生所、医务室	**Clinic**	**451**	
十九、社区卫生服务站	**Community hygiene service station**	**13**	

Health Institutions,Beds and Peasons(2003)(Continued)

人员合计(人) Number of Medical Personnel (Person)	卫生技术人员 Total Number of Medical Technical Personnel	其他技术人员 Other Technical Personnel	管理人员 Management Personnel	工勤人员 Logistics Workers
102	80	2	8	12
562	**281**	**4**	**115**	**162**
3748	**3301**	**41**	**237**	**169**
562	467	12	38	45
3186	2834	29	199	124
2329	**1945**	**38**	**174**	**172**
178	**112**		**22**	**44**
204	**137**	**7**	**23**	**37**
1092	**868**	**27**	**136**	**61**
285	**181**	**31**	**28**	**45**
1325	**1027**	**30**	**116**	**152**
189	**121**	**2**	**28**	**38**
145	**93**	**13**	**18**	**21**
588	**183**	**229**	**95**	**81**
50	**8**	**17**	**22**	**3**
312	**144**	**9**	**29**	**130**
2840	**2840**			
1765	**1765**			
85	**85**			

17-11 各区县卫生机构、床位及人员数(2003年）

Health Institutions、Beds And Peasons by Region（2003）

区县名称	Region	机构数(个) Number of Institutions (unit)	床位合计(张) Number of Beds (unit)	人员合计(人) Number of Medical Personnel (Person)	卫生技术人员（人）Total Number of Medical Technical Personnel
全　市	**Total**	**2495**	**33518**	**50423**	**40129**
新城区	Xincheng	292	5511	9233	7220
碑林区	Beilin	276	4733	8575	6546
莲湖区	Lianhu	235	4091	6180	4945
灞桥区	Baqiao	225	1462	2552	2167
未央区	Weiyang	132	1736	2491	2072
雁塔区	Yanta	321	6829	8487	6726
阎良区	Yanliang	63	1251	1441	1176
临潼区	Lintong	221	1975	2779	2095
长安区	Chang'an	329	2476	3292	2622
蓝田县	Lantian	131	719	1305	1183
周至县	Zhouzhi	84	720	1324	1077
户　县	Huxian	109	1554	2222	1822
高陵县	Gaoling	77	461	542	478

17-12　卫生机构各类人员数

Number of Employed Personnel in Health Institutions by Type of Occupation

单位：人　　(person)

指　标	Item	2000	2001	2002	2003
人员总数	**Total**	**53111**	**52607**	**50751**	**50423**
卫生技术人员	Medical Technical Personnel	41836	41686	40493	40129
执业医师	Licenced Doctors	16146	16065	14646	14496
执业助理医师	Licenced Assistant Doctors	2604	2513	2093	2178
注册护士	Certified Assistant Doctors	14344	14352	12979	13005
药剂人员	Pharmaceutical Personnel	3475	3451	3169	3101
检验人员	Laboratory Personnel	2179	2222	2112	2212
其他	Others	3088	3083	5494	5137
其他技术人员	Other Technical Personnel	855	783	1171	1122
管理人员	Managenment Personnel	5647	5636	4963	4933
工勤人员	Logistics Workers	4773	4503	4124	4239

17-13　卫生部门卫生机构各类人员数

Number of Employed Personnel in Health Institutions under Heath Department by Type of Occupation

单位：人　　(person)

指标	Item	2000	2001	2002	2003
人员总数	**Total**	**23895**	**23849**	**26421**	**25117**
卫生技术人员	Medical Technical Personnel	17687	17990	20092	19346
执业医师	Licenced Doctors	6522	6533	6863	6608
执业助理医师	Licenced Assistant Doctors	950	947	1091	1064
注册护士	Certified Assistant Doctors	6128	6312	6528	6256
药剂人员	Pharmaceutical Personnel	1404	1394	1532	1462
检验人员	Laboratory Personnel	1120	1175	1168	1236
其他	Others	1563	1629	2910	2720
其他技术人员	Other Technical Personnel	536	469	794	607
管理人员	Managenment Personnel	3045	3006	3007	2835
工勤人员	Logistics Workers	2627	2384	2528	2329

17-14 医院、卫生院诊疗人次及诊疗情况(2003年)

名 称	Name of Medical Institution	诊疗人次数 总计 Total	合计 Count
总 计	**Total**	**13170524**	**12520766**
一、医院	**Hospitals**	**11244929**	**10690479**
综合医院	General Hospitals	9415851	8921189
中医医院	Hospitals of Chinese Medicine	1100020	1071826
中西医结合医院	Hospitals Integrating Traditional Chinese	26422	23384
民族医院	Nationalities Hospitals		
专科医院	Specialized Hospitals	702636	674080
口腔医院	Stomatological Hospitals	117161	114550
眼科医院	Ophthalmological Hospitals	26715	20317
耳鼻喉科医院	Ear-Nose-Throat Hospitals	4504	4504
肿瘤医院	Tumor Hospitals	11550	11550
心血管病医院	Cardiovascular Hospitals		
胸科医院	Thoracic Hospitals		
血液病医院	Hematonosis Hospitals	61200	61200
妇产（科）医院	Gynaecological and Obstetrical Hospitals	20767	16814
儿童医院	Children's Hospitals	347666	333020
精神病医院	Mental Hospitals	42478	42466
传染病医院	Infections Disease Hospitals	4299	4299
皮肤病医院	Dermatological Hospitals		
结核病医院	Tuberculosis Hospitals	20391	20391
麻风病医院	Leprosarium		
职业病医院	Occupational Disease Hospitals		
骨科医院	Orthopaedics Hospitals	19578	19393
康复医院	Rehabilitation Hospitals	7300	7290
整形外科医院	Plastic Surgery Hospitals		
美容医院	Beauty Hospitals		
其他专科医院	Other Specialized Hospitals	19027	18286
护理院	Nursing Centers		
二、卫生院	**Health Centers**	**1925595**	**1830287**
街道卫生院	Urban Township Health Centers	360773	325566
乡镇卫生院	Rural Township Health Centers	1564822	1504721
中心卫生院	Certral Health Centers	640247	616568
乡卫生院	Township Health Centers	924575	888153

Statistics on Hospital Patients and Diagnosis in Hospital and Health Centers(2003）

Number of Hospital Patients			观察室	Observing room
其中:门、急诊人次数 Out-patients and Emergency Patients			收容病人数（人） Hospital Admissions(person)	死亡人数（人） Number of Desth (person)
门诊人次数 Number of Out-patients	急诊人次数 Number of Emergency Patients 小计 Count	内：死亡人数 Death		
11622608	**898158**	**919**	**913316**	**181**
9850556	**839923**	**883**	**836762**	**177**
8202658	718531	858	659149	175
1030893	40933	20	25317	2
20812	2572		3600	
596193	77887	5	148696	
112440	2110			
20152	165		1428	
4504				
11534	16			
61200				
16632	182		1866	
260593	72427	5	143187	
42288	178		45	
3862	437			
18264	2127		20	
19350	43			
7290			1650	
18084	202		500	
1772052	**58235**	**36**	**76554**	**4**
307902	17664	4	12924	
1464150	40571	32	63630	4
597478	19090	19	34282	3
866672	21481	13	29348	1

17-15 医院、卫生院床位及病人治疗情况(2003年)

Basic Statistics on Beds and Patients Hospital and Health Center (2003)

名 称	Name of Medical Institution	实有病床数（张） Number of Actural Beds (unit)	平均开放病床数（张） Utilization Rate of Beds (unit)	治愈率(%) Rate of Healing (%)	好转率(%) Recovering rate (%)	死亡率(%) Mortality Rate per 100 Infectious Disease Patients(%)
总计	**Total**	**30778**	**26708**			
一、医院	**Hospitals**	**28251**	**24644**	**63.37**	**32.60**	**1.40**
综合医院	General Hospitals	22980	20597	64.42	31.57	1.52
中医医院	Hospitals of Chinese Medicine	2105	1659	49.71	46.16	0.87
中西医结合医院	Hospitals Integrating Traditional Chinese Therapeutics with Western Therapeutics in Practice	144	1	85.20	14.43	
民族医院	Nationalities Hospitals					
专科医院	Specialized Hospitals	3022	2387	61.94	33.55	0.70
口腔医院	Stomatological Hospitals	96	82	91.78	6.69	
眼科医院	Ophthalmological Hospitals	119	42	98.84	1.16	
耳鼻喉科医院	Ear-Nose-Throat Hospitals	32	32	81.11	18.57	
肿瘤医院	Tumor Hospitals	400	400	55.36	33.64	2.67
心血管病医院	Cardiovascular Hospitals					
胸科医院	Thoracic Hospitals					
血液病医院	Hematonosis Hospitals	30		55.00	30.00	
妇产（科）医院	Gynaecological and Obstetrical	20	20	99.45	0.55	
儿童医院	Children's Hospitals	405	399	68.92	28.31	0.34

17-15 医院、卫生院床位及病人治疗情况(2003年)(续)

Basic Statistics on Beds and Patients
Hospital and Health Center (2003) (Continued)

名　称	Name of Medical Institution	实有病床数(张) Number of Actural Beds (unit)	平均开放病床数(张) Utilization Rate of Beds (unit)	治愈率(%) Rate of Healing (%)	好转率(%) Recovering rate (%)	死亡率(%) Mortality Rate per 100 Infectious Disease Patients(%)
精神病医院	Mental Hospitals	560	549	59.17	38.20	0.03
传染病医院	Infections Disease Hospitals	292	246	45.08	47.74	1.19
皮肤病医院	Dermatological Hospitals					
结核病医院	Tuberculosis Hospitals	315	288	6.81	88.22	1.04
麻风病医院	Leprosarium					
职业病医院	Occupational Disease Hospitals					
骨科医院	Orthopaedics Hospitals	355	97	48.74	42.62	
康复医院	Rehabilitation Hospitals	240	168	24.44	62.96	1.48
整形外科医院	Plastic Surgery Hospitals					
美容医院	Beauty Hospitals					
其他专科医院	Other Specialized Hospitals	158	63	82.02	16.53	
护理院	Nursing Centers					
二、卫生院	**Health Centers**	**2527**	**2064**	**87.22**	**11.15**	**0.10**
街道卫生院	Urban Township Health Centers	677	489	84.12	14.64	0.07
乡镇卫生院	Rural Township Health Centers	1850	1575	87.50	10.84	0.11
中心卫生院	Certral Health Centers	1121	980	84.50	13.36	0.16
乡卫生院	Township Health Centers	729	595	92.24	6.86	0.02

17-16 县（区）村卫生室基本情况(2003年)

单位：个、人

指 标	Item	总计 Total	村办 Run by Village
机构数（个）	Number of Institutions	2530	549
执业（助理）医师（人）	Licenced (Assistant) Doctors(person)	240	124
乡村医生和卫生员（人）	Country Doctors and Medics (person)	4141	1038
乡村医生数	Number of Country Doctors(person)	3909	984
#大专及以上学历	Collage Graduates and Above	290	113
中专学历及中专水平	Specialized Secondry School Graduates	2501	762
在职培训合格者	Qualified in Service Trainees	1103	99
卫生员	Medics	232	54
诊疗人次数	Person-times of Patients	5746587	1455026
孕产妇检查人次数	Person-times of Pregnant Women Examination	11854	5969
接生人数	Number of Children Delivered	2065	14
儿童疫苗接种人次数	Person-times of Vaccine Inoculation for Children	537829	108894

The Market Circumstance of the Consumer Goods Wholesales（2003）

(unit，person)

按设置/主办单位分 Grouped by Setering/Owner				按行医方式分 Grouped by Medical Mode		
乡卫生院设点 Division of Township Health Center	联合办 Collectively	私人办 Privately	其他 Others	西医为主 Mainly Western Medicine	中医为主 Mainly Chinese Medicine	中西医结合 Integrating Chinese Medicine with Western Medicine
	306	270	1405	1894	133	503
	11	8	97	131	15	94
	587	321	2195	3198	176	767
	584	274	2067	3058	164	687
	26	12	139	203	18	69
	452	241	1046	1874	100	527
	106	19	879	970	46	87
	3	47	128	140	12	80
	955337	841835	2494389	4586587	170492	989508
	326	1469	4090	9259	442	2153
	21	875	1155	1708	150	207
	50125	76270	302540	385232	25137	127460

17–17 社会福利事业单位基本情况(2003年)

Basic Statistics on Social Welfare Insititutions（2003）

指 标	Item	院数（个）Number of Homes (unit)	工作人员（人）Number of Staff (person)	床位（个）Bed (unit)	年末在院人数（人）Number of Persons Housed at the Year-end（person）
一、社会福利院情况	**Statistics on Social Welfare**	**56**	**543**	**2736**	**1627**
1.社会福利院	Social Welfare Homes	15	191	927	436
2.儿童福利院	Baby Welfare Homes	1	61	460	460
3.精神病人福利院	Psychopathy Welfare Homes	1	146	450	399
4.收养性老年福利机构	Adopting Elderly Welfare Units	39	145	899	332
城镇	Urban	12	103	674	238
农村	Rural	27	42	225	94

17–18 社会福利事业单位机构、人员数

Number of Social Welfare Institutions and Employed Persons

单位：个、人 （unit，person）

项 目	Item	2000	2001	2002	2003
一、机构	**Institutions**				
烈士纪念建筑物管理单位	Building of Commemorate Martyr Management Unit	2	2	2	2
救助类单位	Collection and Repatriation Station	8	8	8	8
殡仪服务单位	Funeral Sevice Unit	18	19	19	20
殡仪馆	Funeral Home	4	4	4	4
公墓	Cemetry	12	13	14	14
殡葬管理单位	Funeral and Interment Management Unit	2	2	1	2
二、人员	**Staff**				
烈士纪念建筑物管理单位	Building of Commemorate Martyr Management Unit	43	46	45	47
收容遣送站	Collection and Repatriation Station	99	106	114	111
殡仪服务单位	Funeral Sevice Unit	613	570	589	636
殡仪馆	Funeral Home	164	165	170	174
公墓	Cemetry	425	376	401	436
殡葬管理单位	Funeral and Interment Management Unit	24	29	18	26

17–19 福利企业单位基本情况(2003年)

Base Statistics on Socical Welfare Enterprises（2003）

单位：个、人 （unit，person）

指 标	Item	单位数 Number of Units	年末职工人数 Number of Staff and Workers at the year-end	残疾职工 Disabled Persons	残疾职工中:女性 Among Disabled Persons:Female
社会福利企业总计	**Number of Social Walfare Enterprises**	**298**	**10041**	**4601**	**1398**
国有社会福利企业	Run by Governments	11	631	218	65
集体社会福利企业	Run by Collective Units	260	8593	4019	1153
民办社会福利企业	Run by Private units	27	817	364	180

17–20 各区县优抚对象人员情况(2003年）

Statistics on Persons Enjoying Favoured Treatment by Region（2003）

单位：人 （person）

指 标	Item	全市 Total	新城区 Xincheng	碑林区 Beilin	莲湖区 Lianhu
合 计	**Total**	**16369**	**674**	**578**	**825**
1.革命伤残人员	Number of Disabled Veterans	4695	613	530	738
2.烈军属人员	Number of Family Members of Martyrs and Soldiers	1222	40	29	41
3.在乡红军老战士	Old Red Army Men in Hometown	26		3	1
4.在乡复原军人	Demobilized Soldiers in Hometown	9770	21	16	45
5.在乡退伍军人	Veterans in Hometown	656			

17–20 各区县优抚对象人员情况(2003年）（续 1）

Statistics on Persons Enjoying Favoured Treatment by Region（2003）(Continued 1)

单位：人 （person）

指 标	Item	雁塔区 Yanta	未央区 Weiyang	灞桥区 Baqiao	阎良区 Yanliang	临潼区 Lintong
合 计	**Total**	**747**	**542**	**1125**	**655**	**2276**
1.革命伤残人员	Number of Disabled Veterans	516	210	242	120	312
2.烈军属人员	Number of Family Members of Martyrs and Soldiers	38	29	68	37	179
3.在乡红军老战士	Old Red Army Men in Hometown	1			3	5
4.在乡复原军人	Demobilized Soldiers in Hometown	187	300	648	475	1617
5.在乡退伍军人	Veterans in Hometown	5	3	167	20	163

17–20 各区县优抚对象人员情况(2003年）（续 2）

Statistics on Persons Enjoying Favoured Treatment by Region（2003）(Continued 2)

单位：人 （person）

指 标	Item	长安区 Chang'an	户 县 Huxian	周至县 Zhouzhi	高陵县 Gaoling	蓝田县 Lantian
合 计	**Total**	**2419**	**1542**	**1759**	**974**	**2177**
1.革命伤残人员	Number of Disabled Veterans	414	272	289	112	251
2.烈军属人员	Number of Family Members of Martyrs and Soldiers	275	79	150	57	200
3.在乡红军老战士	Old Red Army Men in Hometown	3	3	3	1	3
4.在乡复原军人	Demobilized Soldiers in Hometown	1712	1146	1267	731	1605
5.在乡退伍军人	Veterans in Hometown	15	42	50	73	118

17-21 计划生育和婚姻情况(2003年)

Conditions of Birth Control and Marriage Registration(2003)

地区	Region	晚婚率(%) Late Marriage Rate	计划生育率(%) Family Planning Rate	综合节育率(%) Cntraceptive Rate
全市	**Total**	**67.00**	**97.82**	**91.08**
新城区	Xingcheng	94.43	99.89	86.35
碑林区	Beilin	97.87	99.91	90.94
莲湖区	Lianhu	91.17	99.89	87.87
灞桥区	Baqiao	76.27	99.89	92.65
未央区	Weiyang	50.15	99.81	91.82
雁塔区	Yanta	71.89	99.60	88.29
阎良区	Yanliang	71.69	98.91	87.47
临潼区	Lintong	78.88	96.70	93.71
长安区	Chang'an	49.79	96.70	92.36
蓝田县	Lantian	68.61	96.60	89.99
周至县	Zhouzhi	51.26	96.80	94.14
户 县	Huxian	45.42	97.00	91.34
高陵县	Gaoling	50.43	96.48	91.16

17-21 计划生育和婚姻情况(2003年)（续）

Conditions of Birth Control and Marriage Registration(2003)(Continued)

地区	Region	独生子女领证率(%) Only-child Certificate Rate	结婚对数（对） Marriages (coaple)	再婚数（人） Remarriages	离婚对数（对） Divorced (coaple)
全市	**Total**	**23.01**	**44510**	**9871**	**10670**
新城区	Xingcheng	49.87	3931	1168	1409
碑林区	Beilin	57.57	4032	998	1563
莲湖区	Lianhu	60.18	4600	1197	1698
灞桥区	Baqiao	30.40	2658	1336	657
未央区	Weiyang	42.46	3303	606	823
雁塔区	Yanta	48.83	4303	1609	1200
阎良区	Yanliang	22.60	1641	330	288
临潼区	Lintong	7.25	3233	324	791
长安区	Chang'an	7.68	6039	1121	536
蓝田县	Lantian	3.15	3248	284	543
周至县	Zhouzhi	1.59	3360	90	408
户 县	Huxian	7.97	2948	710	594
高陵县	Gaoling	7.47	1198	96	158

17-22 离休、退休、退职人员情况(2003年)

Statistics on Retired and Resigned Persons (2003)

单位：人 (person)

类别	Item	合计 Total	离休 Dimission	退休 Retire	领取定期生活费的 Number of people who quit working but enjoy regular allowance for living
总计	**Total**	**520166**	**21391**	**488997**	**9778**
一、企业	**Enterprises**	**403103**	**11835**	**383428**	**7840**
(一)内资企业	Domestic Funded Enterprises	402766	11835	383159	7772
1.国有企业	Stated-Ownde Enterprises	322966	10831	308067	4068
2.集体企业	Collective-Owned Enterprises	60015	493	56077	3445
3.其他企业	Other Enterprises	19785	511	19015	259
(二)港、澳、台商投资企业	Enterprises with Funds from HongKong, Macao and Taiwan	285		217	68
(三)外商投资企业	Enterprises with Foreign Funds	52		52	
二、事业	**Institutions**	**98832**	**6706**	**90592**	**1534**
三、机关	**Departments**	**18231**	**2850**	**14977**	**404**

17-23 离退休、退职人员保险福利费用构成情况(2003年)

Composition of Social Insurance and Welfare Fund of Retires (2003)

单位：千元 (1 000 yuan)

类别	Item	合计 Total	离休金 Pensions for Termination	退休金 Retirement Pensions
总计	**Total**	**5253027**	**419723**	**4039862**
一、企业	**Enterprises**	**3390888**	**201714**	**2706080**
(一)内资企业	Domestic Funded Enterprises	3388428	201714	2704161
1.国有企业	Stated-Owned Enterprises	2987220	188682	2355437
2.集体企业	Collective-Owned Enterprises	274113	6667	242728
3.其他企业	Other Enterprises	127095	6365	105996
(二)港、澳、台商投资企业	Enterprises with from Funds HongKong, Macao and Taiwan	1450		1355
(三)外商投资企业	Enterprises with Foreign Funds	1010		564
二、事业	**Institutions**	**1473831**	**123669**	**1076984**
三、机关	**Departments**	**388308**	**94340**	**256789**

17-23 离退休、退职人员保险福利费用构成情况(2003年)(续)

Composition of Social Insurance and Welfare Fund of Retires (2003) (Continued)

单位：千元 (1 000 yuan)

类别	Item	退职生活费 Resignation Allowances for Living Expenses	医疗卫生费 Medical Care Expenses	其他 Others
总计	**Total**	**23540**	**529852**	**240050**
一、企业	**Enterprises**	**21231**	**351449**	**110414**
(一)内资企业	Domestic Funded Enterprises	21224	351225	110104
1.国有企业	Stated-Owned Enterprises	11727	329657	101717
2.集体企业	Collective-Owned Enterprises	9019	9892	5807
3.其他企业	Other Enterprises	478	11676	2580
(二)港、澳、台商投资企业	Enterprises with from Funds HongKong, Macao and Taiwan	7	74	14
(三)外商投资企业	Enterprises with Foreign Funds		150	296
二、事业	**Institutions**	**1600**	**153196**	**118382**
三、机关	**Departments**	**709**	**25207**	**11254**

17-24 律师、公证及调解基本情况

Basic Statisics on Lawyer、Notaries and Mediation

指 标	Item	2000	2001	2002	2003
一、律师工作	**Lawyers**				
律师事务所（个）	Number of Law Offices (unit)	46	54	58	62
律师（人）	Lawyers(person)	534	529	670	766
#专职（人）	Full-time(person)	469	488	624	721
兼职（人）	Part-time(person)	65	41	46	45
聘请担任法律顾问（家）	Legal Advisors(unit)	754	751	851	949
民事案件诉讼代理（件）	Agent of Civil Cases(case)	4283	4018	4017	4555
刑事诉讼辩护及代理（件）	Defender and Agent of Criminal Cases (case)	1322	1319	1536	1670
经济案件诉讼代理（件）	Agent of Economic Cases(case)	2969	2761	2441	2714
行政案件诉讼代理（件）	Agent of Administrative Action(case)	296	282	225	256
非诉讼法律事务（件）	Agent of Non-Litigious Legal Affairs (case)	1088	1606	2202	2985
二、公证工作	**Notarization**				
公证处（个）	Number of Notary Offices(unit)	14	14	14	14
公证人员（人）	Notarial Personnel(person)	158	168	184	196
#公证员（人）	Notaries(person)	96	105	106	107
办理公证件数	Number of Notarized Documents Issued (case)	79199	71687	75798	82149
国内（件）	Domestic(case)	62060	50315	53282	60191
民事（件）	Civil(case)	24576	20060	23588	21018
经济（件）	Economics(case)	37484	30255	29694	39173
涉外（件）	Foreign-related(case)	16990	21238	22408	21790
涉港、澳、台（件）	Hong Kong 、Macao and Taiwan related (case)	149	134	108	168
三、人民调解工作	**Number of People Mediations**				
已建调委会数（个）	Number of Mediation Committees(unit)	4379	3936	3771	3850
调解人员数（人）	Number of Mediators(person)	13059	12721	13856	13576
调解纠纷数（件）	Number of Civil Disputes Mediated(case)	34212	30558	29631	28063
#调解成功数（件）	Number of Cases Successfully Mediated(case)	31574	28430	27317	25947

17-25 共青团组织情况

Basic Facts on Communist Youth League

指 标	Item	2000	2001	2002	2003
一、基层团组织(个)	**Grass-root Youth League Organisations(unit)**	**10323**	**10323**	**10053**	**8103**
二、共青团员(人)	**Youth League Members(person)**	**278165**	**295663**	**283826**	**289994**
#女团员	#Female Youth League Members	134289	152906	144697	117585
三、专职团干部(人)	**Full Time Youth League Cadre(person)**	**845**	**837**	**621**	**598**

17-26 各级妇联基本情况

Basic Statistics on Women's Federation at All Levels

单位：个 (unit)

组 织	Organizitions	2001	2002	2003
妇女联合会	Women□s Federation	233	195	196
市级	Urban Levels	1	1	1
区县	District and County Level	13	13	13
乡(街)妇联	Township/Sub-district level	219	181	182
基层妇代会	Grass-root women□s representatives Committee			
城市(社区妇联)	Urban (Women□s Federation)	415	383	454
农村(妇代会)	Rural Women□s Representatives Committee	3145	3145	3145
团体会员	Member of Societies and Committees			
女职工委员会数	Number of Employee Committee for Women	3730	4545	1000
民政部门登记注册的妇女社团	Registered Societies for Women	2	2	2

17-27 妇联工作情况

Basic Facts on Women's Federation

单位：人、个 （person，unit）

项　　目	Item	2003
一、双学双比活动	**Double learning and double competition activities**	
(一)科技培训	Scientific and technical training	
接受技术培训人数	Number of people accepting technical training	73550
获绿色证书人数	Number of people gaining Green Certificate	174
女农民技术员人数	Women-famer Technicians	**1709**
妇代会主任中农民技术员数	Number of Farmer Technicians Among the	**466**
(二)巾帼扶贫	Woman aid-the-poor project	
脱贫户数	Households lifted out of Poverty	1843
扶贫项目数	Number of Poverty Alleviation Projects	12
二、巾帼建功活动	**"Women Make Achievements"**	
(一)巾帼建功	"Women Make Achievements"	
评选巾帼建功标兵数	Number of Pacemakers	274
巾帼建功先进工作者数	Number of Advanced Workers	160
巾帼建功先进协调单位数	Number of Advanced Supporting Units	85
巾帼文明示范岗数	Model Workers	291
(二)社区妇女工作	Community women work	
妇联建立及管理的巾帼社区服务实体数	Units Providing Services for Women founded	214
三、三八红旗手	**Model of Women**	**72**
四、三八红旗集体	**Model of Women Group**	**24**
五、实施春蕾计划	**Carrying out of CHUNLEI project**	
资助女童入学或返校数	Helping Women Children Enter School or	745
社会捐资总额(万元)	Amount of Money That Social Attribates	50.69
六、来信来访处理情况	**Incoming letter and incoming visit settled**	
来信件数	Letters	381
来访人次	Visits	2787
来电咨询数	Telephones	1056
重大案件(起)	Big Cases (case)	8

17–28 交通事故情况

Statistics on Traffic Accidents

指　标	Item	2000	2001	2002	2003
次 数(起)	Number of Traffic Accidents (case)	4099	4192	4073	4688
死亡人数（人）	Number of Deaths (person)	589	566	511	545
受伤人数（人）	Number of Injuries (person)	2884	3087	3161	3008
直接财产损失（万元）	Direct Property Loss (10 000 yuan)	1116	1154	1147	1352

17–29 火灾情况

Statistics on Fires

指　标	Item	2000	2001	2002	2003
次 数（起）	Number of Fires (case)	1040	1139	1571	1539
死亡人数（人）	Number of Deaths (person)	17	5	9	10
受伤人数（人）	Number of Injures (person)	12	18	9	13
直接财产损失(万元）	Direct Property Losses (10 000 yuan)	472	298	196	261

17-30 安全生产情况

Data on safty in production

指　标	Item	2003	2003年 比2002年增长（%） 2003 increase over 2002 (%)
全市合计	**Sum of erntire city**		
起数（起）	Number of cases (cases)	6302	-0.2
死亡人数（人）	Number of deaths (person)	609	4.8
受伤人数（人）	Number of injured (person)	3055	-4.4
损失（万元）	Economic loss (10 000 Yuan)	1919.4	7.5
道路交通事故	**Road accidents**		
起数（起）	Number of cases(cases)	4688	13.1
死亡人数（人）	Number of deaths (person)	545	6.2
受伤人数（人）	Number of injured (person)	3008	-5.1
损失（万元）	Economic loss (10 000 Yuan)	1352	15.2
火灾事故	**Fire accidents**		
起数（起）	Number of cases(cases)	1539	-2.0
死亡人数（人）	Number of deaths (person)	10	11.1
受伤人数（人）	Number of injured (person)	13	44.4
损失（万元）	Economic loss (10 000 Yuan)	261	33.5
农机事故	**Farm machinery accidents**		
起数（起）	Number of cases (cases)	30	-11.8
死亡人数（人）	Number of deaths (person)	3	持平
受伤人数（人）	Number of injured (person)	14	-6.7
损失（万元）	Economic loss (10 000 Yuan)	8.4	32.3
工矿商贸事故	**Accidents in industry, mine, business and trade**		
起数（起）	Number of cases (cases)	45	-8.0
死亡人数（人）	Number of deaths (person)	51	-12.0
受伤人数（人）	Number of injured (person)	20	-4.8
损失（万元）	Economic loss (10 000 Yuan)	298	-19.9

17-31 公安局刑事案件情况

Data on criminal cases from public security bureau

指　　标	Item	2002	2003
一、案件数情况	**Data on number of cases**		
立案数（起）	Number of registered cases (cases)	35254	25876
破案数（起）	Number of cleared up cases (cases)	14505	12126
破案率（%）	Percent of cleared up cases (%)	41.1	46.9
抓获作案人员（人）	Number of criminals caught (person)	12517	9767
二、查获犯罪集团情况	**Data on hunted down and seized criminal gangs**		
查获犯罪集团个数（个）	Number of hunted down and seized criminal gangs(unit)	306	282
查获犯罪集团人数（人）	Number of members of hunted down and seized criminal gangs (person)	1226	1060
涉及案件（起）	Number of cases involved (cases)	1411	1658
三、涉枪案件情况	**Data on cases with guns involved**		
立案数（起）	Number of registered cases (cases)	71	48
破案数（起）	Number of cleared up cases (cases)	70	41
破案率（%）	Percent of cleared up cases (%)	98.6	85.4

17-32 公安局治安案件情况

Data on public order cases from public security bureau

指　　标	Item	2002	2003
案件数情况	**Data on number of cases**		
受理数（起）	Number of accepted (case)	40485	38176
查处数（起）	Number of investigated and prosecuted (case)	37540	35347
查处率（%）	Percent of investigated and prosecuted cases（%）	92.7	92.6
查处违法犯罪人数（人）	Number of investigated and prosecuted laws breakers and crime committer (person)	47827	45810

17–33 公安局分区县刑事、治安案件情况(2003年)

Data on criminal cases and public order cases from public security bureau grouped by districts and counties(2003)

单位：件 (cases)

区 县 Region	刑事案件 Criminal cases			治安案件 Public order cases		
	立案数 Number of registered cases	破案数 Number of cleared up cases	破案率 Percent of cleared up cases (%)	受理数 Number of accepted cases	查处数 Number of investigated and prosecuted cases	查处率 Percent of investigated and prosecuted cases(%)
新城区 Xincheng district	4788	2177	45.5	3207	2996	93.4
碑林区 Beilin district	4737	2206	46.6	3298	3054	92.6
莲湖区 Lianhu district	4627	1310	28.3	3119	3101	99.4
未央区 Weiyang district	1622	1052	64.9	3305	2978	90.1
雁塔区 Yanta district	2870	1681	58.6	6248	6211	99.4
灞桥区 Baqiao district	885	510	57.6	1969	1795	91.2
阎良区 Yanliang district	372	225	60.5	540	538	99.6
临潼区 Lintong district	1283	510	39.8	3896	3875	99.5
长安区 Chang'an district	1135	526	46.3	3089	2560	82.9
户　县 Huxian county	1105	499	45.2	965	897	93.0
周至县 Zhouzhi county	389	286	73.5	691	681	98.6
蓝田县 Lantian county	341	278	81.5	1149	1094	95.2
高陵县 Gaoling county	98	65	66.3	382	356	93.2

17-34 西安市人民检察院案件受理情况(2003年)

Data on acceptance of cases of Xi'an people's procuratorate(2003)

指　标	Item	受　案 Acceptance of cases
总　计	**Total**	**6401**
一、贪污贿赂案件（件）	**Cases about corruption and bribery(cases)**	**585**
二、渎职、侵权案件（件）	**Cases about misprision and tortious(cases)**	**142**
三、审查逮捕（件）	**Examination and arresting(cases)**	**2552**
决定逮捕贪污贿赂犯罪嫌疑人（人）	Suspects of corruption and bribery to be arrested(poersons)	108
决定逮捕渎职、侵权犯罪嫌疑人（人）	Suspects of misprision and tortious to be arrested(poersons)	10
批准逮捕刑事犯罪嫌疑人（人）	Suspects of criminal to be arrested (poersons)	2434
四、刑事立案监督、侦查活动监督（件）	**Supervision of acceptance of criminal cases and investigation(cases)**	**155**
五、审查起诉（件）	**Examination and prosecution (cases)**	**2967**
起诉贪污贿赂犯罪被告人（人）	Prosecution of corruption and bribery defendants(persons)	180
起诉渎职、侵权犯罪被告人（人）	Prosecution of misprision and tortious defendants(persons)	32
起诉刑事犯罪被告人（人）	Prosecution of criminal defendants（persons）	2755

17-35 西安市中级人民法院案件基本情况（2003年）

指　标	Item	陪审员参加人数（人）Number of jurors partcipating (person)	回避（件）Withdrawn (cases)	诉讼财产保全（件）Preserving of property of lawsuit (cases)	先予执行（件）Execute in advance (cases)	审委会讨论（件）Under discussing of judicial board (cases)	法律援助（件）Legal aids (of cases)
合　计	**Total**	**1564**	**3**		**4**	**742**	**67**
一、刑　事	**Criminal**	**693**				**321**	**67**
二、婚姻家庭继承	**Marriage, family and inheritance**	**437**				**32**	
三、合　同	**Contract**	**244**	**2**		**2**	**214**	
四、权属侵权及其他民事案件	**Tort and other civil cases**	**170**	**1**		**2**	**113**	
五、行　政	**Adiministration**	**19**				**26**	
六、申诉、申请再审	**Appeals, apply for retrial**	**1**				**17**	
七、司法赔偿	**Judicial indemnification**						
八、执　行	**Execution**					**19**	
合计中	Collegiating						
海事海商	Maritime affairs & business						
知识产权	Intellectual property						
一　审	First instance	1563	3		4	621	67
二　审	Second instance					1	
审判监督	Trial supervision					84	

Xi'an intermediate people's court Basic data of the law cases(2003)

合　计	Total	中级人民法院 Intermediate people's court		基层人民法院 Primary people's court		其中人民法庭 Courtroom	
结　案 Wound up cases（cases）	诉讼标的总金额（万元） Amount of lawsuit object (10 000 yuan)	结　案 Wound up cases（cases）	诉讼标的总金额（万元） Amount of lawsuit object (10 000 yuan)	结　案 Wound up cases（cases）	诉讼标的总金额（万元） Amount of lawsuit object (10 000 yuan)	结　案 Wound up cases（cases）	诉讼标的总金额（万元） Amount of lawsuit object (10 000 yuan)
49955	**944005.33**	**6959**	**704481.39**	**42996**	**239523.94**	**7766**	**7247.05**
3711	**1114.02**	**779**	**109.63**	**2932**	**1004.39**	**114**	**35.56**
10538	**4799.03**	**491**	**835.00**	**10047**	**3964.03**	**3854**	**990.71**
13789	**381044.99**	**2529**	**286985.91**	**11260**	**94059.08**	**1396**	**2289.87**
7166	**173230.44**	**1170**	**130554.94**	**5996**	**42675.50**	**2301**	**3741.34**
780		**210**		**570**		**780**	
1667		**1241**		**426**		**1667**	
18	**9.93**	**8**	**6.85**	**10**	**3.08**		
12286	**383806.92**	**531**	**285989.06**	**11755**	**97817.85**	**101**	**189.56**
73	617.28	64	490.58	9	126.70		
31506	492558.50	919	352136.81	30587	140421.69	7665	7057.49
4153	64630.80	4153	64630.80				
325	2999.19	107	1717.87	218	1281.32		

主要统计指标解释

文化事业机构 指从事专业文化工作和为专业文化工作服务的独立建制的单位。不包括这些单位另外举办独立核算的其他机构和各部门的业余文化组织。

艺术表演团体 指从事戏曲、音乐、舞蹈、杂技等专业艺术表演，有独立帐户的单位，不包括半工半艺、半农半艺和民间职业剧团。

电影放映单位 指具有放映机器设备、固定或不固定的放映场所与专职或兼职的放映技术人员，经有关部门登记批准，经常为一定的观众对象放映电影的机构。包括经批准对外开放进行营业，并与电影发行放映管理机构分帐的专用放映单位和军委系统租片单位。

艺术表演观众人数（人次） 指售票、包场演出或民族地区免费演出的艺术表演观众人次数，不包括彩排审查和内部观摩演出的观看人次数。

等级运动员人数 指经考核正式批准授予等级运动员称号的人数。运动员等级分为国际级运动健将、运动健将、一级运动员、二级运动员、三级运动员、少年级运动员。

等级裁判员人数 指经考核正式批准授予等级裁判员称号的人数。裁判员等级分为国际裁判、国家级裁判、一级裁判、二级裁判、三级裁判。

体育场 指有400米跑道（中心含足球场），有固定道牙，跑道6条以上，并有固定看台的室外田径场地。体育场按看台容纳观众人数分为:甲级25000人以上，乙级15000-25000人，丙级5000-15000人，丁级5000人以下。

体育馆 指有固定看台，可供篮球、排球、羽毛球、乒乓球、体操等项目训练比赛活动用的室内运动场地。体育馆按看台容纳观众人数分为:甲级6000人以上，乙级4000-6000人，丙级2000-4000人，丁级2000人以下。

医院 指设有固定床位，能收容病人住院并能为病人提供医疗、护理服务的医疗机构，包括县及县以上医院、农村乡卫生院和其他医院三部分。医院按所属性质不同分为卫生部门、工业及其他部门和集体经济单位三类。县及县以上医院按业务性质不同分为综合医院和专科医院。

卫生技术人员 指卫生事业机构支付工资的全部职工中现任职务为卫生技术工作的专业人员，包括中医师、西医师、中西医结合高级医师、护师、中药师、西药师、检验师、其他技师、中医士、西医士、护士、助产士、中药剂士、西药剂士、检验士、其他技士、其他中医、护理员、中药剂员、西药剂员、检验员和其他初级卫生技术人员。

医生 指经卫生部门审查合格，从事医疗工作的专业人员。分为中医医生和西医医生。包括卫生技术人员中的中医师、西医师、中西医结合高级医师、中医士、西医士和其他中医。

社会福利事业单位 指集中收养社会孤老、残、幼的机构，包括由民政部门管理的社会福利院、儿童福利院、精神病人福利院和城镇集体举办的福利院及农村集体举办的敬老院。

社会福利事业单位收养人数 包括民政部门管理和城镇、农村集体举办的社会福利事业单位中收养的老人、少年儿童、缺乏生活自理能力的残疾人员和精神病人。

社会福利企业单位 指以安置城镇有一定劳动能力的盲、聋、哑和肢体残疾人员就业为目的，享受国家减免税待遇的国有或集体企业。包括福利工厂、福利商业和服务业、假肢厂和安置农场等单位。

律师 指受聘参加法律顾问处工作，担任法律顾问、刑（民）事代理人、刑事辩护人，办理非诉讼事件、解答法律询问，代写法律事务文书等主要从事律师业务的专职法律工作者和兼职律师。

公证人员 指在国家公证机关依法办理公证事务的司法人员，包括公证员、助理公证员和在公证处工作的其他人员。

办理公证文书 指公证处在一定时期内办结的公证文书件数。公证文书按司法部规定或批准的格式制作，包括国内公证和涉外公证两部分。国内公证分为经济合同公证和民事法律关系公证两大类。

调解人员 指在人民调解委员会担负调解民间一般民事纠纷和轻微违法行为引起纠纷的工作人员，包括调解委员会的委员和调解小组的调解员。

调解民间纠纷 指调解委员会依照法律规定，根据自愿原则，用说服教育的方法调解民间发生的有关民事权利和义务的争执，促成当事双方达到协议和谅解，解决纠纷。包括婚姻家庭纠纷，财产权益纠纷等，不包括法院受理调解的民事案件数。

受理劳动争议案件数 指劳动争议仲裁委员会根据

国家有关规定，对劳动争议当事人的申请予以审查，符合受理条件而正式立案、准备处理的劳动争议案件数。

立案 指检察机关对犯罪线索进行初步调查后，认为存在职务犯罪事实并需要追究刑事责任时，依法决定作为刑事案件进行侦查的诉讼活动，是追究犯罪的开始。

离休、退休、退职人员 指正式办理了离休、退休、退职手续，并享受相应的离休、退休、退职待遇的人员。

保险福利费用 指企业、事业、机关单位在工资以外实际支付给职工和离休、退休、退职人员个人以及用于集体的劳动保险和福利费用。

Explanatory Notes on Main Statistical Indicators

Cultural Institutions refer to units which have their own organizational system and independent accounting system and specialize in or serve cultural development. They exclude other establishments run by these cultural institutions and amateur cultural groups established by various departments.

Art Troupe refers to the troupe which is engaged in drama, opera, music, dance, acrobatics or other art performance, opens independent accounts with banks and has self-supporting accounting system; excluding the troupes which are engaged partly in industrial or agricultural activities, partly in art performance and the professional troupes organized by the people.

Film Projection Units refer to units with film projection equipment, full or part time projectionists, permanent or non permanent places, approved by related administrative departments to show films regularly for certain groups of audience, including those film projection units which have been approved to give commercial shows and run business with independent accounting system as well as those film-renting units of the military system.

Number of Spectators at Art Performance refers to the number of attendants at commercial shows, completely booked shows or free shows given in minority national areas, and does not include the number of spectators at rehearsals for examination and internal shows for study.

Number of Athletes in Grades refers to the number of athletes who have been given titles through examination. The titles of athletes include international masters of sports, masters of sports, first-grade, second-grade and third-grade sportsmen and young athletes.

Number of Referees in Grades refers to the number of referees who have been given titles after examination. They are classified as international referees, national referees and referees of the first, second and third grades.

Stadiums refer to stadiums for track and field events with six lane 400-meter tracks around soccer fields, permanent track marks and permanent bleachers. Stadiums are classified according to seating capacity. They include: Class A stadiums seating 25000 people each. Class B stadiums seating 15000 to 25000 people each. Class C stadiums seating 5000 to 15000 people each, and Class D stadiums seating fewer than 5000 people.

Gymnasiums refer to indoor sports grounds with permanent seats in which basketball, volleyball. badminton, table tennis and gymnastics competitions can be held. Gymnasiums are classified according to seating capacity. They include Class A gymnasiums seating over 6000 people. Class B gymnasiums seating 4000 to 6000 people. Class C gymnasiums seating 2000 to 4000 people, and Class D gymnasiums seating fewer than 2000 people.

Hospitals refer to medical institutions with permanent hospital beds, which are able to take in patients and provide them with medical and nursing services. Hospitals are classified into three categories: hospitals at or above the county level, hospitals of rural townships, and other hospitals. According to their ownership, hospitals can be classified into three categories: hospitals under the public health departments, hospitals under industrial and other departments and collective-owned hospitals. Hospitals at or above county level are divided into comprehensive and specialized hospitals.

Medical Technical Personnel refers to all medical staff and workers employed by medical institutions, including doctors of Chinese and Western medicine, senior doctors who integrate traditional Chinese therapeutics with Western therapeutics in practice, senior nurses, pharmacists of Chinese and Western medicine, laboratory specialists, other specialists, paramedics of Chinese and Western medicine, nurses, midwives, druggists in Chinese and Western medicine, laboratory technicians, other technicians, other practitioners of Chinese medicine, nursing attendants, pharmacological workers of Chinese and Western medicine, laboratory workers, and other primary medical personnel.

Doctors refer to qualified professional medical workers approved to practice by public health departments. They are classified into doctors of Chinese medicine, doctors of Western medicine, senior doctors who integrate traditional Chinese therapeutics with Western therapeutics in practice, paramedics of Chinese medicine and Western medicine, and other specialists of Chinese medicine.

Social Welfare Institutions refer to institutions taking care of old people without children, handicapped people and orphans. They include social welfare institutions run by civil affairs departments, children welfare institutions, social welfare institutions for mental patients, and collective-owned old peoples homes in rural areas.

Number of People Taken in by Social Welfare Institutions refers to the number of old people, children, totally dependent handicapped people and mental patientsTaken in by social welfare institutions run by civil affairs departments and those run by collective units in urban and rural areas.

Social Welfare Enterprises are collective owned enterprises which employ the blind, deaf-mute, and other handicapped people who are able to work in cities and towns and enjoy exemption from state taxes, including welfare plants, welfare commercial services, artificial limb plants and farms, etc.

Lawyers are legal workers who are employed full time by legal counseling firms to act as legal advisers, agents in criminal or civil lawsuits, or defenders in criminal lawsuits, or to handle non-litigious legal affairs, to advise on matters of law or to write legal papers for others. Both full-time and part time lawyers are included.

Notary Personnel refers to judicial workers of the state notary offices handling notarization work according to law. They include notaries, assistant notaries, and other people working for notary offices.

Notarized Documents refer to the documents settled by notary offices in a year. The notary documents are drawn up in accordance with the regulations of the Ministry of Justice, including domestic documents and foreign-related documents. Domestic documents are divided into two major categories, documents on economic contracts and documents on civil legal relations.

Mediators refer to workers on peoples mediation committees responsible for mediating in civil disputes and cases of slight infraction of the law. They include members of the mediation committees and mediators of mediation groups.

Mediation of Civil Disputes refers to mediation committees work in mediating in civil disputes concerning civil rights and duties through persuasion and education in accordance with the provisions of law on a voluntary basis, so as to solve disputes by helping the parties involved come to an agreement and understanding. These disputes include divorce cases and disputes over property ownership, but exclude the civil cases to be handled by the court.

Number of Labour Dispute Cases Accepted refers to the number of cases of labour dispute submitted that, after being reviewed by the labour dispute arbitration committees in line with the relevant state regulations, are accepted and registered for treatment.

Acceptance of Case refers to the decision made by the procurators office to confirm the act of crime after initial investigation and to start legal proceedings of the case as criminal case.

Retired or Resigned Personnel refers to the persons who have formally gone through the formalities for their retirement or quitting work and enjoy the corresponding treatments.

Insurance and Welfare Funds refers to labour insurance and welfare fund paid by enterprises, organizations and institutions to their staff and workers as well as retired and resigned persons in addition to their wages and salaries.

2004 統計年鑑

十八、企业调查

ENTERPRISES INVESTIGATION

简 要 说 明
Brief Introduction

本章资料主要包括重点企业和企业集团的主要经济指标、经营情况以及各行业企业景气调查指数等，由市企业调查队提供。

Data in this chapter consists primarily of the economical data, operational data of the key enterprises and enterprise groups and prosperity survey indices of various industries, provided by Enterprise Survey Crew of Xi'an Municipal Government.

18-1 年主营业务收入亿元以上企业集团经营情况(2003年)

Operation status of Enterprise Groups with over 100 Million Yuan Annual Income of Majar Business (2003)

单位：万元 (10 000 Yuan)

指标 Item	总计 Total	农、林、牧、渔业 Agriculture, forestry, animal husbandry and fishery	制造业 Manufacturing	建筑业 Construction Industry	批发与零售业 Construction	住宿和餐饮业 Communication	房地产 Real Estate	租赁与商务服务业 Tenancy and business service
企业集团总数(个) Number of Enterprises Groups(unit)	56	1	31	3	12	1	4	4
年末资产总计 Total Assets at the Year-end	12955163	129777	7884914	2113687	826126	88472	1348980	563207
年末负债合计 Total Liabilities at the Year-end	8311316	63666	4706953	1513587	627452	59574	1018371	321713
主营业务收入 Income of Major Business	5929648	46702	3899653	561672	812037	32904	433601	143079
其他业务收入 Income of Other Business	111905	591	75152	22834	11682	0	1143	503
新产品销售收入 Income of New Product Sales	540564	0	540449	0	0	0	115	0
出口销售总额 Total Sum of Export Sales	303645	4282	248557	0	40062	0	6594	4150
利润总额 Total Sum of Profits	189836	1148	204821	5811	-47496	3208	21617	727
固定资产投资完成额 Investment of Fixed Assets	977875	19685	333912	576112	32524	0	3047	12595
研究开发费用 Expense of Development and Research	150894	182	149942	0	56	0	614	100

18-2 重点企业建立现代企业制度企业主要经济指标(2003)

Major Economic Indicators on Establishing Modern Enterprise System of Key Enterprises(2003)

单位：万元、人 (10 000 Yuan, person)

指 标	Item	2003	2002	增减(%) Increase(%)
企业个数	Number of Enterprises	60	60	□ □
年末资产总计	Total Assets at the Year -end	13133859	11285875	16.37
固定资产原价	Original Value of Fised Assets	4907091	4703200	4.34
累计折旧	Accumulated Depreciation	1662394	1523585	9.11
无形资产	Intangible asset	626607	510880	22.65
累计对外投资	Accumulated Investment to Foreign Countries	653874	514312	27.14
长期投资	Long-term investment	772082	630617	22.43
存货	Inventory	2063168	1767248	16.74
流动资产年平均余额	Annual Average Balance of Circulating Funds	6459755	5735207	12.63
年末负债合计	Total Liabilities at the Year-cnd	8646315	7358004	17.51
年末股东（所有者）权益合计	Shareholder (Creditors) Egnity at the Year-end	4487544	3927871	14.25
股本（实收资本）	Capital Stock (Total Capital Hold)	2363674	2148650	10.01
主营业务收入	Income of Major Business	6515245	5332128	22.19
#主营业务成本	Major Business Cost	4976191	4093043	21.58
新产品销售收入	Income of New Product Sales	875687	628768	39.27
出口销售总额	Total amount of exports	304911	202025	50.93
存货跌价损失和营业、#管理、财务等费用合计	Summation of Inventory Shrinkage Loss and Expenses	975653	845568	15.38
利润总额	Total Sum of Profits	350734	278481	25.95
固定资产投资额	Fixed assets investment	1041217	785978	32.47
研究开发费用	Expenses for Research and Development	94161	86838	8.43
年末从业人数	Number of Employees at the Year-end	263654	271801	-3.00
#在岗职工	Fully Employed	259804	267866	-3.01
从业人员劳动报酬	Remuneration of Employees	426876	391975	8.90
#在岗职工	Fully Employed	423717	388540	9.05
从业人员人均月工资（元）	Average Monthly Wage of Employees(Yuan)	1349	1202	12.23
#在岗职工（元）	Fully Employed(Yuan)	1359	1209	12.41

18-3 企业景气指数(2003年)

Business Climate Index(2003)

指标	Item	一季度 First Quarter	二季度 Second Quarter	三季度 Third Quarter	四季度 Forth Quarter
企业景气指数	**Business Climate Index**	**127.57**	**105.72**	**124.97**	**126.25**
按行业门类分	Grouped by Sector				
工业	Industry	129.08	121.14	130.15	127.49
建筑业	Construction	110.06	124.46	137.06	122.22
交通运输、仓储及邮政业	Transport,Storage,Post and Telecommunication	136.71	74.23	111.97	122.46
批发和零售业	Wholesale,Retail Sales and Catering Business	116.45	97.95	103.54	118.26
房地产业	Real Estate	124.11	125.28	136.21	133.58
社会服务业	Social Services	142.57	38.76	86.66	97.40
信息传输、计算机服务和软件业	Information transmission, computer service and software service	147.28	115.37	153.80	161.41
住宿和餐饮业	Accommodation and catering trade	129.56	19.16	97.46	113.66
按企业登记注册类型分	Grouped by Registration				
国有企业	State-Owned Enterprises	113.27	106.15	122.43	122.70
集体企业	Collective-Owned Enterprises	96.00	102.31	100.00	120.00
股份合作企业	Share-holding Cooperative Enterprises	115.79	100.00	121.05	127.78
联营企业	Joint Ownership Enterprises	150.00	150.00	150.00	100.00
有限责任公司	Limited Liability Corporations	137.55	114.19	126.33	125.75
股份有限公司	Share-holding Corporations Ltd.	164.08	100.93	132.42	140.79
私营企业	Private Enterprises	80.00	60.00	120.00	120.00
外商及港、澳、台投资企业	Enterprises with Foreign Investment and Investment from Hong Kong,Macao and Taiwan	130.34	95.27	120.20	126.71
按企业规模分	Grouped by Size of Enterprises				
特大型企业	Super-Large-size	155.67	131.88	149.13	145.56
大型企业	Large-size	149.40	135.36	148.68	147.86
中型企业	Medium-size	121.43	94.97	111.86	119.32
小型企业	Small-size	98.18	80.00	101.83	101.87
特殊分组	Special-Grorped				
国家重点企业	State Key Enterprises	149.94	144.57	144.19	153.17
国家试点企业集团成员	Member of Stats Experimental Enterprises Group	151.32	136.54	133.19	160.62
乡镇企业	Town\township Enterprises	128.57	114.29	100.00	85.71
上市公司	Companies with Securities listed	158.26	93.78	128.96	151.19
国有控股企业	Enterprises that State holds Majority Shares	124.62	109.65	125.42	123.46
生产总量	Total Output	96.58	113.41	132.89	123.04
盈利(亏损)变化	Profit(Loss) Change	92.08	87.35	110.18	116.65
流动资金	Circulation Funds	73.86	70.25	76.19	73.34
货款拖欠	Loan Credit Default	91.91	87.42	95.47	94.62
劳动力需求	Demand of Workforce	89.31	88.52	96.55	97.92
固定资产投资	Investment of fixed Assets	92.75	101.81	100.58	105.43

18-4 企业家信心指数(2003年)

Entrepreneur Expectation Indicator(2003)

指 标	Item	一季度 First Season	二季度 Second Season	三季度 Third Season	四季度 Fourth Season
企业家信心指数	**Entrepreneur Expectation Indicator**	**131.24**	**112.15**	**126.72**	**127.95**
按行业门类分	Grouped by Sector				
工业	Industry	131.93	125.19	131.50	133.89
建筑业	Construction	135.95	111.95	140.88	136.98
交通运输、仓储及邮政业	Transport,Storage,Post and Telecommunication	151.92	113.92	127.29	130.23
批发和零售业	Wholesale,Retail Sales and Catering Business	112.38	95.91	108.25	109.22
房地产业	Real Estate	153.11	137.73	149.25	133.20
社会服务业	Social Services	117.17	31.98	77.57	82.24
信息传输、计算机服务和软件业	Information transmission, computer service and software service	122.98	115.84	137.27	144.26
住宿和餐饮业	Accommodation and catering trade	125.74	59.45	94.01	96.79
按企业登记注册类型分	Grouped by Registration				
国有企业	State-Owned Enterprises	118.57	102.57	123.15	122.04
集体企业	Collective-Owned Enterprises	125.65	120.00	128.00	128.00
股份合作企业	Share-holding Cooperative Enterprises	78.95	89.47	94.74	100.00
联营企业	Joint Ownership Enterprises	200.00	200.00	200.00	100.00
有限责任公司	Limited Liability Corporations	140.82	118.34	122.27	126.88
股份有限公司	Share-holding Corporations Ltd.	162.43	123.45	143.61	145.20
私营企业	Private Enterprises	100.00	100.00	100.00	100.00
外商及港、澳、台投资企业	Enterprises with Foreign Investment and Investment from Hong Kong,Macao and Taiwan	134.11	104.92	125.37	128.82
按企业规模分	Grouped by Size of Enterprises				
特大型企业	Super-Large-size	149.13	131.88	149.13	139.02
大型企业	Large-size	153.19	126.03	141.16	151.56
中型企业	Medium-size	125.68	106.15	120.90	119.32
小型企业	Small-size	100.00	93.64	103.67	99.07
特殊分组	Special-Grorped				
国家重点企业	State Key Enterprises	162.14	137.44	155.53	155.53
国家试点企业集团成员	Member of Stats Experimental Enterprise Group	153.67	134.59	156.86	159.89
乡镇企业	Town\township Enterprises	128.57	114.29	114.29	114.29
上市公司	Companies with Securities listed	154.92	108.56	152.96	149.25
国有控股企业	Enterprises that State holds Majority Shares	125.88	107.62	126.15	124.80

主要统计指标解释

景气指数：是根据企业家对本企业综合生产经营情况所作的判断与预期（通常是对“良好”、“一般”、“不佳”的选择）而编制的指数，用以综合反映企业的生产经营状况。企业景气指数也称“企业综合生产经营景气指数”。

企业家信心指数：是根据企业家对企业外部市场经济环境与宏观政策的认识、看法所作的判断和预期（通常是对“乐观”、“一般”、“不乐观”的选择）而编制的指数，用以综合反映企业家对宏观经济环境的感受与信心。企业家信心指数也称“宏观经济景气指数”。

景气指数的表示方式：景气指数的表示范围在0～200之间，其含义：100为景气指数的临界值，表明景气状况变化不大；100～200为景气区间，表明景气状况趋于上升或改善，越接近于200，状况越景气；0～100为不景气区间，表明景气状况趋于下降或恶化，越接近于0，状况越不景气。

国家重点企业：是指1999年10月经国务院批准确定的520户国家重点企业。

国家试点企业集团成员：是指由国务院批准组建的国家试点企业集团的成员。

上市公司：是指所发行的股票经国务院授权的中国证券监督管理委员会批准、在境内外证券交易所（包括上海、深圳、香港、纽约、东京等证券交易所）内上市买卖其有价证券的股份有限公司。

Explanatory Notes on Main Statistical Indicators

Prosperity index of enterprise it is an index worked out according to the judgment and anticipation (normally a choice from good , ordinary , not good) of entrepreneurs made based on synthetic productive and operational situation of the enterprise. It is used to reflect synthetically the productive and operational situation of the enterprise. It is also referred to as synthetic productive and operational prosperity index of enterprise .

Confidence index of entrepreneur it is an index worked out according to the judgment and anticipation (normally a choice from optimistic , ordinary , not optimistic) of entrepreneurs made based on their understandings and views of the market and economic environment outside the enterprise and the macro policies. It is used to reflect synthetically the confidence and feelings of the entrepreneurs to the macro economic environment. It is also referred to as macro-economy prosperity index .

The way to express prosperity index the range of prosperity index is from 0 to 200; 100 is the critical value, and means prosperity situation didn't change largely; from 100 to 200 is the interval of prosperity; and from 0 to 100 is the interval of not prosperity, meaning prosperity situation is going down or worse, the closer to 0, the worse the prosperity situation.

Key enterprise of the state it refers to the 520 key enterprises of the state authorized and confirmed by State Department in Oct., 1999.

Member of state experimental unit enterprise group refers to the members of state experimental unit enterprise groups authorized and formed by State Department.

Company on the market refers to the limited companies with stock authorized by China Securities Regulatory Commission which is authorized by State Department, and their securities can be deal on the market in stock exchanges (include exchanges of Shanghai, Shenzhen, Hong Kong, New York and Tokyo) inside and outside P.R. of China.

2004

統計年鑒

十九、附　录

APPENDIX

附录1：　全国各省、市、自治区国民经济主要指标（2003年）

Appendix Ⅰ:Main Indicators Of National Economy By Province , Municipality And Autonomous Region (2003)

地 区	Region	地区生产总值（亿元）Gross Domestic Product (100 million yuan)				地区生产总值增长率（%）Gross Domestic Product Growth Rate(%)			
		合 计 Total	第一产业 Primary Industry	第二产业 Secondary Industry	第三产业 Tertiary Industry	合 计 Total	第一产业 Primary Industry	第二产业 Secondary Industry	第三产业 Tertiary Industry
北 京	Beijing	3611.94	95.30	1298.47	2218.17	10.5	3.3	11.9	10.0
天 津	Tianjin	2386.94	89.70	1212.34	1084.90	14.5	6.1	17.8	11.5
河 北	Hebei	7095.39	1064.33	3675.38	2355.68	11.6	5.9	14.2	10.0
山 西	Shanxi	2445.58	213.28	1400.12	832.18	13.2	2.7	18.4	8.6
内蒙古	Inner Mongolia	2092.86	421.86	947.89	723.11	16.3	5.0	26.9	11.0
辽 宁	Liaoning	6002.54	622.47	2852.60	2527.47	11.5	7.1	12.2	11.7
吉 林	Jilin	2521.78	488.80	1140.78	892.20	10.2	6.1	12.9	9.1
黑龙江	Heilongjiang	4433.12	513.12	2532.45	1387.55	10.3	2.5	11.9	10.1
上 海	Shanghai	6250.81	92.98	3130.72	3027.11	11.8	2.3	16.1	8.0
江 苏	Jiangsu	12451.75	1106.78	6782.25	4562.72	13.5	-0.1	17.2	11.7
浙 江	Zhejiang	9200.00	722.00	4830.00	3648.00	14.0	2.7	16.6	13.2
安 徽	Anhui	3973.20	749.10	1780.60	1443.50	9.1	-3.0	14.0	10.2
福 建	Fujian	5241.73	705.49	2495.63	2040.61	11.5	3.3	16.1	9.2
江 西	Jiangxi	2830.00	560.00	1227.00	1043.00	13.0	2.7	24.4	7.4
山 东	Shandong	12370.00	1505.00	6590.00	4275.00	13.3	5.6	16.1	11.9
河 南	Henan	7025.93	1237.00	3550.47	2238.46	10.5	-2.5	17.0	9.1
湖 北	Hubei	5395.91	792.55	2580.58	2022.78	9.3	5.0	10.2	9.7
湖 南	Hunan	4633.73	885.87	1793.71	1954.15	9.6	3.6	12.6	9.6
广 东	Guangdong	13449.93	1051.60	7048.05	5350.28	13.6	1.2	18.0	10.8
广 西	Guangxi	2733.21	628.18	1005.92	1099.11	10.2	3.9	14.6	10.0
海 南	Hainan	677.54	257.12	150.93	269.49	10.5	9.0	18.9	7.7
重 庆	Chongqing	2250.11	343.07	975.95	931.09	11.4	4.2	15.9	9.4
四 川	Sichuan	5456.32	1128.60	2266.06	2061.66	11.8	5.5	16.5	10.1
贵 州	Guizhou	1344.31	294.53	571.91	477.87	10.1	4.6	13.2	10.1
云 南	Yunnan	2458.80	498.95	1067.76	892.09	8.6	5.0	10.4	8.6
西 藏	Tibet								
陕 西	Shaanxi	2398.58	320.03	1133.56	944.99	10.9	5.1	14.8	8.5
甘 肃	Gansu	1301.06	240.00	607.62	453.44	10.1	6.0	12.2	9.4
青 海	Qinghai	390.16	47.00	184.26	158.90	12.1	3.8	16.4	9.7
宁 夏	Ningxia	384.92	55.50	191.72	137.70	12.2	2.5	18.7	8.3
新 疆	Xinjiang	1849.82	388.00	795.51	666.31	10.8	8.2	12.3	10.3

附录1：全国各省、市、自治区国民经济主要指标（2003年）（续1）

Appendix Ⅰ:Main Indicators Of National Economy By Province , Municipality And Autonomous Region (2003)(Countinued 1)

地区	Region	国有及其它固定资产投资（亿元）State-owned and other enterprises fixed assets investment(100 million yuan)	增长率（%）Growth Rate (%)	规模以上工业增加值（亿元）Value Added of Industry investment (100 million yuan)	增长率（%）Growth Rate (%)	社会消费品零售总额（亿元）Total Retail Salesof Consumer Goods investment (100 million yuan)	增长率（%）Growth Rate (%)
北京	Beijing	1986.19	18.1	970.80	12.3	1916.70	14.5
天津	Tianjin	923.64	31.3	1027.80	20.1	922.27	10.9
河北	Hebei	1619.28	39.4	1810.30	20.1	2177.90	10.7
山西	Shanxi	931.73	37.8	882.20	24.2	729.30	13.7
内蒙古	InnerMongolia	1052.36	70.2	509.70	31.5	726.76	12.6
辽宁	Liaoning	1664.89	26.5	1764.30	18.5	2330.80	12.3
吉林	Jilin	849.42	22.5	806.70	17.9	1110.30	10.1
黑龙江	Heilongjiang	1014.60	11.9	1380.20	13.6	1376.40	10.1
上海	Shanghai	2213.23	12.3	2767.10	22.0	2220.64	9.1
江苏	Jiangsu	3664.76	58.0	4670.60	22.7	3566.48	13.7
浙江	Zhejiang	3057.10	33.1	3194.00	23.7	3157.09	10.9
安徽	Anhui	1093.92	38.1	834.70	19.8	1331.25	9.8
福建	Fujian	1182.02	22.6	1461.40	23.9	1740.45	12.8
江西	Jiangxi	975.40	59.5	440.30	21.0	923.21	11.7
山东	Shandong	3564.79	55.8	4695.20	22.7	3670.13	13.9
河南	Henan	1553.95	39.2	1754.10	19.9	2426.41	10.8
湖北	Hubei	1460.77	16.0	1356.20	12.5	2358.69	10.8
湖南	Hunan	1160.24	27.9	886.50	20.7	1816.31	10.8
广东	Guangdong	3835.22	26.9	5606.30	21.9	5587.20	11.4
广西	Guangxi	717.50	29.9	436.90	17.6	1124.15	9.6
海南	Hainan	237.82	26.2	86.40	24.9	191.64	10.8
重庆	Chongqing	970.19	31.8	477.90	21.1	835.52	9.5
四川	Sichuan	1788.57	27.0	1156.00	21.0	2091.05	10.8
贵州	Guizhou	653.59	23.9	331.90	13.5	458.76	10.2
云南	Yunnan	775.64	26.6	719.70	9.1	782.46	11.0
西藏	Tibet	134.75	23.2	11.00	9.5		
陕西	Shaanxi	1007.65	34.2	664.70	16.8	795.22	9.2
甘肃	Gansu	536.18	19.5	389.80	13.0	474.60	9.5
青海	Qinghai	225.02	9.7	95.50	15.9	102.70	11.5
宁夏	Ningxia	245.89	42.0	105.10	17.5	116.49	11.0
新疆	Xinjiang	833.21	19.0	463.20	10.8	421.17	11.1

附录1：全国各省、市、自治区国民经济主要指标（2003年）（续2）

Appendix Ⅰ:Main Indicators Of National Economy By Province , Municipality And Autonomous Region (2003)(Countinued 2)

地 区	Region	进出口总值（亿美元）Total Imports and Exports (100 million USD)	增长率(%) Growth Rate (%)	出口总值（亿美元）Exports (100 million USD)	增长率(%) Growth Rate (%)	合同外商直接投资（亿美元）Contracted Foreign Businessman Direct Investment (100 million USD)	增长率（%）Growth Rate (%)	实际利用外商直接投资（亿美元）Direct Foreign Investment Actually Used(100 million USD)	增长率（%）Growth Rate (%)
北 京	Beijing	684.63	30.4	168.52	33.6	32.71	16.5	21.47	19.8
天 津	Tianjin	293.59	28.7	143.65	23.5	35.13	74.3	16.33	62.9
河 北	Hebei	89.79	34.7	59.28	29.0	19.65	53.6	11.16	35.3
山 西	Shanxi	30.84	33.4	22.66	36.4	3.48	26.7	1.34	1.1
内蒙古	Inner Mongolia	28.29	16.2	11.56	43.3				
辽 宁	Liaoning	265.61	22.2	146.31	18.3	97.02	35.0	55.83	42.6
吉 林	Jilin	61.72	66.7	21.62	22.3	7.26	26.7	3.18	0.3
黑龙江	Heilongjiang	53.29	22.5	28.74	44.7	13.95	24.2	10.29	8.9
上 海	Shanghai	1123.57	54.7	484.60	51.3	110.64	23.5	58.50	30.1
江 苏	Jiangsu	1136.70	61.7	591.40	53.7	308.07	56.6	158.02	52.4
浙 江	Zhejiang	614.22	46.4	416.03	41.5	120.50	77.5	54.49	72.4
安 徽	Anhui	59.43	42.1	30.64	24.9	10.24	15.4	3.91	4.1
福 建	Fujian	353.35	24.4	211.40	21.7	47.73	22.4	40.75	5.2
江 西	Jiangxi	25.27	49.1	15.05	43.1	23.31	52.0	16.12	48.3
山 东	Shandong	446.41	31.6	265.59	25.8	134.14	86.7	70.94	48.9
河 南	Henan	47.12	47.1	29.80	40.6	18.26	79.0	6.97	38.3
湖 北	Hubei	51.10	29.3	26.56	26.6	25.45	153.9	15.57	11.1
湖 南	Hunan	37.33	29.8	21.46	19.5	20.75	58.2	14.89	44.4
广 东	Guangdong	2836.46	28.3	1529.44	29.1	217.89	34.7	155.78	18.8
广 西	Guangxi	31.86	31.1	19.70	30.7	6.72	36.5	4.56	9.3
海 南	Hainan	22.78	22.0	8.69	6.1	2.92	26.5	5.81	13.5
重 庆	Chongqing	56.39	26.2	32.13	18.5	5.53	10.1	3.11	10.8
四 川	Sichuan	25.95	44.7	15.85	45.3	11.47	10.7	5.82	13.5
贵 州	Guizhou	9.84	42.4	5.88	33.1	1.99	5.3	0.56	52.1
云 南	Yunnan	26.68	19.8	16.77	17.3	5.44	63.3	1.68	46.0
西 藏	Tibet	1.60	22.8	1.22	49.8				
陕 西	Shaanxi	27.84	25.2	17.35	26.1	8.34	0.0	4.66	13.5
甘 肃	Gansu	13.28	51.3	8.78	59.9	2.45	121.9	0.39	-25.7
青 海	Qinghai	3.39	72.5	2.74	81.4	2.86	18.3	1.69	14.7
宁 夏	Ningxia	6.53	47.5	5.12	56.0	0.34	-59.2	0.32	44.1
新 疆	Xinjiang	47.72	77.3	25.42	94.3	1.61	4.6	0.40	-7.6

附录1： 全国各省、市、自治区国民经济主要指标（2003年）（续3）

Appendix Ⅰ:Main Indicators Of National Economy By Province , Municipality And Autonomous Region (2003)(Countinued 3)

地区 Region	地方财政一般预算收入（亿元） Local Financial Revenue of General Budgetary (100 million yuan)	增长率（%） Growth Rate (%)	城镇居民人均可支配收入（元/人） Per Capital Annual Disposable Income of urbam Househdds (yuan/person)	增长率（%） Growth Rate (%)	农村居民人均纯收入（元/人） Per Capita Net Income Residents of Rural (yuan/person)	增长率（%） Growth Rate (%)
北京 Beijing	592.54	11.0	13883	11.4	5752	6.6
天津 Tianjin	204.52	19.1	10313	10.4	4566	6.7
河北 Hebei	335.48	11.1	7239	8.4	2853	6.3
山西 Shanxi	185.95	23.4	7005	12.4	2297	6.8
内蒙古 Inner Mongolia	138.39	22.7	7013	15.9	2268	8.7
辽宁 Liaoning	446.39	11.9	7241	11.0	2934	6.7
吉林 Jilin	153.97	17.1	7005	11.9	2530	10.0
黑龙江 Heilongjiang	248.84	7.3	6679	9.5	2509	4.3
上海 Shanghai	886.14	25.0	14867	12.2	6654	6.9
江苏 Jiangsu	798.03	24.0	9262	13.2	4239	6.1
浙江 Zhejiang	706.50	24.6	13180	12.5	5389	9.1
安徽 Anhui	220.46	10.1	6778	12.4	2127	0.4
福建 Fujian	304.65	11.6	10000	8.8	3734	5.5
江西 Jiangxi	167.40	19.2	6901	8.9	2458	6.6
山东 Shandong	712.83	16.8	8400	10.3	3150	6.9
河南 Henan	337.72	13.9	6926	10.9	2236	0.9
湖北 Hubei	259.57	6.7	7322	7.9	2567	5.0
湖南 Hunan	268.53	16.2	7674	10.3	2533	5.6
广东 Guangdong	1313.32	9.4	12380	11.2	4055	3.6
广西 Guangxi	203.53	9.3	7785	6.4	2095	4.1
海南 Hainan	51.34	11.0	7259	6.4	2588	6.8
重庆 Chongqing	161.40	28.1	8094	11.8	2215	5.6
四川 Sichuan	336.33	15.4	7042	6.5	2230	5.8
贵州 Guizhou	124.49	15.0	6569	10.5	1565	5.0
云南 Yunnan	228.95	10.8	7644	5.6	1697	5.5
西藏 Tibet	8.15	11.5	8765		1562	6.8
陕西 Shaanxi	177.27	18.2	6806	7.5	1675	4.9
甘肃 Gansu	86.72	13.6	6657	8.2	1673	5.2
青海 Qinghai	24.02	13.9	6745	9.3	1794	7.5
宁夏 Ningxia	29.99	13.4	6530	7.6	2043	6.6
新疆 Xinjiang	128.23	10.3	7174	4.0	2106	13.0

附录2:　　全国重点城市主要经济指标（2003年）

Appendix Ⅱ:Main Economic Indicators in Major City (2003)

城市　　City	行政区划（个）Administrative Division(unit)		土地面积（平方公里）Area (10 000 sq.km)	年末总人口（万人）Total Population (10 000 persons)	地区生产总值（亿元）Gross Domestic Product(100 million yuan)	第一产业(亿元) Primary Industry(100 million yuan)	第二产业（亿元）Secondary Industry(100 million yuan)		第三产业（亿元）Tertiary Industry(100 million yuan)
	辖县数 Number of districts	辖区数 Number of counties						#工业（亿元）Industry(100 million yuan)	
常　州 Changzhou	2	5	4375	346	901.42	47.18	520.25	468.91	333.99
无　锡 Wuxi	2	7	4788	443	1901.22	54.02	1093.02	992.74	754.18
苏　州 Suzou	5	7	8488	591	2801.56	75.75	1771.86	1586.61	953.95
南　京 Nanjing	2	11	6582	572	1576.20	65.10	804.40	659.40	706.70
杭　州 Hangzhou	5	8	16596	643	2092.00	127.00	1081.00	935.00	884.00
石家庄 Shijiazhuang	17	6	15848	911	1377.94	188.07	664.79	585.93	525.08
唐　山 Tangshan	8	6	13472	706	1295.32	193.74	715.06	668.81	386.52
呼和浩特 Huhehaote	9	4	17224	214	406.17	37.26	174.71	128.03	194.20
包　头 Baotou	3	6	27768	238	450.19	23.74	253.37	203.60	173.08
沈　阳 Shenyang	4	9	12980	689	1603.38	84.87	758.71	681.83	759.80
鞍　山 Anshan	3	4	9252	345	801.31	55.50	438.59	389.39	307.23
抚　顺 Fushun	3	4	11272	226	314.84	24.24	184.30	168.00	106.30
长　春 Changchun	4	6	20571	718	1338.04	157.33	630.30	542.29	550.41
吉　林 Jilin	5	4	27120	432	600.10	84.63	260.86	188.75	254.61
哈尔滨 Haerbin	12	7	53068	954	1414.80	222.02	524.52	421.29	668.26
齐齐哈尔 Qiqihaer	9	7	42469	541	350.17	78.45	123.79	87.97	147.93
合　肥 Hefei	3	4	7498	457	477.78	40.81	238.33	184.78	198.64
福　州 Fuzhou	8	6	11968	605	1347.68	143.70	681.56	566.57	522.42
泉　州 Quanzhou	7	4	10866	663	1380.11	85.53	734.83	657.97	559.75
南　昌 Nanchang	4	5	7402	451	641.02	52.82	324.16	250.95	264.04
济　南 Jinan	4	6	8177	583	1365.33	103.30	599.68	494.55	662.35
淄　博 Zibo	3	5	5939	413	1003.38	49.30	611.92	538.66	392.16
郑　州 Zhengzhou	6	6	7446	661	1102.28	49.25	571.53	459.53	481.49
武　汉 Wuhan		13	8494	781	1662.40	95.13	741.80	598.80	825.47
长　沙 Changsha	4	5	11820	602	929.49	83.29	393.67	268.28	452.52
南　宁 Nanning	7	5	22293	642	502.53	95.65	148.46	103.09	258.42
海　口 Haikou		4	2305	139	228.86	20.86	76.10	53.96	131.90
成　都 Chengdu	9	10	12390	1044	1870.80	153.18	859.07	670.43	858.56
贵　阳 Guiyang	4	6	8034	345	380.92	28.81	191.94	151.62	160.17
昆　明 Kunming	9	4	21111	501	812.00	59.07	376.66	294.54	376.27
西　安 Xi'an	4	9	9983	717	941.60	50.72	415.68	309.94	475.20
兰　州 Lanzhou	3	5	13086	304	440.08	18.38	232.61	179.13	189.09
西　宁 Xining	3	4	7665	181	144.83	9.46	67.75	46.20	67.62
乌鲁木齐 Wulumuqi	1	7	12000	182	408.58	6.07	144.94	99.90	257.58
银　川 Yinchuan	3	3	9170	133	156.60	14.37	75.03	48.70	67.20
太　原 Taiyuan	4	6	6988	327	515.59	17.77	265.96	204.73	231.86

附录2：　全国重点城市主要经济指标（2003年）（续1）

Appendix Ⅱ:Main Economic Indicators in Major City (2003)(Countinued 1)

城 市	City	人均生产总值（元）Per Capita Product Gross Domestic（yuan）	地区生产总值增长率（%）Growth Rate of GDP（%）	规模以上工业总产值（亿元）Gross industrial Output Value (100 million yuan)	增长（%）Growth Rate（%）	客运量（万人）Passenger Traffic (10 000 persons)	货运量（万吨）Freight Traffic (10 000 tons)
常州	Changzhou	26149	14.5	1527.28	30.9	11413	5437
无锡	Wuxi	43155	15.4	3284.73	29.4	15877	7097
苏州	Suzou	47693	18	4976.51	43.6	24132	7520
南京	Nanjing	27307	15.9	2509.38	27.2	16800	15147
杭州	Hangzhou	32700	15	3202.52	33.4	21348	16815
石家庄	Shijiazhuang	15188	12.5	1198.15	24.1	6112	1003
唐山	Tangshan	18387	13.2	1213.92	31.0	4614	15713
呼和浩特	Huhehaote	18789	24.9	240.78	50.1	3420	4538
包头	Baotou	19089	31.5	431.78	36.7	9298	15617
沈阳	Shenyang	23271	14.2	1064.36	37.2	6612	14636
鞍山	Anshan	23226	13.1	633.68	20.5	5682	7358
抚顺	Fushun	13912	12.6	431.28	18.8	2695	4093
长春	Changchun	18705	14.2	1511.53	22.9	7064	10892
吉林	Jilin	13816	16.5	454.41	30.4	4194	5298
哈尔滨	Haerbin	14872	13.5	721.51	24.5	6458	9517
齐齐哈尔	Qiqihaer	6354	5.1	176.49	8.2	4625	4909
合肥	Hefei	10562	13.3	534.86	19.0	6034	4640
福州	Fuzhou	20520	14.1	1285.69	31.8	9553	8247
泉州	Quanzhou	18414	14	1139.80	32.1	8699	5330
南昌	Nanchang	14446	15.5	414.92	27.3	4523	3926
济南	Jinan	23658	14.5	1318.54	27.3	5810	14354
淄博	Zibo	24319	16.6	1413.70	33.0	15725	6085
郑州	Zhengzhou	15913	14.8	927.05	26.2	16042	21581
武汉	Wuhan	21460	12.1	1334.90	17.5	11882	16610
长沙	Changsha	15527	14	533.93	27.8	10609	10632
南宁	Nanning	7874	10.9	208.38	19.6	7017	5894
海口	Haikou	16730	12.8	202.56	61.3	13284	3305
成都	Chengdu	18051	13	970.10	27.6	72793	28798
贵阳	Guiyang	10962	13	356.94	18.8	18511	5318
昆明	Kunming	16308	10.3	580.96	14.3	5125	12334
西安	Xi'an	12233	13.5	638.66	18.7	11413	9392
兰州	Lanzhou	14540	11	526.67	12.9	2209	5581
西宁	Xining	7110	13.7	114.90	23.7	2788	2037
乌鲁木齐	Wulumuqi	19899	12.7	311.09	2.6	2211	12757
银川	Yinchuan	11890	14.2	146.49	19.8	2146	2127
太原	Taiyuan	15873	15.5	518.32	31.9	4003	23421

附录2: 全国重点城市主要经济指标（2003年）（续2）

Appendix Ⅱ:Main Economic Indicators in Major City (2003)(Countinued 2)

城市 City	邮政业务总量（万元）Amount of post service (10 000 Yuan)	电信业务总量（万元）Amount of telecommuni cation Service(10 000Yuan)	全社会固定资产投资完成额（亿元）Total Investment in Fixed Assets (100 million yuan)	社会消费品零售总额（亿元）Total Retail Sales of Consumer Goods (100 million yuan)	进出口总额（亿美元）Total Exports and Imports (USD 100 million)	出口（亿美元）Imports (USD 100 million)
常州 Changzhou	28615	252039	446.59	280.65	52.51	35.30
无锡 Wuxi	53462	398720	893.32	487.06	143.81	73.25
苏州 Suzou	66696	648904	1408.93	526.05	656.63	326.34
南京 Nanjing	62572	397902	954.05	600.24	147.12	76.65
杭州 Hangzhou	60735	680846	1006.74	587.52	182.38	109.55
石家庄 Shijiazhuang	42340	464557	534.98	456.61	16.93	13.52
唐山 Tangshan	22950	233442	314.86	307.38	10.31	4.48
呼和浩特 Huhehaote	16789	177429	206.00	123.00	4.90	3.64
包头 Baotou	12654	42401	237.93	139.30	5.00	3.21
沈阳 Shenyang	43803	938029	582.61	721.54	42.60	20.04
鞍山 Anshan	13237	210451	175.44	171.15	7.75	4.10
抚顺 Fushun	8507	125503	78.46	140.28	3.55	2.50
长春 Changchun	36166	320427	389.64	438.32	52.18	15.52
吉林 Jilin	17916	135078	311.08	250.03	2.58	1.72
哈尔滨 Haerbin	59042	470958	435.96	624.17	19.05	9.09
齐齐哈尔 Qiqihaer	17080	55096	0.00	135.70	0.65	0.35
合肥 Hefei	30432	242238	255.11	207.43	30.18	18.18
福州 Fuzhou	61873	943095	425.72	490.98	82.96	46.43
泉州 Quanzhou	40668	421300	288.15	409.33	27.25	19.16
南昌 Nanchang	26285	286698	235.00	201.18	13.42	10.04
济南 Jinan			504.88	533.17	20.16	8.35
淄博 Zibo	22069	211799	365.91	254.86	19.30	10.09
郑州 Zhengzhou	44417	522442	0.00	479.89	14.11	8.72
武汉 Wuhan	61832	643909	645.06	853.99	31.36	14.81
长沙 Changsha	43437	503262	494.97	452.00	20.44	10.98
南宁 Nanning	24263	167386	190.39	254.98	6.58	5.11
海口 Haikou	15168	196281	103.40	86.14	9.80	2.67
成都 Chengdu	50000	758000	862.97	771.50	25.17	13.55
贵阳 Guiyang	17199	318563	241.87	153.67	8.52	5.23
昆明 Kunming	29111	487000	361.65	328.41	17.79	10.06
西安 Xi'an	50270	607634	478.10	440.05	23.09	14.03
兰州 Lanzhou	21652	185718	210.64	206.53	7.50	6.00
西宁 Xining	8339	109252	85.42	63.58	2.90	2.39
乌鲁木齐 Wulumuqi	20960	335900	180.52	172.14	9.57	4.20
银川 Yinchuan	10758	139536	143.39	61.30	2.88	2.28
太原 Taiyuan	26690	302859	204.45	185.37	20.05	15.17

附录2:　全国重点城市主要经济指标（2003年）（续3）

Appendix Ⅱ:Main Economic Indicators in Major City (2003)(Countinued 3)

城市　City	地方财政收入（亿元）Local Financial Revenue (100 million yuan)	城乡居民储蓄存款余额（亿元）Outstanding Amount of Saving Deposits in Urban and Rural Areas(100 million yuan)	在岗职工平均工资（元）Average Wage of Staff and Workers (yuan)	城市居民人均可支配收入（元）Per Capita Annual Disposable Income of Urban Households(yuan)	农民人均纯收入（元）Per Capita Net Income of Rural Residents(yuan)
常　州 Changzhou	78.54	622.92	17259	11303	5550
无　锡 Wuxi	149.71	997.75	18927	11647	6329
苏　州 Suzou	220.31	1470.50	19790	12361	6681
南　京 Nanjing	191.78	1133.62	22190	10196	4923
杭　州 Hangzhou	150.39	1589.96	24668	12898	5740
石家庄 Shijiazhuang	0.00	1044.49	12306	7741	3394
唐　山 Tangshan	57.37	723.04	11632	8068	3790
呼和浩特 Huhehaote	21.36	255.45	13092	8230	3169
包　头 Baotou	29.76	243.46	13417	9216	3435
沈　阳 Shenyang	103.52	1422.96	14965	7961	3818
鞍　山 Anshan	35.73	484.06	12732	7434	4000
抚　顺 Fushun	16.83	287.60	12025	6393	3308
长　春 Changchun	45.97	831.36	13867	7905	3411
吉　林 Jilin	24.88	392.44	10610	7700	2931
哈尔滨 Haerbin	85.05	1153.70	10175	7907	2943
齐齐哈尔 Qiqihaer	15.44	280.90	10081	5774	2847
合　肥 Hefei	35.87	359.25	13900	7785	2384
福　州 Fuzhou	83.66	876.22	15052	10179	4402
泉　州 Quanzhou	50.03	711.35	13132	12691	5195
南　昌 Nanchang	33.46	482.80	13914	7793	2808
济　南 Jinan	85.60	758.35	16027	11013	3619
淄　博 Zibo	0.00	479.32	13405	8720	3902
郑　州 Zhengzhou	72.47	1048.49	13537	8647	3631
武　汉 Wuhan	99.71	1285.53	13729	8525	3497
长　沙 Changsha	79.33	704.85	16987	9933	3745
南　宁 Nanning	36.24	451.50	13172	9162	2231
海　口 Haikou	13.71	284.37	14820	8350	3271
成　都 Chengdu	108.30	1494.42	15275	9641	3655
贵　阳 Guiyang	43.72	344.95	12182	7985	2510
昆　明 Kunming	62.95	708.53	14296	7979	2581
西　安 Xi'an	72.86	1285.38	13504	7748	2838
兰　州 Lanzhou	20.57	468.38	13489	7094	2398
西　宁 Xining	9.13	174.93	14632	7024	2054
乌鲁木齐 Wulumuqi	46.15	420.30	16509	9087	4154
银　川 Yinchuan	16.06	193.08	13496	7245	3087
太　原 Taiyuan	0.00	660.13	12679	8264	3356

中国统计出版社最新资料书简目

中国统计年鉴-2004
中国统计摘要-2004
2004年中国发展报告
中国城市统计年鉴-2003
中国农村统计年鉴-2004
中国劳动统计年鉴-2004
中国人口统计年鉴-2004
中国工业经济统计年鉴-2004
中国市场统计年鉴-2004
2003中国城市发展报告
中国建筑业统计年鉴-2003
中国价格及城镇居民家庭收支调查统计年鉴-2004
国际统计年鉴-2004
中国对外经济贸易统计年鉴-2003
中国基本单位统计年鉴-2003
中国民政统计年鉴-2004
中国高技术产业统计年鉴-2004
中国房地产行业名录

北京统计年鉴-2004
天津统计年鉴-2004
河北经济年鉴-2004
山西统计年鉴-2004
内蒙古统计年鉴-2004
辽宁统计年鉴-2004
吉林统计年鉴-2004
黑龙江统计年鉴-2004
上海统计年鉴-2004
江苏统计年鉴-2004
浙江统计年鉴-2004
安徽统计年鉴-2004
福建统计年鉴-2004
江西统计年鉴-2004
山东统计年鉴-2004
河南统计年鉴-2004
湖北统计年鉴-2004
湖南统计年鉴-2004
广东统计年鉴-2004
广西统计年鉴-2004
海南统计年鉴-2004
重庆统计年鉴-2004
四川统计年鉴-2004
贵州统计年鉴-2004
云南统计年鉴-2004
西藏统计年鉴-2004
陕西统计年鉴-2004
甘肃年鉴-2004

青海统计年鉴—2004
宁夏统计年鉴—2004
新疆统计年鉴—2004
新疆生产建设兵团统计年鉴—2004
石家庄统计年鉴—2004
唐山统计年鉴—2004
邯郸统计年鉴—2004
呼和浩特经济统计年鉴—2004
鄂尔多斯市统计年鉴—2004
包头统计年鉴—2004
赤峰统计年鉴—2004
沈阳年鉴—2004
大连统计年鉴—2004
鞍山统计年鉴—2004
长春计年鉴—2004
吉林市社会经济统计年鉴—2004
四平统计年鉴—2004
延吉统计年鉴—2004
哈尔滨统计年鉴—2004
齐齐哈尔经济统计年鉴—2004
牡丹江统计年鉴—2004
大庆统计年鉴—2004
黑龙江垦区统计年鉴—2004
上海蒲东新区统计年鉴—2004
南京统计年鉴—2004
苏州统计年鉴—2004
无锡统计年鉴—2004
常州统计年鉴—2004
徐州统计年鉴—2004
南通统计年鉴—2004
盐城统计年鉴—2004
镇江统计年鉴—2004
杭州统计年鉴—2004
宁波统计年鉴—2004
绍兴统计年鉴—2004
台州统计年鉴—2004
舟山统计年鉴—2004
温州统计年鉴—2004
金华统计年鉴—2004
嘉兴统计年鉴—2004
丽水统计年鉴—2004
福州年鉴—2004
厦门经济特区年鉴—2004
福州经济技术开发区年鉴—2004
南昌经济社会统计年鉴—2004
九江经济统计年鉴—2004
济南统计年鉴-2004

青岛统计年鉴—2004
潍坊统计年鉴—2004
郑州统计年鉴—2004
洛阳统计年鉴—2004
三门峡统计年鉴—2004
平顶山统计年鉴—2004
南阳经济统计年鉴—2004
武汉统计年鉴—2004
宜昌统计年鉴—2004
十堰统计年鉴—2004
荆州统计年鉴—2004
广州统计年鉴—2004
东莞统计年鉴—2004
惠州统计年鉴—2004
深圳统计年鉴-2004
南宁统计年鉴—2004
桂林经济社会统计年鉴—2004
柳州经济统计年鉴—2004
来宾统计年鉴—2004
河池地区经济社会统计年鉴—2004
海口统计年鉴-2004
成都统计年鉴—2004
贵阳统计年鉴-2004
昆明统计年鉴—2004
西安统计年鉴—2004
兰州年鉴—2004
西宁统计年鉴—2004
银川统计年鉴—2004
乌鲁木齐统计年鉴—2004
巴音郭楞统计年鉴—2004
吐鲁番统计年鉴—2004

New Published Statistical Yearbook by China Statistics Press